THE PAPERS OF
WOODROW WILSON
VOLUME 21
1910

NEW JERSEY STATE EDITION

THE PAPERS OF
WOODROW WILSON

The Gubernatorial Years

ARTHUR S. LINK, *EDITOR*

DAVID W. HIRST AND JOHN E. LITTLE
ASSOCIATE EDITORS

JOHN M. MULDER, *ASSISTANT EDITOR*

SYLVIA ELVIN FONTIJN, *CONTRIBUTING EDITOR*

M. HALSEY THOMAS, *CONSULTING EDITOR*

Volume 21 · 1910

PRINCETON, NEW JERSEY
PRINCETON UNIVERSITY PRESS
1976

FOREWORD

PERHAPS the best way to begin a foreword to a volume of the Papers of Woodrow Wilson is to let our thirty-eighth Governor speak for himself. Addressing a campaign audience in Newark in 1910, Wilson exhibited the eloquence and the inspiration that led millions in the ensuing decade to follow him: "Nobody who cannot speak of the common thought, who cannot move the common impulse, is any man to speak for America, or for any of her future purposes." It is this eloquence and deep concern for social and economic justice and equality that make this volume and the other four that are concerned with Wilson's term as Governor of New Jersey so eminently readable.

Wilson merits our study today for many other reasons than his eloquence. In his remarkable entry into politics from the presidency of Princeton University, Wilson came to embody the progressive ideals that swept over the nation prior to the First World War. In two short years as Governor, he persuaded the legislature to accept the people's will by effectuating a comprehensive fundamental reform of the institutions of New Jersey government. The proud list of accomplishments includes public regulation of the utilities and other powerful corporations, direct popular election of United States senators, a system of workmen's compensation, and enactment of a stringent corrupt practices act governing political activity.

Wilson best expressed the spirit behind these reforms during his campaign for the governorship in 1910: "It is because the law is the poor man's friend when it is justly administered that I stand for the law."

It is not enough to say that Wilson's record in New Jersey is relevant only because of his successes. These volumes are relevant also because they record his efforts to grapple with complex issues that have continued to plague the people of New Jersey to the present time. Wilson sought to shift the burden of taxation from the poor to those better able to bear it, to reorganize and achieve economy in administration, to reform the financing of political campaigns, and to establish open and honest government constantly responsive to public needs.

As I write these words, I take pride that we have at last succeeded in making a start toward achieving the first objective, but we continue to struggle to achieve the other three goals for which Wilson vainly fought. New Jersey has made progress, but Wilson's ideals have not yet been attained, nor has his great vision been entirely fulfilled.

I am privileged to express in this foreword my admiration for Woodrow Wilson. Through the cooperation of Princeton University Press and the Editor of the Papers of Woodrow Wilson, Professor Arthur S. Link of Princeton University, the state has been able to donate sets of Volumes 21-25 of the Papers to 500 of the major libraries in New Jersey. I commend our state legislature for recognizing the educational value of these historic papers, published during our nation's Bicentennial era, and for appropriating the necessary monies to carry out the project.

These volumes clearly establish Wilson's identity with and love for New Jersey and demonstrate how he left his mark upon this state. They do it from his own university and from the pen of the foremost Wilson scholar, Arthur Link, and his colleagues.

BRENDAN BYRNE
GOVERNOR

Trenton, New Jersey
September 15, 1976

INTRODUCTION

T HE opening of this volume finds Wilson about to enter politics, having just signified his willingness to accept the
Democratic nomination for the governorship of New Jersey. That
nomination comes to him on September 15, 1910, from a state
convention controlled by James Smith, Jr. and Robert Davis,
Democratic bosses of Newark and Jersey City. Wilson wins over
the progressive Democrats, who have bitterly opposed his nomination, by the sincerity and simple eloquence of his acceptance
speech. During the coming weeks he wins the support of a large
number of independents by his forthright endorsement of reform measures and by his assertion that he wants to be the
spokesman of the whole people as well as the leader of his party.
In a supreme bid, in a public letter to a Jersey City progressive
Republican, he denounces Smith and Davis and promises that
they will not control affairs if he goes to Trenton. Adding thousands of independent and progressive Republican votes to the
normal Democratic turnout, he sweeps the state on election day,
November 8.

We think that readers will find the documents in this volume
richly revealing of an important event in Wilson's career. From
the letters printed herein we can see Wilson reacting day by day
to an aroused public opinion, moving from ambiguity to advanced
progressivism, giving voice to popular demands, and then striking
out to put himself at the head of a people in revolt against bossism. Even more remarkable are Wilson's speeches. The scholar
of politics and institutions is all at once plunged into the world
of affairs. With the state as his classroom, he tries highmindedly
and patiently to educate the people of New Jersey: politics is
the vehicle of life and the means of change; the state can act to
reorder social and economic affairs; public opinion if rightly led
can have its way in the reconstruction of society. Most of all, he
calls upon the people to awaken and assume the responsibilities
and high privileges of citizenship.

All of Wilson's speeches, except for the main portion of the
acceptance speech, were extemporaneous, and we are completely
at the mercy of reporters for versions of what Wilson actually
said. One shorthand reporter, Frank Parker Stockbridge, recorded
most of Wilson's important addresses. However, Stockbridge was
a poor reporter, did not edit his transcripts, and many times
missed or simply did not try to record portions of speeches. Even
so, when the Stockbridge transcript was the most complete version of a speech available, we regarded it as the basic text. Fortu-

nately, Stockbridge was not the only reporter on the scene. Clarence Sackett recorded Wilson's concluding speeches in full; his transcripts are in the New Jersey Historical Society. Reporters for the New York, New Jersey, and Philadelphia newspapers set down long but incomplete versions. By assembling all the known extant texts, we were able to correct and fill out most portions of those Stockbridge transcripts which we used. However, we were unable to correct some portions of Stockbridge's garbled texts; they must remain garbled although Wilson, who was usually able to construct a clear and grammatical sentence, would be horrified to read them. In many other cases, we were able to begin with the full texts in the newspapers published in the cities and towns in which Wilson delivered these speeches. Here again we corrected these basic versions from variant texts, including Stockbridge's, insofar as possible.

We have reproduced in full all of Wilson's major speeches. They are to some degree repetitive, but it is better so than to mangle highly integrated texts. For the rest of the speeches we have contented ourselves with news reports, aiming to give comprehensive coverage of the campaign. If the reader thinks that we have been partisan in our selection of news accounts, let him remember that all of the important independent New York, New Jersey, and Philadelphia newspapers, upon which we relied most heavily, strongly supported Wilson and printed the fullest accounts of his campaign. We have examined the few New Jersey Republican newspapers that existed in 1910. Highly partisan and small in circulation, these newspapers paid little attention to Wilson.

Wilsonian text is reproduced in this volume as it appears in the sources. We have occasionally removed needless commas and infrequently changed other punctuation when we thought the changes facilitated reading and promoted clarity. On the other hand, we corrected typographical and spelling errors in square brackets only when necessary for clarity and ease of reading. In short, we have adhered as much as possible to our rule of printing documents *verbatim et literatim*.

Readers are again reminded that *The Papers of Woodrow Wilson* is a continuing series; that persons, events, and institutions that figure prominently in other volumes are not re-identified in subsequent ones; and that the Index to each volume gives cross references to fullest earlier identifications.

THE EDITORS

Princeton, New Jersey
May 28, 1975

CONTENTS

Introduction, vii
Illustrations, xvii
Abbreviations and Symbols, xix

The Papers, July 15, 1910–November 9, 1910

Interviews
    Three interviews on Wilson's candidacy, 14, 98, 220
    On publicity of campaign funds, 120
    On tariff, corporations, and conservation, 125
    On trusts, 134
    On labor, 179
    On political graft, 477
    About campaign issues, 522
Edmond Kelly, excerpt from *Twentieth Century Socialism*, 175
Letters, Collateral
    Frank Obadiah Briggs to James Richard Nugent, 291
    Cleveland Hoadley Dodge to Henry Burling Thompson, 435
    David M. Flynn to James Kerney, 542(2)
    Moses Taylor Pyne to William Cooper Procter, 434
Letters from Wilson to
    Charles Dexter Allen, 171
    Board of Trustees of Princeton University, 362, 492
    Herbert E. Bowen, 53
    Harry Laity Bowlby, 90
    Robert Bridges, 337
    Calvin Easton Brodhead, 84
    Edwin Grant Conklin, 136
    Winthrop More Daniels, 178, 337
    Cleveland Hoadley Dodge, 139, 295
    Zephaniah Charles Felt, 36
    David Paulson Foster *et al.*, 470
    Harry Augustus Garfield, 429, 559
    Robert Garrett, 25
    Harold Godwin, 444
    Edward Field Goltra, 17
    Charles Henry Grasty, 102
    Joseph Finch Guffey, 623
    George Brinton McClellan Harvey, 5, 24, 35, 40, 41, 46, 61, 88,
        89, 90, 148, 245, 297, 338, 435
    James Calvin Hemphill, 579
    Joseph Stanislaus Hoff, 102
    Edward Howe, 51
    David Benton Jones, 162
    James Kerney, 34
    Wilson B. Killingbeck, 288
    Abbott Lawrence Lowell, 143
    Charles Williston McAlpin, 13, 471
    Cyrus Hall McCormick, 543
    David L. MacKay, 297, 336
    Isaac Wayne MacVeagh, 152
    John Bassett Moore, 559

Walter Hines Page, 5, 579
Alfred L. Parker, 24
Mary Allen Hulbert Peck, 26, 38, 50, 64, 163
Dan Fellows Platt, 22, 36, 58, 149, 436
Henry Smith Pritchett, 39, 160, 492
Adolphus Ragan, 14
George Lawrence Record, 296, 407
James Slocum Rogers, 153
Charles Scribner, 144
James Smith, Jr., 590
George Hammond Sullivan, 543
Charles Andrew Talcott, 590
Samuel Huston Thompson, Jr., 149
Edwin Augustus Van Valkenburg, 164, 241
John Wesley Wescott, 137, 152
William Royal Wilder, 150
Walter Maurice Wilkins, 102
Edgar Williamson, 59
Lawrence Crane Woods, 444
Frederic Yates, 87
Letters to Wilson from
Edwin Anderson Alderman, 595
Archibald Stevens Alexander, 6, 18, 112, 380
Caroline Bayard Stevens Alexander, 150
Henry Eckert Alexander, 8, 9, 22, 26, 33, 37, 54, 57, 62, 158, 167,
  200, 219, 225, 243
Lucien Hugh Alexander, 328
Charles Dexter Allen, 168
Yorke Allen, 300
Alfred Brittin Baker, 117
Simeon Eben Baldwin, 133
Daniel Moreau Barringer, 603
Clarence Hughson Baxter, 158
Edgeworth Bird Baxter, 577
Sylvester Woodbridge Beach, 597
Edward Webster Bemis, 617
William Blackburn, 335
James Gillmor Blauvelt, 260
Benjamin Boisseau Bobbitt, 324
Edward William Bok, 118
Robert Gunn Bremner, 133, 153
Robert Bridges, 298, 591
Calvin Easton Brodhead, 83
Herbert Bruce Brougham, 97
William Swan Plumer Bryan, 201
Edwin Camp, 451
Edward Capps, 166
Hunsdon Cary, 117
Benjamin Bright Chambers, 336
Edwin Grant Conklin, 116
Charles Allen Culberson, 580
Richard Heath Dabney, 138, 597
Winthrop More Daniels, 10, 174, 321

Frank Miles Day, 618
Joseph Albert Dear, Jr., 23, 116, 580
Walter Moore Dear, 450
William Henry Steele Demarest, 620
Alfred Lewis Dennis, 592
Arthur Granville Dewalt, 103
John DeWitt, 442
Clinton Roy Dickinson, 169
Bessie Louise Dickson, 587
Thomas H. Dillow, 82
Cleveland Hoadley Dodge, 137, 292, 385, 591
Henry Nehemiah Dodge, 354
Ralph Waldo Emerson Donges, 577
Thomas Marcus Donnelly, 451
Joseph Dorsey, 156
Matthias Cowell Ely, 540
Charles Apffel Eypper, 464
Thomas P. Fay, 299
Zephaniah Charles Felt, 12
William T. Ferguson, 21, 28, 47, 162, 238, 275, 292
James Fairman Fielder, 97, 442
Henry Burchard Fine, 112
Charles Joel Fisk, 614
David M. Flynn, 541
Henry Jones Ford, 606
John Franklin Fort, 605
Raymond Blaine Fosdick, 238
John Watson Foster, 600
Philip Hilton Fraser, 519
David Ruddach Frazer, 366
William Goodell Frost, 579
Harry Augustus Garfield, 558, 609
James Rudolph Garfield, 609
Robert Garrett, 3
Lindley Miller Garrison, 587
Christian Frederick Gauss, 111
William Cavanagh Gebhardt, 110, 156, 558
Otis Allan Glazebrook, 98
Harold Godwin, 442
Henry Mayer Goldfogle, 618
Marie Louise Norris Gollan, 556
Samuel Gompers, 379
Charles N. Grandison, 171
Edward Herrick Griffin, 586
John Ralph Hardin, 610
Samuel Allen Harlow, 110
George Brinton McClellan Harvey, 17, 27, 40, 52, 85, 87, 166, 243,
    292, 320, 327, 433
Azel Washburn Hazen, 107
James Calvin Hemphill, 539
Robert Randolph Henderson, 599
Henry Lee Higginson, 612
Joseph Stanislaus Hoff, 97

Joseph Howell, 443
William Bailey Howland, 620
James Alfred Hoyt, Jr., 588
William Hughes, 145, 213
Theodore Whitefield Hunt, 377, 602
William Burhans Isham, 602
Melancthon Williams Jacobus, 6, 30, 142, 321, 578
Caesar Augustus Rodney Janvier, 588
Robert Underwood Johnson, 109
David Benton Jones, 29, 132, 144, 173, 593
Harry Pratt Judson, 144
Francis Fisher Kane, 266, 604
Edward Lawrence Katzenbach, 132
James Kerney, 31
John Thompson Kerr, 592
Wilson B. Killingbeck, 267, 351, 386
Darwin Pearl Kingsley, 621
Eugene Francis Kinkead, 213
George Mason La Monte, 610
Franklin Knight Lane, 586
Adolph Lankering, 295
John Holladay Latané, 613
David Lawrence, 608
William C. Liller, 587
Richard Vliet Lindabury, 140, 274, 378, 388, 449
Job Herbert Lippincott, 145, 274
Edgar Odell Lovett, 159
Abbott Lawrence Lowell, 109
William Gibbs McAdoo, 265, 298
Charles Williston McAlpin, 13, 49, 463, 536
Robert Harris McCarter, 131
Thomas Nesbitt McCarter, Jr., 139
George Brinton McClellan, 599
William Frank McCombs, 294
Walter Lee McCorkle, 105
Cyrus Hall McCormick, 10, 518, 519, 594
Nettie Fowler McCormick, 556
David L. MacKay, 287, 322
John Bach McMaster, 609
Isaac Wayne MacVeagh, 293
William Francis Magie, 406
Theodore Marburg, 614
Erwin E. Marshall, 106
Howard Marshall, 324
Franklin Marx, 86
Victor Louis Mason, 586
William Hunter Maxwell, 161, 617
James Cowden Meyers, 107
Raleigh Colston Minor, 585
John Alexander Montgomery, 104
John Bassett Moore, 557
William H. Morrow, 476
Franklin Murphy, 212

Joseph M. Noonan, 42, 54, 63, 85, 108, 265
James Richard Nugent, 106, 173, 290
Joseph L. O'Connell, 239
Alexander Thomas Ormond, 603
William Church Osborn, 155, 172
William Osler, 618
Thomas Nelson Page, 602
Walter Hines Page, 576
Charles Henry Parkhurst, 621
W. C. Payne, 616
Mary Allen Hulbert Peck, 48
Bliss Perry, 406
Magnus Fraser Peterson, 619
Dan Fellows Platt, 11, 56, 140, 172
Edgar Allan Poe, 600
Henry Smith Pritchett, 20, 160, 540, 596
A Progressive Republican, 347
Moses Taylor Pyne, 353
George Lawrence Record, 259, 338, 596
Charles Alexander Richmond, 146
John Augustus Roebling II, 450
Leo Stanton Rowe, 614
William W. St. John, 581
Edward Seiler Salmon, 105
Charles Scribner, 104
Edward Wallace Scudder, 175
Michael Welsh Scully, 131
Rudolph Edward Schirmer, 617
Jacob Gould Schurman, 611
Albert Shaw, 300
Joseph Bernard Shea, 81
Robert Elliott Speer, 334
James Cresap Sprigg, 62
Edwin Augustus Stevens, 198, 601
Bayard Stockton, 131
Edward Casper Stokes, 503
Moorfield Storey, 386
Isidor Straus, 613
Nathan Straus, 18
George Hammond Sullivan, 541
William Sulzer, 616
Charles Andrew Talcott, 578
Henry Burling Thompson, 49, 104, 299, 593
Samuel Huston Thompson, Jr., 130
Edwin Augustus Van Valkenburg, 198
Walker Whiting Vick, 115
Oswald Garrison Villard, 58
Williamson Updike Vreeland, 154
John Milton Waldron, 387
John Wanamaker, 601
Henry Burt Ware, 463
William Henry Welch, 129
John Wesley Wescott, 103, 604

William Royal Wilder, 129
John Sharp Williams, 557
Edgar Williamson, 55, 115
John Adams Wilson, 161
Joseph R. Wilson, Jr., 114
William Lawrence Wilson, 20
Sarah Macdonald Winans, 30
Henry Otto Wittpen, 155
Josiah Townsend Woodhull, Jr., 16
Marion Woodville Woodrow, 581
Charles Albert Woods, 128
Hiram Woods, 555
Lawrence Crane Woods, 157
John Joseph Wynne, 612
Frederic Yates, 59
George Green Yeomans, 611

News Items

Announcement of the marriage of Margaret Randolph Axson and Edward Elliott, 84

Wilson's resignation from Princeton University, 101

Princeton University: Documentary Material

Proposed resolution of the Board of Trustees of Princeton University, 353

Minutes of the Board of Trustees of Princeton University, 364

Petition by the Class of 1912, 381

Princeton University: Meetings and Addresses

Report of Opening Exercises, 151

Reports of addresses to the Philadelphian Society, 169, 176

Report of a talk to Princeton students, 289

Public Statements and Addresses

Report of a religious address, "The Function of the Country Church," Old Lyme, Conn., 4

Address to the American Bar Association, "The Lawyer and the Community," Chattanooga, Tenn., 64

Speech accepting the Democratic gubernatorial nomination, Trenton, N.J., 91

Report of remarks to the Democratic State Convention, Trenton, N.J., 118

Report of a speech to Die Wilde Gans Club, Jersey City, N.J., 147

The Gubernatorial Campaign

Address opening the gubernatorial campaign, Jersey City, N.J., 181

Campaign speech in Plainfield, N.J., 193

Campaign speech in Newark, N.J., 202

Campaign speech in Red Bank, N.J., 213

Report of a campaign address in Long Branch, N.J., 227

Campaign address in Trenton, N.J., 229

Campaign speech in Woodbury, N.J., 245

Report of a campaign address in Burlington, N.J., 269

Report of a campaign speech in Bridgeton, N.J., 276

Report of campaign speeches at Cape May Court House and Wildwood, N.J., 281

Report of a campaign address in Paterson, N.J., 301

Address to the Democratic Union in Caldwell, N.J., 306
Report of remarks at Caldwell, N.J., 309
Campaign address in Atlantic City, N.J., 310
Report of speeches in Ocean County, N.J., 325
Campaign address in Asbury Park, N.J., 328
Remarks to the Democratic leaders of Mercer County in Trenton, N.J., 349
Report of campaign speeches in Bound Brook and Somerville, N.J., 354
Campaign address in Flemington, N.J., 369
Report of a campaign speech in Flemington, N.J., 381
Report of a campaign tour in Warren County, N.J., 382
Report of a campaign speech in Phillipsburg, N.J., 390
Campaign speech in Newton, N.J., 396
Report of Wilson's itinerary for the last two weeks of the campaign, 412
Report of campaign addresses in Camden, N.J., 413
Campaign speech in Salem, N.J., 423
Report of a campaign speech in New Brunswick, N.J., 436
Report of three campaign addresses in Bergen County, N.J., 446
Report of a campaign address in Hackensack, N.J., 452
Campaign address in Elizabeth, N.J., 454
Report of an after-dinner talk in Elizabeth, N.J., 464
Report of three campaign addresses in Hudson County, N.J., 471
Report of a campaign address in Elizabethport, N.J., 465
Report of a campaign address in Bayonne, N.J., 485
Campaign address in Passaic, N.J., 493
Report of a campaign speech in Carlstadt, N.J., 507
Campaign address in Montclair, N.J., 508
Report of a campaign address in Orange, N.J., 520
Report of campaign addresses in Madison, Dover, and Morristown, N.J., 525
Campaign address in Morristown, N.J., 527
Campaign address in Perth Amboy, N.J., 543
Report of a campaign address in Carteret, N.J., 560
Report of four campaign addresses in Essex County, N.J., 561
Campaign address in Newark, N.J., 564
Victory statement, Princeton, N.J., 589
Telegrams from Wilson to
    Simeon Eben Baldwin, 590
    An unknown person, 577
Telegrams to Wilson from
    William Jennings Bryan, 600
    David Bryant, 583
    Richard Heath Dabney, 597
    Josephus Daniels, 585
    Robert Davis, 442
    Cleveland Hoadley Dodge, 112
    John Franklin Fort, 605
    Eugene Noble Foss, 610
    Robert Garrett, 622
    Franklin Potts Glass, 588
    Edward Field Goltra, 294

Charles Henry Grasty, 102
John Maynard Harlan, 266, 389
George Brinton McClellan Harvey, 585
William Hughes, 603
Robert Stephen Hudspeth, 607
Melancthon Williams Jacobus, 109, 594
Thomas Davies Jones, 599
Frank Snowden Katzenbach, Jr., 96
Robert Lansing, 607
Vivian Murchison Lewis, 591
Thomas Bell Love, 584
William Gibbs McAdoo, 108
William Frank McCombs, 108, 607
Cyrus Hall McCormick, 140
Norman Edward Mack, 102
Thomas Riley Marshall, 603
Charles Wellman Mitchell, 599
Roland Sletor Morris, 584
Alexander Mitchell Palmer, 604
Joseph Pulitzer, 595
Ashton Cokayne Shallenberger, 622
Edward Wright Sheldon, 594
George Sebastian Silzer, 585
Roger Charles Sullivan, 584
Charles Andrew Talcott, 583
Joseph Patrick Tumulty, 589
Joseph Patrick Tumulty and Mark Anthony Sullivan, 433
Frederick Jackson Turner, 602
Walter Whiting Vick, 608
Brand Whitlock, 607
Walter Maurice Wilkins, 98
Ellen Axson Wilson, 101
Henry Otto Wittpenn, 434
Writings
Life and Education, 32
Platform of the New Jersey Democratic Party: proposed platform,
    43; final draft, 94
Index, 625

ILLUSTRATIONS

Following page 324

Woodrow Wilson
Princeton University Library

George Brinton McClellan Harvey
Princeton University Library

James Smith, Jr.
Newark Evening News

James Richard Nugent
The Political Education of Woodrow Wilson, *by James Kerney*

Robert Davis
New Jersey State Library, Archives

James Kerney
Princeton University Library

George Lawrence Record
Princeton University Library

Woodrow Wilson, with Vivian Murchison Lewis on his right, and John Franklin Fort on his left
The Political Education of Woodrow Wilson, *by James Kerney*

TEXT ILLUSTRATIONS

Outlines of Wilson's campaign speeches:
  Sept. 28, 1910, Jersey City, 182
  Sept. 29, 1910, Plainfield, 192
  Sept. 30, 1910, Newark, 203
  Oct. 5, 1910, Woodbury, 246
  Oct. 6, 1910, Burlington, 270
  Oct. 8, 1910, Wildwood, 282
  Oct. 19, 1910, Somerville, 355
  Oct. 20, 1910, Flemington, 368
  Oct. 21, 1910, Phillipsburg, 391
  Oct. 22, 1910, Newton, 397
  Oct. 24, 1910, Camden, 414
  Oct. 25, 1910, Salem, 422
  Oct. 26, 1910, New Brunswick, 437
  Oct. 27, 1910, Bergen County, 445
  Oct. 28, 1910, Elizabeth II, 455
  Oct. 28, 1910, Elizabeth I, 466

Oct. 29, 1910, Hoboken, 472

Oct. 31, 1910, Bayonne, 486

Nov. 1, 1910, Passaic, 494

Nov. 2, 1910, The Oranges—Montclair, 509

Nov. 3, 1910, Morristown, 528

Nov. 5, 1910, Glen Ridge—Bloomfield—East Orange, 562

Third page of the first draft of Wilson's letter to George Lawrence Record, 410

ABBREVIATIONS

ALI	autograph letter initialed
ALS	autograph letter signed
CCL	carbon copy of letter
CS	Clarence Sackett
FPS	Frank Parker Stockbridge
hw	handwriting, handwritten
hwLS	handwritten letter signed
hw MS	handwritten manuscript
MS	manuscript
S	signed
sh	shorthand
T	typed
T MS	typed manuscript
TCL	typed copy of letter
TL	typed letter
TLS	typed letter signed
WW	Woodrow Wilson
WWhw	Woodrow Wilson handwriting, handwritten
WWsh	Woodrow Wilson shorthand
WWshLS	Woodrow Wilson shorthand letter signed
WWT	Woodrow Wilson typed
WWTCL	Woodrow Wilson typed copy of letter
WWTLS	Woodrow Wilson typed copy of letter signed

ABBREVIATIONS FOR COLLECTIONS AND LIBRARIES

Following the National Union Catalog
of the Library of Congress

CtY	Yale University
DLC	Library of Congress
MH	Harvard University
MH-Ar	Harvard University Archives
NcD	Duke University
NjHi	New Jersey Historical Society, Newark
NjP	Princeton University
PHi	Historical Society of Pennsylvania, Philadelphia
PP	Free Library of Philadelphia
RSB Coll., DLC	Ray Stannard Baker Collection of Wilsoniana, Library of Congress
UA, NjP	University Archives, Princeton University
WC, NjP	Woodrow Wilson Collection, Princeton University
WHi	State Historical Society of Wisconsin, Madison
WP, DLC	Woodrow Wilson Papers, Library of Congress

SYMBOLS

[July 16, 1910]   publication date of a published writing; also date
                   of document when date is not part of text
[[Sept. 15, 1910]] delivery date of a speech if publication date differs
[*July* 20, *1910*]   composition date when publication date differs

THE PAPERS OF

WOODROW WILSON

VOLUME 21

1910

From Robert Garrett

My dear President Wilson: [Baltimore] July 15, 1910.

. . . I appreciate deeply the confidence in me that you show in asking my advice upon the subject of the political service that you may be called upon to perform.[1] I hesitate greatly to respond to your request, for I feel that you know vastly more about the subject in all its details and in its bearings than I do, and then, too, my judgement in such a matter is not very mature. But since you seem to want an expression of opinion from me, I shall give it frankly.

If, in the event of your nomination and election, you could attend properly to the duties of the governorship and at the same time at least direct affairs at Princeton (and still hold a fair degree of health!), I should consider it an excellent thing to accept the unsought nomination. But if, on the other hand,—as I suppose would be the case,—you would have to resign the presidency of Princeton, I should regard the move as a great mistake. I believe you can accomplish more for the country by working out,—and, when necessary, fighting out,—Princeton's problems, than you could as governor of New Jersey or as the incumbent of any other high public office.

And especially now, when you have won the main issue in the recent very trying controversy, it would in my judgement be deplorable to withdraw and perhaps leave the control of Princeton's future in the hands of a group of men some of whom are incompetent while the rest have false notions in academic matters or are swayed by prejudice or other petty feelings.

I know the present situation is not altogether as you would have it, but I earnestly hope you will find it possible to stay on, for sooner or later you will surely succeed in all your aims.

I trust I have not said too much or spoken too frankly. It would be much more satisfactory to talk these matters over face to face, but that is hardly possible. . . .

With best regards,

Faithfully yours,   Robert Garrett.

ALS (WP, DLC).
[1] See WW to R. Garrett, July 9, 1910, Vol. 20.

A News Report of a Religious Address

[July 16, 1910]

The New Church at Old Lyme

On the night of July 3, 1907, the church building at Old Lyme, Ct., was burned to the ground. Typical of the best of New England meeting houses, beautifully situated upon a spacious street and finely screened by stately old elms, it had stood for ninety years as the chief center of the social and religious life in a noted country town. Here representative families in state and nation, worshiped and went forth into the world's life nurtured by its gracious influence.

Lovers of the former structure have watched with growing joy the replica of the church that was taking shape daily before their eyes. They are now heartened to say that "that which passeth away was with glory, much more that which remaineth is in glory." . . .

Dr. G. Glenn Atkins of Central Church, Providence,[1] preached a masterly dedication sermon. Scarcely could Paul's text upon the laying of Jesus Christ as the foundation be more effectively treated from Christian history and Christian inspiration. Prof. B. W. Bacon of Yale Divinity School, a former minister,[2] made the prayer. Special exercises of the Sunday School followed in the new parish house which has been the place of worship for a year and a half. At the Lord's Supper in the afternoon, thirteen united with the church, nearly all of whom were young people who joined on confession. The address of the evening service was given by Pres. Woodrow Wilson of Princeton.

His subject was The Function of the Country Church. Every part of the life of New England communities in other days centered in the church. Of late years people have sought the cities as the centers of stirring life. The country town and the country church has been deserted or weakened.

The country church with its minister as leader will find renewed supremacy and strength through guiding in friendly ways the reorganization of country life. As these mutual interests are molded by friendliness, wise oversight and counsel, as the country church teaches a religion that penetrates the competitive problems of business transactions and all workaday motives, she will gain her oldtime authority and power. The true minister of this church[3] will be the friendly leader and counselor of men, a man of broad culture and the spirit, able to touch men and women in their common interests with the hand of unselfish love.

Printed in the Boston *Congregationalist and Christian World*, xcv (July 16, 1910), 88-89.

[1] The Rev. Dr. Gaius Glenn Atkins, pastor of the Central Congregational Church of Providence, R. I., since January 1910.

[2] The Rev. Dr. Benjamin Wisner Bacon, pastor of the Old Lyme Church, 1884-89, Professor of New Testament Criticism and Exegesis, Yale Divinity School, since 1897.

[3] The minister at this time was the Rev. Edward Mortimer Chapman, Yale 1884, B.D. 1890.

To George Brinton McClellan Harvey

My dear Colonel Harvey,   Lyme, Connecticut, 16 July, 1910.

The interviews in the World of yesterday[1] forced my hand. I therefore telegraphed to The True American and to The Newark Evening News the statement which appears in this morning's papers. It seems to have made a lively impression, and to have made some persons very angry. I judge that the other aspirants for the nomination will not be quite as easy to handle as was anticipated. I would be the more sorry to have made trouble because my own position is so simple and I could myself so easily retire, if within a week or two the confusion should seem to be greater than the simplification.

On the assumption that things will clear a little in the near future, I will try my hand at the formulations of some resolutions for the consideration of the Resolutions Committee of the convention, should they care to consider them.

Evidently the cue is to be to represent me as put up by The Interests, as Judge Parker[2] was said to be, and to quote me as the enemy of organized labour; but no doubt I could take care of myself on those heads, if nominated with the proper unanimity.

Always,   Faithfully Yours,   Woodrow Wilson

WWTLS (WP, DLC).

[1] A news report (not an interview) headlined "Woodrow Wilson Is Candidate for Jersey Governor" appeared in the New York *World*, July 15, 1910. It consisted chiefly of a brief but essentially accurate account of Wilson's conference with Democratic party leaders of New Jersey held at the Lawyers' Club in New York on July 12, 1910, about which see the Editorial Note, "The Lawyers' Club Conference," printed in Vol. 20.

[2] Alton Brooks Parker, Democratic presidential candidate in 1904.

To Walter Hines Page

My dear Mr. Page,   Lyme, Connecticut, 16 July, 1910.

Your kind letter of the eleventh[1] has been forwarded to me here. I am likely to be here continuously for the next five or six weeks, and it would be a real pleasure to see you at any time. If you would be kind enough to telephone (Saybrook, 151, ring 12) beforehand, you could make sure of not missing me. I may, of course, be unexpectedly called away.

You have probably seen in the papers that I have got into trouble politically, and my sincere desire for the present, until I see whether the thing is really going to "come off," is to keep as silent as possible. To go into print just now would seem like trying to draw opinion to myself. But I dare say what you have in mind does not involve an early indiscretion on my part![2]

With much regard,

Sincerely Yours,   Woodrow Wilson

WWTLS (W. H. Page Papers, MH).
    [1] It is missing.
    [2] Page's son, Arthur Wilson Page, wrote an article, "Are the Colleges Doing Their Job?" *World's Work*, xx (Sept. 1910), 13,431-39, which included material indicating (p. 13,436) that he had had an interview with Wilson.

From Melancthon Williams Jacobus

My dear President Wilson: Watch Hill [R. I.] July 16, 10

Your note announcing the conclusion at which you had arrived in the proposition placed before you by Colonel Harvey, reached me here, forwarded from Hartford after I had written you.

I can easily understand the position in which you find yourself placed and feel you are doing the only thing which is really consistent with your well known views on one's duty to public affairs.

I cannot express what it has been to me to be associated with you in the consideration and working out of the problems of modern University education. It is sad to me to think of your laying aside your leadership in these affairs; but I wish you all the God-speed I am capable of in your new undertaking. May it be blessed not only to yourself, but what is far more important, to the political life of the country

Ever yours faithfully   M. W. Jacobus

ALS (WP, DLC).

From Archibald Stevens Alexander[1]

My dear Dr. Wilson,   Hoboken, N. J. July 16 [1910].

You probably don't remember me at Princeton, where I graduated in 1902, but after reading last night's Newark News, relative to your willingness, under certain circumstances, to run for Governor, and being myself much interested in New Jersey politics, particularly Democratic politics, I venture to write you in order to add my small voice to those that are urging you to run.

I myself have tried since I retired from the Legislature in 1907 to keep in fairly close touch with State politics, and I sincerely believe that with you at the head of the ticket we would be certain to carry the State this fall, and very probably control the Assembly. Almost all the independent voters of Essex, Bergen, Hudson & Passaic counties who are normally Republicans have lost all confidence in those who now control that party, and are only waiting till the Democrats nominate someone whom they can depend upon to be an improvement on their old leaders, to transfer their allegiance to the Democratic party, or at least to vote for a Democrat for Governor. You are, in my opinion, the only person in our party who can attract these voters in sufficient numbers to be elected. Both Wittpen[n] and Silzer[2] are close personal and political friends of mine, both are absolutely honest and free from the domination of either bosses or corporations, but neither can unite the Smith & Davis wings of the party, and neither's reputation is big enough to draw the Independents to him in sufficient numbers to win. Your powers as a speaker would enable you to explain the issues to the voters as no one else could, and we have several issues upon which to go before them. The extravagence, incompetence & neglect of duty of the various state departments, as disclosed by the Hahn Investigating Committee of 1907,[3] have not yet been corrected, the failure to enact a Railroad Bill with a clause therein giving power to regulate rates would appeal to the commuters in Essex, Bergen & Passaic, and the gross undervaluation of railroad property by the State Board of Assessors has stirred up Hudson County tremendously.

The Republicans have no one who would have a chance to beat you. Lewis[4] & Frelinghuysen[5] are the political bosses of their respective counties, Johnson's[6] association with corporations would kill him, besides I think many New Ideaites[7] would support you, secretly if not openly.

I hope therefore that you will permit your name to be used, and will accept the nomination, even if others may have some support in the convention.

Please excuse my inflicting my views on you. My excuse is that in your interview, as published, you said your final decision depended on the wishes of the members of the party, and I can vouch for the fact that many other Democrats all over the state feel as I do. Trusting that if I can be of service to you, now or during the campaign, you will call upon me,

            Faithfully yours,   Archibald S. Alexander

ALS (WP, DLC).

[1] Princeton 1902, member of the Hoboken law firm of Besson, Alexander & Stevens.

[2] George Sebastian Silzer of New Brunswick, jurist and Democratic state senator since 1907.

[3] Under a resolution of the lower house of the New Jersey legislature of April 12, 1907, a special committee of five assemblymen was chosen to investigate "charges of waste and extravagance in the expenditure of the appropriations for the various State departments and for the State capitol," which had been "freely made in the public prints." Under the chairmanship of Simon Hahn, Democratic assemblyman from Essex County, the committee carried on its investigations and presented majority and minority reports to the Assembly on June 20, 1907. The three Democratic members declared in the majority report that, in spite of the limited time available for the investigation, they had found in many departments and agencies "a studied indifference and disregard of official duty, as well as wanton, wasteful and reckless expenditure of public funds—in some instances involving moral obliquity and corrupt practices—matters which call for immediate correction at the hands of the Legislature." Among the specific abuses they described were failure by many state officials, including the State Treasurer, to deposit state monies in interest-bearing accounts, inadequate general supervision of the disbursement of funds by state departments and agencies, absenteeism among "high-salaried" state officials, and widespread plural officeholding. The majority made numerous recommendations for the combining of boards, commissions, and departments with overlapping functions, as well as the outright abolition of some which they considered entirely unnecessary. They further revealed much collusion and fraud in the construction of public buildings, most notably in the building of additions to the State House, for which all the planning had been done by a single architect and all the construction by a single contractor, both of whom were specifically charged with mismanagement and fraud. Finally, the majority members of the committee charged that the legislature itself had been guilty of extravagance in employing unnecessary clerks and doorkeepers and in purchasing "supplies" ranging from toothbrushes to typewriters.

The minority report of the two Republicans on the committee, while not denying that many serious abuses existed, disagreed with a number of the specific criticisms and recommendations made by the majority. See *Minutes of the Votes and Proceedings of the One Hundred and Thirty-First General Assembly of the State of New Jersey* (Trenton, N. J., 1907), pp. 1084, 1235-61.

[4] Vivian Murchison Lewis of Paterson, Passaic County, State Commissioner of Banking and Insurance, who was being mentioned as a possible Republican candidate for Governor.

[5] Joseph Sherman Frelinghuysen of Raritan, Somerset County, Republican state senator.

[6] William Mindred Johnson, Princeton 1867, of Hackensack, a lawyer associated with banking, insurance, and other corporations. Long active in New Jersey Republican politics, he was state senator, 1895-1900, and First Assistant Postmaster General of the United States, 1900-1902.

[7] The progressive wing of the Republican party in New Jersey.

Two Letters from Henry Eckert Alexander

Dear Dr. Wilson: Beach Haven, N. J. July 17, 1910.

I am spending the week-end at Beach Haven.

Your "statement" was exactly the thing. In my opinion it prepares the way for your unanimous nomination and election —and then! It means a political revolution in New Jersey and every man who has any political sense so understands it.

I do not regard the Jersey City complication as serious. Within a few days I hope to see the Mayor[1] or to communicate with him and I believe that I can make a demonstration to his mind that he cannot help himself but on the contrary will hurt himself by persisting in a candidacy that can bring only humiliation and discredit. *He doesn't have even a gambler's chance.* I assume that he has been badly advised and that he doesn't understand the political game.

Of course every Payroll Republican who has access to the newspapers (and they are numerous) will seek to disparage your candidacy but I believe that you are a philosopher as well as historian and that you will take the bitter with the sweet, particularly as there will be so little of the former and so much of the latter.

I have been testing sentiment. It can be shaped into something tremendous for you and your ideals.

Sincerely yours,   Henry E. Alexander.

1 That is, Henry Otto Wittpenn.

Dear Dr. Wilson: Trenton, New Jersey July 18, 1910.

As a matter of policy, so far as possible we speak of you as plain Woodrow Wilson, eliminating "the President" and "Dr." The True American editorial for tomorrow will be "the Job Holders vs. Wilson." It points out that the payroll beneficeries of the Republican machine are the only people hostile to the Wilson movement.

I talked with Mr. Van Valkenburg[1] over the phone tonight and he told me that the North American will say something editorially tomorrow.[2] He did not say what the line would be and as a Republican paper, *at this time* I do not care for it to go too far, but as he knows the political game pretty well we can trust him to help in every way.

It is refreshing to find that in spite of the opposition of the political crooks and time-servers, the people are rising to the occasion. Party lines are ignored in the demand for such a candidate.   Sincerely yours,   Henry E. Alexander.

My paper is read every day in the homes of 700 clergymen in New Jersey. That ought to count for something.

ALS (WP, DLC).
1 Edwin Augustus Van Valkenburg, editor and publisher of the Philadelphia *North American*.
2 The editorial in the Philadelphia *North American*, July 19, 1910, discussed the regeneration of the Democratic party with the emergence of such figures as Judson Harmon of Ohio, Mayor William J. Gaynor of New York, and Wilson.

From Cyrus Hall McCormick

My dear Woodrow: Chicago 18 July 1910.

Your letter of 14 July is received.[1]

I felt, at the conference with Messrs. Jones and McIlvaine when we sent you that telegram, that it was quite possible you might feel your duty as indicated in your present letter, and I sympathize with you most cordially in the way you look at the matter.

Since the Democratic Party left so fine a man as Grover Cleveland, I have not been able to vote for the Democratic ticket, as I should like to have done; and I am therefore, in a very good position to know the great service you would render the country if you should be elected as Governor of New Jersey and thus be placed in a position as a leader in the councils of the Party.

Whatever be the outcome, I shall stand gladly with you in any action that you feel it your duty to take with regard to this whole momentous question; and I appreciate more than I can express, the sentiments of friendship and affection which you send me in this letter, as you have already signified them so many times before.

With most cordial regards to you and Mrs. Wilson, I am,
Yours,   Cyrus H. McCormick.
S.

TLS (WP, DLC).
[1] WW to C. H. McCormick, July 14, 1910, Vol. 20.

From Winthrop More Daniels

My dear Wilson: Princeton, N. J. July 18, 1910

. . . I have seen an abridged copy of your statement as to the Governorship, and do not see how it could have been bettered. It is not necessary for me to say that I hope you may be spared to us at Princeton; but I am quite clear in my mind that no obligation rested on you to exclude the very possibility of a nomination. As a mere matter of mathematical probabilities, I feel that the lesser (State) office is likely to afford only a small chance of capturing something larger in 1912—so many contingencies obtrude —but the small chance, while hazardous, is the only avenue of approach to the larger one. Knowing practically nothing of the overtures you doubtless have been receiving, my advice is worth but little, but my most sincere wishes for success are yours. It occurs to me only to suggest, that should the nomination seem likely to materialize, it would add immensely to your peace of mind to retain as a confidential adviser some capable, clear-headed, and clear sighted man—I have Fulton McMahon in mind —who could be relied on to decide the *modus operandi* in many a juncture when you ought not to allow yourself to be perplexed with any but the broader issues pertinent to the campaign. Could you not retain McMahon in the capacity of private counsel? I am tolerably sure he is a Democrat, and our local troubles have demonstrated his sagacity and his attitude towards your educational policy.

With very best regards,   Yours ever,   W. M. Daniels.

ALS (WP, DLC).

From Dan Fellows Platt[1]

Dear Dr. Wilson,   N. Y. City July 18. 1910

"Princeton for the Nation's service"—as exemplified in your attitude toward the Governorship—puts heart into every Democrat who loves his party, who realizes its present opportunity and the fact that that opportunity is a lost one unless both men and measures come to the call.

I realize your attitude of not courting a nomination—and so will say what I have to say on a tentative basis, so far as you are concerned—and yet at the same time stating that I put the matter in this way only because I want to spare you any burden that you may want to be spared.

Bergen County is to have a Democratic County Convention this year—somewhat informal in its selection of delegates—as the direct primary fills the Convention's place. Bergen has of late years been rather strongly Republican, owing to the influx of anti-Tammany commuters. We Democrats have trouble in assimilating these as fast as they pour in upon us. As a Republican county, it has been rather hard to get able men to run for the legislature on the Democratic ticket. I realize the evils of the Convention system, but we have no "machine" in our party in Bergen, & we feel that a Convention called for the purpose of urging good men to run, will be all right. This Convention will be held in Hackensack on the afternoon of Saturday, Aug 20th & afterwards there will be a dinner with four or five hundred present. I write as Chairman of the Committee on Arrangements to ask if you can come and talk to us at that time. I feel certain that events are so shaping themselves as to make your nomination inevitable and we want our standard bearer to come to us and show our county that he is what a goodly number of our Princeton Bergenites already know him to be. . . . If, in say a couple of weeks from now, you find things shaping toward your nomination—will you not take the burden upon yourself of coming to us? We'll give you a royal welcome, and if I might keep you for the night in Englewood, it would add to our pleasure. If you care to send an answer now, even though you wish to make it conditional, I'll be glad of it.

Yours sincerely   Dan Fellows Platt ('95.)

ALS (WP, DLC).
    [1] Princeton 1895, of Englewood, N. J., gentleman of independent means, former lawyer and Mayor of Englewood, 1904-1906, at this time Democratic state committeeman from Bergen County.

From Zephaniah Charles Felt

My dear Wilson,   Seaview, Wash July 18, 1910.

I am away out here on the Pacific Coast near the north bank of the Columbia River with my family for a summer vacation. In a press dispatch sent out from Newark, I read that you may accept the nomination for Governor. Now I don't want to keep always offering suggestions to you, but my excuse is my interest in and admiration of your self and what you have already done and are yet to accomplish. Last spring, one of your bitterest opponents unfolded to me quite at length the plans they hoped to carry into effect to get you out of Princeton. And one of these was to convince you that it was *your duty* to accept the nomination. Whether you were elected or not was immaterial—they planned that the nomination would be sufficient to get you out. And it looks to me as if these plans they are now seeking to carry into effect. This information was not given to me in confidence, but even if it were, considering the infamous methods adopted by the opposition, I would still consider that I was justified in communicating it to you. I left Denver just before Com[mencement]. and have been travelling so much that I have had no news whatever of P'ton matters. I understood that growing out of the Wyman bequest came a renewal of the Procter offer and a general peace making. However this may be, I am sure that the ambitions of certain parties remain just the same. If you wish to write me, a letter addressed to Seaview, Wash, will reach me. With kindest regards in which Mrs. Felt[1] joins most cordially, believe me,   Yours sincerely   Zeph. Chas. Felt

ALS (WP, DLC).
    [1] Nora Belle Harker Felt.

From Charles Williston McAlpin

My dear Dr. Wilson: [Princeton, N. J.] July 19, 1910.

I enclose a letter from Dean West[1] for your consideration and shall be very glad to carry out your suggestions in the matter. Would it not be a good plan to send another letter to Professor [Augustus] Trowbridge in view of the condition of the original letter, referred to by Dean West.

It is with a heart full of sadness that I write to say that Miss Thompson[2] died on Sunday morning after an illness of a few weeks. She was operated on on Wednesday of last week but did not have sufficient strength to rally from the effects of the operation.

Everything seems to be quiet in Princeton and the change from the hot weather of last week is most refreshing.

Mrs. McAlpin[3] and I are planning to spend August at St. Hubert's Inn,[4] and I shall try to clean up matters here before leaving in order that I may devote my time to rest and recreation while I am away.

With kindest regards to Mrs. Wilson and yourself,
        Ever faithfully and sincerely yours,   [C. W. McAlpin]

CCL (McAlpin File, UA, NjP).
    [1] The enclosure is missing, and its contents are unknown.
    [2] Suzanne Dawes Thompson of Trenton, confidential secretary to McAlpin, died on July 17, 1910.
    [3] Sara Carter Pyle McAlpin.
    [4] In the Adirondacks.

To Charles Williston McAlpin

My dear McAlpin,   Lyme, Connecticut, 20 July, 1910.

It grieves me deeply to hear of Miss Thompson's death. She seemed a fine, trustworthy woman. I fear you will miss her greatly, and that her death will for some time to come add to your work and care. I hope that [Gilbert Fairchild] Close will stand you in good stead at this turning point.

I would be very much obliged to you if you would be kind enough to have the letter prepared which West suggests. We ought to be in the polite class. I am very much obliged to you for attending to the matter.

I hope you have not been grieved by what I have felt obliged to do about the governorship. It cost me many an anxious hour before I could see what appeared to be my duty; and I may have mistaken it. What made me most loath was the thought of the

men, like yourself, whom I *might* be losing my close associations
with.   Affectionately Yours,   Woodrow Wilson

WWTLS (photostat in RSB Coll., DLC).

To Adolphus Ragan[1]

My dear Mr. Ragan,   Lyme, Connecticut, 20 July, 1910.

Your letter of July fifth[2] is most kind and generous, and I want
to thank you for it very warmly. It cheers and reassures me.

I was in great doubt as to what it was my duty to do with regard to the suggested nomination for the governorship. I did not
know where my duty lay, at Princeton, where a great work remains only half done, or in the larger field of politics. The people
of the State will have to decide for me. I have always taught the
men in my classes that educated men owed it to the country to
take advantage of every legitimate opportunity to serve the country politically. I could do no less than follow my own teachings.

With warmest appreciation,
                    Sincerely Yours,   Woodrow Wilson

TCL (RSB Coll., DLC).
  [1] An accountant of New York and member of the New York Southern Society.
  [2] It is missing.

An Interview

[*July* 20, *1910*]

WILSON—PLAIN, BUT DIGNIFIED; GENIAL, BUT WISE;
A DEMOCRAT IN EVERY SENSE OF THE WORD

Intimate Interview with Jersey's Most Widely
Known Citizen.

Lyme, Conn., July 20.—Woodrow Wilson, prospective Governor of New Jersey and President of the United States, and at
present one of the most-talked-of men in the east, is a revelation
to those who meet him for the first time as plain citizen Woodrow
Wilson, one of the most democratic and readily approachable
big men of today.

As an educator, as a master of all the leading issues of the
present time and one who possesses an apparently prophetic view
of what the near future has in store, the president of Princeton
University needs no introduction to the people of this State or any
other section of the country.

Gauged by that standard, some who oppose the nomination of

Dr. Wilson as Democratic candidate for Governor and have no other reason for their opposition, declare that Woodrow Wilson is too big a man for the office of Governor of New Jersey.

Dr. Wilson's view, tersely expressed to your reporter yesterday, is: "There is no man 'too big' for the office of Governor of New Jersey, the highest within the gift of its electorate. As for myself, I am, and will always remain, Woodrow Wilson regardless of what office my fellow citizens may call upon me to accept."

As the man who many believe will undoubtedly be the next Governor of the State, made that assertion on the porch of his summer home at Old Lyme, Conn., yesterday, he looked and acted exactly what he said. Unaffected, dignified, the very essence of democracy in his demeanor, affable and ready to discuss any subject other than himself or political issues at the present time —that is Citizen Woodrow Wilson of today.

Well informed on every move in the political maneuvers of both parties in this State, made as they are decidedly interesting for the first time in many years because of the injection of his name, with his own consent, Dr. Wilson is neither perturbed nor elated over the comments his expressed willingness to accept the nomination, if tendered, have provoked.

In response to a query as to whether he had anything further to say in regard to his prospective nomination, Dr. Wilson said he preferred not to do so at the present time. Urged to talk about himself, Dr. Wilson pleasantly dismissed the proposition with: "That is something I am always averse to doing. I prefer to leave that to others, and the task seems to be pretty well taken care of at present."

Dr. Wilson made no effort to conceal the fact that he is pleased with the favorable view of his candidacy, expressed by some of the leading papers of the country. Neither did he attempt to withhold the fact that he is anxious as well as ready to become the nominee of his party, if the majority thereof in convention so declares.

"For the present," said Dr. Wilson, "I prefer to stand on the statement already issued. It was my effort to make that statement as lucid and positive as seemed necessary at the time. To add to it by discussing important issues or answering implied criticisms of any of my previous utterances, would place me in the position of a candidate seeking the nomination.

"That would be contradictory, and place me in a position I am not ready to assume. The active candidates for the nomination, as well as the people of the State, know just exactly where I stand.

"Prior to issuing my statement[,] Mayor Wittpenn, who is among the list of candidates for the nomination, called here and informed me of efforts that were being made to have him withdraw in favor of my candidacy.

"I assured Mayor Wittpenn that I entertained no desire to have him or any other aspirant retire on my account, and added that I was in a receptive mood, and stood willing to accept the nomination if the party decided to tender it."

That Dr. Wilson is very much in earnest and actually expects —as almost everybody else does—that he will be the nominee was made apparent, indirectly, by the evident interest he displays in the still unsolved problem of who is likely to be the Republican nominee for Governor.

"There is some talk of Chancellor Mahlon Pitney being the Republican nominee," remarked Dr. Wilson, "and if that should occur and I were his opponent the contest would be an interesting one. We were classmates at Princeton, and gradutaed [graduated] at the same time, 31 years ago."

For a moment or two Dr. Wilson was thoughtful, as though outlining a plan of campaign. Then he resumed:

"It would be an interesting contest in many respects, and a warm one, the very kind I like, having been through many of them, and I am not worried as to the outcome."

Printed in the Trenton *True American*, July 21, 1910; some editorial headings omitted.

From Josiah Townsend Woodhull, Jr.[1]

Dear Dr. Wilson,   San Antonio, Texas. July 20, 1910.

It is with the same diffidence that I have always approached you in person that I now do in writing. For my request is so petty in comparison with the demands which are made upon you, that I dislike the office which forces upon me the duty of making it. Yet the gracious way in which you have received me in the past, makes it possible for me to again address you.

The matter in hand is the contribution to The Nassau Literary Magazine from your pen. You consented to my rather trembly request on the night of the Press Club Banquet; and if it is still convenient for you to write the article, Mr. Porter,[2] the managing editor instructs me that we would like to have it by September 25.[3]

Dr. van Dyke contributed to the May issue,[4] and a short sketch —an "appreciation" of his work—written by one of the editors appeared in the same issue.[5] I have been appointed to write an article on you, provided that this is not displeasing.[6]

I hope that this request will to no degree keep you from spending a pleasant and recreative vacation, though to be frank, I fear that it may be a good deal of an inconvenience and a bore to you. I think, however, that there will be satisfaction for you—knowing the interest with which everything from you is read by the students and the helpful influence it exerts—in thus reaching them and at the same time helping greatly so worthy a feature of our undergraduate life as the Lit.

I am very respectfully yours,   J. T. Woodhull, Jr.

ALS (WP, DLC).
  [1] Princeton 1911.
  [2] James Jackson Porter, Princeton 1911.
  [3] Wilson's article, "Life and Education," is printed at Aug. 1, 1910.
  [4] Henry van Dyke, "Brief Thoughts on Large Themes," *Nassau Literary Magazine*, LXVI (May 1910), 73-74.
  [5] Robert Shafer, "Henry Van Dyke—An Appreciation," *ibid.*, pp. 75-78.
  [6] He did not publish an article about Wilson.

To Edward Field Goltra

My dear Mr. Goltra: Lyme, Connecticut, 21 July, 1910.

Thank you most warmly for your letter of the seventeenth,[1] which has been forwarded to me here. It was an act of most thoughtful kindness on your part to write it.

I feel very queer adventuring upon the sea of politics, and my voyage may be brief; but after what I have been preaching to my classes all these years about the duty of educated men to accept every legitimate opportunity for political service, I did not see what else I could do.

With much regard,
Sincerely Yours,   Woodrow Wilson

WWTLS (received from David W. Steck).
  [1] It is missing.

From George Brinton McClellan Harvey

Dear Mr. Wilson,   New York July 21 [1910].

There is little new. Most of the inevitable steam from advocates of personal friends seems to have been blown off and things are settling down. [Eugene Francis] Kinkead was so eager to get himself into the limelight as a real leader that he talked too much and too soon. But perhaps it's just as well to have the little splutter over. The story in the Newark Star[1] was bully.

I inclose a few clippings,[2] some of which are amusing.
Sincerely Yours   G H

ALS (WP, DLC).
[1] The interview printed at July 20, 1910, had also appeared in the *Newark Evening Star* on that day.
[2] They are missing.

From Nathan Straus[1]

My dear Dr. Wilson,   Oberhof i. Th. [Germany], July 21, 1910.

I read with great pleasure in yesterday's paper that you had signified your willingness to accept the nomination for Governor of New Jersey, if the Democrats of that state should ask you to be their candidate. It would be a good thing for the Democratic party of New Jersey, as well as of every other state, to put into office a man of your type, of whom unfortunately we have not many. It is to the well trained, vigorous young men of to-day that the party must look for its regeneration. And New Jersey will have gone a long way in the march of civic progress, if she makes you her Governor. Your candidacy is an honor to the party and your election would be an honor to the state. I look for the nation to call you to the greater honor of the presidency.

I congratulate the Democrats of New Jersey on their choice no less than I congratulate you on your acceptance.

                    Very sincerely,   Nathan Straus

HwLS (WP, DLC).
[1] Philanthropist and owner and partner (with his brother Isidor) of R. H. Macy & Co. of New York and of Abraham and Straus of Brooklyn. Brother of Oscar Solomon Straus.

From Archibald Stevens Alexander

My dear Dr. Wilson: Hoboken, N. J. July 22, 1910.

Your very kind letter of July 20th reached me yesterday and it goes without saying that if any matters come to my attention which may be of interest to you I shall be only too glad to inform you of them for whatever such information may be worth.

We have a rather peculiar local condition here in Hoboken which explains the Observer's[1] attitude towards you. Last fall, Mr. Lawrence Fagan, who controls the policy of the Observer, and who has been for years the bitter foe of Robert Davis, defeated the Davis candidate for the Democratic nomination for Mayor at the primaries, but was himself defeated on election day by the Republican candidate. Since Hoboken has not gone republican for twenty-six years, Fagan very naturally attributes his defeat to the disloyalty of the Davis wing of the Party, and is waiting for a chance to get even. The Anti-Davis democrats are in a small majority in Hoboken and the Democratic City Committee has recently declared its independence of the Davis County Committee.

In Jersey City last year, Wittpenn was renominated by Davis for Mayor, not because Davis wanted him, but because Wittpenn had made such a good record that his renomination was imperative in order to beat Mark Fagan, the New Idea Republican candidate.[2] Since Wittpenn's election he has broken with Davis completely and has done what he could to build up an organization of his own. His candidacy for governor is most distasteful to Davis and has therefore given an opportunity to the Fagan element of the Democratic Party in Hoboken to retaliate for their defeat last fall. They are making the most of this and will undoubtedly combine with the Anti-Davis democrats of Jersey City and other parts of the County to elect delegates to the State Convention which will be pledged to Wittpenn. I believe that they will carry Hoboken and Bayonne, but the rest of the County will elect Davis delegates and will therefore give Davis at least a two-thirds majority of the Hudson County delegation.[3]

I have maintained an absolutely neutral attitude so far and although I voted for the Davis candidate for Mayor at the primaries last year, I supported Fagan after he was nominated and presided at the big meeting that was held here for him. My sympathies however, entirely aside from your candidacy, are with Davis. He never asked me to do anything which I did not want to do when I was in the legislature and never has since. Although as a local boss he is no better or no worse than the average boss, he is, I think, distinctly better than the average, when it comes to dealing with the legislative delegation from this county, which is apparent when one reviews the legislative career of men like Hamill,[4] Kinkead, Sullivan[5] and Tumulty.[6] While I think that one of his objects in supporting you for Governor is because he thinks you are the strongest candidate for him to use in order to beat Wittpenn, yet I believe that he will sincerely support you after you are nominated. I also think that the Observer will support you after the primaries, as they think nothing of making the most acrobatic changes politically.

I am going away a week from to-day for three weeks vacation. Upon my return I hope to devote myself more or less to politics and shall be a candidate for delegate to the State convention from my district in Hoboken, although I shall probably be defeated by the Fagan people.[7] However, even if I am I shall try to be of whatever use I can to you in other ways, both before and after the primaries.

I cannot too strongly express my admiration for the public spirit and dignity which you have shown and which I have heard favorably commented upon on all sides (except by the Observer). You have probably noticed that your candidacy has already alarmed the Republicans, as may be seen from the talk of Chancellor Pitney as a candidate against you instead of Vivian Lewis.

Again thanking you for your kind letter,

Sincerely yours,   Archibald S. Alexander.

TLS (WP, DLC).
1 The Hoboken *Observer*.
2 Mark Matthew Fagan, Mayor of Jersey City, 1902-1907.
3 Alexander's prediction was correct.
4 James Alphonsus Hamill, lawyer of Jersey City, at this time United States representative from the 10th congressional district, which included part of Jersey City and vicinity.
5 Mark Anthony Sullivan, lawyer of Jersey City; New Jersey assemblyman, 1907-1910. He was appointed judge of the New Jersey Court of Errors and Appeals on December 6, 1910.
6 Joseph Patrick Tumulty, lawyer of Jersey City, member of the New Jersey Assembly, 1907-1910.
7 The Editors have been unable to discover whether Alexander was elected to the New Jersey state Democratic convention.

From Henry Smith Pritchett

Teignmouth, S. Devon.
My dear President Wilson,   July 22, 1910

I have just seen with great interest your statement in the New York Press concerning the Governorship of New Jersey. Whether you decide to become a candidate or not I am certain your decision will be upon the most sincere and patriotic grounds. Personally I believe it would be enormously for the good of the country if men like you would stand for political office. With sincere good wishes,   Faithfully yours,   Henry S. Pritchett

ALS (WP, DLC).

From William Lawrence Wilson[1]

My dear Doctor Wilson: Chicago, July 22nd, 1910.

Please allow me to congratulate you upon your decision to consent to be a candidate for the Governorship of New Jersey.

I am sorry that I am not a citizen of that State, so that I could work for you, because nothing would give me greater pleasure. I hope, however, that two years from now I may have an opportunity of doing this work, when you will stand for national honors.

Incidentally, you have a very strong following in the city of Chicago among all classes. I am not speaking of the small circle of Princeton men by any means, but of the entire respectable class. I have talked with a great many people in different walks of life about your possible candidacy for presidential honors, and you have always been spoken of in the highest terms. You would be astonished to know how exceedingly well known you are in this district; especially when the fact is taken into consideration that you have only appeared in public here twice. The better class of men, Republicans and Democrats, are almost unanimously for you, and will watch the Elections in New Jersey this fall with great interest.

Although I cannot imagine my being able to help you from this distance, I promise you to do everything I can, should the opportunity present itself.

With very best wishes for your success, and with kindest regards, I remain,

Yours truly,   William L Wilson "03"

TLS (WP, DLC).
[1] Princeton 1903, salesman for the Aluminum Company of America in Chicago.

From William T. Ferguson[1]

Dear Sir: Washington, D. C., July 22, 1910.

I am a member of an organization of colored men known as the Independent League. We realize that our political past was ill advised. We also realize that all democrats are not our enemies nor are all republicans friends. We intend to support men and principles in the future.

Our annual convention meets at Atlantic City August 4th and 5th and I would be pleased to circulate the information that you were not unfriendly to our people and that if you were the next nominee for governor that you would welcome the support of colored men.

I will not quote *you* unless you permit me.

May I have the pleasure of so doing?

Very respectfully,   Wm. T. Ferguson

TLS (WP, DLC).
[1] A "messenger" of 1420 Pierce Place, Washington, and secretary of the National Independent Political League, with headquarters in the national capital. The National Independent Political League, founded in 1908 as the Negro-American Political League, was largely an outgrowth of the National Afro-American Council and the Afro-American League, formed in 1898 and 1890, respectively. The leaders of the Negro-American Political League were Bishop Alexander Walters of the African Methodist Episcopal Zion Church; William Monroe Trotter, editor of the Boston *Guardian*; William H. Scott, president of the Boston

Suffrage League; and J. Milton Waldron, who served as the N.A.P.L.'s first president. The organization opposed Booker T. Washington's leadership and proposed a militant style of protest. It also attempted to persuade black voters to defeat Republicans and especially William Howard Taft in the election of 1908. Finally, it tried to combat the growing prominence of William E. B. Du Bois and his Niagara Movement. After the defeat of William J. Bryan in 1908, the N.A.P.L. reorganized in 1909 as the National Independent Political League. Walters and Trotter were its most prominent leaders, and it continued to try to break down the traditional Republican allegiance of most Negro voters. For additional identification of Du Bois, the Niagara Movement, and the leaders of the N.I.P.L., see W. T. Ferguson to WW, Oct. 7, 1910, notes 1, 3, 4, and 5.

To Dan Fellows Platt

My dear Mr. Platt,   Lyme, Connecticut, 23 July, 1910.

Your letter of the eighteenth, which reached me only last night (having gone astray under a wrong address), gratified me very deeply, and reassured me in matters which I have not felt clear about. I have been in great doubt as to my duty in this whole political matter, as compared with my unfinished tasks at Princeton.

I wish most unaffectedly that I could say Yes to the interesting invitation it conveys. The task you have in hand in Bergen appeals to me most strongly, to the fighting instinct that is in me and which makes the uphill business the really interesting one. But it is my very clear judgment that the best impression on the voters of Bergen, as of all other parts of the State, so far as I am concerned, would be made by my keeping off the stump until the convention has met,—by my keeping consistently in the background. I cannot afford to do anything inconsistent with my published "statement," even if I were inclined to. Nothing less than a very clear judgment in this matter would make me feel justified in declining an invitation such as this your letter brings; but the conviction is very clear.

I can only thank you very heartily, therefore, and again say how much I have been reassured by your view of what I have ventured to do.

With warmest regard,
Faithfully Yoors,   Woodrow Wilson

WWTLS (photostat in RSB Coll., DLC).

From Henry Eckert Alexander

Dear Dr. Wilson: Trenton, New Jersey July 23, 1910.

You will see by Monday's True American that a labor leader— one Michael McIntire—attacked you in the Saturday issue of the

Times.[1] Now, McIntire fought Mayor Madden[2] at the last election so his Democracy's is not worth much here.

The *Times* has done much to encourage Mr. Katzenbach,[3] whom the *Times* has never liked. My guess is that Kerney,[4] editor of the *Times*, is expecting Senator Smith to "see" him and that he feels "miffed" that this has not been done. . . .

As to the Hoboken Observer man,[5] I know nothing directly. I am told that he opposed and criticized Katzenbach three years ago and that he is as independent as that New York policeman who said: "I bate you, not because I hate you, but to show my aut'ority over you."

Meanwhile every Republican gangster is seeking to make trouble for they know that your election will follow your nomination and then "house-cleaning!" The proofs of your strength are increasing every day.

Sincerely yours,   Henry E. Alexander.

ALS (WP, DLC).

1 Michael F. McIntyre, president of the Central Labor Union, a Trenton organization with a membership of over 7,000, issued a statement which was printed in the *Trenton Evening Times*, July 23, 1910. In it, he declared that Wilson not only would "not receive the support of organized labor, but we will be found in the field fighting him for his well known antagonism to the union wage worker." He also predicted that the state-wide federation of labor would take some action against Wilson. Finally, he gave his personal endorsement to the candidacy of Frank Snowden Katzenbach, Jr., identified in n. 3 below. Henry Eckert Alexander reprinted McIntyre's statement in the Trenton *True American*, July 25, 1910, as part of a news story in which he sought to belittle McIntyre's importance as a leader of organized labor and charged that he was a disappointed office-seeker. He also attacked McIntyre and defended Wilson's position on labor in an editorial in the same issue.

2 Walter Madden, M.D., a practicing physician and Mayor of Trenton, 1908-11.

3 Princeton 1889, Mayor of Trenton, 1902-1906, unsuccessful Democratic candidate for governor in 1907, and again, in 1910, a leading contender for the gubernatorial nomination.

4 James Kerney, editor of the *Trenton Evening Times* and vice-president of the Trenton Times Co.

5 That is, Lawrence Fagan.

From Joseph Albert Dear, Jr.

My dear "Governor"   Jersey City, N. J. July 23d, 1910.

I hope you will not think this rude even though you may regard it as somewhat crude. At any rate I can assure you "them's my sentiments."[1]

If you have anything to say at any time in regard to any of the questions at issue in the coming campaign I hope you will take advantage of the columns of the Jersey Journal which you will always find open to you.

And by the way when you start to stump for votes just recollect that any time you are in Jersey City, the latch-string on the Jersey

Journal sanctum hangs on the outside and there is always a warm welcome within awaiting you.

Yours sincerely,   Joseph A Dear

TLS (WP, DLC).

¹ The enclosure, "Must a Democrat Be an Ass?" appeared in the Jersey City *Jersey Journal*, July 22, 1910. Dear declared that, with Woodrow Wilson now a gubernatorial candidate, the Democratic party in New Jersey had a rare opportunity to select as its standardbearer "a man whose very candidacy would shed lustre upon his party and upon the State, and whose name upon the ticket would result either in a Democratic victory or the election of a Republican at least comparable in public esteem to the distinguished man who presides to-day over Princeton University." Yet, Dear continued, within the New Jersey Democracy there were those who were attempting to discredit Wilson in order to further other "would-be candidates of much smaller calibre." He went on to defend Wilson's controversial statements on organized labor and his well-known lack of enthusiasm for William Jennings Bryan as a three-time presidential candidate. Dear concluded with a series of rhetorical questions challenging the party to seize its opportunity to nominate Wilson.

To Alfred L. Parker¹

My Dear Mr. Parker: [Lyme, Conn., c. July 24, 1910]

I warmly appreciate the kind invitation conveyed in your letter of the 20th,² which reached me in this somewhat inaccessible place only last night. It would give me real pleasure to accept if I did not feel bound by an engagement already made for the 27th from which I cannot in courtesy and fairness withdraw.

Please express to the committee of the League my warm appreciation and sincere regret.

With much regard,

Sincerely yours,   Woodrow Wilson.

P.S.—May we not hope that after this "outing," our party may soon have an "inning."   W. W.

Printed in the Trenton *True American*, July 26, 1910.

¹ Secretary of the Democratic League of Trenton, an organization of progressive Democrats.

² It is missing; however, it conveyed an invitation to Wilson to attend an outing of the Democratic League in Trenton on July 27.

To George Brinton McClellan Harvey

My dear Colonel Harvey,   Lyme, Connecticut, 26 July, 1910.

Here is a letter that has just come to me to-night from Mr. Alexander of the TRUE AMERICAN.¹ I think that you ought to see it.

I do not understand this Katzenbach busines[s] at all.² I thought that the matter of his candidacy had been disposed of before my willingness to be considered was announced, and I begin to fear that I may be put in a rather ridiculous position.

I of course declined to attend the rally at Trenton to-morrow. To have accepted the invitation would have been to get into the competition for popular favour, which is just what I said I would not do, by plain implication, in my statement to the papers.

I am keeping a quiet mind; but I fear that you will be caused a great deal of trouble and anxiety before the tangle in N. J. is unraveled.

With warmest regard,

Faithfully Yours,   Woodrow Wilson

WWTLS (WP, DLC).
 1 It is missing.
 2 That is, that the movement in Mercer County for Katzenbach was gaining rather than losing momentum.

To Robert Garrett

My dear Mr. Garrett,   Lyme, Connecticut, 26 July, 1910.

I want to thank you most warmly for your letter of the fifteenth, and especially for the perfect frankness with which it is written. You could not give me a better proof of your friendship.

What you say about the possibility of my leaving Princeton has made a deep impression upon me. I must admit that it has made me quite unhappy; for I had gone too far, in agreeing to let my name be considered for the gubernatorial nomination, to draw back, and yet I felt very keenly that what I had done seemed to one of my best friends, and one of the most valued of them all, a great mistake.

When I review the circumstances it again seems to me that I could not have done otherwise, in view of my well known principles about public service on the part of informed and educated men, but nothing grips me like the opinion of those I trust and believe in, and I find myself wishing that things had not moved so fast and that I had not been obliged to commit myself before consulting you.

The only comfort I take from it all is that you evidently value my services to the University very highly. It is delightful, at any rate, to be regarded as in some degree indispensable.

I wish I could regard our recent fight at Princeton as virtually won. I could, if West were not left in a position of extraordinary power in respect of the development of the graduate school. He can break any man's heart who tries to administer the thing in the true university spirit. It seems more than ever impracticable to put aside a man who has wrecked one administration[1] and done all in his power to neutralize the work of another.

With warmest regard, and genuine gratitude for your real kindness,

Cordially and faithfully Yours,   Woodrow Wilson

WWTLS (Selected Corr. of R. Garrett, NjP).
[1] Of his predecessor, Francis Landey Patton.

To Mary Allen Hulbert Peck

Dearest Friend,   Lyme, Connecticut, 26 July, 1910.

I am hoping to be in New York tomorrow, to attend the meeting of the Mutual Life Board. I shall lunch with the Board and then hurry up to see you. I shall hope to be at No. 39[1] by (say) two o'clock or a little after. I must take the five o'clock train back.

I hope that this dreadful heated spell has not made you ill or pulled you down. I shall be anxious to see how you look after it.

My warmest regards to Mrs. Allen and your son.

In haste,   Your devoted friend,   Woodrow Wilson

WWTLS (WP, DLC).
[1] Her apartment at 39 East 27th St., New York.

From Henry Eckert Alexander

Dear Dr. Wilson: Trenton, New Jersey July 27, 1910.

I have seen some of our friends potent in political matters and I am sure that nothing important will be overlooked looking toward effective management and organization.

Our conversation over the telephone was "not only difficult; it was impossible."

All that I meant to say was a suggestion as to your letter of regret,[1] but it was not important.

The "outing" was a great success, but the powder had been burned and so the "tremendous ovation"[2] didn't count for much.

I learn that the *owner*[3] of the Hoboken Observer is hostile to Davis and so the poor *editor*[4] takes it out on you. It is pretty hard for a gentleman to act as "the goat" but there you are! I understand that the owner is to be taken in hand.

As to the general situation, I am sure that it will work out splendidly. . . .

Sincerely yours,   Henry E. Alexander.

ALS (WP, DLC).

¹ That is, that he could not attend the Democratic outing in Trenton. See WW to A. F. Parker, July 24, 1910.

² Although neither newspaper used the phrase "tremendous ovation," both the Trenton *True American* and the *Trenton Evening Times* agreed that Frank S. Katzenbach, Jr., received by far the most enthusiastic reception from the crowd at the outing.

³ That is, Lawrence Fagan.

⁴ Matthias Cowell Ely.

From George Brinton McClellan Harvey

Dear Mr. Wilson,   New York Thursday [July 28, 1910]

I have your letter of the 26th, inclosing Alexander's. As it happened, on the same day Alexander had spent the morning with me at Deal. He is a good fellow but not a heavy weight. His fretting was more on his own account than on yours. Tom Mc-Carter[1] was threatening to shut off his electrical power, as he was somewhat in arrears, etc. It was all very cheap and McCarterish, but easily disposed of. Alexander's suggestion about "working up from the bottom" related to the use of boiler plate stuff in the little papers. It is a notion drawn from Ohio and of little moment but I told him to go ahead.

Katzenbach has simply been playing fast and loose. He told Gallegher,[2] the Mercer state committeeman, he was definitely out and then two days later put out his silly statement with his most injured air.[3] What he had really hoped was that he would be implored to take the nomination without being asked to contribute to the campaign fund. His mother,[4] I believe, objected to playing the angel a second time. Gallegher says she was disgruntled also because her boy wasn't appointed a full Professor at Princeton.[5] It sounds like small potatoes and so it is and has to be because it's small potatoes we're dealing with. But it doesn't amount to a hill of beans and will work itself out with the froth stirred up by the Republicans who know they are gone if you become the nominee.

I saw Senator Smith this morning. He says everything is working along as satisfactorily as it is quietly. He talked with Davis yesterday about a somewhat audacious proposal of mine to hold our convention *first*—chiefly to make a predicament for Pitney. Davis approved and we plan now to hold the convention on the 15th of Sept., just two days after the primaries.

Of course, politics is "mighty onsartin" but I cannot see the remotest possibility of your finding yourself in a position anywhere approaching ridiculous. The chaps who feed at the public crib and write for little papers will try to nag you and make trouble as heretofore, but all their fiddling *won't change a vote.*

We are not feeding the flames for them naturally, but simply keeping things in hand and letting them beat their heads against the wall. I can't see that you have anything to do but stand pat. You may and doubtless will continue to be berated somewhat on account of the friends you have made, but I guess you can stand that. The situation surely can, since nobody has the hardihood to asperse yourself. Of course, you couldn't go to the absurd picnic. Nobody expected you to. Your note in response was bully.

I inclose a few clippings and a proof of a piece I am printing in next week's *Weekly*.[6]

As ever   Faithfully Yours   George Harvey

ALS (WP, DLC).

[1] Thomas Nesbitt McCarter, Jr., Princeton 1888, president of the Public Service Corporation of New Jersey.

[2] Charles Henry Gallagher, in the coal business in Trenton and a member of the Democratic State Committee for Mercer County.

[3] Katzenbach issued a statement to the press on July 25, 1910, in which he considerably modified his earlier assertion that he was not a candidate for the governorship. While still claiming that he did not want the nomination, he said that if the "contingency" of his being nominated should actually occur, he would accept. "No loyal Democrat would fail to respond to a draft by his party," he continued. "If drafted, being neither insensible to nor ungrateful for past honors, I would respond to the call." Trenton *True American*, July 26, 1910.

[4] Augusta Mushbach (Mrs. Frank Snowden) Katzenbach.

[5] Edward Lawrence Katzenbach, Princeton 1900, had been Instructor in Political Economy at Princeton, 1902-1903. At this time he was practicing law in Trenton.

[6] Harvey's editorial, "The Effect of a Candidacy," appeared in *Harper's Weekly*, LIV (Aug. 6, 1910), 4. The main thrust of its argument was that Wilson's mere announcement that he would accept the gubernatorial nomination had immeasurably elevated the character of politics in New Jersey and elsewhere. The "managers" of both major political parties now found it necessary to present superior rather than "average" candidates for all offices. Thus, something important had been accomplished even if Wilson was not elected or even nominated for Governor of New Jersey.

From William T. Ferguson

My dear Sir,   Washington, D. C., July 28, 1910.

Yours of the 26th. inst. is very gratifying and if I were near you I would grasp your hand and thank you for your manly words. I will regard your letter as personal until the time comes when I may tell my people what your sentiments are and what you hope for from them. If you are the nominee, you will not get all of the colored vote. There are yet a great many of my people who are deaf to all reason but we are making good headway among the middle aged and younger element. With the assistance of gentlemen of your standing we expect to be worthy of notice by the next presidential campaign. . . .

Champion our cause whenever you can, Professor, and I assure you that the states that our votes made solidly republican will not be so any more.

When I return from Atlantic City I will tell you of our plans and how we hope to execute them.

Your humble servant,   Wm. T. Ferguson

TLS (WP, DLC).

From David Benton Jones

My dear Doctor: Chicago July 29th, 1910.

I have before me your note of the 14th instant.¹ It has not been easy to feel glad, nor does it seem right to feel sorry. I do not see how you could have done otherwise. The situation is one so pregnant with changes of far-reaching importance that the clearest thinking will be found none too clear, and the most steadfast none too steady to remain cool and firm amid the contending elements of the time.

The general principles upon which government and business must be conducted for the next generation are likely to be formulated, or at least indicated, during the next few years.

It is a great surprise to most people to find your announcement considered a matter of such importance by the press. The references to it in the western papers are growing more frequent, and they all recognize in it the potentiality of a regenerated democracy.

There is one element of great importance which is likely to work strongly in your favor as against Harmon: the rising discontent and insurgency in the west is certain to cause a very disquieting state of mind on the part of thinking men in the east. As between two men equally acceptable even, they will, I think, take the one who seems to be a little more removed from the full tide of revolt and so less likely to be swept along into dangerous, or as they see it, destructive measures. This should tell heavily in your favor. "The interests" are as far seeing as they are cruel and remorseless.

The issues rank with those of fifty years ago in moral consequences, and transcend them on the industrial and political side. I only hope your health and endurance will be equal to the strain. I also hope the duties of the governorship, should you be elected, will leave you time to study the charts and to make up your mind what courses to take in the "nasty weather" which we are certain to encounter.

Very sincerely yours,   David B. Jones.

TLS (WP, DLC).
    [1] WW to D. B. Jones, July 14, 1910, Vol. 20.

From Sarah Macdonald Winans

My dear President Wilson   Princeton, N. J. 29th July '10

I wish I knew how to thank you for the two kind letters you have sent us since Mr. Winans' illness began.[1] It will always be a deep grief to me that he could not have enjoyed the one you wrote to him. Your words of appreciation would have meant much to him for he cared a great deal for your personal esteem. He was a man of few words but among your many friends and admirers you had none more loyal than he.

I want to thank you too for your message of sympathy to myself and my family. I wanted very much to have you one of the honourary bearers but hesitated to ask you lest you might perhaps feel obliged to be present, and I would not on any account have had you make the long journey in the heat; but I have taken the liberty of having your name printed in the list. I felt sure you would be willing to pay that respect to my dear husband. With warmest regards to you all, and thanking you again for your sympathy

                    Most sincerely yours   Sarah M. Winans

ALS (WP, DLC).
    [1] Samuel Ross Winans, Professor of Greek and Instructor in Sanskrit, died on July 25, 1910, at the age of fifty-five.

From Melancthon Williams Jacobus

My dear President Wilson: Watch Hill, R. I. July 29, 1910

The unexpected news of Professor Winans death was to me a sad reminder of the changes which are taking place even in the younger Faculty which I knew when I came on the Board.

His loss is without question a serious one to the Teaching Staff of the University—a fine scholar, a worker unsparing of himself, a broad minded man of the tastes and sympathies which go to make the democrat in Education. We shall not find it an easy task to fill his place.

This task, however, must be taken up and should be begun as soon as possible. I have no doubt the men in the Classical Department have names to suggest. We should aim at nothing less than one [who] will keep company with the sort of men we have recently brought to Princeton in Classics.

Does Mrs Winans need her husband's salary until a new professor is chosen?

You will be interested in President Tucker's article in this week's Congregationalist, which I enclose.[1] You may be assured of the joy it is to me to count myself of your kind, whether the companionship be the close one of the University life—or the broader one of the country's living. I can never lose my interest in your career, wherever that career may accomplish itself.

Yours cordially   M. W. Jacobus

ALS (WP, DLC).

[1] The enclosure is missing, but it was William Jewett Tucker, "Aristocratic Tastes and Democratic Sympathies," Boston *Congregationalist and Christian World*, xcv (July 30, 1910), 139-40. Tucker was President of Dartmouth College, 1893-1909. His article was inspired by Wilson's speech to Princeton alumni in Pittsburgh on April 16, 1910 (about which see the news reports printed at April 17 and 20, 1910, Vol. 20). After a handsome tribute to Wilson's intellectual and oratorical powers, Tucker devoted most of his article to a discussion of the antipathy between democracy and "men of taste" and to ways in which such men might develop their "democratic sympathies."

From James Kerney

Dear Sir: Trenton, New Jersey July 30, 1910.

Because of the intense interest that New Jersey is naturally taking in your receptive candidacy for the gubernatorial nomination, the Times respectfully asks that you grant an interview on the following points:

Do you favor a Public Utility Commission, with rate making powers?

Do you favor the direct primary for Governor and Congressman, as well as for the county and city offices?

Do you favor an employers liability law, and along what general lines?

Do you favor the election of United States Senators by the people?

Do you favor stringent legislation against campaign contributions by office holders, including judges?

In the event of your home county being against you in the state convention, would your position as a receptive candidate remain unchanged?

These are matters that, we believe, the people of the state are much interested in, and upon which they would like to be informed. The Times will be very glad to transmit you[r] views to the other newspapers of the state, for simultaneous publication, if you so desire.   Yours respectfully,   James Kerney

TLS (WP, DLC).

An Educational Credo

LIFE AND EDUCATION   [*c. Aug. 1, 1910*]

Life is every man's real school, and every boy's, too; and if he does not make the work of school and college a part of his life, he gets no education from them. He may have got a certain amount of discipline and a certain confused store of information of what passes for knowledge, but he has got no education. That comes from what he puts into his life or receives by sympathy and infection from the experiences amidst which he lives. He takes his education from the men and circumstances about him, from what he finds it necessary to do and to be if he would hold his own in the world in which he lives, retain the respect of those whose esteem he covets, enjoy the pleasure of being put upon an equal footing with those whose companionship and admiration he desires. Nothing becomes part of his habit that is not part of his life from day to day; nothing develops his powers that does not stimulate him to use them freely and for the sake of mastering something. He grows no older, he gets no further than those about him from whom he takes example and inspiration.

That is, for me, the philosophy of education. By that standard I judge colleges and assess the value of what they do. If in them life and study are natural parts of one and the same thing, they are vital and sure to turn out men of training and quickened capacity. If study is merely the formal exercise of the classroom, on the contrary, and everything that makes the place beloved by the undergraduates and the graduates alike is found in that part of the life of the place which has little or nothing to do with intellectual tasks and pleasures, they are mere formal treadmills and will mean education and development to only a hand-full of young men who are unlike their fellows and take little or no part in their life.

I do not wonder that college life has become the theme of eulogy, and the sole theme of eulogy by graduates and patrons of our colleges. The intellectual tasks of college are never eulogized. They are regarded as merely the necessary subtraction from the sum of happiness that makes up college days, the discipline to which all fallen men must submit as the price of comradeship and pleasure. The vital thing is the life from day to day, the life of the playing field, the campus, the clubs, the college rallies, the pleasure expeditions here and there, the amateur dramatics, the music and leisure, the fresh and friendly companionships. Classroom exercises only interrupt these and give them their necessary foil of grim and sober background.

The eulogists are not perverse. They do not despise learning or mean to disparage it. They are only writing of facts as they really are. Life and learning are divorced in our colleges, but of course it is life that is interesting, not these merely formal companionships. Learning is in fact interesting only when it is part and parcel of life and shares its color, its energy, its variety.

It can do this only when life and learning are actually combined in the daily experiences of the university. It cannot do it so long as undergraduate life, for example, is separated and independently organized, so long as its organization is a thing not effected by the university itself, into which the older men of the university, those to whom learning is vital, thought a thing of energy and pleasure, are not drawn as natural and essential parts. At present our undergraduates merely attend our universities. They are not parts of them. Their life does not touch in any intimate family relationship the life of the older men whose stimulation is essential to their education.

The organization of our university life, therefore, must sooner or later be reconsidered, recast from top to bottom, must be rid of the past, of the vast variety of independent organizations which spring, not out of the essential activities of the place, but out of the distractions of the place. It must be simplified and drawn together by the building up of a common life for teacher and pupil, a close association between men young and old, a natural comradeship in things of the mind as well as in the things which fill leisure with pleasure and amusement and constitute the vital sports of life.

Practical programs by which these objects can be accomplished are perfectly feasible, but this is not the place to enter into them. I can only set forth here as plainly and simply as possible my fundamental faith and my confident prediction.[1]

Printed in the *Nassau Literary Magazine*, LXVI (Oct. 1910), 167-69.
[1] There is an undated WWsh draft of this essay in WP, DLC.

From Henry Eckert Alexander

Dear Dr. Wilson: Trenton, New Jersey Aug. 1, 1910.

Trenton seems to be the storm center for New Jersey politics.

It is very plain to me that Mr. Katzenbach has lost ground steadily since his "statement" was issued and the True American failed to encourage a fight in his behalf. A rather adroit effort was made to bring this about but it did not succeed and I find a real desire on the part of some of our Mercer county leaders to "get on the band wagon."

A man may not be a hero to his valet but he may be a hero to his barber and to those who believe that even as Governor he will permit if not encourage familiarities.

Charles H. Gallagher, Mercer county's state committeeman, has helped to bring about a situation here that is very encouraging. He said: "Senator Smith nor any other man has strings on me. I am for Woodrow Wilson and am proud to be for him. His nomination and election as Governor mean the triumph of decent politics in New Jersey."

Mr. Gallagher inspired the editorial which appeared in the Sunday Advertiser. I knew that it was coming. We reproduced it in the True American but you may like to have the original.[1]

Sincerely yours,   Henry E. Alexander.

One of Mr. Katzenbach's close friends warned me that my attitude was taking away business from my paper. Well, the True American has *gained* 900 subscribers in two months.

ALS (WP, DLC).

[1] The editorial, "The Democratic Outlook," *Trenton Sunday Advertiser*, July 31, 1910, said that it was obvious that Katzenbach had no inclination to be a gubernatorial candidate and that in the circumstances it would be improper to force him into the fight. "The conviction grows," it continued, "that Woodrow Wilson is the man of destiny to lead the ensuing campaign. His traducers have pretty nearly exhausted their ammunition and a reaction is setting in, which, in the judgment of calm critics, will wind up in widespread popular enthusiasm once President Wilson has an opportunity to show on the platform how broad are his sympathies, how high are his political ideals, and how thorough[ly] progressive are his views with respect to the rights of the masses as against special privileges for the few. He is a new kind of candidate for the Democracy whose taste has been vitiated by the loud-mouthed utterances of demagogic leadership, and it is therefore not surprising that at first blush many of the rank and file do not recognize his magnificent running qualities in the political crisis which at the present moment threatens to break down old party lines in the State and nation. . . ."

To James Kerney

My dear Sir,   Lyme, Connecticut, 2 August, 1910.

Allow me to acknowledge with thanks your letter of the thirtieth of July.

I am sorry to be obliged to say in reply that I am granting no interviews just now. To do so would be inconsistent with the statement I have published with regard to my attitude toward the Democratic nomination for Governor. I of course meant exactly what I said in that statement. I spoke entirely without reservations of any kind. To grant interviews to the newspapers now would clearly be open to the interpretation that I was seeking the nomination.

Very truly Yours,   [Woodrow Wilson][1]

WWTCL (WP, DLC).

[1] Kerney had sent, *mutatis mutandis*, a copy of his letter to Wilson of July 30, 1910, to some or all of the gubernatorial aspirants. Kerney printed Wilson's reply, together with the questions he had asked, in the *Trenton Evening Times*, Aug. 5, 1910. On the following day, he printed an editorial, "Dr. Wilson's Silence," in which he strongly criticized Wilson's refusal to answer the questions. "The thoughtful Democrats of the State," he said, "are asked to pass upon the candidacy of a man who is unwilling to let them know his views. He has never taken an active part in New Jersey affairs, never had the slightest experience in public life, and is an absolute stranger to the great body of the voters. Democrats have no evidence that he is a Democrat: in fact, in such public utterances as he has made there is nothing to show that he is in sympathy with that party."

"Other candidates, in both parties," Kerney continued, "have either announced platforms of principles on which they sought party favor, or by their public service given substantial evidence of their positions on these issues. Dr. Wilson stands mute. In effect he says: 'Take me on the endorsement of J. Pierpont Morgan, George B. Harvey and Richard V. Lindabury, whose affiliations and corporation connections you know. . . .' He does not even refer to his past expressions on the subject of government regulation of corporations, the disinclination of workingmen to earn their wages, or his decidedly undemocratic view that the people are incompetent to select their servants, but should select only a few of the more important to appoint the others."

"The majority of the thoughtful Democrats in New Jersey," Kerney concluded, "have shown no inclination to accept Dr. Wilson as their standard-bearer. His refusal to declare himself will alienate many who were inclined to be friendly because of his high reputation as an educator. . . ."

Of the other candidates, only Frank S. Katzenbach, Jr., and George S. Silzer seem to have replied to Kerney's questions; at least theirs were the only other replies printed in the *Trenton Evening Times* (Aug. 11 and Aug. 16, 1910, respectively). Both answered affirmatively all of the first five questions asked Wilson, making brief general comments where called for.

To George Brinton McClellan Harvey

My dear Colonel Harvey,   Lyme, Connecticut, 3 August, 1910.

It is very kind of you to keep me posted. I appreciate your little notes very much indeed.

I am more or less pursued by reporters, but it is coming to be generally understood, I think, at last, that I will not grant interviews until after the convention meets. I am looking on with keen interest, and keeping tolerably well informed as to the shifts and intimacies of the game. I find that I take it all with a light heart, the main question of my duty in the matter having been decided.

My favourite paper, The Springfield Republican, announces, very sapiently, that Senator Smith's papers are making a concerted attack upon me, to prevent my nomination!

With warmest regard,

Faithfully Yours,   Woodrow Wilson

WWTLS (WP, DLC).

To Dan Fellows Platt

My dear Mr. Platt,   Lyme, Connecticut, 3 August, 1910.

I am sorry to say that I know of nothing that will take me to New York in the near future. It seems a shame to bring you out to this rather inaccessible place; but if you will be kind enough to come I shall be glad to see you on any day you may choose next week. If you will telegraph or telephone (Saybrook 151 ring 12) me a little while beforehand, you can make certain that nothing unforeseen has called me away. I will be happy to confer with you about anything you wish to discuss, and am obliged to you for the practical interest you are taking.

With warm regard,

Sincerely Yours,   Woodrow Wilson

WWTLS (photostat in RSB Coll., DLC).

To Zephaniah Charles Felt

My dear Zeph.,   Lyme, Connecticut, 3 August, 1910.

I am deeply indebted to you for your letter of the eighteenth of July. It is a proof of your friendship which touches me and gratifies me more than I can say.

I knew very well that a certain sort of alumnus was doing what he could by fostering plans to get me out of the presidency of the University by way of politics; but I did not think that I ought to allow that to influence my decision in what appeared to be a question of public duty.

All my life I have been preaching just this duty on the part of educated men: to avail themselves of every honorable opportunity for political service. This opportunity came to me in a very convincing way (as I am sure you would think if you could hear the details) and I did not see how I could decline to let my name be considered.

There is every evidence that the thing will come to a head. I think that the nomination will be offered me, and I shall try to win the election. My heart, of course, is with the University. It will be heartbreaking to be taken away from my tasks there. But there is this consolation: it would be heartbreaking to remain. That man West will break any president's heart sooner or later, and under the Wyman will he has the power to make the presidency all but impossible. I did not allow this to form an element of my conclusion, but it is a comforting thought so far as my personal fortunes are concerned.

Thank you with all my heart.

Faithfully Yours,   Woodrow Wilson

WWTLS (WC, NjP).

From Henry Eckert Alexander

Dear Dr. Wilson: Trenton, New Jersey Aug. 5, 1910.

Nothing serious has developed in the situation. The True American's editorial of two days ago was ample notice to the Katzenbach boomers what they had to expect in this quarter.[1]

Tonight they had a secret meeting of the county committee and adopted resolutions endorsing Katzenbach.[2] In my opinion this is done as the basis of finding a place to land, for I can find nothing substantial in the Katzenbach movement outside of the professional politician element.

I sent marked copies of the True American editorial to every Democratic and every Independent paper in the state.

Sincerely yours,   Henry E. Alexander.

ALS (WP, DLC).

[1] Alexander actually referred to the editorial, "Vain Republican Hope," printed in the Trenton *True American*, Aug. 4, 1910. This was the editorial written for Alexander by Colonel Harvey, referred to in G. B. M. Harvey to WW, Aug. 6, 1910, and in WW to G. B. M. Harvey, Aug. 8, 1910.

The editorial asserted that Republican leaders were deeply concerned about the possibility that Wilson would be the Democratic candidate for governor, hence their efforts to prevent Wilson's nomination by spreading reports of dissension in Democratic ranks. This was a perfectly natural and legitimate Republican strategy, the editorial continued, but what of the Democrats who were aiding these reports by advocating other men for the nomination? The editorial suggested that the motives of such Democrats was "purely selfish" and further intimated that the prospective candidates did not fully understand their own positions in the contest. George S. Silzer was a "good Democrat": "His time may and probably will come, but it is not now. . . ." Would he not serve his own future better by withdrawing from the contest? H. Otto Wittpenn, the editorial rather uncharitably suggested, was really seeking control of the Hudson County Democratic organization, and it warned him that he would be held "strictly accountable" if he permitted this lesser contest to destroy Democratic hopes for a "Governorship and a possible Presidency."

The longest portion of the editorial was addressed to Frank S. Katzenbach, Jr.: "Mr. Katzenbach has declared over and over again that he is not a candidate for and does not want the nomination. And yet his friends persist in proclaiming him a candidate. Why? Is it because they are convinced that he could get the independent votes essential to success that would surely go to Wilson? Or is it because they think his candidacy would strengthen the local ticket only and be pleasing to themselves, with all their natural pride in Mr. Katzenbach as a leader?. . .

"But the real question confronts Mr. Katzenbach himself. Is his reputation for breadth and generosity likely to be enhanced by the over-zealous conduct of his friends? True, as we believe, he is not a party to the movement, but the determination to pledge the Mercer delegation to Mr. Katzenbach can only serve to discredit Wilson's candidacy. Whatever the intention may be, that, if any, will be the effect."

² The Mercer County Democratic Committee unanimously endorsed Katzenbach. See the *Trenton Evening Times*, Aug. 6, 1910.

To Mary Allen Hulbert Peck

Dearest Friend,   Lyme [Conn.], 6 August, 1910.

We jumped a little out of our rut last week. On Thursday our friends, the Dodges, (Cleveland Dodge, my classmate, a wholly dear fellow, and his wife¹) came to the mouth of the river here and took us for a little run of twenty-four hours or so in their yacht. The boat is a perfect beauty. She was one of the last sea-going boats built to defend the cup.² She is as stately and graceful as a swan, and as comfortable as a cottage; moves in the lightest air; and is, altogether, a thing to love. We cruised up and down the Sound and a little way to sea, spent the night quietly at anchor in Gardiner's Bay, and were brought back to our own landing in the launch. It was most refreshing and delightful, and all too short: for we are very fond of the Dodges and love the water. On Saturday the [Frank A.] Vanderlips, who have a place on the Hudson, between Tarrytown and Ossining, sent their motor for us and we had a wild ride through rain and thunder storm and sunshine, all in succession, for one hundred and eight miles to as beautiful a spot and as nice a home as one could wish to see. We spent Sunday with them, in delightful quiet, meeting only a few people who were easy to talk to, and came back, by train, on Monday. The connections in New York were too close, alas! to give us time to come down to Twenty-seventh Street to see you. We had only half an hour in the city.

The two little outings together interested and freshened us very much. The visit to the Vanderlips was a little more strain than the trip on the yacht, because we know them less intimately, they live rather elaborately, we had to meet strangers and keep dressed up, and we were eager to get back to our own,—our own thoughts and our own people; but it gave spice to the week's end; they are exceedingly kind and very interesting; and this quiet haunt had all the more flavour when we came back to it.

We are all having the pleasurable excitement now of seeing Madge in love. Mr. [Edward Graham] Elliott is here. They have been friends for a long time: we did not know that it was to go farther until we got here. It is a novel sight to see Madge surrender, and show all the tender signs of sentiment, and it is as delightful as it is novel. I think I told you who Mr. Elliott is. He is Professor of Politics at Princeton and Dean of the College. He is, I suppose, about thirty-five. I have been intimately associated with him for years (he began at Princeton as my assistant) and can vouch for his being a singularly fine fellow. He arrived here yesterday, and is to stay a few weeks. They may marry before we go home,—in order to escape the elaborate goings-on they would have to have if they married at Princeton, and, what is much more important, to have time for a honeymoon before the university term opens.

Politics continue very much mixed in New Jersey. My own county has endorsed another man, who has personal grounds, of the pettiest kind, for being opposed to me, and who was the last (defeated) candidate of the party for Governor. It mortifies me a good deal to be treated so in my own home, but I dare say there is more personal politics in it than representation of the people. It will not, I believe, change the result.

I am very hungry for news of you. It seems a long time since I saw you, and I would be very grateful for a letter, as full as possible of personal details.

All join me in affectionate messages to you all, and I am, as always,   Your devoted friend,   Woodrow Wilson

WWTLS (WP, DLC).
  1 Grace Parish Dodge.
  2 That is, the America's Cup races. Dodge's yacht was the schooner *Corona*.

To Henry Smith Pritchett

                                                      Lyme, Connecticut,
My dear President Pritchett,   6 August, 1910.

Thank you most sincerely for your kind letter of the twenty-second of July. It was characteristically generous and thoughtful of you to write it.

I do not yet know what the New Jersey Democrats are going to do; but I felt, when responsible men approached me in the matter, that I had no choice but to consent to allow my name to be presented for the nomination, because I have all my life preached the duty of educated men to render political service when called upon.

It went hard, none the less, to make the decision. I have just won a substantial victory at Princeton, and my position there has just been greatly strengthened by a heavy vote of the alumni, in an election to a representative seat in the Board.[1] It is a most inopportune time for me to leave. But the other thing came to me in a form which seemed to make my duty clear.

It is delightful that you should have thought of it where you are!   Faithfully Yours,   Woodrow Wilson

WWTLS (H. S. Pritchett Papers, DLC).
[1] He was referring to John W. Barr's victory over Adrian H. Joline in June 1910 in a contest for an alumni trusteeship. There are numerous references to this test of strength in Vol. 20.

From George Brinton McClellan Harvey

Dear Mr. Wilson,   Deal, N. J. Saturday [Aug. 6, 1910]

I have your note, and hope your golf is improving. Mine isn't.

As anticipated, the Mercer Committee endorsed Katzenbach. *That* is all right, but presently K. himself will begin to look a bit silly. I wrote a piece for Alexander (inclosed)[1] to give him the beginning of something to think about.

Could you conveniently run in to Boston for a night along about the 19th? I expect to be there about then and there may be things to talk over, resolutions, etc.

Sincerely Yours   George Harvey

ALS (WP, DLC).
[1] See H. E. Alexander to WW, Aug. 5, 1910, n. 1.

Two Letters to George Brinton McClellan Harvey

My dear Colonel Harvey,   Lyme, Connecticut, 8 August, 1910.

Thank you for your note of Saturday. I take the TRUE AMERICAN and had seen the editorial you were kind enough to enclose. It struck me as extremely well conceived and as expressed just in the right terms, when I read it. It is calculated to put things in the light in which they will show most certainly for just what they are.

I dare say I can make it convenient to be in Boston for a night when you are there. Let me know just when it will be and I will take pleasure in fitting my plans to yours. I am thinking over the matter of resolutions.[1]

No, my golf is not improving, I mourn to state. If I am to be observed at play I must play better than this!

Faithfully Yours,   Woodrow Wilson

[1] Wilson and Harvey did meet in Boston about August 19, 1910. Once again, the only account of what took place is that of William O. Inglis, "Helping to Make a President," *Collier's Weekly*, LVIII (Oct. 14, 1916), 12-13.

According to Inglis, the principal topic of discussion between Wilson and Harvey was the proposed platform of the New Jersey Democratic party. The two men conferred for several hours and apparently had no difficulty in settling all points except that concerning the popular election of United States senators, which was included in Harvey's proposed draft. Inglis recalled that Wilson stated flatly, "I am opposed to that." Harvey is said to have replied: "So am I, and I will keep it out if I can, but I fear they [the Democratic state convention] will insist upon it."

There then ensued a discussion of the persisting rumors that James Smith, Jr., would seek to return to the United States Senate with Wilson's and Harvey's assistance, if Wilson was elected governor. Wilson was especially disturbed by a cartoon in the *Newark Evening News* (reproduced in Inglis's article) which suggested that this would be the case. Harvey's reply, as Inglis recalled it, was significant: "You must make up your mind for more of that, for it cannot be avoided. I have the senator's authority to withdraw him absolutely whenever, if at all, I should consider it necessary, but I don't dare do it before the convention. That is a purely party matter, and the senator is going to need all the help he can get from the workers who want him but are not enthusiastic over you. It may become necessary to ask him to stand aside after the nomination, but not before. There is nothing to do but grin and bear it."

Finally, Inglis remembered that on the following evening, probably August 20, Wilson, Harvey, and he had dinner at the Union Club in Boston with Robert Winsor of the banking firm of Kidder, Peabody and Company. This occasion was arranged, according to Inglis, so that Wilson and Winsor could assess each other, with a view to Wilson's possible presidential candidacy in 1912.

My dear Colonel Harvey,   Lyme, Connecticut, 8 August, 1910.

I would very much like your advice upon a matter which has just come up to-day.

Mr. Dan Fellows Platt, of Engelwood, a former pupil of mine, a member of the Democratic county committee of Bergen County, and a keen politician on our side, finds a good many embarrassments in my silence amidst many questionings as to what my views are on questions like the creation of a public service commissions [commission] with full powers of regulation, direct primaries, etc. He came out to see me to-day. I told him my views, but he is afraid things will go astray unless I state them publicly,— at any rate in his part of the country. He proposes, therefore to have his county Committee, which is to meet to-morrow evening, write me a letter containing certain questions and ask a reply, on the principle that they have to decide what their attitude will be and have a certain right, on public grounds, to expect me to answer.

I fear that to reply would open me to the suspicion of having arranged the opportunity to reply to my critics, and that, what is more serious, their letter may give rise to others, from less friendly quarters, from other committees, in which I will be asked questions which will be set as traps: as, for example, on the liquor question, on which no wise opinion can be expressed without a long, carefully argued reply. On the other hand there are certain manifest advantages in issuing a sort of creed on pending state issues. What do you advise. I should very much like to know, for

I am perplexed. I hate timidity, but I do not wish to make a blunder, and feel myself inexperienced.

With warm regard,

Faithfully Yours,   Woodrow Wilson

WWTLS (WP, DLC).

From Joseph M. Noonan

Dear Mr. Wilson: Jersey City, N. J. August 8. 1910.

Although I am doubtful as to the propriety of paying any special attention to the antics of the Wittpennites, their attitude became so truculent and offensive that it was deemed prudent by many of your friends here to make some answer to, and comment on, their proclamations and proceedings; and, accordingly, the letter which, with all its imperfections, I send to you was published on July 30th, in the Jersey Journal of this City,[1] in the hope, which thus far has not been disappointed, that it might have a chastening effect upon the Mayor and his somewhat flamboyant boomers. But, while they are keeping quiet, they are secretly trying to create the impression that, however estimable you may be personally, you are on principle opposed to any practically effective regulation of corporations, especially railroads, and to the just demands of the labor unions. In support of this propoganda they are quoting alleged utterances on these topics, which, they say, have been culled from some of your addresses. I should be grateful to you if you would send to me, or tell me where I can obtain, copies of your addresses in which these topics are discussed so that I may be prepared, should the occasion arise, to correct their distorted reports. I understand that you intend to publish, before the primaries, a statement defining your position with respect to these and all other questions of public interest; but in the meantime it might be well for your friends to be able to quote you by the book on these subjects. If I may venture a suggestion, let me say that there is, in this State, a very numerous commuters vote, which is normally republican, but which next November will be cast for the party whose candidate for Governor will afford the best guarantee to voters of this class that, in the event of his election, their reasonable demands will be satisfied. The present difficulty in dealing with their grievance—arising from the Inter-State nature of the traffic—could very easily be gotten rid of by a proper enactment authorizing the Public Utilities Commission to require each of the several railroads, in New Jersey, to sell commutation tickets between stations on its route within this State, so that, for example, commutation tickets that are now sold between points in New Jersey and New York City should be sold, if desired, between the former points and Jersey City, Hoboken, Weehawken and other terminal stations within this State and nearest to its confines. But, of course, the whole corpus of the public utilities legislation needs to be recast into a progressive but reasonable form that will meet the just expectations of the people while respecting the legitimate rights of the corporations. The commuter of northern New Jersey, as I hear him daily talking on the trains on my trips between this City and Oakland, is heading politically in your direction, not because he knows definitely what your views may be about his real or imaginary grievances but because of his knowledge of your character and his profound confidence in your ability and integrity. I may add, as a "straw" indicating how the wind is blowing, that in the house at which I am presently staying in the country there are four republicans—one a retired silk manufacturer, another the cashier of the Paterson National Bank, another a patent lawyer and the fourth a wholesale merchant of Paterson—who are friends of Vivian Lewis, and each of these tells me that if you are nominated he will vote for you even as against Lewis. Mr. Davis, to whom I mentioned the other day this declared purpose of my four Oakland acquaintances, assured me that he was hearing the same sort of good news from every section of the State. So that my hopes of that 50,000 majority are growing.   Very sincerely,   Jos. M. Noonan

TLS (WP, DLC).
  [1] Joseph M. Noonan to the Editor, printed in the Jersey City *Jersey Journal*, July 30, 1910. Noonan asserted that Wittpenn himself was guilty of many of the dubious political tactics which he had accused Wilson and "the bosses" of employing.

A Proposed Democratic State Platform

[Aug. 9, 1910]

Suggestions for platform resolutions, September, 1910.

The Democrats of New Jersey, in presenting to the voters of the State a candidate for Governor, present also the following declaration of the objects to which they will devote themselves should they be entrusted with the direction of the administration and legislation of the State:

  1. A thorough administrative reorganization, in order to make the administration of the State's business at once as economical and as efficient as possible. This would involve the abolition of all unnecessary offices, boards and commissions, a concentration of functions upon the model of the best business organizations, and a careful coordination of the several parts of the public service. The government of the State should be so systematized and simplified and such methods of public accounting should be established and enforced as would secure unmistakable individual responsibility on the part of every officer entrusted with authority or the handling of public funds. All appropriations of public moneys should be based upon as careful a consideration of the burden of taxation imposed upon the people as of the object sought to be served by the expenditure, economy being as essential to honest government as any consideration of efficiency.

2. The equalization of taxation, both in law and in practice, particularly as between individuals, and railway and other corporations, with regard to the valuation of property and the assessment of taxes upon it; the removal from the State's system of taxation of all elements of obscurity or injustice; and the adoption of such administrative changes as may prove to be necessary in order to make those reforms effective.

3. The preservation intact of the school fund[1] and its prompt and systematic distribution for the purposes for which it was intended.

4. The taxation of the franchises of public service corporations at a rate proportioned to their true and fair value to those to whom they have been granted.

5. The careful conservation for the benefit of all the people of the State of all water rights and of all natural resources still within the control of the State by provisions which will effectually prevent their control or exhaustion by individuals or by single localities.

6. The establishment of a public service commission with ample powers under explicit rules to regulate rates, secure an adequate and suitable service, inflict penalties, require the filing of all traffic agreements and the submission to its examination of all tariff rates before they take effect, and to reject or adjust the same if found to be unjust,—so far as such legislation may be consistent with the power of Congress to regulate commerce between the States.

[1] The principal of the State School Fund was derived almost entirely from the sale and rental of lands under water belonging to New Jersey. The principal could not be used for any purpose, and the income could be used only for the support of public schools. This income amounted to $200,000 in 1910. This sum was apportioned among the counties by the State Superintendent of Public Instruction on the basis of the total days' attendance of pupils in the public schools.

7. The enactment of an employers' liability act which will satisfy the just demands of labour and secure safety and efficient sanitation in all manufacturing processes and employments.

8. The enactment of a law establishing eight hours as the limit of the working day in all public work.

9. The control of such corporations, combinations, or trusts as are not naturally to be regarded as public service corporations by legislation which will define and forbid those acts and practices on their part and those methods in the organization and control of business which have proved destructive of free competition and detrimental to the people's interest, and which will visit the penalties prescribed upon individuals, the individuals responsible for such acts or practices.

10. Such changes in the laws of the State respecting the incorporation of business undertakings as will effectually prevent the abuse of the privilege of incorporation which has in recent years brought discredit to the State, and will properly regulate and restrict, under explicit rules, the issue of securities by companies seeking incorporation and the corporations acting under the authority of the laws of the State.

11. The enactment of an explicit and effective corrupt practices act which will determine what campaign expenses are to be regarded as legitimate and which shall provide for the compulsory publication, in detail, under heavy penalties, of the campaign expenses of every candidate for public office, including the persons or sources from which the money to defray them came.

12. The enactment of such laws with regard to the manufacture and sale of spiritous liquors as will best secure local home rule in this fundamental matter of police regulation.

13. Such a simplification of the electoral machinery of the State as will make possible the effectual exercise of the right of direct nomination on the part of the voters, and the enactment of laws which will secure to them that right in the most effectual manner.

14. The extension of the principle and practice of civil service reform throughout the central administrative service of the State not only, but also throughout the service of municipalities and other local governments, so far as the State has constitutional jurisdiction.

15. The enactment of laws with regard to the use of automobiles within the State which will grant the same rights and privileges to the owners and drivers of machines from other States that are accorded the citizens of this State in the States from

which said owners and drivers hold their licenses; and which will tend to establish a proper reciprocity of responsibility as between the license greanting [granting] authorities of the several States.

In regard to the administration of the federal government we declare our conviction that the tariff legislation of recent years has become, not a means of protection, but a means of patronage, designed, not to effect a general and healthy economic development or an equitable extension and equalization of the opportunities of the people, but to secure profits to particular classes and combinations of producers who, by means of the modern combinations in the field of industry, can absolutely command prices within the United States, if shielded against foreign competition; that the maintenance of our present leadership in the economic world demands the revival by proper legislation of our merchant marine, destroyed under the influence of the mistaken protective legislation of the Republican party; that the federal regulation of corporations should follow the lines we have indicated for state legislation; and that there should be enacted a federal corrupt practices act as explicit and imperative as that we have favoured for the State.[2]

T MS (WP, DLC).
[2] There is a WWsh draft and a WWT draft with WWhw and WWsh emendations of this document in WP, DLC.

To George Brinton McClellan Harvey

My dear Colonel Harvey,   Lyme, Connecticut, 9 August, 1910.

Here are some suggestions for a set of platform resolutions. I should like to know what you think of them. They constitute a first draft and are meant as a basis for discussion. We might have a preliminary skirmish on them before our meeting in Boston, so that we may then come to a definite conclusion.

With warm regard,
                         Sincerely Yours,   Woodrow Wilson

P.S. The question I put in my letter of last evening comes, in sum, to this: Shall I issue a statement of any kind as to my views before the primaries; if so, when, how, and to whom?
                                      Yours,   W.W.

WWTLS (WP, DLC).

From William T. Ferguson

Dear Sir: Washington, D. C., August 9, 1910.

Our meeting at Atlantic City[1] proved to be quite a success notwithstanding the fact that the mayor[2] and some of his white and colored friends, with the assistance of Mr. Charles W. Anderson, collector of internal revenue for the 2nd, dist. of New York, tried to divert the attention of our people with a brass band, barbecue and a celebration of the Emancipation. The first of our two public meetings was crowded. At the second we did not have so many, but the attendance was of that character to show the class of people who were giving aid and encouragement to our efforts. They were the substantial class. When the subject "What action shall we take in the coming State campaigns" was discussed I suggested that it would be wise for us to espouse the cause of such men as you and Mr. Thomas M. Osborne[3] of New York. I explained to our delegates that I had made some effort to find out the calibre of these gentlemen and that I believed that I could truthfully say that you both were friends of our people. I also stated that I did not know how far your friendship would extend in case you were honored by being elected governors of your respective States, but that I sincerely believed that we would fare better than under past Republican governors. I hope that I spoke the truth, for it will be upon my report, in many instances, that the League will take concerted action, and I want to be known as one whose word can be taken. If you are the nominee and I can get in touch with the campaign manager right away I will arrange to have our forces cover New Jersey in a systematic way and I believe that the colored vote will be pleasing to you and your friends. I would like also to talk with you so as to be able to answer querries that will of course be asked.

Hoping that this finds you well,

I am sincerely yours,   Wm. T. Ferguson

TLS (WP, DLC).

[1] The National Independent Political League met in Atlantic City, August 4, 5, and 6, at Price Memorial African Methodist Episcopal Zion Church. Forty delegates attended, and the meeting was significant because of the presence of W. E. B. Du Bois and the selection of a nine-member committee to organize Negro support for Democratic candidates friendly to black people. Du Bois, N.I.P.L. president Alexander Walters, and other speakers attacked Roosevelt and Taft, and, by including Du Bois, the convention succeeded in portraying a united anti-Republican front to Negro voters. The question of explicit endorsements for Democratic candidates was postponed until the N.I.P.L.'s meeting on October 6, 1910, about which see W. T. Ferguson to WW, Oct. 7, 1910. For news reports of the Atlantic City meeting, see the Boston *Guardian*, Aug. 6, 1910; Washington *Bee*, Aug. 13, 1910; and Baltimore *Afro-American Ledger*, Aug. 13 and 27 and Sept. 10, 1910.

[2] Franklin Pierce Stoy, Mayor of Atlantic City, 1894-97, 1900-1911.

[3] Thomas Mott Osborne, prison reform leader, Mayor of Auburn, N. Y., 1903-1906.

From Mary Allen Hulbert Peck

Dearest Friend: Pittsfield, Mass. August 10th [1910]

Your good letters came just as I was leaving N. Y. last Sunday. I am here visiting my friends Miss Learned and Miss Watson[1] for a week (that is until Monday next) and trying to make the house and grounds at 211 East St.[2] look less desolate and forsaken. Last night we spent at the Farm[3]—where there was a small dinner party. . . . It was *too quiet* for me to sleep, so I laid listening to the watchdog padding about, to the rustling leaves and the distant cock crows, the steady roar of the city still in my ears. This morning we all had our breakfast trays in Miss Watsons room, and afterward we planned a tea house and verandah, reared a pergola or two just to fill up a spare moment and were off to the Wednesday Morning Club at 10.45 to hear Mr. Burgess the first occupant of the Roosevelt Chair in Germany,[4] give a talk on the subject. I thought of you and the day when you spoke before that august assemblage.[5] Dr. B. was quite charming but his address was highly laudatory as to Germany—a pean [paean]—her institutions, her ideals, and as for her Emperor—*he* is "the most magnificent specimen of manhood I have ever seen!" (long impressive pause) "The most misrepresented man, the most misunderstood of all the world." Which is *I* think *"going some."* The Kaiser he told us, was the one of all the kings who strove always to maintain the peace of Europe, and the late King of England was the disturber of peace. If he could have had *his* way all Europe would have been involved in bloody war. Dr. B. feels at home in Germany—always has—but has just discovered *why*. Not so in England—because the English are Germans with a veneer of Norman French. The American thanks to freedom-environment loses the veneer—remains the German. Hence the Americans are closer to the Germans in sympathy, ideals, etc. etc. than any nation of the earth. I was interrupted last night & ink & pen not being accessible I must finish this hurriedly in pencil this morning. What you tell me of your lovely Madge is delightful—do give her my warmest congratulations & good wishes. Can you tell me anything as to the whereabouts of Mr. Junius Morgan? I am asking for a friend, and do not wish the inquiry known. The air is heavenly this morning after a soaking rain all day yesterday. Harriet[6] was here visiting other friends when I came, & preparing to take the plants & arbours from the garden for her new home in Magnolia! Still most antagonistic to me—alas! Write me here just a line. With kindest remembrances to your family

I am   Yr. devoted friend   Mary Allen Peck.

ALS (WP, DLC).

1 Florence J. Learned, proprietress of Elmwood Court, the Pittsfield estate at which Mrs. Peck was staying; and Gertrude Watson. Both ladies were active in Pittsfield civic affairs and in philanthropic work and, in addition, Miss Watson was an amateur pianist and a patron of musical activities in Pittsfield.

2 The Peck residence in Pittsfield.

3 Miss Watson's home, Onota, in Pittsfield.

4 The Theodore Roosevelt Professorship of American History and Institutions at the University of Berlin was established in 1905 by James Joseph Speyer, German-American international banker and philanthropist of New York. Appointments were made annually by the Prussian Ministry of Education, with the sanction of the German Emperor, upon nomination by Columbia University, although appointments were not limited to members of Columbia. The incumbent was to lecture in the German language. John William Burgess, Ruggles Professor of Political Science and Constitutional Law at Columbia, was the first holder of the chair during the academic year 1906-1907.

The Prussian Ministry of Education in turn established at Columbia the Kaiser Wilhelm Professorship of German History and Institutions, also beginning in 1906-1907.

5 See the announcement and news item printed at Oct. 6, 1908, Vol. 18.

6 Her stepdaughter, Harriet Peck Snitcher.

From Henry Burling Thompson

My dear Wilson   Hotel Adlon, Berlin W. August 10 1910

While in Edinburgh two weeks past, I received your letter,[1] but the exigencies of rapid travel seem to have made an answer impossible until to day. Your letter raises conflicting emotions. I am afraid sorrow at the possibility of your severing relations with the University, is stronger than the feeling of gratification at the possibility of your usefulness in a National field. I want you to stay at Princeton, but I can not say, stay, in view of the larger call.

It gives me much pleasure to reread your kind words, and I can assure you, I shall always value the friendship, and it pleases me to think, that my position during the past winter, has been of some help to you.

We are having a most delightful trip.

We have just left Sir William Mather after a short stay. He was much interested in all our affairs. Please give my kind regards to Mrs Wilson and your daughters

Yours very sincerely   Henry B Thompson

ALS (WP, DLC).

1 WW to H. B. Thompson, July 14, 1910, Vol. 20.

From Charles Williston McAlpin

St. Huberts, P. O.

My dear Dr Wilson   New York, August 10, '10

I received your kind letter of July 20 and have carried it about with me ever since, intending each day to answer it. We are settled here for the rest of this month and I am beginning to pull myself together. I find that I needed a rest and change more than I realized and I think we have come to the right place to get them.

Personally, I regret what you did about the governorship, although you did the right thing because you did your duty. But the recurring thought in my mind is, what will Princeton do? and I can't find the answer. You can always count on me as your firm supporter in whatever you do, for I know that whatever you do will be the right thing

Faithfully & sincerely yours   C. W. McAlpin.

ALS (WP, DLC).

To Mary Allen Hulbert Peck

Dearest Friend,   Lyme [Conn.], 12 August, 1910

It was delightful to get your letter, and it had the sweet tone of the country in it. Even if you did not sleep the first night after you got to the country it was because of the excitement of the release. I could not imagine a canary or a mocking bird, released from a cage in a city room and given the freedom of the hills again, sleeping its first night on the bough. I should expect it to flutter all the night through with a sweet excitement and wonder, as you, a true child of the countryside, did. You do not take anything dully, as a matter of routine, but everything as a matter of life; and there is always the quickness of life where you are. This letter, written from the country, and from the home of old, congenial friends, has so much more the tone of your real self in it than any you ever wrote me from the city, where your spirit is caged and you do not think naturally. And so it cheers me to read it. I am so happy to think where you are, and how employed, —except for the dreary work at 211, which must be very depressing. And what a hateful piece Mrs. Snitcher is! I cannot understand or excuse her. By the way, is that the name (Harriet's)? I am never sure. Do you still mean, a little later, to go to 211 and camp out for a while, if you can rent the flat at No. 39?

Everything goes quietly and normally with us here. Nothing seems ever to have stirred politics to quite such a preliminary heat and excitement before in New Jersey as have been created by the possib[i]lity of my becoming a candidate for the governorship. *Some*body is raising heaven and earth to prevent the nomination,—the men who expect to be hard hit if I get a chance at them, undoubtedly, and the Republicans who expect defeat; but it does not disturb me, and will not, I feel quite sure, prevent anything now on the cards. I still look on with a singular power of disengagement which I must say I did not expect of myself. It interests and amuses but does not seem to touch me. I begin to hope that I shall feel a certain impersonal zest in the game, should I be put into office; and that I can keep my constituents interested, too.

I am occupying such time as I can spare from letter writing (I am without a secretary here and grind away at the letters all by my lee lane) and from Golf with revising some seven or eight of my essays for republication in a volume which the Harpers want to bring out this autumn.¹ It is odd how hard I find it to fix my attention upon them. I have to read many sentences again and again. They seem part of my own past consciousness, not like the sentences of a book and it is hard to regard them objectively enough to criticise them. And so the task goes very slowly. The only parts I enjoy are the quotations! I find it very true, as Mr. [Augustine] Birrell once said, that one cannot greatly enjoy one's own writings unless they are written wholly or in part by somebody else!

About the nineteenth I shall be going up to Boston on an errand. Then on the last, or rather the fourth, Wednesday of the month I shall attend a meeting of the Trustees of the Mutual, in New York, on my way down to Tennessee to deliver the annual address to the American Bar Association.² I shall pick up my silk hat and frock coat at Princeton on my way back from Tennessee and hurry back here to the wedding on the eighth of Sept.³

We are all well, and all join in warmest messages to you. The oftener you write the happier I shall be. I think of you as much as you could wish, and wait for the letters.

Your devoted friend,   Woodrow Wilson

Please give my regards to Miss Watson and Miss Learned.

WWTLS (WP, DLC).
  ¹ This volume was never published.
  ² Wilson's address is printed at Aug. 31, 1910.
  ³ That is, of Margaret Randolph Axson and Edward Graham Elliott.

To Edward Howe

My dear Mr. Howe,   Lyme, Connecticut, 12 August, 1910.

Thank you for your letter and for your prompt attention to the little matter of business I wrote about. It was kind of you to give your personal attention to it.

We are without a bank here. May I trouble you to have one

hundred and sixty dollars (160.00) sent to me in cash by express? The enclosed cheques cover that amount. It is an awkward way of banking, but our only alternative is to use the cash resources of our local Guinn,[1] one Sterling!

It contents us to think of Stock being with you. We know how he enjoys it and how good it is for him to be with such genuine and enjoyable friends.

With warmest regard,

Faithfully Yours,   Woodrow Wilson

WWTLS (received from the Princeton Bank and Trust Co.).
   [1] Walter Guinn, a Princeton hackman, who obliged in cashing small checks in emergencies.

From George Brinton McClellan Harvey

Dear Mr. Wilson: New York August 12, 1910.

I feel quite certain in my mind that there is no immediate occasion for you to set forth explicitly your views on State or other issues. So far as Mr. Platt is concerned, it seems to me that you covered the situation fully. You conversed with him frankly and doubtless authorized him to acquaint his fellow committeemen with your views. That seems to me to fill the bill. Answering one set of questions now would be only to invite others and to lay yourself open to all sorts of trouble. Moreover, since Katzenbach made himself ridiculous by answering the disingenuous questions which the Trenton Times put to you, your present reserve appears all the more becoming. I can detect no signs of sincere demand for more definite utterances from you—only the enemy seems to be disturbed. Incident[al]ly, Mr. Platt need not lose any sleep over Bergen County in the Convention. It is all right.

I might add that I consulted with Senator Smith on this point last evening, and that his judgment confirms my own opinion. If the time should come, and of course it may, that something more explicit should seem essential or desirable to our minds we will let you know and suggest a way; but for the present the "stand-pat" policy is working too well to justify interference. The situation is well in hand; there are no breaches in the walls.

I am off to-night to Vermont to make a couple of speeches and will take along your proposed resolution which thus far I have had barely time to glance at. Such little examination as I have been able to make has left most favorable impressions.

I expect to reach Boston on Thursday or Friday of next week but will inform you definitely from Vermont.

On the whole, I think it would be a good idea to scatter a sort of character sketch of yourself amongst the small country weekly papers of the State. We have all sorts of folk in Jersey, and I dare say that there is in the minds of some of the backwoodsmen an impression that you are a man who makes whiskey or sewing-machines, and they do not know the difference between Princeton and Carlisle.[1] A sort of personal introduction in any case could do no harm. My suggestion is that Inglis go up to Lyme for a day or so early next week and do such a sketch which perhaps you could fetch to Boston for me to look over before sending it out. If this proposal meets with your approval, will you kindly drop a note to my secretary here, Mr. Herbert E. Bowen, fixing a date when it would be convenient for you to chat or play golf with Inglis, who is an adept at the kind of work I have indicated.

I am ever   Faithfully yours,   George Harvey

TLS (WP, DLC).
[1] The United States Indian Industrial School at Carlisle, Pa., then well known because of the exploits of the Indian athlete, James Francis Thorpe (Wa-Tho-Huck, or Bright Path).

To Herbert E. Bowen

My dear Mr. Bowen,   Lyme, Connecticut, 13 August, 1910.

Colonel Harvey has asked me to drop you a line as to when it would be convenient for me to see Mr. Inglis here, with the idea of having him prepare a personal sketch of myself.[1] He no doubt left a memorandum of the suggestion with you and with Mr. I.

It would be perfectly convenient for me to see Mr. Inglis the first of next week. If he will let me know when he can come, I will make a point of being accessible, unless something now wholly unforeseen should turn up.

I wish that you would be kind enough to make a note, for Colonel Harvey's eye when he returns, That a Miss Anne McIlvaine,[2] whom I know very well, was up here for a couple of weeks on a visit and was trying her hand, when she left, at just such a sketch, meaning to get it into either the Trenton or the Newark *News*. It promised to be a very clever and effective thing.[3]

Sincerely Yours,   Woodrow Wilson

WWTLS (WP, DLC).
[1] As subsequent documents will reveal, Inglis did write the sketch, but Henry Eckert Alexander thought that it was inadequate, and it was never published.
[2] A woman of independent means, born in Wadesboro, N. C., who lived in Trenton. She was active in club work and civic affairs and seems to have taken an active interest in politics. She organized the Trenton branch of the Y.W.C.A. in 1903.
[3] See n. 1 to the following document.

From Henry Eckert Alexander

Dear Dr. Wilson: Trenton, New Jersey Aug. 16, 1910.

The Times today prints the enclosed as "communicated."[1] I have an idea that it is from Miss McIlvaine. She wrote to Mrs. Alexander[2] who replied very enthusiastically, offering to help in every way. We are particularly anxious to have the "snap shot" taken by Miss McIlvaine if it can be reproduced well.

I think that Mr. Inglis "knows his business." I have written Colonel Harvey asking that "President," "Dr." and even plain "Mr." be eliminated as far as possible from the sketch. "Woodrow Wilson" sounds good. "Wilson" will do until we make it "Governor Wilson."

I met Mr. Katzenbach's ablest lieutenant this afternoon. His name is George [B.] LaBarre.[3] Naturally he feels pretty keenly the attitude of the True American which, of course, made the Katzenbach "coup" an impossibility. I invited him to take a good seat on the Wilson band wagon. . . .

I never explained to you the "policy" of the True American. I have refrained from printing many political editorials because our *1300* brand new Trenton subscribers haven't gotten "acquainted" with the paper. People are interested in other things besides politics just now and prefer to read about other things. When the campaign opens it will be different. With continued best wishes I am,   Sincerely yours,   Henry E. Alexander.

ALS (WP, DLC).
  [1] The enclosure is missing, but it was [Anne McIlvaine] "Woodrow Wilson's Home Life," *Trenton Evening Times*, Aug. 15, 1910.
  [2] Elizabeth Kirkwood Alexander.
  [3] In the investment securities, real estate, and insurance business in Trenton. He was also city assessor of Trenton.

From Joseph M. Noonan

My dear Mr. Wilson: Jersey City, N. J. August 17. 1910.

That you should be "very much puzzled what, if anything, to do in the circumstances" referred to in your letter of the tenth instant I can very readily understand. It is perfectly natural that a man of your intellectual and moral tone should shrink from even the appearance of seeking a nomination. But you are, I venture to think, taking a too personal and one-sided view of the situation. For your reluctance to make a public "statement," lest it might seem inconsistent with your determination not to seek the nomination, is, in its very root and essence, nothing else than an extreme form of sensitiveness. If, as you admit, the voters of the State are "clearly entitled to know," before the primaries, your "opinions on all pending questions" then the reciprocal duty is laid upon you to put those voters in possession of that knowledge. And the only way this can be done is by a public statement. To do this is not to "seek" the nomination. It is incontestably to the interest of the commonwealth that its people should intelligently, wisely and conscientiously determine who shall be their nominee for Governor; and, it seems to me, the inevitable corollary of this postulate is, so far as you are concerned, that you should do what you reasonably can to enable the people thus to determine that question.

In making a "statement" that should correct the false reports that are being circulated as to your views, especially in regard to corporations and labor unions, you would not be seeking or advocating your nomination in any sense that is inconsistent with your expressed determination not to solicit the nomination. You would simply be telling the truth about yourself to the people who do not now know it and who have a right to learn it from yourself. The immediate personal justification of this course, as well as its public justification, is to be found in the fact that while adhering to your purpose not to seek the nomination you believe that, in justice to the people whose nomination you are willing to accept if it should come to you unsolicited, you cannot remain silent while your views on some most important questions are being publicly and grossly misrepresented.

It affords to me a novel sensation, and must look to you like an amazing impertinence, for me to lecture the President of Princeton in this fashion on the subject of political ethics. But I feel I can trust your kindness to forgive my candor; nor am I so conceited as to suppose or desire that you will take any step in this delicate business merely because it is recommended by—

Yours very sincerely,   Jos. M. Noonan

TLS (WP, DLC).

From Edgar Williamson[1]

Dear Sir: Orange, N. J. August 18, 1910

At the recent convention of the New Jersey State Federation of Labor held in Newark N. J. August 15 and 16, a resolution was passed condemning you as a foe to organized labor.[2]

I stoutly fought for a resolution to appoint a committee to interview you for your views in the matter, but the substitute resolution was defeated.

I maintain that you should be heard on this subject.

I am to publish a large edition of my paper for Labor Day and would be pleased to have your views for publication.

Very truly yours   Edgar Williamson

ALS (WP, DLC).
[1] Publisher of the Orange, N. J., *Labor Standard.*
[2] "Whereas, The financial interests of Wall Street, New York, are endeavoring to have Woodrow Wilson, president of Princeton University[,] nominated as a candidate for Governor of the State of New Jersey; and
"Whereas, In his baccalaureate address to the students of Princeton University in 1909 Woodrow Wilson again strongly expressed his antagonism to organized labor: therefore be it
"Resolved, By the New Jersey State Federation of Labor in convention assembled, this fifteenth day of August, 1910, that this Federation be placed on record as opposing the nomination of said Woodrow Wilson as a candidate for Governor, that it urges every trades unionist and wage earner in the State of New Jersey to oppose his nomination; and also urges that, should the Wall Street financial interests succeed in having Woodrow Wilson nominated to act as the tool or agent of said Wall Street's interests, if he should be elected, that every trades unionist and every wage earner in the State of New Jersey do their unmost [utmost] to defeat him and to teach the financial interests of Wall Street, New York, that the honest voters and trades unionists of the State of New Jersey are perfectly capable of selecting their own Governor." *Trenton Evening Times,* Aug. 17, 1910. This resolution was actually adopted on August 16.

From Dan Fellows Platt

Dear President Wilson: N. Y. City Aug. 18, 1910.

Although I had the County Comm. appoint me chairman of a committee with discretionary power as to writing to one or more of the candidates for governor asking for a statement of beliefs, I have done nothing in the matter as, on thinking things over, I decided that I had made myself altogether too much of a "butter-in" in my talk with you. I hold my opinion more than ever, as to the desirability of a manifesto from you, but I admit the awkwardness of the situation as to the issuance, at present, of a statement, as a volte face from your attitude maintained even more firmly since our talk, than before. On the chance that you haven't seen it, I enclose a clipping from yesterday's Newark "News."[1] I deplore such action as is therein taken because I feel that a previous statement by you would have precluded it. A large number of laboring men are bound to be influenced by this action, and the longer their antagonism to you remains undissipated, the harder it will be, in the end, to get rid of it.

Talking with Nugent yesterday—he of course expressed the certainty of your nomination and seemed to think that it was good politics for you to say nothing until after your nomination. I don't believe that is good democracy. I believe that *no man* should be taken on faith alone. Nugent is emphatic in his statement that you'll have to meet the labor & liquor questions anyway —& as the other questions are easy—I feel like making you this argument.

There will be a time before Sept 15 when it will be a moral certainty that your name is to be presented to the convention; when that time arrives, why not say that you recognize its arrival, and therefore, in justice to the delegates, now feel that you are obligated to state your position? I had a long talk with Mark Sullivan yesterday, & I know he feels as I do. He is a pretty fine man. I urged him to write you when he said he had been thinking of doing so. He was minority leader in the Assembly.

Congressman Hughes[2] says he is anxious to meet you and wants, as soon as you are nominated, to have you inspect his ideas as to a liquor plank. I'm dropping him a line asking him to write you now, instead.

Yours sincerely   Dan Fellows Platt

ALS (WP, DLC).
    [1] The enclosure is missing, but it reported the action of the New Jersey State Federation of Labor opposing Wilson's nomination.
    [2] William Hughes, United States representative from the 6th congressional district of New Jersey, 1903-1905, 1907-12; United States senator from New Jersey, 1913-18.

From Henry Eckert Alexander

Dear Dr. Wilson: Trenton, New Jersey August 19, 1910.

I attach no importance or weight to the resolutions passed by the State Federation of Labor. The resolutions do *not* "represent any considerable body of opinion among the laboring men."

I confess, however, that I find myself impatient and even indignant that our friends permit some of these things to be done. They ought to know and do know that the New Jersey Republican machine sees its finish in your nomination. Their one chance is to prevent your nomination. There is nothing too low or vile or criminal that they will not do along this line. I am sure that they will fail in their attempt but failure would come all the more quickly if we would use a little wisdom and a little courage and a little well-directed activity *right now*.

I have been trying to get the names of 500 or 1000 active Democratic workers over the state but I haven't gotten them. If I had them I know that I could print two or three editorials aimed straight at them and sent directly to them in marked copies that would "set them by the ears." I have asked Senator Smith to see that these names are sent to me and he has promised to have

Nugent send them. This is just one of the annoying things that I refer to.

As I told you, I have carried at my own expense for more than a year seven hundred ministers of various denominations all over the state. For months they read your addresses and references to you, but until the right time I never permitted any political reference to be made to you in the columns of the True American. From those seven hundred centers of quiet and thoughtful influence it is not hard to guess what is happening now and what will happen later when there is a call to arms. We will make history, not write it.

Sincerely yours,   Henry E. Alexander.

ALS (WP, DLC).

To Dan Fellows Platt

My dear Mr. Platt,   Lyme, Connecticut, 22 August, 1910.

Thank you for your letter of the eighteenth. I have been away from Lyme for a few days, and so have been delayed in replying.

It relieved me of a real difficulty that the committee did not write to me, and I appreciate the consideration shown me in the matter very much indeed. I think, with you, that I shall have to speak out in meeting pretty soon, in fairness to those who are kind enough to support me for the nomination. I shall watch the movement of things at home as carefully as possible, and shall try to take advantage of some right time or occasion to do so. My little talk with you did a great deal to clear my thoughts about the situation, and I am your debtor for a genuine kindness.

With warmest regard,

Cordially and sincerely Yrs.   Woodrow Wilson

WWTLS (photostat in RSB Coll., DLC).

From Oswald Garrison Villard

Dear Mr. Wilson: New York August 22, 1910.

I come back from my vacation delighted to find that from all reports the tide in New Jersey is running very strongly in your direction. This emboldens me to ask you whether I might come up to see you soon, perhaps next Sunday, or during the Labor Day holidays, in order to talk over with you the whole New Jersey situation. We want to exert a greater influence in New Jersey than ever before, in your behalf, and then I am eager to get the inspiration of a direct consultation with you. Believe me, nothing has so inspired and invigorated us here in the office for a long time as the prospect that we may have the pleasure and satisfaction of battling for you for the Governorship of New Jersey.

Faithfully yours,   Oswald Garrison Villard.

TLS (WP, DLC).

From Frederic Yates

Dear Dr. Woodrow Wilson,   [London] 22 Aug 1910

I am coming on the S.S. of 14th Sep and am not sure yet if Mr. Vanderlip will sit or not. I have another string to my bow in New York[,] Mr. Sweny[1] (Oil Standard). He asked me to paint him—but one never knows, they change their mind sometimes. The fault didn't really rest with me about the Vanderlips because he was ill—and during that time while I was waiting to hear from him, a lot of work turned up here—so I took it. Should there be nothing in New York for me from either quarter I shall leave my baggage at some hotel & make a flying trip up to Princeton—see all you dear people—and then be off to Los Angeles. I am booked by way of Grand Canon—Santa Fé Route. Will you keep any letters that come for me.   Fred Yates

Wife[,] Mary[2] & I starting for Paris & Chartres on Friday, 26th Aug

ALS (WP, DLC).
    [1] Perhaps William H. Sweny, a New York lawyer with offices at 35 Wall St.
    [2] His wife, Emily Chapman Martin Yates, and his daughter, Mary.

To Edgar Williamson

My Dear Mr. Williamson: [Lyme, Conn.] August 23, 1910.

I warmly appreciate your kind letter of the eighteenth of August.

The gross misrepresentations of my views with regard to organized labor which some newspapers have printed have given me no concern. They were wilful and deliberate misrepresentations, and such things take care of themselves. The papers that stoop to them will in the end be found out and lose credit altogether.

I was distressed that the New Jersey Federation of Labor should have allowed itself to be imposed upon—not because its members are likely to remain deceived in this matter, but for the opposite reason: because they are sure to discover their mistake and to feel the mortification of having taken unjust and hasty action. I was not hurt, because I knew that no injustice was intended. I was simply sorry. It is a pity to see things so handled.

I had, of course, intended to let the incident pass in silence—for two reasons. First, because I knew the whole matter would right itself; and, second, because I have not been seeking the nomination for Governor at the hands of my party, and to argue the matter would seem to be arguing for my nomination. But your letter puts a compulsion upon me of an entirely different kind. You urged the Federation to inform itself about my views and wait until it could be sure that it was acting justly, and, having failed in that, you turn to me and frankly ask me what I really think. Your friendliness and candor leave me no choice but to reply. I do so with pleasure.

I have always been the warm friend of organized labor. It is, in my opinion, not only perfectly legitimate, but absolutely necessary that Labor should organize if it is to secure justice from organized Capital; and everything that it does to improve the condition of workingmen, to obtain legislation that will impose full legal responsibility upon the employer for his treatment of his employees and for their protection against accident, to secure just and adequate wages, and to put reasonable limits upon the working day and upon all the exactions of those who employ labor, ought to have the hearty support of all fair-minded and public-spirited men. For there is a sense in which the condition of labor is the condition of the nation itself.

I have criticised some of the things organized labor has occasionally done; but I have criticised them as a friend and because I thought them harmful to the laborers themselves and harmful to the country. I know of no other standard by which to judge these things than the interest of the whole community. The laboring man cannot benefit himself by injuring the industries of the country. Many thoughtful laboring men are themselves critics, and very outspoken critics, of many things which the unions do, and I stand with them and with all other right-minded Americans in saying what I honestly think. If I am mistaken, it can easily be shown that I am, and I shall always be glad to have it shown.

I am much more afraid that the great corporations, combinations and trusts will do the country deep harm than I am that the labor organizations will harm it; and yet I believe the corporations to be necessary instruments of modern business. They are good things so long as they act in the common interests, and very bad things when they do not. Joint stock corporations, by putting into one enterprise the money of many thousands of persons, concentrate in their managers the power of thousands, a very dangerous power, which should be closely watched and regulated. Sharp criticism should keep them amenable to public opinion. Strict law should restrain them. The principle is the same for all of us.

But our object, in the one case as in the other, should not be hostile. There has been hostility enough all around. What we need now is to take common counsel as to what is for the common benefit, for the good of the country and of the several communities in which we live and earn our bread, not only, but also our happiness. We need frank, outspoken, friendly opinion. We need criticism which is not intended to damage but to create a better understanding all around. I have tried in everything that I have said on public questions to contribute to this friendly process of criticism, in order to assist in bringing on better days, and a state of opinion in which all men and all interests shall receive their due. To have any fear or favor in the matter is to be untrue to every standard of public duty.

If all editors and writers and public speakers will deal frankly and fairly as you have done, we shall soon hit upon a just and common policy with regard to the many things that perplex us.

With much respect and appreciation,

Sincerely yours,   Woodrow Wilson.[1]

Printed in the Orange, N. J., *Labor Standard*, Sept. 2, 1910; with minor corrections from the text in the Trenton *True American*, Sept. 2, 1910.
[1] There are WWsh and WWT drafts of this letter in WP, DLC.

To George Brinton McClellan Harvey

Lyme, Connecticut,

My dear Colonel Harvey,   23 August, 1910.

I found the occasion[1] waiting for me when I got back. The enclosed letter seemed to me clearly entitled to a reply, and I have sent the enclosed. Will you not be kind enough to return letter and reply to me when you have read them? What I send was my draft. It is to be printed, you observe, on Labor Day.

I greatly enjoyed my visit to Boston.

Always,   Faithfully Yours,   Woodrow Wilson

WWTLS (WP, DLC).
[1] That is, the opportunity offered by Williamson's letter of August 18, 1910.

From Henry Eckert Alexander

Dear Dr. Wilson: Trenton, New Jersey August 23 [1910].

I am terribly disappointed in our friend's sketch. It is exactly what I do *not* want. I can all the more appreciate old Simon Cameron[1] when he referred to "them d - - - literary fellers." It is all very well for those who know you on equal terms to read such an article, but how about the people who don't know you at all? They don't know whether you ever had an idea about God, man or the Devil and it is for their information that I have tried to get this sketch in hand. Forty-eight newspapers will use a suitable sketch but for my purposes Mr. Inglis's document is pretty wide of the mark. Miss McIlvaine sent today some matter containing far more suggestion and substance. I have had my associate editor, Mr. [Forrest R.] Dye, hard at work cooking up something that may be useful. I hope to have it shaped up tonight and that it will pass muster.[2]

The [Trenton State] Gazette had a line this morning that made me laugh. It said: "Mr. Lewis is neither a demagogue nor a pedagogue."   Sincerely yours,   Henry E. Alexander.

ALS (WP, DLC).
   [1] United States senator from Pennsylvania, 1845-49, 1857-61, 1867-77; Secretary of War, 1861-62.
   [2] This was the article which appeared in the Trenton *True American*, Aug. 26, 1910, under the headline, "A Plain Man of the People." As the headline suggests, the article sought to portray Wilson as a Lincolnesque character.

From James Cresap Sprigg[1]

My dear Dr. Wilson: Caldwell, N. J. August 27, 1910.

The receipt of yours of 24th inst. afforded me much pleasure.

Referring to the Gubernatorial situation, I beg to assure you that the independent voters of this state are practically unanimous in their desire to elect you. Unfortunately the political bosses are in control of the various organizations and are a serious menace to the success of every honest undertaking; they are keenly alert at this moment and endeavoring to effect such compromises as will enable them to garner the entire crop of grain expected from a Democratic harvest. Smith, Harrigan[2] and Davis to adjust their differences is the latest fairly well authenticated report. Harrigan for Governor, Smith for Senator and Davis for dollars. Political tricksters trying to influence probable delegates to the convention and spreading such lying reports as—that you are unfavorable to labor, opposed to the regulative powers of the public utility commission, the government of primary elections etc.

If you will write a letter for publication, or issue a statement, I will see that it is given the widest publicity through the associated and State press and in other ways. Your friends would be pleased—and it would do much good at this juncture. . . .

Assuring you of my highest regards, I beg to subscribe

Yours faithfully,   J. C. Sprigg.

TLS (WP, DLC).

[1] Chairman of the Democratic Union of New Jersey, an ephemeral organization which attempted to unite independents and progressive Democrats.

[2] William Harrigan, Sheriff of Essex County.

From Joseph M. Noonan

My dear Mr Wilson: Warwick, N. Y. Aug 28/10

Your letter of 23 inst was forwarded to me here and I am grateful to you for your appreciation of my motives in what I have written to you about your candidacy.

Mr Warren Dixon, Corporation Counsel of Jersey City, an appointee and supporter of Wittpenn, was in Warwick last week and called upon me here. He is a lawyer of high professional standing, intelligent but somewhat narrow. As I know him very well we talked quite frankly over the political situation; and here are some of the things I learned from him about you: he insists, and I really think he believes, you are (1) opposed to the regulation of railroads &c, (2) that you are hostile to the labor unions, (3) that you are a *Socialist* and (4) that you are a prohibitionist. In support of this indictment he referred me to your speeches and published articles, extracts from which, he says, are being published in the Wittpenn press. When I asked him how, if you are a Socialist, he could account for your opposition to labor unions and to effective state regulation of railroads he said it was for you to explain, if you could, the inconsistency of your position.

Now this kind of talk is merely a specimen, and a moderate specimen, of the propaganda that the Wittpennites are carrying on against you. These allegations, while utterly ridiculous, must inevitably have a tendency to unsettle the public mind if they are not answered.

The Davis Association[1] has its annual outing on Sept 7 and on that occasion there will be gathered together about 5000 Democrats and every section of the state will be represented. If your statement could be made before that date it could be used very effectively at that outing.

I am not urging haste for I know what a difficult and delicate task it is to frame a statement of this important nature. Yet delay is harmful. Why cannot the Chairman of the Democratic State Committee invite each of the several candidates for the governorship to place in his hands, for simultaneous publication, an explicit statement of his views on pending political problems &c? At any rate I hope some way may be found, and soon, to silence the enemy.   Very Sincerely Yours   Jos. M. Noonan

ALS (WP, DLC).
1 That is, the Democratic association of Hudson County.

To Mary Allen Hulbert Peck

Dearest Friend,   Chattanooga, Tenn. 31 August, 1910

If you have never been to a meeting of a numerous association, you cannot realize how impossible it is for a guest, who is also a public character, to write letters. But it is not impossible for him to think of his best friends with deep affection throughout all distractions. I think of you and think from hour to hour of a score of things with which I could divert and please you. These men are *very* human and *very* amusing!

I am well—and, if the Southern Road is faithful to its schedule, I will see you Saturday forenoon.
                    Your devoted friend   Woodrow Wilson
ALS (WP, DLC).

An Address in Chattanooga, Tennessee,
to the American Bar Association

[Aug. 31, 1910]
THE LAWYER AND THE COMMUNITY

The whole history of society has been the history of a struggle for law, for the definite establishment and continuance of such relationships as seemed to those who had the choice to be best suited to the support of their own influence and to the maintenance of the community over which they presided. Law is simply that part of the established thought and habit which has been accorded general acceptance and which is backed and sanctioned by the force and authority of the regularly constituted government of the body politic. The whole history of liberty, that history which so quickens our pulses as we look back upon it and which so sustains our confidence in the power of righteousness and of all the handsomer, nobler impulses of humanity, has been a struggle for the recognition of rights not only, but for the embodiment of rights in law, in courts and magistrates and assemblies. Such must always be the form of every high endeavour made in the interest of men and of the ideals of political life.

We do not fight to establish theses. We do not pour our blood out to vindicate a philosophy of politics. There are two great empires of human feeling, the realm of religion and the realm of political aspiration. In the one realm we work spiritually, our liberty is of the thought; in the other we work structurally, our liberty abides in institutions, is real only when it is tangible, a thing that can be put into operation,—not in our own souls merely, but in the world of action outside of us as well. A right in the field of politics is a power to command the action of others in our own behoof; and that is also a right in law. Religions are mighty forces of belief, and the church, when it has its genuine and entire liberty, lies outside the state; but political liberty lives and moves and has its being in the structure and practice of society. The two fields are not, indeed, sharply separated: religious freedom must be safeguarded by institutional arrangements, but religious freedom is the right to be ungoverned, political freedom the right to be governed justly and with equity as between man and man. We fight for law as well as for faith because we fight not only for the right to think but also for the right to be and to do what we will within the limits of a just and equal order.

I remind you of these things at the beginning of my discourse because I wish to say a good deal about our present struggle for law. The old order changeth,—changeth under our very eyes, not quietly and equably, but swiftly and with the noise and heat and tumult of reconstruction. The forces of society contend openly with one another, avow their antagonisms, marshal and discipline their hosts, and are keen to win, not very willing to accommodate their differences and come to a common understanding which will be for the common advantage.

I suppose that all struggle for law has been conscious, that very little of it has been blind or merely instinctive. It is the fashion, too, to say, as if with a superior knowledge of affairs and of human weakness, that every age has been an age of transition and that no age is more full of change than another; but in very few ages of the world has the struggle for change been so widespread, so deliberate, or upon so great a scale as this which we are taking part in. The transition we are witnessing is no equable transition of growth and normal alteration, no silent, unconscious unfolding of one age into another, its natural heir and successor. Society is looking itself over, in our day, from top to bottom, is making fresh and critical analysis of its very elements, is questioning its oldest practices as freely as its newest, scrutinizing every arrangement and motive of its life, and stands ready to attempt nothing less than a radical reconstruction, which only frank and honest counsels and the forces of generous coöperation can hold back from becoming a revolution. We are in a temper to reconstruct economic society as we were once in a temper to reconstruct political society, and political society may itself undergo a radical modification in the process. I doubt if any age was ever more conscious of its task or more unanimously desirous of radical and extended changes in its economic and political practice.

I do not speak of these things in apprehension, because all is open and above board. This is not a day in which great forces rally in secret. The whole stupendous programme is planned and canvassed in the open, and we have learned the rules of the game of change. Good temper, the wisdom that comes of sober counsel, the energy of thoughtful and unselfish men, the habit of coöperation and of compromise which has been bred in us by long years of free government, in which reason rather than passion has been made to prevail by the sheer virtue of candid and universal debate, will enable us to win through still another great age without revolution. I speak in plain terms of the real character of what is now patent to every man merely in order to fix your thought upon the fact that this thing that is going on about us is not a mere warfare of opinion. It has an object, a definite and concrete object, and that object is Law, the alteration of institutions upon an extended plan of change.

We are lawyers. This is the field of our knowledge. We are servants of society, officers of the courts of justice. Our duty is a much larger thing than the mere advice of private clients. In every deliberate struggle for law we ought to be the guides, not too critical and unwilling, not too tenacious of the familiar technicalities in which we have been schooled, not too much in love with precedents and the easy maxims which have saved us the trouble of thinking, but ready to give expert and disinterested advice to those who purpose progress and the readjustment of the frontiers of justice.

You cannot but have marked the recent changes in the relation of lawyers to affairs in this country; and, if you feel as I do about the great profession to which we belong, you cannot but have been made uneasy by the change. Lawyers constructed the fabric of our state governments and of the government of the United

States, and throughout the earlier periods of our national development presided over all the larger processes of politics. Our political conscience as a nation was embedded in our written fundamental law. Every question of public policy seemed sooner or later to become a question of law, upon which trained lawyers must be consulted. In all our legislative halls debate thundered in the phrases of the written enactments under which our legislators and our governors exercised authority. Public life was a lawyer's forum. Laymen lent their invaluable counsel, but lawyers guided, and lawyers framed the law.

I am not speaking of the dependence of our political movement upon the judgments of courts. That has not been altered, and cannot be. So long as we have written constitutions courts must interpret them for us, and must be the final tribunals of interpretation. I am speaking of the prominence and ascendancy of lawyers in the practical political processes which precede the judgments of the courts. Until the civil war came and the more debatable portions of our fundamental law were cut away by the sword, the very platforms of parties centred upon questions of legal interpretation and lawyers were our guiding statesmen. I suppose a more intensely legal polity never existed.

So long as passion was excluded it was a tonic way of life. Statesmanship necessitated precise thinking. Every policy that was proposed had to be explicitly grounded upon precedent. At every step there was a re-examination of the fundamental principles which were alleged to justify or sustain it. Thought of the long history of English constitutional practice and of the avowed purpose with which government had been set up in America constituted the atmosphere in which everything was done. Every ancient, every recent contest for liberty threw its light forward upon the debates of Congress and of state legislatures. The newest State shared with the oldest the long tradition, and all alike were thoughtful of what had been designed and hoped for by the men whose sacrifices had given life to our freedom. No doubt it stiffened the action of government. No doubt there was a formality and a scrupulous regard for the letter in the conduct of legislation better suited to a young country just finding itself and face to face only with large problems of simple and obvious character than to an older country, whose life has grown complex and confused and whose questions of exigency square with no plain precedents of constitutional practice. Lawyers will construct for you a very definite polity, and construct it to admiration; they have not often shown themselves equally fitted to liberalize it or facilitate the processes of change. But the leadership of lawyers at least meant a repeated re-examination of principle and precedent, and was very instructive even when it was least enlightened. It prevented fluidity. A reason had to be given for every step taken,—a reason which would commend itself to the courts after it had commended itself to statesmen. The statesman and the lawyer were clients and consorts, and the legal conscience of the people was constantly refreshed and strengthened. These are great influences. They make for character and for the solidity of institutions.

But they are gone. You have only to recall the many extraordinary interpretations of the interstate commerce clause of the constitution upon which serious debate has been wasted in Congress in recent years to be convinced of it. Our lawyers themselves are not carefully trained as they used to be in the principles of our constitutional law. It does not stand in the foreground of their study or practice, but in the background, very vague and general, a thing to be resorted to only upon rare occasion. Our legislatures now listen to debates upon constitutional questions with ill-concealed impatience, as tedious and academic. The nation has grown keen after certain practical objects and will not willingly brook the impediments set up by constitutions. The temper of the age is very nearly summed up in a feeling which you may put into words like these: "There are certain things we must do. Our life as a nation must be rectified in certain all-important particulars. If there be no law for the change, it must be found or made. We will not be argued into impotency by lawyers. We are not interested in the structure of our governments so much as in the exigencies of our life."

There are many reasons why this change of temper and of point of view has occurred. I will venture to mention one or two of the more obvious. It is not by chance that statesmanship has grown bigger than the bounds of mere legal precedent.

In the first place, the debates and constitutional struggles of the first seventy years of our political history settled most of the fundamental questions of our constitutional law. Solid lines of decided cases carry the definite outlines of the structure and make clear the methods of its action. We seemed after the civil war to be released from the demands of formal definition. The life of the nation, running upon normal lines, has grown infinitely varied. It does not centre now upon questions of governmental structure or of the distribution of governmental powers. It centres upon economic questions, questions of the very structure and operation of society itself, of which government is only the instrument. Our development has run so fast and so far along the lines sketched in the earlier day of constitutional definition, has so crossed and interlaced those lines, has piled upon them such novel structures of trust and combination, has elaborated within them a life so manifold, so full of forces which transcend the boundaries of the country itself and fill the eyes of the world, that a new nation seems to have been created which the old formulas do not fit or afford a vital interpretation of itself. The confusion has clearly come about without intention. We have been engaged in enterprises which the law as we formerly looked at it was clearly not meant to prevent or embarrass. We pushed them forward, therefore, without thinking of the effect they might have upon older conceptions of our legal processes. They seemed to spring out of the normal and necessary uses of the great continent whose riches we have been exploiting. We did not think of the legal consequences one way or the other, and therefore did not need or seek the advice of constitutional lawyers.

Constitutional lawyers have fallen into the background. We have relegated them to the Supreme Court, without asking ourselves where we are to find them when vacancies occur in that great tribunal. A new type of lawyers has been created; and that new type has come to be the prevailing type. Lawyers have been sucked into the maelstrom of the new business system of the country. That system is highly technical and highly specialized. It is divided into distinct sections and provinces, each with particular legal problems of its own. Lawyers, therefore, everywhere that business has thickened and had a large development, have become experts in some special technical field. They do not practice law. They do not handle the general, miscellaneous interests of society. They are not general counsellors of right and obligation. They do not bear the relation to the business of their neighborhoods that the family doctor bears to the health of the community in which he lives. They do not concern themselves with the universal aspects of society. The family doctor is himself giving place to a score of specialists; and so is also what one might call the family solicitor. Lawyers are specialists, like all other men around them. The general, broad, universal field of law grows dim and yet more dim to their apprehension as they spend year after year in minute examination and analysis of a particular part of it; not a small part, it may be, perhaps the part which the courts are for the time most concerned with, but a part which has undergone a high degree of development, which is very technical and many-sided, and which requires the study and practice of years for its mastery; and yet a province apart, whose conquest necessarily absorbs them and necessarily separates them from the

dwindling body of general practitioners who used to be our statesmen.

And so society has lost something, or is losing it,—something
which it is very serious to lose in an age of law, when society
depends more than ever before upon the law-giver and the courts
for its structural steel, the harmony and coördination of its parts,
its convenience, its permanency, and its facility. In gaining new
functions, in being drawn into modern business instead of standing outside of it, in becoming identified with particular interests
instead of holding aloof and impartially advising all interests, the
lawyer has lost his old function, is looked askance at in politics,
must disavow special engagements if he would have his counsel
heeded in matters of common concern. Society has suffered a
corresponding loss,—at least American society has. It has lost its
one-time feeling for law as the basis of its peace, its progress, its
prosperity. Lawyers are not now regarded as the mediators of progress. Society was always ready to be prejudiced against them;
now it finds its prejudice confirmed.

Meanwhile, look what legal questions are to be settled, how
stupendous they are, how far-reaching, and how impossible it
will be to settle them without the advice of learned and experienced lawyers! The country must find lawyers of the right sort
and of the old spirit to advise it, or it must stumble through a very
chaos of blind experiment. It never needed lawyers who are also
statesmen more than it needs them now,—needs them in its
courts, in its legislatures, in its seats of executive authority,—
lawyers who can think in the terms of society itself, mediate between interests, accommodate right to right, establish equity, and
bring the peace that will come with genuine and hearty coöperation, and will come in no other way.

The specialization of business and the extraordinary development of corporate organization and administration have led to
consequences well worth the lawyer's consideration. Everyone
else is considering them, and considering them with deep concern. We have witnessed in modern business the submergence
of the individual within the organization, and yet the increase to
an extraordinary degree of the power of the individual,—of the
individual who happens to control the organization. Most men are
individuals no longer so far as their business, its activities or its
moralities, is concerned. They are not units, but fractions; with
their individuality and independence of choice in matters of
business they have lost also their individual choice within the field
of morals. They must do what they are told to do, or lose their
connection with modern affairs. They are not at liberty to ask

whether what they are told to do is right or wrong. They cannot get at the men who ordered it,—have no access to them. They have no voice of counsel or of protest. They are mere cogs in a machine which has men for its parts. And yet there are men here and there with whom the whole choice lies. There are men who control the machine as a whole and the men who compose it. There are men who use it with an imperial freedom of design, whose power and whose individuality overtop whole communities. There is more individual power than ever, but those who exercise it are few and formidable, and the mass of men are mere pawns in the game.

The present task of the law is nothing less than to rehabilitate the individual,—not to make the subordinate independent of the superior, not to turn corporations into debating societies, not to disintegrate what we have been at such pains to piece together in the organization of modern industrial enterprise, but to undo enough of what we have done in the development of our law of corporations to give the law direct access again to the individual, —to every individual in all his functions.

Corporations do not do wrong. Individuals do wrong, the individuals who direct and use them for selfish and illegitimate purposes, to the injury of society and the serious curtailment of private rights. Guilt, as Governor Harmon has truly said, is always personal. You cannot punish corporations. Fines fall upon the wrong persons, more heavily upon the innocent than upon the guilty, as much upon those who knew nothing whatever of the transactions for which the fine is imposed as upon those who originated and carried them through,—upon the stockholders and the customers rather than upon the men who direct the policy of the business. If you dissolve the offending corporation, you throw great undertakings out of gear. You merely drive what you are seeking to check into other forms or temporarily disorganize some important business altogether, to the infinite loss of thousands of entirely innocent persons and to the great inconvenience of society as a whole. Law can never accomplish its objects in that way. It can never bring peace or command respect by such futilities.

I regard the corporation as indispensable to modern business enterprise. I am not jealous of its size or might, if you will but abandon at the right points the fatuous, antiquated, and quite unnecessary fiction which treats it as a legal person; if you will but cease to deal with it by means of your law as if it were a single individual not only but also,—what every child may perceive it is not,—a responsible individual. Such fictions and analogies were innocent and convenient enough so long as corporations were comparatively small and only one of many quite as important instrumentalities used in business, only a minor item in the economic order of society. But it is another matter now. They span society, and the responsibilities involved in their complex organization and action must be analyzed by the law as the responsibilities of society itself, in all its other aspects, have been.

The corporations now overshadow partnerships altogether. Still more do they overshadow all individuals engaged in business on their own capital and separate responsibility. It is an arrangement by which hundreds of thousands of men who would in days gone by have set up in business for them-selves put their money into a single huge accumulation and place the entire direction of its employment in the hands of men they have never seen, with whom they never confer. These men, these quite autocratic managers, are thereby made, as it were, multiple individuals. In them are concentrated the resources, the choices, the opportunities, in brief the power, of thousands. They could never of themselves, of their own effort and sagacity, have accumulated the vast capital they employ, and employ as if it were their own; and yet they have not the full legal responsibilities of those who supplied them with it. Because they have the power of thousands they have not the responsibility common to those whose power they use! It is an extraordinary anomaly!

A modern corporation is an economic society, a little economic state,—and not always little, even as compared with states. Many modern corporations wield revenues and command resources which no ancient state possessed, and which some modern bodies politic show no approach to in their budgets. The economic power of society itself is concentrated in them for the conduct of this, that, or the other sort of business. The functions of business are differentiated and divided amongst them, but the power for each function is massed. In some instances even the functions are not separated. Railroad companies have been known to buy coal mines. Manufacturing combinations have been observed to develop a score of subsidiary industries, to spread a network of organization over related enterprises, and sometimes even over enterprises whose relation to their main undertakings it is difficult for the lay mind to perceive. Society, in short, has discovered a new way of massing its resources and its power of enterprise, is building up bodies economic outside its bodies politic which may, if we do not find the means to prevent them, the means of disclosing the responsibilities of the men who compose them, dominate bodies politic themselves.

And these huge industrial organizations we continue to treat as legal persons, as individuals, which we must not think of as consisting of persons, within which we despair of enabling the law to pick out anybody in particular to put either its restraint or its command upon! It is childish, it is futile, it is ridiculous! One thinks of the old Confederation, which we had to abandon because it tried to govern States and could not command individuals. As well treat society itself as a unit; insist that it impose a fine upon itself for every wrong done, no matter how notorious it may be who did it; suggest that it embarrass all its processes of action and even break itself up into its constituent parts and begin all over again when the persons whom it has trusted prove depraved or selfish. It is not even interesting to continue such an experiment.

Society cannot afford to have individuals wield the power of thousands without personal responsibility. It cannot afford to let its strongest men be the only men who are inaccessible to the law. Modern democratic society, in particular, cannot afford to constitute its economic undertakings upon the monarchical or aristocratic principle and adopt the fiction that the kings and great men thus set up can do no wrong which will make them personally amenable to the law which restrains smaller men: that their kingdoms, not themselves, must suffer for their blindness, their follies, and their transgressions of right.

It does not redeem the situation that these kings and chiefs of industry are not chosen upon the hereditary principle (sometimes, alas! they are) but are men who have risen by their own capacity, sometimes from utter obscurity, with the freedom of self-assertion which should characterize a free society. Their power is none the less arbitrary and irresponsible when obtained. That a peasant may become king does not render the kingdom democratic.

I would not have you think that I am speaking with a feeling of hostility towards the men who have in our day given the nation its extraordinary material power and prosperity by an exercise of genius such as in days gone by was used, in each great age, to build empires and alter the boundaries of states. I am drawing no indictment: no indictment that I could draw would be just. No indictment that has been drawn has been just, but only exaggerated and disquieting. The time for hostilities has gone by. The time for accommodations, for common understandings, for a surcease of economic warfare and the inauguration of the peace that will come only by common sacrifices and concessions, has come. I am simply trying to analyze the existing constitution of business in blunt words of truth, without animus or passion of any kind, and with a single, clear purpose.

That purpose is to recall you to the service of the nation as a whole, from which you have been drifting away; to remind you that, no matter what the exactions of modern legal business, no matter what or how great the necessity for specialization in your practice of the law, you are not the servants of special interests, the mere expert counsellors of this, that, or the other group of business men; but guardians of the general peace, the guides of those who seek to realize by some best accommodation the rights of men. With that purpose in view, I am asking you to look again at the corporation.

It is an indispensable convenience; but is it a necessary burden? Modern business is no doubt best conducted upon a great scale, for which the resources of a single individual are manifestly insufficient. Money and men must be massed in order to do the things that must be done for the support and facilitation of modern life. Whether energy or economy be your standard, it is plain enough that we cannot go back to the old competitive system under which individuals were the competitors. Wide organization and coöperation have made the modern world possible and must maintain it. They have developed genius as well as wealth. The nations are richer in capacity and in gifts comparable to the higher gifts of statesmanship because of them and the opportunities they have afforded exceptional men. But we have done things in pursuit of them, and have nursed notions regarding them, which are no necessary part of what we seek. We can have corporations, can retain them in unimpaired efficiency, without depriving law of its ancient searching efficacy, its inexorable mandate that men, not societies, must suffer for wrongs done. The major premise of all law is moral responsibility, the moral responsibility of individuals for their acts and conspiracies; and no other foundation can any man lay upon which a stable fabric of equitable justice can be reared.

I call your attention to the fact, therefore, that it is perfectly possible to have corporations and serve all the necessities and conveniences of modern society by means of the great combinations of wealth and energy which we have found to be so excellent, and yet dispense with a large part of the quite outworn and now in many respects deeply demoralizing fiction that a corporation is an indivisible person. Of course we must continue to regard it as an artificial person so far as is necessary to enable it to hold such property as may be proper for the execution of its charter purposes, to sue and be sued, and to conduct its business through officers who speak for it as a whole, and whose signatures and orders are, under its by-laws and resolutions, binding upon it. It must act and live as a person, and must be capable of enjoying, what individuals cannot enjoy, a certain perpetuity of power and authority, though individual men within it come and go, live, die, resign, or are translated. But there its unity should stop.

In respect of the responsibility which the law imposes in order to protect society itself, in order to protect men and communities against wrongs which are not breaches of contract but offenses against the public interest, the common welfare, it is imperative that we should regard corporations as merely groups of individuals, from which it may, perhaps, be harder to pick out particular persons for punishment than it is to pick them out of the general body of unassociated men, but from which it is, nevertheless, possible to pick them out,—possible not only, but absolutely necessary if business is ever again to be moralized. Corporations must continue to be used as a convenience in the transaction of business, but they must cease to be used as a covert for wrong-doers.

The managers of corporations themselves always know the men who originated the acts charged against them as done in contravention of the law; is there no means by which their names may be disclosed to the officers of justice? Every act, every policy in the conduct of the affairs of a corporation originates with some particular officer, committee, or board. The officer, the committee, the board which orders an act or originates a policy contrary to the law of the land or intended to neutralize or contravene it is an insurgent against society: the man or men who originate any such act or policy should be punished, and they alone. It is not necessary that the corporation should be broken up. It is not fair that the stockholders should be mulcted in damages. If there are damages to be paid they should be paid out of the private means of the persons who are really guilty. An analysis of the guilt is perfectly feasible. It is the duty of lawyers, of all lawyers, to assist the makers of law and the reformers of abuses by pointing out the best and most effective way to make it.

It seems to me absurd, for example (let me say by way of parenthesis), to extend the law of libel to corporations, to suffer one publishing corporation to sue another for defamation. Somebody in particular has uttered the libel, somebody in particular has been libeled. Character cannot be incorporated; writing cannot be corporately done. Are lawyers so incapable of ascertaining the facts that they cannot find out who it is that did the thing or who it is that has been injured in his reputation?

I know that the matter is not as simple as it sounds. I know that some corporations are in fact controlled from the outside, not from the inside: that it often happens that some man or some small group of men who are not even in its directorate dictate its policy, its individual acts, its attitude towards law and society, and that the men who act within it are little better than automata. But are they really beyond discovery? On the contrary, is it not generally matter of common knowledge who they are? Would it take extraordinary acumen and intelligence to devise laws which would reach them also? What we are after, of course, is to obtain laws which will prevent the use of corporations to the public hurt and disadvantage. We know that the man who shoots his enemy was not in the gun, that he simply used it, and that no part of the mechanism of the gun itself is criminally liable. We can generally discover who used the gun and how he used it, whatever his cunning and secrecy. We can also find out who uses the corporations against the public interest; and we can punish him, or them, if we will, whether they belong to the actual nominal organization of the corporation or not. Our processes of evidence may have to be considerably altered, but we can alter them; our formal conception of parties in interest may have to be extended, but it is easy to extend it; our makebelieve that we can see nobody in the transaction but those who are avowed and formal members of the organization may have to be discarded, but that ought to be a relief to our consciences. We have allowed ourselves to be ridiculously limited and embarrassed by the theory that a corporation is an indivisible person not only but that nobody outside of it, no matter how intimate his use and control, may be brought into the suit by any genteel lawyer bred in the orthodox schools of law. A corporation is merely a convenient instrument of business and we may regulate its use as we please, and those who use it. Here is merely an artificial, a fictitious person, whom God did not make or endow, which we ourselves have made with our own hands and can alter as we will. I see no law of nature in our way, but only some laws of evidence and of corporate theory which we have outgrown.

You will say that in many instances it is not fair to pick out for punishment the particular officer who ordered a thing done, because he really had no freedom in the matter: that he is himself under orders, exercises no individual liberty of choice, is a dummy manipulated from without. I reply that society should permit no man to carry out orders which are against law and public policy, and that, if you will but put one or two conspicuous dummies in the penitentiary, there will be no more dummies for hire. You can stop the traffic in dummies, and then, when the idea has taken root in the corporate mind that dummies will be confiscated, pardon the one or two innocent men who may happen to have got into jail. There will not be many, and the custom of the trade will change!

There are other corporate matters worthy of your attention, but they do not intimately concern my present theme. I think you must admit, for example, that the position of the minority stockholder is, in most of our States, extremely unsatisfactory. I do not wonder that he sometimes doubts whether corporate stocks are property at all or not. He does not seem to enjoy any of the substantial rights of property in connection with them. He is merely contributing money for the conduct of a business which other men run as they please. If he does not approve of what they do, there seems nothing for it but to sell the stock (though their acts may have depreciated its value immensely). He cannot even inquire or protest without being told to mind his own business,—the very thing he was innocently trying to do! There are many things which are not satisfactory about this putting the money of many men into one pile for the use of a board of directors, and to my mind it is clearly your task as counsellors of society to make them satisfactory. It is the duty of our profession to see to it that no man's powers exceed or lie outside of his legal and personal responsibilities,—that the corporation be made a mere convenience of business and not a means of irresponsible mastery, its interior and all men within it as accessible to the law as its exterior and the scattered individuals who have no corporate ambush from which to work their will.

I have used the corporation merely as an illustration. It stands in the foreground of all modern economic questions, so far as the United States are concerned. It is society's present means of effective life in the field of industry. Society must get complete control of its instrument or fail. But I have used it only as an illustration of a great theme, a theme greater than any single illustration could compass,—namely, the responsibility of the lawyer to the community he professes to serve.

You are not a mere body of expert business advisers in the field of civil law or a mere body of expert advocates for those who get entangled in the meshes of the criminal law. You are servants of the public, of the state itself. You are under bonds to serve the general interest, the integrity and enlightenment of law itself, in the advice you give individuals. It is your duty also to advise those who make the laws,—to advise them in the general interest, with a view to the amelioration of every undesirable condition that the law can reach, the removal of every obstacle to progress and fair dealing that the law can remove, the lightening of every burden the law can lift and the righting of every wrong the law can rectify. The services of the lawyer are indispensable not only in the application of the accepted processes of the law, the interpretation of existing rules in the daily operations of life and business. His services are indispensable also in keeping, and in making, the law clear with regard to responsibility, to organization, to liability, and, above all, to the relation of private rights to the public interest.

The structure of modern society is a structure of law rather than of custom. The lawyer's advice is more than ever necessary to the state, therefore. Communities as well as individuals stand in constant need of his guidance. This used to be commonplace doctrine amongst us; why does it now need to be preached again? Is it mere accident that the relation of the legal profession to affairs has changed? Is it merely because the greater constitutional questions seemed for a time to be settled and legal debates gave place to industrial enterprise, a great age of material following a great age of political development? Has it been merely a change of circumstances, or has it been a change of attitude and spirit as well on the part of the profession itself? Has not the lawyer allowed himself to become part of the industrial development, has he not been sucked into the channels of business, has he not changed his connections and become part of the mercantile structure rather than part of the general social structure of our commonwealths as he used to be? Has he not turned away from his former interests and duties and become narrowed to a technical function?

Whatever may be the cause, it is evident that he now regards himself as the counsel of individuals exclusively, and not of communities. He may plead the new organization of politics, which seems to exclude all counsel except that of party success and personal control; he may argue that public questions have changed, have drifted away from his field, and that his advice is no longer asked; but, whatever his explanation or excuse, the fact is the same. He does not play the part he used to play; he does not show the spirit in affairs he used to show. He does not do what he ought to do.

For there never was a time, in fact, when his advice, his disinterested and earnest advice, was more needed than it is now in the exigent processes of reform, in the busy processes of legislation through which we are passing, with so singular a mixture of hope and apprehension. I hear a great many lawyers join the cry of the business men, that it is time legislators left business alone, allowed it to recover from the confusion and distraction of regulative statutes, altered tariffs, and supervising commissions, find its natural methods again, and go forward upon a way of prosperity which will not be beset by fear and uncertainty. But the cry is futile, the impatience which gives rise to it is selfish and ignorant. Nothing is settled or can be let alone when it is known to be wrong until it is set right. We have settled nothing in our recent reform legislation. That is the reason it is so unsatisfactory, and why some prudent and thoughtful men grow tired of it. But that is only another reason for seeking out and finding what will be the happy and successful way of setting our economic interests in order. There has been no satisfactory settlement, but there must be one. Public opinion is wider awake about these matters than it has been within the memory of any man living, and it is not going to turn away from them until satisfactory reforms of the law are found. There will be no peace until a happy and honourable basis of peace has been hit upon. Lawyers may come into the settlement or stay out of it, as they please, but a settlement there must be. For one, I hope that they will not stay out. I fear that it would be disastrous for them to do so,—disastrous to them and to society. I covet for them their old and honourable leadership in public counsel.

Just because they have so buried themselves in modern business, just because they have been so intimate a part of it, they know better than any one else knows what legal adjustments have and have not been made,—know the practices that circumvent the law, even the existing law, and the provisions of statute and court procedure that might put a stop to them or square them with what the interests of the whole community demand, theirs is the special responsibility to advise remedies. Theirs has been the part of intimate counsel in all that has been going on. The country holds them largely responsible for it. It distrusts every "corporation lawyer." It supposes him in league with persons whom it has learned to dread, to whom it ascribes a degree of selfishness which in effect makes them public enemies, whatever their motives or their private character may be. And the lawyer,—what does he do? He stands stoutly on the defensive. He advises his client how he may make shift, no matter how the law runs. He declares that business would go very well and every man get his due if only legislators would keep their hands off! He keeps his expert advice for private persons and criticizes those who struggle without his countenance or assistance along the difficult road of reform. It is not a promising situation.

Our reforms must be legal reforms. It is a pity they should go forward without the aid of those who have studied the law in its habit as it lives, those who know what is practicable and what is not, those who know, or should know, if anybody does, the history of liberty.

The history of liberty is a history of law. Men are not free when they have merely conceived what their rights should be. They are not set free by philosophies of right. Their theories of the rights of man may even lead them astray, may make them break their hearts in pursuit of hopes they can never realize, objects they can never grasp, ideals that will forever elude them. Nothing is more practical than the actual body of liberty. It consists of definitions based upon experience, or, rather, of practices that are of the very essence of experience. A right is worth fighting for only when it can be put into operation. It can be put into operation only when its scope and limitation can be accurately defined in terms of legal procedure; and even then it may amount to nothing if the legal procedure be difficult, costly, or complicated. Liberty of speech is defined in the law of slander and of libel, and becomes mere licence against which there is no protection if the law of slander or of libel be difficult or costly or uncertain to apply. Liberty of the person is defined only when the law has carefully enumerated the circumstances in which it may be violated, the circumstances in which arrests and imprisonments and army drafts, and all the other limitations upon which society may insist for its protection or convenience, will be lawful. Its reality, its solidarity consists in the definiteness of the exceptions, in the practicality of the actual arrangements.

And it is part of its definiteness and reality that liberty is always personal, never aggregate; always a thing inhering in individuals taken singly, never in groups or corporations or communities. The indivisible unit of society is the individual. He is also the indigestible unit. He cannot be merged or put into combination without being lost to liberty, because lost to independence. Make of him a fraction instead of an integer, and you have broken his spirit, cut off the sources of his life. That is why I plead so earnestly for the individualization of responsibility within the corporation, for the establishment of the principle by law that a man has no more right to do a wrong as a member of a corporation than as an individual. Establish that principle, cut away the undergrowth of law that has sprung up so rankly about the corporation and made of it an ambush and covert, and it will give every man the right to say No again, to refuse to do wrong, no matter who orders him to do it. It will make a man of him. It is in his interest no less than in the interest of society, which must see to it that wrong-doing is put a stop to.

We are upon the eve, gentlemen, of a great reconstruction. It calls for creative statesmanship as no age has done since that great age in which we set up the government under which we live, that government which was the admiration of the world until it suffered wrongs to grow up under it which have made many of our own compatriots question the freedom of our institutions and preach revolution against them. I do not fear revolution. I do not fear it even if it comes. I have unshaken faith in the power of America to keep its self-possession. If revolution comes, it will come in peaceful guise, as it came when we put aside the crude government of the Confederation and created the great federal state which governed individuals, not corporations, and which has been these hundred and thirty years our vehicle of progress. And it need not come. I do not believe for a moment that it will come. Some radical changes we must make in our law and practice. Some reconstructions we must push forward which a new age and new circumstances impose upon us. But we can do it all in calm and sober fashion, like statesmen and patriots. Let us do it also like lawyers. Let us lend a hand to make the structure symmetrical, well proportioned, solid, perfect. Let no future generation have cause to accuse us of having stood aloof, indifferent, half hostile, or of having impeded the realization of right. Let us make sure that liberty shall never repudiate us as its friends and guides. We are the servants of society, the bond-servants of justice.[1]

T MS (WC, NjP); with two corrections from *Report of the Thirty-Third Annual Meeting of the American Bar Association . . .* (Baltimore, 1910).
  [1] There is a WWsh draft of this address dated July 25, 1910, in WP, DLC, and a WWT draft in WC, NjP.

From Joseph Bernard Shea

Dear Mr. President: Pittsburg, Pa. Aug. 31, 1910.

The enclosed clipping from the New York Evening Post,[1] is the reason for this interruption of your vacation.

Now that it seems that Princeton men are expected to work for your nomination for Governorship of New Jersey, it would seem as though those who do not want to see this happen, have their day in court.

While I recognize what a splendid thing it would be for New Jersey if you should take this position, yet I cannot forget the loss it would be to Princeton, and having no particular feeling of obligation towards New Jersey, I am the more in a position to urge the claims of Princeton.

I know, of course, your great affection for Princeton, and I realize that it must have taken a great deal of pressure to make you even go as far as you have in agreeing to run, provided it was the wish of a "decided majority of the thoughtful Democrats of the State," that you should take the nomination. At the same time, as a very sincere friend, although at times an unwilling opponent, may I suggest the strains, the worry, and the almost impossible condition which would surround a man of your high type in such a public position. I hope you will not take it amiss when I say that they would break your heart, and to my mind, now that things are, as I see it, started again on another era of good understanding, I feel that Princeton needs you, and I sincerely trust that the matter will so arrange itself that you will remain there.   Yours very truly,   J B Shea

TLS (WP, DLC).
    [1] The enclosure was a clipping from the New York *Evening Post*, Aug. 30, 1910. With an August 30, Trenton, dateline, it reported that a circular letter had been sent to all of the 1,400 Princeton alumni living in New Jersey, urging them to work for Wilson's nomination for the governorship. The brief article concluded with the statement: "Many of the alumni are enrolled already in the Princeton Alumni Wilson League and it is expected that all Princeton men who vote in the State will join."

From Thomas H. Dillow

Dear Sir   Orange. N. J. September 1/10

The State Federation of Labor (as I suppose you are aware) has passed a resolution condemning your nomination by the Democratic Party for the Office of Chief Executive. Now Sir as one of your admirers, a Union man, and a Democrat, and also one who takes an active part by speaking thro Essex and Hudson Counties at each Fall Election, I take the liberty of asking you as to wether you have been correctly reported in the New York papers as antagonistic to organized Labor. I hope you will not think this presumption upon my part, as I can assure you that it is prompted by pure good will toward your candidature. Noted public men like yourself are often misquoted as you are aware, and often misguided and malignant individuals foist canards upon the unsuspecting citizens to further the ends they have in view.

Secretary Hilfers[1] of the Federation, charges that you in a speech at New Rochelle N. Y. declared that "The Labor unions reward the shiftless and incompetent at the expense of the able and industrious."[2]

If you would care to answer this individual appeal to you by some definite declaration, I should be most happy to have the same published in our local papers, if you so desired together with my letter to you. Of course Sir I do not know wether you have the ambition to fight this battle or not, but this much I do know the chances were never better than they are this year for a Democratic victory, and I believe an explanation upon your part would insure your nomination and Election.

Very Faithfully   Thos. H. Dillow   Carpenter
B. C. 429

ALS (WP, DLC).
[1] Henry F. Hilfers, cigarmaker of Newark, N. J.
[2] About this address, see the news report printed at Feb. 27, 1905, Vol. 16.

From Calvin Easton Brodhead[1]

Dear Sir: New York Sept. 2d, 1910.

As a Jerseyman and being deeply interested in your nomination for Governor, I read with great pleasure this morning your letter to Mr. Williamson on the Labor question. I might say in the first place that I am running for the Assembly on the Democratic Ticket from Union County[2] and I also expect to be a delegate to the Gubernatorial Convention. We Union County Democrats do not believe we have a ghost of a show to be elected unless you head the ticket. Therefore I have a selfish interest in your nomination. I have been thinking for some time that you ought to make some statement as to your attitude on the Labor question for the reason that a good deal of misrepresentation has been cunningly sent broadcast by those who prefer that you should not be nominated. We who are familiar with your character and writings and speeches knew how unfounded and nonsensical all this talk was as to your being against Labor. We knew that whatever you had stated was only in the way of friendly criticism, and in substance what a great many labor leaders and labor men generally believe themselves. Your letter to Mr. Williamson is clear cut and definite and clears up the situation.

I want to express to you my gratification (and I think it is the feeling of the vast majority of thoughtful Democrats) at your willingness to run for the Governorship. It puts new life into us, and is a fine example of public spirit and a willingness to help work out some of the problems of Government that we know you are so eminently fitted for. It is going to rehabilitate the Democracy of New Jersey, and will help the party to a wonderful extent all over our Country.

I do not believe there is the slightest doubt of your nomination and election. The vast majority of the people of the State want you. I live in Plainfield and all the delegates from that section I am sure will vote for you. We expect the sentiment to crystallize in your favor in the next ten days so that when the Convention comes there will be practically no opposition.

I spent some four years at Lawrenceville, and it was my pleasure to hear you make a great many public addresses, and I must say that I never listened to a finer speaker, or a man with such wonderful mentality.

With best wishes, I am

                    Very sincerely yours,   Calvin E. Brodhead

TLS (WP, DLC).
    1 New York sales agent for the Scranton Bolt and Nut Co., he lived in Plainfield, N. J.
    2 He was elected.

A News Item

                                        [Sept. 3, 1910]
    Mr. and Mrs. Woodrow Wilson have issued invitations for the marriage of their sister, Miss Margaret Randolph Axson to Mr. Edward Elliott, on the afternoon of Thursday, September 8, at four o'clock, at the Congregational Church of Old Lyme, Conn. Mr. and Mrs. Elliott will be at home after November 1 at Princeton.

Printed in the *Princeton Press*, Sept. 3, 1910.

To Calvin Easton Brodhead

                                    Lyme, Connecticut,
My dear Mr. Brodhead,   5 September, 1910.
    I am deeply obliged to you for your kind letter of the second, and would have acknowledged it sooner had I not been absent from Lyme when it came.

It heartens me greatly in the new things I am undertaking to have a man like yourself feel as you do. Your letter has not only given me great pleasure but also great reassurance. It was an act of thoughtful kindness on your part to write it.

I am particularly glad that you think that my letter to Mr.

Williamson successfully clears away the misrepresentations that have been so assiduously circulated.

With sincere regard and appreciation, and the hope that I shall be associated with you in active political work,

Very truly Yours,   Woodrow Wilson

WWTLS (received from William E. Brodhead).

From George Brinton McClellan Harvey

Dear Mr. Wilson   New York Monday [Sept. 6, 1910]

I was not surprised to see your statement. It was inevitable. You would have been pestered to death otherwise. And, as the Evening Post said, it could not have been better. You surely should feel flattered by its reception. There has never been anything like it.

There will be no difficulty with the little candidates. It would have been a mistake to let them all go up in smoke at once. Some animation is necessary to keep up interest especially in the Democratic party. But they will disappear peaceably one by one.

There will be some harping of course on the labor business by papers like the Journal,[1] but I guess you can handle that. The talk about the Interests is wholly ignorable up to date.

The World is interviewing everybody on National issues and doubtless will be after you. I should duck. Your position now is perfect and so need not be subjected to explanation or chance interpretations. Clouds will appear undoubtedly, but there is not one in the sky now.

I shall keep you informed of current happenings.

Sincerely yours   George Harvey

ALS (WP, DLC).
[1] He meant William Randolph Hearst's *New York Evening Journal.*

From Joseph M. Noonan

My dear Doctor: Jersey City, N. J. Sep. 8. 1910.

Your letter of the fifth instant was forwarded to me here. Your speech at the Bar Association and your Williamson letter have, I think, set you completely right before the people in these parts. I have heard several men, who previously seemed quite indifferent about your candidacy, express themselves as entirely satisfied with your statement in respect to your attitude towards labor and towards corporations. The feeling at the Davis Outing, yesterday, was very manifestly and very strongly in your favor and you may rely upon it that Mr. Davis and your other friends here, will leave nothing undone, that may properly be done, to secure for you an overwhelming majority of the delegation from this County.

When you return to Princeton I shall be very glad to call on you.

Sincerely yours,   Jos. M. Noonan

TLS (WP, DLC).

From Franklin Marx[1]

Dear Sir: Newark [N. J.] September 8, 1910.

I have been a delegate to every State Convention but one, since 1877, when McClellan was nominated.[2] I expect to be one at the coming Convention that will nominate the next Governor of this State. I have no opposition in my election district, and I am branded "regular" after nominations are made. I even took two doses of Bryan, but at the third dose, my weakened political stomach revolted.

I suppose you wonder why I, unknown to you, am writing this. I will tell you. I don't pose as a great factor in shaping future events for our Party, but I am like thousands of other Democrats in this State, who are anxious to see the State in the hands of honest, unselfish and sane administrators. I have thoughtfully read all your public utterances that have come to my notice though the press, and am finally convinced that you are "The Man of The Hour." At first I thought you a theorist, but your recent letter on Labor, convinced me otherwise. My ideal public man was Grover Cleveland. I not alone admired him; I worshipped him. I believe you to be constructed on his lines. At present we need such men. The people are tired of demagogues, quacks and cure-alls, in both parties and are prepared to vote for men that do not apply the modern methods of politicians; to wit: promising everything and accomplishing nothing.

We want you for our candidate, and as our candidate we will elect you Governor, and then we will see.

Sincerely yours,   Franklin Marx

TLS (WP, DLC).
   [1] Insurance agent of Newark, N. J.
   [2] When George Brinton McClellan was nominated for Governor of New Jersey. He served from 1878 to 1881.

To Frederic Yates

My dear Fred,   Lyme, Connecticut, 9 September, 1910.

This is just a line to say how happy we are at the prospect of seeing you; that you must come at once to Princeton and stay as long as possible; and that the best quiet, comparatively inexpensive hotel we know in New York is The Collingwood, 45 West 35th. Street.

Madge Axson was married yesterday (a quiet, simple country wedding) to my colleague Edward Elliott who is Dean of the College. They will be in their own house when you get to Princeton.

Things are thickening about me politically. It seems probable at this writing that I shall be nominated for the office of Governor in New Jersey by the Democrats of the State at their convention on next Thursday, the fifteenth, and I must take it if it comes.

There are too many things to talk over to even mention in a hurried note, rushed to catch the post. Come straight to us and at once. How I wish the other dear ones were coming too.

All join me in heartfelt messages of love.
                    Your sincere friend   Woodrow Wilson

WWTLS (F. Yates Coll., NjP).

From George Brinton McClellan Harvey

Dear Mr. Wilson   New York Friday [Sept. 9, 1910]

I have had several pow-wows over the platform, as the committee[1] had prepared an old-time "view with alarm"—"point with pride" (at what? I asked) sort. But on the whole I had less difficulty from the pride of paternity than I had anticipated. Last night the inclosed draft was accepted,[2] subject possibly to some minor suggestion. I think you will find it all right, but if you have anything to propose let me know, as there is still time. We cut out all reference to local option, etc., as it is not an issue. The other verbal changes you will understand.[3]

The nomination will be made on Thursday afternoon and the plan is for the Chair to appoint a committee to fetch you before the convention, which will consist of about 2600 workers—delegates and alternates. My notion would be for you not to make a set address, but perhaps take the platform and touch briefly upon the various planks. That of course is only a suggestion and might not suit your method. Afterwards you will be expected to shake hands for a while.

You should be in Princeton Wednesday. Perhaps it would be advisable for you to come to Deal Tuesday and spend the night and I can send you over in a motor Wednesday. The Senator[4] who will be within easy reach at Elberon likes this idea. He will go to Trenton Wed. morning.

We have no question of the result. We had Davis declare himself yesterday and, to provide against any possible contingency in Hudson, we have a fairly satisfactory understanding with Wittpen. All reports are good. There will be only one ballot.

I should like to receive word from you here Monday morning.

Faithfully yours   George Harvey

ALS (WP, DLC).

[1] He was referring to the platform committee of the Democratic State Committee.

[2] The enclosure is missing.

[3] A comparison of Wilson's proposed platform, printed at August 9, 1910, with the platform adopted on September 15, 1910 (printed at that date) reveals that several "verbal changes" were indeed made by the platform committee. Wilson's plank calling for the taxation of the franchises of public service corporations at rates proportioned to their true and fair value was dropped entirely by the committee. His plank on the conservation of water rights and natural resources was modified to read that such rights and resources should not be controlled or exhausted "by private corporations." The plank on the establishment of a public service commission omitted Wilson's proviso about the legislation being consistent with Congress's power to regulate interstate commerce and replaced it with one "giving . . . to capital a fair return." Wilson's plank calling for changes in the state laws respecting the incorporation of business undertakings was deleted, and his call for a state corrupt practices act was made more general and vague, while the reference to "heavy penalties" was omitted. Wilson's plank on local option was eliminated, as Harvey states.

The concluding paragraph on national issues was also modified. Where Wilson stressed the purpose of recent tariff legislation and who benefited therefrom, the final platform accused the Republican party of responsibility, by its tariff legislation, for the high cost of living. Wilson urged the restoration of the American merchant marine; the platform ignored this. Wilson wanted federal regulation of corporations along the lines he proposed for the state; this, too, was omitted from the final platform. Finally, the platform as adopted urged that a constitutional amendment for the election of United States senators by popular vote be submitted to the people; Wilson had not mentioned this in his draft.

[4] James Smith, Jr.

To George Brinton McClellan Harvey

Lyme, Connecticut,

My dear Colonel Harvey,   10 September, 1910.

Thank you for the copy of the platform, and for your suggestions about Thursday. I am content with the changes in the platform (though I do not yet catch the point of No. 14), and think the idea you have of what I should do when called to the convention in every way excellent.

I am sorry to say I cannot come to Deal on Tuesday. I have made all sorts of engagements based on the original plan: that

I should remain here until Wednesday morning and then go direct to Princeton, reaching there that evening. I am in the thick of preparations for the opening of college and cannot just now be too movable. I wish I were free to come, as you suggest.

Apparently my letter on the labor question came at the right moment and made a good impression. I have heard from it from various sources.

With warmest appreciation,
                    Faithfully Yours,   Woodrow Wilson

WWTLS (WP, DLC).

Two Letters from George Brinton McClellan Harvey

Dear Mr. Wilson   New York Monday [Sept. 12, 1910]

I have your note. Have just returned from the Adirondacks where I went to try to rid myself of a nasty cold. My suggestion about coming to Deal was merely precautionary, of course—in no sense essential.

❡ 14 means this: Assemblymen are now elected by *counties*. Under the former Democratic regimes they were elected by assembly *districts*. Essex for example now elects a solid Republican or Democratic delegation on a single ticket. Formerly there might have been and often were 6 of one party and 7 of the other. Our wiseacres say the old method is far more popular. It certainly seems more democratic.[1]

Also, many State and county officers who used to be elected by the people are now appointed. Here again it is deemed wise and popular to urge reversion.[2]

I am to have my final talk with the committeemen about the platform tonight and, unless you hear from me to the contrary, you may assume that it stands.

Oh, yes, the labor letter was precisely timed and wholly effective. A trifling difficulty arose from the fact that our friend Mr. Williamson hadn't printed a paper since Labor Day 1909 and couldn't pay the typestickers to get out this one. However, it appeared in its regular annual form.

I will keep you informed of my movements and anything new that may transpire. As ever   Yours   G H

[1] This plank was omitted from the final platform.
[2] This plank, presumably the thirteenth, was also deleted.

Dear Mr. Wilson   New York Tuesday [Sept. 13, 1910]

All quiet and satisfactory. We had a round-up of the northern tier of counties yesterday and they are solid, as expected.

Senator Smith also had a talk with the Mercer committeemen and told them there would be no interference with them. They could go for Katzenbach or anybody they liked. They were not needed at the convention or at the polls. Your nomination and election were certainties. If they wanted to continue to hold a Mayoralty and Shrievalty of greater importance than a Governorship or Presidency, they could do so and take the consequences. This was the right way to deal with them. They went away saddened to think it over.

The Wittpen outfit in Hudson County is making some noise but Davis says that is all it amounts to. He generally knows what he talks about.

Kean[1] and Murphy[2] are naturally trying to get Stokes[3] to run, but the reason is too obvious and our information is to the effect that he is going to stick for the Senatorship. We shall know more definitely in a few days.

It still looks like Lewis, the man we want.

Sincerely Yours   George Harvey

Bishop McFaul[4] is "wid us."

ALS (WP, DLC).

[1] John Kean, for many years a leader of the G.O.P. in New Jersey; United States representative, 1883-85, 1887-89; United States senator, 1890-1911.

[2] Franklin Murphy, Governor of New Jersey, 1902-1905; president of the Murphy Varnish Co. of Newark, N. J., and chairman of the Republican State Committee.

[3] Edward Casper Stokes, Governor of New Jersey, 1905-1908, banker of Trenton, resident of Millville. Stokes was a candidate for the United States Senate in 1910, winning a narrow plurality in the Republican preferential primary in September.

[4] The Most Rev. James Augustine McFaul, Roman Catholic Bishop of Trenton.

To Harry Laity Bowlby[1]

My dear Mr. Bowlby: Princeton, N. J. September 15th, 1910.

I have just received your generous letter of yesterday.[2] I want to thank you for it most sincerely.

It does look, as I write this morning, as if the convention which meets in Trenton at noon today will nominate me for the governorship. I look forward to the prospect with many misgivings, but with no doubt as to what my duty in the case is. Nothing rejoices me more than that men like yourself and other Princeton men who have written to me should feel as they do about my candidacy and the possibility of my serving the people in some substantial way. It keeps me in heart and makes all that I attempt easier to do.

Always cordially and faithfully yours,

Woodrow Wilson

TLS (received from H. L. Bowlby).
  1 Princeton 1901, pastor of the First Presbyterian Church, Altoona, Pa.
  2 It is missing.

A Speech Accepting the Democratic Gubernatorial Nomination

[[Sept. 15, 1910]]

You have conferred upon me a very great honor.[1] I accept the nomination you have tendered me with the deepest gratification that you should have thought me worthy to lead the Democrats of New Jersey in this stirring time of opportunity.

Even more than the great honor of your nomination I feel the deep responsibility it imposes upon me. For responsibility is proportioned to opportunity.

As you know, I did not seek this nomination. It has come to me absolutely unsolicited. With the consequence that I shall enter upon the duties of the office of Governor, if elected, with absolutely no pledge of any kind to prevent me from serving the people of the State with singleness of purpose. Not only have no pledges of any kind been given, but none have been proposed or desired.

In accepting the nomination, therefore, I am pledging myself only to the service of the people and the party which intends to advance their interests. I cannot but regard the circumstances as marking the beginning of a new and more ideal era in our politics. Certainly they enhance very greatly the honor you have conferred upon me and enlarge the opportunities in equal degree.

A day of unselfish purpose is always a day of confident hope. I feel confident that the people of the State will accept the promises you have made in your platform as made sincerely and with a definite purpose to render them effective service. That platform is sound, explicit and businesslike. There can be no mistaking what it means. And the voters of the State will know at once that promises so definitely made are made to be kept, not to be evaded.

Your declaration deserves and will win their confidence. But we

  1 Wilson had just been nominated for governor on the first ballot after a bitter floor fight in the Taylor Opera House in Trenton. For details, see Arthur S. Link, *Wilson: The Road to the White House* (Princeton, N. J., 1947), pp. 162-66.

shall keep their confidence only by performance, by achievement and by proving our capacity to conduct the administration and reform the legislation of the State in the spirit of our declarations not only, but also with the sagacity and firmness of practical men who not only purpose, but do what is sensible and effective.

It is towards this task of performance that my thoughts turn as I think of soliciting the suffrages of my fellow citizens for the great office of Governor of the State. I shall do so with a very profound sense of the difficulty of solving new and complicated problems in the right way. I take the three great questions before us to be reorganization and economy in administration, the equalization of taxation and the control of corporations. There are other very important questions that confront us as they confront all the other States of the Union in this day of re-adjustment; the question of the proper liability of employers, for example, the question of corrupt practices in elections, the question of conservation, but the three I have named dominate all the rest.

It is imperative that we should not only master them, but also act upon them, and act very definitely.

It is first of all necessary that we should act in the right spirit. And the right spirit is not a spirit of hostility. We shall not act either justly or wisely if we attack established interests as public enemies. There has been too much indictment and too little successful prosecution for wrongs done; too much talk and too few practicable suggestions as to what is to be done. It is easy to condemn wrong and to fulminate against wrong-doers in effective rhetorical phrases; but that does not bring either reform or ease of mind. Reform will come only when we have done some careful thinking as to exactly what the things are that are being done in contravention of the public interest and as to the most simple, direct and effective way of getting at the men who do them. In a self-governed country there is one rule for everybody, and that is the common interest. Everything must be squared by that. We can square it only by knowing its exact shape and movement. Government is not a warfare of interests. We shall not gain our ends by heats and bitterness, which make it impossible to think either calmly or fairly. Government is a matter of common counsel and everyone must come into the consultation with the purpose to yield to the general view, the view which seems most nearly to correspond with the common interests. If any decline frank conference, keep out, hold off, they must take the consequences and blame only themselves if they are in the end badly served. There must be implacable determination to see the right done, but strong purpose, which does not flinch because some must suffer, is perfectly compatible with fairness and justice and a clear view of the actual facts.

This should be our spirit in the matter of reform, and this our method. And in this spirit we should do very definite things. It is obvious even to the casual observer that the administration of the State has been unnecessarily complicated and elaborated, too many separate commissions and boards set up, business methods neglected, money wasted, and a state of affairs brought about of which a successful business concern would be ashamed. No doubt the increase of State expenditures, which marked the last decade has been in part due to a necessary and desirable increase of function on the part of the State. But it is only too evident that no study of economy has been made, that a careful reconsideration and reorganization of the administrative processes of the State would result in a great saving and enhance responsibility on the part of those who are entrusted with the important work of government. Our system of taxation is as ill-digested, as piecemeal and as haphazardous as our system of administration. It cannot be changed suddenly or too radically, but many changes should be inaugurated and the whole system by degrees reconsidered and altered, so as to fit modern economical conditions more equitably. Above all the methods of assessment should be changed, in order that inequality between the taxes of individuals and the taxes of corporations, for example, should be entirely eliminated. It is not necessary for the maintenance of our modern industrial enterprises that corporations should be indulged or favored in the matter of taxation and it is extremely demoralizing that they should be. Such inequalities should be effectually removed by law and by the action of the tax assessing authorities of the State and of the locality. This is a matter which will require dispassionate study and action based, not upon hostility, but upon the common interest. The question of the control of corporations is a very difficult one, upon which no man can speak with confidence; but some things are plain. It is plain, as far as New Jersey is concerned that we must have a Public Service Commission with the amplest powers to oversee and regulate the administration of public service corporations throughout the State. We have abundant experience elsewhere to guide us in this matter, from the admirable commission so long in successful operation in Wisconsin, to the latest legislation in sister States. We need have no doubt of our right course of action here.

It is the States, not the Federal authorities, that create corporations. The regulation of corporations is the duty of the State much more directly than it is the duty of the government of the United States. It is my strong hope that New Jersey may lead the way in reform; by scrutinizing very carefully the enterprises she consents to incorporate; their make-up, their objects, the basis and method of capitalization, their organization with respect to liability to control by the State, their conformity to State and Federal statutes. This can be done and done effectually. I covet for New Jersey the honor of doing it.

It is so also, gentlemen, with every other question we face. Let us face it in the spirit of service and with the careful, practical sense of men of affairs. We shall not ask the voters of the State to lend us their suffrages merely because we call ourselves Democrats, but because we mean to serve them like honest and public-spirited men, true Democrats because true lovers of the common interest, servants of no special group of men or of interests, students of the interest of the people and of the country.

The future is not for parties "playing politics," but for measures conceived in the largest spirit, pushed by parties whose leaders are statesmen, not demagogues, who love not their offices, but their duty and their opportunity for service. We are witnessing a renaissance of public spirit, a re-awakening of sober public opinion, a revival of the power of the people, the beginning of an age of thoughtful reconstruction that makes our thought hark back to the great age in which Democracy was set up in America. With the new age we shall show a new spirit. We shall serve justice and candour and all things that make for the right. Is not our own ancient party the party disciplined and made ready for this great task? Shall we not forget ourselves in making it the instrument of righteousness for the State and for the nation?[2]

Printed in the Trenton *True American*, Sept. 16, 1910; editorial headings omitted; with minor corrections from the text in the *Jersey City Herald*, Sept. 16, 1910.
    [2] There is a WWT draft of this address in WP, DLC. For Wilson's impromptu remarks extending this speech, see the news report printed at Sept. 17, 1910.

The Platform of the New Jersey Democratic Party

[Sept. 15, 1910]

The Democrats of New Jersey, in presenting to the voters of the State a candidate for Governor, present also the following declaration of the objects to which they will devote themselves, should they be intrusted with the direction of the administration and legislation of the State.

1. A thorough administrative reorganization, in order to make the administration of the State's business at once as economical

and efficient as possible. This will involve the abolition of all unnecessary offices, boards and commissions, a concentration of
functions upon the model of the best business organizations, and
a careful co-ordination of the several parts of the public service.
The government of the State should be so systematized and simplified, and such methods of public accounting should be established and enforced as would secure unmistakable individual
responsibility on the part of every officer intrusted with authority
or the handling of public funds. The increase in State expenditures from less than two million dollars, under the last Democratic administration, to more than five million dollars last year,
is grossly excessive. All appropriations of public moneys should
be based upon as careful a consideration of the burden of taxation imposed upon the people as of the object sought to be served
by the expenditure, economy being as essential to honest government as any consideration of efficiency, and equalize the burdens
of taxation.

2. The equalization of taxation, both in law and in practice,
particularly as between individuals and railway and other
corporations, with regard to the valuation of property and the
assessment of taxes upon it; the removal from the State's system
of taxation of all elements of obscurity or injustice, and the adoption of such administrative changes as may prove to be necessary
in order to make those reforms effective.

3. The preservation intact of the school fund and its prompt
and systematic distribution for the purposes for which it was
intended.

4. The careful conservation for the benefit of all the people of
the State of all water rights and all natural resources still within
the control of the State by provisions which will effectually
prevent their control or exhaustion by private corporations.

5. The establishment of a public service commission with ample powers under explicit rules to regulate rates, secure an
adequate and suitable service, inflict penalties, require the filing
of all traffic agreements and the submission to its examination of
all tariff rates before they take effect, and to reject or adjust the
same, if found to be unjust, giving, however, to capital a fair return.

6. The enactment of an employers' liability act which will
satisfy the just demands of labor and secure safety and efficient
sanitation in all manufacturing processes and employments.

7. The enactment of a law establishing eight hours as the limit
of the working day in all public work.

8. The control of such corporations, combinations or trusts as

are not naturally to be regarded as public service corporations by legislation which will define and forbid those acts and practices on their part and those methods in their organization and control of business as have proved destructive of free competition and detrimental to the people's interest, and which will visit the penalties prescribed upon the individuals responsible for such acts or practices.

9. The enactment of an efficient act against corrupt practices at all elections, limiting expenditures by or on behalf of candidates and requiring the prompt publication thereof.

10. Such a simplification of the electoral machinery of the State as will make possible the effectual exercise of the right of direct nomination on the part of voters and the enactment of laws which will secure them that right in the most effectual manner.

11. The extension of the principle and practice of civil service reform in all administrative departments of the State, county and municipality.

12. The enactment of laws with regard to the use of automobiles within the State which will grant the same rights and privileges to the owners and drivers of machines from other States that are accorded the citizens of New Jersey in the States from which said owners and drivers hold their licenses, and which will tend to establish a proper reciprocity of responsibility as between the license granting authorities of the several States.

In regard to the administration of the federal government:

We charge that the Republican party, through the unfair tariff laws devised not as a means of protection, but as means of patronage, is largely responsible for the high cost of living now burdening our whole people, and we demand an intelligent revision, downward, of the present tariff in the interest of all the people.

We insist that there should be enacted a federal corrupt practices act, as explicit and imperative as we have favored for the State, and that our citizens should be given an opportunity forthwith to pass upon a constitutional amendment providing for the election of United States senators by popular vote.

Printed in the Trenton *True American*, Sept. 16, 1910.

From Frank Snowden Katzenbach, Jr.

Trenton N. J. Sept. 15 [1910]

Accept my congratulations upon your nomination

Frank S. Katzenbach Jr.

T telegram (WP, DLC).

From Joseph Stanislaus Hoff[1]

My dear Sir: Princeton, N. J., Sept. 15th, 1910.

I desire to congratulate you on your nomination & assure you that you will have the undivided support of the Mercer County Democratic Committee.

I shall make every effort to properly organize the party in this County, and use every honorable means to elect you Governor of our state.

I sincerely trust that our state will be once more enrolled in the Democratic colume.

Your very truly,   Jos. S. Hoff

ALS (WP, DLC).
[1] Meat, vegetable, and fruit dealer of Princeton, chairman of the Mercer County Democratic Committee.

From James Fairman Fielder[1]

My dear Sir   Jersey City [N. J.] Sept 15 1910

The news of your nomination by our State Convention, has just reached me. Because of my long acquaintance and service in the Senate with Senator Silzer, he has had my support, but I cheerfully accept the judgment of the delegates and pledge my whole efforts toward your election. Your nomination means success for our party and you can count on an old time democratic majority from Hudson County.

Yours   James F. Fielder

ALS (WP, DLC).
[1] Democratic state senator from Hudson County, 1908-13; Governor of New Jersey, 1913-17.

From Herbert Bruce Brougham

Dear Dr. Wilson: [New York] Sept. 15, 1910.

The State of New Jersey has acted nobly in this nomination which practically makes you its next Governor-elect. It assures you of an opportunity for service not only as the head of a great State but as a leader of the Governors of all the States in the work of making their Governments truly representative of the people. You have long foreseen that it is from the States that the inspiration of reform must spring. I believe that this call to leadership finds you prepared.

If during the campaign you can show me how to be of service

to you, pray do so. The Times, as you know, already warmly supports your candidacy.

Yours sincerely,   H B Brougham

TLS (WP, DLC).

From Otis Allan Glazebrook[1]

My dear Dr. Wilson,   Elizabeth, N. J. Sept. 15, 1910.

I am just back from Trenton where I had the great pleasure of witnessing your nomination. I was also near you when you signed your acceptance & tried to speak, but the crowd in general & a burly policeman in particular were too much for me.

I want to write just a line to say that our party is to be congratulated on the wisdom of its choice & I feel sure you will lead the Democracy to a great victory in November. Such is my devout prayer & I beg you to command me if in my humble way you may find me of service.

With kindest regards,

Most sincerely,   Otis A. Glazebrook

ALS (WP, DLC).
[1] Rector of St. John's Episcopal Church in Elizabeth, N. J. He opened the convention by praying so fervently for Democratic success that the convention applauded at the end of his prayer.

From Walter Maurice Wilkins[1]

[Sept. 15, 1910]

Heartiest congratulations from the Class of 1910 upon your nomination for Governor. New Jersey's gain will be Princeton's loss.

Printed in the Princeton, N. J., 1910 Locomotive, 1 (Nov. 8, 1910), 14.
[1] Secretary of the Princeton Class of 1910. Wilkins was about to enter Harvard Law School.

An Interview

[Sept. 16, 1910]

DR. WILSON DECLARES HE NEVER HAD WALL STREET CONNECTIONS

Princeton, Sept. 16.—"It is a humiliating and absurd thing to say that I am the Wall Street candidate for Governor of New Jersey," resentfully exclaimed President Woodrow Wilson on his return here last night after carrying off the nomination at Trenton.

"I never have had any affiliations with Wall Street or Wall Street people. If I had perhaps I would be richer or poorer. I think any one who has read my speeches will bear me out in saying that whenever I have discovered any Wall Street evils I have assailed them. I believe in attacking evils themselves and correcting them if possible, rather than attacking the men, who may or may not be responsible for them. As I said in my speech accepting the nomination for Governor, we shall not act justly or wisely if we attack established interests as public enemies. There has been too much indictment and too little successful prosecution for wrongs done; too much talk and too few practical suggestions as to what is to be done."

"The fact that former Senator James Smith has been the chief promoter of your campaign for the nomination and reports that you have been urged by National Committeeman Roger Sullivan of Illinois, and other corporation men, to run for Governor as a stepping stone to the Presidency, perhaps provoked the impression that Wall Street desired your selection," it was suggested.

"While it is true that Senator Smith has been very active in my behalf, I will say that neither he nor any other man, corporation or anti-corporation man, has asked the slightest pledge from me. As for Roger Sullivan, I think I have met him once only and I do not recall that we exchanged a word on politics. I never sought this nomination, and if I am elected, as I expect to be, I shall be free and untrammeled to serve the people and the State. I repeat that no promises have been asked, much less exacted of me," said President Wilson with fervor.

"You declared today that you stand on every plank of the platform approved by the convention."

"I did."

"Why do you favor State rather than Federal control of corporations?"

"Because the corporation is the creature of the State. Should I be elected I shall make it my task to ascertain exactly and justly the abuses which it is alleged corporations are practicing and send through legislation and a public service commission to regulate and curb them."

"What do you regard as the grossest abuse of which corporations are guilty?"

"I should say over-capitalization or watering of stock. With adequate legislation and supervision this and other wrongs might be stopped. How they are to be stopped, or, rather, how in detail I shall not attempt to say just now. But I have my ideas, and they will materialize if I have a chance to put them into execution.["]

"How does it happen that New York and other corporations which fail to secure franchises from the local government flee to New Jersey and thus give the State the name of 'mother of corporations?' "

"It is not because they know they are assured of protection in New Jersey. I have personal knowledge of this, but as I told the convention today, I covet the honor of New Jersey reforming corporations and compelling them to comply with the Federal and State statutes."

"The direct nominations plank in the platform on which you are running was declared today to be a makeshift. It employs the word 'possible' as if the party were afraid to meet the issue squarely.["]

"I think the plank a very good one. It declares distinctly for such a simplification of the electoral machinery as will make possible the effectual exercise of the right of direct nominations for all elective offices. It seems to me this is plain and explicit."

"What specific plan of direct nominations do you favor?"

"That is a matter of detail to which I have not given much serious attention as yet. But I shall. My information is that twenty different kinds of direct nominations are in operation in twenty different States. I favor the most practicable scheme that can possibly be devised to guarantee the voters, and not the bosses, the right to name candidates for office."

"You declare for equalization of State taxation. Just what do you mean?"

"That the people and the corporations should bear their proportionate share of the State's burdens. I have given serious thought to this. But I am not just ready to divulge my plan in detail."

"Is it your intention to sever your connection with Princeton University now that you have been named for Governor?"

"That is a matter for the Board of Trustees to determine. I surely could not serve as president of the university and as Governor simultaneously. Whether I shall wait until I am elected Governor or resign soon I cannot tell until I talk the matter over with the university authorities. I shall probably meet them next week. Then, perhaps, this question will be definitely settled.["]

"Do you intend taking the stump?"

"I shall place myself in the hands of the Democratic State Committee. I shall do whatever that committee thinks best and wise."

Printed in the *Trenton Evening Times*, Sept. 16, 1910.

A News Report

[*Sept. 16, 1910*]

WILSON TO RESIGN AS PRINCETON'S HEAD

PRINCETON, N.J., Sept. 16.—President Woodrow Wilson of Princeton University announced this afternoon that he would offer his resignation to the Board of Trustees of the university at their meeting on Oct. 20.

What the Trustees will do as a result is a matter of speculation. They value his services highly as President, and would regret to lose him, even in the event of his election to the Governorship. The board may hold the resignation in abeyance until after the election, about three weeks later than the meeting of the board. . . .

Scores of telegrams found their way to the desk of President Wilson following his nomination for Governor. Many came from Georgia, his old home, and from other sections of the South. A telegram of congratulation which pleased Mr. Wilson very much came from his strongest opponent for the Governorship—Frank S. Katzenbach, Jr., former Mayor of Trenton and a defeated candidate for Governor. Another was from Norman E. Mack, Chairman of the National Democratic Committee.

President Wilson will not make a great many speeches.

"The field to be covered," he said, "is not very large unless I should go into the tariff, but I believe that National issues, like the tariff, will not be injected into the campaign. When running for Governor of New Jersey one should run for Governor."

President Wilson will leave his campaign work largely to the Democratic State Committee, and active work will begin soon after the Republican Convention next Tuesday.

Printed in the *New York Times*, Sept. 17, 1910; some editorial headings omitted.

From Ellen Axson Wilson

Lyme Ct. Sept. 16 [1910]

Congratulations from all the house hold   love from the family.

E. A. W.

T telegram (WP, DLC).

To Walter Maurice Wilkins

My dear Mr. Wilkins: [Sept. 16, 1910]

It was an act of thoughtful kindness on your part to send your telegram of yesterday and I appreciate it most highly.

Always cordially yours,   Woodrow Wilson.

Printed in the Princeton, N. J., *1910 Locomotive*, 1 (Nov. 8, 1910), 14.

From Charles Henry Grasty[1]

Baltimore Md. Sept. 16 [1910]

Congratulations and best wishes. If the Sun can be of service to the case, demand [command] us.

Charles P. Grasty.

T telegram (WP, DLC).
[1] Controlling owner and editor of the Baltimore *Sun*, 1910-1914.

To Charles Henry Grasty

My dear Mr. Grasty: Princeton, N. J. September 16th, 1910.

Thank you sincerely for your telegram and particularly for your kind suggestion that The Sun be advised of any service it can render in our approaching campaign. I shall remember the offer with gratitude and interest and may have occasion to avail myself of it.

Cordially and faithfully yours,   Woodrow Wilson

TLS (RSB Coll., DLC).

From Norman Edward Mack

Buffalo N. Y. Sept. 16 [1910]

The democratcy of New Jersey is to be congratulated on the wi[s]dom of it's choice for Governor personally I send you hearty congratulations. Victory is assured.

Norman E. Mack.

T telegram (WP, DLC).

To Joseph Stanislaus Hoff

My dear Mr. Hoff,   Princeton, N. J. September 16, 1910

Thank you very heartily for your kind letter of yesterday. I appreciate very much the assurances of support it conveys. You may be sure that I have never had any doubt about the readiness of the Mercer County Democratic Committee to accept the decision of the party and to work with their accustomed energy in the campaign. I only regret that circumstances should have made it appear that I was in some way a rival of Mr. Katzenbach's. Happily, it was not by any action of mine that the unfortunate situation arose.

With much regard,

Sincerely yours,   Woodrow Wilson

TCL (received from H. W. Bragdon).

From John Wesley Wescott[1]

My dear Sir   Allentown [Pa.] Sept 16, 1910

I am a Yale man, '72 Academic, '76 Law. Mr. Katzenbach was nominated by me yesterday. That circumstance, I trust, will not prevent an early interview, at your convenience, for the purpose of a frank discussion about the campaign in South Jersey. The day is at hand when vast progress can be made in the social and political life of the State.   Sincerely,   John W. Wescott

TLS (WP, DLC).
[1] Lawyer of Camden, N. J., and Philadelphia. Actually, Wescott seconded Katzenbach's nomination in a fiery speech in which he roundly denounced Wilson and the bosses.

From Arthur Granville Dewalt

My dear Sir   Allentown [Pa.] Sept 16, 1910

Permit me as State Chairman of the Democracy of Penna to congratulate the Democrats of New Jersey on their selection of a Standard Bearer in their contest for the election of Governor

The party has honored itself and lived up to its best traditions and renewed hope is given to every advocate of Constitutional Government and safe and sane methods

Declamation & *Proclamation* are to be succeeded by performance and deeds worthy of the cause for which we are all enlisted

The preservation of the rights of all under the law with special privileges to none

Your platform is an epitome of good doctrine irrespective of party affiliation and the candidate who stands upon it can justly appeal to all citizens for their support.

Predicting your election & the triumph of sane Democracy

I am very Resptly Yours   Arthur G Dewalt

ALS (WP, DLC).

From Henry Burling Thompson

My dear Wilson   Paris September 16 1910

Todays papers announce your nomination for Governor of New Jersey. Permit me to congratulate you, for I assume your election is assured. As I wrote you before I can not say this with unqualified pleasure, for the more I think about losing your services to Princeton, the less reconciled I become to the idea. I do not like it. I am finishing up my trip here and hope to be home by October 7th, when I shall soon see you in person.

Yours sincerely   Henry B Thompson

ALS (WP, DLC).

From Charles Scribner

My dear Dr. Wilson: Morristown, N. J. Sept. 16th 1910

Please accept my hearty congratulations on your nomination. The Party has honored itself in selecting you as leader and as a Jerseyman I am proud of my state. It is fine to see such recognition of unselfish ability.

Yours sincerely   Charles Scribner

ALS (WP, DLC).

From John Alexander Montgomery[1]

My dear Dr Wilson,   Trenton, N. J. Sept 16, 1910.

Allow me to congratulate you not only on your nomination but upon your most able address which was appreciated by every person in the Opera House. Two or three speeches of the kind will put Mercer County in the Democratic colume.

I am the candidate on our ticket for State Senator,[2] and although (with our other delegates) I went to the Convention to support Mr Katzenbach, yet I now feel sure that the Democracy of New Jersey did wisely in nominating you, and I am convi[n]ced that you will be our next Governor.

I will be in Princeton within a few days & will then do myself the honor of calling on you.

Yours Most Sincerely   John A. Montgomery

ALS (WP, DLC).
[1] Princeton 1886, lawyer of Trenton.
[2] He was defeated.

From Walter Lee McCorkle[1]

My dear Dr. Wilson: New York September 16th, 1910

As a fellow Virginian born in the County of Rockbridge and as a member of Phi Kappa Psi Fraternity, and as one of your enthusiastic admirers, I desire to extend to you my heartiest congratulations upon receiving the nomination as Governor of New Jersey, and I do hope that the campaign will not be too great a strain upon your strength. I feel confident that your success as governor is bound to follow this nomination.

Our country is in great need of men of your stamp and while I know it is not to your liking to be in a conspicuous position, yet I do realize that you cannot withstand the demand of the public upon you, and I hope God in his wisdom will endow you with strength to carry out the great work that is before you.

With every good wish for your success, believe me to be
Faithfully and sincerely yours, Walter L. McCorkle.

TLS (WP, DLC).
[1] A Wall Street lawyer, active in the New York Southern Society.

From Edward Seiler Salmon[1]

Respected Sir, New York, 16th Sept. 1910

I am a Divinity student of this Seminary, and had the priviledge of hearing your lecture, delivered to the student-body, and Professors of this Seminary in early Spring of this year.[2]

I have been greatly impressed, and many are the lessons I learnt from your most opportune oration, and for this reason, naturally, you always occupy a prominent position on my mind, having won my highest estimation as a lecturer.

Seeing now that you have have [sic] won the approbation and implicit confidence of friends and fellow-citizens, so that they have been moved to promote you unsolicitously to the Governorship of the State, I am moved thro' an impulse of respect, coupled with a spirit of admiration and eulogy toward the movement. I therefore respectfully desire that, you be pleased to accept my heartiest congratulations, with the hope, you will "top the poll" at the election.

Your noble administrative ability, excellence of character, and high literary attainments have qualified you, to such an extent, that a better man than yourself cannot be found. If honour has been conferred in the selection, then it seems to be mutual, as your constituents in doing you honour are sharing the same with you by your accepting the appointment.

I am a British Subject & so cannot share in the election, and though a humble coloured man, yet I feel sanguine you will not ignore the kind feelings I am exhibiting toward you.

I have the honour to be,

Respected Sir,

Your obedient Servant,   E. Seiler Salmon.

ALS (WP, DLC).

[1] A student at the General Theological Seminary.

[2] Wilson's address at the General Theological Seminary is printed at April 6, 1910, Vol. 20.

From Erwin E. Marshall[1]

Dear Sir: Trenton, N. J. Sept. 16th, 1910.

I beg to extend to you my congratulations upon your nomination as the Democratic Candidate for Governor of New Jersey and to express my best wishes for your success. While a strong sentiment prevailed among the Democrats of Mercer County for the nomination of Mr. Frank S. Katzenbach, Jr., whose sterling worth and integrity has greatly endeared him to us, we are, nevertheless, pleased with the outcome of the convention, and as Chairman of the County Executive Committee, I beg to assure you that the Democratic Organization will give to you, as the nominee of the convention, the same earnest and loyal support which would have been given to Mr. Katzenbach had he been nominated. From this time until the election is over we will conduct a vigorous campaign for your election.

I shall be very pleased indeed, to receive any suggestions you may have to make in regard to the plan of campaign for Mercer County.

Believe me,

Very sincerely yours,   Erwin E Marshall

TLS (WP, DLC).

[1] Lawyer of Trenton, secretary and treasurer of Scott's Drug Stores, and secretary of the Democratic League of Trenton, as well as chairman of the Trenton Democratic Committee and of the Democratic County Executive Committee.

From James Richard Nugent

My dear Sir: Newark, N. J., September 16, 1910.

On account of my duties as State Chairman, making it necessary for me to finish the business connected with yesterday's convention, I was unable to congratulate you personally upon your nomination, so I take this means of doing so.

I would be pleased to meet you either at Princeton, or any other place you may suggest, on Monday next, to discuss with you some important matters connected with the campaign.

Again offering you my sincere congratulations, I remain

Yours very truly,   James R. Nugent

TLS (WP, DLC).

From Azel Washburn Hazen

Middletown Connecticut

My dear Friend,   16 September [1910].

Permit me the pleasure of congratulating you in view of the honor which came to you yesterday. It gave me sincere joy. This not only is a just tribute to your own character, but as an evidence that better days are coming in politics. I wish I were a citizen of New Jersey long enough to cast my ballot for the next Governor of the State. However, I am hoping to vote for you as the candidate for a still higher office!

It was a grief to me to miss you at Lyme in June by only a few hours.

In the mountains last month I met Mrs. Woodroe of W. Va., who used to know your wife in Savannah[.] This fact, and the rare enthusiasm with which she spoke of the lovely woman, commended her to me at once.

Mrs Hazen[1] joins me in love to yourself and Mrs Wilson, as well as your children.

Ever Affectionately Yours   A. W. Hazen

ALS (WP, DLC).

[1] Mary Butler Thompson Hazen.

From James Cowden Meyers[1]

My dear Dr. Wilson: New York September 16th, 1910.

I rejoice at your nomination for Governor and, as a political prophet of some reputation, I venture to predict your election.

In a modest way I have been identified with the progressive movement in the Republican party and I think that you should get a large part of that vote in New Jersey. I wish that I could have an opportunity to talk to you about how *not* to alienate it. Party ties are very loose today and there are many men in each party who recognize the fact that they are out of harmony with many of their party associates and realize their political kinship with men of like mind in the other party. We are all striving to destroy the dominance of special privilege and to restore democracy. We differ in details and methods but we are united in a common high purpose.

With earnest wishes for your success, I am,

Faithfully yours,   James Cowden Meyers

TLS (WP, DLC).
[1] Princeton 1891, lawyer of New York.

From Joseph M. Noonan

My dear Doctor: Jersey City, N. J. Sep. 16. 1910.

I wish to congratulate you on your unanimous nomination[1] for the Governorship. I was present in the Convention and had the pleasure of hearing you speak. From the remarks which I afterwards heard I am entirely satisfied that you converted all the delegates who had at first opposed your nomination into enthusiastic champions of your candidacy. It was a very noble speech and the unmistakable tone of sincerity that ran throughout it was its crowning glory. With best wishes for your success and with increased expectation of that fifty thousand majority, I am, very sincerely,   Your friend,   Jos. M. Noonan

TLS (WP, DLC).
[1] Wilson's nomination was made unanimous after the first ballot.

From William Frank McCombs[1]

New York Sept 16 1910

New Jersey is to be congratulated on your nomination for Governor. The people will bear witness to the wisdom of the choice on election day. Princeton has produced the next president of the United States.   Wm F. McCombs.

T telegram (WP, DLC).
[1] Princeton 1898, a New York lawyer who became manager of the Wilson preconvention presidential campaign in 1911 and chairman of the Democratic National Committee in 1912.

From William Gibbs McAdoo[1]

New York Sept. 16 [1910]

May [My] heartiest congratulations and best wishes for your success   W. G. McAdoo

T telegram (WP, DLC).

¹ At this time president of the Hudson & Manhattan Railroad Co.; builder of four transportation tunnels under the Hudson River; vice-chairman of the Democratic National Committee in 1912; and afterward Secretary of the Treasury in the Wilson administration.

From Abbott Lawrence Lowell

Dear Wilson,   Cambridge [Mass.] September 16, 1910

So you have gone and done it! Are not the seas of university management boisterous enough that you must seek the storms of politics? Of course I wish you success, and yet at the same time I shall feel a personal loss if you were elected and leave the Presidency of Princeton. I shall also feel that one of the main stays of the progressive college education has gone. But you will do good wherever you are, and I think you have always had a desire to get a hand upon the wheel of the Ship of State.

Sincerely yours,   A. Lawrence Lowell.

TLS (WP, DLC).

From Robert Underwood Johnson¹

Dear Dr. Wilson: New York Sept. 16, 1910

I rejoice at your nomination for Governor of New Jersey and heartily congratulate you.

It is indeed a new era when conventions have to go to the Academy & Institute² for candidates—and get such good ones as Baldwin³ & yourself. With best wishes for your success

Faithfully yours   R. U. Johnson

ALS (WP, DLC).

¹ Old friend of Wilson's and associate editor and editor of the *Century Magazine* for many years.

² The American Academy of Arts and Letters and the National Institute of Arts and Letters. Wilson and Johnson were members of both organizations, and Johnson was secretary of the former from its founding in 1904 until his death in 1937.

³ Simeon Eben Baldwin, former Chief Justice of the Supreme Court of Errors of Connecticut, who had recently been nominated as the Democratic gubernatorial candidate in Connecticut. He was a member of the National Institute of Arts and Letters.

From Melancthon Williams Jacobus

Cromwell Conn, Sept 16 1910

Congratulations upon your nomination and your speech of wise statesmanship.   M. W. Jacobus.

T telegram (WP, DLC).

From Samuel Allen Harlow[1]

Bethlehem White Mountains, N. H.

My dear Tommy,   Sept. 16th, 1910.

Up here among these beautiful mountains the papers bring me the news of your nomination on the Democratic ticket, for the high position of Governor of New Jersey. I want to send you my congratulations—hearty and sincere as a member of '79 can make them. I wish you all success. I always have voted the Republican ticket, but I shall be glad to see you the next Governor of your state. I will not bother you, now, with any convictions I may have as to the political situation, your time is too precious for that. I do want to say, however, that the situation is amazing, mystifying almost. Many of us are tired of the big stick. We want illumination. A man of lucidity, sanity, with the power of interpreting to the country it's best, highest hopes and feelings—it's real life—it's confused visions—this is what the land needs. And may I honestly say that I do think you have a power of penetration, of insight, of lucid statement, which we need. It is one thing to agitate. It is quite another to clarify the situation. The hour calls for luminous and constructive statesmanship. This nation can never, in the long run, be lifted to it's noblest level through repeated whacks. It must be lifted through noble visions—through large and sane conceptions of it's perils and it's possibilities. Inspiration is the great need of the day—I think.

I wish you great success—large and increasing usefulness in our country's life.

I have been having a delightful rest among these beautiful hills. I trust you are refreshed by the summer's vacation.

With best wishes and regards, I am,

Very sincerely yours,   Samuel A. Harlow.

ALS (WP, DLC).
[1] Wilson's classmate at Princeton, at this time pastor of the Congregational Church of Grafton, Mass.

From William Cavanagh Gebhardt[1]

Dear Dr. Wilson: Jersey City [N. J.], September 16, 1910.

Please accept my congratulations upon your nomination for Governor by the Democratic State Convention yesterday. I am at your service for the campaign and shall be glad to assist you in any way I can. As you are probably already aware, I have, for the last three years particularly, been in the thick of the fight for a Public Utilities Bill, a Direct Primary Bill and a Corrupt Practices Bill, and am, therefore, more, or less, familiar with these bills.   Very sincerely yours,   Wm. C. Gebhardt

TLS (WP, DLC).
1 Lawyer of Clinton, N. J., and Jersey City and Democratic state senator from Hunterdon County.

From Christian Frederick Gauss

My dear Dr. Wilson: Princeton [N. J.] Sept 16 '10

As an 'old' democrat and a member of your faculty, I cannot refrain from sending you my heartiest congratulations on your nomination to the governorship of New Jersey. Your entering upon the public service will of course mean to us at Princeton a private and a personal loss, yet our sense of pride in your leadership increases as we see you assume the larger responsibility.

My convictions having made me a democrat, for some years I have gone into the election booth with a little of that feeling with which a conscientious convict might enter his cell. I could not trust its republican 'principles,' nor yet the wisdom & judgment of my own party leaders, and sought solace with the socialists who at least had a sincere and honest program with much of which I am in sympathy. I could not, however, bring myself to vote their ticket, for fear lest I be siding with a class, even tho' the largest class, as against the nation. This same fear of siding with a class, tho' in that case with the smallest class as against the nation, kept me from any alliance with the republican party and machine. Such a state of affairs tended to give me that sickening feeling that citizenship in the republic was after all not the highest and noblest function of manhood, but for an honest man a rather distressing accident in the system of machine party government.

As I read this morning's account of your nomination and your direct & unequivocal address to the convention, I felt that a new political dawn was breaking. It is not you, however, but the state that is to be congratulated on this new day. Tho' as a professor I must regret your going, as a citizen and I hope I dare say, friend, I do wish to thank you for this sense of relief and the privilege you give me of again casting a ballot with dignity, with confidence, and with pride.

With all good wishes,
          Yours, very sincerely,   Christian Gauss.

ALS (WP, DLC).

From Henry Burchard Fine

My dear Tommy,   Mantoloking, N. J. Sept. 16th, 1910

I congratulate you heartily on the great vote of confidence which you received at Trenton yesterday. To me it seems a very wonderful thing that one who has kept wholly aloof from "practical politics" should win such a victory. I have believed all along that were you to be nominated you would be elected, since in the interval there would be the opportunity for you to be seen & heard by the voters of the state, but I have thought that there were many chances against your nomination. I wish you all the joy and success which you so richly deserve in the political career which began so brilliantly yesterday. I return to Princeton early Monday morning (unless something should occur requiring my presence there earlier than that) and will at once call you up by telephone in order that I may have an opportunity to make my congratulation in person and to talk over certain matters of University business which the occurrences of yesterday affect.

Sincerely Yours,   H. B. Fine

ALS (WP, DLC).

From Cleveland Hoadley Dodge

Saranac Inn, N. Y. Sept. 16 [1910]

Heartiest congratulations   Cleveland H. Dodge.

T telegram (WP, DLC).

From Archibald Stevens Alexander

My dear Doctor Wilson: Hoboken, N. J. September 16, 1910.

I cannot refrain from writing you a line to tell you how splendid I think your speech yesterday was and to show you that I am not the only one the Hoboken delegates who as you know were opposed to you and very strongly in favor of Wittpenn, have returned here to-day full of enthusiasm for you and are spreading this enthusiasm throughout the City. I assume this is happening all over the state. Your speech seems to have put new life and hope into the Party everywhere.

As you were kind enough to suggest some time ago that I write you if anything occurred to me with relation to the campaign, I am going to burden you with my ideas on one or two matters and I sincerely hope that you will not think I am presumptuous in so doing or that I expect you to give any particular thought to them. I believe however, that these opinions are those of some of the other younger men in the Party who have been trying for the last few years to establish a good legislative record for the Party.

I do not know what your plans are in relation to the campaign, but I sincerely hope that you will make as many speeches as you are physically able to make.

What with the Observer[1] and other papers opposed to you and with the efforts of your opponents in the Convention, false impressions of you have been created. As far as those present at the Convention yesterday were concerned, I believe that these impressions were absolutely dispelled by your speech, but of course, there are still a great many people who believe that the word "scholar" necessarily implies someone cold and far away from the people. All anyone who has such a feeling needs to have that feeling removed is to hear you speak, but reading your speeches will not be sufficient and therefore no matter how much newspaper support you have these people will not be reached unless they hear you themselves or their friends hear you and tell them about it.

In this particular locality the two things which have been circulated to injure you are your alleged opposition to labor and your alleged strict views on the liquor question. As to the former, a good big meeting here organized by labor men and addressed by you in person would remove any impression that has been created. As to the liquor issue, I do not believe that you could afford to express views which would be liberal enough to satisfy the Germans of Hudson and Essex counties, but on the other hand, if you could devise some statement which would indicate that you did not intend to be narrow and believed in the utmost personal liberty consistent with the enforcement of the law, such a statement might be of some help, especially as the Republican candidate, whoever he may be, certainly cannot afford to take a liberal attitude on this point. However, this question is the most difficult one in the campaign and I do not feel that my advice is of any importance on it as this community is probably more opposed to rigid liquor laws than any community in the state. I think however, that some announcement on the subject is better than silence as is proved by the defeat of the last Democratic candidate.

It strikes me after seeing the impression that you made on the delegates yesterday, that if you made a speech-making tour of the state, it should be timed so that you follow Lewis, or whoever the Republicans nominate,[2] and follow him within a day or two, as the contrast cannot fail to be very striking and to win you many votes.

I trust that you will forgive me for imposing these views upon you and that you will not try to answer this letter as your correspondence is probably overpoweringly heavy, but if at any time I can do anything for you I hope that you will send me word, as your action has shown us all that we have a civic duty to perform this year and that other matters should be set aside in order to perform it, however small may be our part in helping you to make the Democratic Party "the instrument of righteousness for the state and for the nation."

Yours sincerely,   Archibald S. Alexander.

P.S. Would it be possible for you to have sent to me copies of any speeches that you have heretofore made which could be construed as favorable to union labor and also the context of the speech that is being quoted against you as showing an attitude opposed to union labor.

TLS (WP, DLC).
[1] That is, the Hoboken *Observer*.
[2] Vivian Murchison Lewis was nominated for governor on September 20, 1910, by the Republican state convention in the Taylor Opera House in Trenton.

From Joseph R. Wilson, Jr.

My dear brother: Nashville, Tenn. Sept. 16, 1910.

I must stop long enough in my rush of the day to offer my sincere congratulations over your nomination for governor.

As you remember I said to you when you were recently with us in Nashville,[1] personally I would have preferred to have you remain out of politics. It seemed unavoidable, however, that you should get into the game and my hope is that you may win by the biggest majority ever given a gubernatorial candidate in New Jersey. All day I have been receiving the congratulations of friends here over your nomination, the people of Nashville saying many kind things which I appreciated and I know you would appreciate if you could hear what was said about you. The universal hope is expressed here that you will win. The boys in the office here were considerate enough to wire you this morning as my friends.[2]

You cannot know how we enjoyed having you with us recently. It did me good all over for I do so long at times to be with you, to be able to see more of my own blood. Please as soon as you can write me fully about yourself and the political situation in New Jersey. I am so anxious to know it all.

Kate and Alice join me in great love to you and yours.

Your aff. brother,   Joseph.

TLS (WP, DLC).
1 After delivering his address to the American Bar Association in Chattanooga, Tenn., on August 31, 1910.
2 "Friends of Joe on the Banner" to WW, Sept. 16, 1910, T telegram (WP, DLC).

From Edgar Williamson

My dear Doctor Wilson   Orange N. J. Sept. 16, 1910

I am sorry that I have not the proper learning to express to you my sincere thanks for your kind, frank and manly letter which I received from you August 23d. I am pleased to inform you that your letter to me has made for you thousands of friends who were before hostile to you through misunderstanding.

You are to be congratulated on the splendid testimonial you received at Trenton on 15th and New Jersey is to be congratulated that she possesses a man of your character to be Govenor of this great Commonwealth

Again, Doctor Wilson, I thank you for condescending to write me that grand letter that is sure to make history by placing you in the position now occupied by W. H. Taft

With a grateful heart, and sincer[e] wishes for your every success,   Sincerely Yours   Edgar Williamson

ALS (WP, DLC).

From Walker Whiting Vick[1]

My Dear Sir: [New York] September 16th 1910.

I certainly feel that New Jersey is to be congratulated upon her Democratic candidate for the Gubernatorial chair, and as a resident of Bergen County I wish to tender you my sincere support.

Am a transplanted North Carolinian and a former attendant of the First Presbyterian Church of Wilmington, having been baptised by your Father. You may recall some of my family, especially my Grandmother—Mrs. Laura P. Rothwell.

We have several North Carolinians in Rutherford; and while personally I have religiously refrained from participating in political matters since my residence in the North still I wish to offer my services for such work as I may be able to do on your behalf.

With every good wish for your success which I believe will mean the redemption of New Jersey from the cancerous bacilli that have controlled its political fortunes for several years past, believe me, with respect and esteem,

Very truly yours,   Walker W. Vick

TLS (WP, DLC).
[1] A resident of Rutherford, N. J., engaged in various business enterprises in New York.

From Joseph Albert Dear, Jr.

My dear Doctor   Jersey City, N. J. Sept 16/10

I want to let you know how pleased I am over your nomination. Of course you are to be congratulated for the great compliment your party has paid you, but the party also is to be complimented for the excellence of its judgment and for the fine quality of the candidate it has been able to place at its head.

Should you be elected, and just now I do not see how any other result is possible, I want to assure you of my best wishes for a most successful administration.

Yours very sincerely   Joseph A. Dear

ALS (WP, DLC).

From Edwin Grant Conklin

My dear President Wilson   Princeton [N. J.], Sept. 16, 1910.

I know not whether first to congratulate you or to commiserate Princeton on your nomination for the governorship of this state. Certainly I congratulate you with all my heart on the prospect of large and important public service which lies before you; and the state and nation are to be congratulated that men of your type are willing to go into politics.

On the other hand the prospect for the immediate future of Princeton seems to me very dark. When I wrote you from Rome[1] I had been led to hope that a way out of our University troubles had been found; later I learned that all was not so lovely as had been reported; now it seems to me that we face disaster.

Personally I shall feel your loss here more keenly than I can express. I came to Princeton largely because of my admiration for you and your ideals, and if these are lost I shall feel that the spirit has gone out of the place. But however much I lament your loss to Princeton I recognize that you have done the right thing in turning from a hopeless situation here to one full of promise elsewhere. As the obituary notices usually say (and I feel very much that this is *our* funeral), 'What is our loss is his gain.'

Mrs. Conklin[2] and I arrived on this side of the water last Sunday. We had a very pleasant and profitable sojourn abroad and return in excellent health. I hope I may have a chance to see you and talk with you before the rush of the campaign is on you.

Ever sincerely yours,   E. G. Conklin

ALS (WP, DLC).
[1] E. G. Conklin to WW, June 26, 1910, ALS (WP, DLC).
[2] Belle Adkinson Conklin.

From Alfred Brittin Baker[1]

Dear President Wilson   Princeton [N. J.] Sep 16th [1910]

It is with a very mingled feeling that I congratulate you upon the nomination to the high office which was made yesterday in Trenton, but I do most sincerely and fully congratulate the State upon the prospect of splendid service which the nomination opens to it, and I earnestly pray that the bright vision may be fully realized. With very great esteem and affection believe me

Sincerely Yours   Alfred B. Baker

ALS (WP, DLC).
[1] Princeton 1861, rector of Trinity Episcopal Church, Princeton, 1866-1914.

From Hunsdon Cary[1]

Dear Dr. Wilson,   Richmond, Virginia Sept. 16th., 1910.

Permit me to express my deep gratification at your nomination as Governor of New Jersey. I sincerely trust that you may be elected, and that you will receive the democratic nomination for the Presidency at the next National Convention. It seems that at last the Democrats are coming to their senses and offering the right kind of men for public office. We have had enough of howling dervishes and imitation statesmen, and it does my heart good to see men like yourself and Judge Baldwin placed at the head of the Democratic ticket in northern states. You won my high esteem when I first met you in 1897 at the meeting of the Virginia State Bar Assn. at the Hot Springs,[2] and the passing years have only added to it. May your ripe scholarship and wisdom enable you to render a great service to our nation, and lead it along paths of sober judgment and peace, and away from the strange gods it has followed. I feel that what I write might seem almost patronizing were it not for the fact that it is spoken with deepest earnestness, but I trust you to know and understand.

If the political situation in Virginia is ever of interest to you, I shall be glad to render you any assistance or information in my power.   Sincerely yours,   Hunsdon Cary.

ALS (WP, DLC).
    1 Lawyer of Richmond, Va.
    2 When Wilson delivered "Leaderless Government" on August 5, 1897. His address is printed at that date in Vol. 10.

From Edward William Bok[1]

My dear Doctor Wilson: Philadelphia September 16. 1910

Republican as I am, may I congratulate you, and particularly the people of New Jersey? I wish I lived in your State. May you be elected with a majority that shall speak.

Very cordially yours,   Edward Bok

ALS (WP, DLC).
    1 Vice-president of the Curtis Publishing Co. and editor-in-chief of the *Ladies' Home Journal*.

A News Report of Impromptu Remarks to the Democratic State Convention

[Sept. 17, 1910]

Dr. Woodrow Wilson's versatility was fittingly shown during his great speech to the Democratic Convention on Thursday. Dr. Wilson occasionally departed from the text of his prepared speech and the extemporaneous matter was fully as cogent and effective as the former.

After Dr. Wilson had delivered his set speech, he stated that he would stop as the delegates had been through a gruelling six hours' struggle, and should be given an opportunity to adjourn. But the delegates were so deeply impressed by Dr. Wilson's oratory and were so desirous of hearing more of it that he was greeted with many cries of: "Go on!" and "You're all right." From that point to the end of his address Dr. Wilson spoke extemporaneously and uttered some of the best passages of his entir[e] speech.

After stating that he had made no pledges of any kind, Dr. Wilson departed from his set speech by saying: "If I should be elected Governor of New Jersey, as I expect to be, I am absolutely free to serve the people of this State with singleness of purpose.

And I shall have to serve the State very well, indeed, to deserve your confidence."

Mr. Wilson, following his discussion of the platform, branched off from his set ad[d]ress, and said: "The best pledge you can give the people is the explicitness and definiteness you can give to your promises. You will win the confidence of the people with the platform, but you can only keep this confidence by performance."

Again, after declaring that questions involving established interests established interests [sic] should not be settled in a spirit of hostility, Dr. Wilson strayed from his prepared speech, saying: "It is nonsense to declare that the Democratic party is an enemy of business. We must come to a common understanding, pool our interests, and be guided by those standards that make for the whole interest."

Discussing the creation of a Public Service Commission, with rate-making powers, Dr. Wilson said that the State needs the power to control corporations, not the power to advise.

"Will you control them?" asked Dr. Wilson.

"With your help," shouted a delegate.

Further digressing from his formal speech Dr. Wilson said: "You should see that your State has the power to control its corporations. New Jersey creates a great many corporations, but it has not been controlling its own creatures. For New Jersey, I covet the honor of showing the other States how corporations can be controlled."

This last sentence was nearly all impromptu. The line as it appeared in the prepared speech read: "I covet for New Jersey the honor of doing it."

Continuing his impromptu remarks, Dr. Wilson said: "New Jersey can find out if a corporation is organized to elude the law or to obey the law."

Most of Dr. Wilson's impassioned and eloquent peroration was extemporaneous.

Following his statement that the time had gone when one could fool the American people and play politics. He added: "I pray God that it has gone forever. It is now a case of put up or shut up. Parties must show that they are not looking for office, but for results."

After referring to the Democratic landslide in Maine,[1] he concluded extemporaneously as follows:

"We must reconstruct, by thoughtful processes, economic society in this country, and by doing so will reconstruct political organization. This reconstruction will be bigger than anything in American history.

"America is not distinguished so much by its wealth and material power as by the fact that it was born with an ideal, a purpose to serve mankind. And all mankind has sought her as a haven of equal justice.

"When I look upon the American flag before me I think sometimes that it is made of parchment and blood. The white in it stands for parchment, the red in it signifies blood—parchment on which was written the rights of men, and blood that was spilled to make these rights real. Let us devote the Democratic party to the recovery of these rights."

At the conclusion of his masterly effort Dr. Wilson was mobbed by the delegates, and he had to be rescued by the police, who went to his aid and cleared a way to the stage door where an automobile was in waiting to convey him to Princeton.

Printed in the Trenton *True American*, Sept. 17, 1910.
1 In the election held in Maine on September 12, 1910, the voters had elected a Democratic governor for the first time in thirty years, as well as two Democratic congressmen out of a delegation of four from the state. In addition, the Democrats won substantial majorities in both houses of the legislature, thus ensuring the election of the first Democratic United States senator from Maine since 1853.

Two Interviews

[Sept. 17, 1910]

DR. WILSON STRONG FOR PUBLICITY OF CAMPAIGN MONEYS

In an interview with a reporter for the Trenton Evening Times yesterday, Dr. Woodrow Wilson emphatically expressed himself in favor of the widest publicity for all campaign contributions, further elucidated the stand he took at the convention on Thursday, for the regulation of corporations, and freely expressed himself on a number of other issues that he regards as vital to the people of New Jersey.

Dr. Wilson added that it was his desire to come to Trenton again and make another speech, during the pending campaign, and plans are under way for a big meeting here.

Chairman Joseph S. Hoff, of the Mercer County Democratic Committee, who lives in Princeton, has already taken up with Dr. Wilson the question of such a meeting, and it is expected that former Mayor Frank S. Katzenbach, Jr., will preside. It is the desire of Dr. Wilson to visit every county in the State, and make an address to the voters, and he has so expressed himself to the Democratic State Committee. He will hardly attempt a "whirlwind" tour, meeting voters from early morning until late at night, such as has been the custom of late years, but will content himself with dispassionate presentations of his policies.

He wants a public utilities law that will be full and complete and incontrovertible, and will insist upon the adoption of such legislation as will absolutely guarantee equal taxation. All this was said in unmistakable English—without any "ifs" or "ands."

It was with a kindly, genial smile that Dr. Wilson declared that he had not acquired the art of being interviewed. Maybe it was this fact, or possibly a surprising naturalness in an aspirant for public office, that made the president of Princeton University seem so strangely human.

Turning upon his questioner a countenance serenely clear, considering the momentous questions that must of necessity confront him, he said that it would be his single purpose, if elected Governor of New Jersey, to give to the people an advanced administration, in the interest of all, with special privileges to none.

There was no equivocation in this or any other of his statements, no hesitation in his speech. No studied pause, presaging secret calculation, characterized a single answer to questions pertaining to the public weal. Dr. Wilson said what he meant and, by every extraordinarily strong line in his face, meant what he said.

And when Dr. Wilson says anything he looks you straight in the eye. He speaks very pleasantly, in well modulated tones, with a voice that is wholly convincing. There is about his features that which precludes any possibility of doubting the earnestness of either his desire or determination. Indeed he proposes telling the people of New Jersey just what he thinks.

It is the impression of the Democratic Gubernatorial nominee that he is not thoroughly understood in Trenton. He says that when he agreed in the early summer, that his name might be used in connection with the candidacy since unanimously conceded him, he had no idea that the friends of Farnk [Frank] S. Katzenbach, Jr., intended favoring the lat[t]er for another nomination, or that Mr. Katzenbach would either consider or accept the opportunity. The President of Princeton, when interviewed, had just concluded a letter of thanks to his greatest rival for the honor, in answer to a telegram of congratulation.

"I think a great deal of Mr. Katzenbach," he volunteered, sitting comfortably on a long, low lounge on a shaded side porch of his handsome home, in the center of the famous campus of Old Nassau. "It was not my purpose to become the rival of anybody for the nomination," he added. "The vote of the convention came without my seeking, and so, as a result, I am free to pledge the people as I please, and to plan for the carrying forward of every promise.

"But I don't believe in talking at random," Dr. Wilson quietly continued. "It is possibly not well to criticise generally, but rather to put your finger on one thing at a time and point out its defects and the remedy. When you get out your shellalah [shillelagh], don't cast about indiscriminately, striking everything in sight; make every blow tell."

Asked immediately how he would control the corporations, Dr. Wilson replied that he would first compel the filing of detailed reports with the Secretary of State, showing the origin of every phase of the company's management, including the authority of officers and departmental heads, and when overt acts were committed, prosecute the individuals. "Of course, it will be argued, and rightly," he observed, "that 'dummies' perform all functions of questionable character and are always found to have given the necessary orders. But after a few of the 'dummies' are sent to the penitentiary, a substantial supply of them will cease."

"Yet I would go even farther," it was insisted, "for juries sometimes refrain from punishing these tools, and make the law allow additional latitude in the introduction of testimony that might tend to show the criminality of hidden conspirators, and I would put in the power of the prosecuting attorney the privilege of altering indictments to include offending officials who crawl to cover and might be located were the laws of evidence more elastic."

Asked if he would restrict swollen fortunes, Dr. Wilson replied that a part of the question indicated the necessity of some sort of an operation. " 'Swollen,' " he said, ["]suggests something extraordinary. But we are not concerned so much with whether or not these fortunes should be surgically treated; rather with the means to be employed. No one grudges [Thomas Alva] Edison a penny of his honest earnings. In building up the industries of the country, and thus enhancing the welfare of all, there can be no objection to the resulting income. The quarrel is with the man who masses millions through illicit manipulation and acquires tremendous fortune without really adding to the nation's growth or development. Don't declare that all rich men are thieves, for it isn't true; say that John Smith, who is rich, is a rascal, and prove it."

Dr. Wilson has already concluded to tender his resignation to the trustees of the University, and says he is preparing to present it at the October meeting, on the 20th. In the meantime he will have opened the term with the largest class the institution has ever known and will have already entered upon a campaign that will begin with the nomination of his Republican antagonist, next week.

There will be no speaking by the Democratic nominee, however, until after the Democratic State Committee completes his itinerary in accordance with his county to county suggestion, or otherwise. When he consented to accept the nomination, if it should come to him, it was his purpose to clear his calendar for September in order to make way for possible political exigencies. And so he is not scheduled to talk anywhere before he takes the stump. He will open his campaign in Mercer County, probably after the Congressional nomination has been made.

"It will be a novel experience for me," he said, "to go out and solicit votes. But I like to meet people and I want to become acquainted through the state. For this reason, in addition to a desire to make my views more universally understood in New Jersey, I will seek to reach each county, individually, and not attempt to confine the campaign to the greater or more populous centres."

"And you have confidence in general Democratic success through the country this year?" was asked.

"Oh, I don't know that we can intelligently forecast such events, altogether," he replied. "There would seem to be no doubt of it, so far, considering the present political unrest in the country, which condition will never be quieted, in my opinion, until some actually tangible result is obtained. The people are taking a greater interest in affairs of state," he explained, "than, to my mind, they ever evidenced heretofore, and on every side there are signs of the times.

"For instance, it was always looked upon as a practical impossibility to pry loose a Republican vote in Maine. A crow-bar was required, and yet they were secured this fall without violence. That the voters in all sections of the United States are seeking different government is shown in the fact that men not previously publicly identified with politics, notably in Connecticut, are being drawn into the present primaries."

This led to a question of the Princeton President's idea of New Jersey's existing primary law.[1] He admitted that he was not sufficiently familiar with its operations to publicly pass upon its popular efficacy. "Though you may be assured," he asserted, "that out of the eixsting [existing] chaotic character of our political government there will come some satisfactory result

1 About this matter, see n. 10 to the address printed at Oct. 5, 1910.

to the people. I know how they feel. I have talked with them, indiscriminately; on the trains, in railway stations—and I get all over the country at times—and there is a widespread dissatisfaction."

"Do you think the Republicans will be able, through the insurgent movement, to accomplish the great reforms that are sought?" was inquired.

"Of course, we can't tell that. They must first get their house in order." And to further interrogations anent the Republican party, Dr. Wilson said he had a very warm feeling towards President Taft, and that he was being sufficiently criticised within his own party.

If Dr. Wilson is not entirely acquainted with a subject, he frankly owns it. He said that he had not read very many of Colonel Roosevelt's speeches; that he had not seen the letter of Secretary Norton,[2] explaining that the President, having withheld the patronage that might have been allot[t]ed the insurgents, would restore it;[3] that his time was too much occupied to read any more current literature than was absolutely essential and that his principal recreation, besides being a lover of the great out-of-doors, was the study of politics and government.

He willingly admitted an early inclination towards politics, but said that without an independent fortune, and no particular reputation, he would be subjected to certain temptations which he believed were best unassailed by youth. And being asked if he now felt a financial independence, he replied:

"Mercy, no. Yet I am now inclined to the belief that, were I thrown out of politics, at any time, for any reason, I might be able to get a job."

Dr. Wilson looks the big man he is. There is something in his makeup that suggests the timber of which superior men are made. A gentleness, an easy grace, a firm step and gesture, and a fine physique proclaim him, together with a noticeable forehead, nose and chin, above the average person in physical and mental equipment.

Readily approachable, willingly interrogated, there is a warmth

[2] Charles Dyer Norton, Secretary to President Taft.

[3] On September 15, 1910, a letter dated September 15 and signed by Norton was made public at President Taft's summer residence at Beverly, Mass. The name of the addressee of the letter was never made public, but the *New York Times*, Sept. 16, 1910, stated that it was sent in response to a query from "a Republican in Iowa." In this remarkable document, the President in effect admitted publicly that, as was generally known or suspected, he had withheld federal patronage from insurgent Republican congressmen and senators in an effort to enforce party discipline, conceded that this policy had been a failure, and promised to dispense patronage thereafter in accordance with the customary rules. The letter appeared in the *New York Times*, Sept. 16, 1910.

in his handclasp that is not found every day. There is sentiment, too, in his system and a ready appreciation of the ridiculous. In every way he presents an interesting personality, perfectly composed. He says he has not had time to rearrange his library, since moving into the President's home, at Princeton, and that he therefore has done little regular reading recently. He plays golf in the mornings, adn [and] otherwise spends considerable time in the open, when there is time at hand.

He is fond of the opera and the drama, though complains that transportation facilities preclude attendance at the New York theatres and that as a result he has recently refrained from such entertainment. But he gets to New York often, to Philadelphia less frequently, and to all the large cities of the East and West on odd accasions [occasions]. His life is seemingly quiet and peaceful, singularly removed from the stress and strife of campaigning. This situation has nothing daunted his duty or determination in connection with the possibilities of his party and, though not inclined in the direction of a steam roller canvass of the State, said, at parting, that in this respect, he was wholly in the hands of the Democratic State Committee.

Printed in the *Trenton Evening Times*, Sept. 17, 1910; some editorial headings omitted.

◊

WILSON VIEWS ARE CLEAN-CUT

Tariff Revision, Regulation of Corporations and Conservation Are All Vital Issues.

HIS PLANS OF CAMPAIGN

Special Correspondence of the News.

PRINCETON, Sept. 17.—The views of Woodrow Wilson upon public questions are well defined. His method of campaigning for the Governorship of New Jersey, for which office he has been nominated by the Democratic party, is not so well settled. It will be decided after further study of the field and conference with the State committee. Interviewed yesterday, Dr. Wilson spoke freely of the position he will assume with reference to what he considers vital issues.

There will doubtless be no uncertainty in the terms he will use in telling the voters the Republican party is responsible for the high cost of living. Dr. Wilson stated to the News representative that, in his judgment, the three most important questions before the people are the regulation of corporations, the reduction of the tariff and the conservation problem. These are the questions the nation must face and settle, and, according to the view of Dr. Wilson, the Democratic party is to be asked by the people to bring about a new era.

In reply to a query he stated that the property held by citizens is paying an undue tribute to the State, while the corporations, especially the railroads, are escaping taxes which should be imposed upon them. The question was one of methods of assessment, and if the candidate becomes the Executive at the November election, he states this question will receive immediate and vigorous attention.

It is the judgment of Dr. Wilson that the State should regulate the corporations it makes.

The high protective tariff made and continued by the Republican party is one of the several causes that have produced the present high cost of living. The affiliations of the Republican party with special interests has enabled the interests to control the cost of necessary products, and it is the opinion of the Princeton president this will continue so long as the Republican party, with its Payne-Aldrich tariff and its trust connections, remains in control of the National Government.

On the conservation question, so far as it concerns New Jersey, the candidate stated that he was for "State control," rather than "national control." He said that "in the West, there are vast domains of government land which the federal authorities should control," but in this State the question was one which concerned the State alone. "I do not believe that a single privilege should be ceded by the State to any individual or corporation, and if elected the careful conservation, for the benefit of all the people of this State, of all water rights and natural resources, shall have my immediate and constant attention."

That the candidate has decided personal views concerning the direct primary, the corrupt practise act and the manner in which public business should be conducted was clearly indicated.

A very thorough discussion of the direct primary resulted from the query, "Do you believe in the extension of the direct primary to the selection of Congressmen, United States Senators, and Governors?"

"This entire question of whether we shall have a representative or delegated government," declared Dr. Wilson, "leads back to the primary discussion of whether the legislator should be a mere deputy, going to Washington or Trenton to act as directed by his constituents at a distance shall dictate, or whether he will be allowed to exercise his own judgment, after first hand information has been gained through exhaustive and informing debate in the legislative halls. Personally," declared the candidate, "I think the legislator should be allowed to do his own thinking and that the voters should take care to elect men to office whom they can trust."

When pressed for a statement of his position regarding the direct primary, his answer was: "I think the statement of the platform regarding that a very excellent one. It declares for such a simplification of the electoral machinery as will make possible the effectual exercise of the right of direct nominations for all elective offices. The forms of the direct primary are so various that with my limited knowledge I cannot be specific, but it is my intention to give the entire problem careful consideration. I understand thirty States have some form of direct primary expression. The principle is certainly a most excellent one, but the method of expression, which is of first consequence, is not, by any means, settled."

Closely allied to the problem of the direct primary in the mind of the nominee was the matter of limiting the amount of money that could be used in both the primary and general elections. "There should certainly be a very explicit act, obliging every candidate to publish in careful, tabulated form all his expenses in both elections and the sources from which the money is derived. County and State committees should do the same. In response to the question, "Will you urge the Democratic State central committee to make such a statement?" the candidate's terse answer was, "I certainly will."

In answer to the query, "Just what did you mean in your convention speech when you stated, 'the business of the State has been conducted in a haphazard manner?'" Dr. Wilson said, "I used that word in a general sense and did not imply that there has not been thought given to administration and efficiency sought in the service of the State. It is my personal conviction, though I have not made any personal inquiry in the matter, that there could be a co-ordination of services between boards of administration which would considerably lessen the number of men needed and the expense involved in administration. If elected, I shall certainly oppose during my term the creation of new commissions which public conditions do not strongly demand."

When reference was made to the assertion of his convention speech "that the people want honesty in government and they do not think the government is being conducted as honestly, as economically and as wisely as it should be conducted," Dr. Wilson instanced Maine as an illustration of the awakening of the voters to that truth. "Much of the work undertaken by the government is undertaken unnecessarily and could be dispensed with without injury to efficient administration. What is true of the nation is, also, true of the State. If the executive power is conferred upon me by the voters, it will be my object to administer affairs in an honest, economical and wise manner."

Dr. Wilson wished it to be stated most emphatically that the nomination came to him Thursday afternoon practically unsought. You may state that "no promises have been asked, much less exacted of me."

Replying to questions relating to the conduct of his camp[a]ign, Dr. Wilson spoke freely. No definite plans have been announced to him concerning his notification or plan of campaign. He will consult with the State committee as to details. His present idea would include the campaigning of the entire State, with at least one speech in every county, preferably at the county seat, and additional speeches in the more populous counties. This would enable him to meet the voters face to face, and familiarize himself with the needs of the people. Dr. Wilson said he anticipated with no small degree of pleasure this "swing around the circle."

On next Tuesday evening, September 20, Dr. Wilson will deliver a non-political address at a dinner to be given in Jersey City to celebrate the opening of the new courthouse.[1] After that function he will rest until summoned to enter upon the active work of the campaign.

Printed in the *Newark Evening News*, Sept. 17, 1910.
  [1] A news report of this affair is printed at Sept. 21, 1910.

From Charles Albert Woods[1]

My dear Doctor: Tate Spring, Tenn. Sept. 17th, 1910.
    I feel impelled to express to you my conviction of the deep significance of your willingness to accept a nomination for the office of Governor. It means much of benefit to the people & much of usefulness to you. May your example lead others of like character to serve the country in this hour of need & may your venture result to you in the award of still higher honors & nobler service.
                Very sincerely,   C. A. Woods.

Mrs. Woods[2] & I deeply appreciate your kind letter from Chattanooga.

ALS (WP, DLC).

¹ An old friend and lawyer from Marion, S. C., justice of the Supreme Court of South Carolina since 1903, whom Wilson had met on shipboard in 1896.
² Sally Wannamaker Woods.

From William Royal Wilder

My dear Wilson,   New York September 17th, 1910.

I have been on the verge of 'sticking in my oar' and writing you this summer. I have not done so for I knew that my love for Princeton would have led me to advise a postponement of your entry into politics. I felt sure it was coming, but I hoped for the sake of Princeton that another year would elapse before the occurrence of what has just happened. Princeton, after all, can afford to lose you if the State and the Nation get you. As an old friend and classmate I foolishly feared that you might fall between the stools. Not in our lifetime have the times been riper for the public appearance of a man like yourself. Cleveland was not worse needed in the early Nineties. I need not describe my feelings as a Democrat, to say nothing about my personal friendship for you. As a Mugwump, Free-trader and Democrat I voted three times for Cleveland. Since then I have been obliged to hold my nose with one hand while I voted with the other,—when I voted at all. 'The scholar in politics' and the honest man in politics will prove an invincible combination,—and you are *it*.

My heartiest congratulations! I am sorry I am not a voter in New Jersey. I will respond to any call from the Treasurer of your campaign committee to my utmost dollar, and from now on shall proceed on the theory that I shall be of more service to you in 1912 than I can be now.

With Roosevelt and the Republican party behaving as they are now, it ought not to be difficult for a sane, sound and sober Democrat to become president.

I am, as heretofore,

Cordially yours,   Wm. R. Wilder

TLS (WP, DLC).

From William Henry Welch

                                        Norfolk Connecticut
Dear President Wilson,   September 17 1910.

I wish to send you my hearty congratulations and best wishes, even if my feelings are somewhat mixed on the subject of your nomination for the Governorship. For one as much interested in education as I am, it is hard to balance the loss to the cause of higher education with the gain to political life and your state and very likely our country which your acceptance of the nomination to the Governorship implies.

Princeton needs you, but so does the country, and always and everywhere my best wishes for your success and happiness accompany you.

With most cordial regards to yourself and Mrs. Wilson, I am,
Faithfully yours,   William H. Welch.

I am returning to Baltimore next week.

ALS (WP, DLC).

From Samuel Huston Thompson, Jr.

My dear Mr. Wilson: Denver, Colorado September 17, 1910.

I noted yesterday, in our Denver papers, that you had been nominated by the Democrats of New Jersey for Governor. I hardly know whether to congratulate you or not. Although a Republican, I certainly can congratulate the Democrats of New Jersey, but, as for you personally, I appreciate the task you will have on your hands if you are elected. To drive out the grafters and the truckling politicians is a task not to be envied. But I believe that you are the man to do it. My only suggestion is to jump on them hard from the very start.

Another announcement, that you had offered your resignation as President of Princeton, almost makes me sick and, to my mind, is a calamity. I hope the "yapping" monied interests are satisfied and that they will rue the day they ever made an attack on you.

I have just finished building a home on Congress Park, in Denver. From it I can see two hundred miles of the Rocky Mountains and seven peaks with an altitude of over fourteen thousand feet. My den will be in orange and black. It would please me very much if I could have your autographed photograph to place in the position of honor.

Deeply regretting your offered resignation but congratulating the Democrats, and in fact all the people of New Jersey, on your nomination, I remain,
Your sincere friend,   S. H. Thompson Jr.

TLS (WP, DLC).

From Bayard Stockton

My dear Dr Wilson: London, S. W. Sept 17, 1910.

The English papers tell us this morning of your nomination, and I hasten to offer my services in your campaign in any way that you may be able to use them.

From this distance the outlook is most favorable, and I trust that we may be able to bring a triumphant success to our colors at last.

I sail for home on Wednesday next, and will be ready for service by the 29th.

With earnest congratulations to the Jersey Democrats, rather than to you, I am   Yours very truly   Bayard Stockton

ALS (WP, DLC).

From Michael Welsh Scully[1]

Dear Sir: Somerville, N. J., September 17th, 1910.

The battle for the Gubernatorial nomination has been fought and your friends have triumphed. The rules of the Convention were most fair and just, leaving no room for fault finding or criticism. This in its self gives to the successful candidate a good send-off.

I have the honor to be the County Chairman of Somerset County, and though divided on the day of the convention as to a choice, to-day we are a unit for you. Our nominee for the General Assembly, Mr. George Mason LaMonte of Bound Brook, is a gentleman of high character, fine business ability and executive qualifications. Our nominee for Sheriff, Mr. Frank Mobus of North Plainfield, is a vote getter and it is my opinion that we will carry the County this fall for the whole ticket.

Hoping to have the pleasure of meeting you in my County during the campaign, I am,

Very truly yours,   M. W. Scully

TLS (WP, DLC).
[1] Secretary of the Hillsboro Fire Assurance Co. of Somerville, N.J., and chairman of the Somerset County Democratic Committee.

From Robert Harris McCarter

My Dear Tommy   Little Silver, New Jersey 17 Sept. 1910

You have my warmest and sincerest congratulations on your new honor. As I look back thirty five years to the two wing rooms in Mrs Wright's Boarding House,[1] and recall the modest lad who occupied the one next to my own, and also remember some of those midnight talks we used to have, I imagine I can foresee your great future.

I hope to see you soon[.] Meantime believe me as ever
Your sincere and delighted friend   Robert H McCarter

ALS (WP, DLC).
  [1] About Mrs. Wright's boarding house, see n. 1 to "Two Items from a Wilson Notebook," Sept. 7, 1875, Vol. 1.

From Edward Lawrence Katzenbach

Trenton, N. J.,
My dear President Wilson: September 17, 1910.

Having been abroad during the greater part of the past summer, I have not been conversant with political affairs at home. I wish, however, to assure you how thoroughly pleased I am personally to have your name at the head of our ticket this fall. I shall give to you all the support which I could possibly give to any man, with knowledge that in the event of your success the affairs of our State will be most faithfully administered.

Very sincerely yours,   Edward L. Katzenbach

TLS (WP, DLC).

From David Benton Jones

My dear Doctor: Chicago September 17th, 1910.

If you can do something to keep the stars in view, in the welter and whelm of present day conditions, Princeton's loss will be the country's gain. I am sorry to confess my interest in Princeton lags with the loss of your leadership. I find a gain, however, in the increased personal interest I feel in politics. I shall follow the situation with great enjoyment and I hope with growing encouragement. It is fortunate Roosevelt started his roaring so early. It seems to have reduced President Taft to imbecility, judging by the recent Norton letter. The more Roosevelt roars, the greater will be the call for someone who still believes in conserving representative government. It may come to that in the future, but the carrying on of representative government as now understood, cannot be done by roaring, and that is the only thing Roosevelt can do.

I wish there was some way I could be of any service.

Very sincerely yours,   David B. Jones.

TLS (WP, DLC).

From Robert Gunn Bremner

My dear President Wilson,   Passaic, N. J., Sept 17 1910

In the general acclaim—the most enthusiastic since the shouts of the rejoicing Greeks stunned the birds overhead—we add our voice.

I enclose clippings[1] with hesitation, for I know you are over-burdened with such matter, but as I wrote you about a month ago and I received such a kind reply,[2] I do this to show how we stand today.

You must come to Passaic. When could you come do you think? You recall when you were here at the Board of Trade banquet.[3] An even warmer welcome awaits you this time.

Scores of Republicans will vote for you—they flock into the office to tell me so. Our weak point so far is the "labor" vote but I dare say you are planning to give emphasis to the appeal to labor.

What is enclosed is but an earnest of every issue till election day.

Any suggestions will be much appreciated. Will be glad to give you any Passaic county information confidential or otherwise.

Sincerely yours   Robt G. Bremner

ALS (WP, DLC).
  [1] They are missing.
  [2] R. G. Bremner to WW, July 5, 1910, and WW to R. G. Bremner, July 9, 1910, both in Vol. 20.
  [3] A news report of Wilson's address at this affair is printed at Dec. 3, 1903, Vol. 15.

From Simeon Eben Baldwin

My dear President Wilson   New Haven, Conn., Sept. 17 1910

It gave me great pleasure to see how heartily the Democrats of New Jersey ratified the suggestion of your nomination as their leader, this Fall.

Connecticut, we think, will follow Maine and join New Jersey in supporting the revolt against legislating for the protection of special interests at the expense of the people.

I hope that your election as Governor will be the prelude to your election to the Presidency of something greater even than a great university.   Yours sincerely   Simeon E. Baldwin

ALS (WP, DLC).

An Interview

[Sept. 18, 1910]

CRIME OF TRUSTS IS INDIVIDUAL, SAYS DR. WILSON

Admitting That Combination of Capital Is Necessary, the
Democratic Nominee for Governor of New Jersey Declares That
If Elected He Will Put in Jail the "Dummies" and
the Men Behind Them Later.

"This cry for quiet and peace is quite futile. These things will
not be settled until the people are convinced that they have been
settled rightly."

Woodrow Wilson made this statement to a reporter for The
World at Princeton Friday, the day after he was nominated for
the Governorship of New Jersey by the Democratic State Convention. Corporations, railroads, the tariff, swollen fortunes and
the high cost of living had been touched on and Dr. Wilson had
said that a great reformation was going on in the country: a
swift reformation that means much.

From what the nominee said and from the manner he said it,
it was evident that the State that has been called "the mother of
corporations" will see many reforms of its own in the next two
years, if Dr. Wilson be elected. If he carries out the reforms he
has in mind it seems highly probable that "the mother of corporations" will not know her own children when he gets through.

Sitting on the porch of his home in the grounds of Princeton
University, Dr. Wilson expounded his views on many things. But
in the course of an hour he reverted time and time again to
corporations, the necessity of their [there] being government
supervision and the absurdity of regarding corporations as individuals. These things he has studied and it is quite obvious that
if he be elected, it will be to them that he will devote much of his
time and thought. In fact he says as much.

The President of Princeton, who is still called "Doctor" there,
though they will be calling him "Governor" when the campaign
gets fairly started, is an old-young man. Seeing him walking in
the college grounds with students all about, one might easily mistake him at a little distance for a senior. His carriage is erect, and
his step elastic. He is tall and somewhat spare, but his shoulders
are broad. Seen at close range he appears at first glance to be forty
or thereabouts. He is fifty-four.

There is a story to the effect that Dr. Wilson once told a
photographer that if his picture were taken it would be found that
the negative had been smashed. The doctor asserted that he was

the homeliest man in the world. He isn't. He has what is sometimes called "a strong face." The brow is both high and broad; the
blue eyes deep set, the nose long and the mouth quite straight and
not very large. The whole face is long and somewhat narrow and
the lines at either side of the mouth are very deep. The most
noticable feature are the ears. They are very large, protrude, and
have very long lobes. The doctor's dark hair is turning gray and
is quite thin.

When first addressed Dr. Wilson turns sharply and his eyes
flash directly into those of the speaker. The glance is penetrating,
but not challenging. It is a look of expectancy, and while talking
he smiles frequently, but seldom laughs heartily. His enunciation
is remarkably clear and he talks rather quickly, thoughts
evidently following each other rapidly and in proper sequence.
His tongue never is at a loss for a word. He is a powerful and
persuasive public speaker. He looks scholarly and can speak very
learnedly, but in general conversation, and sometimes in his
speeches, he uses colloquial terms and even slang, as witness his
remark at the close of the Trenton convention:

"The time when you could play politics and fool the American
people has gone by. Now it is a case of put up or shut up."

This from the pedagogue to the politician; from the man who
may be elected to the highest office in a State renowned for its
machine politics.

"I have always wanted to go into politics," said Dr. Wilson to
The World's representative. "As a young man that was my ambition. But I came to the conclusion that it was not the place for a
man who was not independent. Such a man would have to consider the possibility of remaining in office, and that consideration
might move him to do things he should not do.

"So I studied law. And the law, as Coke says, 'is a jealous mis-
tress.' If you take up other things you soon find you have no
clients."

It was in response to a question whether he thought financially
independent men were being called more and more into politics
that Dr. Wilson said a great reformation was going on.

"I travel about a great deal and I frequently talk with men I
meet on the train; chance acquaintances," he said. ["]It is surprising to find that they have views on all great public questions; that
they are doing their own thinking. Of course they get fooled, but
not always. And they have come to believe that party does not
make as much difference as they used to think it did. Why, a few
years ago, it would have necessitated the use of a crow-bar to

turn Maine Democratic. Yet the recent election was managed witho[u]t violence. It's astonishing how many detachable votes there are these days." . . .[1]

The conversation turned to the recent utterances of Mr. Roosevelt.

"To tell the truth," said Dr. Wilson, "I haven't read them. I haven't had time. I know in a general way what he has been talking about. He is very voluminous."

Once again the Doctor smiled. He will probably read the Roosevelt speeches before he takes the stump, but the matter of time is one that has been bothering him evidently for quite a while.

"I haven't had time in the last eight years, since I came here," he said, "to arrange my library. About one-third of it is in order but the rest is in confusion. I don't have time, either, to keep up with the present books, though I get some idea of the best of them from what my friends tell me. You see, I have really spent two half lives. I spent one half learning how to write, and the other half I have had to spend learning how to manage business affairs here at the University.

"When I go on a vacation I spend my time out of doors. When I have time I ride horseback. If I haven't time for that I play golf. I started too late to be much of a golf player, but I enjoy it, and my friends get a lot of fun out of beating me. When I haven't time for golf I take a walk." . . .

Printed in the New York *World*, Sept. 18, 1910; some editorial headings omitted.
[1] Certain paragraphs in this interview have been omitted because they duplicate those in interviews already printed in this volume.

To Edwin Grant Conklin

Princeton, N. J.
My dear Professor Conklin,   18 September, 1910.

It was a great pleasure to see your handwriting under the heading "Princeton" again; and I can assure you that no letter I have received has given me more pleasure than this of yours. What you say of your feeling about me and about my relations to the University give me more than pleasure: they touch me very deeply. It causes me a great pang to think of leaving Princeton, unhappy as the last few years have been for me here, and at the centre of every thought I have of it stand men like yourself who have honoured me with your trust and confidence. I hope and believe that the Trustees will see to it that nothing substantial that we have accomplished amongst us shall be impaired or taken away from. They have perhaps learned something in recent months, and I think they will be very careful about their next move.

I shall hope to see you very soon and to have the pleasure of a talk with you.

With warmest regard,
Your sincere friend,   Woodrow Wilson

WWTLS (E. G. Conklin Papers, NjP).

To John Wesley Wescott

Princeton, N. J.

My dear Judge Westcott,   18 September, 1910.

I sincerely appreciate your kind letter of the sixteenth. You may rest assured that the fact that you thought Mr. Katzenbach better fitted for the office of Governor of the State than myself will have not the slightest effect upon my feelings or my attitude towards you. On the contrary, I respect no men so much as those who act upon their own sincere judgment and act upon it with outspoken candour.

It will give me real pleasure to see you at the earliest possible opportunity, and I shall greatly value your advice as to they [the] way in which the campaign should be conducted in South Jersey.

With much respect,
Sincerely Yours,   Woodrow Wilson

WWTLS (J. W. Wescott Coll., NjP).

From Cleveland Hoadley Dodge

Dear Woodrow   Saranac Inn N. Y. Sept 18th [1910]

Off in the woods for a few days, the papers are more interesting than even during the football season & I rejoice with all my heart that everything has gone so well in New Jersey. Your Convention speech was splendid & unless all signs fail, you ought to carry the State by a large majority. As it has to be, I am very happy that the country has taken your entrance into politics with such real enthusiasm. What will it be, when you get full speed on?

I see that [John Huston] Finley is already in the field for Princeton[1] & Geo McClellan too. If the friends of both get to work it will make a nice split.

Have just had a letter from Harry Thompson, who met Parker Handy in Switzerland. He says that we can count on Parker.

God bless you old man. Don't wear yourself out

Ever affly   C H Dodge

Don't answer this as I shall be home in a few days.

ALS (WP, DLC).

¹ That is, for the presidency of Princeton.

From Richard Heath Dabney

Dear Woodrow: [Charlottesville, Va.] 18 Sept., 1910.

Three cheers and bully for you!

Whoop-la-whoop! Whoop-la-whoop!

The G.O.P. is in the soup!

I felt confident that you were going to be the nominee of the New Jersey Democrats, and I feel equally confident that you will be the next governor of the State. And what is more, there may easily arise conditions and contingencies that will land you in the White House on March 4th, 1913. So mote it be! When it happens, I shall make a mighty effort to leap o'er the Rotunda, cracking my heels together with glee as I fly through space. That is, I'll do that when I hear of your election. But, when you actually take your seat in the chair of George Washington, I'll not be close enough to the Rotunda to jump over it. For you can bet I'll be a spectator of the inauguration. I've never seen one yet, but I shall not miss *yours*!

But, to return from this pleasing prospect of the future to the present, and the period that lies just ahead of us, I predict that you will be elected Governor of New Jersey; and by way of fortifying my pretensions to being a political prophet, I will mention that I predicted the recent Democratic victory in Maine. You have got a big fight ahead of you, but then I know you are going to prove a big fighter! And I firmly believe you will win.

I wanted to write to you as soon as I heard of your nomination, but have been up to my eyes in the work of registering students for the session that began on Thursday. Only today did I get a breathing spell, & I use my breath to shout "Hurrah for Governor Wilson"!   Faithfully yours,   R. H. Dabney.

ALS (WP, DLC).

To Cleveland Hoadley Dodge

Dear Cleve.,   Princeton, N. J. 19 September, 1910.

Thank you with all my heart for your message.[1] I am deluged with messages, but yours stands out from all the rest, because it goes straight to my heart.

Always,

Faithfully and affectionately Yrs.   Woodrow Wilson

WWTLS (WC, NjP).

[1] Dodge's telegram of Sept. 16, 1910.

From Thomas Nesbitt McCarter, Jr.

My dear Dr. Wilson: Newark, N. J. Sept. 19. 1910.

I write not so much to congratulate you as to felicitate the democracy upon your nomination. The party has acted wisely. With you as a candidate, under existing conditions, success is indeed quite possible. The old names of "republican" and "democrat" do not seem to mean very much any more; rather we are drifting toward radicalism and conservatism as the alternatives; when I must choose between these two, it will not take me long to act.

I have had considerable experience with the political side of life and much of it is unpleasant. After a generation spent in a scholarly and academic atmosphere, I shall be surprised if you like it.

The platform is in one or two respects more strenuous than I should suppose one of your habit of mind would approve. I may be old fashioned but I am opposed to government by bureauocracy and the tendency to destroy representative government.

As you know I am the head of one of the largest of the so called "wicked corporations." They are no better and no worse than the individuals, who dominate them, cause them to be. My experience is that, while sometimes they may yield to blackmail imposed by political highwaymen—as does the individual when surrounded by bandits—they do not voluntarily seek to corrupt; on the contrary they are for the most part managed by self-respecting, honest men.

Very truly yours,   Thos. N. McCarter.

ALS (WP, DLC).

From Cyrus Hall McCormick

Boston Mass Sept 19 1910

Great enthusiasm in our family for splendid success   hope see you next week.   Cyrus H. McCormick.

T telegram (WP, DLC).

From Richard Vliet Lindabury

My dear Mr. Wilson: Newark, N. J. September 19, 1910.

I am this morning in receipt of your letter of the 16th inst. I was sorry to miss you at the Convention on Thursday but the crowd was so large that it seemed impossible to reach you without an unprofitable amount of elbowing. Besides, that day belonged to "The Boys" and I thought I could see you more satisfactorily some other time.

I am writing now in particular to congratulate you both upon your nomination and upon your speech of acceptance. The latter did not surprise me although it gratified me exceedingly. It confirmed the view which I had already formed that you know how to deal with the masses and to lead them. Really I feel and certainly trust that this is the opening for you of a great career. You do not need either instruction or guidance from me. At the same time, if during the campaign or your administration which will succeed it I can give you any information or suggestion which I think would be of value, I shall not hesitate to do so. Generally, I would say that your views with regard to the important issues before the people are in exact accordance with my own. Corporations ought not to be hectored or destroyed. They, however, should be regulated and controlled and made to serve and not oppress the people. It has been a number of years since I have had the heart to do much political work. Now, however, I shall take off my coat and go in with great heartiness.

I am,   Sincerely yours,   R. V. Lindabury

TLS (WP, DLC).

From Dan Fellows Platt

Dear Mr. President: N. Y. City Sept 19th 1910.

I owe it to you to pass on to you the congratulations that were handed to me by anti-Wilson delegates as soon as you had concluded your speech to the convention. The effect you produced on the delegates is the same effect you are going to produce on the voters of the State of New Jersey. I know that they aren't going to be able to get away from you!

In talking with Nugent as to your campaign plans, he said you would surely come to Bergen County & to Englewood. In that case I'll probably have charge of arrangements. I don't believe that the candidate should have put upon him such a strain as three years ago when we autoed Frank K[atzenbach]. from one end of the county to the other—with a big meeting at the finish. We can do as effective work by limiting ourselves to three places—but one of these will be Englewood. As you know, we have a good Princeton contingent there. We can cram the "Lyceum" full of Republicans when you speak—something that hasn't happened in a good many years—for a Democratic speaker. "I speak first" now on the proposition of taking care of you, at dinner & for the night. I want the Bergen County leaders to know you and I think the best way would be by all coming to dinner. Nugent's idea was to have you speak say at 5 o'clock at Rutherford—which will just catch the commuters—& to have meetings at Englewood & Hackensack—which are only ten minutes apart—in the evening. That would give us plenty of time for dinner. It will not be possible for you to get back to Princeton that night—& if not Princeton—why not Platt's?

I had a talk in Trenton with Martin Devlin[1]—the Labor man. I was much interested in what he had to say and hope that you'll get into touch with him before long. I don't see how you & he are going to disagree on *fundamentals*. I don't like his opposition to you as I regard it as *unnecessary*. Ex-Senator James Smith Jr. tried to tell me on Thursday that, in our efforts to put definitely in the platform the plank for direct election of U.S. Senator & for direct primaries in re Governor & Congressmen, we were fighting *you*. I told him I had it from your own lips that you were for these reforms. I regard the plank as to constitutional amendment for U. S. Senatorial Election as a very weak one—just the sort of a subterfuge that is indulged in by people who are at heart opposed to the direct election. So many states now get on without the constitutional amendment that they will be backward in helping us get it. There should be added to the plank a statement calling for the strengthening of our present law along Oregon lines.[2] I was particularly glad of your statement that "States learn too slowly from their sister states." Afterwards, Jo Tumulty (than whom no better man has for years been in the Assembly) threw his arms about me & said "Dan—this is one of the happiest days of my life—the Wisconsin R. R. law!—the best in the country

—if Wilson stands for legislation of that calibre, Jim Smith will find that he has a 'lemon.' " Excuse the quotation—but I want you to know how you impress a progressive who had been offish owing to Smith's espousal of your cause.

You are a busy man—but some day in the future you & I are going to have it out on the question of initiative & referendum. I am for representative government. I don't believe in a pure democracy; but the man who puts a fire escape on his house doesn't believe in fire! So long as corruption pays lobbyists—you'll have an incentive for corrupt men to go to the legislature. If you've got a surer method of sending honest men to the legislature—than the removal of paying corruption, I'm for it. But have you?

I'm writing Nugent to try & fix on the 21 of October for Bergen Co. That is Friday.

Our friend Winton[3] isn't any too well thought of in Bergen County—by Democrats, at any rate. I wouldn't say this did I not think it might be well for you to know it. It is no secret in the County.   Yours sincerely   Dan Fellows Platt.

ALS (WP, DLC).
[1] Martin Patrick Devlin, Trenton lawyer, liberal Democrat and labor leader, and political ally of James Kerney, editor of the *Trenton Evening Times*.
[2] The Oregon law put strong political pressure on candidates for the legislature to pledge themselves, if elected, to vote for the nominee of the senatorial primary.
[3] Henry D. Winton, Democratic state senator from Bergen County, 1890-1895, and former editor and proprietor of the Hackensack, N. J., *Bergen County Democrat*. At this time he was a tax commissioner in Hackensack.

From Melancthon Williams Jacobus

Cromwell, Connecticut.
My dear President Wilson: September, nineteenth [1910]

My telegram to you last week was a sincere expression of my gratification in the hearty endorsement given you by your Party and especially of my delight in the practical statesmanship of your admirable address. At no time have the people of the country so needed common-sense in the great questions which have forced themselves upon them for settlement

If no settlement can be given these questions without the overturning of our Constitutional Government, then American Democracy is a failure and we might just as well confess it and try some other form

You can do the country immeasurable service in pointing out to them the safe road of progressive politics that will conserve what our country stands for before the world. May every success attend you in the effort

Now to the matters of immediate concern before our Board of Trustees. The papers say you will present your resignation at the October meeting. Have you any idea that the Opposition will move for a forcing of its acceptance at that time? It seems to me that no action would be dignified which does not contain a provisional acceptance conditioned upon & to issue in case of your Election as Governor of the State.

Also, have you any knowledge of the candidate, or candidates whom the Opposition is intending to present to the Board to fill your vacancy? I wrote Mr Sheldon soon after my conference with you at Lyme, suggesting the need of a getting together of the Administration members of the Board to consider whom it would be best to propose & support for the office; but he seemed to think there was plenty of time & I have not heard from him since

It seems to me most unwise, through lack of early action on our part, to give the Opposition chance to impress the minds of "uncertain" members of the Board with a candidate of their own choice & possibly secure the promise of favorable action from them before we have had a chance to be heard

I am here for a few days rest before the opening of the Seminary, and would be glad to hear from you—providing there is anything to say

With all good wishes for your future

Cordially yours   Melancthon W Jacobus

ALS (WP, DLC).

To Abbott Lawrence Lowell

My dear Lowell: Princeton, N. J. September 20th, 1910.

Yes, I have gone and done it and am already experiencing many pangs of doubt as to whether I have done the right thing or not but apparently there was nothing else for it in the circumstances and I shall start out upon the new career as bravely as possible.

I shall see less of you and feel less close to you in the work of each day but I shall hope to have many opportunities to strengthen myself by consulting with you on public affairs and I shall not lose my grip on university affairs, if I can help it.

With warmest regards,

Faithfully yours,   Woodrow Wilson

TLS (A. L. Lowell Papers, MH-Ar).

To Charles Scribner

My dear Mr. Scribner: Princeton, N. J. September 20th, 1910.

Allow me to thank you very heartily for your kind letter of September 16th and the very gracious congratulations which it conveys. I feel very highly complimented that you should feel as you do about my nomination and candidacy.

Cordially and sincerely yours,   Woodrow Wilson

TLS (Charles Scribner's Sons Archives, NjP).

From David Benton Jones

My dear Doctor   Chicago [c. Sept. 20, 1910]

I want you to use the enclosed in any way you can to minimize the wear & tear incident to the work ahead of you. Many burdens will fall upon you and it is not right that these should be borne by you in addition to the work which must be done.

At this distance it is the only thing I can do & I find it a joy to be able to do any thing. The work of redemption is the duty of all. May I ask that you say nothing about it to any one.[1]

Very sincerely   David B. Jones.

ALS (WP, DLC).
[1] Wilson's reply is printed at Sept. 25, 1910.

From Harry Pratt Judson[1]

My dear President Wilson: [Chicago] September 20, 1910

I am very much gratified to learn of your nomination to the Governorship of the State of New Jersey. While of course I regret anything that will take you from the educational work in which you have been of so great service, at the same time I cannot help feeling that our public life is still more in need of you. It has been one of the great misfortunes of the country for a dozen or more years past that the opposition party has not been a coherent body with a definite list of sane policies and led by men in whom thoughtful persons could feel it safe to repose the trust of the government. I am highly gratified, therefore, to see the Democratic party adjusting itself to larger things in the nomination of such men as Judge Baldwin in Connecticut and yourself in New Jersey. In the wise administration of such good men as Governor Harmon in Ohio and Mayor Gaynor in New York is the promise of better things for the republic. I can say this with the more assurance as I am a lifelong Republican. Party names, however, count for little in the question of good government.

Wishing you all success, I am,

Very truly yours,   Harry Pratt Judson

TLS (WP, DLC).
[1] President of the University of Chicago.

From William Hughes

My dear Dr. Wilson: Paterson, N. J., September 20, 1910.

Permit me to extend to you my most sincere congratulations upon your nomination. The press of delegates about you was so great at Trenton that I despaired of getting an opportunity to congratulate you in person. I was compelled to leave home early the morning after and have only just returned, therefore I trust you will pardon this tardy expression of my feelings. Then again I did not desire to write you a short hasty note, but to tell you of the deep impression you made upon me by the extremely happy speech in which you accepted and thanked the convention for your nomination. I have heard a great many efforts of this kind and have been guilty of a few myself, but I can sincerely say that I have never listened to a more effective utterance by a candidate in all my experience. There were many men in that convention who were opposed to your nomination before you commenced to speak, but there were few, if any, who would have changed candidates by the time you had finished. It is a long time since our party has had the good fortune to be represented in a campaign by such a man as yourself. I sincerely hope that you will be elected, and I am becoming more and more confident every day that you will be.

If there is anything I can do to be of service to you please do not hesitate to call upon me.

Very truly yours,   Wm. Hughes

TLS (WP, DLC).

From Job Herbert Lippincott[1]

Dear Sir: Jersey City [N. J.], Sept. 20, 1910.

Allow me to extend to you my sincere congratulations on your nomination for Governor of New Jersey. While I was opposed to your nomination in the convention through a combination of local conditions which made it necessary for us to support another candidate, I am none the less gratified that New Jersey has done itself the honor to name you as a candidate for Governor. I also wish to assure you of my most hearty support.

On Saturday, September 24th, the Democratic State Auxiliary Committee will hold a meeting at State Headquarters, No. 772 Broad St., Newark. The meeting will be called to order at three o'clock. We would be very much pleased if you could be present. I assure you that there will be a representative gathering of Democrats at this meeting.

There are a number of things in the work of the Committee in which your advice at this time would be of the greatest value.

Trusting that I may have an opportunity to discuss these matters with you in the near future, I am,

Very truly yours,   Job H Lippincott

TLS (WP, DLC).
   [1] A bank teller at the Commercial Trust Co. of New Jersey; president of the Board of Excise of Jersey City; president of the Board of Police Commissioners of Jersey City; and chairman of the Democratic State Auxiliary Committee.

From Charles Alexander Richmond

Schenectady, New York
My dear Dr. Wilson: Sept. 20th 1910.

I hear of your nomination with mixed feelings: First one moment I feel that your place is in Princeton: At another moment that you ought not to refuse this high call; but all moments I am confident of your high purpose and of your great capacity for usefulness. I believe you will be elected. I lunched with Governor Hughes day before yesterday, and he expressed what we all feel, that it was very encouraging to see men of your type entering the field of political life. I need not tell you that you have my cordial, may I say, my affectionate good wishes. My hope is that the Trustees may still be able to hold you in the service of Princeton if by any chance you should fail of election. Talk about a successor does not give me comfort.

I have a letter this morning from my old father[1] who lives in East Orange, New Jersey; He is Eighty Eight years of age and is a Republican bigot: He says for the first time in his life he proposes to vote for a Democratic Governor.

Remember me most kindly to Mrs. Wilson and believe me,

As ever your friend,   Charles Alexander Richmond

TLS (WP, DLC).
   [1] Archibald Murray Richmond.

A News Report of a Speech in Jersey City

[Sept. 21, 1910]

WOODROW WILSON RAPS ROOSEVELT'S COURT CRITICISM

Dr. Woodrow Wilson, President of Princeton University, and Democratic candidate for Governor of New Jersey, took notice of Col. Roosevelt's new nationalism and his views on the Supreme Court of the United States[1] in a speech in Jersey City last night. Dr. Wilson did not mention Col. Roosevelt's name, but those who heard his speech understood his references and applauded him heartily.

"You cannot accomplish anything with a mob, save destruction," said Dr. Wilson. "When I think of the processes of politics I believe that the object of politics is law. If you think of what the people are clamoring for it is law—better law, new law or laws to correct abuses which the people believe to exist. We are always seeking order and we know that the instrumentality of order is law.

"When, therefore, public men flout at the law they decline the needs of progress. Our courts may be imperfect, and some of them undoubtedly are; some of our judges may be imperfect, but they are the instrumentalities of law and the moment you flout at the instrumentalities of law you flout at the instrumentalities of order and therefore at the instrumentalities of progress.

"Progress is not proportioned to the capacity for revolution, but it is proportioned to the capacity for law. Are we growing impatient at the progress of law? Are some of our leaders growing impatient at the slow progress of law? The characteristic of all great governing peoples has been poise, patience and ability to make for progress by these virtues."

Dr. Wilson's speech was to the members of the Die Wilde Gans Club, which celebrated the opening of the new Hudson County Courthouse in Jersey City yesterday. He was introduced to the diners by former Supreme Court Justice Gilbert Collins,[2] who described him as "a many sided man, a publicist and an educator who is to tread the unknown path of practical politics."

In his address the President of Princeton deplored the tendency of judges to follow precedents blindly.

"It is the tendency of courts to exaggerate precedent," he said. "It is a labor-saving device for one thing; it saves trouble to assume that a problem has been wisely worked out and that it is needless to work it out again.

"When I was a younger man I lectured in the New York Law School on constitutional law.[3] My classes displayed considerable impatience with me when I would ask them if a decision of the

Supreme Court was valid in reason and law. They did not like the question. What they asked was: 'What does the Supreme Court say? For what the Court says is law.' They regarded me as an opinionated young man who dared to question a decision of the Supreme Court.

"But law has an infinite capacity for adjustment, providing those who administer the law have a capacity for adjustment, and it is the constant application of the law and its own adjustment that creates the true precedent and the one which ultimately becomes law."

Printed in the New York *World*, Sept. 21, 1910; one editorial heading omitted.

¹ Theodore Roosevelt set out in late August 1910 on a tour of sixteen western states. In a series of speeches, most notably one in Osawatomie, Kansas, on August 31, he called for a vast increase in the power of the federal government—a "new nationalism"—through a graduated income and inheritance tax, regulation of the labor of women and children, thoroughgoing revision of the tariff, and strict regulation of all corporations engaged in interstate business. Before the legislature of Colorado on August 29, he attacked the United States Supreme Court as a barrier to social progress and for creating a twilight zone in which no state or federal regulation was possible. See George E. Mowry, *Theodore Roosevelt and the Progressive Movement* (Madison, Wisc., 1946), pp. 142-44, and William H. Harbaugh, *Power and Responsibility: The Life and Times of Theodore Roosevelt* (New York, 1961), pp. 390-392.

² Prominent Hudson County Republican; Mayor of Jersey City, 1884-86; justice of the New Jersey Supreme Court, 1897-1903; and at this time partner in the Jersey City law firm of Collins and Corbin.

³ About these lectures, see the Editorial Note, "Wilson's Lectures at the New York Law School," Vol. 7.

To George Brinton McClellan Harvey

My dear Colonel Harvey,   Princeton, N. J. 21 September, 1910.

I have been answering letters at the rate of about one hundred and fifty a day since last Thursday, but the flood has slackened a little bit to-day, and I take advantage of the lull to write at least *one* letter I want to write.

I have always had an odd shyness, of which I am not a little ashamed, in expressing my feelings when they are really deep, and so now I do not know just how to express to you my sense of obligation for the unselfish work you have been doing in my behalf. I have admired very deeply your disinterested part and your true friendship in the whole matter, and I want to say how thoroughly I have admired it all. I do not deserve to be so ideally served in the matter of my public career; but, if I cannot justify it, I can at least be sincerely grateful for it, and give in return my deep admiration.

With warmest regard,

Faithfully and Sincerely Yours,   Woodrow Wilson

WWTLS (WP, DLC).

To Dan Fellows Platt

My dear Mr. Platt: Princeton, N. J. September 21st, 1910.

Thank you sincerely for your kind letter of the 19th. I shall be only too glad to put myself in your hands with regard to the arrangements for my speaking in Bergen and what you suggest commends itself to me entirely.

There is only one matter about which I find I am getting myself into difficulties. Let me say to you confidentially that I am being invited to dine with certain persons whom I think it would be a mistake to dine with. It occurs to me, therefore, that the only safe thing for me to do is to decline to be privately entertained by anybody on my travels. I know that you will understand this and will appreciate the political reason for it and that you will not deem me ungrateful for your own personal kindness in inviting me to stay with you.

I shall be very glad to "have it out with you" some time about the initiative and referendum!

Always cordially and faithfully yours,

Woodrow Wilson

TLS (photostat in RSB Coll., DLC).

To Samuel Huston Thompson, Jr.

My dear Mr. Thompson: Princeton, N. J. September 21st, 1910.

Your kind letter of the 17th has given me a great deal of pleasure. You may be sure that I would not have turned away from Princeton for anything which did not seem a superior duty. If I could tell you the circumstances of my nomination, I think you would see that it was a call of duty which I could not escape.

I hope with all my heart and believe that there is force enough in the Board of Trustees to prevent any serious reaction of policy, but I must admit that I have latterly spent a very unhappy life under the attacks which have been made upon me by some Princeton men.

How I wish I could see your new home and sit with you in its orange and black room. It will give me the greatest pleasure to send you a photograph so soon as I can get a decent one.

With warmest regard,

Cordially and faithfully yours,   Woodrow Wilson

TLS (S. H. Thompson, Jr., Papers, DLC).

To William Royal Wilder

My dear Wilder: Princeton, N. J. September 21st, 1910.

It pleases me very deeply that you should feel as you do about my entering politics and I want to stop, even in the midst of my present rush of engagements, to thank you with all my heart for your kind letter of the 17th.

Cordially yours,   Woodrow Wilson

TLS (W. R. Wilder Coll., NjP).

From Caroline Bayard Stevens Alexander[1]

My dear President Wilson,   Hoboken, N. J., Sept. 21st 1910

I want to add a line of congratulation to the many names you have doubtless already received on the occasion of your nomination. The congratulations however should really go to the Democratic party, to the State of New Jersey and to the cause of higher ideals in politics all over the country.

I have been for many years deeply interested in the politics of New Jersey and have felt many times as if there was no hope of improvement in either party but now I feel with many thousands that a better day is at hand. I hope you will allow me to do anything in my power to assist in carrying out one of your policies, that of efficient economy in the running of State Institution[s]. I think I may say that my connection as a Manager of two State Institutions[2] for many years and my relations with the last three Governors with reference to these matters have made it possible for me to collect information which might be of service to you and which it might be rather difficult for you to obtain from the officials connected with the Institutions.

I hope you will let me go to Princeton and talk these matters over with you when the election is over. If there is anything in the world that I can do it will be a pleasure to me.

Yours sincerely,   Caroline B. Alexander.

TLS (WP, DLC).

[1] Assistant probation officer of Hudson County, former wife of Archibald Alexander, and daughter of Edwin Augustus Stevens and Martha Bayard Dod Stevens.

[2] At this time she was a member of the Board of Managers of the Village for Epileptics in Skillman Station, Somerset County. Until 1909, she was a member of the Board of Managers of the Home for Feeble-Minded Women in Vineland. In 1910 she was also serving as president of the New Jersey State Board of Children's Guardians and a trustee of the State Board of Industrial Education for Hoboken.

A News Report About Remarks Opening
Princeton University

[*Sept. 22, 1910*]

PRINCETON'S 164TH YEAR

President Woodrow Wilson Delivers
Address at Opening Exercises.

Princeton, New Jersey, Sept. 22—The opening exercises of Princeton[']s one hundred and sixty-fourth year were held this afternoon at 3 in Marquand Chapel.

President Woodrow Wilson, Democratic candidate for Governor, gave the address of the afternoon, and he said among other things:

"The spirit of scholarship grows from year to year; there is a growth in the spirit of learning, the desire for it and the comprehension of what it means. It is the spirit of enlightenment, which has no object for itself but to remove the scales from the eyes of the student so that he can see the world as it is. It dispels the whimsical terrors and doubts that surround the man who does not know.

"With the growth of the spirit of learning here in Princeton we have established a spirit of comradeship between the teach[e]r and the pupil. There is no longer any artificial line between the two. We have tried to keep our hold on boyhood spirit, to see the point of view of youngsters, and to preserve a spirit of comradeship between the teacher and those being taught.

"I wish we knew some means by which to give you entering men some intuition of the spirit of this place and communicate the contagion of it. There is play and fun and comradeship here, but the basis of it all are the serious contentions of men. No one enters here who cannot put off the spirit of childhood and work here the works of serious men.

"We here are only the temporary embroidiments of a very ancient institution. For, although 160 years is not very long for a nation that has existed for centuries, it is a long time for one that is just attaining its maturity. The years that Princeton has existed are the most prophetic in the history of the world, and in the growth of nations.

"Here in this place has dwelt from the first the new life of the nation. Princeton has always stood for the spirit of manhood, for patriotism, for sound learning and true religion and highest of all, the fear of God."

President Wilson spoke in the highest terms of the late Professor Winans who served the university most efficiently for a period of 30 years.[1] President Wilson and Moses Taylor Pyne, a trustee, led the academic procession. Other trustees present were: Cyrus McCormick, of Chicago; Bayard Henry, of Philadelphia; Wilson Farrand, of Newark, and Henry W. Green, of Tren[t]on.

Printed in the Trenton *True American*, Sept. 23, 1910; some editorial headings omitted.
[1] There is a WWhw outline of these remarks, dated Sept. 22, 1910, in WP, DLC.

To John Wesley Wescott

Princeton, N. J.
My dear Judge Wescott: September 22nd, 1910.
Allow me to acknowledge the receipt of your letter of September 21st[1] and to thank you for it.
Did you intend to suggest meeting me in *Trenton* on Saturday evening next? Perhaps it was a slip of the pen for Princeton. Unhappily, it will be impossible for me to be in Trenton on Saturday evening because there is a college function scheduled for that evening which I must attend, but I shall be free during the late afternoon and it would give me great pleasure if I could see you here at that time.   Sincerely yours,   Woodrow Wilson

TLS (J. W. Wescott Coll., NjP).
[1] It is missing.

To Isaac Wayne MacVeagh

Princeton, N. J.
My dear Mr. Mac Veagh: September 22nd, 1910.
I have read your letter of September 19th[1] with the warmest gratification and interest. I think that we are certainly upon common ground in our feelings about public affairs. I enter the chaos with many misgivings, but with the hope that it may be possible to accomplish a little.
I wish that I could look forward to seeing you at the meeting of the Mutual Board[2] next week, but that is the day appointed for the opening of my campaign and I fear that it will be out of the question for me to attend. Do you not think, by the way, that in the circumstances it would be best for me to resign my seat upon that Board? I should greatly value your candid opinion upon that question.

Cordially and sincerely yours,   Woodrow Wilson

TLS (I. W. MacVeagh Papers, PHi).
[1] I. W. MacVeagh to WW, Sept. 19, 1910, ALS (WP, DLC).
[2] That is, the Board of Trustees of the Mutual Life Insurance Co. of New York.

To James Slocum Rogers[1]

My dear Mr. Rogers: Princeton, N. J. September 22nd, 1910.

I have read your letter of September 19th[2] with a great deal of interest and appreciation.

I do not think that we are, after all, seriously at odds in our opinion regarding the control of corporations. It is a field of action in which it seems to me the States which create corporations may very properly act, without at all excluding Congress from such legislation as is possible and proper under the Inter-State Commerce Clause of the Constitution. I do not agree with you in thinking that state control need be ineffectual, but I realize the very great danger and difficulty of regulation of that kind because of the diversity it may produce with regard to undertakings which cover the whole country. The division of the field between the state and federal governments should be very carefully studied and I believe it can be eventually satisfactorily determined.

I need not tell you how warmly I appreciate what you say about the affairs of the University, and I need not tell you either that I turn away from them with many pangs of sincere regret.

With warmest appreciation,

Sincerely yours,   Woodrow Wilson

TLS (PP).
[1] Princeton 1893, a lawyer of Philadelphia.
[2] J. S. Rogers to WW, Sept. 19, 1910, ALS (WP, DLC).

From Robert Gunn Bremner

Dear President Wilson: Passaic, N. J., Sept. 22, 1910

I thank you for the invitation to drop you suggestions as they may arise.

(1). In regard to the wrong impressions which have been so diligently circulating about your attitude towards labor, I think it would be well if you could make some arrangement whereby Martin Devlin, a Trenton lawyer, would make speeches and write letters for you. No man in the State has more influence with so many labor organizations. If you do not care to treat with him personally, I would suggest that John Dullard[1] be authorized to make some arrangement with him.

(2). Would it be possible for you to attend the Congressional Convention of the Sixth District which will be held in Paterson on Tuesday the 27th? No doubt Congressman Hughes has written to you allready. If not, I will have him do so, probably tonight.

As Hughes is very strong with the laboring men, there will be a great many of them at the convention to "whoop it up for Billy." He will be renominated without opposition.

(3). What have you done towards organizing an efficient Press Bureau? I think it is infinitely important that you send out advanced copies of set speeches that you purpose to make. (I might add that we had Roosevelt's speeches delivered in Paris, Berlin and Oxford, before he left Cairo for home. We had all his western speeches before he started on the trip at all. I quote this, not to hold Roosevelt up as an example, but merely as a proof of how he values newspaper space, and of the ways he is able to get it.) There are some excellent and energetic newspaper men, well acquainted with the State and the papers in it, who would be only too glad to take charge of such a bureau. Having the matter come from New York is not wise.

(4). Can I not announce that you will come to Passaic? It is not necessary, as yet, to fix the date, but everyone has such pleasant memories of your board of trade speech, that I think it would do a world of good for you to come back again. This is a strong republican city, and we hope to hold Lewis's majority down to a minimum.   Very truly yours,   Robt G Bremner

P.S. We have a new high school auditorium here that seats 1400. It would be a splendid stroke if you could accept Branson's invitation to speak there.[2] I told the teachers committee who came to see me about it that I would most heartily recommend it to you. It would be better than any political meeting

TLS (WP, DLC).

[1] John Power Dullard, veteran Trenton newspaperman, at this time Trenton correspondent of the Associated Press and Trenton City Assessor.

[2] Roswell H. Branson, listed in the Passaic city directories of this period as a teacher. His letter of invitation is missing.

From Williamson Updike Vreeland

Dear Dr. Wilson: [Princeton, N.J.] Thursday Sept. 22, 1910.

I have talked the political situation over so frequently with you during our golfing days that I don't suppose a formal letter of congratulation is necessary. You know how all your friends feel and how sorry we are at the thought of losing you at Princeton. I don't think I ever did tell you how much of a mistake I at first thought you were making in consenting to be dragged into politics. No president has ever done so much for Princeton as you have, and it did seem to me that your services to the state could not offset the great loss to Princeton. But I have brought myself to look upon the state as bigger than Princeton, and we, your friends in the faculty shall have to try to reconcile ourselves to the thought of Princeton's loss by bearing in mind the principle of "the greatest good to the greatest number.["] We can assure you of our entire loyalty through everything, and wish you the success which we know will be yours.

Faithfully yours   W. U. Vreeland

ALS (WP, DLC).

From Henry Otto Wittpenn

Jersey City, N. J.

My dear Doctor Wilson: September 22nd, 1910.

Please accept this expression of my sincere congratulation upon your nomination, as well as my best wishes for your success at the coming election.

Be assured that I shall do all that lies within my power toward insuring a splendid victory.

Most respectfully,   H. O. Wittpenn

TLS (WP, DLC).

From William Church Osborn[1]

My dear Doctor Wilson: New York, September 22nd, 1910.

As a consistent Democrat, I am greatly delighted with your nomination for the Governorship. I feel confident of your election, and that you[r] administration will revive the true spirit of popular government.

In common with all other Princetonians, I realize the immense gap that your going will leave in the management of the University, and I look with apprehension to the choice of your successor.

I read with much interest the platform declaration on the subject of "Corrupt Practices at Elections," as I have for the last five years or so been the Treasurer,[2] and I may say confidentially, an extremely active spirit in forwarding that reform in this State. When we took the subject up, we consulted with Mr. Borden,[3] a prominent member of Parliament for Canada, and he told us that the real success or failure of a Corrupt Practices Act lay in its enforcement. An experience of considerable activity for the last five years satisfies me that his observation is fundamentally correct.

I am sending you by separate envelope two or three copies of our Year Book for this year, and I add herewith a few brief hints on such legislation. If I can be of any service to you in this, or in any other way, in connection with your campaign, I trust that you will call upon me. I think that in a short conversation, I could give you the results of a good deal of experience in Corrupt Practices Work.

Believe me with confident best wishes for your success,
Very sincerely yours,   Wm. Church Osborn

TLS (WP, DLC).
    [1] Princeton 1883, a New York lawyer active in many reform and philanthropic organizations.
    [2] Of the Association to Prevent Corrupt Practices at Elections.
    [3] Robert Laird Borden, a member of the Canadian Parliament since 1896 and leader of the Conservative party in the House of Commons since 1901. Prime Minister of Canada, 1911-20.

From Joseph Dorsey[1]

Honored Sir,   Baltimore, Md., Sept 22 1910

I congratulate you on your nomination and shall be glad to aid in your election.

I can render valuable aid in your elevation among my people, in The Columns of The Crusader.

With best of wishes,

I am Obediently   Joseph Dorsey

ALS (WP, DLC).
    [1] Editor of the Baltimore *Crusader*, a black newspaper.

From William Cavanagh Gebhardt

Dear Doctor Wilson: Jersey City [N. J.], September 22, 1910.

I am in receipt of your nice letter in reply to mine, and in answer will say that I am very gratified to learn from the newspapers that you will begin speaking as early as the 28th instant. I got a previous impression to the effect that you were not going to begin until well along in October and I was about to write you to begin as quickly as possible. The sentiment of the State is surely going strongly our way at this time, but your presence throughout the State will help very much indeed. I am just now exceedingly busy and will be until the latter part of next week. If, however, a day, or a part of a day, comes when I can get away, I shall call you on the 'phone and try to arrange to go down and see you. I have been in practical politics since 1896 and am more thoroughly convinced than ever that the Direct Primary should be extended to Congress and to Governor.

Wishing you the utmost success in the pending struggle, I am,
Very sincerely yours,   Wm. C. Gebhart

TLS (WP, DLC).

From Lawrence Crane Woods

My dear Dr. Wilson: Pittsburg, Penna. September 22, 1910.

I would like to have even a small part in the campaign not so much for your election as governor of New Jersey, because I cannot but feel that this is nothing that you would personally seek or your friends seek *for you*, but in the cause of good government, sanity and honest politics throughout our nation. You will do me a great favor, therefore, if you will permit me to make this small contribution towards the great expense that you will be under in this campaign. I fully appreciate that as far as you can control it the campaign expenses will be reduced to those of the most legitimate character, but even they are great. If you could use this for the numerous little personal expenses to which you will be subject and which you might not feel could be properly included in your drafts upon the campaign funds proper, it would give me still greater pleasure. Limitations of purse, not of heart or mind, prevent its being a hundred times more.

I spent last Thursday and Friday in New York and talked with ten or a dozen friends of mine who live in New Jersey. All of them were formerly Republicans in the old meaning of that word. Everyone of them is going to vote for you in spite of the fact that you are a candidate of the so-called Democratic party, whatever that means nowadays. You will see from this that I have drifted far away from party lines myself, as I think most people in this country have. It is difficult to tell a Democrat from a Republican now. It seems to me as tho the country were divided into "progressives" and "insurgents" on the one hand and "stand-patters" and "reactionaries" on the other. I know of no one who embodies a spirit of progressive conservatism better than you do. I only hope that you may be strengthened physically and in every other way to stand the strain of the campaign and your incumbency of office, as I believe there could be today but little doubt that you will be overwhelmingly elected.

Pray do not bother to answer this letter or any others I may write to you from time to time. Save all your strength and every moment of your time for those who do not know you as I do.

Very sincerely yours,   Lawrence C Woods

TLS (WP, DLC).

From Clarence Hughson Baxter[1]

My Dear Mr. Wilson: Paterson, N. J., Sept. 22 191[0]

Permit me to personally congratulate you upon your nomination. Your election as Governor, which seems assured to those who study the signs of the times, will mean the dawn of a new day for Democracy in New Jersey, during which you can do much to restore belief in its principles, regain the prestige which has been lost, and make it once more a party truly representative of popular government.

In anticipation of your coming visit to Paterson, I want to ask if the state committee intends to send out advance copies of the speeches which you will deliver in the different cities?

The Guardian desires to make a special feature of your visit to this city, the home of your opponent, Mr. Lewis. I presume that you will perhaps consider this visit one of the most important of your campaign; worthy, perhaps, of extra effort in the form of a special speech.

If this proves to be your intention, can I secure an advance copy of your Paterson speech? If you intend to talk without special preparation, I will arrange for a stenographic report.

Yours Sincerely,   Clarence H. Baxter.

TLS (WP, DLC).
[1] Managing editor of the *Paterson Guardian*.

From Henry Eckert Alexander

[Trenton, N. J.]

Dear Mr. Wilson: Friday night [Sept. 23, 1910]

I am just in from Philadelphia at midnight and scribble this note before going home.

I saw Mr. Van Valkenburg of the North American. He had seen something purporting to come from you and feared that you were not "right." Now, all I could say was for him to wait for your speeches. He is the ablest newspaper man in Philadelphia and one of the ablest in the country. He is afraid (1) that you will not show your interests and sympathies are with the *people* (that you may place property rights above human rights) (2) that in defining your views on state rights you may afford a roosting place for the despoilers. I think not. I think that you can and should amplify that declaration we printed under your picture Sept. 16. "Good laws are desirable but good men are essential. And good men may make even bad laws yield pure and righteous government."

This is quoted from memory but I think that it is of the utmost importance to make it plain that you are a man with sympathies and that they are in the right direction.

I hear complaints from many quarters that the state committee in arranging the campaign is hedging you around with "dignity" so that only so many "*big*" meetings shall be held.

I am sure that you will find, as your speeches are printed and the meetings are described in the newspapers, a tremendous demand from the country people in the little towns and hamlets to *see you* and hear *a few words* from you. It seems to be that it can be arranged to do this without wearing you out.

My associate editor, Mr. Dye would like to make an early appointment with you just to form his own impressions.

Sincerely yours,   H. E. Alexander

ALS (WP, DLC).

From Edgar Odell Lovett

Dear Mr Wilson   Houston, Texas. 23 September 1910

I have been slow in joining the P-rade, but then gosh-ding-dang-dong it! I told you not to do it. However here are my congratulations and they are most hearty. You will of course win, and in a walk, but it has occurred to me that inasmuch as I have not yet voted in this state I could be useful in New Jersey on the day of the election, if not alone and single handed perhaps with a hundred Texas Rangers, experienced in assisting at the polls, and every man of them on a mount capable of breaking the record of your spin from Princetown to Trent-en. If these ideas seem impracticable, a hint for the campaign fund might prove less so: I have it on good authority that all the funds of the Astronomical Expedition to the Southern Hemisphere are available and at the disposal of your campaign committee. These suggestions completely exhaust my resources. If they fail to appeal to you, just save a stump where I can beat a drum and holler.

Faithfully yours   Edgar Odell Lovett

ALS (WP, DLC).

From Henry Smith Pritchett

PERSONAL.

My dear Wilson,   New York September 23, 1910.

I learned on landing yesterday that you had been nominated for the office of governor of New Jersey and that you had resigned from the presidency of Princeton and entered upon the campaign. Your action in all this matter has seemed to me most admirable. I never before felt that I would like to be a citizen of New Jersey but at the moment I feel that I should very much enjoy being a citizen this year and thus have the pleasure of voting for you in November, and I have not cast a Democratic vote since the last time that Mr. Cleveland ran for President. You have my best wishes and I believe that you are to achieve a splendid success. No one of your friends will anticipate this with more pleasure than myself.

I venture to make one suggestion which is probably a wholly unnecessary one. To a man of your training and thinking, many of the things which Theodore Roosevelt does offer an opportunity for a telling attack. It may be that some time or other you may need to give Theodore a mild tap, but the time is not now for two reasons; first of all, Roosevelt in spite of his mistakes is an enormous influence against political corruption and in favor of decent government; secondly, the men who are going to throw aside party ties and vote for you in November are, in a large measure, Roosevelt's friends also.

Please do not take the trouble to answer this because I know you are overwhelmed with work.

                    Faithfully yours,   Henry S. Pritchett
TLS (WP, DLC).

To Henry Smith Pritchett

My dear Pritchett: Princeton, N. J. September 24th, 1910.

I need not tell you how warmly I appreciate your letter of September 23rd. I particularly thank you for the warning and suggestion. Happily I was wise enough to see that point in advance, and I shall be very careful throughout my campaign not to attack individuals but to confine myself to principles and purposes.

It was thoughtful of you to write me.

With greatest appreciation,

Always cordially and sincerely yours,

                    Woodrow Wilson
TLS (H. S. Pritchett Papers, DLC).

From William Hunter Maxwell[1]

Honorable Sir: Newark, N. J., Sept. 24, 1910.

Since it is that you are a candidate for Governor of the state of New Jersey, and if elected will preside over the governmental affairs of the whole people of the state, will you please be so kind as to inform me as to your attitude toward the Negro people of our state?

I ask you this on behalf of a large number of intelligent and respectable Negroes.

I herewith enclose a sheet[2] containing the answers of the recent Progressive Republican Candidates, practically to the same question; this will give you an idea as to my meaning.

I endeavored to get an expression in the Republican platform, but to no avail. And I now feel that we have been slapped in the faces by our so-called friends and I am determined to stand it no longer. I am for men rather than parties, but I like to know my ground before I attempt to set foot upon it. An early reply will be greatly appreciated and may be of advantage to you.

Very Truly Your's,   Wm. H. Maxwell.

TLS (WP, DLC).
   [1] Jeweler and president of the Newark Negro Council and of the Negro Progressive Republican League.
   [2] *Shall We Work or Be Worked? Being an Appeal to the Colored Republican Voters of Essex County . . . Together with the Sentiments of the Progressive Republican Candidates for Nomination Regarding the Negro* (n.p., 1910).

From John Adams Wilson

My dear Woodrow: Franklin, Pa. Sept. 24th. 1910

While I congratulate the Democrats of your State in nominating you I am sorry you are getting into the political game. It is a dirty mess, to say the least. To most of the opposition you will be anything but what you really are and you will do nothing without some bad motive. I am fifty nine years of age to-day and have associated with politicians all my life. During the war it was politics all the time and for a Democrat to get what really belonged to him was out of the question. All my family were Democrats and all who were of sufficient age went to the front. My mother's family were also of the same political stripe and they also went to the front. The first political cpeech [speech] I ever heard was from our front steps in Erie, Pa., when Stephen Douglass, talked to a crowd that had come to give him a serenade. That was during the hot fight with Lincoln. During the war I met, as a boy, about all the big ones and was well acquainted with Lincoln, being a playmate of his son Tad.[1] Of the whole lot, on both sides, of those engaged in political fights I never saw a really happy looking man. More lives have been wrecked and more fortunes destroyed by this same game than by war or any other agency.

There is only one thing to do, be true to yourself and let the rest go hang. Keep your skirts clean: make no promises to any one and do not let any one make promises for you. Write no letters on any political matter and take nothing for granted when it relates to your opponent or to your own chances. I shall drop in and have a talk with you soon and think I may be able to do you some good in your fight. That you will win I have not the slightest doubt and that you will also be the candidate of your party for President in 1912 I also really think. Hope you will not worry nor work yourself to death.

With love from us all to all your family

Affectionately yours   Jno. A. Wilson.

TLS (WP, DLC).
[1] Thomas Lincoln, 1853-71. John A. Wilson's father, Edwin Clinton Wilson, had been adjutant general of the State of Pennsylvania and spent a good deal of time in Washington during the Civil War.

From William T. Ferguson

My dear Sir: Washington, D. C. Sept., 24/10

I intended to suggest to you that if the manager of your campaign deemed it unwise to let it be known that the Democratic organization was encouraging colored independents that *you* have some personal friend look after the matter. We have no promises to exact. We know you to be a high class American gentleman and trust to your honor. If you have a personal friend who will confer with us as to our plan have him arrange to see me as soon as possible.   Sincerely Yours,   W. T. Ferguson

ALS (WP, DLC).

To David Benton Jones

My dear Friend,   Princeton, N. J. 25 September, 1910.

I have been overwhelmed with letters that were very encouraging to receive but that did not matter. Yours does matter, and I have had to wait till Sunday to get the leisure of heart and mind to reply to it as I wished,—in a letter written by myself, with this mechanical pen of mine.

I know that you will forgive me for returning the cheque, because I know the spirit in which it was sent, and hope that I know the trust and affection it stands for. I do not remember anything that ever touched me more or made me happier. You have treated me as you would have treated your own brother. I feel as I never did before the value and the beauty of the friendship you have honoured me with.

But I want to say, if possible, that I paid every cent of my own personal expenses in this campaign out of my own pocket. I do not think that they will run above a few hundred dollars; and I have arranged to deliver three addresses after the election[1] which will net me five hundred dollars in fees. I made the engagements with the express purpose of earning the money for that object. Friends at every turn are putting their automobiles at my service; I shall have only hotel bills, the fares for short railway journeys, and the fees for extra stenographic services to pay. It will not come to much, all put together. If I get stuck, I will not hesitate to call on you for what I cannot do. You have made that possible by the way you have done this and by what I see between the lines of your generous letters.

I only hope that I shall prove worthy of such trust and friendship. It warms my heart securely against the chills and discouragements that are sure to come in this distracted field of politics. I am grateful with a deep gratitude that I hope will make me a better man.

I am booked for twenty-seven speeches in the next four and a half weeks; but if you are to be East I simply must have a talk with you about what is to be done here.

Please give my warmest regards to your brother.

Gratefully and affectionately Yours,   Woodrow Wilson

WWTLS (Mineral Point, Wisc., Public Library).
    [1] Two lectures in Milwaukee and one in Chicago. A news report of Wilson's speech to the City Club of Milwaukee is printed at Nov. 17, 1910, Vol. 22; his public lecture in the Pabst Theatre in Milwaukee is printed at Nov. 17, 1910, *ibid.*; and a news report of his address in Chicago, sponsored by the Business Service Lecture League, is printed at Nov. 19, 1910, *ibid.*

To Mary Allen Hulbert Peck

Dearest Friend,   Princeton, New Jersey 25 September, 1910.

This is really worse than I expected even: there has not been a half hour, or any other fraction of an hour, that I could call my own since the nomination. Even to-day (Sunday) I have been besieged. I have thought of you constantly through it all; but it has been literally impossible for me to write. I have been dictating some hundred and fifty letters a day (to two stenographers), but that is another matter! To write a letter myself was simply impossible! I hope I shall never go through such another ten days again: letters by the hundred, newspaper men, photographers, friends, advisers, committees, beggars,—I thought that I had been distracted before!

To-night I have been trying to get you on the 'phone, but they tell me at central that they can get no answer at 2712, Madison Square. Late as it is, I must send you, instead these hasty lines, to say that I am well, that I am very happy that you have rented the appartment on such good terms,[1] that I hope that the packing is over, and that you are resting and getting strong again, —resting your mind and feeling the burdens a little lightened. I am so sorry I could not have heard your voice and in turn told you these things!

On Wednesday I start out, to try to carry out the speaking engagements made for me by the State Committee as shown on the enclosed clipping. I hope that I shall survive! I mean to make it as much of an amusement as possible, and not let it become too strenuous, but it is a severe initiation.

Be gracious and let me here [hear] from you at short intervals. I shall be anxious otherwise. It will refresh me and help me to know how you are faring and feeling. I am all right.

Your devoted friend,   Woodrow Wilson

WWTLS (WP, DLC).
    [1] That is, her apartment at 39 East 27th Street, New York, which she had sublet. This letter was addressed to the Brayton, Madison Avenue and 27th Street, where she was staying before leaving for Bermuda.

To Edwin Augustus Van Valkenburg

Personal and Private.

[Dear Sir: Princeton, N. J. Sept. 25, 1910]

Mr. Alexander has spoken to me more than once of your kind interest in my candidacy for the governorship of the State, and also of pertinent questions you have from time to time raised as to my position upon essential issues now at stake in our politics, not only in New Jersey but throughout the country. I so sincerely respect the stand you take for the best things in our life and set so high a value upon the opinions of the North American that I am going to give myself the pleasure of stating to you directly my visions and hopes as I look forward to the responsibilities that may fall upon me.

It has distressed me that so much credence has been given to the statement that I was out of sympathy with the point of view of the plain people, that I put conventional property rights above human rights, as it were, and hold a sort of stiff and academic view of the things that go to the rights of life. Nothing could be further from the truth. Those who really know me would laugh at such a picture of me, and say that their difficulty with me had generally been just the opposite, that my sympathies were so broad as holding of views sometimes a bit radical. But that will take care of itself, when I have a chance to talk directly to the voters from the stump.

What I want to speak about more directly is my view of the function of the States and of the Federal government with regard to the regulation of corporations. I am not a preponderant state rights man: I desire the energetic cooperation of the several law-making powers of our system in the common undertaking of re-form. To insist on state rights beyond a certain point—to insist, that is, that their right in this matter excludes that of the Federal government—would be to create an impossible condition. The field of operation of modern corporations is as wide, in most cases, as the country itself. In no case, probably, is it as narrow as a single State. It would be just what some of the men who are most to be feared would like, to be free from the danger of such uniform and immediate regulation as the Federal government could effect and left to deal with the legislatures of the several States. That must be avoided. But this does not mean that the States have no duty in the matter (we will not speak of rights) or that their duty can be as well performed by some other authority. They create corporations. It is within their power and it is their duty to redirect and reform the processes by which they create them: to scrutinize their business, the character of their organization, and above all things else, the basis of their capitalization. These duties lie at the basis of all reform.

They are not the exclusive powers of the Federal government. That lies in the field of the general interest of the country as a whole. The interests of interstate commerce furnish abundant ground for their exercise and suggest with sufficient clearness the lines upon which they should be exercised.

I need not elaborate. You will read the particulars into this general statement. My object is attained when I express to you my great respect, my desire to be understood by the North American, and my essential motives and principles of action in these fundamental matters.

With much respect,   Woodrow Wilson.

Transcript of WWshLS (WP, DLC).

From George Brinton McClellan Harvey

Dear Mr. Wilson   Deal, New Jersey. Sunday [Sept. 25, 1910]

I want you to know that I deeply appreciate your most generous and really beautiful letter—though I have to confess that there has been little of the personal in my somewhat persistent purpose until comparatively recently. An old friend—Elihu Root—was wont to identify me for years with genial speech as an "ideal chaser." I never minded much—certainly never less than now.

There is not a cloud in the sky. The pebble chucked into the pond has produced, not ripples, but waves. Your majority will surpass all expectations. And, most happily, is it not gratifying that everyone who has participated with much trust and no little magnanimity is not only satisfied but proud?

I am off tomorrow to Saratoga and Rochester—but am in close touch with the situation here and have hatching various suggestions which we may talk over in about a week.

Meanwhile, so far as I can see, "all's well."

Faithfully Yours   George Harvey

ALS (WP, DLC).

From Edward Capps

My dear President Wilson,   Athens, Greece. Sept. 25, 1910

The Paris Herald of the 19th inst. has just reached Athens, with the announcement of your nomination by the Democratic Convention for the governorship of New Jersey. I congratulate you most heartily and wish you overwhelming success at the polls. Alas that I can't be there to contribute my vote!

But in spite of my satisfaction on your account, that you are given the opportunity of a wider field of service, I am naturally distressed and full of forebodings as regards the situation at Princeton. I have a feeling that you would not have decided to stand for the nomination if you had considered the prospects of a peaceful development of your policies encouraging after the events of Commencement Week. I know very little about what happened then, beyond the elections to the Board—which I assume were favorable to you—and the announcement of gifts, and nobody has given me a political diagnosis of the situation as it then stood. But in any event your resignation will oblige me this year, I think, to reconsider carefully my own position. I realize that I have become an object of hostility to a considerable element in the community and that this hostility will continue to make itself felt by me and my family. All this I shouldn't mind much in a good stubborn fight for a principle with you to lead it. But without you I am afraid that we shall find ourselves giving in a little here and a little there until we are at last virtually beaten through our sheer inability to fight all the time against the kind of odds that oppose us. And after that I would have no joy in my work nor happiness in my life at Princeton.

I do not mean to do anything rash, in fact nothing at all before my return. But at present both Mrs. Capps[1] and I are thinking that it will probably be foolish to wait much longer. Just now I am sure that I could have the professorship once offered me at Yale and also at Harvard, but the opportunity is not likely to be open much longer. I can wait to see what the next turn of the wheel at Princeton will be, and then I must make my final decision.

You will be so full of affairs when this reaches you that I cannot ask you for counsel in my own personal concerns. But it is a satisfaction to have laid them frankly before you, and to have told you, tho indirectly, how vital to me has been your leadership at Princeton and how keenly I shall miss you there. It is not my intention to take anybody else into my confidence until the time for a decision comes—and I still faintly hope that it may not come.[2]

Mrs. Capps joins me in cordial greetings to Mrs. Wilson and your daughters, and in the hope that they and you, after the first painful experiences, when you leave your beautiful home at Prospect, are over, will find yourselves happily established and surrounded by congenial friends elsew[h]ere.

Ever faithfully yours   Edward Capps

ALS (WP, DLC).
[1] Grace Alexander Capps.
[2] Capps remained as Professor of Greek at Princeton, retiring in 1935. He died in Princeton on August 21, 1950.

From Henry Eckert Alexander

Dear Mr. Wilson: Trenton, New Jersey Sept. 25, 1910.

I suggest that you write Chairman Marshall at Trenton and ask him to furnish you *briefly* the part the Democratic Committee or League has had in the fight against the use of money in elections. The request will be promptly and solemnly communicated to Dullard and La Barre and the information furnished.

If you denounce the use of money to corrupt voters you will "catch" the Trenton Democrats. If you say that the man who

buys a vote is worse than the man who sells a vote it will please
our people, but if you heap infamy on the head of the man who
stands back of the vote-buyer—the rich man who furnishes the
money with full knowledge of its use—the man "higher up" who
shields himself behind supposed respectability and yet who is the
beneficiary of the corrupt practices which he sets in motion,
it will count. It is notorious that from $25,000 to $50,000 has
been spent by the Republican machine in a single election in
Mercer County.   Yours truly,   H. E. Alexander.

ALS (WP, DLC).

From Charles Dexter Allen[1]

My dear sir,   Montclair, N. J. 25 Sept. 1910

I want to send my hearty word of gladness that you are taking
the nomination for Governor of this State. Though counted as
Republican, and mostly so voting, I shall vote for Woodrow Wilson this year, and have a hope of being able to do so for another
office in 1912. For twenty years the "New York Evening Post"
has been a delight to me. Last evening's articles[2] about you are
the kind one delights to read.

You will not remember me, but I have in my files a program of
"The Owl Club" of Hartford, where I used to live, which brings to
mind a talk you gave to us and our friends, when you were at Middletown, away back in 1888: it was on the 17th of May and you
spoke on "Comparative Politics" to an interested audience.[3] I was
secretary of the club, which has since languished—through
removals and the growth of different associations of Hartford
men.

I must know when you are to speak in this vicinity, for I want
to be present.

Hoping for the success of your canvass,

I am sincerely,   Chas. Dexter Allen

TLS (WP, DLC).

[1] Book collector of Montclair, N. J., specializing in book plates, and the author
of a literary column for the *Montclair Times*.

[2] These were three articles about Wilson in the New York *Evening Post*,
Sept. 24, 1910. The first, "Wilson's Views," included a long series of quota-
tions from his earlier statements and addresses; the second article, "Woodrow
Wilson Prophet," was a long biographical sketch; the third, "Dr. Wilson's
Campaign Tour," was a report on his projected campaign schedule as released
by the Democratic State Committee.

[3] Actually, Wilson spoke to the Owl Club on May 17, 1889. His address is
printed at May 10, 1889, Vol. 6, and a news report of the event is printed
at May 18, 1889, *ibid*.

From Clinton Roy Dickinson[1]

New York City

My dear Mr. Wilson: September twenty-fifth Nineteen ten

At this late hour when you are probably in the midst of your campaign preparations, and have received hosts of letters, I wish to add my humble but most sincere congratulations and best wishes for the outcome.

As former business manager of the "official college daily" and toastmaster at the '09 Princetonian banquet I had the very great pleasure of knowing you and hearing you speak. This year I cast my first vote in New Jersey, and in the face of a rockbound Republican family it is to be for Woodrow Wilson, and as a matter of fact I'll have all the male members of my family voting the same way when the time comes. Every Princeton graduate who knew you, regardless of party is an organization in himself, and the successful outcome of your campaign I feel confident is assured. Again congratulating you upon your success so far and expressing the earnest hope that this is merely the start of a wonderful political carreer, believe me to be

Very Sincerely Yours   C. Roy Dickinson 09

ALS (WP, DLC).
     [1] Princeton 1909, direct descendant of Jonathan Dickinson, first President of the College of New Jersey. At this time, Clinton Roy Dickinson lived with his family in Newark and was assistant advertising manager of *Cosmopolitan Magazine*.

A News Report of an Address to the Freshman Class

[Sept. 26, 1910]

ENTERING MEN LEARN OF COLLEGE ACTIVITIES

Freshman Class Enjoys Hospitality of the Philadelphian
Society at Annual Reception Saturday Evening.

The annual reception given by the Philadelphian Society to the members of the Freshman Class was held last Saturday evening in Murray-Dodge Hall. The class first assembled in Murray Hall where they were addressed by several of the upperclassmen on the various phases of undergraduate life and by President Woodrow Wilson '79. after which they adjourned to Dodd [Dod] Hall where refreshments were served. . . .

The final address of the evening was given by President Woodrow Wilson. His address in part follows:

"It is now thirty-five years since I was in your place, and twenty of those years I have been living and working in this university. In those thirty-five years I have never lost the feeling that I had when I came here as a Freshman,—that feeling as if the world were beginning for me.

"You have heard a series of speeches this evening, in which various activities have been outlined, and it is my singular function to remind you that all these are associated with a university. There is the very diverting work of the musical clubs; there is the valuable work of the Halls; and there is the very fundamental work of the Philadelphian Society. But these would not be here, if it were not that there is a university in Princeton. The faculty occupies a position of strategic importance. These gentlemen whom you have heard to-night can *invite* you to play football, and so forth; but we can *require* you to study.

"It is really necessary, if you will stay here, that you should study. It is a sort of a qualifying heat. It is something you must do as a foundation for these other things that are in themselves very delightful. With the exception of public speaking and the Philadelphian Society, these things are temporary.

"These things belong to that interesting period of your life when you are undergraduates. The word *undergrad[u]ate* describes your humble estate. You are below the life of those men who have got out of the shell. Upon the great field of the world these undergraduate activities don't count for very much. They are for our leisure hours and they serve to limber our faculties, but little more.

"Nothing now can be slovenly done. Every man must have the training that underlies mastery. We should try to make our minds instruments of precision. Command your faculties, and then you are fit for the competition of the modern world. In this country of ours, this beloved country which depends for its prosperity and its very existence upon the average intelligence and capacity of the men who make it up, every man should qualify from this time until he is called away, for the duties of a true citizen. This is the place where you begin to qualify.

"If you engage in these activities, you must realize the atmosphere in which they take place,—the atmosphere of intellectual endeavor. The man who does not work while he is in college will some day say to himself, 'What an unfathomable fool I was.'

"I would fain hope that this day shall not come to any one of you. Our love for Princeton is not a love for her beauty and comradeships. We remember that there are generations and generations behind us and coming after us. We would not have the history of Princeton have any blemish during the time that we are in college and you will not want it to be said that any class of any year did the university more good than your class did, in your year."

Printed in the *Daily Princetonian*, Sept. 26, 1910.

To Charles Dexter Allen

My dear Mr. Allen: Princeton, N. J. September 26th, 1910.

Your letter of September 25th has given me a great deal of pleasure and I want to thank you for it most sincerely.

I remember with a great deal of interest my visit to the Owl Club of Hartford and I am sorry to hear that so interesting a club should have lost its vigor.

My speaking engagements in Essex County are: Newark, the 30th of September; the Oranges November 2nd (exact place not yet determined, so far as I know); and Newark again, November 5th.

With much respect,
Sincerely yours,   Woodrow Wilson

TLS (WC, NjP).

From Charles N. Grandison[1]

Dear Sir: Atlantic City, N. J. Sept. 26, 1910.

I trust you will pardon the liberty I take of addressing you, and I beg to assure you that nothing but a sincere interest in you and the cause you represent and an earnest desire for the triumph of righteousness and civic decency could induce me to obtrude myself upon your notice.

Speaking one day last week to an influential colored man of this city, a man of my own race, about the coming election in this State this fall, I remarked to him that I intended to give my public and private support to the ticket which you so worthily head. He replied by saying that Princeton University would not admit to its academic department a Negro student and that you, being a Southern man, was in sympathy with the policy of excluding Negroes from the academic department of that institution, and had so expressed yourself. I told him I could not believe that statement, unless it came from one less partisan in his views than he. I can not bring myself to believe that a man of your breadth of vision and of your high moral ideals would be willing to close the door of opportunity in the face of any aspiring human being, whatever his race or nationality; and I write imploring that I may have direct from you, in brief but unequivocal terms, your attitude on the race question as it manifests itself in this country.

It may interest you to know that I was in the great fight in Philadelphia five years ago against the Durham ring and in the interest of the City Party, and it is said that my services contributed considerably to the defeat of the "gang."[2] Hoping an early and favorable reply, I am

Yours truly,   (Rev.) C. N. Grandison.

ALS (WP, DLC).
[1] President of Bennett College, Greensboro, N. C., 1890-1892; pastor of Ezion Methodist Church, Wilmington, Del., 1893-94; deserted his church on January 7, 1894; afterward an occasional lecturer and itinerant minister.
[2] About this matter, see G. L. Record to WW, Oct. 17, 1910, n. 6.

From William Church Osborn

My dear President Wilson: [New York] September 26, 1910.

I am sending you a booklet of the more striking Corrupt Practices Act[s] of this country.[1] This was issued a few years ago and is not down to date. The English and Canadian system provides for the loss of office of the offending candidate. That system is not applicable to this country, as the offense is committed by the party and not the candidate. The statutes of this country have all adopted publicity as their keynote. Our statute in New York has added to the publicity provisions an opportunity to any disaffected citizen to make an inquiry on his own account. The cure for corrupt practice lies in a roused and vigilant moral tone in the community. The better citizens do not suspect its widespread character.

Sincerely yours,   Wm. Church Osborn

TLS (WP, DLC).
[1] The enclosure is missing.

From Dan Fellows Platt

Dear Mr. President,   N. Y. City Sept. 26. 1910

Just a hurried word as to something that comes to me through a good source. One "Andy" Knox, New Idea man from Hudson[1] —a very fine man—who intimates that he is going to vote for you —will probably speak out at your Jersey City meeting to ask you how you stand on direct primaries & their extension. This is to say that the man is *high class* & is *friendly*. As to your Bergen

County engagement I hope to have a chance to talk with you before Oct. 27th. Please don't bother to acknowledge this.

Yrs sincerely   Dan F Platt

ALS (WP, DLC).
[1] Andrew Knox, grocer and member of the Board of Street and Water Commissioners of Jersey City.

From James Richard Nugent

My dear Sir: Newark, N. J., September 26, 1910.

I have answered all the enclosures received from you up to date.

As stated in the itinerary sent you Saturday last by special delivery, the campaign will open at Jersey City on Wednesday evening, September 28th, at eight o'clock.

With their usual lack of foresight, the Hudson County Committee have failed to arrange to entertain you previous to the meeting. However, this gives me the opportunity of having an hour with you to discuss some important matters and enjoy a quiet dinner. You will therefore kindly start from Princeton on the train leaving at 4:50 P.M. I will meet you at the Newark station on the arrival of the train at 6:15.

After our conference and dinner we will proceed to Jersey City in an automobile which I have provided for your use during the entire campaign. By using the auto you will be able to return to Princeton almost every night if you so desire.

I will have the auto at your residence at Princeton at twelve o'clock on Thursday, so that you may attend the Fair and in the evening motor over to Plainfield. The distance is short and preferable to travelling on the railroad and changing routes.

Kindly send me an immediate answer so that I may complete the above arrangements.

Yours very truly,   James R. Nugent

TLS (WP, DLC) with WWhw and WWsh notation.

From David Benton Jones

My dear Doctor,   Chicago Sept 27 1910

I fully appreciate the situation which made the return of the Draft seem best.

There is something wrong however when those who have the power to lead must also bear the burden incident to leadership for the general good.

I do not want you to "get stuck," but in case you do I shall rely on your promise to let me know, not only this Autumn, but *at any time in the future*. It will not only be a joy, but bring a sense of relief—you have conferred distinction on Princeton and Princeton men and we are all in debt to you—money debt for value received.

You are now entering on more important work still, while most of us comfortably go our way and what is worse will complacently accept our share of the general good that will result from your labor and your sacrifices.

If that is right I want to be in the wrong.

Very Sincerely   David B. Jones.

I beg of you not to reply in any way to this. I hope to see you in November if not sooner.

ALS (WP, DLC).

From Winthrop More Daniels, with Enclosure

My dear Wilson: Princeton, N. J. Sept. 27, 1910.

Ever since returning I have wanted a talk with you but I realize how busy you are, and starting the Departmental work has kept me pretty busy also. What I wanted to say was that I shall be more than glad to undertake any work in the campaign that I could be advantageously entrusted with. To my mind it is a question whether it might not provoke criticism for your Faculty to "stump" for you. Three years ago I made two short addresses for Katzenbach which might seem to give me a pretty fair right to repeat the performance this fall. But frankly, I do not rate myself very high as a stump speaker, my voice is not resonant enough; and hitherto I have been confining my effort to the printed page, as Stock[1] has probably intimated. At all events, if you find anything which you think I can do, I hope you will call freely on me.

I am enclosing a citation from Edmond Kelly's last book entitled "Twentieth Century Socialism"[2] which can be made very effective on the public platform, because it so neatly and dramatically demonstrates the true inwardness of "downward revision," without puzzling the ordinary hearer with schedules, rates, classifications, and the like. I hope you may find it useful. If supplemented with newspaper citations, as Kelly suggested, —especially from Republican journals,—it would be very telling.

Yours ever,   W. M. Daniels.

TLS (WP, DLC).
1 That is, Stockton Axson.
2 Edmond Kelly, *Twentieth Century Socialism; What It Is Not; What It Is; How It May Come* (New York, 1910).

E N C L O S U R E

An Excerpt From Edmond Kelly's *Twentieth Century Socialism*

"Again, after Taft had, on three separate occasions, solemnly promised the people, if he were elected, a revision downward of the tariff, the same lobby secured a revision of the tariff upwards. We are assured by Messrs. Aldrich and Payne that the revision is a revision downward. How, then, will they explain the extraordinary haste with which ships sought to reach this port before the new tariff came into effect?* Were these ships hurrying to port in order to escape the payment of a low tariff? . . . It is seldom that the Interests have gone so far as to elect a presidential candidate on a definite promise and deliberately, as soon as the candidate was elected, to violate their promise. But the Interests have at this moment such control over our politics that they can do this; and it seems very doubtful whether this treachery will ever be materially punished."

*(Footnote.) See any daily paper between March 16, 1909, when the bill was introduced in the House, and Aug. 6, 1909, when the law went into effect.

Kelly also calls attention to an article "The Payne-Aldrich Tariff" In the Review of Reviews For Sept. 1909, as indicating the extent of the upward revision.

T MS (WP, DLC).

From Edward Wallace Scudder[1]

Dear Sir: Newark, New Jersey September 27th, 1910.
    I am afraid, from my rather hasty and careless wording of my telegram of yesterday,[2] you may have misunderstood my purpose.
    My intention in wiring to you was to send by one of our editorial staff the skeleton of an editorial under preparation, in which we were thinking of attempting to show how "New Na-

tionalism" and your views, as I have understood them, were supplementary to each other rather than mutually exclusive, together with some effort to show where the two could meet in what is well termed "the twilight zone."

From your telegram of this morning, which I may have misunderstood, I take it that perhaps in your view, the two ideas are largely mutually exclusive as far as "the twilight zone" is concerned.

I would appreciate it very much, therefore, if you could grant our Mr. Haney,[3] a member of our staff in whose discretion I have great confidence, an interview to be confidential—not to be published at least as coming directly from you—on these matters.

The News, as you are doubtless aware, has the most emphatic desires to play fair as far as our knowledge and information go. We do not desire to misrepresent either you or Mr. Roosevelt on these questions, and it was for the sake of gathering information that could be used for later editorials that the interview was requested.

I hope, in view of this explanation, you can grant us an interview at some early date.[4]

Yours very sincerely,   Edward W Scudder

TLS (WP, DLC).
    [1] Princeton 1903, editor of the *Newark Evening News.*
    [2] It is missing.
    [3] Conrad Haney, editorial writer for the *Newark Evening News.*
    [4] One can only conjecture that Wilson probably did grant the interview to Haney.

A News Report of a Religious Address

[Sept. 28, 1910]

TRUE UNIVERSITY SPIRIT

Princeton Must Maintain Its Lofty Ideals
of Sound Scholarship and Service To the Nation.

On the eve of opening his campaign for governor, President Wilson '79 addressed a large audience of undergraduates in Murray Hall last night. It was the first meeting of the Philadelphian Society for this term. President Wilson's address was particularly forcible. He took as his text a portion of the second chapter of the second Epistle to Timothy. He spoke as follows:

"The words I want to speak from are these: 'Thou therefore endure hardness as a good soldier.' I suppose that a great many of us regard religion as wholly a matter of doctrine, a matter of what men believe, not realizing that what men vitally believe is what they steer by. When a man once gets a principle of action into his thinking, he is governed in the processes of his life by that principle.

"Now I suppose that men at your age hardly realize that there is nothing in the world that is not a warfare; not a warfare in the sense of harboring hostility in your hearts against anything except evil; but nothing is come at easily,—without toil, without struggle. The only thing that keeps us alive is putting our capacities to some strain. The man who never puts his muscles under any strain, never has any muscles. The man who never puts his character under any strain, never has any character.

"You know we sometimes attempt to surround ourselves with all sorts of protections against evil. Now we must all surely come into contact with evil, and if we are not able to grapple with it, it will overcome us. It is interesting to find the writers in the Bible taking the simile of battle so frequently.

"Don't go about seeking to associate only with good people. Endure hardness. Match your principles with your temptations, and see whether your principles are capable of standing the strain of your temptations. The man who is worthy is the man who goes out and joins battle. He doesn't allow himself to be turned aside by immaterial things, but keeps his eye on the main point that he seeks to gain, and cuts his way to that. This is not a mere warfare of blind battling, without aim, without definite movement forward in a particular direction. A man must have a certain degree of circumspection. He must be careful how he makes this or that kind of promise. He must be careful to see that he is always in fighting trim, and fighting, fighting, fighting, in the right direction.

"What commends the Christian religion to red-blooded men is its combination of robustness and tenderness. The Christian must have both strength and tenderness. It is a religion to quicken the pulse of strong men. But it is also an infinitely tender religion, the basis of which is love, in which we fight not because we want to injure anybody, but because we want to deliver everybody from the thraldom of evil. The spirit of infinite love and sympathy gives life to Christianity.

"The reason I have always been interested in the University, is that its service has been to the spirits of men. It is a place to which men come that their minds and their understandings may be opened. I know of no reason why we study literature, if it is not as the expression of the spirit of individuals and races. And a university justifies its existence only in proportion as it breeds nobility and enlightenment in the human spirit. Unless its members are willing to work always in order that the truth may prevail, it is not a university.

"I have often thought if there were a single university in this fullest sense of the word, it would not have to have its history written. Its voice would command the world. Its graduates would be marked and picked men wherever they went.

"I hope that I shall often be with you again. I do not think of any possibility in the future as separating me from my spiritual connection with Princeton. And I shall always feel, it may be a partiality, it may be a tender fondness for this place where twenty years of my teaching life have been spent. But I have a firm belief that there is an impulse planted in this place that will presently lift it to a position that not even our love has ever contemplated; that the men of this place will from one college generation to the other see the true interests of the University. I have fought for certain things here which you understand in a very considerable degree, and I am not afraid to turn away from the task. I believe that the things that are best for the University are already comprehended by her men. These are ideas originated by no one man, but which have grown in the breath of the place.

"Endure hardness, for the sake of the University, for the sake of yourself, and for the sake of the truth. Don't entangle yourselves too much with the play, the immaterial things of college life. Make war upon the things that drag the University down, in order that you may please Him who hath chosen you to be His soldier."

Printed in the *Daily Princetonian*, Sept. 28, 1910; two editorial headings omitted.

To Winthrop More Daniels

My dear Daniels: Princeton, N. J. September 28th, 1910.

You are always generous and I particularly appreciate the generosity of your letter of yesterday offering to help in the campaign.

It gives me a chance to say how warmly I appreciate what you have done already, which has been a great deal. I am a perfect novice in the matter of campaigning and do not feel that I can yet form a judgment as to what it is possible for men like yourself to do, but I am going to talk the matter over with the more experienced men, for it would be a real delight for me to know that you had made speeches in my behalf.

Your excerpt from Kelly's Twentieth Century Socialism is most interesting and apposite, and I am sure I shall find real use for it.

Always cordially and faithfully yours,
Woodrow Wilson

TLS (Wilson-Daniels Corr., CtY).

An Interview

[*Sept. 28, 1910*]

Lie Nailed By Woodrow Wilson
Uses Plain Language In Stating Labor Views.

GIVES FRANK TALK

By S. M. Christie[1]

Princeton, New Jersey, Sept. 28.—Woodrow Wilson, the Democratic nominee for Governor, discussed vital issues in his usual frank and fair manner when interviewed by me today.

During the course of our talk, I suggested that some persons had been a little doubtful as to the wisdom of supporting his candidacy on account of some of the men identified with it.

"I am not used to being nominated for Governor," said Mr. Wilson, "but I know that no man ever ran for the office who was so free from pledges and promises as I am. I rather anticipated that I would be approached and asked as to my views on certain questions, and as to what I would do in certain contingencies, but I was not. Everything seemed to be taken for granted. It puzzled me, and I asked a friend what it meant.

" 'It means,' said my friend, 'that the Democratic State leaders, after 15 years of leading a minority, want to elect a Governor. They will gain in prestige and will gain incidental advantages, and they know that while you will only appoint fit men to office you will not discriminate against Democrats, and they have been discriminated against for 15 years, you know. And they expect also to reap incidental advantages from the house cleaning you will, if elected, be enabled to make, and the economies of administration you will undoubtedly effect.' "

Bringing the discussion to Mr. Wilson's attitude on labor matters, I asked him if he had ever said that a dollar and a half a day was enough for any workingman?

"It does not seem that it should be necessary for me to answer such questions," said Mr. Wilson, "since I have given by [my] views publicity many times.

"The statement that I said a dollar and a half a day was enough for any workingman is an absolute lie.

"In my letter to Mr. Williamson I said that 'It is, in my opinion, not only perfectly legitimate, but absolutely necessary that labor should organize in order to secure justice from organized capital.' Surely that is plain language.

"A little while ago the New York Press published a statement that I had said that only college men should hold public office. That is not only a lie, but an absurd lie.

"How could any sane man, who knows anything about American history say such a thing? What are the two names that stand out most prominently in American history—George Washington and Abraham Lincoln. And neither Washington nor Lincoln went to college.

"Friends of mine called my attention to that statement, and urged me to reply to it, but what is the use? Lies are eventually shown to be lies, and hurt only those who resort to them.

"And while I know little about campaigning for public office, I know enough about it to realize that if I try to reply to all the lies that will be told about me I will have time for nothing else.

"I feel like the farmer who said to his son: 'Son, if you hear some pretty bad things about me, and I pay no attention to them, you may be sure that they are lies. But if you hear some things about me, and I immediately get mad and deny them, you may be sure they are touching a sore spot, and that what they say is true.' "

I suggested to Mr. Wilson that, not being a college man myself, I had been much interested in reading one of his addresses to the alumni in which he said: "Most of the masters of endeavor in this country have not come through the channels of universities; but from the great rough-and-ready workers of the world."

"The importance of a college education," said Mr. Wilson, "is overestimated, and it is most frequently overestimated by those who have not had it. The self-educated man has the advantage of having had to put forth greater effort to obtain what he has obtained.

"Reforms do not begin at the top of the social strata, they begin at the bottom. A recognition of that fact has been one of the great sources of strength of the Catholic Church. In the Middle Ages the Catholic Church kept alive the democratic idea. A peasant could not hope to be king or emperor, but the humblest peasant knew that it was possible for him to become the Pope at Rome, and to dominate kings and emperors. This country cannot afford to drift away from democracy."

Mr. Wilson talks frankly, freely on all subjects, dodging no issue, but apparently convinced that the only right thing for him to do is to open his mind without reserve to the people of the State. He seems to be under the impression that on any matter which will come within his executive control the people are entitled to know his views.

Printed in the Trenton *True American*, Sept. 29, 1910; some editorial headings omitted.
 ¹ Samuel M. Christie, former reporter for the *New York Herald* and later owner of the Christie Press of New Brunswick, N. J., and publisher of the *New Brunswick Spokesman* and the New Brunswick *South River Spokesman*.

A Speech in St. Peter's Hall in Jersey City Opening the Campaign

September 28, 1910.

I am sincerely obliged to you for the generous reception you have given me, and you have relieved me of great embarrassment. I never before appeared before an audience and asked for anything, and now I find myself in the novel position of asking you to vote for me for Governor of New Jersey.

I do not want to give you any personal reason why you should vote for me. If I were in your place and you were in mine I am sure I would be at a loss to give any personal reasons whatever. I am [not] going to give those persons who are generous enough to believe in me the reason why you should choose me in particular.

What I want to give you to-night are some reasons why you should believe the Democratic party in this State a suitable party to serve you at this juncture in your affairs, for, gentlemen, we have come to a point where any individual cannot ask for a favor from his fellow citizens, unless he can give reasons that will satisfy the public in general that a real service would be rendered in return.

Some gentlemen on this platform can tell you more specifically than I can that I did not seek the nomination as Governor. They were generous enough to offer it to me, and, because they offered it to me, they were generous enough to let me understand that I was under no obligations to any individual or group of individuals.

But I am now asking you to vote for me for Governor, and I particularly want to confess to one obligation. If you should vote for me for Governor I shall be under obligations to you, I shall be obedient to the people of this State, to serve them and them only.

I wish to be your servant, not because I recognize any partic-

~~Newark~~ Jersey City, 28 Sept., 1910.

Glad to meet so many fellow Democrats

Do not come to ask your votes for me, but
  for a change of programme.

Take it for granted you wish a change of programme, because something seems to have
  happened to the capacity and the intentions
  of the Republican party!

Why [shorthand]?

Because 1) [shorthand]

2) [shorthand] insurgents [shorthand]

3) [shorthand]

You know the [shorthand]
How can you [shorthand]?
  1) [shorthand]
  2) [shorthand]?
  3) [shorthand]

ular qualifications in myself above those of scores of other men who might have served you just as well, but because I believe to the bottom of my heart that the time has come when the Democratic party can be of real service to the State of New Jersey and to the nation to which we belong.

I believe I can take it for granted here to-night, gentlemen, that you want a change of program. I believe I can take it for granted that you believe, as I believe, that those who have been attempting to govern this State have in some degree lost their capacity.

I am not now indicting a great party. I hope sincerely that you will never hear me in the course of this campaign saying anything against that great body of our fellow-citizens who have believed in the principles of the Republican party. What I want you to understand me as doing is this: I believe that that great body of citizens is now led by persons who are not capable of realizing in a proper public spirit the great principles of the Republican party any more than they can win the acquiescence of those persons who believe in the great principles of the Democratic party.

I believe we want a change of government, and what I want you to-night to believe is that the Democratic party can give you the kind of change of government that is desired. I fully realize when I ask you to believe that, that I must give you sufficient reasons. The reasons I shall give you are modest enough reasons. I don't believe that the virtue of public service rests with any particular group of men, but I do believe, gentlemen, that, in order to see what the public interest is, it is necessary that you should be detached for some considerable length of time from the temptations of office.

I believe those who have had the offices of the State in their possession for a long time are induced to look upon it as a private gain, rather than a public gain. And it is necessary, as the sailor would say, to "get your offing to know what you are about."

I hope you will not think me guilty of audacity for what I am about to claim for the Democratic party. I think I have no more gall than my fellowmen and I am in the pitiable condition of the colored man who went sound asleep in the train, with his head way back and his mouth wide open, and a man nearby, who had some powdered quinine in his pocket, went up and dusted a lot on the darky's tongue. He slept on quite unconscious of what happened, and presently closed his mouth and waked up with a start, and called in great excitement to the conductor: "Is there a doctor on this train, boss? I done busted my gall."

I have not quite busted my gall, but I haven't the audacity to go too far in claiming any particular virtue for any particular party. I simply want you to listen to me while I give a candid set of reasons.

In the first place, although the Democratic party has, first and last, made some blunders, and, although the same political party has sometimes wandered this way now and then another, it is the party, speaking by the book—historically speaking—it is the party which has longest and most intently maintained its connections with the great body of the plain people.

At most, the Democratic party is the party that does not study how to advance particularly [particularity], but it has always had principles as great and as broad as the great body of the people itself. I have had a great deal to do, first and last, with the plain people. I myself have all my life long been a poor man. I know what it is to be careful in living, careful in expense, observant of the conditions that affect great bodies of men. Moreover, gentlemen, I know this—that nobody who has ever read the pages of history can fail to notice that the real wells of strength and sources of renewal are in the great body of the people.

Every great state is like a great tree. It does not receive its nourishment and renewal from its fruit and branches. It is received from its root, and every great state is rooted in that great soil, which is made up of all the vast body of unnoticed men, the great masses of toilers, the men who never emerge to the general view, the men who go quietly, painfully on, from day to day, from month to month, from year to year, from generation to generation, and sustain by their labor the whole economics of a political body. There is the sap of the nation, and the glory of America has been that again and again—not rarely, so as to make any singular circumstance, but again and again,—plain men have arisen from the ranks in order to be, first, the captains of the things they found immediately to do, and, after a while, the captains of the country itself.

I found a gentleman to-day with whom I was talking who did not know that one of the most celebrated characters of our history gained his elevation by arduous effort just in that way —no less a person than George Washington. He could not afford more than a common school education, had to go out in the rough country that surrounded his home to serve as a surveyor, had to endure all the hardships of a frontier and struggle for an education which he gained from practical affairs, and never to the end of his life could he spell correctly.

This great figure, that all the world turns to as the typical figure of America, was rooted in the common soil of everyday life of the country where he lived; and so I say that party which has, so far as I have known it, always felt the keenest, intensest sympathies for the greatest body and mass of citizenship, is the party which I wish to work with, and, I believe, in the long run, can serve the people best.

Then there is another reason—a reason which concerns the Republican party. It has a very distinguished history, and I would not want to take away from its laurels in any respect, but from circumstances I need not stop to narrate to you, the Republican party has in one circumstance and another identified itself with policies which were meant to sustain special interests in this country. I say that because of changes in economic policies; it has been at pains to serve the particular economic interests which sprung up from generation to generation; it has established a partnership which it cannot break. By saying it cannot break it, I am not suggesting corrupt reasons why it cannot break it; it cannot honorably break it. If it has tied itself up in its policies with certain dominating interests in the country, I leave it to you, is it honorable for it to break it to get the votes of a large number of citizens?

And I say that the Republican party has identified itself with particular interests from which it cannot be expected to divorce itself in a single generation.

You will say that the Democratic party has not done so because it has not had the chance. I do not think that is a fair judgment at all, but let us assume that is the case. The Democratic party has not formed these alliances and the Democratic party is therefore free to go in any direction it pleases to go in the service of the country. I think, for my part, that is a very good reason for choosing my own party lines. Not that I would have you believe that I am just choosing them, for I have been a Democrat ever since I was born. I was first a Democrat because I was born that way; then I became a Democrat because I believed that way. Now I am giving you the reasons why I believe that way. I want to belong to a party which at present, at any rate, is free to serve the country without too many entangling alliances.

Because there are a great many things that it is necessary to do and only men free from such alliances can do.

This is not an easy time in which to live, gentlemen. I do not wonder that great mistakes of policy have been made. I could point out to you the tremendous economic changes which have occurred in this country within a single lifetime, aye, in some instances in a single decade, that have changed the whole face of economic endeavor. Fifteen or twenty years ago, for example, business was conducted by partnership, by individuals, by small groups of men, and now, as everybody knows, the great sorts of business are conducted by corporations, are conducted by big combinations of men, not controlled by any one group, including the means and savings and investments of hundreds of thousands of persons. And look what has followed! A very peculiar thing has followed. The board of directors of a joint stock corporation is using more money in the business than the board of directors could ever through their own separate endeavors have collected and amassed.

They have piled up in one enterprise the small contributions of hundreds and thousands of stockholders. They have, therefore, yielded [wielded] enormous economic power. And yet we find this singular circumstance that if I did this by myself, with my own small accumulations, the law always knows who I am and where to find me when I am responsible. If I am a member of a board of directors—the most influential of a board of directors—and am possessed of millions of dollars which I could not possibly accumulate by myself, then the law does not know where I am. The law cannot find me; I am in ambush; I am under cover, because the law has a pretty theory—you may not know that I was bred in the law, therefore, I can speak by the book in this matter—the law has a very pretty theory that a corporation is a person, a legal person, and you cannot dissect a person.

You cannot find out which piece of a person did a thing. You have to take the person as a whole. I demur from that theory. Everything that any corporation does was originated by somebody in particular, and I say that the immediate task of the law is to find the person. I liken the modern corporation to a powerful motorboat, such as is common in these waters. In order that the boat may have sufficient strength it must, of course, be knitted and held together in all its riven parts—for it is generally of steel,—and in order that it may not be overwhelmed by the water, as it forces its ways with tremendous rapidity through it, it has to be decked over in front, covered up, so that it will not take its own wash; but because the boat has to be thus knitted together, because the modern corporation is thus knitted together as the motor boat is, it is not necessary that the crew should be covered over. I am perfectly willing that the forepart of the corporation should be decked over, but not the hind part; I want to see who is running the boat responsible.

Our modern corporation law is like the law of some States

with respect to automobiles, or rather like the law as I have heard it proposed in respect to automobiles. I have heard it proposed that it should be the law with respect to automobiles that when the law was broken the best thing to do was to seize the automobile and lock it up.

Now, that might inconvenience the owner, and, as we say in the South, "learn him sense," but we want to use the automobile. Because a reckless person misuses it is not any reason why a sensible person should not use the automobile. Therefore, I say get the man who is running the automobile and teach him to behave and do not take the automobile away; the automobile is not to blame.

If I get a gun and shoot somebody, whom I would dearly love to shoot—and I could name several—I am seized, and not the gun. There is not known to the law any process by which the gun can be indicted. I may be never so cunning in the arrangements I make; it may be ever so hard to find out for certain whether I fired the gun or not; but nobody pays the slightest attention to the gun, except as an item of evidence.

If the gun is found in a place where it is probable that I put it, it is a useful piece of evidence; but the gun is not blamed for the difficulty. Therefore, with that gun which we call a corporation, I do not blame the gun, but I do blame the men behind the gun; and what I am trying to illustrate for you is that all of this thing with regard to personal responsibility and tremendous accumulated power has arisen within less than a generation and the mere fact of the matter is that the law does not fit it; the law was made in an age when these corporations did not exist, and that is the only trouble with our law.

Then, what do we need? We need some party, some group of men, some set of leaders, who are free to throw over this old idea so that the new idea of the law can be adapted to the new and extraordinary circumstances of the day. They must be free, because they must be unprejudiced, and they must be fair.

The air in recent years in this country has been surcharged with excited rhetoric. It has sometimes been so surcharged with excited rhetoric that you could not breathe without asphyxiation. I have heard so many sermons about how good we ought to be that I am entirely convinced that we ought to be good.

Well, I can sit down in my room at any time and determine, in general terms, to be good. I find there is no trouble about that. But the trouble is when the next morning comes and I go out about my affairs to determine how I am going to be good in each circumstance that arises. I tell you very frankly that I am not interested in general programs of being good. I am intensely interested in every program of how to be good. It is the idea, from what I suppose are credible sources, that there are a great many rich crooks in this country—an idea that there are a great many poor crooks—and, I suppose, there are crooks also, in order to be fair, of medium means.

I have not found that poverty or riches or mediocre circumstances have much to do with crookedness. Some men are born that way and cannot help it, and some men diligently educate themselves to be crooks; their economic circumstances do not have much to do with it. But a rich crook is more dangerous than a poor crook, and, therefore, he is more conspicuous. But I [am] not interested in analyzing my fellow men and setting them, the goats on one side and the sheep on the other. I must admit that sometimes I do not know a goat from a sheep, I mean among my fellow men. I hope I do know one from the other in the animal kingdom. The business of classification may be interesting: but, as the Scotchman said about charity, it don't set you any forward[er]; you do not get anything out of it; therefore, I am tired of hearing, in general terms, what ought to be our duty toward the things that are wrong and toward the things that are right.

Let us cultivate, if we can, a different source of atmosphere. Let us try to clear the air of accusations and counter accusations, of prejudices that pull us this way, and of prejudices that pull us that way. Let us be fair and look each other in the eyes and admit the facts, and then get down to business and see how we can correct them. Let us have men in our places of leadership and power, if we can; let us have men who will be approachable by all sorts of persons and perfectly willing to hear all sides; but men whom we can depend upon to be fair in the final decision.

I would not have any part or lot with a plan to put any party in to serve any particular side. What we need more than anything else in this country is some body of men who do not recognize sides and are ready to do the right thing, no matter who is concerned in the questions that are raised from time to time.

Therefore, gentlemen, you will see that in order to do this, in order to get this, gentlemen, you have got a big program ahead of you. We have arranged in this country—and I have no quarrel with it—a very intricate constitutional system, and it is very difficult to clear the way for action because of the intricacies of that constitutional system.

If you want a change of program, what have you to do? You

have got to elect a Democratic Legislature, you have got to elect a Democratic Governor, and you have got to elect a Democratic Congress. You have got to go the whole way, if you want to change the policy. It will be very gratifying to me, for example, personally, privately, very gratifying to me, if you merely put me in as Governor and should do nothing else; but, if you did that, you would not accomplish anything. The Governor cannot make the laws of the State; the Governor cannot effect the changes of policy, which, it seems to me, it is necessary to effect.

You might put a figurehead up and say: "We will give you a complimentary vote and go in and look as handsome as you can, and talk as handsome as you can, but we wouldn't help you out in any other way." It would be a very lonely isolation; it would be a very uncomfortable job.

I do not know how to do anything by myself. If there is one thing that I have studied more than any other, it is how to attach myself to bodies of men who are trying to accomplish great objects. I want to attach myself to some great body of Democrats who have received the approval of the citizens of the State of New Jersey, who are all bound together in common enterprise to serve the State of New Jersey. If I felt that I was coming to this meeting to-night, or going to any other meeting to oppress you with my eloquence; if I thought that I was coming here or going to any of these other meetings, with the sole picayune idea of speaking for myself, I would go home and have a good comfortable sleep and I would not come to another meeting.

I do not understand that that is the program. The program that I am engaged in is the election of a body of Democrats who can change the policy of the State. I am not speaking for myself; I am speaking for what I have been privileged, by the action of the convention that nominated me, to represent. I regard myself as the representative of a great idea, of a great purpose, which I hope will turn out to be the purpose of the people of New Jersey. I want to say just this about the means which we are to use to accomplish the ends that are ahead of us. I know, gentlemen, that recently a great many persons have talked as if they were impatient of the law—as if they were impatient of those slow processes by which legal remedies are effected. I know that there are a great many persons who wish that it were possible, just by vote, to put out everything that is wrong and to put in everything that is good; but if you had that sort of an arrangement you would not accomplish anything at all. You might just as well wish that we were all disembodied spirits and did not have to submit to trammels of legs and hands and all those mysterious things that give us so much trouble inside.

You cannot accomplish anything except through the instrumentality of the law. Now, the law is a rough-and-ready instrument. Law cannot adapt itself to very minute conditions or circumstances. It has to consist of general rules, and somebody is going to get pinched by the general rules. It has got to be unfair to somebody, but not to most people. If it is properly arranged, the general rule will be for the benefit of everybody, but it will not be for the benefit of any particular person.

What I want to insist on to-night is that the law is the poor man's friend. It has been part of my business to study history. I have read the records of many revolutions. I could recite the many occasions when law was absolutely flouted and set aside, and in every instance the record of the bloodshed and of the wrong done would be the record of blood that the poor shed and of the poor who were wronged; because in a state of anarchy, when the law is dethroned, it if [is] the privileged, the unscrupulous who escape, and the common man is without protection.

It is because the law is the poor man's friend when it is justly administered that I stand for the law. I was bred a lawyer. I do not believe that the law, as a profession, breeds a particularly liberal temper on the part of those who follow it. I say this with great respect to the lawyers, but I do not believe that the lawyers supply us with the only thing that holds the ship of State steady, with that solid ballast that is the bottom of the ship, without which she could not stand up straight and carry the canvas.

I believe that this structure of the law, which we sometimes find so painfully inconvenient, is, nevertheless, the only safe thing in which to brave the waves and the waters. Therefore, the thing that I want to preach—and I would preach the salvation of society—is respect for law but with the free determination to change it in such ways as may be necessary to serve the general interests.

By preaching the efficacy of the law, now, I am not urging that the law should be left as it is, but that these prop[o]sed changes of the law should not be made in hot temper, on sudden impulse. There are things to be changed in the body of the law, but those changes should not be made by resolution of boards of directors.

There is another singular contrast in the history of the Democratic party speaking historically. The Democratic party has always been a party of the widest sympathy, and I think is [it] has always, in a certain sense, been a conservative party, not a radical party. I would like to illustrate for you, if I know how to illustrate it sufficiently, just what I mean. I do not mean a party which tries to hold men back, a party which does not progress, because nothing is so conser[va]tive as progress.

If any tissue of my body stopped growing it would die. If any part of the body politic were to lose its impulse for progress, it would die. The only thing that is conservative is growth.

I remember meeting a certain member of the United States Senate recently, who opened up to me on the subject of the Interstate Commerce clause of the constitution, and he said: "Well, the constitution must grow." "Yes," I said, "that is very true, but there are different kinds of growth." "Have you heard the latest theory about cancer?" he said. "No, I had not," I said. "The latest that I have learned about cancer is this: that cancer is not a deterioration of the particular tissue affected, but it is the setting up of a growth in the surrounding tissue that extends as fast as the growth of a child in the womb, and that tissue around it, being unable to stand the attack upon it, becomes a destructive growth set up in one spot."

Now, I do not want the interstate clause of the constitution to be a cancer, but I do want that clause in the constitution and every other clause in the constitution to be a progressive growth, and I call myself, on that account, a conservative, a conservative because a progressive.

But there are different ways of progressing. I know of some men who think that if they go around in a circle they are conservative. I know of some men who think that movement is progress. I know of some men that don't know where they come from nor where they are going to. I can recall the picture of a poor devil of a donkey on a treadmill. He keeps on tramping, but never gets anywhere, but there's a certain elephant that's tramping, too, and how much progress is it making?

And so I have made my first political appeal. I leave my case in your hands. I feel that it is a trustworthy jury and with its verdict I shall be content.[1]

FPS T transcript (WP, DLC) with additions and corrections from the partial texts in the *Trenton Evening Times*, Sept. 29, 1910, and the *Philadelphia Record*, Sept. 29, 1910.
[1] Following this address, Wilson spoke in a similar vein in St. Patrick's Hall and in Grand View Hall, both in Jersey City. For a news report of these addresses, together with portions of the text of the former, see the Jersey City *Jersey Journal*, Sept. 29, 1910.

Plainfield, 29 Sept., 1910.

"Democratic opportunity," my theme when I was last here

Opportunity to do what? Are the programmes of parties very different? [shorthand symbols]

Opportunity to do definite things, to ~~pull~~ draw the various thinking elements of the State and nation together and form and execute a common object.

1) Think, and secure Common Counsel, free from party prepossession

2) Frame measures with regard to the things with regard to which we have formed definite judgments. — E. g. —

Regulation of public service corporations
Preventing corrupt practices
Recasting Taxation
Employers' liability. — These can be handled with some certainty of touch.

A Campaign Speech in Plainfield, New Jersey[1]

[[Sept. 29, 1910]]

You put me very much at ease by your cheering, for that is the atmosphere in which I live at college, and yet I am haunted by the fear, as I face this audience in the dignified joy now there is upon me, that there are a good many Princeton men in it.

I am cheered by the fact that I stand here as the representative, as I conceive, of a great body of men who have very definite hopes and purposes with regard to the reformation of government in New Jersey.

There never was a time, I am convinced, when party bonds were quite so loose as they are at this moment in this country. There never was a time when there was more independent thinking being done than is now being done in this country. What is more, there never was a time when that thinking was more generally based upon a sympathy with the common needs of all classes of men. I have had men say to me, in very recent days, that they were ashamed of the things that they themselves had been engaged in in pushing on the great economic interests of this country. They said: "It seems to us as if the scales had fallen from our eyes, and we have at last realized the significance of the things we have been doing." It is an extraordinary moment in public affairs in this country.

Men are not stopping now to examine party labels; they are beginning to examine candidates; they are beginning to examine programs; they are beginning to ask whether they can rely upon definite promises; and if they are convinced upon these points they are ready to thrust aside all antecedent connections and prepossessions and vote for the man and the things that they believe in.

The Democratic party has strayed on at different times through many devious paths, but it has never forgotten its sympathy with the great bodies of toiling men; and it is that sympathy which will sustain and renew any party that continues true to it; for the Democratic party is renewed in our day, not by the rise of new men but by the impulse of a new time, which naturally expresses itself in new men. If I were asked to fit the old party cries and shibboleths to the present state of politics, I should say at once that I did not see how it was possible; and the difficulty with the party which I am now trying to play my part in displacing is that it has stuck to old cries and shibboleths and has not noticed the change of the times.

[1] Delivered in Reform Club Hall.

Why is it that there is a great insurgent movement in the Republican party? It is because great bodies of thoughtful men inside their party are beginning to perceive how that party has, not by movement, but by inertia, not by new policies, but by old, separated itself from the enlightened interests of the present moment. The proof of the Democratic argument is the action of these great, powerful bodies of insurgents within the Republican ranks.

A gentleman who is an importer asked this question of a Republican friend of mine the other day. The Republican friend was one of those credulous persons who is willing to argue that the recent revision of the tariff was a revision downward. It takes an ingenious mind to construct the argument, but it can be constructed. He was asked by the importer if that is true, if the Payne-Aldrich tariff lowered the duties, why was it that every captain of a steamship was sent a wireless message to hurry into port before the act went into operation.

You know how the ships were hurried to get into port. Now, if it is true that the Republican party is still carrying the true standards of the interests of this country why is it that thousands of its own are rebelling against their master? The reason is that they know that the best traditions of that party are being violated and that by holding to policies which are outworn and unstable the Republican party has forgotten to keep up with the movement of the time.

We are thinking of a great many things and we are talking about a great many things, but it is interesting to note that we are not doing anything in particular.

All this insurgency is built upon negative lines; it is a movement of discontent. Now, mere discontent does not produce anything positive.

Did you ever think how many things we have had abundant experience about and how many things we could now go forward with with a good deal of confidence to act upon? We are in the presence of very complicated problems, but a great many of them are not due to act upon. For example, all through this country there have been set up public service commissions intended for the regulation of the railways and other public service corporations.

It is not necessary to stop to make inquiries.

All of that is told in a field in which there is abundant experience to guide us. There is no longer such complexity of thought that we cannot safely act upon established models of legislation.

Take, for instance, the Employers' Liability Act. There is no mystery about acting there; there has been legislation going on for years and years in Germany, in England and in various states of the United States along that line.

And speaking about the Direct Primary Law, why, there has been a direct primary law, such as Governor Hughes of New York advocated[2] in evidence in other states. I am saying all this in illustration of the fact that we don't seem to know that other states have been acting on this subject for a long period of time. That is also true with regard to the Employers' Liability Act.

The time when the luxury of talk is all that is sufficient in politics is at an end. We talk about corrupt practices in politics. There are corrupt practices on both sides of the water. If you want to stop corrupt practices you can stop them, but not by merely talking about them, but by putting laws on the books that can be carried out and then carrying them out, and that is the only way you can ever do it.

The scandal of great sums of money can be stopped tomorrow by right statutes, because we have courts in this state, thank God, that administer the statutes. I say that New Jersey has just right to be proud of the reputation of her incorruptible courts. If you give our courts the chance they will show you whether it can be stopped or not, because under a proper corrupt practice act it is the privilege of any citizen who knows anything to lay the thing before the proper tribunal and bring the whole thing to a stop if they were prosecuted in the courts under an efficient corrupt practice act. There are societies organized suitable to do this, but there is no law by which it can be done. I could go on and illustrate, but the point is that we hold back and do not know why we do not go forward.

Corruption in politics is a very subtle thing: it isn't all corruption of money; it is corruption of understanding. The trouble is that a batch of men representing different corporations can meet in any room and arrive at an understanding. No papers are drawn; no act of incorporation is asked for; there is nothing to show authority; the air of the room has not recorded what is spoken. Is it possible that there are compacts against the public?

I have found already in this campaign that people that know the least about me are the people who say the most about me. I have heard all sorts of things about me for the first time since this campaign began. I shall, I dare say, know a great deal more about myself before the campaign is over. I have heard of myself that I said nobody but a college graduate should be appointed

2 See A. C. Ludington to WW, Feb. 4, 1909, ns. 4 and 6, Vol. 19.

to office, and I think it is also reported that I once wrote a history of the United States. I think everyone knows that the two greatest figures in history were the figures who never were inside of a college—George Washington and Abraham Lincoln. And you could increase that roll by scores and hundreds.

If, therefore, I did say that I am either a fool or an ignoramus. Now, inasmuch as I believe I am neither a fool nor ignoramus, I prefer to say that I did not say it. I have no recollection in any sane moment of my life saying anything of the kind. But that is merely by way of digression. It just shows how absolutely free you are to talk about things you don't know anything about. The corporation should have things pointed out to it that it hasn't any means of learning.

The point that I want to drive home is that when we get down to business we shall dispense with reckless and irresponsible criticism and come out on a basis of fact and propose definite things to be done that can be done. There are a great many things that are wrong that we do not yet see the way to set right, and those are not the things we ought to make a shouting about. As I said to the Democratic convention the other day, it is now either a case of putting up or shutting up. We have already discussed the point: the time now is to act in hearty co-operation with each other.

The Public Service Commission is not intended merely to regulate rates; it is meant to regulate rates by a fair and judicious inquiry; it is not meant merely to register complaints, but to correct abuses with regard to corporations as well as the public; not merely to serve one side, but to serve both sides by pointing out what parts of the community need an extended service.

I believe the tariff can be reformed in a way that will not disturb business too much and will meet the necessary and just demand. There is one argument that comes to me forcibly in this country which cannot be answered. There are various causes for the increase in the cost of living, but one cause which makes it rise more rapidly in America than anywhere else. Now, what is that cause? That cause is the tariff wall that has been built so high that business concerns, being absolutely free against the danger of foreign competition, can get together and control prices and cost. It is not the just and reasonable protection the Republican orators used to talk about of putting them in competition with foreign merchandise, but in such a position they can get together and command our fortunes by establishing a rate of price and also the amount of production.

You know what happens when prices get too low, when the

product is too abundant, then the amount produced is curtailed by a common agreement. If there were normal foreign competition they would not dare curtail it. That is the tariff. And so all along the line; the minute you get down to a dispassionate businesslike discussion of the questions at issue you realize you don't remember whether you are a Republican or a Democrat, and are ready to act in the general interest of the country.

We have, therefore, to ask you as Democrats, do you believe that the Democratic party in New Jersey as at present constituted and under its present nominees for office is going to be a suitable instrument in your hand for the reformation of abuses in New Jersey?

I want to say that if you gentlemen do not believe it, then I most candidly hope that you will not vote the Democratic ticket, but if you do believe it, I ask you without distinction of party to vote the Democratic ticket, and when I say vote the Democratic ticket I don't mean the Democratic ticket for Governor. I don't wish to enjoy any kind of splendid isolation. It would be a dead easy thing for me if you would—if you would pick me out on the Democratic ticket and elect me Governor and make the Legislature Republican. Don't you see what an enormous advantage I would have?

I have been praying and talking all my life, and you would set me apart from my present characteristic job, and I could talk and talk and say the things I would have done if I had only a Democratic Legislature back of me and nobody could disprove it. I can say I intended the public welfare. I knew what had to be done, but these hide-bound Republicans in the Legislature could not see the point. Moreover, I was a Democrat and they were of the opposite party, and they wanted to spite me anyway.

I am here to argue for the election of the Democratic ticket, and I want to say that the Democratic ticket does not stop at the state line. If you believe the Democratic party is under new leadership and ready to serve you, then give us Democratic Congressmen, too. It is a pretty serious thing to propose that because you give us Democratic majorities in the Legislature and Democratic majorities in Congress so far as it is possible, don't you see what a burden of proof is put upon us? You will say we promised you thus and so; the means are in your hands, and let us see you do them. Look at the penalties. Party lines are obscured—party lines have gone to pieces. Less than two years ahead of us lies the presidential election.

Give us the power, and if we misuse it, if we lose our opportunities, we should lose all opportunity to elect a Democratic

President of the United States. It is not an easy thing to be asked to be put to test. It is not a prudent thing to be asked to be put to the test, but for my part I am not interested in the game unless we can test ourselves and try ourselves out. I am tired of talk. I wish performance, and if we cannot deliver the goods, then I am satisfied for one to take a back seat.

I am here merely to plead for what I believe to be a cause—a cause of reform and of good government, and it pleases me to conceive that back of all this lies that ideal impulse of the American people which has so characterized us among the nations of the world.

Printed in the *Trenton Evening Times*, Sept. 30, 1910, with one correction from the FPS T transcript in WP, DLC.

From Edwin Augustus Stevens

My dear "Tommy,"   Hoboken, N. J. Sept. 29th, 1910.

I have just returned from a two and a half months' trip abroad, and have been informed of your nomination for the Governorship. Having had a little experience in running for office, I am inclined rather to commisserate with you than to congratulate you. The parties really to be congratulated are—first, the people of New Jersey, and second, the Democratic Party, and as I am a member of both of these bodies, I would hereby tender you an expression of my appreciation for the service you are doing the Party and the State.

I am sorry I was too late to attend the meeting at which you were present in Jersey City.

If I can be of any service to your cause, I trust you will command me, and you may be sure you will have my heartfelt wishes for your success in November. I hope you will not hesitate to call upon me if I can in anyway contribute to so desirable a result.

Sincerely yours,   E. A. Stevens

TLS (WP, DLC).

From Edwin Augustus Van Valkenburg

My dear Doctor: Philadelphia, September 29th, 1910.

It is with peculiar gratification that I acknowledge your letter of September twenty-fifth, because it carries with it so high a compliment to the newspaper which I have the honor to direct. Recognition from a man holding the public relations which you hold, of The North American's aim to serve well the interests of the public, is a tribute of unusual value.

While your letter is marked "Personal"—and will, of course, be kept confidential—I regard it of such importance that I have discussed it carefully with the editorial council, and my reply may be taken as an expression from that body.

I understand perfectly that it would be impossible for a man to formulate a complete platform within the compass of a brief letter, and that the expression of your views on certain vital matters is intended merely as a very general outline. Nevertheless, I think I have arrived at a fair comprehension of the principles for which you stand, an understanding which will doubtless become clearer with study of your writings and of your public utterances, past and future.

You are perhaps familiar enough with The North American's attitude to realize that one of your declarations has a most favorable sound. Your repudiation of the theory that "property rights" are superior to "human rights" is thoroughly in line with the policy upheld by this newspaper.

With equal readiness, no doubt, you will mark where we diverge; as, for instance, was shown in your statement Wednesday[1] that the movement of recent years had resulted in no progress—that it was, in fact, like the labor of a treadmill.

But, after all, the most direct and important passages of your letter have to do with the overshadowing questions of Federal and State control of corporations. These paragraphs have been read with great care and discussed freely in the light of recent events and the strongly conflicting views of adherents of both policies.

Frankly, it would be difficult for The North American to challenge the position you take—unless, as I have intimated before, other utterances of yours, in the past or the future, should indicate other views as to principles or methods than those which appear in your letter now before me. And as a matter of fact, this is one of the great public questions which is unfolding day by day as new problems arise. The North American does not stand where it did ten years ago; perhaps you do not, either; and therefore possibly the fair procedure would be to await clearer development of your views as you may express them from time to time. Unquestionably much may be said for both sides, and one may readily imagine scores of problems where it would be difficult justly to determine whether federal or State power should be invoked. But on one point we are perfectly clear: that system is faulty and must not endure which, because of conflict in interpretation, leaves a "twilight zone" of refuge for lawbreakers.

Probably the easiest way to arrive at a clear conception of your position would be the framing of questions touching some of the leading issues in the matter of Federal vs. State control:

For instance:

"Would physical valuation of the railroads, under Federal direction, as a basis of determining interstate rates, be regarded as an infringement upon the rights of the States in the matter of regulating the capitalization of corporations created by the States?"

"Should water-power sites and other natural resources still in the public domain be controlled by the States, or by the Federal government working in conjunction with the States, for the purposes of conservation and development?"

Your own tender of confidence provokes my desire to have a clearer understanding of your position on these very important questions. I am all the more desirous because of my appreciation of the benefit to the nation to have men of your high type of personal and intellectual character coming into public life.

Assuring you of my gratification in this fact and in the compliment of your letter, I beg to remain,

Sincerely yours,   E. A. Van Valkenb'g

TLS (WP, DLC).
[1] At the end of his speech in St. Peter's Hall in Jersey City.

From Henry Eckert Alexander

Dear Mr. Wilson: Trenton, New Jersey Sept. 29, 1910.

I don't like the attitude of always projecting unasked for advice, but I have seen so many fine political situations muddled by the interjection of matters not fully considered. I want to urge upon you the importance of simply *reserving* an expression on *two* subjects to everybody—without exception—until you have determined exactly what should be said *if the necessity for a declaration should arise.*

I refer to local option and to the senatorial succession.[1]

As to the former, my suggestion is that you say to any inquirer that so far in the campaign the excise question has not arisen; every body admits that the liquor traffic has its evils and that they must be regulated. Opinions vary as to how these evils should be regulated. You will give consideration to the subject when it is presented to you, and *later* will state your views as clearly and as directly as possible. Meanwhile, you will listen *without expressing an opinion* to any one's honest opinions.

I am very sure that you will see the wisdom of this. The people respect any one who will *consider* a question first and then seek to solve it *afterwards* without evasion.

As to the senatorial situation, if the Democrats fail to carry the legislature there will be no situation. It seems to me that you cover the case when that you say that no one ever suggested personal obligation growing out of the nomination and that your only pledge is to the people. That is broad enough to satisfy any reasonable person.

Personally you have never seen the baser side of politics. You will find that plausible men will come to you and seek expressions from you in order to use them against you. I am anxious that no mistake shall be made in this campaign for if this goes on as it has started it will be "a peaceful revolution" in New Jersey.

With best wishes always,

Sincerely yours,   Henry E. Alexander.

ALS (WP, DLC).
¹ That is, the successor to Senator John Kean. Rumors had already begun to circulate that James Smith, Jr., planned to return to the Senate if the Democrats won a majority in the legislature.

From William Swan Plumer Bryan[1]

My Dear Dr. Wilson: Chicago Sept. 29, 1910.

I write to say that it is with profound regret that I read of your purpose to resign the presidency of Princeton University. I have followed your course ever since you became President with deep interest and have approved of the steps which you have taken for the elevation of educational standards and for deepening in the young men under your care the sense of personal responsibility both during their course of study and in after life. My son is a member of the present Sophomore Class[2] and for purely selfish reasons I could wish that he might be under your administration until his graduation, and for reasons of general educational interest, I will deeply regret your withdrawal, however important may be the political exigencies to which you have yielded.

With very kind regards and best wishes, and fresh memories of the days in Columbia and at Davidson, I am

Faithfully yours,   W. S. Plumer Bryan

TLS (WP, DLC).

1 An old friend from Columbia, S. C. and Davidson College. At this time pastor of the Presbyterian Church of the Covenant in Chicago.
2 Alison Reid Bryan, Class of 1913.

A Campaign Speech in Newark[1]

September 30, 1910.

You do me great honor by giving me so great and generous a reception and I thank you for it from the bottom of my heart.

As I was coming to this meeting and passing through the crowds that lined the sidewalks, I kept asking myself, what is it that draws these people away from their homes?

(A voice—"Wilson.")

I would feel very much complimented if I could believe that, but that was not the answer that came into my mind. Men do not flock after a man they do not personally know unless they believe that he stands for something in particular, and one of the most delightful and inspiring things about the American people is that they believe in causes: they believe in principles and they believe in ideas, and they flock after a man who they hope and believe represents those things. These are not demonstrations of honor to an individual; they are manifestations of a very stirring impulse on the part of the people of this city and State with regard to the political affairs that lie immediately ahead of them.

You want from me, I am sure, gentlemen, a confession of faith, and I am ready to make it.

I hope that you have all read the very sound and explicit platform put forth by the Democratic convention that did me the honor to nominate me, and I say to you now, as I said to them, that I stand absolutely without any equivocation for every plank in that platform.

I also stand for some more planks that are not in the platform, because it is impossible for a body of men to exhaust in any statement of principles the subjects which really lie at the very bottom of all political thought and welfare in every American community. There is one plank I would have liked to have seen in that platform. I do not pretend to criticise anybody who had any part in the making of that platform because it is not there. But my own thought would be this:

I am very proud of being a citizen of the State of New Jersey and I am very proud of New Jersey, and I wish there were nothing to be sorry for in connection with her very recent

1 Delivered in Krueger Auditorium.

Newark, 30 Sept., 1910.

A new age, in wh. many old formulas
    are inapplicable

Not as little power for the government as
    possible, but any amount used in the right
    way: the use, not the amount important. As
    much as may be needed for safeguarding _and_
    developing the national life

No pedantic distinction between state and federal
    power, but a sound practical division and co-
    operation.

After all, the main question that of Corporations,
    their relation to the law
        Corporations vs. Gov't = general control
What objects should we seek?
    1) General development
    2) Safeguarding of those who cannot guard them.
    3) The interests of labour, — the foundation as
    4) The interests also of Capital.
Deal with individuals

Revival of the people's rights   9/30/10.

political practice. And yet there is something to be sorry for. New Jersey has earned a certain reputation throughout this country because of her too great and hospitable care of any or all corporations, good or bad; and I wish with all my heart that the citizens of this State might interest their Legislature to the extent of putting the law of incorporation upon another footing, so that the men who come to New Jersey seeking the privilege to do business in the way of corporations will be obliged to go through a severe scrutiny as to the purposes of the corporations.

I believe that the great body of the people have the right of direct nomination for office.

I believe that the people of this State are entitled to a public service commission which has full power to regulate rates.

I believe it would be wise to do what New Jersey has already once done, pass an act in favor of a constitutional amendment allowing the people to vote directly for their Senators.

I believe in each and ev[e]ry plank of the Democratic platform, but I am not going to go over that platform plank by plank and discuss it to a great audience like this whose heart is moved by great issues. It is not necessary that I should go into this discussion or into the details of legislation by which we are to carry each plank out. Suffice it to say that it is our bounden obligation, myself included, if we are put into office, to carry out candidly and to the full extent every principle and every project laid down in that platform. You could not wish it made more explicit than that.

Now, I have said that involves great issues. Why is it, gentlemen, that you come to a super-heated hall like this—super-heated by yourselves? Why is it that you should come and sit uncomfortably in a crowd for an hour together to hear men speak—who, it may be the best of them are good speakers but who are not worth, any of them, myself included, a solid hour of discomfort? Why do you come and stand up, some of you for an hour together, if it [not] be that there is something behind all this that is deeper that [than] mere curiosity to see an individual or mere curiosity to hear him talk, or mere curiosity to see what he looks like?

The truth is that, deeper than all this, you know that your happiness as citizens, that your prosperity as men of business and workmen, depend on the things that are going to be discussed in this meeting, and depend on the clarity with which it is discussed and the sincerity of the purpose of the men that you are going to listen to.

We do not come to meetings like this for amusement. Ther[e] are things more amusing. We do not come for entertainment; we do not expect to be entertained. We come to hold council together upon the most serious matters of our public welfare. Let us do so, therefore, and find out what it is that we are about.

Now, I take leave to believe that there is one singular question that underlies all the other questions that are discussed on the political platform at the present moment. That singular circumstance is that nothing is done in this country as it was done twenty years ago.

The old party platforms of twenty years ago read like documents taken out of a forgotten age. We are in the presence of a new organization of society. We are eagerly bent on fitting that new organization, as we did once fit the old organization, to the happiness and prosperity of the great body of citizens; for we are conscious that that order of society does not fit and provide the convenience or happiness or prosperity of the average man.

We are not legislating in this country for exceptional men; we are not legislating for the rich; we are not legislating for the poor; we are not legislating for any class. We are trying to find out what is for the common interests of every living soul, providing he lives honestly and strives honorably in the profession to which he has devoted himself. America does not consist of the men who get their names in the newspapers; America dose [does] not consist politically of the men who set themselves to be political leaders. America does not consist of the men who talk and speak for her—and they are important only so far as they speak for that great voiceless multitude of men who constitute the great body and the saving force of the nation.

Nobody who cannot speak of the common thought, who cannot move the common impulse, is any man to speak for America or for any of her future purposes. So, we seek to conform all the policies of this country to this great body of American citizens, the men who go about their business every day, the men who toil from morning to night, the men who go home tired in the evenings—too tired to think about things sometimes, the men who are carrying on that thing that we are proud of.

You know how it thrills our blood sometimes to see how all the nations of the earth wait to see what America is going to do with her power—her enormous resources, her enormous wealth, her power to levy innumerable armies and build up armaments which might conquer the world. And the nations hold their breath to see what this still young country will do with her young unspoiled strength; and we are proud that we are strong.

But what has made us strong? The toil of millions of men, the toil of men who do not boast, who are inconspicuous, but who live their lives humbly from day to day, and this great body of workers, this great body of toilers, constitute the might of America.

What is the manifest duty of all statesmanship, therefore? It is to see that this great body of men who constitute the strength of America are properly dealt with by the laws and properly nurtured and taken care of by the policy of the country.

Well, what hinders? What stands in the way? Why, you know that everything really worth discussing comes to the question of the corporations. Now, I do not want you to expect from me any invective against the corporation. I was bred a lawyer, but I do not know how to draw up an indictment against a whole nation. If you will give me the facts I will indict one man at a time.

There are some men, who, I admit, it would be a great pleasure to indict upon some proper occasion. I may name them just for the pleasure of naming them and then put it up to them whether they will stand trial or not, but I am not going to indict my fellow-citizens, who are conducting business. I am not going to utter invectives against the modern instrumentalities of business, but to discuss the improper and unfortunate uses to which these instrumentalities have been put.

Everything comes down to that—what is the matter with the tariff? That is a long story and there is a great deal the matter with it.

If you go through the tariff schedule you will find some "nigger" in every woodpile, some little word put into almost every clause of the act which is lining somebody's pocket with money, but that is too long a story and too complicated for one evening.

The main trouble is that it has been an ambush, a covert, a forest in which all men who wanted to get illegitimate profit have been able to get it. So that the tariff question is not a question of individual manipulation, but a question of what has been exemplified in building up the Sugar Trust, and in building up the American Tobacco Company; what part the tariff has had in building up this, that and the other concern[s] which could not have been built up in that fashion if it had not been for the protection afforded by that legislation.

I am not objecting to the size of these enterprises. Nothing is big enough to scare me. I am not objecting to the extent of the business, and last of all I am not objecting to the people getting rich from conducting business with prudence, but what I am objecting to is that the government should give them exceptional advantages which enables them to succeed and does not put them on the same footing as other people.

Of course, size has something to do with that. I think those great touring cars, for example, which are lab[e]led "Seeing New York" are too big for the streets. You have to walk almost around the block to get out of the way of them, and size has a great deal to do with the trouble if you are trying to get out of the way. But I have no objection on that account to the ordinary automobile properly handled by a man of conscience who is also a gentleman. Many of the people I see handling automobiles handle them as if they had neither conscience nor manners. I have no objection to the size and beauty and power of the automobile. I am interested, however, in the size and conscience of the men who handle them, and what I object to is that some of these corporation men are taking joy rides in their corporations.

You know what men do when they take a joy ride; they sometimes have the time of their lives and sometimes, fortunately, the last time of their lives. Now these wretched things are taking joy rides in which they don't kill the people that are riding in them, but they kill the people they run over. So the tariff has to do with corporations. Corporations have to do also with all those things I have discussed in the platform of our party.

The Public Service Commission is set up because we find corporations that are called railways or street railways or gas companies or water companies are getting so big that we don't know how to control them, and know that they ought to be controlled in some way and their service regulated to the convenience of the public right, with just compensation for their efforts.

We ought to set up a commission to govern. To govern what? Why, to govern the great aggregations of capital that we call the corporations. I am entirely in favor of that; I think it absolutely necessary.

I think that such a commission ought to be set up and given the fullest power possible.

I think our present commission[2] is entirely harmless; I have

2 The New Jersey legislature in 1907 had created a Railroad Commission; however, it had no authority to determine railroad rates and no jurisdiction over public service corporations. In March 1910, as a result of continued agitation, the legislature passed a bill which, while retaining the existing Railroad Commission, changed its name to the Board of Public Utilities Commissioners and

no objection to the members of that commission amusing themselves by drawing their salaries. But the real objection is, as the Scot[s]man said, it doesn't set us any forwarder; we don't get anything from it except a lot of very interesting opinions. In fact, I am receiving a salary, for that matter; I am just as prolific as the commission. My own opinion and personal objection is that I cannot get people to pay for them.

This commission I speak of ought to have power to put their notions into force, because their notions concern us. We know how to regulate, but the fact is that New Jersey is lagging away behind the procession. There is nothing difficult, nothing complicated or nothing impossible about it, but that is a corporate question. Sooner or later the question of taxation must be settled. I believe it is the fact that in this State corporations are not equally taxed. Now, that is a very complicated question. I believe that is true, but it will take a long time to find out about it, and when we do find out about it, we will make the thing equal.

Competition is being done away with. You are still in the personal modern organization of business; not one bit of legislation has been passed to meet these essential circumstances. What are we going to do then? Why, you know what a corporation is. It is in the terms of the lawyer, an artificial person. The law gives it the right to hold property, to bring suits, also to sue and be sued, notwithstanding that the individuals who compose it change and the officers are not always the same; whereas, an individual's business ceases with his death or incapacity. But they are regulated by statute, and statute can do anything that it pleases with them, therefore, but that statute cannot do anything it pleases with me; it cannot say that my liver has to work this way or that; it cannot go inside of me and arrange this dreadful and vital arrangement which surgeons are so curiously anxious sometimes to explore, or to do anything on the inside of me.

You can do anything you please with the inside or outside of a corporation, and because a corporation is given a tremendous advantage in the conduct of its business and a tremendous convenience, the law can impose any kind of taxes it pleases. If this same body of men is given personally the same conveniences to conduct business, then it is perfectly fair to tax them for the full value of that privilege which they enjoy. So the corporation

---

extended its jurisdiction to other utilities. However, the board still had no power to fix rates or make physical valuations and had no adequate power to enforce its orders. See Ransom E. Noble, Jr., *New Jersey Progressivism before Wilson* (Princeton, N. J., 1946), pp. 100-104, 112.

is specially favored in regard to its taxation in its very character and existence.

I was born with a certain arrangement that passes for the operation of the brain, or a good working imitation, but I am not indebted to any lawmaker for that. Nobody gave me leave to exercise its powers. Therefore, it is not fair to tax one man more than another, because perchance, he has greater capacity of thought. But it is perfectly fair to tax people for anything you give them in the way of prosperity. That is the reason you can tax them for the privileges which the law affords them, in order that they may be able to support the other law which enables them to do those things. That is the principle of taxation.

Now, all of this leads to one conclusion. I have said, and I do not believe that it can be contradicted successfully, that legislation in recent years has not met the difficulty. If you make a law about something that I am concerned in and I do not know whether that law is going to hit me personally or not, I will take the chance and do as I please. But if I do wrong the minute it is discovered I will catch it then. So that I am going to be a very respectable citizen.

The trouble with all legislation in regard to corporations is that in respect of our punishments we treat them as persons, like individuals, and they are not persons, they are not individuals.

Don't you know that it is true that everything any corporation does was originated by some person in particular, or some body of persons, some board of directors, or some officer or some employee of a corporation? Do you suppose that there is any corporation whose business is so badly handled that the officers of the corporation could not tell you who originated any particular act of the corporation? If there is such a corporation, it is on the verge of bankruptcy, and if the officers who ordered the thing done don't know who did it, then they don't know their business. They do know who ordered it done, and the man who ordered it done is the man the law ought to punish.

I said just now that I am not jealous of the power and speed of the automobile, but I am very critical of the man sitting at the wheel. I am not critical of corporations so long as they conduct their business honestly, but I am very critical of the men at the wheel. And we know there are individuals—we sometimes actually know their names—who go scot free when the stockholders of their corporations are fined for the things they do.

Look what a corporation is! It affords you an opportunity to put your money into a thing that you could not do by yourself.

Here is some big undertaking which you have not the money to carry on individually, but here are its stocks and bonds for sale, and by putting your money into them you can share in the profits of the big business which they do, which you could not do individually with the money that you put into those stocks and bonds, and so hundreds of thousands of men put their money together until in the aggregate it makes a vast sum, and thus we find small groups of men conducting the corporations with this money.

The man who misuses a corporation is the man who misuses you and your investment; it is not fair when he misuses your money to punish you and not to punish him.

I told you a moment ago that I was bred as a lawyer, and yet I must smile at the apparent innocence of some lawyers. I have seen small trials dragged out for a week to determine whether a man was guilty or not when he was not guilty, when every man in the case knew he was not guilty and knew he was not under indictment, knew that he was outside of the corporation altogether: that because he controlled a group of corporations or was of great influential power he could use these corporations just as you use a pawn in a game of chess. They knew what his name was, but they went around with dark spectacles and said they did not see anybody. Well, that is not the fault of the lawyers; it is the fault of the law; the law wears the dark spectacle.

Now the point is we must change the law in order that we may do the remarkable thing of finding the man who really is guilty. Don't let's go around then, barking up the wrong tree; don't let's go put up the bars after the animal has left long ago; let's get down to business in the regulation of our corporations and find out what we do want and then do it. Then, when we find somebody that has done that thing that he ought not to do, even though he was authorized to do it by the corporation, put him into jail. Our jails are used to a great advantage, but the philanthropy might be extended; the moralizing effect of the jail ought not to be withheld from certain classes of the community.

I am not saying all this in any spirit of vindictiveness, for I honestly believe that most of these men have simply been using a great system without thinking thay [they] were crushing and doing an injustice to their fellow men.

I know a great many men who do things that are wrong who, I am perfectly convinced, do not see the wrong; therefore, I am not going to be hypocritical enough to criticise them personally, but the law ought to take the scales from their eyes; the law ought to say who are going to do these things for which they are responsible.

Now, all those difficult questions cannot be handled in any kind of detail before a vast audience like this; therefore, I can only speak generally of the general idea that underlies it all.

We are tired of seeing legislation in favor of special interests and want legislation for the general interests. When I say that we are tired, I mean that the American people are tired, and they are going to show it in the next decade in a way that will make some gentlemen's heads swim.

I was told today that I had disappointed one of my audiences because I had not given fits to the Republican party. [The Republican party] as a whole consists of a very large body of our fellow citizens, and I do not know how to give fits to a very large body of our fellow citizens. But I am perfectly willing to tell those very fellow citizens how they are being led and who they are being led by. They have been led in a way that is deserving of condemnation, and the best proof of that is that a very large section of their party is telling them so.

A friend of mine was walking down the street in Wilkesbarre, Pa., one day with two friends of his, who were lawyers, in very earnest conversation, and he asked one of them, "What are you talking about?" He replied, "We are discussing who is the leader of the Lucerne County bar." "Why," the other said, "I am." "How do you prove it?" he was asked. He replied, "Why, I don't have to prove it; I admit it."

Now that is the case with the Republican party; it admits it, and I am not going to jump on the poor thing when it is down. Since it is going all over the country saying, "We have sinned and done wrong in thy sight," I am not going to jump on it; I am going to say, "All right; come over and we will show you how." And I believe honestly that we can show them how to do it. For one thing, we have been out of business a good while and have had time to think about it, and not being too close to the matter we have held it off at arm's length and studied its proportion. Moreover, we are not embarrassed; we are not split up into warring factions in the Democratic party; we are all standing together; whereas they are reading each other out of the different sections of their party. And that is a very demoralizing process. Each part of it is trying to lead the other part of it out of business. Therefore it is bankrupt as a party; they must have somebody to take it over, and now we intend to act as receiver. We don't have to ask for any order of the court; we will leave it to the jury.

Why should a man try to persuade his fellow citizens that he is a fit man to serve them? It is a very immodest part to take. No man with any sense of proportion—no man with any sense of any kind—could stand up and pose as the savior of his fellow citizens. He would go away with a permanent bad taste in his mouth for having made such an unfathomable ass of himself.

But it is perfectly worthy and perfectly dignified to stand up and say: "Gentlemen, let us all get together and try to understand our common interest." Because we are not working for today; we are not working for our own interests; we are all going to pass away. But think what is involved. Here are the traditions and the fame and the prosperity and the purity and the peace of a great nation involved. For the time being we are that nation, but the generations that are behind us are pointing us forward to the path and saying, "Remember the great traditions of the American people." And all those unborn children that will constitute the generations ahead of us will look back at us, either as those who served them or as those who betrayed them.

Will any man in such circumstances think it worthy to stand and not try to do what is possible in so great a cause to save a country, to purify a polity, to set up vast reforms which will increase the happiness of mankind? God forbid that I should be either daunted or turned away from a great task like that!

FPS T transcript (WP, DLC) with corrections and additions from the partial text in the *Newark Evening News*, Oct. 1, 1910.

From Franklin Murphy

My dear Doctor Wilson: Newark, New Jersey Sept. 30th, 1910.

If I have not sooner sent you a word of congratulation on your nomination for Governor, it is not because I have not rejoiced that you have been willing to leave the tranquil shades of the scholarly and enter the turmoil of the politician—always interesting, sometimes absorbing, and never dull. Frequently rewarding devotion and sacrifice with a lemon, and occasionally with a few leaves of laurel that we receive with a gentle feeling of content, for then we know that the Country has recognized a statesman and a patriot.

Your nomination weakens a little my Republican confidence in the Democratic Party to do the wrong thing, but it is well for the Nation when men like you are willing to stand up in an emergency and say "here I am!"

Sincerely yours,   Franklin Murphy

TLS (WP, DLC).

From William Hughes

My dear Doctor Wilson: Paterson, N. J., September 30, 1910.

Permit me to thank you for your congratulations upon my re-nomination, and to thank you for your good wishes. I hope to have the pleasure of meeting you many times during the campaign, and want you to feel that if there is any way in which I can promote your interests that you have only to call upon me.
                    Sincerely yours,   Wm. Hughes

TLS (WP, DLC).

From Eugene Francis Kinkead

My dear Doctor: [Jersey City, N. J.] September 30, 1910

Thank you very much for your good letter of congratulation of the 28th instant. I know that your nomination will mean a great deal in my district towards rolling up a big Democratic vote. I want you to feel that I am at your service at any time that you think I could help you during the campaign.
                    Sincerely yours,   E. F. Kinkead

TLS (WP, DLC).

A Campaign Speech in Red Bank, New Jersey[1]

[[Oct. 1, 1910]]

I have one pleasure in being late, and that is that it afforded you an opportunity of hearing my friend Mr. Katzenbach. It is a great pleasure for me, ladies and gentlemen, to appear before you, not because it affords me satisfaction alone for my own personal selection [delectation], but because every issue that presents itself in this campaign must be left to the sober judgment of the voters of the country.

I believe the American people know of the very difficult problems they are to solve and that they will solve them with soberness and deliberation. They see what is happening all over the country. The man you have just elected as your congressional candidate[2] is an admirable selection, the selection of a man with whom I really deem it a distinct pleasure to be on the ticket.

What is the battle we are fighting? What are we fighting for? Well, you know; there has been a long history of administration

---

[1] Delivered in the Frick Lyceum.
[2] Thomas Joseph Scully, Mayor of South Amboy, N. J., and president of the Scully Towing and Transportation Co. He was elected.

of the Republican party in this state, and all over the country. Not, I want always to say, because the Republican voters were less public-spirited and patriotic than the Democratic voters, but because the Republican leaders have been to blame for the new policies they have followed. You know the traditional history of the Republican party, and the trouble is that they have become so traditional that the time has come when the only thing they can do is to stand pat. They have so lost their originality and the power of adaptation that they have nothing new to-day, and all the older men whom I need not name, who have controlled their party in the last few years, are standing still.

Now, we are not standing still and we cannot stand still. If these gentlemen do not know that the country is moving and moving fast, it is time that they wake up and find out. We cannot stand still. You know that one branch of the Republican party[3] is now fighting for control of this state. There are two branches of the Republican party in this state, but one branch is not Republican to hurt and the other branch[4] is so intensely Republican that it has forgotten the movement of the calendar and doesn't know what year it is. It is still moving along in those halcyon days when the high tariff was invented, the time when the country supposed that the Democratic party stood for reaction and chaos.

But those days have long gone by; we have proved that the Democratic party has moved faster and in a better direction than the Republican party, so we are gathered here to discuss this simple question and the things we desire done.

You know what happens to a party long in power; they cannot be long in power without forming all sorts of complicated associations, and one of the complicated questions that perplexes us to-day is a thing like a tariff. They have tied strings to every industry in the country. Every industry in the country is saying "We are depending on you to see that our business don't suffer." And it says, "All right, you may depend on us; you have always depended on us and you can continue to depend on us."

It is because the Republican party has tied itself up, and perhaps in honor, to those associations that it cannot be expected reasonably to break with them.

I have always been opposed to the policy of protection, but, be that as it may, there are some things that may be said in favor of the protective policy, and, historically speaking, the protective tariff has not in the past very greatly increased the cost of living.

---

[3] The New Idea progressive Republicans.
[4] The regular organization Republicans.

But in recent years and months it has greatly increased the cost of living. Why? Because it is a protective policy? No, not especially that, but because the wall of protection has been so high that the great domestic industries have been able to form great combinations behind them, knowing that anybody with whom they could not come to an understanding would break in and hurt the game, and so they have been able to limit the product and increase the price.

Now look at what the Republican party has done in the so-called revision of the tariff. The only thing that it has done is to change the tariff, and that is the only way they have revised the tariff. It is like the woman who, when she changes her good overdress, works the seams different so that she has, as she thinks, revised the dress; but it is the same old dress, the domestic circle at any rate is not deceived by it.

Now, this is the same old tariff adjusted, not in accordance with the demands of the nation, not at all. I believe that the tariff of to-day was made in Rhode Island,[5] and there is a certain gentleman whose name is well-known, who lives in Illinois,[6] who co-operated in standardizing this fashion. So it is not the American people, but it is the dictates of the pattern bureau that patterns the fashion of the tariff. And what are the standards of these gentlemen in Rhode Island and Illinois?

Do you know that the Republican party undertakes to guarantee profits to the industries of this country? Do you know what that means? It means that the poorest factories are drawn in with the best, that the least economically managed factories are united with the most economically managed, and that a level is struck, so they will all make a profit. And that is another premium offered in this country on the system these gentlemen have fashioned.

I was interested, for example, not personally, though I am to a slight extent interested, in the hosiery scale. We all know that man's interest in that is very brief. But I was interested because I had a number of friends engaged in manufacturing stockings and half hose of all qualities, all of which I don't know much about, and there was one concern that had been looking forward to a probable revision of the tariff, and got its business in such shape that it could afford to have free trade under ordinary conditions, because they had the sense to take their employes in to share the profits of the business; and there were profits to share.

[5] By Senator Nelson Wilmarth Aldrich, chairman of the Senate Finance Committee.
[6] Joseph Gurney Cannon, Speaker of the House of Representatives.

Now these gentlemen were ready to see the duty taken off of stockings because they had had the sense to get ready for it. But the other men were not because that tariff wall was there, and they knew their profits would be cut off because they could not make stockings as good as they could make them in Germany. That's the reason.

One summer when I was abroad, for example, I got some socks in the town of Aberdeen, Scotland, and those miserable things never yet have worn out; I am tired of them; the color didn't suit me to begin with. But the American socks I have bought within the time, I have worn out so fast that the household is constantly employed in darning them. Now that is not because Americans do not know how to make stockings and have not the stuff to make them of, but because they do not have to make that sort because of the policy of the country. That is the reason.

You know that the farmer has been made to take care of himself; he was abundantly able and he has always taken care of himself. The other industries of the country have been assured of the profits and the farmer has been helping to assure the profits of the other fellow. I say that there was enough and to spare and they could do it, but the real stuff upon which this country has prospered is its great soil and the intelligent men who till it, and the great advantage of this country has been that its soil was fertile and that it was inexhaustible in its other sources.

I do not begrudge the assistance, because I believe in my heart, opposed though I am to the protective system now, that the protective system was necessary. It was necessary to build up those infant industries that have met with such a coarse growth and have grown to such eminent manhood. We have at last come to the point that we must ask ourselves have we had enough of this? Are you going to stand about and forget all about these changes? Are we going to alter the policy? Are we going to get things done on a business basis and serve the common interests of everyone?

Men are making a cover of the tariff and a cover of the corporations, so all the men that we want to get out of control are covered. Now we have got to organize a great hunt; we have got to find their burrows and smoke them out. I am not interested in the burrow; I am interested in the animal that is in it.

You know the story of the Irishman who went to digging a hole and he was asked, "Pat, what are you doing, digging a hole?" And he replied, "No, sir; I am digging the earth and leaving the hole." It is also like the same Irishman that was digging around the wall of a house, was asked, "Pat, what are you doing?" And he answered, "Faith, I am letting the dark out of the cellar."

Now that's exactly what we want to do, let the dark out of the cellar. We want to discover the persons who are responsible and make them know that this country is for the people, and not for a party standing for corporations and trusts. Now that can be done. You say how? Well, I know lawyers by the score who know how. They haven't said how, but they know exactly what is going on and they could produce the man. Now let us give our lawyers some inducement to help us out with their advice.

I once asked a learned Judge if the object of the Courts was to do justice, and he said, "God forbid. The object of the Courts is to follow precedent." He said that if the object was to do justice they would get in the most terrible confusion, so they have to follow the lines that have been laid down. Now there is a great deal to be said on that. Therefore, in order to break it up you must better it from the outside, not from the inside. That is the reason we have had to have so much legislation to alter the law and the jury to determine the alteration of the law.

You know the great Italian writer, Dante, wrote a great poem on Hell, and in it he described a great many persons who were there, but the interesting part of it was that he described a great many persons as already in Hell who were yet living. Thus illustrating what I have ever believed to be true, that all a man's Hell is with him while he lives.

I cannot prove that the Democratic party would have done something if it had the power, because it has not been in power, but I don't have to prove that the Republican party has done nothing, because everybody knows it.

Now, if I had one riding horse that did not suit me and I was offered another, I would at least take the chance at the other horse.

And we are not crossing a stream either. You can swap horses; it is perfectly safe to swap horses; all the conditions are very favorable for the swapping of horses, and the question you want to answer for yourselves is which horse is the better horse?

I have nothing personal against the Republican party. I had the pleasure the other day of meeting my Republican opponent at the great Trenton Fair, merely for exhibition purposes. I was pleased with him and I am sure he is a very estimable gentleman. I have been informed that he has a good deal the best of me in looks. Now, it is not always the most useful horse that is most beautiful. If I had a big load to be drawn some distance I should select one of those big, shaggy kind of horses, not much for beauty, but strong of pull. So it is not a question, I hope, of looks; I hope it is a question of serviceability. And I hope it is not a question between individuals. It would distress me very much to think it was. It is that plus the backing you have got, and I have already pointed out to you that the backing that the other candidate has is the backing of the stand-pat element of the Republican party.

Do you want to stand pat? Do you want to stand still? Do you want all the things that have been safeguarded against or do you want to do what is so characteristic of the American people—to turn bravely about? There are some people to whom a little change always brings things that are not beneficial. But we are a marked race, a marked people among the people of the world. We did not start out merely to be rich, we did not start out merely to show what material power we could build up, what armies we could recruit and what navies we could put afloat. We did not start out to show the world how those things that the world has always been doing could be done over again upon a slightly larger scale. That does not satisfy our ambition. That is not what America is for. America set out to show the nations of the world an example of justice and of a people made happy by fair and equal laws. That is what we started out to do. Our object was not the profits of the rich man but the welfare of the poor man, the welfare of the ordinary man. Let others say: "You may believe it is possible to have nothing but the deep valleys of sorrow,["] but we believe that we can lead to a place where there may be the high tablelands of the common enjoyments of the benefit of law and of the fruits of the earth, where the air is full of honey for every man, and every man may go happy and peaceful to his bed at night. Shall we give up the search for these uplands which we set out to discover? Shall we depress some of our fellowmen into those dark valleys of distress and let the others walk the sunlit heights, or shall we persist in believing as I do believe that these uplands are just ahead of us;· that a little courage, a little persistence, a little faith, a little self-sacrifice, will presently allow us to debouch like a great army upon that land of promise?[7]

Printed in the *Freehold*, N. J., *Transcript*, Oct. 7, 1910, with additions and corrections from the partial texts in the *Philadelphia Record*, Oct. 2, 1910, and the Jersey City *Jersey Journal*, Oct. 3, 1910.

[7] Upon finishing this address, Wilson went to nearby Long Branch, where he spoke in the evening. A news report of this address is printed at Oct. 3, 1910.

From Henry Eckert Alexander

Dear Mr. Wilson: [Trenton, N. J., c. Oct. 1, 1910]

I enclose the pledge made by Lewis as to his conduct if elected.[1] I think that you should read that pledge to your audience and then declare that you do no[t] wish any one to vote for you who agrees with Mr. Lewis, because if *you* people (address them directly in second person) elect me as your Governor and bring me to Trenton to serve you, I pledge myself to do precisely what Mr. Lewis says that he will not do.

Criticise his position freely and declare that in taking this view Mr. Lewis is mistaken when he asserts that he is forbidden by the *constitution* to fight for *you* people, in seeking for instance, to have the elected legislature redeem party platform pledges. It is not the constitution that forbids Mr. Lewis, it is the bosses who prefer for him to remain inactive while they do the business, it is the *Board of Guardians*,[2] (correct designation) that remarkable body of leading Republican machine politicians who are not provided for by New Jersey's constitution and yet who invaded Trenton to enforce their demands on a subservient legislature.

If elected and your interests are threatened by failure of legislature to redeem pledges, I intend not to sit inactive by by [but] I intend to take off my coat and roll up my sleeves and use all the power that you people have voted to me and to use all the strength that God has given me to defend your rights, and I will appeal to *you* people to help me, etc.

In your reference to corrupt practices, you should praise Mercer County Democrats for taking initiative. They deserve praise, and on that platform they elected Mad[d]en and Berrien[3] to city offices and won a sweeping victory in the city of Trenton.[4] Hoff can tell you about this.

Please refer to denunciation of Aldrich-Cannon tariff by Republicans—Cummins, Dolliver, Beveridge, Fowler, et all.[5]

You must be the spokesmen for people in denouncing these wrongs under which they *suffer now.*

Hastily   H. E. Alexander

ALS (WP, DLC).
[1] Lewis's pledge, made in his speech accepting the Republican gubernatorial nomination on September 20, 1910, follows:

"Aside from the suggestion by message of measures to the Legislature and the right to compel, by veto, the reconsideration of legislation already passed, the Governor has no right or power to interfere with the representatives of the people in the exercise of their exclusive right to make the laws under which we live. If elected I shall enter the executive chamber with a firm purpose of observing the constitutional limitations placed upon the authority of the Governor's position. I shall conscientiously perform the duty laid upon the Executive of recommending to the Legislature, as forcibly as I may be able, such measures as in my judgment may be necessary for the welfare of the State, and shall, if occasion seems to demand, exercise without hesitancy the right by veto; but, aside from these constitutional methods, if the people of New Jersey see fit to indorse your choice of a Governor, there will be no executive interference with the work of the Legislature. The power incident to the Governor's office will never be used to coerce the Legislature into subordinating its judgment to my own. The law-making power will remain where it has been placed by the organic law of the State—in the hands of the elected representatives of the people." *Newark Evening News*, Sept. 21, 1910.

² The "Board of Guardians" was the opprobrious title given by the liberal New Jersey press to the conservatives who controlled the executive committee of the Republican State Committee. The term was first used in early 1909 during the administration of Governor John Franklin Fort, who began to espouse some of the programs of the New Idea wing of the Republican party. The state committee instructed the executive committee to render "assistance" to the legislators in considering Fort's proposals, and, as one historian has put it, the group became "the perfect symbol of reaction." The most prominent and powerful members of the "Board of Guardians" were Franklin Murphy; Senator Frank Obadiah Briggs, chairman of the executive committee and assistant treasurer of the Trenton wire manufacturing concern of John A. Roebling's Sons Co.; Senator John Kean; Edward Casper Stokes; and David Baird of Camden, powerful South Jersey political boss, wealthy lumber manufacturer, president of the First National Bank of Camden, and United States senator, 1918-19. See Noble, *New Jersey Progressivism before Wilson*, pp. 108-109.

³ Andrew J. Berrien, Receiver of Taxes for the City of Trenton.

⁴ In the municipal election of 1909.

⁵ Albert Baird Cummins, United States senator from Iowa since 1908; Jonathan Prentiss Dolliver, United States senator from Iowa since 1900; Albert Jeremiah Beveridge, United States senator from Indiana since 1899; and Charles Newell Fowler, United States representative from the 5th congressional district of New Jersey, which included Elizabeth.

An Interview[1]

[Oct. 2, 1910]

WHO WOODROW WILSON IS; WHAT HE STANDS FOR

. . . Dr. Wilson is five feet eleven. He stands squarely and solidly, with the strength of an iron column. His face embodies this idea of strength, and concentrates and intensifies it. It is long and narrow, but the brow is broad and high, and the whole cranium is cast in a large mould.

The visage is what catches and holds the attention of any beholder. It has habitually an expression of seriousness, but relaxes often into the well-known glance over the top rims of his noseglasses—a glance penetrating, sagacious, thoughtful.

When you look at the face in profile it is decidedly aquiline. The nose is large. The mouth is large and full-lipped, but drawn into a straight, firm line. When he smiles he shows fine, large teeth. The eyes are blue-gray, clear and penetrating, undimmed by the glasses. His complexion is brown, the color of tan over a

---

[1] The author of this interview was Charles Reade Bacon, then a reporter for and later editor of the *Philadelphia Record*. Bacon followed Wilson throughout the entire campaign and in 1912 published his dispatches to the *Record* as *A People Awakened: The Story of Woodrow Wilson's First Campaign* . . . (Garden City, N. Y., 1912).

healthy skin. He has brown hair, a little sparse and tinged with gray.

His hand is big, and he has a hard grip when he greets you. His voice is baritone, mellow, manly and sympathetic. He is well-groomed, his appearance suggesting the Southern gentleman. He usually wears a gray suit and a brown Fedora hat, and looks more like a man of affairs than a scholar and university president. He neither drinks nor smokes.

When he walks he has a vigorous, quick, firm tread. It is the very walk of the man of purpose who has work to do and is doing it, using every minute and still not giving any appearance of breathless, precipitate haste.

He is a man who attracts attention wherever he goes, because of the elusive, subtle characteristic which denotes that here is something more than the average. There is certainly no trace of ostentation in his bearing or any consciousness of self. He prefers to go about unnoticed, as do all busy men with real work to do. . . .

I was somewhat surprised, during my visit to Dr. Wilson, at Princeton, for "The Record," when he refused to give utterance to any expression of opinion on national affairs. Largely from curiosity, and also because I saw the news value of such expressions, I had prepared a rather formidable lot of subjects, such, for instance, as immigration, conservation, Cannonism, the referendum, etc., etc. With a half-bewildered glance, as if to question whether I really meant it or not, he paused, turned toward me, and, with his characteristically illuminating smile and a deprecatory wave of the hand, said:

"Please excuse me! I have strong convictions as to what constitutes legitimate methods on the part of a candidate. It is undoubtedly true that an expression of opinion on my part on the topics which you have suggested to me would have a peculiar advertising value; but I do not care to be advertised in that way.

"I am a candidate, I have been nominated by the Democratic party for the Governorship of the State of New Jersey; and I shall take my stand firmly upon State issues. I should feel it unworthy of myself and undignified to express myself upon issues other than State issues at this time. I am persuaded that I have a logical method of procedure in what I undertake, and I believe in handling each difficulty as it presents itself, one at a time. Now, I am not at present in a position to do anything whatsoever toward the solution of the great national problems of Government and administration which confront us.

"It is a waste of time and energy to go about the wholesale reform of institutions which have reached their present proportions through a process of normal growth. It is a difficult matter to remove any existing evil without placing an equivalent good in its place. There are certain public evils existing in the State of New Jersey, but I am not one of those who see in the great corporations an unmitigated evil and who would extirpate them entirely root and branch; to do so would be to put society back 100 years. I do not believe in abusing everything that I do not agree with. It is my experience that real reform has often been impeded by over-zealousness on the part of so-called reformers; in their attempts to bring about reforms they have tried to dragoon the legislators. I do not call into question the good motives of those who would reform society at a stroke, but I do question their good sense. Human institutions are the result of growth and progressive development. There have been periods of arrested development when, for the time being, society has perhaps appeared to stand still and merely mark time. I believe that the evils of the time are often magnified in order to advertise one's self.

"Now don't you see how unworthy, how undignified, it would be on my part to express myself on questions which have no bearing upon the present campaign? I have learned a great deal in the course of my life, especially in the last few years. I find that one who is ready to air his views on every subject without provocation gives the impression that he is frothy and dissatisfied with life. I am a thorough-going optimist; and I venture to hope as level-headed and as satisfied with life as any man has a right to be. While there is much that doesn't square with my views of things, I believe thoroughly in the good sense and good feeling of the average American citizen. He may make mistakes, he may fall behind false leaders, but he is quick to see his errors and quick to forsake those who have betrayed him. He means to do the right thing and, when he is given the opportunity he does it.

"We are living in a period of extraordinary enlightenment on economic, social and political subjects. The time has gone by when it is possible to fool the majority of the people for any length of time. For 20 years now I have been speaking all over the country—as a private citizen discussing public questions—and it is my conviction that politics are cleaner to-day than ever before in the history of the country. This is due in large measure to the thoroughly practical manner in which political and social sciences are taught in our schools and universities. The young blood of the country has been aroused to see the value of citizenship, and it is no longer a difficult matter to induce young men of the highest intellectual attainments and moral responsibility to enter upon a political career. It has been discovered by the young man of to-day that the sure road to political preferment is to go firmly on record as a fighter of abuses."

"Do you believe government by party is a good thing?"

"Party government is necessary," he replied. "The unanswerable argument for it is that under it everybody's power is precarious. In effect, men can hold office only during good behavior. Those in power must 'make good' all the time. I am not inclined to believe that the present widespread eruption within the ranks of the Republican party means the final disruption of that party. I do not think that a new party will rise upon its ruins. One wing or the other will triumph in the test of strength, and that faction of the party coming out on top will fall heir to the party name and the party organization. It is no longer necessary to form a new party in the effort to escape from the odium, more or less deserved, which attaches to the record of a party. It is a distinct step in advance that political parties, as well as individuals, are expected to 'make good' now. It is possible to live down the follies of the past without emigrating to a distant part of the country.

"You ask me why I am a Democrat? Whether I came by my Democracy through inheritance or through conviction? I answer—'both.' My father and my father's father were stanch Democrats, but that is no argument for my Democracy. I am a Democrat by conviction because I am persuaded that it is the party through which the salvation of the country must come. The Republican party has been guilty of forming an unholy alliance with the vast moneyed interests of the country. It is true that so long as there is life in a man he may repent and turn from his wicked ways, but it is far better if a man has formed no evil habits and is not a fit subject for repentance. Now the Democratic party, while it has undoubtedly made its mistakes, has not formed any evil habits. I will go so far as to say that it might have formed the same set of evil habits under the burden of which the Republican party is struggling to-day, but it so happened that Providence in its wisdom directed that the Democratic party should be reserved for a great task. If the Democratic party had been so fortunate as to be in control of the mechanism of Government during the time which the great corporations were growing up and amassing such colossal wealth and exercising such tremendous power, it is possible that it might have been corrupted."

When questioned as to how he came to be made the nominee

of the Democratic party in the State of New Jersey, Dr. Wilson said, with a touch of feeling and a kind of dramatic power that thrilled: "It is really a most extraordinary thing. I had no idea whatsoever that I was to be made the nominee, and the most extraordinary part of it is that there was no intimation at any time of controlling me, in case I should be elected; not only am I absolutely free from any promise, but no promise was asked of me and no influence was brought to bear upon me. That, to me, is of itself most gratifying. I regard it as a distinct recognition of my integrity. This is as it should be. The man who is selected by a party to be its standard-bearer should be so well known for his honesty and incorruptibility that to demand a pledge of him should be regarded as unnecessary. Every candidate for public office should be absolutely above reproach, he should be a man of deep convictions on public questions and he should have the strength of character to stand by those convictions, so long as he believes he is right."

Dr. Wilson's surprise at his nomination was evidently genuine and he was clearly interested in examining the new experiences it had already brought to him.

"During the first week after the nomination," said he, "I received letters at the rate of 150 a day and I answered them all. This somewhat crowded me, for while I do not write out all I have to say in lecturing or making addresses, I devote considerable time to getting it into shape in my head and committing at least some of it to memory."

Concerning many of the questions now involved in New Jersey's political situation, the doctor begged to be excused from making extended comment, and the point he raised in asking for such consideration revealed a fine sense of honor.

"I have the feeling," he said, "that my constituents should be the first to hear and they should hear from my own lips what I have to say on all those State affairs which are to be elucidated from the platform. It is fairer to me, too. A loose and piece-meal expression of only part of my views on questions which are of grave moment would create false inferences. I do not believe in doing anything by halves and a disconnected sentence here and there apart from all that explains it or causes it to be uttered conveys no adequate expression of one's meaning.

"I shall, of course, attack some of the evils under which the State struggles, but I shall attack the system rather than the man in every case. Of course, if that system corrupts the individual and makes him culpable I believe punishment should be visited upon the individual."

The Doctor heartily approves of the proposed ship canal across New Jersey. "I shall do all in my power," he said, "to further the project, and I shall be very glad to see the Atlantic flowing across the middle of the State and joining hands with the Delaware River above Philadelphia."

When it came to submitting to "The Record" photographer Dr. Wilson was manifestly disinclined, and again showed that his candidacy was bringing unusual experiences. He humorously excused his own reluctance, and that of the other members of his family, on the plea that it was "so sudden." "We have been jealous of our privacy," he said, "and we are so used to being unphotographed that it has got to be a habit. I do not think that I had been photographed more than twice in my life before this nomination."

Naturally this brought forth an inquiry as to earlier photographs, and Dr. Wilson was quite sure that none were in existence. With a twinkle in his eye, he accounted for this on the theory of heredity, saying that his mother had also always had a disinclination for pictorial publicity and had doubtless not preserved any earlier pictures.

Here, however, when appealed to, Mrs. Wilson came to the rescue. She remembered and finally produced a photograph of the Doctor when he was 22 years old.[2]

But it must not be supposed that this hereditary distaste for personal portraiture bars the Wilson family from the field of art. Mrs. Wilson is herself a painter in both oils and water colors of no mean achievements, and the walls of more than one of the rooms at Prospect bear evidence of her skill, while one of the daughters[3] is a student of modeling in clay. Lyme, Conn., the namesake of the English place made famous in Jane Austen's novel, consists largely of a colony of artists, and it is there that the Wilsons have spent their summers for some years. . . .

Printed in the *Philadelphia Record*, Oct. 2, 1910; some editorial headings omitted.
    [2] The photograph was reproduced in the interview, and may be found in the illustration section of Vol. 1 of this series.
    [3] Eleanor.

From Henry Eckert Alexander

Dear Mr. Wilson: Trenton, Sept. [Oct.] 2, 1910.

I hope that I am not urging you too strongly to plant yourself squarely on your own position in regard to the right and duty of the governor to fight *for the people* with all the power that they have voted to him. I remember very well *the* [New York]

Sun's arguments on the other side, but you have taken the contrary position and *the people* by an overwhelming majority will sustain that view, while the *Sun* will not try to muddy the waters by making criticism, I am quite sure.

Monday night you begin your second week in the campaign. You have given the voters of the state ample opportunity to size you up and the scrutiny has been all to your advantage. Now you proceed logically to *specifications*.

You may say specifically that if the people elect you governor you will seek to serve them with all the power that they have voted to you, and that you will not sit inactive by and permit Bosses or any Board of Guardians to rule this state.

The people of the whole state will be electrified by such a declaration.

Also when you refer to the Public Utility Commission with full powers you can stir your audience to the depths by asserting that with such legislation it will be *impossible* for any trolley company to take away from the people its strip tickets over night and compel people to pay straight five cent fares or walk.

With such legislation, the people will have adequate service looking to their comfort, convenience and safety or *know the reason why*.

This is a vital issue in Trenton where the trolley company, protected by the Republican machine, brought about last year's revolt at the polls. And feeling is still intense.

In referring to the election of Madden and Berrien, if you say that the Republican local machine was sent to the junk pile, and that "the famous card index["], devised, I believe, by *Mr. Salter*,[1] was sent to the pulp mill—this famous card index which told all about a man's life and family and business, and how much the machine hold up man could take out of his pay envelope.

I am sending you these suggestions for what they are worth. If you will be the spokesman for the distressed and revolting people, betrayed by their leaders.

Sincerely yours,   H. E. Alexander

ALS (WP, DLC).

[1] Harry Broughton Salter, City Clerk of Trenton and prominent conservative Republican. It was rumored that he would succeed Vivian M. Lewis as Commissioner of Banking and Insurance if Lewis was elected governor.

A News Report of a Campaign Address
in Long Branch, New Jersey[1]

[Oct. 3, 1910]

WILSON ON "STANDPAT" REPUBLICANS

Long Branch., Oct. 3.—Declaring that the Democrats will be discredited unless they do the things they have explicitly promised, Woodrow Wilson, Democratic gubernatorial candidate, opened up his South Jersey campaign Saturday with two speeches in Monmouth County.[2] He had some pointed things to say about insurgency and stand-patism in the Republican party during the course of his two speeches. . . .

At Long Branch he said:

"The insurgent is neither fish, flesh nor fowl, politically speaking, so far as his labels are concerned. Some insurgents are very able men. They know what the country wants and know how to get it, but that is not the point; the point is that they have not yet found a label.

"Between a real Democrat and a really progressive insurgent there is very little difference. What has been happening to these insurgents is that they have been catching the Democratic infection. They have been long exposed to the expression of Democratic opinion and Democratic sympathies and principles by Democrats and now, by the grace of circumstances, they are being converted by the things that are happening throughout the country. The men who stand pat are those who simply cover their eyes and will not look at anything.

"It doesn't pay, ladies and gentlemen, to stand pat about anything. If you won't move you are going to rot, or else get destroyed by the rest of the crowd that is moving.

"A friend of mine, having heard of the Florida cracker, as they call a certain very 'ne'er do well' portion of our population in that State, passing through the State in a train, asked a party to point out a cracker to him. His friend replied: 'Well, if you see something in the woods that looks brown, like a stump, you will know it is either a stump or a cracker, and if it moves away it is a stump.'

"Now I call the Republican stand-patters the crackers of the Republican party. I cannot imagine a man living in the world and not knowing that something is going on. And some of these gentlemen have not heard of anything that has happened since the Civil War; their speeches would apply just as well if delivered then as now. When I hear or read some of their speeches it seems like reminiscences of the time when I had to read everything in order to write a history of the United States. There is a strong tinge of reminiscence in everything they say." . . .

Mr. Wilson tapped a new vein of thought in discussing the public service corporations and the need of publicity in governmental affairs. . . .

"Ladies and gentlemen, there is one function which has never been performed for the citizens of New Jersey. The men who have been connected with the government have never told you about it. It sometimes looks as if some of them had got it into their heads that public business is private business. I hold the opinion that there can be no confidences as against the people with respect to their government, and that it is the duty of every public officer to explain to his fellow citizens[,] whenever he gets a chance[,] explain exactly what is going on inside of his own office.

"There is no air so wholesome as the air of publicity, and the only promise I am going to make you, if you elect me Governor, is that I will talk about the government to you as long as I am able. I have made it my business all my life to explain the things I have studied and it has been my habit all my life to talk about the thing I understand. I think you will admit anything that is happening at Trenton, or in regard to the public affairs of this State is something that everybody has a right to talk about.

"There will come a time when the business of many of these corporations will be virtually public business. Those corporations that we call public corporations, that are indispensable to our daily lives and serve us with transportation and light and water and power, for the lighting of our business places and our houses, and the supplying of power by which we drive our machinery—we will say that their business is public business. Therefore, we can and must penetrate their affairs by the light of examination and of discussion. Then it will occur to us that all corporations, whether they are public service corporations or not, exist by the grace and permission of the law. I was pointing that distinction out recently to another audience.

"The law does noth [not] give me as an individual permission to live, but it gives a corporation permission to exist; the corporation could not exist without it. Is the creator not at liberty, then, to investigate the affairs of its creature? Is it not very pertinent that we should ask about these things that we made what they are doing?"

Printed in the Jersey City *Jersey Journal*, Oct. 3, 1910; some editorial headings omitted.
1 Delivered in the Ocean Park Casino on October 1, 1910.
2 The other speech, made in Red Bank, N. J., is printed at Oct. 1, 1910.

A Campaign Address in Trenton, New Jersey[1]

[[Oct. 3, 1910]]

Mr. Chairman and Fellow Citizens of Mercer: I have enjoyed this evening so far more than most of the evenings of my campaigning; then I only heard myself.[2] I feel a great responsibility as I stand here. It is the second time within the last month I have stood upon this platform. I stood here to accept the nomination of the convention, which did me the honor of offering me the nomination as Governor of this State. I now ask you if you approve of that nomination and will support me. (Cries of yes! yes!) The second responsibility is greater than the first. With the generosity which I can only say I did not deserve, the nomination was offered to me.

I am asking you for your votes, and if you give them to me I will be under bonds to you—not to the gentlemen who were generous enough to nominate me.

And that leads me to say something of a sort that I have not said during the campaign. I have sought during the last week to avoid as much as possible all reference to myself and to my personal purposes, and it seems to me appropriate standing upon this platform where both candidates for Governor have so recently stood, to say something that will be definite about what I shall try to do, because my competitor in the race tried to say to the convention that nominated him what kind of a Governor he intended to be.

He said, if you have read the reports of his speech, that he would try to be a constitutional Governor. He went on to define that by that he meant that he would exercise the powers suggested by the constitution, and studiously refrain from exercising any others; that he would send messages to the Legislature reading in the strongest way he knew how the messages that he thought were necessary; that he would if he disapproved of the acts of the Legislature, veto, upon occasion; and require them to be reconsidered by the Legislature; but that beyond that he would not go; that he would not try to coerce the Legislature into doing anything simply because he thought it was in the interests of the people. In other words, he said that instead of talking to the Legislature, he would not talk to anybody. Now, I cannot be that kind of a constitutional Governor. I have formed the habit of talking to other people, and I want you to understand exactly

[1] Delivered in the Taylor Opera House.
[2] Wilson was preceded in speaking by Professor William Libbey of Princeton University, Democratic candidate for Congress, and by Frank S. Katzenbach, Jr., who presided at the meeting.

what kind of a Governor you will be electing, if you elect me. If you elect me, you will elect a Governor, who in the opinion of Mr. Lewis, will be an unconstitutional Governor. There is a kind of pressure that can be brought to bear upon the Legislature which is not only unconstitutional, but immoral. I, for my part, believe that the standards of morals transcend the standards of the constitution.

It is immoral to bring the pressure of patronage to bear upon the Legislature. It is immoral to try to undermine the influence of individual representatives by going into their districts and trying to form machines against them. Those are methods to which no honorable man will resort, but every honorable method of urging upon the legislators of this State things to do in the interests of the people of this State is assuredly constitutional, and will be resorted to by myself, if I am elected Governor. Gentlemen, who have been associated with me in other undertakings[,] have complained of my habit of talking. They have complained that I do not regard anything that concerns the public interests as confidential. I do not. I never shall; and I give notice now that I am going to take every important subject of debate in the Legislature out on the stump and discuss it with the people.

If that is pressure upon the Legislature, then it is the pressure which belongs to popular government—the expression of opinion, and nothing else. If, in these circumstances, the people do not agree with me, it cannot do the legislators any harm. If the people do agree with me, then it will be necessary for the legislators to do something. It is a perfectly even game. The members of the Legislature can talk—some of them with amazing skill.

I am not such a talker as they need be afraid of, and therefore the only thing they need be afraid of is my opinion, and opinions are perfectly "constitutional." Moreover, there is a sense in which this is serving the spirit of the constitution, which relieves the Legislature of certain kinds of pressure which they will find it very welcome to be relieved of.

You know what happens when everybody is very silent, very quiet, when everybody refrains from discussing in public matters that have happened in the Legislature. Even their needs are being said in undertones; their needs are being managed, their combinations are being formed.

I have even heard of an organization called the Board of Guardians, an organization which, I understand, heartily desires what Mr. Lewis regards as a constitutional Governor, a Governor who won't bring any pressure to bear except such pressure as the Board of Guardians brings to bear upon the Legislature.

This Board of Guardians is not elected by the people of New Jersey; this Board of Guardians holds no authority except that of party machinery, and a constitutional Governor, according to the constitution, is not such a Governor as yields to party machinery. If that is the constitution of New Jersey, the constitution of New Jersey ought to be changed. But it is not the constitution of New Jersey. New Jersey's constitution is meant to build every public action upon public approval, upon public discretion—to see to it that every impulse that is a lasting impulse comes from the judgment and opinions of the people themselves.

You will notice that the Governor of this State is the only officer of the State government elected by all the people of New Jersey. Every member of the Legislature is elected by some portion of the people of New Jersey. If the Governor does not talk, therefore, the people of New Jersey, as a whole, have no spokesman.

I am an amateur politician, and I shall, not timidly, as standing outside of the ranks of the profession, tackle the profession. I shall insist in every instance that tackling be done in public and not in private, and I welcome any politician in the State to a debate upon the public platform upon a public question. If you choose me as your Governor, then you will choose me as your spokesman, and upon these terms I shall approach the various questions which are interesting particularly at the present time.

I have said some things which may make you think that the centre and core of our politics is corrupt; the centre and core of our politics, gentlemen, is ourselves, and I do not believe for one moment that the people of this State or of any other State in this Union are corrupt.

I believe that corruption thrives only in secret places, not in public places, and that the reason you are constantly suspicious is that so many things are privately done instead of by public arrangements, and that the politicians themselves—I mean those who have been under suspicion—I am now naturally referring to the Republicans (laughter), will find it to their advantage to have secrecy supplanted by publicity, because in many instances they have been unjustly suspected. What I object to principally in the definition of his principles by my opponent is that he is volunteering publicly a service of a System, and it is a System I object to, and a System I will do everything in my power to break up.

There are corruptions in politics. It would be an empty pretense if I were to try to make you believe that I thought these corruptions were characteristic of one party rather than another. They are, I am sorry to say, in parties which have long been in power. It ought not to be so, and I believe in my heart that it need not be so, but I believe and I am sorry to admit it is so generally. I am not attacking our Republicans as far as they are the rank and file of the Republican party, but that the politics of the State have got into a very bad system, and corruptions have crept in which should not have been permitted.

One thing we need in politics for protection is the corrupt practice act. The corrupt practice act can go and should go into very interesting details. It should specifically state what are the legitimate expenses of a campaign; it should limit the expenses of a campaign to these legtimate objects; it should require that all candidates and all committees should publish in full an account of every cent they have received and from whom they have received it. Then, last of all, it should forbid any person who holds a public office of any kind to contribute one penny to a campaign fund.

I have heard mentioned with much interest in this county a certain machine card index of persons who were expected to contribute to a campaign fund, their personal circumstances, their disposition towards the party, and the amounts they could be expected to contribute. Under a proper corrupt practice act, these things would be impossible and inconceivable. Moreover, I am speaking of men who have been through this business.

I know just as well as you do how the Democrats of this county have taken the initiative in stopping bribery at elections, and that one of the chief fruits of that campaign was to put your excellent Mayor in office, and also your present very efficient receiver of taxes. A league has recently been formed here, non-partisan in character, and the Democratic party has co-operated very heartily with that league, to see that the card index has gone to the pulp mill and a certain Republican machine has gone to the scrap heap, so I am talking to persons who know the joy of victory in this interesting field and who know that the moment that [they] bring all these things into the open they will stop.

There is one very disturbing character in man, and I have experienced it myself, and I dare say you have, when you are a long way from home and see no neighbor from near your home, you give yourself an extraordinary latitude in your conduct, but if you were on the desert of Sahara and met one of your immediate neighbors coming the other way on a camel, you would behave yourself until he got out of sight. (Laughter.)

Publicity is one of the purifying elements of politics. The best thing that you can do with anything that is crooked is to lift it up where people can see that it is crooked, and then it will either straighten itself out or disappear. These, therefore, are matters which touch us.

All last week I was talking about general principles and showing how eloquent I can be, and now this week I am getting down to business. There is another matter that has interested us very much, indeed, and it is the regulation of public utility corporations.

You have tried to do some regulating of these corporations in Trenton, and you know, just as well as I do, that you have not the proper instrumentality through which to control these things. Complaints in the newspapers do not do any particular good. Protests to employes do not do any good. Protests to superintendents and to owners go unheeded. There is no place to which you can go and feel that your protests and suggestions are going to have any weight at all. The object of a public utility commission, such as ought to be set up, with full power in this State, is that every complaint made by a responsible person, by an honest person, will be investigated, and that you can be assured that under the operation of public opinion it will not only be investigated, but that the complaint, if found to be well founded, will be set right, and that the law, rather than whimsical choice on the part of the men governing the enterprise, will govern what they do. So that, if you will allow me to use a local expression, they cannot over night change from a system of strip tickets to cash fares. That, perhaps, is a detail, but it is a detail that illustrates the issue and illustrates it in your own personal and recent experience.

A public utility commission ought to have the right, after thorough investigation, such investigation as will put their action upon a fair footing for the men whose business they are regulating, as well as for the public, to determine the thing that is reasonable and exacted of them in the interests of the public, so that the public will know why their interests and their comfort and their public convenience are not served, if they cannot be served, and so that there will be a mutual protection, a protection on the part of the public utility corporation itself, and a protection on the part of the public.

No man who looks forward to the permanent welfare of a community would wish to see a condition of hostility set up. No man would wish to see unfair things done. If you oblige a public utility corporation to do things by which they lose money, then there is only one honorable thing to do, and that is to take over the business.

If you are going to leave the business in private hands, it is only just and rational that you should make it possible for the private individuals to run it without actual loss. Therefore, I say that it is absurd to discuss these things upon a basis of hostility, as if we were trying to break up public utility corporations. We cannot afford to break them up; we have to use them every day to transport our goods and person. We are trying to break up one thing—we are trying to break up unjust discrimination. We shall break up insufficient service. We shall try to see that these corporations which monopolize the highways, to which are accorded all sorts of extraordinary privileges, to which is given the State's right of eminent domain—we shall try to see that they are operated in the general interests.

Now, in order to do that[,] gentlemen, the program that I began to outline, is a necessary program, and we have to take it up outside of the Legislature as well as inside the Legislature. It is the business of those who represent us to get as many of our fellow citizens together as possible, and go over the facts so that they may with advantage do the just thing.

Then there is another matter to which I shall descend to a bill of particulars. It is the habit to talk about efficiency and economy in the government. A great deal has been said about the increase of expenses in the federal government, and about the increases in the expenses of the State government. My friend, Mr. Libbey, I am sure, would join me in saying that in recent years we have put new functions on our government, and they have necessarily cost more, but we have not managed these matters in a business-like manner, in an economical manner. We have not performed our work as economically as we might. Therefore, the history of the administration needs to be studied from the top to the bottom, and every effort made to put it upon a business basis of efficiency.

Do you know the powers of the Commissioner of Roads of this State? The Commissioner of Roads has the absolute authority to lay out and construct roads and to make contracts for the repair of roads of this State, and he is not under any kind of restraint or control. He is given full power in these matters. You see the position he is in.

He ought not to be subject to temptation—private arrangements with regard to the contracts that he makes. And if you look through every item of the public business you will find some place where the business is run as no sensible man would run his business without loss or without being cheated by his employes.

We are undertaking a big contract, if we are going to run this government on the basis of economy.

If you elect me to undertake it, do not blame me for coming to you after a few months with tedious rows of figures; don't blame me for coming to you, as to a board of directors, to lay before you as I would lay before the university board the budgets, the means, the circumstances, as to where the money is to come from, how the money is to be spent and how it is to be saved. That is what I understand to be the business of the Governor and all other representatives. So that you must get ready to understand what I propose doing if you elect me Governor.

Nine men out of ten vote either the Republican ticket or the Democratic ticket because they have always voted it or because their fathers voted it or because their friends voted it or because they are new in the country they vote the nearest thing that happens.

If you want efficient government it is necessary that you take pains to understand it and vote on some rational basis; and I cannot understand how, at the present juncture of affairs, any man can vote the Republican ticket on a rational basis.

Now, just look at the Republican ticket. There isn't any Republican party. You ask one man what he is and he will tell you he is an Insurgent. You ask another man what he is and he will tell you he is a Standpatter. And you say to the Standpatter, "What do you think of the Insurgents?" and he will answer, "Oh! they are all traitors, trying to break the Republican party up." And you ask the Insurgent, "What do you think of the Standpatter?" and he says, "He's a mossback—a man who doesn't know what year it is; he is living back in a past age." And particularly the Insurgent will say, "The Standpatter is the man who does not know the hundreds and thousands of Insurgents there are in this country."

So, that if I were inclined to vote the Republican ticket, I would want to find out what kind of a person I was, politically speaking. I would not condescend to be a Standpatter, and if I was an Insurgent I wouldn't know whether I was a Republican or not, and I would say, "Here are a lot of men talking as Democrats, talking pretty good sense, who seem to know what they are talking about, and they do not differ in any important particular with the Insurgents of the Republican party."

Now nobody understands the standpatter. Let's all get together. The standpatter is out of court on the testimony of the Republicans themselves—not, unfortunately, in this State. The standpatter, as I understand—I am not one of their company, and, therefore, speak with all deference, but I understand the standpatters ran the convention that nominated my opponent. If so they are an negligible quantity, taking the country as a whole, for the country, as a whole, is going insurgent, whether you call it Democratic or Insurgent; and one of the things that interests me about all political movements, is that the men in whom real progress rests are always Insurgents, whether you call them by that name or not.

Everything that has ever happened in history, has happened because a large number of men kicked—would not submit.

You will remember the old darkey's illustration of the theological doctrine of election. He says it is this way: "The man he vote one way, the devil he vote the other way, and then the Lord comes in and decides the election." And I think that's a pretty reasonable way of deciding the election. The Lord has the casting vote, I imagine, and the Insurgents always have the casting vote; the men who insist upon using their minds; the men who refuse to wear any man's collar.

And the beauty of the present situation, as I see it, is that the Democratic party, having been untrammeled by power for fourteen or fifteen years, have got into an insurgent frame of mind, and they are all free to decide the election.

In such circumstances, it seems to me that our appeal to our Republican friends, if they can find out what Republican means, is to study the practicable method of carrying progress forward in the country at this time, for that is what we are after. We are not after party advantage.

I have conferred with a good many men standing high in the councils of the Democratic party of this country, and I have yet to find the man who, in conference, urged low party political methods. I have yet to find the man who was not conscious of that great power of independent thought rising in America. But you cannot put new wine in old bottles. If a man has been so saturated in controlling things in the wrong way that he cannot control them the right way, we had better get somebody not so saturated.

My objection to the Republican party is the partnership that they have got into without any intent to do the thing for which they are responsible, and one of the things is our perverted sense of thought. For example, if you tell a candidate who desires office that certain interests were instrumental in obtaining the nomination for him, and after he is elected, something comes up that affects those interests, he says: "Now, these men helped me to get that nomination, and although I did not promise them anything,

I know they were influential in obtaining it." Therefore he will let up; he will make concessions.

Now, the beautiful part of the situation, so far as I am concerned, is that I have not been told that anybody was responsible for my nomination. If anybody did bring it about, I am glad to say I do not know who it was. Therefore I am not under that subtle influence to anybody, and I believe that most of the Democratic party throughout the country is purified by the very air that vibrates the country itself, and the party is putting up men for office who do not know anything but the impulse of public service.

How fine a thing it is, then, to be the candidate under such circumstances; how high an honor it is to be trusted, to be trusted by the men who nominated you, to hope you will be trusted by the men who vote for you. What living man could sleep in his bed if, after being so trusted by men upon whom the whole strain and stress of life rests, trusted by men whose interests are involved in every movement of public policy—I say what man could sleep in his bed if, after being so trusted, he betrayed the trust?

It does not require any great imagination to think that high thoughts and purposes in politics are running subtly through every household and every member of every household in this country. It does not need that you should touch elbows, actually touch elbows, with men in the street and men in the shop in order to know the great issues of human happiness that are involved in a great contest like this, for the question of the tariff is not a mere question of policy, it is a question of the rearrangement of the public interests as you touch every household in this country; and how any man, in such circumstances, can hold his head up after he has voted for a special interest without a just conception of the common interests, I, for one, cannot comprehend.

But, whether men can comprehend it or not, help it or not, we all know that the "mills of the gods grind slowly," and they "grind exceeding fine," and the men who now resist this great impulse of reform, the men who impede this great compulsion of public interest, will be ground so fine in some of these mills of the gods that their very dust will be imperceptible.

I am not pleading with you to make me an instrument of retaliation; I am not pleading with you to make me an instrument for the punishment of men; but I am pleading to make me, if you trust me, a representative of these new ideas, a spokesman of these purposes, so that in constant conference with you I may be some humble instrument when men do not entirely think of their own interests, but of the interests of their villages and cities, the interest of their counties, the interests of their states and their nation; that this is the America in which the common man is the representative man.

A few who are distinguished with their names daily in the newspapers are not the real representative citizens of the country; but the man who toils, who goes about his work with a desire to perform it well, to support those who are dependent upon him, to do his duty toward those who trust him, he is the representative American, and it is because he is that America has grown rich and powerful. If American men could not be trusted, if they did not know how to work, America would have neither distinction nor power. And, therefore, in appealing to impulses of this nature we are appealing to impulses that are right, to impulses that will redeem, to impulses that will perpetuate America.

Printed in the *Trenton Evening Times*, Oct. 4, 1910; editorial headings omitted; with minor corrections from the text in the Trenton *True American*, Oct. 4, 1910.

From Raymond Blaine Fosdick[1]

My dear Dr. Wilson: [New York] October 3, 1910.

The pressure of business here in the office makes it impossible for me to take the stump for you as I should like very much to do. Nothing would please me better than to get into the fight for you in New Jersey.

May I take this opportunity to assure you of the moral support, at least, of the Gaynor administration and of my own support as a Princeton man and a lover of good government.

                    Faithfully yours,   Raymond B. Fosdick

TLS (WP, DLC).
    [1] Princeton 1905, at this time Commissioner of Accounts óf the City of New York.

From William T. Ferguson

My dear Doctor: Washington, D. C., Oct., 3d., 1910.

I have just received the following letter and clipping.

                    New York City, Oct., 1, 1910.
    Friend Ferguson:

        Hearing that you are working in the interest of Dr. Woodrow Wilson and under the impression that he is friendly to colored men, I send you this clipping from the New York Age.[1] I dont know anything about him myself, but The Age seems to think that he is not friendly to our people.

Hope this finds you well.

Yours truly   (Signed) H. A. Arnold.[2]

A copy of my reply.

Dear Harry:

Your letter with clipping received and I thank you for same. I have had some correspondence with Dr. Wilson and I am convinced that he is an honorable southern gentleman and he says that he is a friend of our people and wants their support. I believe him, and am doing all I can to help him win. We have been going it blind too long. We have friends among Democrats and would have more if we exercised judgment in casting our votes. It is a crime against our race to let the large number of northern Democrats see that time makes no improvement upon our minds. Our organization is doing all it can do to help Dr. Wilson and if we do not do more it is because the Democrats of New Jersey will not let us.

I have no excuses to offer for my course of action and shall believe that Dr. Wilson is what he says until he proves otherwise.

Very truly yours,   (signed) W. T. Ferguson.

Dr. Wilson:

I hope that you will mention, in one or more of your addresses, the fact that the aid of colored men would be appreciated by you. Our statements to that effect will then be verified and will greatly aid our appeal.

Your loyal supporter   W. T. Ferguson

TLS (WP, DLC).

[1] The clipping was an editorial from the *New York Age*, Sept. 29, 1910, and read as follows: "Before the Negroes of New Jersey give any serious consideration to the candidacy of Woodrow Wilson, we are sure they will carefully examine Mr. Wilson's record on the rights of the Negro race. Mr. Wilson used to think pretty loudly on this matter when he lived in Atlanta, Ga."

[2] Probably Harris A. Arnold, physician of New York.

From Joseph L. O'Connell[1]

Dear Sir: Jersey City [N. J.] Oct 3. 10

I was one of the many interested listeners to your masterly speech in St. Peter's Hall Jersey City when you opened your campaign for the Governorship of this State.

Permit me to remark that while the concensus of opinion of those whom I met after the meeting—even up to the present writing—was that while you made a beautiful speech and was evidently an honest gentleman, it was also remarked that you did not cover any state issues. You did not suggest or name any specific remedies for the evils of the State House Ring &c. In fact all told—it was said you made a lamentably weak *political* speech—one that would draw few votes to you.

I endeavored to the best of my ability to show that a man of your mental equipment was needed to head the Democratic forces of this State.

They could not see you—so to speak[—]as a political factor. In fact you were too nice a man—a schoolmaster rather than a leader—and one whose mode of attack upon the Republican party did not appeal. This feeling has spread to a great extent among the young men of our town & which situation is to be deplored.

Personally I have every hope of your success because (1) I believe a change is necessary & long overdue in State administration. (2) You will improve in your work as the campaign goes on (3) You have the support of the New York papers, which has an undoubted effect on thousands of "independent" Commuters What I am trying to show is that here in this "Democratic" town you need all the votes you can get. You cannot afford to lose any Democratic votes. Every Democratic voter who votes against you, makes a change of two in the result; and the party cannot afford to have any former Democratic voter stray away from the fold at this very critical juncture in its existence.

Now the young men I have previously mentioned are working men, not idlers[,] some mechanics, carpenters, Iron workers, office clerks, electricians & the like. Men who are getting fair salaries are intelligent & up to date so to speak. They pay their own way have no affiliations with the "Machine" in fact *detest* the Bossism feature in both the big parties, and are not afraid or ashamed to openly express their political convictions to anyone.

These men are now what you would call *lukewarm* in the *Wilson proposition*. You made a deep impression on them in your first speech, but not a favorable one from a political standpoint.

They must be brought around for they are Democrats at heart and need only the right kind of treatment to be cured of the hallucination that you wont do.

If you will let me offer a suggestion—offered in all kindliness let me say to you—that when you next pay Jersey City a visit, you change your mode of attack. Give us a ringing speech on all the issues and there are many—in no uncertain language. Let Jersey City know where the Republican party stands, and what it stands for. Just what you propose to do as Governor on questions that now confront the people of the state.

You must be our leader rather than one who is [to] stay in the rank & file. You must show us qualities of leadership—(political I mean)

The party is in sore need of a leader—one with enough magnetic force to bring around such recalcitrants as I have mentioned—to keep the old timers in line to win over the votes of disgusted Republicans. You have all the qualifications necessary to effect this result. Your opportunity is here for a Leadership as well as Governorship and you will be taking a Long Island chance if you do not pursue different tactics in your next set of political speeches in Jersey City, where a whooping big vote awaits you—is here for the asking—if only asked for in the right manner.

Our young men here are not thin skinned. You may put all the red pepper you like in your speeches, so long as you propose doing something for the public good. The day of the old way of voting is past. There is an enormous *independent* vote in this State—the greater part of which was formerly Democratic. Win that greater part & the next Governor of the State of New Jersey will be Woodrow Wilson.

With assurance of my heartiest support and hoping for complete success of the Democratic ticket, believe me

Sincerely yours   Joseph L. OConnell

ALS (WP, DLC).
1 Affiliated with the Williamsburgh City Fire Insurance Co. of New York.

To Edwin Augustus Van Valkenburg

[Princeton, N. J.]

My dear Mr. Van Valkenburg: October 4th, 1910.

I warmly appreciate your letter of September 29th, but particularly regret that the rush of a campaign is so bad a time in which to write letters deliberately and cast them into the shape one would wish them to have in discussing important matters such as those which you propound.

Let me say how interesting it is to me and how reassuring that the discussion upon their merits of great public questions should so obviously lie at the base of your editorial policy. It is a pleasure to discuss things so handled.

I hope that you will feel at liberty at any time to propound any question you please. At present I confine myself to the two which you do ask.

The first I can answer very simply. I do not think that the physical valuation of the railroads under federal direction as a basis of determining inter-state rates should be regarded as in any way an infringement upon the rights of the States in the matter of regulating the capitalization of the corporations created by the States.

In reply to your second question, "Should water power sites and other natural resources still in the public domain be controlled by the States or by the Federal Government working in conjunction with the States, for the purposes of conservation and development?," I would say that if by the "public domain" you mean the property originally controlled by the Federal Government but now within the area of States which have been set up, I should reply that in my opinion such domain should be controlled by the Federal Government working in conjunction with the States. The question is less simple for the older States, like New Jersey, for example. Very little property is really subject to the control of these older States, but it seems to me clearly their duty to legislate in the matter of watersheds, forests, drainage, and like matters in such a way as to serve the public interest as against the selfish operation of private owners. If necessary, the property in question should be acquired by the State and administered in the interest of the whole community.

I do not know whether in my haste I am expressing myself very clearly, or not, but I hope that this constitutes a real answer such as I wish to give to your question.

I entertain no jealousy whatever of federal power. I am merely earnestly desirous of maintaining the vitality and enhancing the responsibility of the States, which I think bring the necessity of action and of right political thinking home to individual communities.

With much respect and appreciation,

Sincerely yours,   [Woodrow Wilson]

CCL (WP, DLC).

From George Brinton McClellan Harvey

Dear Mr. Wilson,   New York Oct 4 [1910].

Can you have your secretary or somebody save up your various speeches as reported and from them make up a composite speech, embodying most of your views, to be put in my hands about a week before your last speech—which I think is to be made in Newark about Nov. 5.

Melville Stone[1] tells me that if I will give him such a document at that time,[2] he will get it into all of the Associated Press papers in the country.

It seems worth while.   As ever   Yours   G H

ALI (WP, DLC).
    [1] Melville Elijah Stone, co-founder of the *Chicago Daily News* in 1875 and the *Chicago Morning News* (later the *Chicago Record*) in 1881; since 1893 general manager of the Associated Press.
    [2] Stockton Axson later put together a long press release consisting of portions of Wilson's various campaign speeches. Dated November 1, 1910, the press release, not reproduced in this series, is a printed document in WP, DLC.

From Henry Eckert Alexander

Dear Mr. Wilson: [Trenton, N. J.] Oct. 4, 1910.

I enclose the *Jersey Journal* editorial[1] and the *Outlook* comment.[2]

No effort was made here to advertise your meeting. What we did was without suggestion from the able committee in charge and even the "band" was kept indoors. Nevertheless you had a great audience and you did business with it. Of course you were at a great disadvantage to be the last speaker and Mr. Nugent should see to it that no such arrangements are made elsewhere for it is the effect of *your* speeches that counts.

My suggestion, if it is not too late to adjust matters is that at Woodbury you make more prominent the revolt of the people against their betrayal by false leadership. A great many Philadelphia business men live at Woodbury and give a certain character to it. You will find that the Philadelphia *North American* has a very substantial circulation through that country—and the *Record.* They have pounded Aldrichism and Cannonism so hard, (with the help of a dozen magazines) that the names of Aldrich and Cannon are names with which to release evil spirits. It will be a great asset for you, I think, to refer specifically to Aldrichism and Cannonism, refering to Aldrich's enforced retirement and to the practical abandonment of Cannon by his late friends and allies *except in New Jersey.*

Then when you raise the question as to insurgency and progressiveness and ask if the rank and file of the Republican party is proud of New Jersey's Aldrich-Cannon representation. *New Jersey* has not yet cast off the Aldrich leadership for Mr. Kean accepts without question the honor awarded to him of having "personally conducted" the recent Republican nomination, including the nomination of Mr. Lewis and the presentation of resolutions, and to make the Aldrich-Cannon line up complete—the chairman chosen for the management of the campaign[3] is Mr. Kean's colleague in the U. S. Senate—the two men who have not a single insurgent or progressive vote in the records of the U. S. Senate, where they were know[n] and lab[e]led as Aldrich men.

Your Burlington address, I take it, will depend largely on what Lewis says in his opening speech, for the people will be interested in watching you meet Lewis *on the spot*

At Bridgeton, you can make a sensation if the accurate facts reach me in time to send you tomorrow about open bribery at recent Republican primaries—105 paid workers in *one* precinct where 163 votes were polled altogether

I do not believe that the real nature of this campaign has *yet* penetrated the amiable gentlemen who are in evidence at the Newark headquarters.

Sincerely yours,   Henry E. Alexander.

ALS (WP, DLC).

[1] The enclosed editorial, "Wilson and the Dough Bag," Jersey City *Jersey Journal*, Oct. 1, 1910, criticized Wilson for failing to come out strongly for a specific law prohibiting corrupt practices in politics. "What has Woodrow Wilson to offer as a remedy?" the editorial continued. "He is an honest man and a man of exceptional ability. The people are disposed to trust him. They look to him and to men of his kind for guidance. Is he in favor of a law that will limit campaign expenses, require publicity of all amounts received and expended for primaries and elections, and prohibit office-holders from contributing to dough bags? If he is in favor of such a law, why does not Mr. Wilson say so? Why does he not say that if he is elected Governor he will demand the enactment of such a law? He is wasting time in merely telling the public that corruption exists and that laws can stop it. The people know all this as well as he does. What they want is a definite cure for the evil. The question is, what does Wilson propose to do about it? The people want to know where he stands upon this matter and upon every other issue in the campaign."

[2] This missing editorial, "Unprogressive New Jersey Republicans," New York *Outlook*, xcvi (Oct. 1, 1910), 246-47, sharply criticized the New Jersey Republican state convention which, it said, had been dominated by "zealous stand-patters" and had selected a candidate who was "intimately allied with the Republican machine" and who had given indication in his acceptance speech of intending as governor to stress more the limitations than the opportunities of the office. The Republican platform, continued the editorial, dealt in "broad and vague generalities" and was "depressingly unprogressive." Proposals offered by progressives had been "curtly and cynically" rejected, and George L. Record, who had presented the minority report of the resolutions committee embodying progressive planks, had been greeted with "jeers and insults." "The Convention," concluded the editorial, "in the opinion of many hitherto stanch Republicans of the State, did a great deal to insure the victory of Dr. Woodrow Wilson in the coming election."

[3] Senator Briggs.

To George Brinton McClellan Harvey

My dear Colonel Harvey: Princeton, N. J. October 5th, 1910.

Thank you very much for the suggestion contained in your letter of yesterday. I shall act upon it at once and shall hope to have a composite speech ready for Mr. Stone's use. It is an excellent idea and does seem worth while.

I hope that you will hand on to me any criticisms in particular that you hear of my campaign, in order that I may profit by them.

In haste, with warmest regard,

Faithfully yours,   Woodrow Wilson

TLS (WP, DLC).

A Campaign Speech in Woodbury, New Jersey[1]

[[Oct. 5, 1910]]

Mr. Chairman and Fellow Citizens of Gloucester County:

I esteem it a great privilege to stand here and press upon you what seems to be some of the most critical issues that have ever had to be faced by the American people. I would not esteem it a pleasure but a mere embarrassment if I felt that I came here to plead in any respect for myself. My privilege here to-night is not to solicit your votes personally, but to represent what I believe to be a cause and to call your attention to what I believe is a turning point in the history of this country politically.

This campaign, gentlemen, upon which we have entered is a campaign when we as neighbors get together to discuss the things we are all interested in and to determine the things we wish to accomplish, and the men through whom we wish to accomplish them. By the very generous choice of the gentlemen who constituted the Democratic convention, I have been chosen as a spokesman by a party who now intends the service of the people. I could not refrain to respond to that call because all my life long I have been interested in the service of the people, and a man can not turn away from that to which his thoughts have for so long a time been directed. I should not like to engage in this campaign if I thought it was a mere party matter, if I thought I would have to answer for the record of one party and attack the record of another. I don't think it would be worth while. There are many things to criticise in the records of both parties, but it has come to be a party matter only in respect to

1 Delivered in Green's Opera House. The news reports do not identify the chairman.

WOODBURY,   5 October, 1910.

A turning point for the whole country. New Jersey's part to
    be determined. A question of parties only because a
    question of men and programmes.

General revolt of the people vs. Aldrichism and Cannonism.
    Except in New Jersey.
            Record of insurgency in New Jersey
            Record of the convention, and its control.
            Futile efforts of Mr. Lewis.
            Reception given Mr. Record and other able and lib-
                eral men
            The two Senators: one (Kean) behind the convention,
                the other (Briggs) behind the campaign. Their
                records.
    Except in New York. The platform. The bitter disap-
        pointment of the progressive Republicans, especi-
        ally in the Middle West.
    The position of the national Administration.
            Identification with the tariff is identifica-
            tion with Aldrich and Cannon.

    The new protectionism, and its meaning.

 The Democratic party offers a definte programme, under free
    leaders. The Republican party offers, what? under what
    auspices?
    The Programme: Thorough administrative reform
                    Equalization of taxation
                    Safeguarding of school fund
                    Conservation
                    Pub. Service Commission
                    Employers' liability

a matter of programme. We are not interested now—I will frankly say[—]in the success or failure of parties, but in the success or failure of policies, in the success of measures for the relief of some conditions which have turned out to be intolerable, and therefore I profoundly believe that the Democratic party is the most suitable instrument for the realization of the policies I hold to be indispensable, and I consider it a proud moment when I recognize that period.

We are coming to a turning point in the affairs of the United States and we are met here tonight not merely for the purpose of discussing the affairs of our beloved commonwealth, but also for the purpose of discussing the affairs which concern the whole country, our choices with respect of which are choices which will concern the whole country, not only of this commonwealth, a leadership in affairs which for a great many years it has declined, yet as fitted as any commonwealth in the country, to exercise leadership. Now, let us think it over calmly and dispassionately, just the position in which we find ourselves. I spoke just now of its being a matter of programme. Have you read the Democratic platform? Have you read the Republican platform? Do you remember how the Democratic platform begins? It begins—I can't quote it exactly—I can't quote anything exactly—but the substance of it is this. That the Democratic party in presenting a candidate for Governor also wishes to make the following statement of what it proposes it should do if entrusted with the government of the State; not what it thinks the Republican party ought to have done. You know how many of the old fashioned platforms read that they pointed with pride to something or other and with condemnation and reprobation of something else that their party had done. There is no pointing with pride and no pointing with condemnation in the Democratic platform; there is a pointing with purpose if you will entrust us with the government of this State, and there are things we shall try.

There is one definite promise that the Republican platform makes, and that is for a public utility commission that will have some power; and that is exactly what the Republican platform promised three years ago. Have you got it? This thing that they call a promise in this platform is regarded as an apology. It says "We promised it once and relied upon your credulity. Now, we are going to promise it again and see if you will be credulous a second time," or else it means: "We promised it once when we did not mean it, now, we beg your pardon for not having meant it, and this time we mean it." One or the other of those two meanings must be the significance of that promise, which was the only promise that they did not dare omit—because that was not a promising convention. I think, from all the indications that I can gather, that it was not even a hopeful convention. And that, ladies and gentlemen, because it did not represent the rank and file of the Republican party. It represented a certain group of interests in control of the leaders of the Republican party and not the people of the State of New Jersey. You will not find me in any speech of this campaign uttering one word of criticism of my fellow citizens who compose the rank and file of the Republican party. I respect them just as much as I respect the men who had voted according to my opinions in past campaigns. But what I am finding fault with is that they have been radically misled by men who have not meant to serve them in the manner in which they promised to serve them in times past, or have not acted in the spirit in which the leaders of the past generations have acted— in sympathy with the people of these communities. I am not one of those silly students of history who can read history all in favor of one party. I know the services that the Republican party have rendered to this country, and I know that that party has rendered such services to this country because they were backed by the sympathy and manhood of the people up and down the counties and states of this Union. I want to make good the things that I have said by calling your attention to certain circumstances. What is happening among the Republicans of this country? Why, this is happening, that everywhere that a progressive impulse shows itself, men are flinging away from the regular organization of the Republican party and calling themselves insurgents, and in some instances they have been so numerous that they have absolutely dominated the political conventions in more than one State, so that if you will read the Republican platform of the State of Kansas you will read one kind of document, and if you will read the Republican platform of the State of Ohio, you will read another kind of document, because it is not the same Republican party that is in control in Ohio that has control in Kansas. Everywhere, throughout this country, men are dissatisfied with the past organization of both parties, to be frank; and the dissatisfaction with the past government of the Republican party has shown itself in one of the most powerful and widespread party movements that has ever been witnessed in this country— I mean the insurgent movement. Now, what encouragement has the insurgent movement received in New Jersey? None whatever, so far as those who are governing the councils of the party are concerned; the voters are another matter. I am now speaking entirely of those who are governing Republican conventions and

Republican councils in this State. There was one insurgent Republican Congressman in New Jersey.[2] What happened to him? He was not renominated. They have substituted another— a very able man whom I respect greatly; I mean Mr. George Record.[3] But, what happened to Mr. George Record in the convention which nominated Mr. Lewis? He was jeered at; the calls were "Put him out." He was not listened to with any degree of patience even, much less with respect; and immediately after that convention Mr. Record himself condemned it as a convention which was a disgrace to the Republican party; but they have had the very good sense, in Mr. Record's congressional district to nominate him for Congress, as he richly deserved to be nominated; and now, Mr. Record is saying that a certain person called Woodrow Wilson is disappointing the "Independents" of this State, because he is not talking more plainly about the issues of the State campaign. Whom is Mr. Record disappointing? Mr. Record who was almost cast out of the Republican convention, now gives it as his opinion that you are to reject the candidate of the persons they represented in the Democratic convention. Who controlled the Republican convention? And, if I represent some of the men who are said to have controlled, but did not control, the Democratic convention, whom, I should like to know, does Mr. Record represent? If he represents what was represented in the convention, you know who engineered that convention. It is common knowledge that that convention was engineered by one of the United States Senators from New Jersey,[4] and the campaign is now being run by the other United States Senator from New Jersey.[5] Can you find anything in the Senatorial record of either of these men except an absolute, stand-pat, support of Aldrichism and Cannonism? Aldrichism, which every public spirited man denies to be true Republicanism at all; Cannonism, which every man of the country despises as an attempt to control in the interest of particular persons, the great national legislature of this country. I am perfectly content to represent the reorganized Democratic party, and I am surprised that Mr. Record should be content to represent the un-reorganized Republican party—an insurgent nominee supporting a campaign backed and originated by the man who was the chief errand boy for Mr. Aldrich in the

[2] Charles Newell Fowler, who had lost his renomination bid in the 5th congressional district. Fowler had served in Congress since 1895 and had opposed Joseph Gurney Cannon, dictatorial Speaker of the House of Representatives since 1903.

[3] Record was running against Eugene Francis Kinkead for the seat from the 9th congressional district.

[4] Senator Kean.

[5] Senator Briggs.

Senate. If this is the tune these gentlemen are singing, let us carry the war into Africa. There is absolutely nothing, so far as the record of that nominating convention is concerned that gives the least encouragement to the progressive Republicans anywhere, either in New Jersey or out of it. Look at the efforts—the very creditable efforts—that Mr. Lewis himself made in that convention to get some liberal planks into that platform. I have the pleasure of knowing Mr. Lewis, and I esteem and respect him. You will find not one word in anything that I have said, except esteem and respect for my opponent. You know how little respect was paid to his wishes to put into that platform anything that had the least tinge or color of progressiveness. Therefore, he is tied hand and foot by the machinery that has nominated him, and he has consented to stay so tied; for, in his speech of acceptance, he said that he would not undertake to force upon his party in the legislature anything that they did not want forced upon them. He said that he would be a constitutional governor, and would punctiliously confine himself to those things that were modest and becoming a man who had nothing of his own to thrust upon anybody. I do not want to be elected, if you should elect me upon any such false pretenses; if that is the definition of a constitutional governor I shall not be a constitutional governor, because there is one thing that a man has to obey over and above the State constitution, and that is his own constitution. I come of a Scotch-Irish stock that cannot help fighting to save its life. I always think I am right, and although I try to be courteous to the men I differ from, I am always sure they are wrong; and if you make me governor, you may expect me to proceed upon that programme, for I heartily believe in all the things that constitute the program of my party and mean to do everything that is honorable, everything that is legitimate, everything that consists in the pressure of reason and persuasion to carry out all the things that we believe in. There is a constitution of Americanism underlying the constitution of New Jersey and the constitution of the United States. Everything that has ever been done in America has been done by the frank conferences of fellow-citizens, has been done by free argument and persuasion, by closing no man's mouth, by being afraid of no man's immoral force. The man who can convince his fellow citizens in this country is the man who is going to rule this country, not because he has the support of the men who would force his will down throats, but because he has the desire to express the impulses and convictions of his fellow citizens; he wishes to be their mouth piece; he wishes the privilege of being their leader, the delight of expressing the impulses which lie in their breasts and which may, if God be willing, find expression in himself. That is the whole spirit of our government; that is the spirit of the constitution of America.

I am not afraid to act upon that constitution, and you are not afraid to see it acted upon, provided everything is done openly and above board. But if you commit yourselves to a system, if you commit yourselves to a board of guardians, if you commit yourselves to a party of gentlemen operating outside the Legislature but not appearing upon the public platform, then what have you done? You have enslaved your representatives in the Legislature.

Many a man whom you elect to the Assembly or the Senate of the State would wish to act with great independence, but if you make everything a process of quiet conference he receives orders from somebody who tells him that all this has been decided upon by the party leaders entirely, "so you do what you are told."

It is supposed that I am a very innocent candidate. I don't know what the people of the State who have seen me think of me, but if they do say these things about me, I can assure them that I am not as big a fool as I look; and I can tell these gentlemen exactly how our politics is operated if they would like to hear the story; but I don't think they would like to hear the story, at any rate, many of them who are now desperately endeavoring to stick to their offices.

Neither has the insurgent cause received any encouragement from New York. There is a singular lethargy, and lack of observation of opportunity on the part of the Republican managers in New Jersey and New York; it looks as if it was necessary for somebody to tell them what year of grace it is, for somebody to inform them of some of the things that have been happening in the rest of the country.

Do you happen to have seen something that appeared in the Des Moines *Leader*? Do you know that one of the most powerful leaders in the insurgent ranks is Senator Cummings, of Iowa; he is supposed to speak through the Des Moines *Leader*, not because he controls it in any way, but because it is his great friend, and the Des Moines *Leader* says that it utterly repudiates anybody who is responsible for the New York State platform of the Republican party. Why? Because that platform stands for a tariff which the great Middle West utterly rejected, because that platform endorses the administration of President Taft, which the Middle West has rejected. And so the leaders in New York who would have posed as leaders of the Republican progressives have been repudiated by the Republican progressives of the Middle West; just as they would reject the Republican leaders of New Jersey.

The present leaders of the Republican party in New Jersey have not been important enough to be rejected by anybody. It has been worth while to reject the present leader of the Republican forces in New York,[6] but it has not been worth while to reject the Republican Senators of New Jersey.

See what a position the national administration is in. All my criticisms are not only without personal point because I know these gentlemen, every one of them, and I have nothing whatever to say against their character and no suspicion to throw upon their motives. I have a very great respect and profound sympathy, I must say, for President Taft. He is in about as unfavorable and awkward a position as a man could get in and it is not his own fault that he got into it. That is the reason that he has my sympathy. If a man walks into a hole he has no sympathy from me, but if he is put in a hole, he has my sympathy. President Taft has my profound sympathy and yet he did make a great blunder himself, he did not see the signs of the times, that little cloud no bigger than a man's hand rising on the horizon in the west; he did not know it was going to spread until it covered the whole face of the western heaven, and so in a very well known speech at a town named Winona—which I am happy to say was not in New Jersey,[—]he declared that the Aldrich-Payne tariff was the best tariff ever enacted by a Republican Congress.[7] I think that is nothing less than libel on previous tariffs. Some previous tariffs have been very reasonable in my opinion, but the Aldrich-Payne tariff was impossible—impossible for rational men to sustain.

I say that there was a colossal blunder. I have just now spoken of being an unconstitutional Governor if I should be elected Governor of New Jersey. I don't know that the Constitution forbids the executives or the President from using his patronage in any way he pleases, but it does forbid him to use it in order to drag men into voting the way he wants them to vote. There

6 William Barnes, Harvard 1888; owner of the Albany, N. Y., *Evening Journal*, and leader of the Old Guard Republicans in New York State. Roosevelt had become embroiled in a battle with Barnes for control of the Republican state convention of 1910. Lloyd C. Griscom, a supporter of Roosevelt and Taft, proposed that Roosevelt should serve as temporary chairman. Barnes countered by advancing Vice President James Schoolcraft Sherman for the post. When the convention met on September 27, Roosevelt was elected temporary chairman, and his candidate, Henry Lewis Stimson, was nominated for governor. See Elting E. Morison, *Turmoil and Tradition: A Study of the Life and Times of Henry L. Stimson* (Boston, 1960), pp. 133-38.

7 At Winona, Minnesota, on September 17, 1909.

is an immorality which is very much more serious than an unconstitutionality, and I am very sorry that this great and honorable man has made this use of his patronage and now he says that he made a colossal blunder and used it on the wrong side. That great body of insurgency is running and rising, and these stand-patters are going to get drowned, because if they can't rise they must drown. They cannot stand pat, for that means to stand still. You have got to get a move on you and the only direction in which to move is in the moving direction. But these gentlemen do not see anything moving; they have not had a new thought in a generation. As old Dr. Johnson used to say, the Scotchman was so slow to see a joke that it took a surgical operation to get it into him. Now, it would take a surgical operation to get it into some of these gentlemen who are standing still. Any fool can stand-pat. As Dean Swift used to say if you want to have the reputation of being a very wise man, always agree with the person with whom you are speaking. Standing pat and saying, "Why, we have this great protective system, the pride of American politics." "Quite so, quite so, quite so; I entirely agree with you." Then he is standing pat. It means having no opinion of your own; it means being unable to contribute anything to the progress of the age.

What is the present protection policy of the Republican party —not the ancient protective policy, to which I would give all credit, but an entirely new doctrine? I ask anybody who is interested in the history of high protective tariff to compare the last Republican platform with the last one that preceded it on this very matter of the tariff. Men have been struck, students of this matter, by an entirely new departure. The true doctrine of the protectionist, says that the Republican party—again I am not quoting exactly—should be the difference between the cost of production in American [America] and the cost of production in other countries, plus a reasonable profit to those who are engaged in industry. Now, that is the new part of the protective doctrine. The Republican party by its last national platform guarantees profit to the men who come and ask favors of Congress; and let us see what the results are. I know that a great many gentlemen here are deeply interested in this matter, because they can see that in the matter of their employment they depend upon it; and I want to argue the matter with them very candidly for a moment or two.

The old idea of protective tariff designs to keep American industries alive and therefore keep American labor employed. But the form of protection has become so permanent that this is what has happened. Men, seeing that they need not fear foreign competition, draw together in great combinations; these combinations include factories, if it is a combination of factories, of all grades, old factories and new factories, factories with antiquated machinery and factories with brand new machinery; factories that are economical and factories that are not economically administered; factories that have been long in the family, which has allowed them to become rundown and factories with all the new, modern inventions. Now as soon as the combination is effected, the less efficient factories are put out of operation generally, but the new process has been put on them by the combination, and therefore you have to pay for the stock they issue for the purchase of them, and the United States Government guarantees profit on the investment in factories that have not been put out of business; and as soon as these combinations see the process failing, they reduce the hours of labor, they reduce production, they reduce wages, they throw men out of employment—in order to do what? In order to keep the prices up in spite of the lack of efficiency in finding the best markets and making the best goods.

There was a time when the tariff did not raise prices, but that time is past, and the tariff is now taken advantage of by the great combinations in such a way as to give them absolute control of prices. Now, these things do not happen by chance. It does not happen by chance that prices are and have been rising faster than in any other country. That river that divides us from Canada divides us from much cheaper living, notwithstanding that the Canadian Parliament levies duties on its importations. But there are not these combinations of factories in Canada that ride our backs like the old man of the sea, to make men really believe that these combinations with capital give them the benefit of the tariff. Don't they know that? They know that if they had gotten the benefit out of anything they have gotten the benefit out by the process of organized labor. I say all honor to the legitimate use of organized labor. I have taken the liberty sometimes, as every man should, to criticise some of the things that organized labor has done, but I have never for a moment ceased to sympathize with those essential objects which have benefited the laboring men, and in order that they may not be deprived of the benefit of increasing profits and increasing prosperity.

One of the things that has drawn our admiration to some of the labor organizations of Gloucester county is that they have known how to manage their own affairs without turmoil, without prejudice, like sensible men, and I greatly respect them for it. They are engaged in industries which require a great deal of skill, a skill that has manifested itself in the persistent intelligence with which they have managed their organizations. The history of wages is the history of organized effort; it is not the history of the tariff. The tariff may have made it an opportunity, but the tariff has not operated directly to raise or lower wages.

I know what has sometimes happened. Sometimes when there have been Democratic Congresses and it has been known what certain manufacturers' duties were going to be, they have deliberately closed their mills and thrown men out of employment in order to prejudice the Democratic policy, an action which is just as inhuman as it is unpatriotic. But you know perfectly well, when you analyze the thing for yourselves, that you do not see wages rise and fall with the tariff. Watch the tariff and see what causes the rise and fall of wages. It is the bank accounts of the men who control these great combinations that regulate the price of labor. And does Congress act equitably and uniformly in the matter? Not at all! Some men who have better organized representation in the national House and better organized representatives and replenished campaign funds get more protection for their products than others get in the way of tariff legislation. If you will get some expert to go through the schedules of the present Aldrich-Payne tariff you will find a "nigger" concealed in every woodpile. Some little word, some little clause, some unsuspected item that draws thousands of dollars out of the pockets of the consumers and yet does not seem to mean anything in particular. And when you see the man who stands there for years, interested, pecuniarily interested, in one of the most important industries, one of the industries that has gotten the largest benefits out of the tariff, you ask yourself in all conscience what is going to be next—are the Republicans of this country going to stand for this? And you answer voluntarily, "They are not going to stand for it."

Aldrich is about to retire from the United States Senate and it is an act of very sagacious discretion.

Other men served Cannon in the House, and if you will call the roll of Republican Congressmen in New Jersey you will find a number of men who have been hand in glove with Cannon. The very men who supported Cannon are now trembling in their boots for fear that Cannonism will catch them in the general cataclysm. I can reassure them, it will. Things are going to happen and there's no use trying to sweep back the sea with a broom.

There is no appeal that I know of that will insure them against the earthquake. I have heard the rumblings of that earthquake and I am trying to keep out of doors as much as possible; that is, I mean I am trying to keep in the open and get in touch with my fellow citizens.

I said the Republican party has a platform. It has. Look at that platform with regard to protection. I dare say you have heard rumors of the way votes are obtained after midnight on election day.

I dare say you have heard of the participation of a State not very far distant, from us, in the State of Pennsylvania, in the elections in New Jersey.

A certain journal which has been very kind to me and whose editors I greatly respect said, "It was all well enough for Wilson to say that he subscribed to all the planks in the Democratic platform, but he should be more specific.["] And then it adds: "What did he say with regard to publication of campaign contributors, the specific means by which corrupt practices are to be prevented?"[8] I am surprised that question should be asked. All of that is in the platform. The platform says not merely that there should be legislation with reference to corrupt practices, but demands that the money subscribed, and the persons from whom it comes, shall be made public in every instance. In the Democratic platform where specifications can be given they are given. Take the plank with regard to employers' liability. It doesn't go into particulars there. Why? I will tell you. They do not, nor do I know, all the particulars that will be wise. I know that the present law in regard to employers' liability[9] is entirely inadequate and entirely unsatisfactory. I know there are many ways in which it can be made satisfactory, and there is a way in which it is worked

[8] The editorial in the Jersey City *Jersey Journal*, Oct. 1, 1910, quoted in H. E. Alexander to WW, Oct. 4, 1910, n. 1.

[9] Prior to 1909, New Jersey had no uniform legal code· for dealing with questions of employers' liability, for it was one of the few states which still adjudicated this problem according to common law rules. The maze of legal intricacies and subtleties was resolved somewhat by legislation in 1909 stipulating employers' liability for injury to workers under two conditions. First, the employer was liable for damages if the worker had been injured due to the negligence of a superintendent or some other person acting in behalf of the employer. Second, the worker no longer lost his right of legal action if he stayed at work under conditions that he knew to be unsafe. Juries would determine whether the employee had exercised sufficient caution. The law of 1909 frustrated passage of a stronger bill sponsored by James Gillmor Blauvelt (identified in J. G. Blauvelt to WW, Oct. 5, 1910, n. 1) and the New Jersey Federation of Labor, which lost by one vote in the Assembly. In 1910, labor and New Idea men in the state legislature continued to agitate for more comprehensive employers' liability legislation, but conservative Republicans deflected the effort by establishing a commission to study the problem. It was the bill drafted by this commission that paved the way for a stronger law in 1911. See Noble, *New Jersey Progressivism before Wilson*, pp. 125-27.

satisfactorily in Germany and England. In Germany it is done by actual insurance, and in England the employer is expected to meet the expenses of accidents incident to the employment, whether the servant is negligent or not.

The thing that should be, the thing that must be investigated before we formulate a statute is, which of these works best for the parties concerned, for you will agree with me, gentlemen, that we don't want an act that will be so hard on the employer that he cannot afford to have employees in their trade. We want an act which will enable men to adequately protect their employees against accident. My judgment is that it is the better plan to consider it at a time when one can sit down and find out what has been the experience under these two systems. That is the pledge I am going to give. I am not going off half-cocked and talk to you as if I knew the thing by rote, for I don't and I would be a hypocrite if I said I did. Moreover, I would like to hear from the Republican side more particulars than I have. Can they say that they know the effect it has had upon German and English labor; can they say that they have consulted the labor organizations and know exactly what the labor men want? Do you want from your candidate anything more than a solemn promise that he will keep an open mind in this matter and consult the persons who ought to be consulted? And not the persons who ought not to be consulted. I am not a quack; I don't go about with a patent medicine for everything that is annoying us. You say there is not equal taxation in this State, and I believe you, but you can't prove it; neither can I. Why? Because we have the most imperfect method of assessment; it is go as you please with every tax assessor in this State, and [if] they never consult with each other, how are you going to tell whether the assessments are equal or not. I have been personally acquainted with a good many of the assessors and I have been assessed, and I know that nine out of ten simply copy the assessments of the last assessor, and if you look in the books you will find that they run ten to fifteen years, and while the values have changed the methods of assessing have not changed. You pay these assessors $10 to $50 a year, a most munificent reward. So you cannot expect any expert assessment, you cannot expect men to give their time to anything toward ascertaining what properties are worth at that figure, so in promising you that we will study to try and reform, try to equalize the methods of taxation in this State, what are we promising? We are promising you that we will study the methods of assessing from the bottom to the top and try to put them upon a rational basis, try to find out where the inequalities are, and then correct them. If anybody else can promise any more than that you had better look into their records for veracity.

Take the matter of direct nomination—why, gentlemen, is there anybody satisfied with the primary law of this State[10] as it exists at the present time; is there any reasonable man satisfied with the methods of voting in this State? Think of a system which involves so many different methods; there have been many types, ringed, straight and streaked, and some of them have worked and some of them have not. What we have got to do is to find out which has worked and then get one for New Jersey which has worked. We are not going to hand you out lemons. Our Republican friends have been great optimists. Somebody defined an optimist as a man who made lemonade out of the lemons handed him. Now, our Republican fellow citizens have been handed out a lot of lemons and they looked as cheerful as possible and I think they have been drinking lemonade, but we wish to improve the beverage. I will not express what it might be, but at any rate we will not give you something you will have to make out of lemons, and so I might go on. If anybody wants particulars I cannot give you all the particulars in every speech. Some of you gentlemen who have been criticising my campaign speeches have not had in mind how many I have to make yet. I have to save something, some very pleasant surprises for those who are criticising and thinking I am an amateur campaigner. I have campaigned before, not in the field of politics, but in the field of some politics, the field of education. There is a lot of politics in education. I cannot establish any relation between education and politics because one of the most distinguished—and I will say one of the most reputable politicians—is a graduate, with the highest honors, from the Harvard University, I mean Mr. William Barnes, of New York. Mr. Timothy

10 The campaign for direct primary legislation in New Jersey went back as far as 1892, when George L. Record proposed a comprehensive law to Governor-elect George Theodore Werts, who recommended its adoption in his inaugural address in 1893. However, it was not until 1903 that the New Jersey legislature adopted the first direct primary law. It established direct primaries for all ward and township offices. An unsuccessful attempt was made in 1906 to extend the direct primary to candidates for Congress, all state offices, and presidential electors. In the following year, the legislature approved an extension of the direct primary to state legislators and county and municipal officers. The legislature in 1907 also passed a compromise law creating a senatorial preferential primary. It stipulated that 1,000 voters of a party could petition to have the name of a senatorial candidate placed on the official primary ballot. Candidates for the state legislature had the option of signing a pledge to support the senatorial candidate who received a majority or plurality of the votes of their party within their county or the candidate who received a majority or plurality of the votes of their party within the state. Neither the legislators' pledges nor the outcome of the primary was legally binding. Further efforts to widen the scope of the direct primary prior to 1911 were unsuccessful. *Ibid.*, pp. 130-137.

Woodruff[11] is a graduate of Yale. For my own sake—if you will excuse me, I am not going to mention any others though there are many in the family. Inasmuch as I have been connected with education—perhaps after that you will not have anything to do with me. If Mr. Barnes graduated with highest honors from Harvard and I have been for twenty years connected with another rival university, perhaps you will say you had better not try the three. I have so far lived in a condition of innocence, and I am soliciting you to try me under the force of temptation. For after all, gentlemen, it comes to this, progressive Republicans, progressive Democrats are all after the same thing. For my part, I cannot tell the difference between them. So far as their purposes are concerned and the motives in which they wish to serve the country are concerned, so the thing they all have to decide, Democrats and Republicans is, which set of men will they use for their purposes. Will you continue to use the set of men who are now in control of the Republican organization of your State, or will you turn to another party and try a new set of men—a set of men whatever may be said of their purpose or character are free to serve you, have no entanglements, have made no promises and formed no partnership in interest of any kind, absolutely untrammeled and unbound? Which will you try? I can't argue that point with you. I cannot commend and esteem my character and my patriotism. You must judge that for yourselves. I cannot argue that to you nor the patriotism and character of my friends running on the same ticket with me. I can only say that we are asking you to choose a programme and the men you prefer to carry that program out.

Printed in the Woodbury, N. J., *Gloucester County Democrat*, Oct. 6, 1910, with minor corrections from an FPS T transcript (WP, DLC) and the partial text in the Trenton *True American*, Oct. 6, 1910.

11 Timothy Lester Woodruff, Yale 1879, Lieutenant Governor of New York, 1898-1903, prominent New York Republican, and political ally of William Barnes; president of the Maltine Manufacturing Co. and Pneumatic Machine Co. of Syracuse, N. Y.

From George Lawrence Record

Dear Sir: Jersey City, N. J. Oct. 5, 1910.

The newspapers announce that you have publicly challenged any politician in New Jersey to debate with you upon the public platform any question of public interest.

I am keenly interested in public questions, and I hope I am enough of a politician to qualify under your challenge.

At all events, I accept your challenge, and am willing to meet you in public discussion at any of your meetings, or at such other time and place as you may suggest.

Very truly yours,   George L Record

TLS (WP, DLC).

From James Gillmor Blauvelt[1]

OPEN LETTER TO DR. WOODROW WILSON.

Dear Sir: Paterson, N. J. Oct. 5, 1910.

You are quoted as having said in your Trenton speech:

"I welcome any politician in the state to a debate upon the public platform upon a public question."

In your Long Branch speech, you are quoted as saying:

"Insurgents are very able men. They know what the country wants and know how to get it. x x x There is very little difference between the real Democratic and real Progressive Insurgents."

Is not this latter statement confusing to the public? Your nomination for the governorship has everywhere been hailed because you have been regarded as the very flower of Democracy in New Jersey and, as such, a welcome figure in the political arena. You are regarded as a "real" Democrat. You have been making speeches for about two weeks, but if you think you have been advocating the matters which the Progressive Republicans have been advocating, I think you will only consider it an act of kindness on my part to call attention to the matters which the Progressive Republicans advocate on which you seem to be either silent or so evasive, indefinite and inexplicit that your position on those same questions is practically unknown.

If you desire to advocate the matters dear to the hearts of the Progressive Republicans, I am sure they would be rejoiced to have you do so, and they would also be rejoiced to have your adversary do so. There are certain principles which the Progressive Republicans seek to write upon the statute book in the form of definite laws. We know we have little to hope from the Republican State Committee, composed of Kean, Baird, Strong,[2]

---

[1] Progressive Republican and prominent trial lawyer who defended the workers in litigation arising out of the Paterson silk strike of 1901. Blauvelt served in the New Jersey Assembly in 1909; the following year he abandoned the practice of law to become president of the Hohokus Bleachery Co. of Hohokus, N. J.

[2] Theodore Strong, a lawyer of New Brunswick and frequently associated with the "Board of Guardians." He served as a state senator from 1901 to 1903 and had been a member of the State Board of Assessors since 1903.

Dalrymple[3] and the rest, but we also know we have no hope from Smith, Nugent, Bob Davis and the crowd that has mismanaged the Democratic party for the benefit of the corporations and themselves. My only hope that any of the Progressive Republican measures may succeed in this campaign is that you or your adversary will rise to the occasion and prove bigger than the bosses of your party that made the party platforms and control the party conventions, and that you will both stand for definite measures for the people's welfare in place of the indefinite, inexplicit, read-them-any-way-you-want, declarations in the party platforms.

As you are to address the voters in Paterson in a few days, may I not ask that you then declare your position upon the Progressive Republican measures outlined below. I do this, as I say, because I do not believe your position is known. I, of course, hope that you will take the same position as we. If, however, we should be so unfortunate as to lose your assistance in advancing these measures, I may then take advantage of your challenge, above quoted, and request you to debate upon the public platform the questions on which you take an opposite view, unless the reasons you may give shall seem to me sufficient.

Direct Primary.

1. The Progressive Republicans favor a state law providing for the choice of party candidates for GOVERNOR and CONGRESSMEN and election of delegates to national conventions by the DIRECT VOTE system.

The present direct primary law relates to all offices, EXCEPT THESE THREE. The platform, as drafted for submission to the Democratic state convention, provided for direct primaries for "ALL elective offices," but—BUT before the platform emerged from the convention these words "for ALL elective offices" were STRICKEN OUT, which raises in our minds the fear that you do not stand for direct primaries for ALL elective offices, and do not stand for them for GOVERNOR and CONGRESSMEN. In several of your speeches recently you said you believe that the people have the right of direct nominations. You have dismissed the subject with this slight reference. Many Progressive Republicans have waited patiently for you to define what you mean by that. Do you mean for ALL elective offices? Do you mean that you favor direct primaries for GOVERNOR and CONGRESSMEN or do you not? And, if not, why not? If you do, what are

[3] Alfred N. Dalrymple, Newark lawyer and member of the Republican state executive committee.

you going to do to bring it about? You are not discussing it in public, although it is the most important question before the public to-day and is aimed to destroy the BOSS control of the two parties. You are creating no public opinion upon direct nominations, and you are making it as EASY as possible, though perhaps not intentionally, for a legislature to refuse to pass such a bill. That is what your SILENCE on this subject means for this measure. It means its death.

What measure will you take, if you favor the direct primaries, to induce the present Democratic legislative candidates to declare now, in advance of the election, that they will vote for such a law? Do you not see that in this respect you can render a real service to New Jersey? And whether you agree with us or not, the public is entitled to know how you and how the Democratic legislative candidates, who must be your main support in the event of your election, stand upon this subject in DETAIL, for, as you said in your speech of acceptance: *"Explicitness is the great test of the sincerity of any pledge."*

Fair Primary Officers.

2. The Progressive Republicans advocate a law for the appointment of IMPARTIAL PRIMARY and ELECTION OFFICERS by the court or some other impartial agency where there is a contest at the primaries instead of the appointment of those officers by the county chairman as at present.

Do you favor that? If so, what measures are you taking to secure votes for it in the legislature? Where have you advocated it? If you are opposed to it, why are you opposed to it?

Public Distribution of Ballots.

3. The Progressive Republicans favor the DISTRIBUTION of primary and election BALLOTS at PUBLIC expense by mail.

Do you favor this? If so, what will you do to advocate it and make it such an integral part of the canvass of yourself and the Democratic legislative candidates as will assure its passage in case you and your associates are elected?

If you are opposed to it, why are you opposed to it?

A Modern Ballot.

4. The Progressive Republicans favor the Massachusetts or BLANKET BALLOT containing the names of ALL candidates with party designations, arranged, not in party columns but under the title of the appropriate office.

Do you favor that? If so, what will you do to make it such an integral part of the canvass of yourself and the Democratic legislative candidates as will assure the public of its adoption in case of your and their election?

If you are opposed to it, why?

Safeguarding Primaries and Elections.

5. The Progressive Republicans advocate a law for PERSONAL REGISTRATION at least IN LARGE CITIES with the voter's signature under a proper description of the voter.

Will you let us know your stand on this, and why?

Popular Selection of United States Senators.

6. The Progressive Republicans advocate a law for the adoption of a plan for actual POPULAR CHOICE OF UNITED STATES SENATORS.

What is your position on the question of United States senators as disclosed by the last primaries? Do you believe that Democratic assembly nominees and Republican assembly nominees, who did not declare what their position would be in reference to that primary, are morally bound to follow the expression of the party will as indicated by the results of the primaries? In other words, are not all the Democratic assembly candidates for the assembly bound to vote for Martine for United States senator?[4] Ought not the Republican legislators vote for Stokes for United States senator[5] unless they announced to the voters a contrary determination before the primaries? Will you use the influence of your office, in case you are elected governor, to induce these legislators to follow the will of the voters in their respective parties as expressed at that primary, or will you advocate the election of some other person and, if so, whom?

Will you advocate a law requiring all candidates for legislative offices to file with their petition for nomination a pledge to vote in case of their ultimate election, for the person for United States senator who secured the largest vote for that office in the party primary?

Public Utilities — Valuation.

7. The Progressive Republicans favor a statute giving the PUBLIC UTILITY COMMISSION the power, unpon [upon] com-

[4] James Edgar Martine of Plainfield had defeated Frank M. McDermit of Newark in the Democratic senatorial primary on September 13. Martine received 48,449 votes; McDermit, 15,573. McDermit, a Newark criminal lawyer, had served in the Assembly, 1887-89.

[5] Edward Casper Stokes had won a narrow plurality in the hotly contested Republican senatorial primary on September 13.

plaint or on its own motion, to FIX RATES, and VALUE ALL PHYSICAL PROPERTY devoted to public service; to ENFORCE ADEQUATE SERVICE and to secure the publicity of the affairs of public utility companies, including steam and trolley railroads, together with adequate means for enforcing the order of such commission.

From my reading of your speeches, I think you agree with most of this. But I nowhere observe any reference in your speeches to the advisability of giving the commission the power to value the physical property of the companies. It is important that stress should be laid upon this power because it is an essential power, and it is one that is going to cost some money to carry out, and, on the pretended ground of economy, or some other pretence, legislators will be persuaded to vote against granting this power with an adequate appropriation unless they have been bound to it properly and definitely before the election. What is your attitude on this particular point?

Economy. Useless Offices.

8. You say in your platform that you are in favor of abolishing USELESS OFFICES AND COMMISSIONS—or words to that effect. The Progressive Republicans were more EXPLICIT. They proposed to ABOLISH the COUNTY BOARDS OF TAXATION. What office would you abolish? Would you favor ABOLISHING the STATE BOARD OF RIPARIAN COMMISSIONERS and casting their duties upon the State Board of Assessors, which has the time and ought to be qualified for the work?

Would you ABOLISH the office of REGISTER OF DEEDS and confer the duties upon the County Clerk, as up to a very few years ago was the practice?

Would you favor making such a change in the law as would prevent Passaic County from passing from the second class counties into the first class counties? As soon as the county becomes a first class county, additional salaries will go to officers who don't earn what they get now and new offices are automatically created. What "explicit" change do you advocate?

As this is a public matter, I have taken the liberty of giving this letter to the press.   Yours truly,   James G Blauvelt

TLS (WP, DLC).

From William Gibbs McAdoo

Dear Doctor Wilson: New York October 5, 1910.

We are particularly desirous to have you with us at the next annual dinner of the New York Southern Society, which is to be held at the Waldorf-Astoria on December 14th next. By the unanimous vote of the Executive Committee of the Society today I have been requested to extend to you a cordial invitation. I hope you will accept and speak on some subject that you may find agreeable. We expect to have other distinguished men among our guests, and you will receive a very cordial welcome, I can assure you.

I am delighted to hear of the splendid progress you are making, and am looking forward to your triumphant success in November next.

Believe me, with warm regards,

Very sincerely yours,

W G McAdoo
President
NEW YORK SOUTHERN SOCIETY.

TLS (WP, DLC).

From Joseph M. Noonan

My dear Doctor: Jersey City, N. J. Oct. 5. 1910.

I had expected to have the pleasure of meeting you and hearing you last Wednesday at St. Peter's Hall, for I had been requested to speak at the same meeting, but a cold which has kept me in limbo for the past ten days deprived me of that pleasure. I read your speech, however, with great interest, and found it admirable in every respect—but one. I enclose an editorial from the Jersey Journal of this City which indicates what that "one" is.[1] I am glad to see, however, from the reports of your subsequent speeches in other parts of the State, that there is no longer ground for criticism on this score. That was a very happy touch of yours in speaking of yourself as a probably unconstitutional Governor when judged by the Lewis standard. That sort of thing makes a great impression on the public mind and a little oratorical slamming around will not do the least harm in the world. The only thing, so far as I can see, that can keep your majority within anything like modest bounds is the apprehension, which is troubling some of your Republican friends, that in the guilelessness of your heart you may not be able to cope with the wily practical politicians with whom you will find your-self in contact. You should have no trouble in disabusing their minds on this score. I see you are after the Board of Guardians and the Overlords. That's good. An occassional intimation that, if you should be elected, there won't be any accomodation for these gentry in the Capitol—not even in the cellar—will prove very stimulating and encouraging to those who are looking for a new era. Another thing that occurs to me is that it might be well for you to make a more direct and almost personal appeal to the young voters. This you can do better than your opponent or than any other man who ever ran for Governor. For you have been devoting the best years of your life to the interests of the young men of the country, have always had the broadest and most intimate sympathy with them and have prepared, or helped to prepare, thousands of them to acquit themselves with honor and distinction in the great battle of life.

Wishing you all kinds of prosperity, except the kind the coun-try is just now enjoying, I remain.

Yours very sincerely,   Jos. M. Noonan

TLS (WP, DLC).
[1] "Dr. Wilson Should Discuss the Issues," Jersey City *Jersey Journal*, Sept. 30, 1910.

From John Maynard Harlan

Chicago Ills. Oct. 5-1910

Have just learned that Illinois Manufacturers Ass'n. has invited you to be its guest at its annual meeting in December. The Ass'n. comprises most if not all of the leading manufacturers in the state. It has always exerted great influence and stood for what it believed to be right. By all means you must accept this invita-tion and give your friends here satisfaction of having you known in this community in the new field upon which you have just entered.[1]   John Maynard Harlan.

T telegram (WP, DLC).
[1] See J. M. Harlan to WW, Oct. 21, 1910, n. 1.

From Francis Fisher Kane

My dear Dr. Wilson: Philadelphia October 6, 1910.

Upon my return to the city a few days ago I found your kind letter in my mail. I am delighted to know that there is something for me to do.

I asked a personal friend of Van Valkenburg's to dine with me last night and secured from him a promise to see "Mr. Van" (as they call him at the "North American" office) to-day. My friend is sure that the editorial in yesterday's issue was not dictated by a hostile spirit. I see another editorial in this morning's issue which perhaps bears this out. I send them both to you.[1]

Tom Wanamaker[2] owned the North American and is dead. I know his widow[3] slightly; calling on her would do no good. Should real hostility develop I can see Rodman Wanamaker[4] (Tom's brother) or write to him. I am afraid he would say that the paper is outside of his control. It's interests require that it should not be Democratic but only Insurgent-Republican.

"Mr. Van" is a vigorous and very ruthless person. I mean that he tramples hard upon anyone that gets into his path and the "North American" must make money. Judge James Gay Gordon is the legal adviser of the paper, and there is not in Philadelphia anybody more malicious and more likely "to turn and rend you," if it suits his purposes. Personally I detest him, and it would be a reason for him to influence the paper against you, if he knew that I was working for you. But I do know an old schoolmate of his, who, I think, will point out the fatuity of the "North American" opposing the man who is bound to be successful in New Jersey.

Your speeches have been glorious. Don't overtax yourself. Your campaign is the greatest cause for congratulation that we have had for many a long year.

Don't of course acknowledge this letter.

Yours very sincerely,   Francis Fisher Kane.

TLS (WP, DLC).
[1] "The Shortsightedness of Woodrow Wilson" and "Another Word to Woodrow Wilson," Philadelphia *North American*, Oct. 5 and 6, 1910. Both editorials were only mildly critical of Wilson. They defended insurgency as a positive political force and pointed out Wilson's inconsistencies regarding various progressive programs.
[2] Thomas Brown Wanamaker, Princeton 1883, who died on March 2, 1908.
[3] Mary Lowber Welsh Wanamaker.
[4] Lewis Rodman Wanamaker, Princeton 1886, vice-president of John Wanamaker's department stores, and executor of the estate of Thomas Brown Wanamaker, which owned both the *Philadelphia Record* and the Philadelphia *North American*.

From Wilson B. Killingbeck[1]

Dear Sir: Orange, N. J. Oct. 6th 10.

At the Trenton Democratic Mass Meeting held on the evening of October 3rd, you assumed that there are grounds for your election that are superior to those of all other candidates and you stated that you would "welcome any politician in the state to a debate upon public platform upon a public question." Sir, this statement does you honor. It is not always that we Socialists can induce candidates of your or the Republican Party to debate with Socialist speakers the question of the day.

I, hereby, accept your offer and will, upon correspondence with you, decide upon a place and date convenient to you where I will meet you to discuss the political situation. There is no doubt that even if your evenings are all engaged, a Saturday afternoon can be used for this purpose, or your next Newark Meeting can be held in a park so that thousands can hear us.

If you will allow us to arrange for the debate, we guarantee to defray the entire cost of the meeting including your expenses.

While considering the acceptance of this offer, please remember that the strange political situation in which a man of your standing is pushed to the front in an endeavor to retain for the Capitalistic system the respectability it is losing is of our creating. We are antagonists worthy of your talents. We alone, of all parties, as everyone acknowledges, have a program and system of industrial, social and political organization to offer in place of the present, that is acknowledged by experts to be the only sane solution of the present evils. The Socialist program becoming known speedily to all men makes them dissatisfied with the atrocious social system, under which the men and women who work in productive ways lack the very things they produce and where the non-producer, by virtue of law and custum [custom], makes for himself a position between the producer and consumer that gains him a parasitic prosperity. Not only that, but the parasite, or middleman, with his retainers, the learned professions, and their economic hangers on, outnumber the real producers of the means of life and are constantly obliged, in order to hold their position, to increase their profits at the expense of the poverty and misery of the masses.

Please to remember also that the word Democracy means far more than you are willing to allow it. Your meaning of it is all right for your hearers and admirers. You speak to and for a class whose formerly profitable occupations of middlemen are being slowly but surely absorbed by the combinations of Trusts. They want liberty to make profits and still more profits out of the producer and consumer, and your kind of a Democracy appeals to them. It means a renewed lease of life for competition.

Our idea of Democracy is that no man should be at the economic mercy of another. That no man should owe his life or living or that of his wife and children to the whim or caprice of an employer. That Government and Legislative Bodies should always be controlled by the use of the Initiative, Referendum and right of recall. That where the economic lordship and power has been achieved in a trade by a combination or Trust; that trade, that business is ripe for the people's ownership and operation. We look to see, as the process of centralization grows to its climax that every intelligent person will see that we have the only sane solution—The public ownership and operation of the means of production, transportation and exchange. Only thus can we achieve a true democracy, Only thus will it be possible to destroy the means of exploitation, through the eliminarion [elimination] of rent interest and profit.

While all classes will be benefited by the new social system, we make our appeal especially to the workers who with mind and muscle are the real wealth producers. They compose the exploited class. They have nothing to lose and much to gain by the change and they are rapidly coming to our standard in every country of the civilized globe. And it is from this vantage ground and as their candidate for Governor of the State that I accept your challenge to discuss the meaning of Democracy. I will be glad to hear from you regarding dates and place of meeting for this debate.

Thanking you in advance for a prompt reply, I am yours for a true Democracy.   Wilson B. Killingbeck

TLS (WP, DLC).
1 Socialist candidate for Governor of New Jersey.

A News Report of a Campaign Address in Burlington, New Jersey

[Oct. 7, 1910]

WILSON WINNING HIS WAY

Attentive Audience Last Night at Burlington

BURLINGTON, N. J., October 7.—About 1,200 men and women gathered in the Auditorium in this town last night to hear Woodrow Wilson speak on the issues of the gubernatorial campaign. Frankly, there were vacant seats in the balcony and gallery, due, in large if not complete measure, to the proximity of the Burlington County Fair, and the fact that yesterday was the grand fête day of the week. Evening, therefore, found Burlingtonians sleepy and tired after their holiday diversions, and not in a mood to whoop things up for anybody or anything.

Burlington, 6 Oct., 1910.

——————— o ——————

What we want is Service of the Common interest
    Items: Conservation — transportation — no monopolizing.
    Means: Regulation and direct popular control.
This the common impulse: this what every liberal man
    stands & strives for.
In New Jersey
    The Rep. leaders do not even pretend to stand for
        these things, and if they did, who would
        believe them? Who are they?
    The Dem. leaders at least new.
The country over:

    A divided Republican house
    Everywhere new Dem. leaders

Other States have forged ahead: New Jersey has
    lagged behind for 15 years, under "constitutional"
    governors and leaders. "Constitutional" = machine
    ~~back~~ led.

6 Oct. 1910

Let it not be understood from this that the meeting, to fall
into the political as well as theatrical vernacular, was a "frost."
It was not. Dr. Wilson had an attentive audience, who caught
his points and applauded them generously. It was only that this
was the first gathering at which people have not been turned
away from the doors by scores and hundreds, and the contrast
last night was striking only because of that. Residents of Burlington said that, as political meetings go here, it was a fine success. . . .

At the meeting which followed Dr. Wilson followed his custom of speaking extemporaneously. Parts of his speech which
were most loudly applauded follow:

"We have done things in this country without great thought.
Nature has given us abundant largess, and so, unceasing, we
have pressed forward to miscellaneous ends until we became
among the richest nations of the earth. Now has come the time
when we have stopped to wonder what has happened. So ardent-
ly, so eagerly, have we pressed forward that we have lost the simplicity of the olden days and are now, to-day, facing a situation
where opportunity is no longer as free as the air and wherein
privileges belong to the few.

"We are now conserving the natural resources of our own
State, facilities in which are in danger of falling into hands of
special interests. Conservation extends beyond natural resources.
There is the conservation of human life; the improvement of
factory conditions, the fight against tuberculosis; in short, the
conserving of our race to the end that our physical force and
mental balance may be preserved."

His reference to the Legislature was received with marked
favor.

"Legislation needs an atmosphere in which to thrive, if the
proper thing is to be done. Legislative matters should not be
passed upon secretly in committee and then acted upon openly
on the floor. We should know all the inducements which tempt
legislators from their duty. This applies to all parties. I am not
a Pharisee. I know that men are engaged in their own affairs
and are not inclined to view conditions which exist outside
of those affairs. But they should be brought to see how far their
own interests affect and are affected by the public good."

Concerning direct primaries:

"Primaries should be direct and primary. Primary, inasmuch
as they should be the first appeal to the people, and direct, inasmuch as they should insure the people's choice as to candidates,
without interference of party leaders."

He had a sharp dig at the Republican leaders of the State:

"The constitutional manner," he said, "in which the Republicans walk has interested me. You have heard of the Board of Guardians, I suppose. I have asked the members of it what they were guardians of, but have never received a satisfactory reply. It is the privately professional name of the Republican State committee, and its object is to see that nothing passes the Legislature that is not approved by the committee. I do not believe the Legislatures of our States are naturally corrupt bodies. America has not fallen so low as that. They follow the tendency to organize under some prevailing influence. I have talked with legislators and know that their desire is to serve in legislative bodies that are free and not bound to anything save the interests of the people."

Of Aldrich he said:

"Mr. Aldrich does not belong to any party. He is not a Republican, and I am glad to say he has never been a Democrat. He has merely used the great name of the Republican party for his private interests."

Leading up to this attack on the Republican leaders Dr. Wilson said:

Legislators ought not to be subjected to the temptations of arranging things privately in committees and passing them without debate on the floor. You know that every bit of regulative legislation touches the interests of some sort of influential persons. We should have it in the most public way, so that we should hear all the arguments used and know all the inducements that are resorted to. I say that for the safety of all parties. I am not a Pharisee.

I know the natural power of self-interest and I know that many an honest man, concentrated in his attention upon his own business, sees nothing but his own business; and it requires that his attention should be drawn to it before he will see his own business is related to the common interest.

I am not only insisting that we should have a corrupt practices act, but I am also insisting against all that which operates when things are done in private. And so I say we have but to do everything which will bring our legislators and legislation into direct contact with the choice of the people. That is the reason it is important to discuss matters like direct primaries, and to find something in the form of direct primary that will be direct; that is to say, first of all resort to the people themselves, and that will be direct; that will not be susceptible to manipulation by persons that ought not to manipulate.

Continuing, he said that all over the country there was an impulse to serve.

Have the Republican leaders served the people of New Jersey as they had promised to serve? Have the present leaders, and by the present leaders I mean the men who organized and conducted the convention, and who nominated the Republican candidate for Governor—do the people understand these gentlemen to have promised them service along the lines that I have indicated, and if they do understand them to have promised that service, do they expect them to keep the promise?

Just as an exercise of memory, if nothing else, go back and read the platform of three years ago. Go over it by item. It is generalized for the most part, but so far as it is itemized, go over the items and see how many of these promises have been kept. These are my witnesses in respect to the keeping of these promises. Republicans themselves are my witnesses. I am now telling you only what Republicans have again and again said in the Republican prints of this State, that the Republican party leaders had not kept faith with the people; had not given them the things they wanted. These same gentlemen who did not keep these promises are the gentlemen who are now giving you new promises.

From the old ones, what is the characteristic circumstance in which you find these gentlemen? You find them tied up with just the same interests which have prevented their keeping their promises in the past. Is there any one of them whom you have observed who has detached himself from the interests which have prevented him from keeping these promises in the past? Is there anything new in the personal make-up of the leadership of the Republican party in this State in this day which gives you hope in this respect?

On our side, what can we say to you? We are at least offering you new men, men who have not been, and could not be, entangled in these alliances. We are at least offering you men who have made it their duty to study these things from an offing, it is [who are] not entangled with the interests which would warp their judgment, and I ask you if it is not more reasonable to expect these men free to keep their promises than the other men?

I am not asking you to believe, for I do not myself believe, that the Democratic candidate for Governor is a more honest man than some of the eminent men who have led the Republican party. That is not the point. I merely want to ask you if you do not believe he is a free man; that he has the fighting qualities which come from his Scotch-Irish blood, and if you believe, moreover, that he is not afraid of the things that he will be expected to fight.

Printed in the New York *Evening Post*, Oct. 7, 1910.

From Richard Vliet Lindabury

My dear Doctor: Newark, N. J. October 7, 1910.

I am just in receipt of a letter from Judge Van Syckel[1] from which I quote as follows:

"I see in the evening papers that Record has offered to meet Dr. Wilson on the stump. It seems to me that Dr. Wilson should decline. If Record adheres to the views he expressed in a letter shortly after Lewis was nominated, Dr. Wilson agrees with him and there is nothing to discuss. If Record has changed his views to secure votes for Congress Dr. Wilson should be unwilling to meet him."

Judge Van Syckel, as you know, is a Democrat of wide experience and great ability and his views are always worthy of consideration. Partly because of this and partly because I entirely agree with him, I am letting you know how the matter strikes him.

Permit me to congratulate you on the splendid canvass you are making. The newspapers are reporting you so fully that I am able to follow your speeches quite closely. Besides, I am constantly hearing from others who have attended your meetings and they tell me that as a campaigner you are a wonder. Judge Van Syckel writes that he heard your Trenton speech and it was "very effective." For the good of the state and the country, I most heartily wish you success and I hope that your majority will be so large as to prove the ability of the electorate to distinguish between sincerity and false pretenses.

I am,   Yours sincerely,   R. V. Lindabury

TLS (WP, DLC).
[1] Bennet Van Syckel of Trenton, Princeton 1846, justice of the Supreme Court of New Jersey, 1869-1904.

From Job Herbert Lippincott

Dear Mr. Wilson: Newark, N. J., Oct. 7/10

I trust you will pardon me for making the following suggestion. I make it for the reason that it may be of use to you, to learn the feeling of the people in Hudson County, in reference to Mr. Record's letter.

I believe that the general run of Independent voters, who have allied themselves with the New Idea faction, are going to vote for you. I believe that it will be a great deal better for you to meet Mr. Record, as I feel that no discussion of the issues in this campaign will alienate this vote from you. I do, however, feel that should you refuse to meet Mr. Record, that you would come in for some criticism from Hudson County.

If Mr. Record attempts to defend the Republican State Platform, he will be forced to go contrary to almost every principle of the New Idea faction. He himself is running for Congress in the 9th District, on a Platform which condem[n]s the Payne-Aldridge Tariff, which the Republican State Platform defends. Our Democratic Platform is far more in accordance with the New Idea principles than the Republican Platform, and I do not see how it is possible for anything but good to come from your meeting Mr. Record.

With kind regards, and best wishes for your success, I am

Very truly yours   Job H Lippincott

TLS (WP, DLC).

From William T. Ferguson

Dear Sir: Washington, D. C. Oct 7/10

With the aid of Rev. Dr. Waldron,[1] I succeeded in having our organization go on record as endorsing your candidacy.[2] I hope that our action will not lose you any white support. I am certain that it will add colored. Dr. Waldron and Dr. Du Bois[3] are the gentlemen whom I hoped to have speak to our colored brethren in New Jersey. I hope the New Jersey papers will report our action of yesterday. We had a rousing big meeting, Bishop Walters[4] and Wm. Monroe Trotter[5] being among the speakers.

Yours truly   W T Ferguson

Mr [Henry Eckert] Alexander did not answer my letter.

ALS (WP, DLC).

[1] John Milton Waldron, pastor of the Shiloh Baptist Church of Washington since 1906 and first president of the Negro-American Political League in 1908. He was one of the founders of the National Association for the Advancement of Colored People in 1909-10 and established and presided over the Afro-American Industrial and Benefit Association, 1899-1905. Educated at Lincoln University and Newton Theological Institution, Waldron was active as a journalist and public speaker urging civil rights for Negroes.

[2] The National Independent Political League met at Galbraith African Methodist Episcopal Church in Washington on October 6. Bishop Alexander Wal-

ters, the N.I.P.L. president, attacked Roosevelt, Taft, and the Republican party for deserting Lincoln's legacy and urged Negroes to support candidates of any party who espoused the welfare of blacks. In New Jersey, the N.I.P.L. endorsed Wilson but also various Republican candidates for the legislature and Congress. In Ohio, the organization advocated the election of the Democrat, Judson Harmon, for governor and a Republican legislature. In New York, the N.I.P.L. supported the Democratic gubernatorial nominee, John Alden Dix, and all opponents of Roosevelt candidates, and in Massachusetts it recommended voting against all members of the legislature favorable to the re-election of Senator Henry Cabot Lodge. The N.I.P.L. also endorsed straight Republican tickets in Delaware and West Virginia. See the *Washington Herald*, Oct. 7, 1910; Washington *Evening Star*, Oct. 7, 1910; *Washington Post*, Oct. 7, 1910; and Baltimore *Afro-American Ledger*, Oct. 29, 1910.

³ William Edward Burghardt Du Bois, one of the leaders of the "Niagara Movement" formed in 1905 to oppose Booker Taliaferro Washington's policies of accommodation with the white establishment and a founder of the National Association for the Advancement of Colored People, at this time editor of the *Crisis*, official organ of the N.A.A.C.P., and director of research and publicity for that organization. In addition to his efforts in the civil rights movement, Du Bois was also one of the leading black intellectuals of the twentieth century. He did his undergraduate work at Fisk University and Harvard University, pursued graduate study at the University of Berlin, 1892-94, and received the Ph.D. in history from Harvard in 1895. His doctoral dissertation was published as the first volume in the Harvard Historical Studies, *The Suppression of the African Slave-Trade to the United States of America, 1638-1870* (New York and London, 1896). He was editor of the pioneering analyses of black culture and society, *The Atlanta University Publications* (16 vols., Atlanta, Ga., 1898-1914), as well as the author of *The Souls of Black Folk* (Chicago, 1903) and *The Philadelphia Negro* (Philadelphia, 1899).

⁴ The Rev. Dr. Alexander Walters, bishop of the African Methodist Episcopal Zion Church since 1892 and former pastor of the historic "Mother Zion" Church of New York. With Timothy Thomas Fortune, editor of the *New York Age*, Walters was one of the founders of the Afro-American League in 1890, which reorganized in 1898 as the National Afro-American Council. He was elected president of this organization seven times, served as president of the National Independent Political League in 1909 and 1910, and established and led the National Colored Democratic League in 1912 to support Wilson's presidential candidacy. In addition to these political activities, Walters was active in various ecumenical causes.

⁵ One of the prominent Negroes opposed to Booker T. Washington's policies during the early twentieth century. Born in Massachusetts and educated at Harvard, Trotter was the editor and publisher of one of the leading black newspapers of the period, the Boston *Guardian*, as well as president of the New England Suffrage League and corresponding secretary of the National Independent Political League, in which he was the dominant force.

A News Report of a Campaign Speech in Bridgeton, New Jersey

[Oct. 8, 1910]

WILSON TAKES HARD FALL OUT OF GRIGGS

Sails Sharply Into the State Water Board

Bridgeton, Oct. 8.—In one of the almost impregnable citadels of the "enemy's country" last night Woodrow Wilson found his way to the hearts of an awakened people in one of the most direct, most pointed and forceful of all the addresses he yet has made. He aroused an immense audience¹ to a wild pitch of

¹ In the Criterion Theatre in Bridgeton.

enthusiasm and it was a plain appeal to the people of the nation, of New Jersey and Cumberland county, to awake and cast off the malign influences of machine politics. Over and over again, as he forced home the plain truths that lie next his great heart, he won a response from the audience which choked the theater entrances which showed that his lofty ideals had reached the spot.

Ex-Governor John W. Griggs, who said at Hackensack, the other night, that Dr. Wilson never offered to serve New Jersey till he had been nominated for Governor, was fairly potted. Without mentioning the name of the author of this criticism, Dr. Wilson referred to it in these words:

"I am told—I did not see it—but I am told that a gentleman who was once Governor of New Jersey says that I never offered to serve New Jersey until I was nominated for a political office. Well, he was elected to a political office and never served New Jersey, and as between the two cases I think mine is the better.

"It at least remains to be shown that, if elected Governor of New Jersey, I cannot serve the state and will sit down and do nothing with a degree of patience, a degree of dignity, a degree of pleasing eloquence which will not discourage the pulsations of the machine in the least."

State commissions also came in for Dr. Wilson's attack, one in particular, the State Water Supply commission, of which ex-Governor Foster Voorhees is president. He said:

"Did you ever reflect upon the water commissioners? They are supposed to do something about preserving the watersheds which supply New Jersey. I never have observed that they have done anything in particular. Every man of the commission draws $2,500 a year. The total cost of the commission, I never can remember figures, but it is over $10,000 a year. They meet very infrequently and then only for a little while and the president, or at any rate one of the members of the board, I believe he is the chairman, is the president of a water company. Now I have no doubt that he likes being water commissioner, but I do not like his being water commissioner."

The recent [Republican senatorial] primary battle in Cumberland county between former Governor Edward C. Stokes and State Senator Isaac T. Nichols in which, it is alleged, barrels of money were spent, gave Mr. Wilson a clue which he used to big advantage, his thrusts being cheered time and again by the crowd.

After declaring for a corrupt practise act that would prohibit campaign contributions from corporations and provide publicity and limitation of election expenditures, he had his audience almost on their feet when he said:

"Do you know how much money was spent in the recent primary contests in this neighborhood? Do you not think that sums of money, obviously too large, were spent, and, likewise, not all spent for legitimate purposes, and do you know that the results were sometimes, not always, but sometime[s] manipulated? You could have legislation to prevent that, but the chief leaders have never allowed such legislation to go through."

Then he spoke in regard to that matter upon which so much attention has been concentrated and about which so many promises have been broken, the regulation of the railway rates, the establishment of a commission with power to regulate rates, not the power merely to talk about rates and report on them, but the power to regulate. That has been done in other states, while New Jersey has hesitated.

"You have in your present leaders the most promising crowd of gentlemen that I have ever heard of," he said. "You have been very indulgent with your present leaders; you have with a simplicity that I thought would be impossible among men, failed to observe the operation of affairs. I congratulate you for your faith in human nature.

"What has interested your leaders, and what only has interested your leaders, is who should be the next candidate for the United States senate. That is what has stirred up the Republican leaders to their real depth. They have not been worried about these questions which affect the welfare, happiness and support of the whole Commonwealth; they have been stirred up by the question as to whose turn it was to go to the United States senate. Were the primaries contested on the ground of great public questions? No, wholly on the ground of a personal choice, and some men, at least one man,[2] offered himself in any contest where anything was to be discussed because he cannot discuss anything.

"I have my private doubts whether he knows what the issues of the campaign are except by label. His name is David, and I do not know that he has any Jonathan. And you have had your primaries upon this interesting question, what was the result,

[2] Wilson was referring to David Baird, Republican boss of Camden County who, although he had not run in the senatorial preferential primary, was already organizing a campaign for election to the Senate if his party won a majority in the next legislature. Baird began his political career in the 1870s as a Camden County freeholder; he next served as county sheriff from 1887 to 1890 and 1896 to 1899. He was a member of the State Board of Assessors during 1895-96 and from 1901 to 1909, serving as president of that agency from 1904 to 1909.

gentlemen, now that the primaries are over and the people of New Jersey of the Republican sort are supposed to have spoken their choice. Nobody knows, if you have a Republican Legislature, whether that choice is going to stand or not. Men have poured out money. There have been many workers.

"In one precinct, not so far away from the sound of my voice, there were eighty-three workers. You have been stirred up to the depths of your souls, and now that it is all over nobody knows whether it counts or not. Money has been spent, energies have been spent, the papers have been filled with letters of crimination and recrimination.

"You would have thought that these gentlemen were leaders [of] opposing hosts, and now that it is all over, I understand petitions are to be circulated asking the Republican members of the legislature whether they are going to stand by the result of these primaries or not. How many times you have been stirred up upon these deeply important personal questions before they are decided, and when you have decided them, to what extent have they affected the welfare of the country in any way? Not in any visible way. Do you know what these gentlemen would do if they went to the senate? You have not asked any of them.

"The principal question upon which you have wasted your time is who should go there and do what he pleases. He is not pledged—nobody is pledged, so far as I am able to understand. No one is pledged to anything in particular or to anything in general. And it is very likely, I should think, from what I hear, that if the Republicans elect a majority upon joint ballots in the coming legislature, you would have to guess over again to know who was going to be elected to the United States senate.

"When you see things like this stirring up great parties, you know what is stirring them. It is not the pulse of opinion; it is the pulse of a machine. You know some machines. For example, take the automobile. I have been, for the first time in my life, riding all over the country in an automobile, and I notice when the crank is started and the machine is stopped it can tremble all over and never go an inch. That is the kind of vitality that is at present stirring the Republican organization.

"It is the pulse of the machine, and the Republican party is not getting anywhere under the impulse of that machine, and the men who cranked the machines are not likely to go to the senate, either. Surely, here is much ado about nothing. Surely, here are things for serious-minded citizens of the great commonwealth to spend their time and energy on."

Continuing, Mr. Wilson said that what he desired to do in

making a campaign was not to elect himself Governor of New Jersey. "Because," he said, "I am engaged in things now, and have been for twenty years, which I thoroughly understand and have managed to do successfully.

"I am venturing out upon new fields. It would be a great deal more comfortable for me not to be Governor of New Jersey, and, therefore, I can say to you in all candor that I am not asking you for an office which I covet. But there is one thing which I do deeply covet, and that is an opportunity to serve the people of New Jersey in some sensible way."

Here he fired the shot at Griggs, the point of which his hearers instantly caught.

"There are very quiet, comfortable and prosperous ways of being Governor of New Jersey," he went on, "that I do not desire. I have said that the rest of the country is going forward, while New Jersey has stood still. This is what attracts my attention, for it mortifies me, as a citizen of New Jersey, while a great commonwealth full of men radiant for the public interest is sitting under a sort of hypnotic influence, believing that they are being served by the men whom they have elected to office.

"I am uncomfortable under these conditions. And while these conditions remain, what is happening, do you suppose, that the rest of the country has not noticed that New Jersey is stalled?"

Pursuing this line of thought he said that one of the functions of a political machine was to create as many offices as possible in order that the machine might be supported.

It was an easy transition to the subject of state extravagance. Then he aimed his blow at the State Water Supply commissioners.

Paying a tribute to independent voters he praised insurgency, which, he said, was merely another word for independence of judgment. All the progress that had ever been made in government, he said, came from men of that stamp. Again he paid his respects to Cannonism and Aldrichism.

"That sort of public man is never respected. He goes into the past," he said. "We shall presently look back upon him as a curiosity, an unpleasant curiosity, just as we might go into a bacteriological museum and look into glass jars at the germs of past diseases, put in glass jars and in alcohol in order that the contagion might not spread."

Discussing employers' liability he said that New Jersey had no efficient law on that subject because the laboring man had been misled by false assurances. It was not the tariff, he continued, but the wise use of organized labor that had carried the rate of wages forward. But for the systematic and organized effort of working men their wages would not have advanced properly.

"The relation between the employer and the employe in respect to liability for accident is very unsatisfactory as the law stands in New Jersey now. We have no satisfactory legislation on this subject. Our legislation stands just where it stood generations ago when the organization of labor was absolutely different from what it is now. I believe, gentlemen, that the most thoughtful of working men in this country desire not an advantage, not an unfair advantage for labor, but justice for labor. What they want is such an employers' liability act as will give the working man proper insurance against accident and relieve him of these subterfuges of technical law which now make it so extremely difficult for him to get any support after an accident has happened."

Printed in the *Paterson*, N. J., *Guardian*, Oct. 8, 1910.

A News Report of Campaign Speeches at Cape May Court House and Wildwood, New Jersey

[*Oct. 8, 1910*]

FORGET STORM AT HEARING WILSON

Cape May County Turns Out Strongly at Two Big Meetings to Welcome Him.

Wildwood, N. J., Oct. 8.—It amazed Woodrow Wilson to discover how many Cape May countians risked the discomforts of a chill, wet day and night to come to see and hear the man who is making the new kind of campaign in New Jersey. And those who came to two large meetings, one at Cape May Court House, this afternoon, and the other here to-night,[1] with one accord expressed with decided emphasis their awakened interest.

It was as though the elements had conspired to cast the candidate for a minor part, but in the play of emotions among his auditors there was no gainsaying the fact that his was a stellar role. In both his addresses Mr. Wilson continued his appeal to the broadest spirit of patriotism and sense of justice lying, as he firmly believes, inherent in the breasts of American citizens. He strenuously attacked Machine politics and its twin evil, a corrupted ballot.

In both his meetings this newly-discovered leader of American manhood and honor received many open assurances of support

[1] In the Hippodrome in Wildwood.

Wildwood, 8 Oct., 1910.

The country in search of remedies for
    Special privilege
    Legal inequalities
    Extravagance, in brief.
    Selfish use of power

Many new men drawn out into service. For what
    To study the new problems, without prejudice
       Or, rather the old problems

The Republican party? New men? New mea-
    sures?

It comes to a choice of sympathies & objects
On the one hand the habits and the alliances
    of Power.
On the other the information & comprehension of
    long disinterested observation and the
    habit of independent thinking

from the people irrespective of parties' ties. Many well-known Republicans appeared and warmly applauded his most telling points, especially as he alluded to the boss system as applied to Cape May county. The meeting here was held in the new Hippodrome, and, despite the steady downpour beating heavily upon the roof and into the open space above the rows of seats, contained fully 500 persons, all deeply interested in the issues in this campaign for better government.

Men in oilskins and some in dusters and women in heavy winter wraps listened with rapt attention to the address of the night, applauding warmly as if no storm beat upon the storm of popular approval of the man upon whom the eyes of a nation are focused. Mr. Wilson stepped out into the ring to get closer to his audience and modestly disclaimed all credit for learning and greatness, as had been claimed for him by J. Thompson Baker's[2] interesting and dramatic introduction. He told the crowd he was not seeking the Governorship and believed that no man should seek public office in his personality, but that he was before the voters standing for principles.

"I believe," said he, impressively, at the conclusion of one of the best addresses he has so far delivered, "that the greatest day of change has dawned upon America, the greatest day-dawning that has ever been seen, and the most dangerous thing would be the election of partisan candidates at this crisis. For America is awakening, and when America awakes the world sees a new play put upon the boards."

The shout of approval which followed the sentiment drowned the roar of the breakers and the throb of the storm.

Referring humorously to the fact that he had been designated as a schoolmaster by former Governor Griggs, Mr. Wilson said: "It is significant in my mind that we are not in an ordinary political campaign. It is perhaps extraordinary in the circumstances that a schoolmaster is on one side. I am proud to be a schoolmaster, and I wish that some of the gentlemen who are opposing the policies I am in favor of had attended school to some purpose. They may some time have known things that would be now to their advantage, but it is interesting that the same gentlemen have not hesitated when the State was in need of money to appropriate part of the school fund in order to pay the running expenses of the government, so that it is no wonder that they look askance at a schoolmaster."

[2] Jacob Thompson Baker, one of the founders of Wildwood and the borough of Wildwood Crest, N. J., and first mayor of the consolidated town of Wildwood in 1911 and 1912.

Returning to the main theme of his address, the return of the old spirit in American affairs, Mr. Wilson said: "There is a new tide in politics, a new tide which is running very strong. It runs throughout the country, and yet, perhaps, it is not a new tide, but the return of the old tide, the tide of the politics of sympathy and of the comprehension of policies which has not run for so long in our politics. We are now feeling the rise of the waters that used to float the Ship of State in America, the time when men were concerned not so much with the success of the parties as with the success of policies.

"You know what has happened throughout the length and breadth of this country in recent years. Opinion has broken away from the parties, opinion has risen supreme, but our politicians in New Jersey are trying to persuade you to conduct your affairs as if there had not been any awakening of judgment on the part of the citizens of the Commonwealth to public interests. But the thing will not do, this opinion is not manageable, it cannot be manipulated, cannot be silenced, cannot be resisted.

"It is not for the benefit of the people that it is necessary that the expenditures of the Government have nearly quadrupled in a period of about 12 years. But that is not confined to New Jersey. The expenses of the Federal Government have increased three times more rapidly than has the population of the United States within those three [sic] years. Everywhere money is being put out like water and we are paying the bills.

"Of course, the money is not spent out of the pockets of those who conduct the Government, but it is spent out of your pockets. What have we gained? Well, we have gained something, not directly out of the expenditure, but out of the things that have resulted from the expenditure. It is a very singular circumstance that a Republican President of the United States[3] called the attention of the whole country to the misuse of power by his own party and by all those who have been concerned in public affairs."

Getting to State conditions, Mr. Wilson said: "What the Republican party of New Jersey is now face to face with is the reckoning brought about by that awakening produced by the voice of a Republican President. The result of that awakening has been that everywhere the Republican party is divided. There is nowhere that I can learn of, except perhaps in the State of Massachusetts, which is extremely well managed, any solid Republican party, so far as leaders are concerned.

"Is there a solid Republican party in New Jersey? Do you

---

[3] He referred to Theodore Roosevelt, whose growing insurgency and criticisms of the Taft administration were threatening to split the Republican party.

know what your leaders have been interested in in recent months? They have not been debating your welfare; they have been debating who should be sent to the United States Senate. They have not been interested in the matters in which they should have been interested, in the matters of change of policy.

"The managers of the country are certain persons who have been interested in party control as the policy for running the Government. It is not a new circumstance; this has happened in past times to the Democratic party. I want you to understand that I am not delivering a partisan speech, and I never shall deliver a partisan speech. I want to say very frankly that this is something in past years has happened to the Democratic party, and the pity of politics is that if you leave men in power long enough to give them the impression that the party machine can at its pleasure command the majority of the votes, then this thing will happen to it.

"They will become indifferent, as they have become indifferent to the real movement of conviction in the ranks of their own party and among their own people. They will assume, as they have assumed, that the interest of the people of New Jersey is to keep certain Republican leaders in charge when the real interest of the people of New Jersey is to serve their best interests by the right policies."

Going after Machine politics, of which Cape May county has a very intimate acquaintance, the speaker said: "A great political Machine builds up its fortunes and success in the midst of things as they are and considers itself under bonds to see that those things are not changed, because they don't know whether they can make their calculations under the changed circumstances or not, and so they are under bonds to the existing order. But the existing order is susceptible in this country only to those who have exceptionally profited by it. It does not achieve justice or bring about the kind of progress that is most desired, and so, throughout our survey of modern conditions, we see how natural it is, I dare say, how inevitable it is, that men in charge of public affairs for years together should allow themselves to be governed by things as they are. I want to be perfectly fair and not insinuate that the grosser kind of corruption is involved in this matter. I don't want to intimate that the public men have yielded to temptation that other men would not have yielded to. I am pointing to circumstances, not making accusations, and they are undisputable as I have stated them.

"Extravagance has for its foundation what? What do you get if you are a member of a political Machine? What do you get by large appropriations out of the public fund? No money to line your pocket with, but new offices for your friends, new opportunities of patronage, the general feeling that people will stand by you and your associates; that there shall be lots of money to spend upon contracts, offices and improvements of various kinds, and therefore the thing to do is to stand by the people who have access to the general fund.

"That is the kind of power that comes out of the expenditure of large sums of money, and the Republican Machine at the present moment has by that calculation four times as much power as the Democratic Machine that it displaced 15 or 16 years ago. That is the most demoralizing sort of power that can possibly exist, because you tie scores of men to you by self-interest, rather than by patriotic conviction."

Mr. Wilson caused a significant titter in the audience, so well acquainted with Senator "Bob" Hand,[4] when he said: "You know a boss when you see him and you know what he does. Now, do you like it? Do you think he is accomplishing anything substantial to your welfare? Do you think he is in business for his health? Do you think he regards it as a public service or private business? I don't have to answer these questions for you. And do you like going through the motions at the bidding of such persons?

"You have recently been through the motions of a primary contest to express your opinion as to who ought to be United States Senator, if there happens to be a Republican Legislature to send one. I don't think there is going to be one, but if there happens to be you have been through the motions of saying whom you prefer of several candidates differing very widely in character. If you have a Republican Legislature are you sure that your preference will be recorded, will be registered?

"I understand at the present moment that it is thought that it will be wise to begin the thing all over again and to circulate petitions to be signed, begging the members of the Legislature to vote for the people's choice. If I were a betting man I would like to wager you that you know who in those circumstances would be United States Senator again. I say 'again' because everybody knows that the other United States Senator is engineering the campaign. It is a family party.

"If you expect in voting for a Republican Legislature to have your preferences recorded you better get up and hump your-

---

[4] Robert E. Hand, state senator from Cape May County, 1898-1903 and 1907-1912. He was a dominant figure in Cape May County Republican circles and was extensively engaged in oyster planting and general contracting and owned large timber holdings in New Jersey.

selves because it may not happen. Now, are you going to indulge in this game any longer on a mere gambler's chance? Do you like it? I have read in the Scriptures praise of faith, hope and charity. Now, I must say and I do not think I am disobedient to the Scriptures, that I think you have exercised the three long enough. Your faith has been betrayed, your hope has not been realized, and your charity must be exhausted because politics in a popular country, I mean under a popular government, is a thing in which the people can be fooled."

This is the way in which Mr. Wilson hit back effectively at the Republican leaders who thought the first week of his campaign had been a failure:

"I spent the first week of my campaign trying to set forth what I considered the principles upon which the Democratic party was trying to act. I noticed that some of my Republican critics have said that I spent that week in glittering generalities. I do not wonder at that, for they have not looked a principle in the face so long that they do not know one when they see it.

"Now, I wish that principles could glitter as generalities until they constituted the sun by which men would guide their steps, in which all should stand in the air of the glitter, the gleam of compelling light of the things that we call principles, and a man that despises principles as glittering generalities has absolutely no compass by which to steer, he is steering by the compass of expediency.

"He says I would like my opponent to get down to particulars so that I could catch him, trip him up on some detail and then I will check him. I cannot meet him. No, I cannot meet him on this field of high ideals. If they cannot meet us upon this field of high ideals then they will be overthrown in the contest, because the American people are now turning back to past policies, to the ideals upon which this government was built up, and chief of all is that ideal which says that Government ought to thrive in every pulse in sympathy for the common people. They are recovering the breath that they had in that day of hope."

Printed in the *Philadelphia Record*, Oct. 9, 1910; some editorial headings omitted.

From David L. MacKay[1]

Dear Sir: Astoria, L. I., Oct. 8, 1910.

In the New York Sun of Oct. 8, which purports to give extracts of your speech at Bridgeton, N. J., you are quoted as follows:

"I believe that labor has been misled for a number of years by false assurances. Labor men have advanced in efficiency in this country because of their unions and because of absolutely nothing else."

Your reported remarks are so directly opposite to those of your baccalaureate sermon of June 14, 1909 that I am led to ask whether you repudiate them. In the latter you said as follows:

"You know what the usual standard of the employe is in our day. It is to give as little as he may for his wages. Labor is standardized by the trade unions, and this is the standard to which it is made to conform. No one is suffered to do more than the average work man can do."

This, it seems to me, is a condemnation of trades unionism based on the belief that it prevents an advance in efficiency. I believe that an explanation is due labor in order that it may not be misled "by false assurances.["]

Though not a voter in the state of New Jersey, nevertheless, being a firm believer in trades unionism, I would appreciate it very much if, in the stress of a political campaign, you could find time to reply.   Very truly yours,   David L. MacKay

ALS (WP, DLC).
[1] A labor union official who served as president of the Central Association of Building Trades in Manhattan during 1909.

To Wilson B. Killingbeck

[Dear Sir: Princeton, N. J., Oct. 10, 1910]

Allow me to acknowledge the receipt of your letter of October 6, which arrived during my absence from home, and to which I have had no earlier opportunity to reply.

I am very much interested in your suggestion that we might come together in debate, but unhappily I have promised every day that is available between now and election for the regular speech-making of the campaign, and discussion of the questions involved in the programs of the Republican and Democratic parties. While I feel that it would be most interesting to discuss with you the things which you believe should be done for the betterment of society, I feel that such a discussion would lead us very far afield, and that it is not practicable for me to depart from the program I have made out for myself.

I know that you will be kind enough to interpret this reply as it is meant and not as in any way intimating the opinion that the matters you suggest are not of the most vital consequence.

[Sincerely yours,   Woodrow Wilson]

Printed in the *Newark Evening News*, Oct. 12, 1910.

A Report of a Talk to Princeton Students

[*Oct. 10, 1910*]

STUDENTS GIVE PARADE FOR WILSON
HE MAKES A SPEECH

Princeton, New Jersey, Oct. 10.—The students of Princeton University took advantage of President Woodrow Wilson's presence at home tonight to give him a demonstration of their esteem and admiration. A big parade formed at the cannon at 8.15 and proceeded to Prospect, where the president delivered an address. The whole student body turned out and the parade was over a square in length. The students were most enthusiastic, and President Wilson was applauded and cheered time and again. He spoke in part as follows:

"I find myself in an interesting position tonight. It is deeply gratifying to me to know that you are making this demonstration in my honor. I am sure that nothing could be more pleasing to me than this mark of approval by my fellow-comrades in this place. Yet it would be a distasteful matter for me to make a political speech to you. I want to explain to you my attitude in this campaign.

"I have been preaching to you youngsters all my life the doctrine that the university man should do his part in the affairs of the world, and when the call came to me I had to listen to the voice of duty. Now I want you young gentlemen to know what is in my heart concerning this matter. There are two qualities that university men should have—sincerity and independence. It is our business to try and find out concerning all issues and then to do the right.

"There are great political changes sweeping over our country. Men are awakening to the importance of progress in dealing with public questions, and will not put up with the 'stand-patters.' I have no respect for the man who does not do his own thinking on public questions, and who does not have the courage of his convictions.

"One of the most interesting things to me has been to see the great interest that the men in the various audiences I have addressed have shown in public questions, and how certain they are in responding to those impulses which have always moved men to do right things. The great events in history have always been carried out by men who rebelled against existing wrongs, and had the courage to rebel against those conditions.

"I want you men to know that it gives me the keenest pang of my life when I think of severing my connection with Princeton. But then it is exactly the same position you will be placed in when, after your graduation, you are going to leave this dear place and take your place in the world, and follow the ideals you have as Princeton men.

"I want you to feel that a university lives not because of her system of teaching, or her magnificent buildings, but lives because of the men which she sends out in the world to take their places and quit themselves like men. It alleviates the pain that I feel at the thought of leaving you when I think that I will have a chance to do things which will reflect honor on the university. I feel that the real work of Princeton has just begun, and that she will have a glorious future.

"I thank you again for the demonstration, and assure you that this token of your esteem is most gratifying."

Printed in the Trenton *True American*, Oct. 11, 1910; some editorial headings omitted.

From James Richard Nugent, with Enclosure

My dear Sir: Newark, N. J. October 10, 1910.

I enclose a letter received today from Frank O. Briggs. You have probably read it in some of the newspapers. Briggs certainly evades the question,[1] and my thought is that we should insist upon a direct answer. However, I will be guided by what you think in the matter. When you arrive at a conclusion, kindly draft whatever reply you may wish sent to him, so that we may attend to the matter when I meet you tomorrow.

Paterson is a very difficult city to reach by railroad, so I will have our automobile meet you at the Market Street, Newark, station of the Pennsylvania Railroad on the arrival of the 4:54 P.M. train, leaving Princeton at 3:32 P.M. At the conclusion of the Paterson meeting, I will have the auto convey you to New York City.

When I meet you tomorrow, I will outline the arrangements made for the Caldwell meeting. My friends got together on Saturday according to the wish expressed by you at Bridgeton and subscribed for one hundred tickets to the Caldwell dinner. This insures a goodly attendance.

Trusting you have recovered from the fatigue of the South Jersey trip, I remain

Yours very truly,   James R. Nugent

[1] After the publication of Record's letter to Wilson of October 5 in the newspapers on the following day, Wilson and Nugent conferred in Burlington, N. J.,

on October 6 concerning the reply to be sent. Speaking for Wilson, Nugent declared in a statement to the press:

"George L. Record's letter to Mr. Wilson, offering to meet the Democratic candidate for Governor in a public discussion of campaign issues, has appeared in the daily press, but Mr. Wilson has not received it, and probably will not receive it until his return to Princeton at the end of the week.

"Mr. Wilson does not wish to leave Mr. Record's letter so long unnoticed. Therefore, he has asked me, as State chairman, to do what in any case he should do before replying to Mr. Record, namely, to communicate at once with Senator Briggs, chairman of the Republican State committee, to ascertain officially if Mr. Record has been or will be designated by the Republican State committee and the Republican candidate as their representative and spokesman. If so, I am authorized by Mr. Wilson to arrange with Chairman Briggs for such joint meeting, or meetings, as may be agreed upon." *Newark Evening News*, Oct. 7, 1910.

"Mr. Wilson, it is stated," the news report in *ibid.* said, "does not fear a debate. All he wants is to hold it with some one who has authority to speak in the capacity of a representative of the Republican party, as he himself speaks, as the representative of the Democratic party."

E N C L O S U R E

Frank Obadiah Briggs to James Richard Nugent

My dear Sir: Trenton, New Jersey October 8, 1910.

Your letter of the 7th inst.[1] was received by me this morning. I have no knowledge of the details of the challenge of Dr. Wilson except what I have seen in the papers. As I remember it Dr. Wilson made a public challenge expressing himself as follows: "I welcome any politician in the State to debate upon the public platform upon any public question." I also learn from the newspapers that Mr. George L. Record has accepted the challenge, and I think there is no one in the State who will claim that Mr. Record does not qualify under the conditions laid down therein.

Assuming the newspaper reports to be correct, it would seem that Dr. Wilson should either withdraw his challenge or be willing to debate with Mr. Record or any other man prominent in the politics of the State who may accept it.

This in my opinion would be better and more straightforward than to attempt to escape the consequences of a somewhat rash remark by asking the Republican State Committee to limit its significance.

Yours very truly,
Frank O. Briggs
Chairman Republican State Committee.

TLS (WP, DLC).
[1] Nugent refused to give out the text of his letter to Briggs but instead issued the statement quoted in J. R. Nugent to WW, Oct. 10, 1910, n. 1.

From Cleveland Hoadley Dodge

Dear Woodrow   New York. Oct. 10th 1910

I knew you would—but you have succeeded beyond even my wildest expectations. It is perfectly bully & I congratulate you heartily.

As I told you in the Summer I want to help out on the sinews of war but have not known how to do it. Now I have the enclosed,[1] & while I am loath to bother you, I *would* like to know whether this is the best channel through which I can help your campaign or if there is any other you prefer, what is it? Morever I have not the slightest idea how much is needed or what it would be best for me to give. Can you advise me?

You certainly are putting up the prettiest fight the country has seen since Lincoln, & I only hope & pray that you are not overtaxing your strength[.] Evidently from the reports you are enjoying it but don't overdo it

                                Ever affly   C. H. Dodge

Just write a line in reply

ALS (WP, DLC).
    [1] It is missing, but it was a circular letter requesting contributions to Wilson's gubernatorial campaign. See WW to C. H. Dodge, Oct. 11, 1910.

From William T. Ferguson

Dear Sir: Washington, D. C. Oct 10/10

I am exceedingly anxious to arrange for some meetings to be addressed by Dr. Du Bois and Rev. J. Milton Waldron.

Mr. Nugent and Mr. Alexander fail to reply. Is there some other friend who might arrange for these meetings and these speakers?

                    Yours very truly,   W. T. Ferguson

ALS (WP, DLC).

From George Brinton McClellan Harvey

Dear Mr. Wilson   New York Monday [Oct. 10, 1910]

I cannot report any criticisms of your canvass because I haven't heard any—only the highest praise—and most amazing reports of how Republicans are going to vote *right*. It is evident that the enemy are beginning a general nagging and "baiting" game in the hope of irritating you. But I suspect that you will not experience much annoyance therefrom or much difficulty in handling their quips to advantage.

My sole apprehension is that you may overdo physically. That must be avoided at all hazards. A tranquil spirit and responses tinged with tolerant good nature may not be a bad prescription—for the next few days.

Record's seeking of the limelight is trifling, of course, but if by any chance you should consider it desirable to meet him later on, it might not be a bad idea for Inglis to slip over to the Congressional library and make transcripts of the more caustic things Record has printed in the Jersey Journal about the Republican bosses, legislature, etc. There would be found an abundance of material with which to convict the blatherskite out of his own mouth. And that would be the way to get it instead of having anybody go through the files in the Journal office, so that the lamb might be led unsuspecting to the slaughter. Perhaps it would be well to have the stuff on hand anyway, in case of emergency, and if you think well of the suggestion I will post Inglis off to Washington immediately.

Meanwhile all looks well to me. No State canvass ever before attracted so much attention throughout the country and you will "win in a walk," so far as that is concerned.

As ever, Faithfully Yours   George Harvey

Of course, you will let me know if you want to see me anywhere at any time   GH

ALS (WP, DLC).

From Isaac Wayne MacVeagh

Personal

Bryn Mawr, Pennsylvania.
Dear Mr. Wilson: October 10. 1910.

I must begin by telling you how delighted I am at the splendid canvass you are making. When I urged you to take "the plunge" if the nomination was offered you I had no doubt you would show the old politicians some new tricks but I confess you are surpassing my expectations. And you are right from the lowest standpoint of "practical politics" so called in lifting your speeches to a high *moral* plane and keeping them there. Years ago I was the rep[.] gad-fly sought for political platforms and I never held up the moral law to any audience without scoring a great success.

But dont *step down* to debate with Record—with Lewis by all means—or even with Stokes perhaps; but dont give Record the notoriety he seeks, as he professes in substance the reforms for which you are pleading. There is nothing material for you and him to wrangle over except party names, which this year mean less than ever.

And now to your question. Dont think of resigning from the Mutual Board until your canvass is over. Then we will have far more light on the subject and can discuss it in the light of the result of the election. At least such is my *clear* view of the matter.

And here's to your success!

Sincerely Yours,   Wayne MacVeagh.

ALS (WP, DLC).

From Edward Field Goltra[1]

St Louis, Mo Oct. 10-1910

Missouri Democrats earnestly desire you make one speech here some Saturday night during campaign, answering Roosevelt who speaks here to-morrow, Tuesday night. You could leave Philadelphia Friday evening eight seventeen arrive St Louis five twenty five Saturday evening, leave St Louis eight forty five Sunday morning arrive Jersey City nine forty five Monday morning, expenses paid. I personally feel it would not only help us but have a good effect in your local canvass. Wire me name of chairman your speakers bureau that I may make arrangements. Speaking will be in Coliseum which accomodates twenty thousand people. Will guarantee to fill the building.[2]

Edward F. Goltra.

T telegram (WP, DLC).
[1] Princeton 1887, prominent in Missouri Democratic circles, and engaged in iron and steel manufacturing in and around St. Louis. He was the organizer and president of the American Steel Foundry Co. of Granite City, Ill.
[2] Wilson was unable to accept this invitation.

From William Frank McCombs

My dear President Wilson: New York October 10, 1910.

Appreciating that the legitimate expenses of your campaign must be large and that contributions from your friends are proper to further it, I am enclosing herewith my check for $100 in this behalf. I would forward the contribution to the person or committee having charge of the matter for you, if I knew where to send it. Wont you please do it for me?

I am tremendously gratified at the success of your campaign thus far and I hear on all sides predictions of your election by a large plurality. I am doing what I can for you among my friends in New Jersey. If you can think of any other way in which I may be of service pray command me.

Yours sincerely,   Wm. F. McCombs.

TLS (WP, DLC).

From Adolph Lankering[1]

Dear Sir: Hoboken, N. J., Oct. 10, 1910.

It affords me great pleasure to send you a copy of the minutes of the meeting of the Officers and the Executive Committee of the State Organization of the German-American Alliance in New Jersey held on Saturday last in the afternoon at Naegeli's Hotel in this city.[2]

Personally I wish to assure you that I will use every effort to secure the same assistance of the Alliance for the success of the coming election, as was rendered three years ago to bring about the election of our mutual friend Katzenbach, at that time the candidate for governor of this State. His defeat was not due to lack of interest on the part of the Alliance. The members of this organization are sincere and will prove to you reliable friends in the hope that after your election you will extend to them such consideration as they are deserving as good American citizens of this State. The Alliance has never demanded of the Legislature or the Administration of this State anything unfair. The members expect only to be treated like all others, equally sharing with them in the consideration that should be extended by the State government and Legislature to all good and law-abiding citizens alike.

Wishing you a grand success, and the election of a majority of the members of the coming Legislature in your favor to make a good popular Administration of this State possible, I remain

Very sincerely and truly yours,   A. Lankering.

TLS (WP, DLC).
[1] President of the German-American Alliance of New Jersey, Hudson County Democratic leader, and Mayor of Hoboken, 1902-1906.
[2] The enclosure is missing.

To Cleveland Hoadley Dodge

My dear Cleve: Princeton, N. J. October 11th, 1910.

Everything that you do increases my affection for you. It is certainly most generous of you to wish to contribute to the campaign fund. I do not quite understand the circular letter which you have received, but the Treasurer of the New Jersey Democratic State

Committee is General D[ennis]. F[rancis]. Collins, and the head-quarters of the committee are 772 Broad Street, Newark. The safest and most direct way would be to send a letter to headquarters, addressed to James R. Nugent, Chairman, and enclosing a check drawn in favor of the Treasurer.

I am trying to take care of myself. The rush is indeed tremendous and the strain very great, but so far I have managed to enjoy it and think I shall pull through without too great physical strain. It is delightful of you to think of me with solicitude and I am delighted that you think I am doing the thing as it ought to be done.

Always affectionately yours,   Woodrow Wilson

TLS (WC, NjP).

To George Lawrence Record

My dear Mr. Record: [Princeton, N. J.] October 11th, 1910.

Senator Briggs' reply to my letter,[1] the object of which I explained to you yesterday,[2] is so evasive and inconclusive that it confirms me in the impression that we shall have to deal with one another as individuals and not as representatives of any organizations of any kind.

I think I am right in assuming that if we were to engage in public debate, the subject of the debate would really be our own individual views and convictions and not the announced programme of either party. Having authorized the Democratic State Committee to fill every date that is available for public use, so far as I am concerned, it seems impossible to give myself the pleasure of such a personal interchange of views in public.

I am very anxious, however, to meet you with absolute candor upon the matters regarding which you are in doubt as to my position. I would esteem it a favor, therefore, if you would be kind enough to state the matters about which you wish to learn my opinion in a letter, to which I would take pleasure in replying, in a letter which you would be at full liberty to publish. From what I know of your views upon public questions, I think it very likely that we are essentially at one in regard to the substance of our views, and probably differ only in practical detail. Debate, therefore, would seem to be less suitable than a frank interchange of views in a form that can be very simply handled.

Very sincerely yours,   [Woodrow Wilson]

CCL (WP, DLC).
[1] These letters are missing and were not published in the newspapers.
[2] Perhaps over the telephone.

To George Brinton McClellan Harvey

Princeton, N. J.

My dear Colonel Harvey: October 11th, 1910.

Your letter of Monday is thoughtful and kind, but I do not believe that it will be necessary to look up Mr. Record's utterances, because I have just written a letter to him in which I say that it is evident that what he wishes to discuss with me is his own opinions and not the programme of either party, and that therefore it seems unwise to arrange a public debate as part of the campaign, but that if he will write me a letter asking my views on the matters about which he is in doubt, I will take pleasure in replying in a letter which he will be at liberty to publish. Some mutual friends of Record's and mine are trying to manage the thing so that there will be no trickery in his letter and that I can give it a frank and honest answer. There is certainly nothing that I need wish to avoid in a mere expression of opinion. Record's own turgid assertions are so well known that that matter, I think, will take care of itself. I found that it would make a very bad impression in Hudson County if I seemed to try to dodge his onset, because of course I am trying for the votes of the New Idea Republicans, with whom he has high standing, I am told.

I am standing the strain, so far, very well but shall be blessed glad when it is over.

Always faithfully and cordially yours,

Woodrow Wilson

TLS (WP, DLC).

To David L. MacKay

My dear Sir: Princeton, N. J. October 11th, 1910.

In reply to your letter of October 8th, I would say that there is absolutely no contradiction between the two sets of remarks you have seen quoted from me regarding the organization of labor. I believe that the organization of labor is absolutely necessary in the face of organized capital and that most of the legitimate advantages which the laboring man has won in recent years in respect of wages and many other matters have been won through the instrumentality of labor organizations. They have been legitimate and useful. At the same time I have once and again criticized the use they have made of their organizations. What you saw quoted from my Baccalaureate Address was a criticism of what I learned from an official government publication some of the unions had done in respect of the regulation of the standard of a day's labor.

Very truly yours,   Woodrow Wilson

TLS (WC, NjP).

From Robert Bridges

Dear Tommy: New York, October 11, 1910.

I heard of your nomination in Dublin and also from Edward Sheldon on the steamer coming home. Since arriving a week ago I have read the account of your great success in the campaign, and the general feeling that you are going to be elected by a good majority. I wanted simply to give you my best wishes and congratulations.

Judge Coxe[1] of Utica told me last night that [Charles A.] Talcott had been nominated for Congress by the Democrats. I knew you would be interested in hearing this and perhaps you might be moved to write Talcott an encouraging letter. It is generally a Republican district, but there are indications that Talcott has a good fighting chance. You may need him in Washington some of these days!

With best wishes always

Faithfully yours   Robert Bridges

TLS (WP, DLC).
  [1] Alfred Conkling Coxe, United States circuit court judge in the second judicial circuit.

From William Gibbs McAdoo

Dear Dr. Wilson: New York October 11/10.

I have your kind letter of the 10th instant. We are only too happy to hold the invitation open until after the 8th of next November, at which time I hope you will be able to accept as the Governor-elect of New Jersey. I believe you will.[1]

I wish I could take a hand in the campaign and help you, but I suppose that a word spoken in your behalf by the President of a "corporation" would damn you, rather than help you.

Believe me, with warm regards,

Sincerely yours,   W G McAdoo

TLS (WP, DLC).
  [1] Wilson accepted and spoke to the New York Southern Society on December 14, 1910. His address is printed at that date in Vol. 22.

From Thomas P. Fay[1]

My dear Sir: Long Branch, N. J. October 11th, 1910.

Your letter in reference to Mr. Bobbitt's[2] editorials received.

Since writing you, the Democratic editors of New Jersey have had a meeting in Newark and Mr. Bobbitt was elected the secretary.

Mr. Bobbitt has become the "bell-wether" of the flock. His editorials are the most quoted throughout the State. He informs me that there has been some change in newspaper sentiment and some activity among our opponents.

He informs me that he will be able to meet you once or twice a week and keep you posted as to the trend on newspaper criticism throughout the State. A half-hours' conference with Mr. Bobbitt once or twice a week might be of advantage to you in meeting the argument of the opposing party.

It is difficult for you to make arrangements in the height of the campaign for any definite place and arrangements should be made to meet your convenience as to time and place.

I am enclosing you the editorials which have been published during the past week.[3]

Very truly yours,   Thomas P. Fay.

TLS (WP, DLC).
[1] Lawyer of Long Branch, N. J.
[2] Benjamin Boisseau Bobbitt, editor of the *Long Branch*, N. J., *Record*.
[3] These enclosures are no longer attached to Fay's letter.

From Henry Burling Thompson

Dear Wilson: [Greenville P. O., Del.] October 11th, 1910.

It is always a disappointment to be in Princeton and not meet you—which thing happened on Saturday—but my disappointment is softened by the great pleasure which I am taking in reading the accounts of your campaigning. I arrived in New York last Thursday morning, and immediately was imbedded in the Sun's news of the New Jersey campaign. It is all delightful reading, and I wish you every success in your new field.

Yours sincerely,   Henry B. Thompson

TLS (Thompson Letterpress Books, NjP).

From Albert Shaw

My dear Wilson: New York October 11, 1910

I have meant to write to you, ever since your nomination, to congratulate you in a more personal and private way, although I have done the thing publicly in the October and also the September numbers of the Review.[1] Of course I hope you will be elected with a rousing majority. My Republicanism is wholly subject to the best political welfare of the country, and nothing could do the Republican party more good than to have the Democratic party nominate and elect men of your qualifications and character. But then you knew I felt that way anyhow, so it is hardly necessary to write it.

William B. Shaw, of our staff, who is much interested in your campaign, wants to go over and make a little article about it for our November number.[2] I am arranging with the American Press Association (of which I, by the way, am a director) to send a photographer to get us a very special lot of the right kind of illustrations. It was their pictures that were published to illustrate the Harmon article we had two or three months ago.[3] No better pictures were ever taken of any public man than those Harmon pictures. I am asking you not to put yourself out but to give the photographer of the American Press Association, who will bear a letter from me, every kind of reasonable facility to get a set of pictures. We shall use them in the right way and we shall get good pictures, so feel that you can entirely trust the man who will bear my note of introduction.

As ever,   Faithfully yours,   Albert Shaw.

TLS (WP, DLC).
[1] "The New Jersey Senatorship," *Review of Reviews*, XLII (Sept. 1910), 268-69, which included a picture of Wilson, and "New Jersey's Next Governor," *ibid.*, Oct. 1910, p. 393.
[2] The unsigned article, accompanied by several photographs, was "Woodrow Wilson and the New Jersey Governorship," *Review of Reviews*, XLII (Nov. 1910), 555-62. In addition, Shaw praised Wilson's candidacy in a short editorial, "The Campaign in New Jersey," *ibid.*, p. 529, and printed extracts from his address to the American Bar Association, "The Lawyer and the Community" (printed at Aug. 31, 1910) under the title, "Woodrow Wilson on the Responsibilities of Lawyers," *ibid.*, pp. 602-603.
[3] Sloane Gordon, "Judson Harmon of Ohio," *Review of Reviews*, XLII (Sept. 1910), 298-309.

From Yorke Allen[1]

My dear President Wilson: New York. October 11, 1910.

I write to give you my very best wishes for your campaign for the Governorship of our State.

For the first time in my life I was obliged the other day to decline to serve as an officer of a meeting to promote the Republican cause. I had to tell them that, though I was going to vote the balance of my ticket Republican, I intended to vote for you for Governor.

I have been following your speeches with the very greatest interest and pleasure.

I know you will be interested to know that I have met a very large number of men who are Republicans who are going to vote for you to be their Governor.

In closing I cannot fail to say how deeply I feel the loss which your leaving the University will be to it. You are ahead of your time in your ideas and you are right. We shall cross many a stream before your fellow can be found to pilot the ship.

Very sincerely yours,   Yorke Allen

P. S. Of course do not bother to reply to this letter. I just wanted you to know how I felt about things.

TLS (WP, DLC).
1 Princeton 1894, a New York lawyer who lived in South Orange, N. J.

A News Report of a Campaign Address
in Paterson, New Jersey

[Oct. 12, 1910]

WILSON TALKS PURE POLITICS

Bumper Crowd in Rival's Home City Greets
Democratic Gubernatorial Nominee.

PATERSON, Oct. 12.—With Congressman Charles N. Fowler an interested auditor in the front row of the balcony, and former Assemblyman Henry Marelli, of the "new idea" forces, in a box, Woodrow Wilson, in the Paterson Opera House last night, presented to the people of his rival's home city his reasons for seeking their votes at the coming Gubernatorial election.

The theatre seats about 1,800 persons, but one of the attaches is authority for the statement that there were 2,500 or 2,600 persons in the place. Among them were several hundred Republicans.

It was anticipated that the Democratic candidate would make some direct retorts to John W. Griggs, but Dr. Wilson did not go as far as that. He did make a few sarcastic comments that could be applied to Mr. Griggs, and dealt with the "Board of Guardians" with which, he had previously intimated, Mr. Lewis had been connected.

Summarizing his speech, Dr. Wilson said at the beginning that he intended to dwell primarily on the purification of politics. Mayor Andrew F. McBride was chairman of the meeting. He first presented Congressman William Hughes, who is seeking re-election. The latter spoke about three-quarters of an hour and received a cordial greeting. . . .

Dr. McBride presented the candidate for Governor in a few simple sentences.

Appreciating the greeting given, Mr. Wilson said he recognized it as an indication that "bodies of men are coming together, not out of curiosity to see an individual, but out of eagerness to hear what can be said in what they know to be a cause."

Congressman Hughes, in his address, had reminded the audience that the meeting was not a "case of Wilson that's all,"[1] but that he (Hughes) also was in a contest. Mr. Wilson, referring to Mr. Hughes's remark, said:

I am glad to say it is literally true, as Mr. Hughes has said so wittily, that it is not a case of Wilson, that is all; if it were a case of Wilson, that is all, I would go home, because I am not interested, and to speak frankly I have never been interested in discussing the personal fortunes even of myself, because a man's fortune is interesting only when it is lifted upon a great tide.

That great tide, which is rising in this country now, no man can mistake and all dishonest men most heartily see it—the tide which is going to float away all the jetsam and flotsam of political machines, and begin to float again those handsome emblems of liberty which have been the bulwark of America.

The cause upon which we are met, ladies and gentlemen, is the purification of politics—is the freeing of politics from the management of machine organizations.

I am not speaking of bribery and the gross forms of corruption. Those things will presently become impossible, they are becoming impossible; they will become so impressed in public opinion that it will not be possible longer to do things of that sort. Men will not dare to receive money to debauch the process of legislation; but that is not what we have to fear.

We have to fear a deeper and more dangerous thing that has taken place. We have to fear making a business of political management in the interests of special groups of persons.

We have to fear that kind of management which does not rest upon public opinion, does not rest upon public discussion, does not rest upon anything except the will and agreement of party managers.

[1] The slogan of a popular whiskey.

Have you never received any intimation that the real managers of legislation in this State were the State committee of the dominant party? Have you ever investigated their management? And did you think that they were managing that legislation in the interest of the Republican party—I mean in the interest of the rank and file of the men who vote the Republican ticket?

In Trenton that group of gentlemen are called the "Board of Guardians." They are the "guardians" of the Legislature, which has not moved without their permission and approval. They are the guardians of the special interests; which, I have no doubt, they believe—many of them conscientiously believe—support the State of New Jersey.

I am trying to wake these gentlemen up to a new conscientiousness. I am not accusing them. I am not bringing an indictment against them. I am calling upon them to wake up and find out what is going on in the world.

It has been said that in some of my speeches I have been indulging in "glittering generalities." I thought I was indulging in the statement of principles, but, if it is so long since these gentlemen looked at principles that they do not know them when they see them, I am not surprised at their calling them "glittering generalities."

Taking up graft, Mr. Wilson referred to the noted distinction made by Senator George Washington Plunkett, of New York,[2] between honest and dishonest graft—honest, or "legitimate" graft, being the taking advantage of information obtained before any one else could take advantage of it. Then, said the candidate:

I must say that many special interests have enjoyed legitimate graft. They have known beforehand what the Legislature was going to do, and have known beforehand what it was not going to do, and have profited accordingly.

They have been perfectly content when any kind of agitation was going on because they knew they were safe in the "Board of Guardians," and the "Board of Guardians" were interested in the

[2] George Washington Plunkitt (1842-1924), New York state senator, 1884-87, 1892-93, 1899-1904; best known as a long-time Tammany Hall district leader and a street-corner political philosopher. His views were expressed in a series of interviews with a journalist, which were published as William L. Riordan, *Plunkitt of Tammany Hall: A Series of Very Plain Talks on Very Practical Politics, Delivered by Ex-Senator George Washington Plunkitt, the Tammany Philosopher, from his Rostrum—the New York County Court-House Bootblack Stand—and Recorded by William L. Riordan* (New York, 1905). It has become a classic textbook on boss rule. The first chapter was entitled "Honest Graft and Dishonest Graft." Dishonest graft, according to Plunkitt, was anything which was explicitly against the law. Honest graft was taking advantage of business opportunities, most frequently those provided by inside political information.

State of New Jersey, and that these gentlemen knew it beforehand and should feel safe.

We have therefore to force our way into the interior sanctuary of our own government and ask these gentlemen if they ever heard that the great body of persons known as the citizens of New Jersey had a right to come in there.

"The way of preventing selfish control of legislation is to appoint somebody to look at what is going on, and appoint somebody to talk about it as much as you can," said Dr. Wilson. "Put in from the outside an intelligent, indefatigable man, who knows a thing when he sees it, and make him promise he will come and tell you all about it.

"I don't want you to employ any self-respecting Democrat as a spy, but I do want you to employ some self-respecting Democrat to go and find out how your business is being conducted and come and tell you."

Further on Dr. Wilson asked:

What do we want legislation about? We want legislation about a number of things. In the first place, in order that there shall not be graft; in order that there shall be economy, we want a revision, a re-examination of our whole tax system, of our whole system of assessments, so that our taxes will be fair and equal, no matter who is taxed.

As to control of corporations, Dr. Wilson wanted to prevent imposition on the public.

"We do not want to break up business, but we do want to break up wrong. We can get at wrong when we get at the wrongdoers, and we cannot get at wrong until we get at the wrongdoers."

Wrongdoers had been caught in the sugar customs fraud,[3] Dr. Wilson said, even though they were the smaller fry. He would have liked to see the big fish caught. The nominee was not sorry for those who had been caught, because, he said, "no man has the right to be a scoundrel at the bidding of any other man."

About the big men, the speaker said they "were never found, and so far as I can observe, were never seriously searched for in the prosecution.["]

I shall feel, for one, that justice has miscarried in this country when it stops short of the top in the investigations. The guiltiest man of all is the man who devised the system and commanded the thing to be done. There is the man in whom is the seed of lawlessness and anarchy, for he has devised cunning means by which the

[3] See n. 2 to Wilson's article, "The Tariff Make-Believe," printed at Sept. 5, 1909, Vol. 19.

law of the country may be set at naught. I have no toleration for anything that exempts him, and the law must find him, or fail.

If that is a glittering generality then let the gentlemen who think it a glittering generality give us the exact program by which they will accomplish that, and we will have something to discuss.

I, for my part, can give you items of it, but not the whole of it. If any man pretends that he can give you the whole of it, don't believe him.

It is easy enough, upon a public platform, before you are clothed with responsibility, to promise "I will do this and that." I am going to absolutely promise nothing except that I will use my ability and my brains the best I can in the solution of these questions.

I don't pretend that I have it absolutely by the wool, as some gentlemen seem to think they have. It is hard to get hold of absolute truth and keep your fingers in the wool.

Presumably having in mind the references to himself as a "schoolmaster," made by John W. Griggs and David Baird, Mr. Wilson said:

Some gentlemen talk about modern universities in a way that convinces me that they have never seen the inside of one. The modern university, let me tell you, is a place where men study the things that are, because modern universities are afraid of nothing so much as the men that know so many things that are not so.

The advantage of living in a university is at least this: that when you know that a thing is not so, and see it, you go out and see that honest men will do their best to get at the actual facts.

But there are other things we want besides the regulation of corporations. The particular kind of corporations that we have in our time—when our eye is red—is the public service corporations. And there are a great many red eyes.

Dr. Wilson declared again that he wanted a rate-regulating public utility commission. It should impartially study the conditions to establish the rates. Dr. Wilson followed this by asking:

"Is that a 'glittering generality?' Can anybody else go any further?"

Mr. Wilson said he felt the same way about the automobile laws, and the employers' liability law. He said that when things were proposed to him he asked the persons proposing them to draft a statute on the subject. That, said the candidate, was not easy. He continued:

To tell the truth, what I am principally interested in is awakening, and keeping awake, the opinion of men in New Jersey about

New Jersey matters. In other words, though I borrow the designation from the other side of the house, I am, and always have been, an insurgent.

We are not insurgents against government, but we are insurgents against privately managed government. If I were to define a "standpatter" I would say that he was a man who always did what the party organization told him to do. If I were to define an insurgent, by way of contrast, I would say that he was a man who wanted to do the thing that the country wanted. That is the reason there are so many insurgents.

In conclusion, Dr. Wilson said he wanted to "bring about in New Jersey a government by public opinion."

Printed in the *Newark Evening News*, Oct. 12, 1910; some editorial headings omitted.

An Address to the Democratic Union in Caldwell, New Jersey[1]

October 12th, 1910.

I[t] has been a very vital experience with me, going up and down this State during the present campaign, because I have never come into contact with the people of the State in the same intimate fashion before. I have taken pains to know what the various parts of the State represented, and I have taken pains to note who the chief figures were in the various sections of the State, but never before have I gone up and down the State and come in contact with hundreds of my fellow citizens of New Jersey when I was bent on learning what was the common interest and which they regarded as being the common interest.

I suppose you feel as I do, that our State is variously composed, it holds a great many elements; and one of the difficulties of New Jersey, from the point of view of politics, is that in either extremity of the State the attention of the people is to some extent drawn away to other States; that the centre of gravity in portions of South Jersey tends in the direction of Pennsylvania and that the centre of gravity in this northern part of New Jersey tends in the direction of New York. Do you know also, that in this northern part of New Jersey the elements of population are very numerous and extremely varied. One gets the impression, therefore, that the State lacks homogeneity; that its elements do not hold together and more than that, and more serious than that, its attention is not sufficiently concentrated on its own affairs. I think that

[1] Delivered at the Monomonock Inn.

these facts are reinforced by others which reassure us in this particular, but they are sufficiently strong and sufficiently noticeable to make the task we are now entered on a very interesting and a very difficult task. I find that it is my experience that varied bodies of men are not so much drawn together by common interests as by common conceptions. I do not believe (though it may sound strange from a man who has spent so much of his life in a university) I do not believe that men are governed by their minds, but I believe they are governed by their affections. It is often said in this age that this is an age in which mind is monarch. Well, if it is it is one of those modern monarchs that reign and do not govern.

The real government of our age, as of all others, is vested in a great house of representatives, made up, for the most part, of passions, and the most that we can achieve is to keep the handsome passions in a majority. Now handsome passion is enhanced by the effects of the imagination. You do not enhance the finer passions by appealing to men's interests; you enhance those handsome passions by appealing to their conceptions. For we are, nowadays, in an altruistic state of mind, which means our conceptions are based upon a love which is very much wider than love of one's self, that extends to the interests of others not only, but to those deep spiritual concerns of others which we know we share with them when we really extend our vision beyond ourselves. What we are now engaged upon, therefore, is enhancing the handsome passions of New Jersey. The underlying passion which holds every country together is the passion that we call patriotism. I believe that the real motives of life are the deep sentiments which make us cling to our homes, to our friends, to our country, to our neighborhoods, to all those older attractions which have bound us ever since we were children. So it seems to me a very vital thing to go about this State and try to gather up the sentiments of it, try to minister to those sentiments, try to speak to that part which I know to be in every man with regard to his country and its institutions.

As I go from one part of this State to another I receive a great deal of excellent advice. I mean that; I was not joking. I do not mean that all of it is excellent—all the advice.

I am advised, for example, when I go to one part of the State that what the people are deeply interested in is this issue or that issue. They desire first that I make a speech about rate-making, then that I make a speech about an employers' liability act, and then about electoral reform, and in another place their interest is in direct primary, and so forth, and so forth. Now all of that is very serviceable to me because I think it is right, indeed I think it is necessary to interest the attention of the voter upon measures which he thinks necessary to serve the interests of the State. But what lives [lies] back of all that is not his own local and particular interests, but the interests of the State, and the particular issues [issue] is merely generally to draw his attention to the great principle that underlies it all; and an issue that does not lead up to a principle is not worth talking about. I do not mean that all public business leads up to principle because that is not true. Many measures have to be enacted in which there lies an expression of politics and not a great conception of government. But the only way to keep the force behind the government is to discuss those things which lead up to principles.

I receive a good many confidences, and I have received confidences from men very high in the financial world which have astonished me; they have repented; that's what happened. If they can manifest their offence without too much public mortification, they are ready to do so. The men who have been engaged in certain questionable transactions in recent years, many of them, men who do [did] not realize that the transactions were questionable, who now see that they were and are ready to help in rendering such transactions in the future impossible, not only for the benefit of the country, but for their own self-protection. They don't want to be led into temptation; they believe in the spirit of the Lord's prayer—"Lead us not into temptation, but deliver us from evil"; and there are ways of delivering oneself from evil that are statutory, and that have a finger that points to the penitentiary.

The only theme I have in mind to-night is the necessity of controlling men, not in a pedantic way, but nevertheless dwelling upon essential principles of public action; and let every man say that what we are at present engaged in is not so much how to rule men personally, but how to rule them on principles that are fair to everybody; in other words let us determine the best way in which to realize justice. It is not a short road; it is a long road. And wh[e]n I see the possibility that a great many of my fellow men may repose their trust in me for the realization of some of the principles of justice, my heart fails me, because I have read the history of our country and of other countries, and it is not possible to go a very long way upon the road of justice in any one generation, it is not possible for any one man to realize large hopes, either his own hopes or hopes centred in him by others; and yet it would be a very cowardly thing to turn away from the possibility of accomplishing anything, though it were ever so little, toward putting our government upon a footing that would be satisfactory to all men.

There is one saying attributed to Washington that ought to suffice to keep us in heart. The saying was not repeated until long after the Constitution of 1787, and I may not be able to couch it in exactly the words Washington used, but it confirms a memory of that convention that recalls early days when the members doubting what its conclusions ought to be, were pulled about by this and that interest, so that they were inclined to lose heart; they were wondering whether this line of action or that would be acceptable; and Washington said: "Gentlemen, we must regard a standard to which the false and the judicious will repair and the event is in the hands of God."[2] If I did not believe that, I would not think that this haphazard game was worth while. I do believe that, and I believe that such a standard, raised sufficiently high, where it will be visible to the eyes of those who hold it, will be the standard around which men may rally in greater and greater numbers, and we will come to an age where men who may look back upon it will be proud.[3]

FPS T transcript (WP, DLC).
    [2] The reporter, Frank Parker Stockbridge, garbled this quotation. Wilson must have come closer to Washington's actual words, which were: "Let us raise a standard to which the wise and the honest can repair. The event is in the hand of God." Max Farrand, ed., *The Records of the Federal Convention of 1787* (4 vols., New Haven, Conn., 1911-37), III, 382.
    [3] Earlier in the day, Wilson spoke at Cleveland's birthplace in Caldwell. A news report of his remarks follows.

A News Report of Remarks at Caldwell, New Jersey

[Oct. 13, 1910]

WILSON TALKS OF CLEVELAND

Caldwell Birthplace of Last Democratic President Scene of Great Demonstration.

Democrats gathered at a shrine of Democracy—the birthplace of Grover Cleveland, in Caldwell—yesterday, and did honor to Woodrow Wilson, the hope of New Jersey's Democracy in the present Gubernatorial campaign. Nor was the gathering confined strictly to those of Democratic political principles, many Republicans being in the throng of "pilgrims." . . .

Colonel James C. Sprigg, head of the Democratic Union, introduced to Dr. Wilson a committee of women, who had prepared a luncheon for the visitors. Following this, Colonel Sprigg escorted the candidate to the little front porch and presented him to the crowd on the lawn as "the next Governor of New Jersey." This was greeted with applause and cheers, which evoked from Mr. Wilson an answering smile of appreciation.

"It is a most unexpected pleasure to me," said Dr. Wilson, "to meet so many fellow-citizens here to-day. I did not know what was in store for me, and I owe you my hearty thanks. Standing in this place I do not and cannot think of myself.

"My thoughts go out to the great Democrat who was born in this house, and whose example of character and moral force—qualities that were inherent in him—must have been due to his early training in this place, and led him later to eminence. He left his mark.

"Of Grover Cleveland it has been said that he possessed no originality or brilliancy. I think, though, that he was original in that originality which comes of slowly accumulating moral purpose. He was original as a great wind in [is] original, one that comes up and dispels the mists and vapors and clears the air so that we see the beauty of the hills beyond. The wind has merely blown the mist away, but in that it was original. And it would be a wholesome thing if every candidate for office could come and spend some time in contemplation in this spot.". . .

Following the reception, Colonel Sprigg took Mr. Wilson to the Kingsley School. When they arrived the school team was near the end of a game of football with the Montclair High School eleven. The automobile was stopped until the conclusion of the match to allow Mr. Wilson to watch it. The Kingsley team was beaten by the score of 18 to 0.

When the boys gathered about Mr. Wilson he told them that he was sorry he could not congratulate the school team on winning, but that they had only to remember that that was of little consequence, as all that was required of them was that they should do the best that was in them.

Printed in the *Newark Evening News*, Oct. 13, 1910; some editorial headings omitted.

A Campaign Address in Atlantic City, New Jersey[1]

October 13, 1910.

Mr. Chairman,[2] Ladies and Gentlemen: You have given me a very gracious welcome, and I appreciate it very much. I do not feel that I can gratify or satisfy the anticipations of an audience like this, but I do want to discuss with you very candidly

[1] Delivered in the theater on the Steeple Chase Pier.
[2] Clarence Lee Cole, lawyer of Atlantic City; Democratic county chairman for Atlantic County.

and simply, indeed, the matters which I know we all regard as of the deepest concern, not only to ourselves individually, but as of much greater consequence to the great commonwealth of which we are citizens.

I find myself now upon the political platform in these recent days in a somewhat peculiar position. When I started out upon this campaign, we were discussing the issues which seemed to be raised by the difference between the platform adopted by the Democratic party and the platform adopted by the Republican party for the state campaign.

In recent days the candidate of the Republican party, a gentleman for whom I have a great respect, has promulgated practically a platform that is one which differs very radically from the platform of the party promulgated in convention, and as he adds item after item in that platform, I find that it very greatly resembles my own. So I experience a sense of relief, therefore, in finding that there is no issue between Mr. Lewis and myself. This eliminates personal considerations. I have nothing in any circumstances except what is complimentary to say about Mr. Lewis, and personal consideration would, so far as I am concerned, never enter in in any case; but I mean that there appears to be no personal issue between me and the Republican party in respect of the sort of legislation we would desire to see adopted in New Jersey.

The question you are called upon to consider, therefore, is whether the Republican leaders standing alongside Mr. Lewis will assist and permit him to carry out his ideas with regard to that government. I do not see how to escape that statement of the question. You have now to determine, in view of what he has recently said, whether you think that he or I is most likely to do the thing which he intends. What are the things that we are interested in? There are a great many of them, and I am not going to be tedious by enumerating all of them. I want to take merely a few specimens, and I want to choose those specimens with regard to what I suppose you have been thinking. For example, you have been thinking about the conferring upon the proper commission—a commission which already exists in name, at any rate, which we call in this state the Public Utilities Commission—a proper set of powers, in order that they can have the power to regulate instead of the power to advise. You know how great a question this is. You know what great interests are involved. You know that what we all want is a commission which has a rate-making power. The rate-making power does not apply merely to railways—either the great steam railways

of this State or the great trolley lines of this State. It applies also
to the rates charged for water and gas, and all those public
utilities, which so nearly concern our convenience and comfort.
We know what happens. You know what happens. There are, for
example, two competing companies supplying a town with gas.
Each is charging fifty cents for gas. The one buys the other, and
the result is a charge of one dollar for gas. That may or may not
be legitimate. It may, for all I know, not have paid either of the
original companies to supply gas at fifty cents, but when they
have combined and are without competition, and have control
of the whole business, we would, at any rate, like to know why it
is necessary that they should charge one dollar. We should like
to have a commission which can find out, and upon some perfectly fair basis—for I am not in favor of confiscating legitimate
profits—find out upon what basis these charges rest; find out with
regard to inquiry, with the right to discover, with the right to
publish the results of their inquiry, with the right to base upon
that inquiry the establishment by their own authority of the rates
which shall be charged; so that there will be a real connection
between what the public has discovered to be the basis of the
business and the public convenience and comfort.

This applies to the railway companies, to the transportation
companies, as well as to the other public utilities. We would like
to know why we cannot go still for five cents to the neighboring
towns. (A voice: Because the Pennsylvania Railroad Company
bought the franchise.) Now, there is a distinct allegation that
the Pennsylvania Railroad Company bought the trolley line. If
we had what we want—a commission with powers to determine,
powers to regulate—that assertion could be carried before them.
They would be obliged to investigate it and tell us exactly what
the cause was; and if non-competitive conditions exist, they
would have the right to give us the benefit of the non-competitive conditions. That illustrates perfectly what we want and what
we mean to have. Very well, then; let us view the situation that
we may determine by our votes on the eighth of November.

Mr. Lewis has also desired that the Public Utility Commission
should have the power to regulate rates, and I suppose he wishes,
as I wish, that it should have the power of determining the basis
of those charges so that the regulation will not be arbitrary or unreasonable. Is it likely Mr. Lewis can bring that about through
the instrumentalities now in charge of the Republican party?
What has been your experience, gentlemen? This same unalter-
able organization that you have now has been in charge of the
Republican party—I don't mean the rank and file of the Repub-

lican party, because they have wished to God they were not in control of the Republican party spoken of as an organization—this same group of men have been in charge of that organization during the last three years and this same promise was made by the party and its candidates in the year 1907. Why has that promise not been fulfilled? And is it any more likely that it will be fulfilled under the present candidate than it was then under the candidate of three years ago?

There is a very practical question for you to answer, and you had better ask that question of some gentleman very near at home, who was the leader of the assembly during those three years.[3] It may be, ladies and gentlemen, that that leader was himself in favor—I don't know—of redeeming that pledge; but the leader of the Assembly is generally the representative of the party organization; he does not act as an individual; he acts as the representative and the spokesman of certain party determinations. Very well, acting whether or not upon his own opinion and impulse, that leader assisted and led in the effort that killed that bill. That is not an understanding; that is a fact. As a certain friend of mine, with whom I got in an argument, said: "I am not arguing with you; I am telling you." And you don't need to be told; you knew it already. If you want to know whether it is likely that the same organization will back Mr. Lewis in doing what it has not backed your present Governor in doing, ask Mr. Edge. He can give you the most satisfactory inside information. It may reveal nothing that is crooked. I am not intimating that; for that is neither here nor there; but he will be obliged to tell you that the organization was against the measure, and it is the same organization now as then. Moreover, the present candidate for Governor, without involving himself in any disrepute of any kind, has been a member of the organization for the past three years, and longer; so he is not an outside party, he is an inside party in the organization. You will have to reckon the probabilities then.

There is another matter, a very practical matter, that we ought to take into consideration. What has happened to all the attempts in the Assembly of New Jersey to pass a corrupt practices act? Every measure of that kind has been smothered or defeated. And why do corrupt practices prevail? Why are registration lists padded? Why is it impossible to detect and expose

[3] Wilson referred to Walter Evans Edge, advertising agency proprietor and newspaper publisher of Atlantic City. Edge entered the Assembly only in 1910 but did serve as Republican majority leader that year. His immediate predecessors in that office were Griffith Walker Lewis of Burlington in 1909 and William Parmenter Martin of Newark in 1908.

the padding of lists? Why, because in every direction where you turn for relief, you find organization men, not the Republican party, resisting you; for I happen to know that there are hundreds, aye, thousands of thoughtful Republicans in this State who are just as anxious as any Democrat can possibly be to correct these very ugly things. But they find no means of correcting them; there are no instrumentalities through which to do the thing; nobody can be brought to act who is in authority. It is impossible to discover why.

One does not like to intimate dishonorable reasons, but the fact is, as I have stated it, that it is impossible to correct these things; that it is common rumor and belief that they exist. Here is a pretty state of affairs! A self-governing people, indeed! A people that have charge of their own affairs, indeed! If they have charge of their own affairs and want them changed, why don't they change them?

The people of New Jersey are just awakening to the fact that they have been balked in this power of theirs, this self-government under which they live; that somehow it is tied up in the hands of somebody, and that they themselves are outsiders in their own business house, where their own affairs are concerned.

Anybody who touches the use of the franchise in this country to debauch it or to pervert it, is a public enemy. If he calls himself a Republican, he is hiding, like a coward, behind a handsome name. If he calls himself a Democrat, he is of the same cult and cut. The great curse of this country is that men in politics, who, no matter by what name they are called, are in it for the sake of the game and for the sake of control.

Now I tell you candidly, ladies and gentlemen, without making any charges of fraud, that this is a campaign to break up the Republican machine, and I believe in my heart that the men who are going to assist with the greatest zest in this matter are Republicans themselves. So what is the cause we are met to discuss? The cause of good government, you will say, yes, the cause of good government, but we are always met to discuss the cause of good government; we are met to discuss something more practical than that, we are met to discuss that means of getting good government. Perhaps you will turn to me and say you are so immodest as to say that the means of getting good government is to elect you as Governor. I say nothing so silly, nothing so futile as that; I simply say that the way to get good government is to get somebody to assist you who knows a thing when he sees it and does not belong to any organization or machine. And let us see about the hopeful task of conducting good government, not by private management, but by public discussion. That is the programme, public discussion. There is nothing in this world to which machine men are so averse as to public discussion. It gives the ordinary politician a chill in the back because he doesn't know which side the chill will come from. Mr. Cole said and said very truly that this is not a campaign that is of partisan color and bias. We are all in the same boat and are trying to find the practical way of releasing ourselves from what has grown intolerable.

The Republican machine illustrates a story which may be familiar to some of you of the mule that was put upon a Mississippi steamboat to be carried down the river, and his destination was marked on a cardboard tag which was tied around his neck. The man who tied it made the string too long, and the mule, being inquisitive, got hold of the tag and chewed it up. One of the deck hands, on seeing the tag gone, called out to the captain, "Our mule done gone eat up where he was gwine to." Now, if the Republican machine thought that it was destined to have a power in this campaign, it has eaten up where it was gwine to; it has chewed its tag and has not noticed that the public was looking on when it chewed its tag.

We must be frank with each other. There are gentlemen connected with the Republican machine whom I know and greatly respect. That is not the point. I am not, as a little girl said, "I am not angry with them, I am sorry for them." These gentlemen believe, if I am to credit them, and I do credit them, they believe the public welfare of this country depends upon the management of the Republican machine. They believe it is necessary to maintain an organization which they have been kind enough to call a Board of Guardians. It is the State Republican committee when concerned with legislation, and that, if you please, is under the control of the Board of Guardians. Nothing can be done in the Capital in Trenton without the consent of our guardians. That puts us all [in] the category of being under age or else non compos mentis. We are either defective mentally or in our minority if we have to be taken care of by a Board of Guardians. I do not know any court of competent jurisdiction to appoint such guardians.

I do not know any constitution under which such a board can be appointed, and if it is self constituted it is odi[o]us.

It is very heartening, ladies and gentlemen, to take part in a campaign like this; for we are not discussing the narrow matters even of our beloved commonwealth. We are discussing a cause which comes to us out of all the broad sides of the country itself. All America is awakening to the fact that it has stumbled into a more complicated age than it ever knew without changing sufficiently the organization of its politics, and that it has been so intent upon private business that it has not discussed sufficiently public affairs. From this time out audiences like this are going to gather from one end of this country to the other, from time to time, not merely to discuss who shall be elected to particular office, but to sit in what in a legislative assembly would be called the committee of the whole on the public safety, to discuss those matters which concern us all and to discuss them intimately, in detail, one measure at a time, so as to find out certain things to find out the question, to find out why it has not been solved before, what means are proposed for solving it, how likely are those means to be effectual, who has been standing in the way of adopting them. That is what we have got to discuss about the character of the powers we are to give to a Public Utilities Commission; that is what we have to discuss about the effectiveness of regulations to prevent corruptive practices; that is what we have to discuss in regard to the control of all corporations, those that are not public service corporations but private undertakings; that is what we have to discuss with regard to the measures that are to be adopted to carry out, and build, and finance, and maintain a great inland waterway, such as we all desire in this State; that is what we have to discuss with regard to the conservation of our water supply and the purification of our water supply with regard to the drainage which is a public question, and the supply of that absolute necessity of life, the water that we drink; and the water that supplies power to the mills which it is necessary for us to drive, and for the great machinery which it is necessary for us to give power to in the conduct of our great industrial enterprises. Those are the things which we must have the patience to discuss and when we have discussed them and made up our minds they will have to be decided, and the legislature at Trenton will register our decision.

That is the program that is before us, and there is a very happy thing to think of in connection with that programme. You know that in recent years we have thought of ourselves, with some concern, because we say that there are so many elements mixed in our population, elements which after they have been mixed for a year are indistinguishable. Here a man bears a name which shows that he is of one nationality; but after a generation we do not see any difference between the two men; they are both Americans. But we are disturbed by the constant influx, the fresh streams of new elements, and we say: "How are we to digest this great body of new people?" There is only one way, ladies and gentlemen, in which a nation becomes unified and single, and that is by giving the same thoughts. The only way by which to bring all America together is the way of thinking, the way of discussion, the way of honor. Our relationship to each other is a spiritual relationship, the relationship of those who think the same thoughts, who have the same impulses, who desire the same things, who love the same ideals. Have you never travelled on the other side of the water and have found yourself very lonely for lack of some American to talk to? Why do you want an American to talk to? There are plenty of intelligent people in any country you may enter on your travels, not only people who are intelligent but people with a vast deal of what is novel and deeply interesting to tell you, but you get very hungry for some American who says to you those things that you expect him to say. You are tired of hearing new things. You want to hear some men whose thoughts will be the same as your own. Some cynical gentleman has said that what we want as the leading editorial in some newspaper is something that we can read and say, "Exactly my own opinion." The celebrated Dean Swift once said: "If you wish to enjoy a reputation of sense you must always agree with the person with whom you are conversing." Now, what distinguishes us as Americans is that upon most fundamental questions we do think alike, and therefore we enjoy in a noticeable degree each other's estimation the reputation of being men of sense. Whereas, foreigners seem to us to have queer notions, to have an odd attitude towards affairs and opinions. And so the vital processes of American politics are the processes of discussion. Those are the processes which draw us together, which make us brethren, which give us a common feeling, and those are the processes which we must nurse if we are to move together.

What is the manifest destiny of America? The manifest destiny of America is not to rule the world by physical force. The manifest destiny of America is not to pile up in vulgar height the mere mass of wealth and outward magnificence. The destiny of America is not in the amount of money she can command and spend, and throw away and burn. The destiny of America and the leadership of America is that she shall do the thinking of the world, and that her thought will not be the thought of the university circle, that her thought will not be the thought of the literary clique, that her thought will not be that of little circles that read unusual books and have unusual experiences, but that there will be throughout her great thought the pulse of the common man, of the average man, of all men—the thought of humanity itself. What gives a man courage to talk in meetings such as I have had the privilege to address in this campaign is that in the audience before him he sees not persons of a particular social stratum, not persons of particular bringing up, but men and women from every circle and rank, the real bulk and substance of America. Then he knows that part of America is before him, the thought of America before him, the future of America stored up in the impulses of the people who sit before him.

I was saying to a little company of gentlemen last evening that what interests me about all government is that it must of necessity rest upon the desires and impulses of the body of the people; and that we are very much mistaken when we suppose that government is an intellectual matter. You hear people say that this is an age in which mind is monarch. As I was saying last night, I take for granted that if that is true, mind is one of those modern monarchs that reign and do not govern, and a monarch which, like other monarchs, is apt once and again to be unseated and rejected. What we are ruled by is our passions, but, mark you, there are different kinds of passions. Hate is a passion; envy is a passion; cupidity is a passion. But love and patriotism and honor may also be passions; and the effort of every great government ought to be to keep those splendid, handsome passions in a working majority so that hate will be rebuked, so that envy will be balked, so that cupidity will be restrained; and men, taking conference together, will serve each other as well as serve themselves, and so let the great impulses of honor, and of patriotism and of love that created America also rejuvenate America. For America, ladies and gentlemen, is not merely a piece of the surface of the earth. America is not merely a body of towns. America is an idea, America is an ideal, America is a vision.

I have heard foreigners laugh at us for boasting of the size of America, and I have heard them very naturally say: "You did not make that continent, and, therefore you have no reason to be proud of its size." I reply: "We have reason to be proud of its size, because a man is as big as the thing that he conquers and masters, and we conquered and mastered that continent. We made it ourselves, and we showed the greatness of our nature by making it arise in unselfish form, by taking possession of it for mankind as well as for ourselves." That is the vision of America—America for the leadership of the world, America for the purification of the world, America for the example of the world.

But, ladies and gentlemen, that all comes back to New Jersey. How are we going to make New Jersey an example, first to America, and then to the world? How are we going to make an example of some gentlemen who have forgotten the vision? You cannot afford to hold up in front of you unsuitable representatives; you cannot afford to allow to act, in your name, men who are doing things which you do not wish to be done in your name. The beauty of all principle is, the beauty of all ideals is, that they are of no account unless they can find practical experience, and that the nation which professes ideals and does not live them is a nation discredited and disgraced. There is no mistaking the great impulse which is now beating in the heart of America. Everywhere that you turn you see that splendid thing that we call "independence."

There never was in America before so numerous a detachable vote as there is at the present moment. There never was a time when the politicians, accustomed to regular seasons, were more hopelessly guessing than they are now. A free nation may almost be defined as a nation which keeps its professional politicians guessing. Independence, as well as eternal vigilance, is the price of liberty. There is nothing higher in the world than independence. You know, ladies and gentlemen, what independence means. I can illustrate it in this way: One great church requires its clergy that they should not marry, and I have sometimes thought that there was a very deep, spiritual justification of that requirement. When a man is married, he has hostages to all the selfish interests that are in him.

Many a man will dare to do right, to abide the consequences, if the consequences descend upon himself, but if they involve the fortunes and the very bread of their wives and the very children he loves, how often will he yield to what seems to be the stern necessity of giving away to temptation. And when you reflect on all the threads and sensitive nerves that connect us, not only with our beloved families, but with our neighbors, with our towns and our cities, and forget how we tremble to break the tender film of those tender nerves, then you know the cost of independence, the cost of standing up ruthlessly and breaking anything rather than give up the independence of your spirit and faith. And if that is the operation of your government, if men will not do that they cannot be free.

You remember that fine story taken out of the middle ages, when, to humble his subjects, David, their king, said to them, "Fools, do you not know that I can have you condemned?" "Yes," they said, "we know you can do it, and we know the result, that

we can die hating you and cursing you." And the monarch knew
that he did not dare to put those men to death, because the terror was in his heart, that if those men were put to death there
would be sown the seeds of hatred and rebellion. He did not dare
attempt violence upon the spirits of independence. And so, if you
are a free people, you will remember that the price of liberty is
independence.

I have preached you a sermon upon a great theme, but what
theme could be greater than our own integrity, the integrity of
our Government, the liberty of our lives, the satisfaction of having thoughts, the integrity of which has not been violated? Do
you want pure and good government? You cannot have it in
perfection under any circumstances. No man dares promise
you more than so much as it is possible for brave men to do in a
single generation, but you must make up your minds by which
road and through which men you can accomplish the most in
your own time.

FPS T transcript (WP, DLC) with additions and corrections from the
partial texts in the New York *Evening Post*, Oct. 14, 1910, and the *Philadelphia
Record*, Oct. 14, 1910.

From George Brinton McClellan Harvey

Dear Mr. Wilson   New York Thursday [Oct. 13, 1910]

Quite so! And the solution seems to me a happy one.

My recollection is that you are to speak at Asbury Park Saturday afternoon & at Freehold in the evening. If you should feel
the need of something fit to eat while en route, my house is on
the road and I shall be there writing pieces. Don't bother to
answer.

The enclosed from Uncle Wayne MacVeagh[1] may amuse you.
It is a genial word, too, from Dr. Helm.[2]

What a job the enemy is having! And what a mess they are
making of it.   As ever   G H

I hope you are going to make the speech advertised at Carnegie
Hall.[3] *Great* would be the reception.

ALI (WP, DLC).
    [1] I. W. MacVeagh to G. B. M. Harvey, Oct. 8, 1910, ALS (WP, DLC).
Among other things, MacVeagh had written, "The real object in writing you
now is to lose no time in applying for a place in President Wilson's Cabinet.
Relying on your giving it to me I will go ahead and free myself from all
entangling alliances by March 5, 1913 without waiting for your reply."
    [2] Nathan Wilbur Helm, principal of the Evanston Academy of Northwest-
ern University, to G. B. M. Harvey, Oct. 10, 1910, ALS (WP, DLC). Helm
congratulated Harvey on the role he had played in Wilson's nomination and

expressed the hope that the Democrats would choose Wilson as their next presidential candidate.
3 The Editors have been unable to find this advertisement.

From Melancthon Williams Jacobus

Private   Hartford, Conn.,
My dear President Wilson: October 13th, 1910.

I knew how busy and over-occupied you were with your new engagements, and have not wondered at the delay in your reply[1] to my letter.

I am exceedingly obliged to you for taking the time you have to write to me, and your statement regarding the feelings of Dodge and McCormick upon the matter of the acceptance of your resignation.

There seems to be a division of sentiment among your friends as to whether or not your best interests will be conserved by holding the acceptance of the resignation in abeyance. Mr. Jones thinks that it might seem as though we were discrediting the likelihood of your election by delaying the acceptance. Others have proposed settling the matter of resignation by granting you leave of absence for two years in case of your election.

We are to have a conference of a few of your supporters at the Hotel Belmont[2] on Tuesday afternoon of next week. If you would care to make any statement to this conference beyond what you have written in your letter to me, I shall be only too glad to present it. The only thing I am especially anxious for is that we shall know what we want to do before we come to the meeting next Thursday, and that in deciding what we want to do, we shall fix upon that which will be most agreeable and of most advantage to you.

I will be at the Hotel Belmont from Monday evening until Wednesday.

With kindest regards and always with best wishes for your enlarging career, I am

Yours most sincerely,   M. W. Jacobus

TLS (WP, DLC).
1 It is missing.
2 In New York.

From Winthrop More Daniels

My dear Wilson: Princeton, N. J. 13 Oct. 1910.

I hope you may not be inclined to make speeches in New York state in the present campaign. It may provoke retaliation, and

I think you may legitimately decline to assume responsibilities not your own. Moreover I am not at all re-assured by the key-notes struck by Dix and Judge Parker[1] in New York State. The "New Nationalism" (T. R. borrows the term from Croly's recent book on "The Promise of American Life"[2] which I read carefully, as I had to review it for *"The Nation"* early this year)[3] may or may not be assailable. If it implies that the Federal Government must essay essential tasks for which economic growth has unfitted the States, we cannot fight against it. And while I fear that Roosevelt may be inclined to reduce the states to convenient administrative satrapies, *until he explicitly proposes to do so,* I feel it dangerous —because merely reactionary,—to pin much hope to the people's willingness to measure everything by the yardstick of a technical constitutional lawyer.

I hope everything is going well with you in the campaign. With best regards, I am,

Ever yours sincerely   W. M. Daniels.

ALS (WP, DLC).
    [1] Alton Brooks Parker, as temporary chairman of the New York Democratic state convention at Rochester, gave the keynote address on September 29, 1910. The Democratic nominee for governor, John Alden Dix, made his acceptance speech at his home in Thomson, N. Y., on October 12, 1910. The two addresses are printed in the New York *Evening Post*, Sept. 29 and Oct. 12, 1910. Both men strongly criticized Theodore Roosevelt and his New Nationalism, particularly his attacks upon the courts.
    [2] See L. Abbott to WW, April 8, 1910, ns. 1 and 2, Vol. 20.
    [3] "The Future of Democracy," New York *Nation*, xc (March 3, 1910), 209-11.

From David L. MacKay

Dear Sir: Astoria, L. I. Oct. 13, 1910.

I wish to thank you for your answer of October 11th. in view of the fact that I have found the critics of trades unionism inclined to ignore a request for an explanation or proof of their remarks, as for example, the editor of The Century[1] who has been criticising labor lately but who has ignored Mr. Gomper's[2] request for proof.

Permit me to say, however, that I fail to get your point, that I still believe the two sets of remarks contradictory. In those at Bridgeton, you said that the laboring man's advance in efficiency i.e., *in his ability to produce more and better work,* is due solely to his union; while in your baccalaureate address, you said that the standard of the trades unionist is to give as little as he may for his wages which would imply that any advance in efficiency was despite his union rather than because of it. Your statement befor the People's Forum, New Rochelle, Feb. 26, 1905, that "the labor unions reward the shiftless and incompetent at the expense of the able and industrious"[3] is but a stronger expression of the same belief. You speak in your baccalaureate address as though the restriction of output was characteristic of trades unionism in general. Nowhere do you point out that it is the practice of but a small minority of unions.

Volume XIX, p. 76, of The U. S. Industrial Commission's Report, tho it cites cases here and there, does not find the practice sufficiently general to warrant them in charging it as a practice of trades unionism in general.

Permit me to point out that in your reply to a request from a member[4] of the composing room chapel of the N. Y. Evening Telegram for your authority, you mentioned no official government publication.

You based your criticism on several cases of buildings in New York city the bricklayers working on which spent one-third of the day sitting around because they had laid the number of bricks to which they were limited for the day; on your own experiences in Princeton "where I once found it impossible, for example, on a very cold evening, to get a broken windowpane mended at the house of an invalid friend"; and on the testimony of friends. "I, of course," you said in concluding, "could not, in the case of more than one or two of these instances, give legal proof of my assertions, but the evidences I have are entirely sufficient to convince me of the general truth of the statement I made."

These are rather narrow grounds to condemn a nation-wide movement upon. The testimony of friends, and your experience in Princeton out of which you can cull but two legal proofs is rather a flimsy foundation for such a broad condemnation of a movement which extends throughout the United States. In your statement regarding the bricklayers you are, I believe, in error. The bricklayer's union in New York city does not restrict the number of brick laid. Competition is so keen and mechanics so efficient that any bricklayer sitting around one-third of the day would be very quickly discharged.

Very truly yours,   David L. MacKay

ALS (WP, DLC).
[1] Robert Underwood Johnson.
[2] Samuel Gompers, president of the American Federation of Labor.
[3] A news report of this address is printed at Feb. 27, 1905, Vol. 16.
[4] See Edgar R. Laverty to WW, June 16, 1909, Vol. 19.

From Benjamin Boisseau Bobbitt

Long Branch New Jersey.

My dear Dr. Wilson: Oct. 13, 1910

In your coming speech at Asbury Park, do you not think it would be good policy to mention the Ocean Highway and Inland Waterway projects, from more or less empty pledges to support which Mr. Lewis is making capital along the coast?

Might not it also lend local flavor and piquancy to the address, too, to make some reference to the mysterious disappearance of the cold storage bill, so-called, from the desk of Senator [Oliver Huff] Brown, of this county,[1] in the closing hours of the legislative session when it was about to be brought up for passage in the Senate after being rushed through the Assembly, where it had been unnecessarily held for many weeks? Also to the smothering in committee—of which committee (Elections) Assemblyman [Monroe Van Brackle] Poole, of this county, was chairman—of the campaign fund publicity measure? Brown was chairman of the Senate Health committee to which the cold storage bill was referred. Both instances have been much commented upon in the county and have tended to alienate many old line Republicans. They certainly don't constitute a flattering commentary on prevailing State House methods at Trenton.

Use or don't use these suggestions in any way you may see fit. I shall not be offended whatever you do. I don't mean to be presumptuous, but only wish to call to your attention material which you might otherwise naturally overlook.

With best wishes I am

Sincerely yours   B. B. Bobbitt

ALS (WP, DLC).
[1] Monmouth County.

From Howard Marshall[1]

My dear sir: East Orange, N. J., October 13th., 1910.

I have observed in the newspapers that you have on several occasions, in discussing the issues of the present campaign, expressed yourself, in a general way, in referring to the question of amendment to the Public Utility Law, as in favor of a "rate-making power[.]" This is a statement which may be so easily misunderstood, unless it be supplemented by some further and more definite expression of your views, that I venture to write you in the interest, and on behalf of a large body of citizens and urge that you will, either in a letter in response to this, or in some

Woodrow Wilson

George Harvey

James Smith, Jr.

James R. Nugent

Robert Davis

James Kerney

George L. Record

Woodrow Wilson, with Vivian Murchison Lewis on his right, and John Franklin Fort on his left

public address, inform the public more fully as to what you regard as properly within your contemplation of the "rate-making power"

You will recall in the original Robbins bill of 1908 that rate-making power was given to the Commission provided that the corporation was not deprived of power to pay dividends on watered stock; and you will also remember in the Pierce bill provision was made for a return on the value of the franchises which the public had donated to the company. Do you favor either of the above kinds of alleged rate-making power, or do you favor a statute giving the Public Utility Commission the power upon complaint, or upon its own motion, to fix just and reasonable rates, which will give a fair return on the value of the property devoted to public service, which is outlined by the decisions of the courts as being the real and the just and constitutional basis of such rate-making? Do you favor an appropriation for the purpose of making a valuation of all the physical property of public utility companies devoted to the public service?

Thanking you in advance for a response at your early convenience, I beg to remain

Very respectfully yours,   Howard Marshall

TLS (WP, DLC).
[1] President of the Commuters League of the State of New Jersey; in the carpet and floorcovering business in New York, he lived in East Orange, N. J.

A News Report of Speeches in Ocean County, New Jersey

[*Oct. 14, 1910*]

Wilson Gets Great Reception in His
Ocean County Tour

Lakewood, New Jersey, Oct. 14.–With two speeches in which he invited the scorn of all sensible men for antiquated registration and voting laws, Woodrow Wilson completed tonight his first day of town-to-town campaigning. He came to Ocean County from Atlantic City at noon, and the three automobiles filled with Mr. Wilson's party, newspapermen and stenographers, stopped at five little coast villages for hand-shaking purposes, and at Toms River for a speech early this evening. At Pleasantville, just outside Atlantic City, there were so many workmen on hand that Mr. Wilson spoke from a store stoop for two minutes. At Tuckerton, where the party got lunch, an automobile arrived from Lakewood to join the procession.

At Toms River there were 800 people from all over the county, some of them coming on special trains to attend the meeting. The crowd was so large that the court house would not do, and Mr. Wilson spoke from its steps. Mr. Wilson knew how to appreciate the turnout in a village where the Democrats have not been able to get more than two dozen together to hear a political speech in years. He made a speech containing little new for him, except his thrusting attacks on the registration laws; yet he spoke more comprehensively of his purposes and beliefs than on any occasion so far.

He told the Ocean County folks he wanted to be what the old Romans called the tribune of the people, and he said with distinctiveness: "If you elect me, and some thing does not happen right away, you may be sure I will never again come before you as a candidate."

"New Jersey's election laws would be ludicrous if they were not so loose and evil," said Mr. Wilson. "Why, the very system of letting a man register by proxy and transfer his registration lends itself to fraud," the candidate exclaimed, "and to have ballots privately distributed and marked so that the buyers of the votes can tell that they get what they pay for, is just as bad."

Mr. Wilson told the Toms River crowd that he thought his advantage lay outside of being a politician.

"They call me an amateur," he said to the crowd, "and I willingly accept the classification. You want amateurs, men who play the game because it is a handsome game, worth playing, for its own sake. A professional in politics or anything else is a man who plays the game for the money there is in it for himself."

The rank and file of the Republicans, Mr. Wilson continued, find they can't accomplish much with their own men in power.

"A stand-patter," he said, "is one who stands still and can't be started; a progressive, one who is started and can't be stopped. The stand-patter thinks he has the people by the wool. He has come to believe that there is no necessity in being perfect."

From Toms River Mr. Wilson hurried by automobile to Lakewood, where a Democratic meeting was being held in a hall over a garage. Facing 2,000 men and women, Mr. Wilson took more thrusts at the Jersey election system. He said that the evil is pretty bad these days. "There has come about in this country one of the most dangerous conditions possible," he cried, "an alliance between political parties and business. That's why, when we lay a finger on the corporations, we find we have disturbed political arrangements. It has been simply impossible to get from the Republican managers in this State any corrupt practice act. Every bill of that sort has been smothered in committee."

Mr. Wilson says he was in favor of a great inland waterway for Jersey, and he does not believe with the Republicans that it should be used only by yachts.

In his speeches today Mr. Wilson spoke as one who took his hearers to an eminence from where they might view for the first time the wreckage of all their fondest plans. He said the assertion of the men on the opposite stump who called him an amateur were true, and he differentiated himself from the professionals as the amateurs are differentiated in college games—as a man not in the game for money or for anything but the sport and glory, and the good of the game itself. His addresses here tonight were notable in a series that have been characterized by a searching vision and an eloquence almost inspired.

"We will let complaining business alone," he said. "When it leaves us alone—if it ever will. Unless we recognize the rising tide of insurging opinion and guide it as men in the West and Middle West are trying to guide it, one day it will overwhelm everything, and destroy the foundations of all that business has built, and after that no living man can tell what will follow."

Printed in the Trenton *True American,* Oct. 15, 1910; some editorial headings omitted.

From George Brinton McClellan Harvey

Dear Mr. Wilson: New York October 14, 1910.

I happened to meet at dinner, the other evening, Congressman [John Joseph] Fitzgerald, the most active-minded of Representatives hereabouts. In the course of the conversation, he remarked that the true status of tariff legislation in Washington had not been made clear by the press and was most imperfectly understood by the public. I asked him to jot down a few facts that might possibly be of some aid to you during the campaign or later. I have just received the enclosed.[1] Fitzgerald, I am confident, was very glad to do it, as he manifested great interest in your campaign. Incidentally, Clark Howell[2] was at the same dinner and declared himself in.

Faithfully yours,   George Harvey

TLS (WP, DLC).
    [1] J. J. Fitzgerald to G. B. M. Harvey, Oct. 6, 1910, TLS (WP, DLC), and a long typed memorandum on the Payne-Aldrich Tariff Act and alleged Republican iniquities in tariff legislation.
    [2] Editor-in-chief and owner of the *Atlanta Constitution.*

From Lucien Hugh Alexander[1]

My dear *Mr.* Wilson   Washington D. C. 14 October 1910

I have concluded I was very ungracious last Sunday on the train not to wish you a more hearty God-speed in your fight. While I am utterly opposed to some of your views *in re* the relations of the national and state government and am myself a Republican I sincerely hope you will win your New Jersey contest for it will be a great aid to good government in every state of the Union to say nothing of your adopted state. Furthermore I believe it will make you the Democratic nominee for the Presidency in 1912 which I believe will also be a splendid thing for the country as it will force to the front for settlement the great issues which in my judgment must be settled before we as a mighty people can develope as we should.

Please note the enclosed.[2]

With sincere regard and hearty wishes for your success in November 1910.

                    Yours truly yrs   Lucien Hugh Alexander

ALS (WP, DLC).
[1] Lawyer of Philadelphia, a leading figure in the American Bar Association for many years.
[2] It is missing.

A Campaign Address in Asbury Park, New Jersey[1]

                                                October 15, 1910.

Mr. Chairman,[2] ladies, gentlemen and fellow citizens: Your greeting is indeed cordial and gracious, and I thank you for it most sincerely. The chairman of the meeting has paid me a very neat compliment. I am not aware of its requiring any courage or involving any particular self-sacrifice to enjoy the privileges of presenting to the people of New Jersey what I believe to be the people's cause. For a man trained as I have been trained to meet and to desire this privilege is one thing, gentlemen, to sit in a quiet study and read the history of liberty; it is another thing and a thing much more equally interesting to take some part, although it be a very small part, in advancing that movement toward the realization of human rights which began for us in Magna Charta and has been gathering force and volume ever since. The real satisfaction of life is not, I believe, in study

[1] Delivered in the Hippodrome.
[2] Samuel Alexander Patterson, lawyer of Asbury Park with the firm of Patterson and Rhome.

but in action. It has not required courage but a privilege to undertake the things I have undertaken. It will remain a privilege whether you elect me to the office of Governor or not. I will at any rate have the opportunity of showing you where my real interest lies.

The speech to which you have just listened[3] has rendered a great service and discussion which it seems to me necessary it should, and we ought to devote our thoughts to it. Mr. Katzenbach's speech was excellent in temper and what he says bears on the fortunes of every man in the state and in the nation, and it seems to me that they [we] should be very frank with each other at the present crisis of affairs in this state; that we should be very frank [and] at the same time very just.

It is not for anyone of us to judge the foundation of character. It is not for anyone of us, in the absence of those grosser forms of corruption which are unhappily displayed, to label this man "corrupt" and that man "bad." That we can safely leave for the final judgment, with which we have nothing to do. And every man, when he searches his own conscience, reflects the motives that have moved him in the conduct of his life, recollects many a day when weakness and degradation, many a day when motives less handsome than others govern the real decisions he made. So we must look at the leaders of the Republican party in a fair historic temper.

They have grown into the things which they have been doing, and because they have grown into them they have become confirmed in them. Nothing confirms like growth. You do not shake off a thing that you have come insensibly into through a long period. So that what we must regard is the history of the situation in which the Republican leaders now find themselves.

I have read with a great deal of interest and with some sympathy the speeches which Mr. Lewis has been making about the Republican party. I do not wonder that Mr. Lewis in his thoughts harks back to the great name of Lincoln, which stands at the beginning of the history of the Republican party, and yet how far back must he go to find typified in the leaders of the Republican party that man of the people, that man who wished nothing so much as freedom, nothing so much as that the individual man should have his shackles and trammels struck away from him, so that every man, every common man, should have his rights in America. There has been a long process of building since then, in which these gentlemen have insensibly been led away from

3 Frank S. Katzenbach, Jr., had spoken briefly.

the ideals and standards of Lincoln. It would be a happy circumstance for America if we should go back to the leadership of men like that, to the leadership of men in whose hearts no motives had found lodgment except the motives which they grew from sympathy with the great mass of men.

But we, alas, have been drawn away from these circumstances, partly by circumstances which we would not wish to reverse if we could reverse them. The great circumstance of modern times is the particular form in which business has grown. It has grown, as Mr. Katzenbach has so admirably pointed out to you, in these artificial forms which we sum up under the general name of corporation, combination, trust, or whatever name you choose to use in connection with the great organization of business which is now so characteristic of our times. And in that process of building up nothing has been more instrumental—I make this by way of a concession, but I think it is a just concession—than the policy of the Republican party. The Republican party, therefore, has come to be regarded—I mean the Republican party leaders have come to be regarded—as the partners of big business. Now, there is no doubt that big business, business on the great scale, business on the corporate scale, organized, united business, has been at the bottom of the building up of the colossal wealth and material power of this country. In the process certain men have come to the top, men of genius, men who in other circumstances would have ruled not merely great business combinations but great states and great empires, men of the stuff that statesmen and kings are made of, but, alas, in some respects also like the great statesmen and kings whom other ages have known, who have centered their thoughts upon their own power and have come to believe that the exercise of that power was one and the same thing with the prosperity of the country. Therefore, these kings and rulers have allied themselves with the leaders of the Republican party, have poured money into their coffers, have stood by them at every critical turning point in their political history, until these gentlemen feel, and very naturally feel, an honorable alliance that cannot be broken between the corporate leaders of the country and the political leaders of the country.

Put yourself in their places. Let yourself be engaged in great business, let yourself be as intimately concerned with big business as the two present senators from New Jersey are both of them engaged, and ask yourself frankly what would your point of view be. Your point of view would be that anything done by the legislature or by Congress that disturbed the plan or impaired the prospect of these great bodies of business would be detrimental to the community as a whole. These gentlemen, I have very little doubt, honestly think that the brains of the country are lodged where the money is used; that the discussion of the country lies where great business has to be overlooked; where the vision extends beyond the boundaries of the United States, to foreign markets, to great international transactions, as great as the transactions of ancient states when they dealt with one another, until these great masters of finance are entertained by foreign monarchs, not as a condescension, but as those who would acknowledge the greatness of their equals—men who are presiding over the destinies of great nations.

I am not impeaching, therefore, the motives of these men, I am challenging their thoughts. I do not believe that these men can do the thinking for the country, and I do not believe that they ought to be suffered to do the thinking for the country. The question you have to face in this campaign is: who shall do your thinking and your governing for you—men who think in the terms of special interests or men who have been engaged away from special interests and think in the terms of no special group of persons whatever? I have nothing, not a syllable, to say against the character or the purpose of my opponent, the Republican candidate for the Governorship. I have only this to say as to his situation—that he has for a great many years been allied with and connected with this group of men who have come to think that they must do the thinking of New Jersey for her, and that it is inconceivable to me that he should be able to detach himself from that connection and think independently and even antagonistically, as it is necessary he should think, to the things which they have intended. Mr. Katzenbach has recited for you some of the broken promises of the Republican party, I mean of the Republican party leaders, for that is what we mean in this discussion when we say the Republican party, the Republican party leaders have done the misleading. Now, why have they misled you, why have they made promises which they do not keep? Because after they had made them they found it would disturb business to keep them, and, therefore, they did not keep them. Their object was and is to retain their leadership in order that existing conditions may not be disturbed. You will find great ramifications of these motives.

It would look as if all they have to do was to prevent legislation which would actually interfere with the business of corporations. I can understand, because it lies on the surface, why they should not keep their promise about the Public Utility Commission, which should have rate-making powers. They did not regulate all public utilities, that is perfectly plain, but why did not they pass a corrupt practices act?

Oh, gentlemen, don't you see that the power of a political organization does not lie actually in the person who determines its policy. A political organization has branches in every community in the country. It is necessary that they should keep the offices in as many communities as possible in order to preserve the integrity of their own power unbroken. Moreover, it is necessary that they should create as many offices as possible, and have as many salaries at their disposal as possible, and, in order that this community should not be able to break this grip upon them, it was necessary that the election should not be too clearly scrutinized by the voters because the spirit of insurgency, the spirit of independence, is alive and even when it seems most to slumber.

Have you read the Democratic platform? It is singularly businesslike and explicit; it enumerates the things it wants; when it says it wants anything it does not [only] say it wants an effective corrupt practice act, but that it wants one which will limit expenses to legitimate expenditures, one that will require publication, including the sources from which the moneys come. When you get that publicity there is going to be great timidity about contributing large sums of money, and you are going to be very much surprised, but as to the amount of expenditure and the character of the expenditure. But don't you see that if a party is fighting to keep power, it cannot afford to have any changes because changes are incalculable. If I am working a scheme I want to know that the conditions to-morrow will be exactly the same as they are to-day. Then I know how to work the scheme. But if you change them for me, then I don't know whether I am expert at the game or not.

One of the difficulties about [the] direct primary is that in some communities in the United States—I won't mention which—methods have been found for working the primary; and when we are framing a direct primary law we should have the light of our own experience throughout the United States. Direct primary adds another election, to all intents and purposes. You must have primary machinery and I am for putting the machine out of business, no matter which one. I want to say parenthetically, that if you find out that I have ever been or ever intend to be connected with a machine of any kind I hope you will vote against me, because, for my part, there wouldn't be anything interesting for me,—I am sorry to say, that this was true even when I was a school boy—there never has been anything interesting for me in doing what I am told to do. The only thing that I have ever found interesting was having something to do and trying, at any rate, to do it in a way I thought was interesting and wise. I have not always been wise—don't misunderstand me, but I have always thought that I was. You have, therefore, this question to decide: It is a question of leadership. It is not a question between parties so much as it is a question between groups of persons representing parties. It is a choice of leaders. Now, I cannot argue that question with you; I couldn't stand up here and argue that I was the kind of leader needed by the state of New Jersey.

I will venture to tell you again a story I told another audience, which you may not have read. An old darky fell asleep in a railroad coach, with his head thrown back and his mouth wide open. Somebody in the coach happened to have some powdered quinine in a bottle, and he stepped up to the darky, and dusted his tongue with it. The darky was entirely unconscious of what was going on about him until the quinine was put on his tongue, when he awakened and asked the conductor, "Say, boss, is a doctor on this train?" And the conductor said, "I don't know, why, what do you want a doctor for." And the darky said, "Because I done busted my gall."

Now, in respect of arguing my own virtues, I have done busted my gall. I cannot do that; I can only ask you a question: "Do you want entangled leaders, or do you want disentangled leaders? Do you want leaders with a countless number of commitments, or do you want leaders with no commitments at all?["] That is a question that you must ask yourselves. Moreover, do you want—and this is the most fundamental question of all—do you want leaders who listen to the voice of business, that is to say, leaders of economic expediency—or leaders who listen to the voice of the people? It is a very radical and a very fundamental choice that has been made thousands of times in the history of the world. The difference between America and other parts of the world is that in America we make such a choice without revolution or bloodshed, whereas the choice used to be made with revolution and bloodshed.

What is the voice of the people? Can any man pretend that he hears the voice of the people? No man can hear any such thing. But some men can pretend because they know whereof they speak, that their hearts are listening, that their minds are attentive, that they have no reason to listen to other voices, that they are dearly promising themselves that when they hear the voice which seems to come from the ordinary home, out of the ordinary shop, from the ordinary toiling masses of men and women they will listen and heed. I say that there are many who can say that they know that, because a man does know his own heart whether he knows his own abilities or not.

And so, gentlemen, I beg that in the great choice that is to be made on the eighth of November next, you will cast out party feeling, that you will cast out partisan prejudice, and say to yourselves that you are choosing a course for your party, and that you will make your choice upon that great basis of sympathy which you may find in one set of men or the other; and you will think of it as a choice between two sets of men, because no man can be a self leader. No one voice can speak loud enough to speak the words of command in a great self-governing community; you must choose a set of men who are working together, in the executive offices of the state, in the legislative halls at Washington, to bring about that new day when men will not destroy or turn back the natural currents of business. Let this be the basis of your choice, for when a man goes to the polls, with that as his conscious object, then he may be trusted to exercise that act of sovereignty, and what he does will be approved by God and man.[4]

FPS T transcript (WP, DLC) with corrections and additions from the partial text in the *Philadelphia Record*, Oct. 16, 1910.
[4] Following this address, Wilson went to Freehold, where he spoke that evening in the Armory Opera House. A brief report of his address appears in the *Freehold, N. J., Transcript*, Oct. 21, 1910.

From Robert Elliott Speer[1]

My dear President Wilson,   New York Oct 15, 1910

You will have been overwhelmed by letters from men in New Jersey telling you of their satisfaction in voting for you for the Governorship and one ought, perhaps, to spare you another, but I cannot forbear telling you how thankful I am for the opportunity both to work and to vote for you, and how good it is for a Democrat to be able to support you and the party with you, and to hope for better things nationally. My only regret[,] and it is a deep one, is that you are leaving the college. I have sympathized with your ideals and, as far as I have understood them, with your policies and I, with many, will have to temper rejoicing in your election as governor with sorrow at your withdrawal from the presidency of the college.

Yours very faithfully,   Robert E. Speer.

ALS (WP, DLC).
    [1] Princeton 1889; secretary of the Board of Foreign Missions of the Pres-
byterian Church in the U.S.A.; author of numerous religious books and studies
of missionary work.

From William Blackburn[1]

Dear Sir,   Camden, N. J., Oct 15 1910

enclosed you will find three (3) circulars sent me from *Trenton*.[2] Will you kindly tell me if they reflect your sentiments toward labor, as I have quite a bundle of them sent for me to
distribute, but being a life long Democrat, I will hold them until
I have your answer. I have voted for every Democratic Candidate
since Seymour and Blair ran for President. I am also a working
man and a firm believer in labor unions. If your answer is satisfactory I will destroy them[,] if not I shall distribute them, and
will for the first time be compelled to vote against our Candidate
for Governor. hopeing to hear from you I am

Yours truly   Wm. Blackburn

ALS (WP, DLC).
    [1] Recording secretary of Machinist Local No. 87, West Jersey Lodge, Inter-
national Association of Machinists, Camden, N. J.
    [2] All three circulars were sent from Trenton by one Luke McKenney, who
signed himself secretary of the Progressive Voters of Labor. The first, com-
prising four pages, was dated October 6, 1910, and entitled *Workingmen, Read
and Reflect! "Reward Your Friends and Defeat Your Enemies" The Deeds of
Lewis The Words of Wilson Compare Them!* Under the heading, "The
Labor Record of Vivian M. Lewis," was listed a number of bills and measures
affecting labor which Lewis allegedly had supported during his three terms
in the Assembly, 1899-1901. Wilson, on the other hand, claimed the circular,
was the "Aristocratic Candidate of Democratic Bosses and Their Wall Street
Allies," and his record was one of "Sustained Opposition to Labor's Welfare."
Quotations from two of Wilson's addresses then followed. The first, dated
February 26, 1905, read: "Labor unions reward the shiftless and incompetent
at the expense of the able and industrious." It was from Wilson's speech to
the New Rochelle, N. Y., People's Forum on that date as reported in the New
York *Sun*, Feb. 26, 1905. The second, much longer quotation, was from Wilson's baccalaureate sermon on June 13, 1909, and included his oft-quoted
remarks to the effect that American workers were rapidly becoming "unprofitable servants." The fourth page concluded with the exhortation, "Make
the Majority for Vivian M. Lewis so large as to leave no doubt of the concrete
judgment of Labor."
    The other two enclosures were single-paged flyers both dated October 12,
1910, and addressed "To the Workingmen of New Jersey." One, entitled *The
Source of His "Wisdom,"* excoriated Wilson for his "warped" views about labor
which were "echoes from the dark past, when kindred theorists urged that
it was God-ordained that the many must toil that the few might prosper." It
called on workingmen to vote for Lewis and help "rebuke the Wall Street
candidate who sneers at American products and condemns American labor."
    The second flyer, *If Wilson only Could and Would*, after quoting once again
Wilson's comments about "unprofitable servants," suggested that if Wilson
would spend a day with a bricklayer on the scaffold "in the boiling sun or the
biting cold," with an ironworker "ten or fifteen stories in the air," or in "some
ship's fire hold shoveling coal," then he perhaps could tell workingmen how
much to reduce their wages a day in order to make themselves profitable.
The sheet ended with a quotation from Shakespeare's *Romeo and Juliet*, "He
jests at scars who never felt a wound."

Both flyers took sharp slaps at Wilson's southern origins. For example, the first began: "Woodrow Wilson draws his inspiration upon labor topics from those who made labor 'profitable' with the lash. His mind was warped, in the 'old regime,' when the black chattel slave gave place to the white child slave, whose father and mother toiled beside it that all might become 'profitable servants' to the same taskmaster. It was under the same regime that the ball and chain and the prison camp were meted out to the labor organizer who dared to protest against such inhuman conditions." The second flyer said that Wilson's statements on labor might have been appropriate "if expressed at the banquet board of an assembly of slaveholders in the Old South sixty or seventy years ago."

From Benjamin Bright Chambers[1]

My dear Dr. Wilson,   Portland, Oregon October 15, 1910.

I hope, although I indeed know that I have taken already entirely too much liberty with your very precious time, that you will vouchsafe me again the privilege of a few lines. I do not write to congratulate you upon your nomination; for rather I would heartily congratulate the State of New Jersey. But I am thinking of Princeton, and knowing of the report that you may probably soon resign from Princeton, I would ask you—if that report be true—if you will not consent to some arrangement, by which you could be temporarily substituted, for it seems almost certain that you will be elected Governor.

Now I trust that you will pardon this seeming trespass, by a very young and inexperienced man, upon what is entirely within your freedom and wisdom to choose. I do not speak with any feeling of authority whatever or any knowledge of the situation that would warrant me in thus writing to you. I simply know that the loss of you would mean the loss of too great an opportunity for Princeton; and I write merely from the impulse which all of her sons must feel, who realize that their Alma Mater is in danger of losing her loved President.

I am,—if I may say with cordial wishes—
Sincerely yours   Benj. B. Chambers '09

ALS (WP, DLC).
[1] Princeton 1909, in the lumber business in Oregon.

To David L. MacKay

My dear Sir: Princeton, N. J. October 17th, 1910.

I am very sorry that I did not make my points clear in my previous letter. It must have been due to the necessary haste in which I write during the engagements of the campaign.

I did not say in my speech at Bridgeton, to which you refer, that labor owed its great increase in efficiency to labor organizations. I said that it owed its ability to get its rights to that organization, that it was entitled to the fullest freedom of organization, and had been greatly benefitted by the assistance organization had been able to give its members.

In the extracts which have been published from my Baccalaureate Address and from my address at New Rochelle the context is entirely omitted. I did say that the things I was criticizing were characteristic of only *some* of the unions. I did not say, or mean to convey the impression, that such limitations of output were characteristic of the labor unions in general. The criticisms I uttered in those addresses were meant entirely as the criticisms of a friend and directed against what seemed dangerous tendencies and a mistaken policy.

I think, therefore, that I am justified in saying that there is really no contradiction between one set of utterances and the other. Certainly there is no contradiction in my own mind, and my own position is consistent with the friendliness and sympathy I have always felt with the labor organizations. I am obliged to you for having given me the opportunity to correct the impression made by my first letter.

Very sincerely yours,   Woodrow Wilson

TLS (WC, NjP).

To Winthrop More Daniels

My dear Daniels: Princeton, N. J. October 17th, 1910.

Thank you sincerely for your letter of the 13th, which I find awaiting me on my return.

I entirely agree with you about my speaking in New York and about the inadvisability of attacking the vague New Nationalism. Your idea as to what is expedient jumps with mine entirely, but I am none the less obliged to you for your kindness in making the suggestion. I hope that you will let me know what you are thinking as often as possible.

Cordially and faithfully yours,   Woodrow Wilson

TLS (Wilson-Daniels Corr., CtY).

To Robert Bridges

My dear Bobby: Princeton, N. J. October 17th, 1910.

Thank you with all my heart for your letter of October 11th, which I would have answered sooner, had I not been away on a speaking trip.

I need not tell you how much pleasure your message has given me. I knew how you would feel, but I love to have you say so.

Thank you also for telling me about Charley Talcott. I am delighted to hear the news and will write to him at once.

In haste,   Affectionately yours,   Woodrow Wilson

TLS (WC, NjP).

To George Brinton McClellan Harvey

Princeton, N. J.

My dear Colonel Harvey: October 17th, 1910.

I am extremely glad to get the data which Mr. Fitzgerald furnishes. It was very kind of you to obtain it for me. I think that we should treat the tariff only incidentally in the present campaign, so far as the gubernatorial question is concerned, but this data would be of great service to me later, I hope. I am taking the liberty of writing a letter of acknowledgement to Mr. Fitzgerald himself.

I was mighty sorry not to be able to get hold of you at the Asbury Park meeting, but it seemed impossible to manage. I hurried in and hurried out. If I had known that you were going to be there, I could have managed it. It is very trying to see a friend so near and yet have him so far away.

In haste, Cordially and faithfully yours,

Woodrow Wilson

TLS (WP, DLC).

From George Lawrence Record

My dear Sir: Jersey City, N. J. Oct. 17, 1910.

I have your two letters declining to meet me in a joint debate, and offering to answer any questions I may put to you in reference to your attitude upon any public question, and to debate in writing any differences between us. You convey the impression in your last letter to me that our views are fundamentally the same upon the principal questions of the day. I hope this is so, because I know of no one in this State who exceeds you in ability to reason, or in power of statement, while your great and justly earned reputation gives weight and authority to whatever position you take.

Before entering upon any debate the first thing is to determine wherein, if at all, we differ. I submit to you a list of questions which show exactly the principles and the program of the Progressive Republicans of this State. These questions are so framed that you can categorically answer yes or no, except where your reasons are requested. I ask you to so answer. When these questions are answered, we can determine upon what subjects we differ and debate accordingly.

I favor the enactment of laws to carry out the following principles, viz:

1. That the public utility commission should have full power to fix just and reasonable rates to be charged by all public service corporations. Do you favor this?

2. That the physical property of each public utility corporation which is devoted to a public use should be valued by the State. Do you favor this?

3. That such physical valuation should be taken as the assessment upon which such corporations shall pay local taxes. Do you favor this?

4. That such valuation should be used as a basis for fixing rates to be charged by these corporations and that such rates should be so limited as to allow them to earn not exceeding six per cent. upon this valuation. Do you favor this?

5. That the present primary law should be extended to the selection of candidates for party nominations for governor, congressmen, and delegates to national conventions. Do you favor this?

6. That United States Senators should be elected by popular vote. Do you favor this?

7. To apply this principle I favor a law compelling all candidates for nomination to the Legislature to file a pledge to vote for that candidate of their party for United States Senator who shall receive the highest number of votes under the present primary law. Do you favor this?

8. That the names of all candidates at elections should be printed on a blanket ballot, and that all ballots shall be distributed to the voter by mail at public expense, or confined to the polling place. Do you favor this?

9. That primary and election officers should be appointed by some impartial agency, like a court. Do you favor this?

10. There should be a drastic corrupt practices act, forbidding all political expenditures except for the objects named in the act, with drastic penalties for the violation of the act; prohibiting the employment of more than two workers or watchers at the polls on primary or election day representing any one party, or group of candidates; prohibiting the hiring of

vehicles for transporting voters; limiting the amount to be expended by candidates; prohibiting political contributions by corporations. Do you favor this?

11. That every industry employing workmen shall be compelled to bear the expense of all injuries to employees which happen in the industry without the wilful negligence of such employees. Do you favor this?

12. That the County Board of Elections law[1] and the Hillery maximum tax law[2] should be repealed. Do you favor this?

13. Does the Democratic platform declare for the choice of candidates for all elective offices by the direct vote system?

There is one other subject, the nature and extent of the boss system in our politics, which I desire to discuss as briefly as I can, as a necessary foundation for some further questions which I request you to answer. My idea of the boss system is that there is a virtual partnership between the great public service corporations, such as the railroad, trolley and gas companies, and the principal political leaders of both party organizations; that the terms of this partnership, express or implied, are these: the corporations in question receive from public officials franchises,

[1] Record, or his typist, undoubtedly made an error here. A comprehensive act to regulate elections, passed by the New Jersey legislature in 1898 and modified in 1905, did include provision for county boards of election. Each was to consist of four members, one to be nominated each year by the state chairman of each of the two major political parties to serve a term of two years. The nominees were then "commissioned" by the governor without further investigation. The county boards in turn appointed, upon nomination by the county chairmen of the two major parties, boards of registry and election for each election district within the respective counties. The two bodies together determined the lists of eligible voters in each district and conducted all elections. See Laws of New Jersey, 1898, Chap. 139, pp. 237-338, and ibid., 1905, Chap. 258, pp. 502-508. This system, obviously open to domination by political bosses, remained in force until 1911 when it was drastically altered by the Geran law, about which see n. 1 to the news report printed at April 14, 1911, Vol. 22.

However, it seems almost certain that Record intended to say "County Board of Taxation law." The Newark Evening News, October 25, 1910, in reprinting Record's letter with Wilson's answers, perhaps after hearing from Record, so reworded the question and repeated the new wording in an editorial in the same issue. The county boards of taxation were established by an act of 1906 in order "to secure the taxation of all property in the various counties of this state at its true value" (see Laws of New Jersey, 1906, Chap. 120, pp. 210-217). Although ostensibly created to equalize tax assessments throughout the state, it was widely believed at the time that the boards were established at the behest of the railroad companies and were intended to force local assessors to raise valuations on private property and thus lower the average rate at which railroads would pay. For a discussion of the rather complex laws and the political realities behind them mentioned in this paragraph and in the following note, see Noble, New Jersey Progressivism before Wilson, pp. 20-31.

[2] The so-called Hillery act, named for Senator Thomas J. Hillery, was passed by the New Jersey legislature in 1905. It fixed a maximum tax rate for country, school district, and local purposes of $1.50 per $100 valuation, or $1.70 per $100 in cities of over 50,000 population. These rates could be exceeded only if approved by a referendum of local voters. See Laws of New Jersey, 1905, Chap. 83, pp. 177-79. Once again, it was commonly believed that this bill had been enacted under the influence of railroad lobbyists.

privileges and advantages, such as street railway, gas and water supply franchises, exemptions in whole or in part from the common burden of taxation, the power to determine for themselves the standard or quality of service they are to render, and the rates they are to charge therefor; that candidates are nominated by the bosses in both parties who can be trusted to do nothing if elected to interfere with these privileges, when granted, and who will help to grant new ones when needed, or who, even if they are forced by public opinion to vote right, or wish to do so, will at least do nothing to overthrow the political power of the boss; that these privileges enable these favored corporations to exact huge sums from the public in excessive rates and exemptions from taxation; that in return for these privileges the corporation managers grant certain favors to the party leaders or bosses; that these favors take the form of either direct money payments, or heavy contributions for campaign expenses, or opportunities for safe and profitable business ventures, according to the standard of morality of the particular boss or leader.

Consider some illustrations. The trolley company in Jersey City obtained from our public officers extremely valuable franchise in our streets. The value of these franchises may be seen by comparing Jersey City with Toronto. Jersey City gets for these privileges not exceeding $60,000 a year; Toronto, a much smaller city, gets some $600,000 a year. Robert Davis, one of your principal backers in the State convention, was then as now, the Democratic boss of Hudson County, influential with officials and powerful in controlling Democratic nominations for office. Subsequently, the son of Davis,[3] and another of his political followers, Congressman Kinkead, turn up as the owners of the very valuable privilege of the advertising in the street cars, not only of Jersey City but of all North Jersey, a privilege said to net these gentlemen the tidy sum of $40,000 a year. Neither Davis nor Kinkead knew anything about this business, nor did they get it by offering the highest bid. That it was a political, and not a business arrangement, is shown by the fact that when Everett Colby ran for Senator in Essex County, Kinkead refused to receive his advertisement, at any price. When this much is done openly, is it not fair to assume that more is done secretly?

Similar examples are coming to light everywhere. Witness the insurance scandals that Hughes exposed;[4] the San Fran-

[3] William J. Davis, oldest son of Robert Davis, associated with Kinkead in the New Jersey Car Advertising Co., which controlled the advertising in the street trolley cars throughout New Jersey.

[4] See WW *et al.* to J. J. McCook and C. B. Alexander, Dec. 29, 1905, n. 1, Vol. 16.

cisco traction graft that Heaney exposed;[5] the Philadelphia gas scandal,[6] where indignant citizens threatened to hang to the lamp-posts the members of the council who were acting for the gas syndicate; the Pittsburg graft;[7] the Croker millions and his cynical "working for his own pocket all the time";[8] wit-

[5] Actually, this was only one part of a much broader investigation of widespread graft in the San Francisco city administration dominated by the political boss, Abraham Ruef. Ruef and numerous other political figures as well as corporation leaders who had supplied bribes were indicted and brought to trial, beginning in late 1906, under the aggressive leadership of Assistant District Attorney Francis Joseph Heney. Eugene E. Schmitz, the Mayor of San Francisco, was convicted of extortion and removed from office, but his conviction was later invalidated upon appeal. The final trial of Ruef was a sensational affair which culminated in the nearly fatal shooting of Heney by an embittered ex-convict in the courtroom on November 13, 1908. Ruef was convicted and sent to prison in December 1908. Though the prosecutions continued into 1911, there were no further convictions. The authoritative study of this complex episode in the economic, social, and political history of San Francisco is Walton Bean, *Boss Ruef's San Francisco: The Story of the Union Labor Party, Big Business, and the Graft Prosecution* (Berkeley and Los Angeles, Calif., 1952).

[6] In the early spring of 1905, the Philadelphia Republican machine headed by Israel Durham proposed, on behalf of the United Gas Improvement Co., a city ordinance which would terminate the existing short-term lease of the municipal gasworks to that company and replace it with a seventy-five-year lease. The proposal was widely regarded as a giveaway to the utility company and caused a public furor. Civic leaders, reform organizations, and several of the city's newspapers denounced the measure. Despite the allowance of only eleven days in which to submit rival bids, a group of business leaders did succeed in securing a bid with terms much more favorable to the city. However, the machine-dominated city councils (select and common) passed the ordinance sought by United Gas on May 18, 1905. This action caused a wave of protest meetings throughout the city and even led to threats of physical violence against some councilmen. Moreover, it led Mayor John Weaver to break with the machine which had elected him by announcing that he would veto the ordinance. Since the councils could override his veto, he moved on May 23 to break the power of the machine by dismissing the heads of the Departments of Public Safety and Public Works, both organization leaders who had been active in the gasworks transaction. These actions by the Mayor, together with the public outcry against the ordinance, forced the city councils to withdraw it on June 1, 1905. See Lloyd M. Abernethy, "Insurgency in Philadelphia, 1905," *Pennsylvania Magazine of History and Biography*, LXXXVII (Jan. 1963), 3-20.

[7] In December 1908, an investigation by the Voters' League of Pittsburgh brought to light the payment of a bribe of $17,500 by a Pittsburgh bank to certain members of the Pittsburgh city councils (select and common) in order to secure a share of the city's deposits of funds for the next four years. The bank's president and four members of the councils were tried and convicted in early 1909. After appeals of these convictions had been refused by the Supreme Court of Pennsylvania, one of the convicted councilmen on March 18, 1910, made a full confession to the Voters' League which revealed that all six banks which had been awarded shares of the city's deposits in June 1908 had paid bribes totaling $102,500. Moreover, the confession implicated 105 of the total of 155 members of the Select and Common Councils, of whom ninety-eight were eventually indicted by a grand jury. As of June 1, 1910, fifty-three councilmen had confessed and been given light or suspended sentences, while six others who refused to confess had been tried and convicted. In addition, seven bank officers had been indicted, of whom five had pleaded *nolo contendere*. For a discussion of this episode, see Charles Edward Russell, "Graft as an Expert Trade in Pittsburg," *Cosmopolitan Magazine*, XLIX (Aug. 1910), 283-92.

[8] It is impossible to make any precise estimate of the wealth of Richard Croker, boss of Tammany Hall from 1886 to 1902. However, it was widely believed that he was worth several million dollars at the time of his retirement from politics. For a discussion of what is known of his financial af-

ness our own coal combine and race-track scandals, with the rumor of the big money that the Democratic leaders got;[9] witness the recent investigation of the New York Legislative Committee, which at the very beginning unearthed $80,000 in graft payments to politicians by the street railways of New York City, with testimony that this is only a small item of the huge sums that were actually paid.[10] Witness Lorimer elected to the Senate by

---

fairs, see Lothrop Stoddard, *Master of Manhattan: The Life of Richard Croker* (New York and Toronto, 1931), pp. 120-129. The phrase which Record put into quotation marks was a paraphrase of a question asked of Croker and his reply during a hearing of a committee of the New York State Assembly investigating politics in New York City in 1899: "Then you are working for your own pocket, are you not?" "All the time; the same as you." The exchange became famous. *Ibid.*, pp. 120, 124-26.

[9] The so-called coal combine was a scheme by which the railroad companies, which hauled most of the anthracite coal used in New York City and vicinity and, through subsidiary mining companies, owned the bulk of the anthracite coal beds in Pennsylvania, proposed to create a monopoly of that market through consolidation of the coal companies. In 1891, the Philadelphia and Reading Railroad Co., which controlled an estimated 50 per cent of the coal supply, attempted to put the plan into effect by creating a dummy corporation, the Port Reading Railroad Co. The Central Railroad Co. of New Jersey (usually known as the Jersey Central Railroad), which controlled another 20 per cent of the available coal, leased its entire assets to the dummy company in January 1892. A bill legalizing the combination was next pushed through the Democratic-controlled New Jersey legislature. However, the public outcry against the "combine" led Democratic Governor Leon Abbett to withhold his signature from the bill after the adjournment of the legislature, thus allowing it to die. The combination was forced to dissolve by an adverse ruling in August 1892 by the New Jersey Chancellor, Alexander Taggart McGill, Jr.

The question of whether horse racing and betting should be legalized in New Jersey was a subject of continuous controversy from 1890 to 1894. Several extra-legal race tracks were set up at this time and were strongly opposed by civic and religious groups. In 1893, the racing interests rammed bills through the Democratic-controlled legislature which permitted towns or counties to license race tracks within their bounds and legalized establishments for betting. Because of the public furor stirred up by the passage of the bills, Democratic Governor George Theodore Werts vetoed them; his vetoes were then overridden. The Republican-controlled legislature of 1894 hastened to repeal the racing and betting laws.

In both of these affairs, it was widely charged that wholesale bribery had been used to influence the members of the legislature. The race track scandal in particular played a sizable role in bringing to an end thirty years of domination of the state government by the Democratic party. The Republican party won an overwhelming victory in the legislative elections of 1893 and, although Governor Werts served to the end of his term in 1896, he was the last Democratic governor until Wilson.

On the coal combine and race track scandals and their political consequences, see William E. Sackett, *Modern Battles of Trenton* (2 vols., Trenton, N. J., and New York, 1895-1914), I, 383-406, 440-456.

[10] As a result of investigations by the New York State Superintendent of Insurance between October 1909 and April 1910, the New York legislature on May 24, 1910, voted to create a joint committee to investigate corruption in connection with state legislation and insurance companies other than those dealing in life insurance. The committee was organized on July 8, 1910; carried on investigations and a series of public hearings in New York City between September 7, 1910, and January 6, 1911; and presented its final report to the legislature on February 1, 1911. The bulk of the committee's work dealt with fire insurance companies and their dealings with state legislators, but it also looked into alleged corruption of legislators by race track interests, dairy and beet

Democratic votes.[11] Witness Tammany congressmen coming to the rescue of Cannon when he was hard pressed by the Progressives.[12]

---

sugar manufacturers, and street railway companies. Some of the early public hearings of the committee in September 1910 brought out the information that the Street Railway Association of the State of New York, whose membership included virtually all the traction companies in the state, had, through its legislative lobbyist, G. Tracy Rogers, made very substantial payments over many years to members of the state legislature from both major political parties in order to secure or prevent passage of bills affecting their interests. Although the surviving records of the stock brokerage firm through which Rogers had operated were fragmentary, the committee was able to establish that payments of $82,475 had been made either by the association or member companies between May 1900 and July 1903 alone, a fact which Rogers was obliged to acknowledge in public testimony on September 22, 1910. The committee's report and a complete transcript of the public hearings is printed in *Report of the Joint Committee of the Senate and Assembly of the State of New York Appointed to Investigate Corrupt Practices in Connection with Legislation, and the Affairs of Insurance Companies Other Than Those Doing Life Insurance Business* (3 vols., Albany, N. Y., 1911). A brief summary of the committee's activities appears in Gustavus Myers, *The History of Tammany Hall*, 2nd edn. (New York, 1917), pp. 347-53.

[11] The Illinois legislature became deadlocked in early 1909 over the election of a United States senator. Congressman William Lorimer, Republican boss of Chicago, was finally elected as a compromise candidate on May 26 on the ninety-fifth ballot. His majority of 108 was composed of fifty-five Republicans and fifty-three Democrats. Lorimer took his seat in the Senate on June 18, 1909, and immediately allied himself with the conservative Republicans. On April 30, 1910, the *Chicago Daily Tribune* printed a sworn statement of an Illinois Democratic assemblyman, Charles A. White, that he had been paid $1,000 to vote for Lorimer and that he had later received an additional sum of money. Subsequently, three other Democratic legislators confessed, under grants of immunity, to having accepted bribes for the same purpose. The affair soon became a national scandal. Lorimer stoutly maintained his innocence and himself called for a Senate investigation of the charges. A sub-committee of the Committee on Privileges and Elections carried on an investigation from September 22 to December 17, 1910, and then reported (to carry this story to its conclusion) that it had found no evidence that Lorimer had engaged in bribery or that his election had been corrupt. The full committee accepted the report by a vote of ten to two, but Senator Albert J. Beveridge presented a minority report and a resolution that Lorimer's election be declared void. After lengthy debates on the question, the Senate rejected the Beveridge resolution on March 1, 1911, by a vote of forty-six to forty. However, an Illinois State Senate investigation of the affair had begun in January 1911, and new evidence brought out in the course of it led Senator Robert M. La Follette to call for a second Senate investigation. A new sub-committee was created on June 1, 1911, and carried on its hearings from June 20, 1911, to February 9, 1912. On March 28, 1912, the committee voted five to three in Lorimer's favor. However, a member of the minority, Luke Lea of Tennessee, again submitted a resolution declaring Lorimer's election invalid. After further debate in June and July, the Senate on July 13, 1912, expelled Lorimer by a vote of fifty-five to twenty-eight. The large shift of votes between the first and second expulsion resolutions was primarily the result of the changed complexion of the Senate as a result of the elections of 1910.

For a full discussion of the Lorimer case, see Joel Arthur Tarr, *A Study in Boss Politics: William Lorimer of Chicago* (Urbana, Ill., 1971), pp. 199-307. Tarr concludes that "whether Lorimer's election was dependent on bribery or whether he was involved in the corruption will probably never be answered." *Ibid.*, p. 303.

[12] On March 15, 1909, at the opening of a special session of the newly elected Congress, the attempt of a coalition of Democratic and insurgent Republican congressmen, led by George W. Norris of Nebraska, to secure major alterations in the rules of the House of Representatives shearing Speaker Joseph

This system is by necessity bi-partisan. It cannot exist in one party alone. In your speeches you declare that the Republican party is allied to the special interests, and that the Democratic party has been regenerated, purged from these influences, and reorganized. When and where did this purification and re-organization take place? Has the party changed its leaders? Have not Smith, Nugent and Davis been its most influential leaders for years, and are they not its leaders now? If the leaders are the same, when did they get purified? When did they cease to represent in politics, or be willing to represent, the special interests? Have you forgotten the race-track and coal-combine scandals, which took place under their leadership? Have you forgotten that President Cleveland denounced the action of Senator James Smith on the tariff bill as "party perfidy"?[13] Or, if all that is too long ago, have you forgotten the record of the Democratic legislature three years ago? Do you not know that its record was disgraceful; that the same difficulty was there encountered in passing all bills aimed to prevent fraud at elections, to make corporations give up these special unjust privileges, as is encountered when the Republican machine controls the legislature; and that on the

Gurney Cannon of some of his dictatorial powers was defeated by an alliance of regular Republicans and a small group of Democrats, most of whom were from New York City or southern states. It was widely believed at the time and later that Cannon and his allies had made a deal by which the Tammany and southern Democrats would support Cannon in return for concessions in the upcoming tariff legislation. Norris and his insurgent Republican-Democratic coalition succeeded in a second attempt in March 1910 by excluding the Speaker from membership in the Rules Committee and depriving him of the power to appoint members of standing committees. See Richard W. Lowitt, *George W. Norris: The Making of a Progressive, 1861-1912* (Syracuse, N. Y., 1963), pp. 146-48, 310 n. 31, 166-82, and Mowry, *Theodore Roosevelt and the Progressive Movement*, pp. 40-43, 90-93.

[13] During the struggle to enact a tariff reform bill in 1894, a group of eight Democratic senators, led by Arthur Pue Gorman of Maryland and including James Smith, Jr., of New Jersey, banded together to demand drastic amendments to the bill passed by the House of Representatives. The effect of the amendments was to nullify virtually all of the moderate reforms of the House measure. Anticipating that a conference committee would have to be formed to reconcile the differences, President Cleveland on July 2, 1894, wrote a letter to Representative William Lyne Wilson of West Virginia, the principal author and advocate of the House bill, urging that the House Democrats stand firm for meaningful reform. Cleveland's lengthy letter included one sentence which became famous: "Every true Democrat and every sincere tariff reformer knows that this bill in its present form and as it will be submitted to the conference falls far short of the consummation for which we have long labored, for which we have suffered defeat without discouragement, which, in its anticipation, gave us a rallying cry in our day of triumph, and which, in its promise of accomplishment, is so interwoven with Democratic pledges and Democratic success that our abandonment of the cause of the principles upon which it rests means party perfidy and party dishonor." After the conference committee became deadlocked, Cleveland's letter was made public on July 19. For the text of Cleveland's letter, see Allan Nevins, ed., *Letters of Grover Cleveland, 1850-1908* (Boston and New York, 1933), pp. 354-57. For its background, see Allan Nevins, *Grover Cleveland: A Study in Courage* (New York, 1947), pp. 563-88,

last night of the session, in order to prevent the passage of some bills opposed by the bosses and corporate interests, the Speaker[14] resorted to the revolutionary course of declaring the legislature adjourned, when in fact it had not adjourned?

There have been individual members of the legislature whom these Democratic bosses could not control, like Hendrickson, Tumulty, Sullivan and Kenny,[15] but that is because we New Idea men have waged such a fierce fight on Davis that he has been compelled to sprinkle among his legislative dummies some good men in order to fool the voters; and these free men have to some extent thwarted the plans of the bosses. But none of these men has ever led a revolt against the Boss, and all are in political life by sufferance of Davis.

I call this the boss system. I do not hesitate to call it the most dangerous condition in the public life of our State and nation today—an evil that has destroyed representative government, for the time being at least, and in its place set up a government of privilege. I say that while this system manifests itself more plainly in the party that is in the majority, in reality the minority organization is always secretly in the game. This system, and this alone, accounts for the Republican "Board of Guardians," under whose leadership bills aimed at corporate privilege are killed or opposed when the Republicans are in power, and the Democratic "Overlords," under whose leadership exactly the same thing occurs when the Democrats are in power.

This is the exact truth. The remedy is to take away the valuable privileges which furnish the money and the motive for corrupting politics. Before the remedy can be applied, we must destroy the power of these bosses, and the way to do that is to abolish conventions, take away their power to control election officers, adopt the blanket ballot and distribute it at public expense, and limit by law election expenses. Why not use your great powers of oratory and of reasoning, and the splendid opportunities of your great meetings in driving home to the people this plain lesson?

In order that your position on this vital question may be made clear, I ask you the following questions:

14. Do you admit that the boss system exists as I have described it? If so, how do you propose to abolish it?

15. In referring to the "Board of Guardians," do you mean such Republican leaders as Baird, Murphy, Kean and Stokes?

14 Edgar E. Lethbridge of Orange, N. J.
15 Charles Elvin Hendrickson, Jr., Joseph Patrick Tumulty, Mark Anthony Sullivan, and Edward Kenny, all of whom had served in the Assembly from Hudson County.

Wherein do the relations to the special interests of such leaders differ from the relations to the same interests of such Democratic leaders as Smith, Nugent and Davis?

16. I join you in condemning the Republican "Board of Guardians." I have been fighting them for years, and shall continue to fight them. Will you join me in denouncing the Democratic "Overlords," as parties to the same political system? If not, why not?

17. You say the Democratic party has been reorganized, and the Republican party has not. Can a political party be re-organized without changing either its leaders, or its old leaders changing their point of view and their political character? Will you claim that either of these events has taken place in the Democratic party? If yes, upon what do you base that conclusion?

18. Is there any organized movement in the Democratic party in this State, which corresponds to the Progressive Republican movement, of which you have favorably spoken?

19. Will you agree to publicly call upon the Republican and Democratic candidates for the legislature to pledge themselves in writing prior to election in favor of such of the foregoing reforms as you personally favor? If not, why not?

Permit me in closing to express the hope that you may attain in the domain of politics the same honorable fame and the same character for distinguished and unselfish service that have characterized your career in the field of literature and education.

I am, with great respect,

Sincerely yours,　George L. Record

TLS (WP, DLC).

From a Progressive Republican

My dear Doctor Wilson:　　　　　　　　October 17, 1910.

As a Progressive Republican, I desire to call your attention to some points in this campaign that are not merely material but to my mind vital, from a moral point of view.

We have been treated to Gubernatorial promises and platform pledges until I believe the people of the State are sick of both, not necessarily because they are sick of the men who, as candidates, made the pledges but because, while the platform contained certain pledges, and the candidates made certain promises in conformity therewith, the sinister influences of the State, Republican and Democratic, have controlled the members of the legislature.

What we must have, if we hope to have real reform are pledges on the part of the candidates for the Assembly and Senate. If you could have any influence whatever with the legislature after they are elected, you can have ten times' more before, by demanding that they follow you in pledges.

I am familiar with the contents of the letter which Mr. Record will shortly write to you, but no human being will ever know that I have written this letter to you. However, since I am convinced that you and I are hoping to have the same things accomplished in the political world of our State, both that we may establish political morality and political honor in the State (there is absolutely none now) and secure a higher degree of equity and justice between the property interests and the citizens of the State, I cannot refrain from making one or two suggestions that I believe you will appreciate as the advice of a true friend and a lover of the State of New Jersey, and a man who, at least, wants to be a patriot.

First: I sincerely hope that your answers to Mr. Record's questions will be as short and unequivocal as the English language and your own views will permit.

Second: You may not have had your attention called to the fact that in the fall of 1907 at the extra session of the legislature, the present law providing for an expression of the public will with regard to the choice of United States Senators was passed by a unanimous vote of the Senate which was Republican, and by a unanimous vote of the Assembly which was Democratic, and signed, of course, by a Republican Governor.

This, then, is a law of the State and calls for the acquies[c]ence and obedience of every citizen, certainly by every such citizen as you are. And this the more because it is the first real positive step toward the purification of the ballot.

I know it seems to very very many of our independent citizens as though you were evading, may I saw [say] actually conniving at disobedience of this law in the interest of Senator Smith, who, I personally like very much, but who, the people of the State, especially such men as you appreciate and whose support you want and must have, regard as a most sinister and unworthy of public confidence.

Indeed, when you recall some of the things that occurred when he was in the United States Senate you must admit that their suspicions and distrust were well-founded.

Now, to the exact point, can you afford to remain silent upon this question of obedience to the law, especially since your own platform this year declares in favor of the popular selection of United States Senators? I do not think so. If you do, it will greatly lower the conception the people now have of you, and this apparent support of Senator Smith may mean ten, possibly twenty thousand votes directly and indirectly.

A personal friend of Senator Smith's told me the other day that Mr. Smith did not want to go back to the Senate. If this is true, to keep up the appearance of your support of a man who is regarded by the great mass of our best people as one of the most sinister and corrupt political bosses of the entire State, it seems to me is a serious blunder, and I am afraid may prove a fatal one.

Notwithstanding all your protestations, there is a general belief that you are playing a political game in his interest because he nominated you and that you are defying and disobeying the law to consummate your understanding with him. This you can readily see is most unfortunate, and I am devoutly hoping that this cloud may be brushed aside and that you will stand in the clear sunlight of an invincible public opinion.

For God and good government, I am with you,

"A Progressive Republican."

TL (WP, DLC).

Remarks to the Democratic Leaders of Mercer County in Trenton, New Jersey[1]

[[Oct. 18, 1910]]

I am very glad to feel that this is an evening when I am with you personally, and can shake hands with you. To tell you the truth I am tired of making speeches; not that I am tired of the occasions which call them forth, for nothing has interested me more as I have gone throughout the various parts of the State than the eagerness with which men have gathered to hear the great questions discussed which it is our duty to discuss. Because a very interesting thing has happened.

We talk a great deal about the machine of this party and that party, and we seem to be very much afraid of machine government. But machine government exists partly because we don't take the government into our own hands, and in blaming the machines we must remember that we have allowed them to do business.

Now I understand from this campaign that the people are resuming control of their affairs, and what gratifies me more than anything else in going about the State is the feeling that if I should be chosen Governor I will be chosen something more than Governor. I will be chosen the spokesman of my fellow citizens in the way in which our government ought to be conducted. I want to be your spokesman. I want, if I may have the privilege, to interpret your interests in respect to legislation and other questions in the State. I want to have the privilege of picking out for you the best office holders that can be found in the State.

I speak of myself on this occasion because this is not a speech-making time, but a time when I want you to understand me as a person. I tell you frankly I am not ambitious of political office. Political office of itself has no attractions for me whatever. But when I think that I may be given an opportunity to do things—things not easy to do, on the contrary, difficult to do, which I will be called upon to do by a large body of my fellow citizens, I feel that whether I want office or not, that will be one of the most distinguished privileges that has ever been accorded an individual. Therefore, I want you to regard me as a person who desires to put himself at your service, and in no other light whatever.

Inasmuch as I am speaking of personal matters, I want to speak of something that has, I will permit myself to say, caused me a good deal of distress.

Ordinarily, I do not think that misrepresentation makes any difference. Ordinarily, I think that lies take care of themselves. But it has distressed me, I will admit, that I should have been so consistently and persistently, and I will take the liberty to say, malignantly misrepresented in respect to my attitude towards labor.

I am not at all afraid that the laboring men of this State will depart from their usual practice. I am not afraid but that they will judge of this matter for themselves, and I am not afraid that they will oppose me.

But I think that at a reception like this I should tell you how false the whole thing is, because to be represented in the light in which I have been represented, when I have been always a consistent friend of the laboring man, has distressed me.

I want to say this to the laboring men. I claim to be a good friend of the laboring men, because I am not afraid to criticise things that they do when I think that they are doing things they ought not to do. I could be what a great many other men have been[,] a cowardly friend who was afraid to say what I thought. But if I were that sort of a person I would kick mylself [myself] around the block.

I have, as you know, criticised a few of the unions for doing some things in regard to the regulation of labor which I thought were inimical to their interests and to the interests of the country, but I take the pains to say that they did not represent the mass of the working men, and I said the things I have said as a friend desirous of promoting their best interests.

And I believe in my heart that that is the kind of friend the workingmen want.

If you want the other kind of friend, the kind represented in the (Republican) headquarters across the street, (Chairman Frank O. Briggs), so far as I am concerned, you are perfectly welcome. You have only to examine their lack of consistency in dealing with other questions and other interests of the people. For their works are written on the pages of the State records. If you think that these gentlemen have always acted in your interest, I beg that you will support them, for I have no jealous feeling in regard to this matter.

Printed in the Trenton *True American*, Oct. 19, 1910.
  1 Delivered in Masonic Hall at a reception given in his honor by the Democratic League of Mercer County.

From Wilson B. Killingbeck

Dear Sir:　　　　　　　　　　　　　　Orange, N. J. Oct. 18, 1910.

I have received your letter of the 11th in which you state that you have no date available for the debate I proposed in answer to your challenge to meet any one to discuss the political issues of the day. I am honest enough to credit men like you with a belief in the truth of your professions.

Pardon me if I suggest that, by implication at least, you place the things I propose as issues and which you ignore altogether in your seeming contest with the republicans, as of minor importance.

Government is supposed to be instituted and administered that the welfare of the greatest number of the whole people be advanced. The things that affect a people's welfare cannot be separated by you along political, social and economic lines and the few things advocated by you in this campaign hardly touch the needs of the people.

We are in the madst [midst] of a political, social and economic evolution that marks a crisis in the history of the world. In these twenty years past and in the twenty years to come methods and practices, laws and customes, hoary with age are being overturned. The right of individuality, the right of initiative, of liberty of action, of liberty of thought and opinion gained for us through centuries of stress and struggle are being lost because nine tenths of our people are being forced to an economic dependence on the other tenth.

Here is where you fail. As a great instructor we have reason to expect from you discussions on issues that are vital and you split hairs with your opponent over an extension of the primary system, the powers of some officials, and lament the inability to reach an evil doer or two. But the economic dependence which threatens the right to a living, the right to work, the right to have a home, wife and children living in comfort are denied to millions through lack of work or through poorly paid work. These are not issues in the campaign, I am to understand.

You are a democrat. But is there not a test for real democracy these days of business imperialism? The initiative, referendum and recall—when and where have you favored these measures? Just where [Everett] Colby and his progressives failed the people, you with the old hungry crowd of "democrats" out of sight behind you, fail also.

I used the word "seeming" in regard to your contest with the republicans, for if anyone were to ask either you or Mr. Lewis for a definition of party faith, not even an expert could tell which was which without the labels. The contest between you is to see if enough republicans can be tempted by your personality and by their disgust with a party long in power to elect you. That is all.

The real issue of this and future campaigns is the breakdown of the wage system and the utter incapacity to better conditions. The industrial and economic system, ever increasingly efficient, cannot be a blessing to mankind unless socially owned. If permitted to run its course unhindered it will destroy this civilization as others have been destroyed. Man! can't you read the signs of the times?

Our industrial system is no longer what it ought to be. It allows over three millions of workers, willing to work, to be idle. It charges an extor[t]ionate price ofr [for] the means of life. It keeps other millions of workers at the edge of starvation. The producers cannot use their own products for their own comfort. The people are driven into degeneracy. Prostitution, crime, idiocy are assuming alarming proportions. Slave camps and slave cities are multiplying all over our land. All this while a few grow rich beyond the dreams of avarice.

Fifty million Socialists with their organizations in every civilized country are banded together to redeem mankind. I am their standard bearer in this state and the masses, the burden-bearers, the producers of wealth are rallying to the Socialist standard.

Our aim is the socialization of the machinery of production and distribution and ours is the only program that can be helpful to mankind in this crisis. This the people of every land are beginning to understand and are steadily and surely coming to support.

I venture to insist that, as you flung your challenge broadcast, you meet me in a debate on your own issue, that of "Democracy."

Yours,   Wilson B. Killingbeck

TLS (WP, DLC).

A Proposed Resolution of the Board of Trustees of Princeton University[1]

[c. Oct. 19, 1910]

Resolution prepared by Mr Cadwalader to be presented by him should the President neglect to present his resignation at the October meeting 1910:

Resolved that, in the judgment of the members of this Board, the position of the President of the University as a candidate for office before the public and the impossibility of the performance of his duties are so inconsistent with the retention of his office as to work to the injury of the University.

Hw MS (M. T. Pyne Coll., NjP).
[1] This resolution is in the handwriting of Moses Taylor Pyne.

From Moses Taylor Pyne

Princeton, N. J.

My dear Woodrow   19 September [Oct.] 1910

Ed Sheldon astonished me yesterday by telling me that Cyrus had quoted me to you and to him as saying that, in the matter of your proposed resignation, I should be guided entirely by your wishes. Of course you must have realized that I could not have made and did not make any such statement. Cyrus must have entirely misunderstood what I did say, for, while I am only too glad to consider your wishes in every way possible, I must always be at liberty to vote according to my duty as Trustee as I may see it.

It is only fair to me and to you that I should make this explanation.

Yours very sincerely   M Taylor Pyne

ALS (WP, DLC).

From Henry Nehemiah Dodge[1]

My dear Sir: Morristown, N. J. Oct. 19th, 1910

I very much appreciate the courtesy of your reply to my enquiry as to your position on the Local Option issue, but regret that you are in doubt on the question—not of prohibition or lisence, but as to the truly democratic principle of letting the people say whether the hurtful liquor trafic shall be permitted or forbidden—a privilege denied to the voters of but three states in the Union, of which trio New Jersey has the unenviable distinction of being one. I hope very much to see you elected, & that you will forward this righteous cause.

Sincerely yours   Henry N. Dodge.

ALS (WP, DLC).
[1] A dentist of Morristown, N. J.

A News Report of Campaign Speeches in Bound Brook and Somerville, New Jersey

[Oct. 20, 1910]

NEW ORDER IN LIFE OF PARTY

Wilson Tells Somerset Voters Organization Has Severed Old Connections.

SOMERVILLE, Oct. 20.—Twice yesterday Woodrow Wilson told audiences that he had not sought office and that in becoming the candidate of the Democratic party he did so only out of a desire to serve the people. The first time was at a reception at Bound Brook, and the second at the big mass meeting held here in the armory. . . .

Both Somerset and Hunterdon County men attended the meeting. Two special trains were run on the Central Railroad from points along the line, and both were crowded. Senator Gebhardt came from Hunterdon and Senator Silzer from Middlesex County. Both of them spoke at the meeting as did Frank S. Katzenbach. From the Bernardsville section of Somerset came former Assemblyman Archibald Alexander and a large delegation of Democrats as well as some Republicans.

Richard V. Lindabury was chairman, and told how Mr. Wilson became a candidate for Governor. He asserted that he was absolutely unpledged.

Continuing, the speaker said:

Now, I happen to know something about how he came to be nominated, and right here I will take a moment to tell you about it.

Somerville, 19 Oct., 1910.

Dem. break with the past, here, there, everywhere, —
    particularly in New Jersey.

Rep. break with the past in some places, notably
    Middle West, but not in New Jersey.

Here old connections, old control, — the old
    leaders in the campaign
    Mixture of business and politics
    No adequate or powerful representation
        of the people.

Here we want Corrupt practices act, —
          Administrative reorganization,
          Public service Commission
          Control of corporations and scrutiny
          Conservation
          Direct nominations

The means of getting them?
    A spokesman
    Publicity
    Leadership

                    10/19/10

I was one of a party[1] of gentlemen, Democrats, to wait upon the man who has since become the candidate and who reported to him that there was a time now in this State for a great public service to be performed; that affairs in our State government had got in the condition that a strong man was needed to lift them above the low level in which they were; that we would have a man of character, a man of independence, a man of strong will and wisdom.

We represented to him that if he would become the candidate, we believed that he would be the Moses that would lead the people to the land promised by our forefathers in our Constitution.

We said to him: "If you will allow your name to be presented to the people it will be with the understanding that you are under no promise or obligation to any boss or any special interest; that your whole undertaking will be to serve the people of this State as a whole, according to the best of your ability as God shall guide you in the work."

The gentleman said that upon that understanding he would take the matter into consideration, and two weeks thereafter announced to us that if the sober thinking people of the party would call him to the candidacy of the office of Governor, he would not feel that he had a right to refuse it. So it was that we got our candidate.

That sort of a man I have now the pleasure of presenting to you. His character, his learning, his honesty is known to you all.

After referring to Mr. Lindabury's statement that the coming election is one of the most important known, Mr. Wilson stated:

I venture to say, gentlemen, that when you come in future years to look back upon this election, you will realize that it afforded you an occasion to take part with the rest of the country in what is little short of a revolution in American politics.

Do you realize what is happening in New Jersey and outside of it? Do you realize that both parties are almost of necessity breaking away from the past?

It is in vain that either party turns to its past record, either for vindication or excuse. Its past record is not pertinent to the matters now in hand.

The corrupt vote was discussed, Mr. Wilson saying that in view of the importance of the present campaign he could not "imagine a man so small, so debased," as to sell his vote. He proceeded:

If it were my function to excuse a party, if it were my task to

---

[1] He was here referring to the meeting at the Lawyers' Club in New York on July 12, 1910, about which see the Editorial Note, "The Lawyers' Club Conference," Vol. 20.

seek an office for the sake of getting an office for a party, I would have nothing to do with the campaign. These things do not interest me.

I believe in my heart that the Democratic party is now offering to serve you, and that it is bidding me to put myself at your service. That is what I am doing. That is what it is my heart's desire and ambition to do.

Later on, the nominee said:

New Jersey has her own special aspect of the general questions, but they are only special aspects of general questions. Now, what is the situation?

The Democratic party has almost everywhere in this country broken its connection with its past and is putting up new men. What is the consequence?

Men who have long been out of the Democratic ranks are coming back to them and men who have never been in the Democratic ranks are listening attentively to see what new things it is that this party purposes.

Look at the Republican party. In many parts of the Union the Republican party has broken with its past, has seen that the policies which it has been pursuing are not suitable to the day in which we live.

Many of the voters, young and old, have arisen to protest against policies and purposes that have prevailed in that party. Particularly in New Jersey has the Democratic party taken a new course, and unprecedented in its history.

It has called from outside party organization altogether not one man, but several, who are to be brought in to speak the views of the new age without respect to any machine connection, without respect to any pledges of any kind, as men who seek to voice the general citizenship in this country. The Republican party has broken with its past almost everywhere except in New Jersey.

Elaborating on this, Mr. Wilson referred to the Republican convention, and then noted:

One of the most distinguished representatives of the Republican organization—I mean former Governor Griggs—has said that he objects to the term "reform" as applied to the Republican party organization. He says the implication of that word is that something has been wrong with the Republican party. He says that the only word he will accept was the word "improvement."

He graciously conceded that there was some room for improvement. He went on to say that he stood, first of all and always, for the organization of the party, the existing organization of the party, the unbroken, unreformed, unimproved organization of the party. In other words, he took pains to declare himself a partisan of the Republican organization.

The Republican "organization," Mr. Wilson declared, had not acted for the true interests of the people, and, he added:

You cannot reform an organization by keeping it in power. If you want any of your friends to reform, take them out of their ordinary surroundings and put them apart, where they can enjoy a period of reflection.

If you want to reform, if you want to teach, if you want to discipline the present Republican party organization, put it where it can go off and think by itself.

You know what we are for, ladies and gentlemen, in this campaign. We are for free and pure politics. And you know that the whole indictment against political machines—against political organizations—is this: That they have got themselves into such connections that the whole difficulty is to distinguish where business stops and politics begin.

It has been the policy of the Republican party in the National Legislature and the State Legislature to promote business, to build up the great business enterprises of the country—and I want to say that for a long period of time they were eminently and honorably successful in doing so.

But when they have built up great business enterprises by the assistance of a great party organization an interesting thing happens; big business enterprises think they own the organization, and the organization knows they are supported by the big business enterprises.

The idea that cannot be gotten into their heads, said Mr. Wilson, is that they build from the top, not realizing that every secure building is built from the bottom up. Big business men are bribed by the existing order of things, and that, asserted the candidate, "is the deepest kind of bribery there is."

As an instance of this, Mr. Wilson told how efforts to prevent the cold storage of eggs, a commodity used by all, by the passage of a statute, were prevented by the Republican organization, working for the storage-business men. Apropos of politico-business affiliations, Mr. Wilson said:

A certain man who was once prominent in New York, made this sage remark: "There ain't no politics in politics." By which he meant political government on the part of the machine is not determined by political questions; it is determined by the question how the organization is to be maintained and how its partnerships are to be preserved.

If you do not smash these partnerships, gentlemen, you might as well not try to smash the machines. The only way you can smash a machine is by first starving it. It will be too lusty and robust to be thrashed if you keep on feeding it. The way to get at the machines is to get at the things they live on.

Mr. Wilson then took up corrupt practises and pointed out that the Republican machine "had killed every corrupt practises act that had been introduced," explaining:

It does not want to open the partnership books to public scrutiny. If it did, it would be too obvious what the game is. That is the heart of a corrupt practises act—the publication of the sources of subscription.

Mr. Wilson said he had lived too long to hope for a "revolution by statute." If corporations were forbidden to contribute they might do so indirectly. Another way to do would be to limit expenditures. It has been done elsewhere, but New Jersey has "been in an air-tight compartment, entirely surrounded by the 'Board of Guardians.'"

As a remedy, Mr. Wilson suggested:

The corrupt practises act ought absolutely to forbid any contributions from any business organization whatsoever, whether it be a corporation or a mere partnership, or any kind of an organized business. It ought absolutely to forbid that.

As to corporations, the candidate said:

It is perfectly legitimate, indeed, it is necessary, to make them pay their just share in taxes not only, but to pay, and pay well, for being corporations; for it is a privilege granted by law. It is not a natural privilege; it is not a privilege that comes to you because you are men; it is a privilege that comes because certain statutes permit, and it is proper that our corporations should pay for the privilege of being corporations.

Of public utility corporations, Mr. Wilson said that as they use governmental powers in the exercise of the right of eminent domain, there is danger of a too close conjunction between them and the government, therefore there should be a public utility commission, "with powers of ratemaking and regulation."

Referring to the watersheds in north Jersey and the canals, Mr. Wilson said of the latter:

It is absolutely necessary that New Jersey should assume control of the things which are necessary public instrumentalities. We cannot afford to let these things slip out of the grasp of the State.

Direct primaries formed the next theme of the speaker, who said the people want them "to break up the machines," and to "get inside of the game." He stated:

The organization names the candidates; the candidates serve the organization who names them. Everybody serves the person who puts them in power, and the organization has its ear to the keyhole of the door where big business is being done. See what a circle that is, what a connection that is. That is the reason that all of our reform desires are strung like beads on one string.

This, in Mr. Wilson's view, was the heart of politics. But he did not expect the millennium could be enacted into effect by statute. Of complete reform, he said:

I have lived a great many years and seen a good many hopeful reformers live and die, and most of the reformers that have died have died disappointed, because in spite of all the statutes they got passed, things were going wrong yet.

I had a confession made by one of these reformers. He was connected with a very important organization which tries to keep in business all the year around. Most reform organizations are spasmodic, but this one tries to remain an organization all the time. He said to me:

"I have made a discovery which is very mortifying to me. For twenty years I have been going up to Albany and exercising every legitimate influence I could bring to bear to get statutes passed which I thought would reform the administration of the State government, and I have been successful in scores of instances, but the State government is no better.

"I have made the mortifying discovery that the way to get good government is to elect good men to office.

"No government is better than the men who administer it. A good man will torture out of all the statutes a reasonably good government. It is the motive force, gentlemen."

Mr. Wilson said the people needed a spokesman to give publicity regarding public matters. He said:

You need a spokesman. You need a representative. You need leadership of your own choosing, not leadership of the choosing of an organization. Now, it embarrasses me very much, gentlemen, to discuss that aspect of the question, because I am at once conscious of the fact that I am offering myself to you as a leader. All I can say as an excuse is, I did not do it. I did not pick myself out.

Further on, Mr. Wilson said:

I would like to have an opportunity of looking into these things for you and coming and telling you exactly what I have seen. I hope it is not immodest to offer myself in that capacity, and I want to say this, I believe that this program would please nobody so much as the members of the State Legislature.

The most galling thing that members of the State Legislatures have to do is, that they must obey orders from an organization which does not appear in public, and which sometimes is not even known by the public to exist.

I know from personal acquaintance with scores of members of legislatures that there is nothing they would welcome so much as the liberty of representing their constituents and not representing a political organization.

The reception at Bound Brook was a unique affairs [affair], one of those things that specially brighten the ordinary work of a campaign by reason of its unusual features. After meeting State Chairman Nugent at Somerville, Mr. Wilson went to the Bound Brook home of Mr. [George Mason] La Monte, the Assembly candidate. It had been arranged that he should there meet any local voters who might desire to call. About 200 men of all classes, including workingmen with their dinner pails in hands still unwashed, besides about a hundred women. Mr. Wilson met the callers at the side of a summer house on the lawn of the property. The presence of the woman [women] gave the affair the aspect of a garden party, and this was further heightened when Mrs. La Monte served lemonade, the women acting as servers to everybody. . . .

After saying the request to talk had come as a surprise to him, Mr. Wilson said:

This is one of the most delightful experiences of my life in meeting earnest people bent upon considering things most vital in men's life. Political meetings generally partake of a more or less hilarious aspect, but that is not so during this campaign. Men are showing that they are interested in the welfare of their commonwealth.

I am not seeking office, but am offering myself to my fellow-citizens for their service, and I desire only to do such service as may accrue to their benefit.

Having studied politics from the outside for many years, I did not obtain an intimate acquaintance with the political leaders, but I will say that those whom I have met during my campaign are bent solely on the welfare of New Jersey.

Printed in the *Newark Evening News*, Oct. 20, 1910; some editorial headings omitted.

To the Board of Trustees of Princeton University

[Oct. 20, 1910]

GENTLEMEN OF THE BOARD OF TRUSTEES:

On the fifteenth of September last the Democratic party of New Jersey nominated me for the office of Governor of the State, and I deemed it my duty to accept the nomination. In view of Princeton's immemorial observance of the obligations of public service, I could not have done otherwise.

Having accepted that nomination, it becomes my duty to resign the presidency of the University I have so long loved and sought to serve. I, therefore, hereby offer my resignation of this great office with which you have honoured me, and venture to express the hope that the Board will see its way to act upon the resignation at once.[1] It is my earnest prayer that the University may go forward without halt or hindrance in the path of true scholarship and thoughtful service of the nation.

Woodrow Wilson[2]

TLS (Trustees' Papers, UA, NjP).

[1] Wilson had publicly announced on September 16, 1910, one day after his nomination for the governorship, that he would offer his resignation from the presidency of Princeton University to the Board of Trustees at their meeting on October 20, 1910. The report in the *New York Times* (printed at Sept. 16, 1910) added the comment: "What the Trustees will do as a result is a matter of speculation. They value his service highly as President, and would regret to lose him, even in the event of his election to the Governorship. The board may hold the resignation in abeyance until after the election, about three weeks later than the meeting of the board."

Melancthon W. Jacobus, upon reading the news reports of Wilson's intention to resign, wrote to him on September 19, 1910 (his letter is printed at that date): "Have you any idea that the opposition will move for a forcing of the acceptance at that time [the meeting of the trustees on October 20]? It seems to me that no action would be dignified which does not contain a provisional acceptance conditioned upon & to issue in case of your Election as Governor of the State." He also suggested that Wilson's supporters on the board should meet to agree on a candidate for the presidency to counter any similar move by the opposition members.

Jacobus then proceeded to take a poll of opinion among Wilson's supporters on the Board of Trustees, perhaps partly by mail and partly by interview. In his letter to Wilson of October 13, 1910 (printed at that date), he reported the results:

"There seems to be a division of sentiment among your friends as to whether or not your best interests will be conserved by holding the acceptance of the resignation in abeyance. Mr. [Thomas Davies] Jones thinks that it might seem as though we were discrediting the likelihood of your election by delaying the acceptance. Others have proposed settling the matter of resignation by granting you leave of absence for two years in case of your election.

"We are to have a conference of a few of your supporters at the Hotel Belmont on Tuesday afternoon of next week. If you would care to make any statement to the conference beyond what you have written in your letter to me, I shall be only too glad to present it. The only thing I am especially anxious for is that we shall know what we want to do before we come to the [trustees'] meeting next Thursday, and that in deciding what we want to do, we shall fix upon that which will be most agreeable and of most advantage to you."

Unfortunately, Wilson's reply to Jacobus's letter of September 19 is missing, as is his answer to Jacobus's letter of October 13, if indeed Wilson replied to it.

The proposed resolution "to be presented . . . should the President neglect to present his resignation at the October meeting 1910" (printed at October 19) makes it clear that at least John Lambert Cadwalader and Moses Taylor Pyne doubted whether Wilson would resign at all on October 20. Pyne's letter to Wilson of October 19 (printed at that date), serving notice that he would be guided by his own conscience in regard to Wilson's resignation, reinforces the belief that the opposition suspected Wilson's and his supporters' intentions.

Pyne explained his position in greater detail in a draft of a letter to Cyrus Hall McCormick dated October 21, 1910 (Hw draft L, M. T. Pyne Coll., NjP). He wrote to correct McCormick's mistaken impression that he, Pyne, was willing "for instance either to accept it [Wilson's resignation] at once, refer it to a committee, even to table it or give him a long leave of absence." Pyne asserted that he "never did agree or could have agreed to any such attitude in view of my oath as Trustee." He recalled that Bayard Henry had suggested calling a special meeting of the board to accept Wilson's resignation, but that John Aikman Stewart advised against it because both Cadwalader and Edward Wright Sheldon were abroad. Pyne also had counseled waiting for the regular meeting on October 20. Once Wilson's resignation was accepted, Pyne continued, he was "in favour of meeting Wilson's wishes as far as possible" in regard to "how long his salary should be continued, the length of time Prospect should be put at his disposal and so on." It is significant not only that Pyne went to such great length to correct the misapprehension, but also that McCormick and Sheldon should have fallen into such an erroneous conception in the first place. It strongly suggests that some of Wilson's supporters, and perhaps Wilson himself, were quite willing that his resignation be in some way held in abeyance pending the outcome of the gubernatorial election.

The only further contemporary reference to the circumstances of Wilson's resignation is Pyne's comment in his letter to William Cooper Procter, October 25, 1910 (printed at that date): "The thing was done, I think, in a very satisfactory and diplomatic way. According to the newspapers he forced his resignation on a reluctant board, although actually he was most reluctant to put it in and had to be told pretty positively that it had to be done."

Wilson Farrand's undated memoir on the Graduate College controversy (typed MS in the Wilson Farrand Coll., NjP) gives a concise retrospective account of the affair:

"That summer Wilson was nominated for the Governorship of New Jersey. There was no meeting of the Board until October, and no definite announcement [this is of course an error], although rumors were plentiful, as to whether he proposed to resign from the Presidency or not. A little before the meeting an intimation came from his friends that his resignation would be presented, but that it would be pleasing if the Board should decline to act on it until after the election. This plan did not meet with approval, for many even of his supporters felt that if he were going into politics he ought definitely to sever his connection with the University, and indeed should have done so as soon as he accepted the nomination. The final conference was held in Princeton the night before the meeting. A sufficient canvass of the Trustees had been made to ascertain the sentiment of the Board, and a definite decision was reached during the evening. Wilson was making a campaign speech out of town and did not return until late. Just before midnight Mr. Stephen Palmer went to his house, and announced the decision, that his resignation must be presented, and would be accepted.

"The next morning as soon as the opening business of the meeting was ended, President Wilson read a brief letter of resignation, asked that it be accepted at once, then turning picked up his hat and coat, and while we all stood in silence, passed from the room and from his connection with Princeton."

There is no reason to doubt the correctness of Farrand's recollection. Certainly it fits well with the other evidence presented in this note. The great gap in the extant evidence is, of course, the lack of any indication whatever as to exactly how Wilson felt about the matter. David Ruddach Frazer to Wilson, October 20, 1910 (printed at that date) is ambiguous, but one can read between the lines that Frazer knew that Wilson had been forced out. It seems reasonable to suppose that prior to October 19, at the very least, he would not have objected had the trustees withheld a final decision on the acceptance of his resignation pending the outcome of the gubernatorial election.

2 There is a WWsh draft of this letter in WP, DLC.

From the Minutes of the Board of Trustees of Princeton University

[Oct. 20, 1910]

The Trustees of Princeton University met in stated session in the Trustees' Room in the Chancellor Green Library, Princeton, New Jersey, at quarter past eleven o'clock on Thursday morning October 20, 1910.

The President of the University occupied the chair and opened the meeting with prayer. . . .

GENERAL ORDER OF BUSINESS SUSPENDED

The President of the University asked that the regular order of business be suspended in order that he might bring before the Board a matter of importance. The request was granted.

RESIGNATION OF PRESIDENT WILSON

President Wilson presented his resignation as follows:

GENTLEMEN OF THE BOARD OF TRUSTEES:

On the fifteenth of September last the Democratic party of New Jersey nominated me for the office of Governor of the State, and I deemed it my duty to accept the nomination. In view of Princeton's immemorial observance of the obligations of public service, I could not have done otherwise.

Having accepted that nomination, it becomes my duty to resign the presidency of the University I have so long loved and sought to serve. I, therefore, hereby offer my resignation of this great office with which you have honoured me, and venture to express the hope that the Board will see its way to act upon the resignation at once. It is my earnest prayer that the University may go forward without halt or hindrance in the path of true scholarship and thoughtful service of the nation.

(Signed)   Woodrow Wilson

PRESIDENT WILSON RETIRES FROM THE ROOM

Having presented his resignation, President Wilson then retired from the room.

THE SENIOR TRUSTEE TAKES THE CHAIR

Mr. John Aikman Stewart, Senior Trustee of the University, in accordance with the requirements of the Charter, took the Chair.

PRESIDENT WILSON'S RESIGNATION ACCEPTED

Mr. Cadwalader offered the following preamble and resolution:

The President having announced that, in view of his nomination as a candidate for the Governorship of the State of New Jersey he has felt it incumbent upon himself to present to the Board his resignation as President of the University, and having expressed the hope that the Board would see its way to act immediately upon his resignation, therefore be it

RESOLVED, That the resignation of the President be accepted with deep regret; that a Committee of Five be appointed by the Chair to prepare and to submit suitable resolutions for adoption by the Board in recognition of the distinguished services of the President to the University; and that when the Board adjourns it be to meet on Thursday, November 3rd, 1910, at 11:15 a.m. to receive the report of such Committee.

After Dr. DeWitt had questioned and Mr. Cadwalader had explained the reason for adjournment until November third, the Board voted on Mr. Cadwalader's resolution, and it was adopted unanimously.

RESOLUTION BY MR. CADWALADER

Mr. Cadwalader then offered the following resolution:

RESOLVED, That the functions and duties of the President of the University, until the further order of this Board, be and the same are hereby devolved upon the Dean of the Faculty.

SUBSTITUTE RESOLUTION LOST

After a discussion of the resolution Mr. Farrand offered the following substitute resolutions:

RESOLVED, That while the University is without a President, the direction of academic affairs shall be vested in the Faculty, under the guidance of an Executive Committee of nine members. The Dean of the Faculty, the Dean of the Graduate School, the Dean of the College, and the Clerk of the Faculty shall be ex-officio members of this Committee. The remaining five members shall be full Professors, elected by the Faculty. This Executive Committee shall appoint all Faculty Committees, shall recommend all new appointments to the Board of Trustees, and shall be the channel of communication between the Faculty and the Board of Trustees. The Dean of the Faculty shall act as Chairman of this Committee and of the Faculty.

RESOLVED, That a Committee of five Trustees be appointed by the Chair to arrange for the carrying into effect of this plan, with power to settle minor details as they may arise. This Committee shall confer from time to time with the Executive Committee of the Faculty as to the general condition of the University, and as to specific matters requiring attention.

After further discussion, Mr. Cadwalader moved to lay the substitute resolutions on the table, and a division having been called for by Dr. DeWitt, the motion was carried, 18 yeas, 8 nays.

MOTION TO POSTPONE ACTION ON MR. CADWALADER'S RESOLUTION LOST

Mr. Henry moved to postpone action on Mr. Cadwalader's resolution until November third, and a division having been called for, the motion was lost, 11 yeas, 15 nays.

SUBSTITUTE RESOLUTION BY MR. PYNE ADOPTED

Mr. Pyne then offered the following substitute resolution:

RESOLVED, That the Senior Trustee, Mr. John A. Stewart, be appointed President of the University, *pro tempore.*

Mr. Cadwalader withdrew his resolution and a vote having been taken, Mr. Pyne's resolution was adopted, and the Senior Trustee of Princeton University, Mr. John Aikman Stewart, was declared elected President of the University, *pro tempore.*

REMARKS BY PRESIDENT STEWART

Mr. Stewart in a few words expressed his thanks to the Board for the honor that had been conferred upon him.

MR. STEWART CHAIRMAN OF THE COMMITTEE ON RESOLUTIONS

On motion of Mr. Sheldon it was voted that Mr. Stewart should be Chairman of the Committee on Resolutions in recognition of the distinguished services of the President to the University. . . .

"Minutes of the Trustees of Princeton University April 1908-June 1913," bound minute book (UA, NjP).

From David Ruddach Frazer

My dear Dr. Wilson,   [Newark, N. J., Oct. 20, 1910]

You are out—& by your own election. My thought was to defer action on the resignation until the next stated meeting.

But some "good friends of yours" made it their business to tell me of your insistence, hence my seemingly cold blooded inquiry when I greeted you this A.M. "do you want to get out." Your affirmative response sealed my tongue. I can appreciate the feeling if you are "tired" & some of these days, when you get thru campaigning & have a breathing spell I will tell you a tale which will show that my sympathy is based upon community of experience. I am revelling in my liberty & growing fat at the expense of monumental liars & cowardly sneaks.[1]

At a dinner of Newark Presby. a kid yelled across the table, "Say, Dr. how are you going to vote for Govr?" "For W. W. 1st last & intermediate" was the sonorous yell in response. To my great surprise & greater delight, there came the practi[c]al reply, "So say we all of us." Only one man dissented & he was from Maryland. I'm glad he wasn't born in Baltimore, the place of my nativity.

Coming on the train this A.M. a quiet man said to me, "I voted my 1st ticket for Genl. Grant & have voted the Republican ticket ever since,—this time I mean to vote for WW. I dont know about the rest of the ticket." I am satisfied that one thing which imperils your election is your necessary connection with the "2 Jims" & "the old gang" back of them. I am very fond of Senator Smith, but others are not & I am persuaded that he would help you immensely should he disclaim any purpose to re-enter the U.S. Senate. Jim Nugent, I hold in supreme contempt & regret that you are compelled to fellowship him by reason of his position as State chairman. It does you harm & you cannot help the harm. I have no fear that "evil communications will corrupt good manners" in this case, but there are many who dread the association.

Stewart of Auburn Semy.[2] made a sweet speech in his insistence that the statement of the action of the Board, in accepting your resignation, was in compliance with your demand.

Well, whatever may be the final output I loved the Princeton Prest. & will continue to love the man, whether he be "His Honor, the Govr." or plain W. W. the man.

Now, dear Dr. W. if you reciprocate these sentiments dont put in one half second in replying to this screed, but give my time to to [the] epistolary correspondence which you have invited.

Yrs Always,   D. R. Frazer.

ALS (WP, DLC).

[1] Frazer, former pastor of the First Presbyterian Church in Newark, had retired in 1909.

[2] The Rev. Dr. George Black Stewart, President of Auburn Theological Seminary and a trustee since 1887.

Flemington, 20 Oct., 1910.

A question of persons.
A question of method:
    The old organization method, or
    The new method of public discussion
       and personal responsibility

A question of objects   and prudence:
    To serve party interests, or
    To solve public questions and effect
       justice.

Get away from the spirit of attack; cultivate
    the spirit of adjustment.
    Break the corporations? No: accommodate
       them a) in action, b) in taxation
    Break parties? No: sober and moral-
       ize them.
The spirit of right and service

A Campaign Address in Flemington, New Jersey[1]

[[Oct. 20, 1910]]

MR. CHAIRMAN[2] AND FELLOW-CITIZENS:—It is very delightful to face an audience like this, and I feel that your greeting is really a welcome. I feel as I have felt before so many audiences in New Jersey, that you really want to hear what I have to say, that you have not come here merely to indulge the natural political instinct of all Americans who like to go to political meetings, but you have come here out of a feeling that something is afoot.

The Chairman has very kindly referred to Princeton. It pleases me as it pleases every Princeton man to remember that nowhere has there been more devotion to the service of the country than at Princeton College, and one of the greatest figures in the history of that college is the history of an old Scot who was once President of Princeton and was one of the leaders of his day. I mean John Witherspoon. No voice sounded more sincere or more strong in the council which guided the Revolution than did the voice of that indomitable old Scot, who really formed the character of that University and gave it the tendency which it has had since until the present day.

Of course, I have not come to speak about Princeton. I have, as the Chairman has just said, severed my connection with the University. I feel very singular. I have been connected with Princeton for twenty years and a little over, and I feel like the man in England whom I asked which party he belonged to, replied, "I can't tell you exactly, I am between sizes." I feel as if I am between sizes in occupation, but nevertheless I have felt I owed it to the people whose franchises I am asking, to disengage myself from other occupations and to devote myself to the serious purposes of this campaign.

And yet I sometimes wonder, when I face an audience like this, what it is that we are discussing. You know some very singular things have happened in this campaign. We started out with marked differences between the programmes of the two parties. The Democratic platform has a great many items in it, all of which are explicitly expressed, the Republican platform has fewer items in it, most of them not specifically expressed, and there are only two important items expressed in it.[3] But the

---

[1] Delivered in the Flemington Opera House.

[2] Abraham Chalmers Hulsizer, Mayor of Flemington and Democratic chairman of Hunterdon County.

[3] Wilson probably referred to planks favoring a public utilities commission with rate-making powers and endorsing the Payne-Aldrich Tariff of 1909. The Republican platform is printed in State of New Jersey, *Manual of the Legislature of New Jersey . . . 1911* (Trenton, N. J., 1911), pp. 164-65.

Republican candidate has added to the principles of his party platform practically everything in the Democratic platform, and therefore it is obvious that what we have come together to discuss is not so much the differences between the professions of the two parties as interpreted by their spokesman [spokesmen], but the difference between persons—the differences as between what is to be expected of the one candidate and what is to be expected of the other.

I am not going to waste your time by discussing that, for I cannot discuss my own merits and demerits; I cannot depreciate in any respect—and do not desire to depreciate—the character of my opponent. You can judge for yourselves which is the better man to carry the programme out—which is the freer man to carry the programme out. I cannot dwell upon that, but I can dwell upon some things that are involved in this question. I can dwell upon the method by which the programme is to be carried out, and I think I can point out to you, without any personal reference to myself, treating myself entirely impersonally, what the difference is in the method, what the necessary difference is in the method.

The Republican candidate has, for a long time, been part of an active party organization. The Democratic candidate has never been part of a party organization. The Republican candidate has, in more than one speech, given a sufficiently clear indication of how he expected to act. You will remember that when he accepted his nomination he said that he expected to be a constitutional Governor, by which he meant that he would punctiliously confine himself to those things that were intimated as his privileges and duties by the constitution of the State, that is to say, he would send messages to the Legislature, make strong recommendations to them, but that if they did not accept his recommendation he would have nothing more to say about it. I, following about a week afterwards, said that if that was the standard, I was going to be an unconstitutional Governor, because if it was unconstitutional to urge upon the citizens of the State, in order that opinion might guide the Legislature, the things that it seemed absolutely necessary the Legislature should enact, then I was going to take the liberty, the utmost liberty, of speech that belonged to me—not merely as Governor, but as an American citizen, to urge upon the people of the State the necessary reforms in legislation and administration. Then Mr. Lewis followed suit and said that he also would do that. But Mr. Lewis, as I pointed out to you, is an intimate part of an organization, and I am not part of any organization at all. The contrast in the programme, therefore, is this: Will you have the things that you want attempted and carried out by the organization methods, or will you have them carried out by the other method which I have suggested to several audiences in this State, by the method of public discussion and personal responsibility? That is what I propose to you as a serious question, gentlemen. Are you, or are you not, tired of the organization process; are you or are you not disappointed with what you have got from party organization, from party machines? I know perfectly well that everywhere, from one end of this State to the other, there is disappointment, and in some cases reaching the point of discussion[,] with the fact that in spite of innumerable promises, in spite of occasional prospects of fulfillment, the organization does not do what it has promised the voters that it will do. And, therefore, men are losing confidence in organizations to accomplish things which ought to be accomplished. And I want to tell you that not only now, but always, it has been proven that the only way to get things done in a self-governing country is by that tremendous power which resides in opinion.

You cannot make opinion over night; you cannot make opinion by merely reading the newspapers; you cannot make opinion by casual conversation on the street; but the way opinion is made and compacted is by parties of men getting together and comparing their views and then to unite in a common determination. If we really went to the polls on a summons through the newspapers or through posters, and declared our opinions or our several opinions upon any public question, there would be the greatest differences of opinion. It would be impossible to make up the common judgment out of a multiplicity of opinions publicly expressed. Opinion must be based, built together; it must be made up of the ideas of united men having a united purpose, and, therefore, public questions, in order to be backed by public opinion, must be discussed in public meetings, must be discussed on the one side and on the other, and then there must be personal responsibility, not organic responsibility, not the responsibility of an organization. An organization is exactly like a corporation, of which it was said long ago that there was nobody to be kicked and that it hadn't a soul to be damned. Therefore, you cannot get at it. You cannot find political organization and punish it; it is spread all over the State. Moreover, most political organizations do not consist, at any rate altogether, of the men who are in office. If you want to find a real boss, you don't look for him among the men who hold office; you look for him among persons who sit quietly apart by themselves and run the machine.

Now, you cannot get at him, you have not elected him to do anything, and you cannot put him out of anything. He has kindly volunteered to run your affairs, and to determine who is to occupy public office from the point of view of the organization. The only way is by holding the man you elect to office responsible for what he does, and if he says he did it at the bidding of the organization, tell him it is none of your business what the organization does. You want to know why, contrary to your opinion and to the interest of the community, he did what he did. That is the only way you will ever get at anything you wish to accomplish in public affairs. I suggest that you therefore elect a Governor who will be responsible to you in his duties as Governor, responsible to you and nobody else, and who will render his account to you and to nobody else.

I suggest that you establish the same direct personal relationship with your Senator and Representatives in the Assembly. I suggest that you call upon them to explain in public meeting their votes, their motives and their ideas of the public interest. I hope that they will tell you once in a while that they do not agree with you. I do not want subservient men; I don't want men to represent me at any rate who do not have minds of their own and form independent opinions. I want them to come out and say if they don't agree with me. We want the relationship to be personal and not the relationship of an organization. We want something to say about the objects to be kept in view. Not only do we want the methods to be personal, but the objects to be divorced from the thing that concerns the organization.

What is a political party? A political party does not exist for its own sake. A political party does not exist for the sake of maintaining an organization and bringing success to that organization. Its only excuse for existing is for trying to serve the people and serve the public and therefore [not] determining as to what will bring the party success at the next election but what would bring the people the most happiness if fought for long enough. I tell you the public in every community should look toward the future and get together in small groups and see these things which are necessary that are based upon justice and [the] real interests of the community, and where you will find a little group that will not be big enough to elect anybody but will preach this thing and fight [for] it and it may be five and it may be ten and it may be twenty years, until some day we have gathered such a host to our banner that we are going to carry an election. Those are the men who deserve in the long run to serve with a spirit of self-sacrifice. I say a party is an instrument in your hand and that man is an unserviceable citizen who serves his party instead of using it as an instrument for serving his community and his people.

What are the objects you are to demand of all your candidates? You are to ask them what are you after. Are you after promoting the interests you belong to or are you after settling public questions? The man who is not after settling public questions is not worth listening to, and a man who is genuinely desirous of coming at a just settlement of such questions is worth listening to whether he is right or wrong, because all force comes from the moral vigor that is in the man, all self-respect comes from his honesty, his real desire to see the truth, and a man who has that desire and is wrong can be convinced and set right. So I say of you, you must demand of your candidates that they specify that their object is to settle public questions in the way they [that] will be just and right and bring about justice in the relation of men to each other in the settlement of their affairs. It is not reasonable that you should demand of them that that should be their attainment. Public questions are complicated things, they cannot be settled in a single campaign, in a single Legislature; they must be thoroughly worked out by long tedious processes of discussion and therefore you must not expect a man can hurry opinions; you must not expect that he can work some miracle of legislation, but you must demand of him what you want him to do is to settle public questions.

In a sense in this campaign we are divorcing ourselves from parties altogether. I have all my life been attached, and I dare say almost all of you have been attached, to the great party called the Democratic party. It is the only party now active in American affairs whose history runs back to the actual beginnings of the republic and ever since this beginning those years have been made illustrious by many a great name, and many a great life, and that would be a singular man who did not feel a certain pride in being enrolled in a party that had such a history, so long a service of the republic that in so many days, dark and bright, it tried to serve public questions in the interest of public right and public happiness[;] but when we come to the decision of public questions and the selection of men to carry them out we must in a certain sense lift ourselves above party, and if we love our party and deem it wrong, we will sometimes vote against it.

You do not want to separate yourselves from the rank and file; you do not want to separate yourselves from the neighbors in whom you believe; but you do want to separate yourselves from the leaders in whom you do not believe; therefore, your test must be of men; your test must be of the way they go to work; your test must be of the things they want to accomplish. Then there is another thing you must be careful about in making your choice. You must be careful about the spirit of the whole thing. You know, gentlemen, that we have been in danger in recent years in this country of undergoing too deep an excitement in political affairs. You cannot settle things right when you are excited, when you are prejudiced, when your hatreds, when your cupidity is excited, you are not in a frame of mind and spirit to settle anything justly and rightly; and, therefore, it seems to me that we ought to face the great complicated public questions that we are facing, not in a spirit of hostility to anybody, but with a desire to reach an adjustment. I wonder if you have ever thought of the principles of force that lie in a great piece of machinery. For example, take a great railway locomotive. You know that the strength and efficiency of that locomotive depends upon nothing so much as upon its adjustment; if the parts are never so slightly thrown out of adjustment with one another, then there is set up friction and that friction will presently heat the machine, and if it is too heated, it will presently buckle the machine and tie it so tight it cannot move in a single joint. I often hold that up to myself as an image of politics. If you over-heat the parts, they won't run with each other, and if you want freedom, if you want justice, if you want the things that are right, the thing to secure is adjustment; so that different interests are properly related to each other; so that one man cannot claim more than is his due, cannot put injustice upon his neighbors, so that all may be sure of being fitted into the community in which he lives, and obtain his rights not patronized by any man, not given favors by any man, merely asking the rights that every man has the right to claim in a just order of government; and so I say that is the spirit in which we ought to approach each question.

Take the great matter of corporations. I have heard a great deal of cheap and easy denunciation of corporations. It is perfectly easy to grow eloquent in denunciation of these great business organizations which we call by that name. And it is perfectly easy by the same token to be absolutely unjust. What we are jealous of is not legitimate business, not the right use of the power of the corporations, because they are a great convenience in the conduct of our complicated modern business; but what we are jealous of is the wrong, the criminal, the unjust use of the corporation. And so all we ask in seeking to regulate corporations—public serving corporations for example and other corporations—is not to break them up, but to adjust them to our interest; and we cannot adjust anything to our interest unless we study the character of the thing itself and the character of our interest as related to that thing. And every step of public policy depends upon inquiry, depends upon understanding, depends upon the comprehension. If you put men into our Legislature who are going to run amuck in modern business, they are not going to do you any service, but if you put in men who intend, no matter who suffers, no matter who is interfered with, that justice is going to be done, nobody need fear what these men may do, at least nobody who is not in fear of the penitentiary. There are many men that live in fear of the penitentiary, but no rightly adjusted man, no just man, no righteous man, is going to be afraid of any proper reform; and, therefore, it is necessary that righteous men should undertake reform.

Now there are two things we want adjusted in respect of our corporations. In the first place, we want to make them act in a way that is fair to us, and in the second place, we want to make them right in the way of taxation. You have heard a great deal, a great deal that is true, about inequalities of taxation in this State, and in the country too, for that matter; and it has been said, and sometimes justly said, that the corporations which enjoy enormous legal advantages, do not pay enough for those advantages, and that the taxes that are levied on their property are not levied in a way that shows equality between the taxes that are levied on their property and the taxes that are levied on the property of private individuals. Now, all of that must be adjusted in a spirit of fairness, not in order to do the corporations an injustice, but in a way to see that everybody gets his rights in a matter of that kind.

I have often gone up and down this great country of ours; I have faced many kinds of audiences in this broad land, and I have never yet found an audience that wanted anything more than what was right. And when I come to this ancient county and know the kind of men I am addressing here, many whose traditions run back generation by generation, many of them to the settlement of this rich and beautiful portion of our State, I know those men are of the real stock of America, and not only that, but that they have the real impulses of America, which are founded upon justice, are founded upon the right, are founded upon not giving any man privilege over another, but upon equality. So I know how safe it is to appeal to an audience like this, on the basis of just action, not partisan action, but to bring justice into existence, so that we may know that the laws are square, so that we may know that the courts are pure, so that those who conduct prosecutions mean to find the criminal, and when they have found him to punish him; and that no man can make himself a public enemy by never so slight a degree without coming under the common public condemnation. That is the public spirit of America; and so it is with parties.

I share, and share very heartily, your jealousy of the secret power of the political machine, and I am just as anxious as you are to break up the power—the secret power—of the political machine. But I am not here to break up parties. I don't think parties ought to be broken up. And I am not here to break up the machine for the fun of breaking it up. I have never been of that excitable temper that I found satisfaction in breaking things up. I have the satisfaction of never remembering having necessarily broken up a piece of furniture. Now political machines, in their legitimate sphere, are useful pieces of furniture, and there is no use of losing your temper and smashing them up just because you have lost your temper and don't know what else to do. And the danger of our attitude toward parties, of our attitude as it is at the present moment, is that we would smash things without knowing why we smash them. There is no fun in destruction; there is merely madness in that kind of passion. We don't want to break parties; we want to save and moralize parties— save them by a sense of responsibility and teach them that right conduct is service of the community and what is right.

Parties respond to other things than the whip. I have never known anything useful done under the whip, but I have known very many useful things done under the kindly warmth of a great principle.

You know the fable of the contest between the wind and the sun. How the wind and the sun wagered with each other that they could make a certain man take off his cloak that he had wrapped about him, and the wind swooped upon him and seemed as if to carry him from his feet; and he only wound the cloak tighter and tighter about him; and the genial sun came out and shed upon him its heat, and he relaxed and threw the cloak from his shoulder.

Now, I believe that that fable can be realized in politics. I have dealt with a great many men in politics; they are of the same stuff we are of. You cannot, by beating, bring them out of their covert and hiding, but sometimes, by the mere warmth and genial influence of a great principle, you can make them turn to you as the flower turns to the sun.

There are forces in our natures which are the fundamental

forces of all human affairs. They are not the forces of mere intellectual controversy, they are not the forces that distract, but they are those deep pulses of moral impulse that beat in us from the time we are children and grow warm and beautiful, suggestive of moral principles, until we grow old and are convinced in our old age that to be right is the only happiness in the world. These are the foundations of life. I know there are cynical men who say that they are not, I know there are men who shrug their shoulders and say "That is all very pretty but it don't work out." I know there are men who cover their springs of action and pretend that they do not care for sentiment, but if you take the pains to break that mask away from them, you will see the gleam of the waters. Every man has deep in him a great sentiment of what is just and right, and it is that we are seeking, to regulate the conscience, in order that men may look back upon this gracious year 1910 and say, "Ah! that was a time when we turned about and recovered some of the ancient, honorable, glorious principles of American politics, where men covered their consciences as citizens, and, through seeking, found him [them], through a way they could realize, in part at any rate, the great impulses of right which underlie all nations."

I beg, ladies and gentlemen, that in the contest to come—for it is a contest—the day of voting, the day for the formation of judgments, in the contest to come you may have a consciousness of what it is that you are doing. This is what America was founded for: America was founded to give every man a right to participate in this sovereign function of choosing who should govern him and under what laws he should be governed—and that thrill goes over every man who votes on the eighth of November—the thrill of the recollection that multitudes of men before him have sought to serve America as he on that day tries to serve her.[4]

Printed in the Flemington, N. J., *Hunterdon County Democrat*, Oct. 25, 1910; with a few corrections from the partial text in the New York *Evening Post*, Oct. 21, 1910.

[4] Following this address, Wilson spoke to an overflow crowd in the Flemington Court House. See the news report printed at Oct. 21, 1910.

From Theodore Whitefield Hunt

My dear Dr Wilson,   [Princeton, N. J.] 10 20 1910

I have just heard of your resignation as President & of its acceptance by the Board of Trustees. One of these days, when your political engagements are less exacting, I will see you personally & talk over the events of the last nine years.

I now write simply to say that you close an administration that has immensely added to the educational repute of Princeton University and to the cause of American Education in general, an administration, in my judgment, second to none in the history of the institution. Personally, Dr Wilson, I can scarcely express to you what is in my heart, for since the old day's when we were neighbors, your friendship has been one of the greatest compensations & inspirations of my life, so true & refreshing in all times of joy & sorrow. The severance of our official relations is to me nothing less than a personal loss, in that in all such relations I have found your counsel and kindly interest invaluable. These conferences I shall sorely miss, but console myself with the thought that your companionship may be still enjoyed[.] I trust that the future may have rewards in store for you commensurate with your brilliant intellectual gifts & your generous & unselfish nature. Success to you in all your plans & aims in life! Upon Mrs Wilson & your children & yourself, may the richest blessings of Heaven rest!

Affly   T. W. Hunt

ALS (WP, DLC).

From Richard Vliet Lindabury

My dear Doctor: Newark, N. J. October 20, 1910.

Will you permit me to make a suggestion? I am inclined to think that the question which is pressing hardest just now upon the mind of the Independent voter in this State is whether or not the return of the Democratic party to power at the coming election would mean much more than the substitution of Smith, Davis and Nugent, as the dominant forces in the government of the State in the place and stead of Baird, Voorhees and Strong, or what is called the board of guardians. You have frequently declared that you do not owe your nomination to any individual, boss or organization, and if elected will be free to serve the people according to your best judgment. I have talked with a number of leading Democrats during the last day or two who fear that this is not going quite far enough and that the wavering voter may conclude that notwithstanding your freedom from pledges, the Democratic leaders and the Democratic organization as such would dictate the policy of your administration, or, in other words, occupy the place of the present board of guardians. My suggestion is that you take an early opportunity to meet this point a little more fully and specifically. It seems to me that you would do well to declare that if elected you will not, either in the matter of appointments to office or the shaping of the policy of your administration, submit to the dictation of any person or persons, special interest or organization; that you will always welcome advice and suggestions from any citizen, whether a boss, leader, organization man or plain citizen, but that all such suggestions and advices will be considered on their merits and that no additional weight will be given to them because of the fact that they happen to come from persons holding the assumed or imputed titles referred to; that no leader or organization man will be ostracized on account of his position as such or his activity in the electoral canvass but that neither such activity nor such position will give to his advice or recommendations a force or power to which they are not entitled on their merits.[1]

I do not doubt that you are considering this matter and perhaps have already formulated in your mind a better way to meet the issue. Be that as it may, I venture the above suggestion with the feeling that it will not at least mislead you and in the hope that it may be helpful.

I am,   Yours cordially,   R. V. Lindabury

TLS (WP, DLC).
[1] In his letter to George L. Record, printed at Oct. 24, 1910, Wilson paraphrased this entire sentence.

From Samuel Gompers

Dear Sir: Washington, D. C., October 20, 1910.

Some weeks ago as you will recall I requested copy of the baccalaureate address you delivered at Princeton on the subject of "Unprofitable Servants."[1] Your Secretary advised me that you were unable to comply with my request, because you had only the manuscript copy of your address.

I am writing to say that if you will be so good as to let me have your manuscript copy I will have additional copies made here in my office, and will return the original manuscript to you together with one or more of the additional copies if you should so desire.

I sincerely trust that you can comply with my request, and beg to thank you in asvance [advance] for your courtesy.

Very truly yours,   Saml. Gompers.

TLS (WP, DLC).
[1] His earlier letter is missing.

From Archibald Stevens Alexander

Dear Dr. Wilson,   Hoboken, N. J. Oct. 20 [1910].

I had hoped to see you for a moment at Somerville last night to express to you what I am about to say in this letter, but did not have an opportunity to do so. I feel very strongly that the turning point in your campaign has been reached, and that your election or defeat depends on your answer to Record's letter. Before he injected himself into the situation it looked as if you would win by 15000. Now I see people everywhere who two weeks ago were for you but who now are wavering. These are New Idea Republicans, of whom there are 6000 in this County, 13000 in Essex & 3000 in Passaic. If you satisfy them in your answer you will get 2/3 of this vote, if not you will get very few. They have confidence in you personally, but they want to be told the difference between your relation to the Democratic bosses & Lewis' relation to the Republican bosses. Your statements so far that you have made no pledges & have been asked for none does not, in their minds, meet the situation. There must be something more in the nature of a specific declaration, which cannot be made too emphatic, that after election you will not give them any more consideration than you would to any ordinary citizen, something which will absolutely differentiate your position from Lewis' in their minds.

I trust that in your answer you will be able to clear up this situation, and that you may also be able to emphasize it in your speeches in Essex, Hudson & Passaic counties. The Boss issue is the overshadowing issue of this campaign—an attack on the Republican bosses only will not overcome the handicap of a normal Rep. majority of 25000 in this State.

I hope you will pardon this letter. I have been speaking & have been meeting all kinds of people all over North Jersey, and I think the tide is turning against you. Feeling this I also feel it my duty to so inform you, as I have no use for the politicians who only see rainbows.

                    Sincerely yours,   Archibald S. Alexander

P.S. Please don't think that I have any other thought or intention but to report to you what I hear. I know that you have repeatedly stated your independence, but some of these people are so used to superlatives that they don't grasp an ordinary statement, and they have been fooled so often that they don't trust anyone, no matter how high his character.

ALS (WP, DLC).

A News Report of a Speech to an Overflow Audience in Flemington, New Jersey

[Oct. 21, 1910]

WILSON ON FEDERAL POWER

The "New Nationalism" As It Appears To Him.

Flemington, N. J., October 21.—Woodrow Wilson last night faced the greatest outpouring of people in all his campaign thus far, in this seat of Hunterdon County, noted for its peaches, cream, applejack, and rock-ribbed Democracy. The Opera House, scheduled as the place of meeting, was utterly inadequate to contain those who wished to hear the candidate, and so the court house was thrown open for an overflow meeting, which Mr. Wilson addressed after he had spoken at the Opera House.

For the first time in his canvass the Princetonian faced audiences entirely friendly to him through principles of party affiliation, and so in large measure he abandoned political issues and preached, as only Mr. Wilson can preach, upon the duties of citizenship and the part that each man should play in public affairs. This, at the court house, turned his mind to the subject of "New Nationalism," which he illumined vividly in at least one of its aspects.

"The new nationalism," he said, "means something. I do not know exactly what, it has been defined so often by various persons and never twice alike, but I can tell you one thing that it means: It means that if States cannot reform certain things we will have to look to the Federal government to do the reforming for us. We talk about centralization of power and say we are jealous of Federal power. Well, somebody has to furnish the power. If you won't furnish it, the government will. It is your duty to take hold of and to familiarize yourselves with your home affairs, and if you do not, why then you need not be surprised if your Congressmen give that power to the Federal government."

Printed in the New York *Evening Post*, Oct. 21, 1910; some editorial headings omitted.

A Petition

[Princeton, N. J., c. Oct. 21, 1910]

We the undersigned, having elected your course in Jurisprudence for our instruction, do hereby signify our regret at the severance of your relations with this course. We further venture to express our sincere desire that it may be within your power, as far as your duties will permit, to resume your lectures so deeply appreciated by us.

Signed: D. Paulson Foster. . . .[1]

T petition S (WP, DLC).
[1] David Paulson Foster, Class of 1912. There were 181 other signatures, three of which were duplicates.

A News Report of a Campaign Tour in Warren County, New Jersey

[*Oct. 21, 1910*]

WILSON READS A NEW LESSON
WARREN WARMS TO HIM

Steadfast Democratic County Gives Him a Welcome Without a Parallel.

Phillipsburg, N. J., Oct. 21.—Woodrow Wilson is a weary but a happy man to-night. Nothing quite so heartening to him has happened in his new kind of campaign as his great reception in Warren county, one of the four of the State that has a fixed habit of presenting majorities to Democratic candidates. A tremendous meeting in Ortygian Hall to-night wound up for him the hardest day of his great battle.

He had made one of those old-fashioned "whirls" by automobile, covering nearly 90 miles of New Jersey's most beautiful country, stopping at eight towns and making seven speeches, six in response to insistent demands, and he was mighty weary when he reached this city to-night. And yet such was the tonic effect upon him of the gathering that he was at his best, bright, earnest and filled with the spirit of his broad patriotism that is carrying him straight to the hearts of the people. . . .

Mr. Wilson's long and arduous day began at 9 o'clock with the start in the touring cars from Flemington. After his great stir of Hunterdon county there was little chance for him to get a breath, so strenuous was the going every minute. The first objective point was Washington, Warren county, and the cars had traversed but a few miles of an excellent, even road when they were halted at a long stretch, where rebuilding was under way and the only thing to do to avoid a sure hold-up was for all hands to get out and walk.

Mr. Wilson was one of the first out and, [as] he climbed rail fences to make the detour through the fields to escape the quagmire made by excavations and recent rains, he showed that he was as nimble as anybody in the party and he was one of the most cheery over the mile walk to Lebanon, where the cars after pushing through the mud, awaited the pedestrians. The way then led through Clinton, Glen Gardner and Hampton, and while one or two short stretches of bad road were encountered, most of the way was good and, despite the delay, Washington was reached soon after 11 o'clock, a half hour after schedule.

There on the sidewalk in front of Baker's Hotel were gathered fully 500 men and Senator Johnston Cornish, the State Committeeman from Warren, had gathered eight automobiles, prettily decorated with flags, for the run through the county. Here, too, were met many prominent men of this "always straight" Democratic county among them former Assemblyman Joseph H. Firth, Mayor of Phillipsburg; former Judge William H. Morrow, Assemblyman George B. Cole, who is going back for another term, and William T. Tuttle, candidate for Congress in the Fifth district, sometimes alluded to as "Fowler's" district.

Much to Mr. Wilson's surprise, he was looked upon to make a speech and was carried almost on the shoulders of the cheering crowd up the narrow stairway to the little hall, into which 500 tried to squeeze, though it will hold only 250. The local managers declared that never had the town beheld anything to equal the unusual demonstration. Mr. Wilson was presented by J. M. Snyder, chairman of the County Committee, and he made a brief address which greatly stirred the gathering, largely composed of workingmen.

"This is an unexpected pleasure," he said. "It is satisfactory and pleasing to me to see so many of my fellow-citizens gathered at this hour of the day. I have gone about in a good many places since the campaign opened and I have been most cordially received. I am not going about seeking office. My only desire is to serve the people of New Jersey to the best of my ability and understanding. You can't depend upon the political machine to give you good government; the members of the machine do not explain or justify themselves. I believe in personal responsibility; you can't hold a political organization responsible; it is too numerous and spread out too much. You can't kick a political organization and you can't punish it in this world or the next. It is the officers who are supposed to serve you, your neighbors, that you must get at. You should require of them that they serve you and give an account of themselves."

The crowd cheered as an earnest affirmation and then pressed in a dense mass about the commanding figure of the candidate as he was placed in Senator Cornish's car and the run begun for Hackettstown, 11 miles away over a splendid macadam road, skirting fine hills and woodlands, the procession of 11 cars making a fine show along the way. At many points workers and drivers recognized Mr. Wilson in the forward car and set up a lusty cheer.

Hackettstown, nicely decorated for the day, was reached soon after noon, and in the street in front of the American House fully 1000 persons had gathered and a noisy demonstration greeted the arriving cars.

So insistent was the demand for a speech from the candidate that he doffed his overcoat and, standing in Senator Cornish's car, he spoke for ten minutes, covering in a general way the points of his previous address, though couching his thoughts in new and attractive wording.

"I do not speak for the machine," he said. "I do not represent any machine, and was not even asked to represent any. I am simply putting myself at the service of the people of New Jersey. It is not office that I desire; I would be just as well pleased to serve you in any other capacity. But the offices of your State have been badly managed, and I want to see if others cannot manage them a little better."

The party had dinner at the hotel, and then drove on to Blairstown, 16 more miles over rather poor roads through some of Warren's most beautiful hills. Mr. Wilson was greatly surprised at the big turnout there, for the population is only about 1200, and it looked as though every man, woman and child in the town, as well as the lads and lasses from Blairstown Seminary, had gathered on the porches, sidewalks and at the windows of houses in the immediate vicinity of the Blairstown Hotel, and they showed how mighty glad they were to see the candidate.

Mr. Wilson made another short speech from the touring car and shook many more hands thrust out eagerly to him. A quick run of six miles over more beautiful hills brought the party to Hope, the quaint old village founded by the Moravians, where a stone building erected in 1781 and long used as a house of worship is now an inn, where good, old Moravian applejack is dispensed to those who can stand the strain.

There as the cars were drawn up on the village green, Mr. Wilson spoke pleasantly and hopefully of the campaign outlook. The next stop was at Oxford, the iron mining and manufacturing centre, where Mr. Wilson addressed 300 more aroused persons gathered on the walk in front of Allen's drug store. Belvidere, the county seat, one of the prettiest of New Jersey's towns, was reached at 5 o'clock, and the waiting crowd jammed into the Court House, where Mr. Wilson spoke for a few minutes to the admiring host. A stop was made at Roxbury for some handshaking, but no speech, and the 12 miles to this city was quickly run, the party arriving at the Lee House at 6.30.

Printed in the *Philadelphia Record*, Oct. 22, 1910; many editorial headings omitted.

From Cleveland Hoadley Dodge

Dear Woodrow   New York. Oct. 21st 1910.

Yesterday's business as it effected you, almost broke my heart,[1] but the last straw will be your hurriedly vacating Prospect. I don't blame you for being mad—you are not half as mad as I am —but for all our sakes, stay on—if you can.

When you do decide it best to move I earnestly hope you will go to Dodge Lodge.[2] Grace's[3] first impulse was to write last night to Mrs. Wilson but I persuaded her to wait so as not to embarrass Mrs Wilson's decision as to Prospect. Anyhow she is as eager as I am, to have you go there, if you will, & she says to tell Mrs Wilson that Lizzie[,] our old caretaker, who has been married again can go down at short notice & get things to rights.

It was "Fine" that Momo's scheme for government by committee was so emphatically squelched[.] His general behavior has had the effect of antagonizing some of his best friends & insofar the general situation is better. How he is going to raise the money for the Proctor condition I do not see, as Stephen [Palmer,] the Joneses & I think Cyrus too, are not very favorably disposed. I only regret that I did not obey my first impulse & decline to contribute until all the others had decided. As it was I was carried away by the harmony of Commencement time.

You are very busy so *please* don't answer this, unless you want Dodge Lodge when you can either telegraph or drop me a line.

Your political fight is perfectly splendid & you are winning golden opinions from all the thoughtful men of the land

                     À Díos   Yrs affly   C H Dodge

ALS (WP, DLC).
    [1] This letter, H. B. Thompson to E. W. Sheldon, Oct. 21, 1910, TLS (Thompson Letterpress Books, NjP), and C. H. Dodge to H. B. Thompson, Oct. 25, 1910 (printed at that date), all make it clear that, following Wilson's resignation and departure from the meeting of the Board of Trustees, there was considerable haggling among Wilson's friends and opponents over how long the Wilsons should occupy Prospect and Wilson's salary should continue, and that they blamed Pyne for it. On the day after his resignation, Wilson told a New York reporter: "The resignation, of course, takes effect at once. I shall remain in Prospect only so long as it takes us to make plans to move elsewhere." New York *Evening Post*, Oct. 21, 1910. Wilson wrote to L. C. Woods on October 27, 1910 (the letter is printed at that date), that, save for the gubernatorial nomi-

nation, he might have broken down under the mortification of what he had discovered to be the real feeling of the Pyne party toward him.

2 That is, his house at 24 Bayard Lane, Princeton.

3 His wife, Grace Parish Dodge.

From Moorfield Storey[1]

Dear Mr. Wilson: Boston 21st October 1910.

I am very much obliged to you for sending me a copy of your address before the American Bar Association, and I have read it with very great interest and cordial sympathy. It so happens that I am going to deliver the Storrs lectures at Yale this year, and I have taken for my subject the necessity of reforming the procedure of the law.[2] Our profession today is, in my judgment, more discredited and its processes more ineffective than at any time in my recollection, and if I can persuade the young lawyers to recognize the danger, the next generation may deal with the subject more effectually than ours has. It is very important that the country should realize the truth of your statement that it is men who commit crimes and not corporations.

I take this opportunity of expressing the interest which I feel in your campaign which seems to be extremely successful, and my sincere hope that you will be triumphantly elected. When such men as you, and Judge Harmon and Judge Baldwin come into power, there is hope that the present incompetent and corrupt office-holders may be driven into their deserved retirement. With high regards,   Sincerely yours,   M. Storey

TLS (WP, DLC).

1 Lawyer, publicist, and reform leader of Boston.

2 Published as *The Reform of Legal Procedure* (New Haven, Conn., 1911).

From Wilson B. Killingbeck

Dear Sir: Orange, N. J., Oct. 21st-10

Yours of the 20th inst. at hand. I want to thank you for your patient and courteous replies to my communications.

I wish to assure you that there was absolutely no feeling of personal animosity towards you as the Democratic nominee, but simply a wish to have discussed matters which to me and the members of our movement are of vital consequence. We are giving our lives for the purpose of trying to forward a movement which we sincer[e]ly believe will be of tremendous value to humanity—the restoration to the people of the means of life, which they lost when the simple hand tools of our fathers, which were owned by the people who used them; but which have evolved and developed into the gigantic and complex tool of the present day and not owned by those who are compelled to use them, but who must subordinate their ideas and thoughts to the tool owners, or run the risk of losing their right to life, or in other words their jobs.

This applies to nearly all walks of life as you know, and it seems to me that there can be no true democracy while these conditions prevail and the recent history of the Democratic Party, especially in the southern states where it is in absolute control, does not hold out the promise of anything better in the future.

I certainly have no wish to enter into a personal controversy, but really believe that in the interests of good government and even for the preservation of our republic, we shall be compelled to seriously discuss this subject.

With best wishes, I remain yours for an improved civilization and a real democracy,   Wilson B. Killingbeck

TLS (WP, DLC).

From John Milton Waldron

My Dear Sir: Washington, D. C., Oct. 21st, 1910.

As you will see from the enclosed newspaper clipping,[1] The National Independent Political League have decided to support you in your candidacy for the Governor of New Jersey. We feel that you are worthy of the loyal support of every liberty loving, fair-minded citizen—especially every manly, independent colored voter.

If our League can be of any service to you in furnishing speakers, organizers, canvassers, etc., please let us hear from you at once.

We are

Yours

For Equal Justice and Fair Play to Every American Citizen,
                J. Milton Waldron, National Organizer.

TLS (WP, DLC).
1 A news story entitled "Colored Voters Adopt Standard," *Washington Herald*, Oct. 7, 1910. See W. T. Ferguson to WW, Oct. 7, 1910, n. 2.

From Richard Vliet Lindabury

My dear Dr. Wilson: Newark, N. J. October 21, 1910.

I have been a little disturbed by the attitude of the Newark Evening News during the last week with regard to your candidacy. In consequence of this, I went over this morning and had a pretty full talk with the editor and chief owner, Mr. Wallace Scudder. He told me that when you were first nominated, practically everybody in the News office was for you but that latterly the spectre of Senator Smith had loomed up so ominously as to put nearly everybody on the fence. He said that if the Smith-Nugent-Davis issue was out of the way, you would be elected by a very large majority but that he feared that the independent voters would sooner see you defeated than Smith sent to the United States Senate. I told him that I had conferred with a number of the leading hold-over members of the Legislature and was convinced that the fears of his people with regard to the senatorship were baseless; that in my judgment it would be quite impossible for Smith to get himself elected to the Senate however large the Democratic majority of the Legislature might happen to be. I also told him that anyhow I thought it unfair to put up to you as a gubernatorial candidate, the question of the Senatorship, and that if you asked my opinion I should advise you not to be drawn into a discussion of that question and that in that respect I wished to particularly criticize the attitude of his paper. He replied that he thought I was right about that matter and that his paper had not been quite fair in that respect and he gave me to understand that upon that subject the attitude of his paper would be changed. He also seemed to be relieved by my assurance of the very great improbability of Mr. Smith being able to accomplish his election even if a Democratic Legislature should be returned. I then referred to the paper's suggestions that while you had denounced the Republican bosses you had not denounced the Democratic bosses and asked him what he thought you ought to do, remarking that, of course, you could not be expected to drive away from your support any person or persons who were intending to vote for you—much less the regular organization of the party which had nominated you. He admitted this but said that he thought you might be a little more explicit in your declarations that you would not be controlled by the bosses in your own party or, for that matter, by the organization. I told him that I was sure you would not be so controlled and I thought you had intended by what you had already said to make this reasonably clear. I told him also that I would let you know how the matter appeared to him as I was sure you would appreciate the views of men of the independent position and character of himself. I left him with a better feeling with regard to the situation and am hopeful that the future attitude of the paper will be a little more satisfactory. You will note that Mr. Scudder's only suggestion as to what as a matter of practical politics you could properly do, is closely in the line of my letter to you of yesterday.

There is no doubt whatever, I think, that the issue at this end of the State is becoming to be Smith, Nugent and Davis. The Republican speakers are discussing nothing else and they admit to me as I meet them that it is about the only thing that they have to talk about. Their hope is to frighten the Independent Republicans back into the fold by the spectre of these men. Of course, you can say nothing with regard to the Senatorship but I do think that it is in your power to convince the voters of the class referred to that they have no reason to fear that you will be dominated by the gentlemen whose malevolent influence they so much fear.

With regard to the "News," I perhaps ought to add what you may, however, already know, that there is no newspaper published within or without the State that has an influence with the independent voters in this part of the State at all comparable with this paper.

I am,   Yours truly,   R. V. Lindabury

TLS (WP, DLC).

From John Maynard Harlan

Chicago Ill Oct 21-1910

The Illinois Manufacturers Assn. can easily remove conflict of dates. The officers of the association are determined to have you here as its guest and they will make their date fit your New York engagement. They have put it up to me to get you here. If I am to live longer in Chicago you must come[.] would Monday the twelfth of December suit you. You can leave here Tuesday on the eighteen hour train and be in New York Wednesday morning the fourteenth. David Jones agrees with me that you could not appear here under any auspices more favorable than the Illinois Manufacturers Association. Please wire me whether the twelfth will suit you. It is understood that your acceptance is provisional as indicated in previous correspondence.[1]

John Maynard Harlan.

T telegram (WP, DLC).
1 Wilson did address the Illinois Manufacturers' Association on December 12, 1910. A news report of his remarks is printed at Dec. 13, 1910, Vol. 22.

A News Report of a Campaign Speech in Phillipsburg, New Jersey

[Oct. 22, 1910]

WILSON STORY CAUGHT CROWD

If Republican Mule Balks Lewis Won't Dare to Twist Its Tail.

PHILLIPSBURG, Oct. 22.—After the most strenuous day since his campaign began, Woodrow Wilson, Democratic candidate for Governor, told a story during his speech in Orbygia [Ortygian] Hall here last night. It was applied to his opponent, Vivian M. Lewis. With his preface, it ran as follows:

There is nothing to say against the character, and I believe nothing to say against the purposes of the Republican candidate for Governor, but he is part, and always has been part, in his public life, of the organization which has been led into mistaken uses of its political power. He is in the position of a former member of the Board of Guardians.

You have to ask yourself: How probable is it that he will try to use the old organization, which is unpromising in itself, to new purposes? I will try to illustrate it to you by a story, which doubtless some of you have heard.

An old colored man in a Southern town went into a drug store and said:

"Boss, will you get 'the colonel' on the telephone for me?"

Everybody knew who "the colonel" was in that town. When the colonel was got, the old darkey said:

"Colonel, that ere mule down in the back road in front of the sto'—"

"Sir?"

"Yes, sir; yes, sir, right here."

"Yes, sir, ah done put dirt in his mouth, but he won't budge."

"What's that, colonel? Yes, sir; he had strings around his ears, but he wouldn't budge."

"Oh, yes, sir; yes, sir; ah put a fire unner him, but it didn't do no good."

"Sir? What's dat, colonel? Oh, no, no, sir; I didn't twist his tail; no, sir."

"One gem'len did twis' his tail. Dat gem'len looked like a No'thern gentleman. Sir, sir! Yes, sir; yes, sir; dey done took 'im

Phillipsburg, 21 Oct., 1910.

A wrong system has prevailed (— — Insurance)
   What do we mean by "the machine"?
    [shorthand]
    Can Mr. Lewis make the Rep. [shorthand] —?
A narrow gateway (Sluice - way).

The remedy? What was the insurance remedy?
   New men, — but chiefly a new point of view.
What is the people's point of view?
   Who are the people?
The trouble has been that there has been no
   Common medium and no communication of in-
     terest as bet. classes. — Negociation rather
     than Community.

   Let everybody look outside (as well as inside)
     his own interest.
   Let all take the common point of view

   And get men who have it
   And make them keep it, — by discussion
     and personal responsibility.

to the hospital. Wat's dat, colonel? No, sir; no, sir; I ain't heard yet."

Now, Mr. Lewis is no Northern gentleman, and he is not going to twist that mule's tail, because he has seen that mule behave before. It would take some inexperienced outsider to risk going to the hospital.

That is what I mean by the improbabilities of this campaign. The improbability is that the Republican candidate ought to— he must know from experience—that it must be not only useless, but dangerous, to twist the organization's tail.

So I am not counseling you to get anybody to twist that Republican organization mule's tail. I think that is hopeless.

I think that mule ought to be put out of business. He always balks, and always balks right in the main street; and he always balks just where he is the greatest obstruction to traffic.

You buy him every three years on the candid promise that he will do certain things; then he stalls and won't do them. You cannot change that mule's point of view. You have got to get a new mule. You've "done put dirt in his mouth," you have done everything that is suggested by ordinary tactics in such circumstances.

That story "got" fifteen or sixteen hundred persons who heard the address, and it was shown by the applause that interrupted it during the telling and at its conclusion. For that matter, the candidate secured attention shortly after he started speaking by utilizing the life insurance methods that were exposed a few years ago as instancing the evils of a combination between business and politics. He declared that New Jersey was a battle centre in this campaign, on which were directed the eyes of the entire country, as attested by newspapers all over the United States.

Labor, however, was the theme that attracted most attention in the town. As in Trenton, Mr. Wilson insisted that he had criticized it only in a friendly way. He said the Republicans have tried to make him the victim of "the most elaborate misrepresentation," and that "one of the most elaborate" was his views concerning laboring people. Although he had made only one criticism, he said the Republicans were finding it profitable in their view to forget all the rest of his life, but he added:

"They are very forgetful anyhow. They cannot remember a promise three years, so that it is natural to forget the rest of my life. I expect that from them, and therefore I forgive."

Every word of this part of his address was listened to with intense interest. A large part of the men present were employed by the railroads and in the shops and factories of the town. That he won their confidence was indicated by applause for his statements. . . .

Among the auditors here were about fifty students from Lafayette College in Easton, across the river, besides a delegation of the faculty. The boys made things lively with college cheers and parodies on popular songs. The cheer leader was Paul Hutchinson, of Bayonne. When Mr. Wilson entered the hall they sang the following:

> "What's the matter with Wilson? He's all right.
> That's the reason we're here to-night.
> He's got poor Lewis on the run;
> He's got the Republicans on the bum.
> He's all right."

In opening his speech, after having been presented by the chairman, Dr. Thomas Barber,[1] he told the boys that, like the man who slapped another on the back, the latter didn't know his name nor his face, but "your manner is very familiar."

Telling of the insurance expose, which showed that the managers of the business had forgotten the fundamentals of it, Mr. Wilson said something similar had happened in the field of politics, both in this State and country, until the people had gotten tired of the political machines. However, political organizations "up to a certain point, are indispensable. Our quarrel is with the use made of the political organizations." Developing this, Mr. Wilson said:

When there is an investigation and bribery is disclosed, what is shown? Who are bribed? Is there miscellaneous bribery? Certainly not. Certain men who find they can control their organization are bribed, and if there is any distribution of the money they distribute it to make sure of what they want. Now, what do they want? They want certain legislation passed at the State capitol.

The speaker instanced the alleged $50,000 fund raised to prevent anti-racetrack legislation in New York. He told also how policemen are prevented from doing their duty by political organizations, the persons enjoying immunity subscribing to the funds of the politicians. He compared political power to the sluiceway of a gristmill, the force going through the sluice driving or stopping the wheels of legislation.

The remedy, as in the insurance companies' cases, was to "change the men who were wrong." And he added:

As I have said, political organization is indispensable, and somebody must supply the motive force. The motive force must come from the outside, instead of from the inside, in what we are seeking to do. You have got to move this machine, and you have got to move it in the right direction and use it for right purposes.

It was at this point Mr. Wilson told the story of the organization mule. In applying the story seriously, he said political machines must take the point of view of the people. The people, it was pointed out, consist of all classes and not of any one class. This led to the statement that Republicans are misrepresenting Mr. Wilson on labor; and he said:

The misrepresentation rests upon this fact—that I never have looked and I never shall look at workingmen as if they were living all by themselves. I have, all my life, been a consistent friend of workingmen and of workingmen's organizations.

But when the workingmen's organizations have done things that I thought were not in the general interest—that is to say, were hurting the general interests of the country and reacting on their own interests—I, of course, have criticized what they did.

I am not ashamed, and I am not afraid to criticize anybody, and I would consider myself a very unfaithful friend if I did not dare to make the criticisms that I think are just.

If you are a man's real friend and he is doing something wrong you will not say to him, "You are all right; you never did a wrong thing in your life; you are all right." If you do that you are an unfaithful friend—and you are a fool besides.

If your friend is doing something that you think is hurtful to him and hurtful to the community in which he lives friendship will dictate and, whether he likes it or not, you will go and tell him the truth. That is the only kind of a friend I care to be. It is not pleasant; it is sometimes very painful.

I have done it very seldom—and, so far as I can remember, I did it but once, and that is what the Republican party is making so much of.

It is profitable to the Republicans to forget all the rest of my life, and they are perfectly welcome to it. They are very forgetful anyhow; they cannot remember a promise three years, so that is natural; I expect that of them, and therefore I forgive even from my friends what I expect.

That illustrates what I am trying to say. I do not think it is just to deal with any class by itself, as if it constituted the community.

Most of the mistakes that have been made, have been by treating the capitalist crowd as if it constituted the community and doing everything for the interest of high finance and the management of "Big Business."

That is a colossal blunder, it is a fatal blunder. Big business is not worth inspiring only as it relates to the general interest.

Here, what have we been doing? Talking about the rights of capital and labor, rights of this and that, as if they had been existing in a[i]rtight compartments and had nothing to do with each other.

They are all parts of the same thing. There cannot be different rights for those different interests and classes. Unless you can tie them together you have not found justice and not found right. They are all tied together and all belonged to one great family.

That is what some of the managers of big interests are finding out for themselves. If they found it out long ago there would not have been any trouble and we would not now have to use a whip to make them behave.

Mr. Wilson then insisted on the need of public opinion to be created by the people themselves. The people must think "outside of their occupations" and select men for office who will be of public service, and he said: "It is a game of matching"—matching men and public opinions. As a reason for forming correct public opinions in this State, Mr. Wilson said:

The attention of the country is concentrated at this moment—to judge by the newspapers from California to the Atlantic Coast—more upon the present contest in New Jersey than upon the contest anywhere else in the United States.

There are editorials being written from one side of this continent to the other about what may or may not happen in New Jersey, and every influential newspaper in the United States—almost without exception—wishes to see the old-fashioned organization at present misguiding the Republican voters of this State put out of business.

There is nothing personal in the thing. It is because they regard this as one of the battle centres, because they know the Republicans in New Jersey have not proposed anything new in their nominations, and that the Democrats in New Jersey have at least proposed something new.

It remains to be seen, after you have voted, whether they will give you something new or not.

Mr. Wilson said that "after all the tall talking I have done there will have to be some tall performing if the lightning should strike me. Nevertheless, I am in for it now and I have to take the risk. This is a very simple one; it is based on probabilities." The probabilities, he said, were as to whether the people were going to be fooled again or not. The people wanted, he believed, a person who "intends the same thing that you intend, who gives the best attention to it, and is free to do it."

Printed in the *Newark Evening News*, Oct. 22, 1910; some editorial headings omitted.
    [1] A physician who practiced with his brother, Isaac, in Phillipsburg. Thomas Barber was elected state senator from Warren County in 1911.

A Campaign Speech in Newton, New Jersey[1]

[[Oct. 22, 1910]]

MR. PRESIDENT,[2] LADIES AND GENTLEMEN. You have given me what I have learned to recognize as a true Sussex welcome, and I am sincerely obliged to you for it. It puts me in heart for the task of attempting to explain to you what it is that we are met together to consider, because this is not, as I have several times said, an ordinary campaign. It is not a campaign in which we are interested chiefly in the personality of the candidates, or in the filling of the offices. We are interested chiefly in what the candidates stand for and what the offices are to be used for. We realize that we are engaged in the people's cause. Nobody, I take it for granted, has ever seriously doubted that the sympathies of the Democratic party were the fundamental sympathies of the people. And the Democratic party, though it may from time to time have lapsed in its duty, has always had in its conscience this close, sympathetic connection with the great body of the people.

For we see stirring about us everywhere in America at this time very remarkable changes. This has been described as a year of Democratic opportunity. It may be described as a year of Republican opportunity, if the Republicans could only see the opportunity. But the difference between the two parties at the present juncture is that the one has and the other has not seen that this is the time for opportunity, particularly in the circumstances a more than ordinary time for opportunity. There never was a time when the voters were so detachable from their parties as they are in this particular year. That means that the old formulas, the principles of the two parties as they were once stated, has [have] not the same significance now that they once had and that men, feeling that the old old ties have not been definitely regulated, are holding themselves free to vote for ideas

    [1] Delivered in the Newton Public School.
    [2] Harvey Sylvester Hopkins, County Clerk of Sussex County and president of the Woodrow Wilson Club of Newton.

Newton, 22 Oct., 1910. –

Object not confined to New Jersey
        To draw the free and thinking Elements of
        the State and nation together to form and
        carry out common purposes.

To prevent Control
        What is graft?

Not jealous of governmental power but of
        Its private, selfish, wrong use

Strong classes can take care of themselves,
        Law must be the friend of the unprotected
                elements of society. *
        Law is the friend of the weak when purely and
        . conscientiously administered

Conservation vs. the strong and selfish.

New men, new measures
        Republican party has neither
                Called to them and they w'd not come.

——————
* Working - men have never controlled "machine"
        Why?

and for individuals rather than for parties. Don't you see how it quickens the pulse to think of such a time when the candidates of the people's favor stand for something besides a party name? Party names are things to conjure with, particularly the ancient name of the Democratic party, which is older than any other party name now in use in this country. But party names have, in some degree, in recent years, lost their magic.

Men will not wear party labels any longer; they attach themselves to causes; they seek to elevate persons who represent those causes. Even insincere men in some parts of this country are now masquerading in the handsome costume of great ideas, for great principles. You can see the things best displayed in the Republican party; you can see it best displayed in that party because that party has been long in power, and has, in the opinion of a growing number of persons in this country, misused its power. Therefore the most notable insurgents in this country are at present made up of Republicans who have seen that their party leaders have been leading them in directions which are not sanctioned by principles of that party any more than they are sanctioned by the principles of the Democratic party.

It does not mean that there are more independent men in the Republican ranks than there are in the Democratic ranks. But it means they are, therefore, the most notable sample of insurgents. Insurgency in the use of principles is displaying itself in the ranks of all parties at the present time. What does the opportunity consist in, therefore? It consists in drawing all free thinking persons together in a common undertaking. It consists in appealing to the men who think in the only way in which they can be appealed to—that is to say, by policies based upon thought, by policies based upon ideas, by policies based upon definite purposes.

I am not able to forecast the future of politics in America, but I know this much, that the party [that] raises the right standard first and raises it with united front and with enthusiasm is going to be the party to draw these free and thinking elements to itself. Some Republicans have sought to raise such a standard, but their party is divided, and they are not united in that handsome purpose.

The Democratic party is not divided, but is united in that purpose and has elevated that standard; and my prediction is, that the people of this country, seeing that circumstance, are going to flock to the Democratic banner, because that is the banner which now represents freedom and progress. That is the situation, a situation in which the country—the free, thinking, sober, ardent men of the country—are going to be drawn together in a common cause. That is the truth of which we are seeking to avail ourselves.

What is it that these people have got tired of? What is the cause in which they wish to be led? They have got tired of control; they have got tired of being dominated by any combination of men for whatever purpose, provided that combination of men shows itself devoted to particular interests instead of to the general interests.

They mean to throw off control which is exercised for the benefit of particular groups or classes of persons.

We talk a great deal about graft in our time. There are cynical persons who believe that graft is present in every walk of our life. Sometimes in moments of discouragement it looks like it, it looks as though every body in this country were looking for some pull, to exercise some influence, to get on the inside of some managing circle. I do not believe, except in moments of discouragement when my liver is out of order, that any such thing as that is true, but there are widespread notions prevailing of the thing which we call graft.

Graft is a big word. What do we mean by it? By graft, do you mean bribery? That is a very small proportion of graft. It springs up and stares us in the face occasionally in great investigations like that going on in the State of New York, and we are particularly interested to find that men should allow themselves to receive money to betray others.

That is, after all, not the principal part of graft, it is the easiest to stop because it is easier to prove, easier to condemn because it is so obvious. There are other kinds of graft that go deeper than that. Graft in its most general form means taking advantage of political power for your own benefit. That is what graft means.

Now, suppose there is no money in the case; suppose you are contributing considerable sums of money to a campaign fund or have contributed large sums of money to a campaign fund, and after the campaign is over you find party managers permitting certain items of legislation to go through unchallenged which are hurtful to your interest. What are you tempted to do? You are tempted to go to those managers and say, didn't I contribute to your campaign fund, why are you acting against my interests? Are you not my friend, and is there not another campaign coming sometime, and are you going to treat me this way? Have you never heard men expressly threatening never to contribute anything if certain things are done? Still, we have not got away from the grosser forms of graft. Graft is living on the public power by reason of your control of it. There is also something else.

Certain gentlemen in political life are what is known as "climbers"; they want to get up in the social scale and play in with the rich and fashionable, and if the rich and fashionable prey upon their political prospects they draw back, because the entree will not exist any longer in this circle that they are seeking. I remember a young man coming to me in college once and explaining to me that he was a very humble member of the college fraternity and did not have any pull. He did not seem to think he was saying anything offensive. I said: "What did you say, that you haven't any pull?" He said, "Yes." I said, "Has anybody got a pull here," and he flushed a little and said he thought some people had. I said, "If they had I didn't know anything about it." I said, "If you will bring me a case where anything has been done for anyone here which you consider in that line, I promise you on my word of honor as a gentleman, it will be corrected. Don't go about saying these things unless you can prove it, and if you prove it, in God's name bring it to me right away; there's no place where it will be more disgraceful in the whole world for a pull to exist than in an educational institution." He was speaking of which I include in the word "graft." Anything that can be privately obtained for a public power in the interest of private individuals or public individuals is graft, no matter what its form is, and it could not be obtained unless a small group of men control things.

You cannot tip off the voters of this State, you cannot go to the voters and obtain the influence you want for your private benefit. In order that there should be an opportunity of that sort, the control should rest in the hands of a comparatively small number of persons from whom you can go and give orders and the orders will issue to the rest. That is why we have come to dislike a political machine, not because it manages politics, but because it mixes in business, because it manages party power in the interest of those who are in business and for convenience.

These, then, are the things that the American people are utterly tired and disgusted about and that they mean to have stopped. Do you wonder that they are tired of this control? Is there anything to be said for it? When we try to control it, however, what is the situation? How are we going to control it?

I have said a great many times that it is a great mistake to set up one interest against another. Politics properly conducted do not constitute a warfare in which one class is waging war against another in order to obtain an advantage. Everything that is done in politics ought to be done in the common interest, looking at the people as a whole, without regard to class, in order that there may be an equality of opportunity and equality of burden. But, while that is theoretically the truth, this is practically true, that the strong classes, by which I mean the economically strong classes, can look out for themselves. I am not even intimating that they ought to be left to look out for themselves, because they are as much entitled to the defence of the law as anybody else is; but you don't have to be anxious about them—they are going to look out for themselves.

Law is intended in most instances to protect the unprotected classes, the classes that cannot look out for themselves. There is, therefore, a sense, gentlemen, in which the law is intended for the poor man, and when properly administered, is first of all and chiefly the poor man's friend; it is his buttress and his only buttress against imposition and wrong.

I want to point out to you a very interesting circumstance. You know that we are syeaking [speaking] constantly of the control which the capitalistic classes exercise over legislation—meaning the control which they exercise over the political machine. Has it ever been stated, even, that organized labor controlled the political machine? I have never heard it before stated. (A voice: Nor anybody else) Nobody has ever even supposed that organized labor could control the machine. But why? Can there be any other explanation than this—that the organizations of labor—even if they had the purpose to do these things, and they have never shown the purpose—do not command the resources which are the real bottom of graft. I mean that where the money is, there is the control, in plain language. And the fact that there has never been even suspected an alliance between organized labor and them shows that organized labor is more in need of the law, its justice, its purity, its integrity and its protection than the capitalistic classes are. Again, I want to say that nobody representing the true principles of organized labor would desire an advantage— an unfair advantage. I tell you frankly that the classes that need protection most are the classes that can exercise the influence— the wrong kind of influence—least. That is what I mean by saying the law should regard itself—and those who make it should regard it—as primarily the poor man's buttress and friend.

If I am trying to accommodate interests, it is not very difficult to find out what the interests are of those who do the most of the talking, but it is difficult to find out what the interests are of those who do very little talking or none at all. Therefore, the chief study of those who are to make a study of adjustment of the law ought to be the study of the silent and unprotected classes; and this whole struggle to overcome control is the struggle to re-establish the levels of the law—to see that the law fits the average man, that it fits the average conditions, that it fits those things that can be expressed in the terms of whole communities and whole bodies. That is the reason that it has become very striking and important; that in this very day of ours, it is these very voices that are beginning to be heard. These voices of the people as against the voices of the special interests.

I am not attacking special interests. I would be violating my own very fundamental principles if I were attacking any interests. I should feel it my duty, if I had any kind of governmental power, to accommodate interests to each other and be fair and just to all of them.

I am now merely expounding to you a set of circumstances and call your attention to the fact that the silent classes are more in need of the services of the law than the vociferous classes. We do not have to be told what the gentleman [gentlemen] who can write to the newspapers, and who can get admitted to the news-papers, want. We have to be told what those want and need, who do not get admitted to the newspapers and do not write, and do not inspire editorials, and do not have anything to do with those voices which are so audible from one end of the country to the other. It would be interesting if we could discuss all these matters.

For example, take the great question of conservatision [con-servation]. We are interested in this state in the preservation of our watershed[s,] their preservation from pollution, so that the watersheds which furnish us with drinking water shall not be polluted. We want to preserve them against deforestration [de-forestation] so that the streams will not go dry. What prevents our preserving them? Why, the selfishness of private owners, cer-tain men, certain water companies, for example—certain interests of one kind or another—that want to get control of these water-sheds and control and distribute and use up and pollute these waters. What does that illustrate? It illustrates the necessity of protecting those who are silent in this matter and have no money with which to buy up these rights and have no other means by which to prevent these things, to stand by them and prevent private selfishness from taking these common advantages away from them.

We want to regulate railway rates, and there is one natural way, in some parts of the State, of regulating railway rates which has been taken away from us. There are at least two great canal systems in this State.[3] Each of these systems has been got control of by a railway system that does not want the cheap transportation of the canals to compete with the more expensive transportation by rail, and those two systems of canals have practically been put out of business. Here is a case of conservation. These very railways are claiming that we do not give them leave to earn enough to multiply their rolling stock, to put in additional tracks, so that they can handle the enormous freightage of the country. Well, if the difficulty is in handling this enormous freightage, why do they put these natural highways of commerce out of business? If it is the service of the community that they seek, why do they try to destroy parallel lines and competition of all kinds? All of these, ladies and gentlemen, are public questions. They are not private questions, and they are questions of the protection of the people against the selfish control of limited numbers of people. Great railway systems are indispensible to the country. We do not want to make their operation unprofitable. We want to reward with a proper profit the men who invest their capital and invest it so intelligently, in most instances, in these great enterprises but we cannot allow them to go beyond that, we cannot allow them to become masters of our business.

The question of conservation, any question that you turn to, is a question of breaking up the control. The question of corrupt practices in elections is a matter of preventing corrupt control. The men who can manipulate an election by any means, by way of marking the ballots and by way of bribing the voter, are maintaining an illegitimate control over you; and it is the illegitimacy of control that excites our envy and excited our determination to break it up. If the voters decide the wrong way, there is nothing corrupt in that. They may change their opinion at some time, but if they have not decided it that way, if votes are found to make majorities after the polls are closed, then who has supplied the majority is the determinable question. Majorities have been fo[u]nd in parts of this State which I can name after the polls were closed. (A voice: "So can I. Burlington County.")

And so, in general terms, ladies and gentlemen, what we are after is to reorganize freedom; we are after recovering for the people, to whom it belongs, the control of the affairs of this country. How are you going to do it? (A voice: "You're all right.")

---

[3] The sixty-seven-mile Delaware and Raritan Canal from Bordentown to New Brunswick, leased to the Pennsylvania Railroad, and the 106-mile Morris Canal from Jersey City to Phillipsburg, leased to the Lehigh Valley Railroad.

Why, you must do it by insisting upon new motives, and in order to be sure that the new methods really are used, by insisting upon new men.

A method is a very tenacious and a very contagious thing. If you have once adopted the habit of using a particular method, it takes a surgical operation to change it. If you want a new method, irrespective of whether you think the men are corrupt or honest, honorable or dishonorable—if you want a new method, you have got to get new men.

What I am saying, and what I am justified in saying, is that the Republican party of this State is offering you neither new methods or new men.

The Democratic party, I make bold to say, is offering you both new methods and new men. If you want to break up the control you have the opportunity to do so. I do not entertain the slightest doubt that Sussex county wants to break it up, but I am very interested in assisting you, if I can assist you, by telling you the way you want to break it up. Not on the principle "turn the rascals out," for there is nothing in that; but on the principle of recovering, in some degree, that control of your affairs which belongs to the traditions of America.

It seems very interesting to me, ladies and gentlemen, that we are constantly illustrating what that old generation represented by the great man whose bust is on my right—and for that matter, whose bust is on my left[4]—was so constantly intent upon. You must remember what you have heard, in patriotic speech after patriotic speech, that the men that lived in that time said it was constantly necessary to refer to independent principles. Now, that sounds like an abstract matter.

You know about what some of the Republican speakers have said of me dealing in generalities and abstract principles. Well, we are built on principles, and if the Republican orators don't know how to handle them, it is because they have not used them in so long. Now, it sounds very abstract to say, in regard to fundamental principles, "What do you mean by fundamental principles?" We don't mean anything strictly intellectual; it is not something you have to reason out. America was not built as an intellectual structure; it was built as a heart structure; it was built on the sympathies of all sorts and conditions of men; it was meant to be an asylum for those who could not get their rights anywhere else; it was meant as a home for men who could not find opportunity anywhere else; it was meant as a gathering

---

[4] A large bust of Washington was on Wilson's right and one of Lincoln on his left.

place for [men] of all nations who wanted to have principles, right and equality recognized and applied in their case. That is what I understand to be the fundamental principle. But that is not intellectual; that is based on the principle of brotherhood, it is based on the principle of what underlies brotherhood, namely, sympathetic understanding.

No man is fit to be a popular leader who cannot put himself at the point of view of every class of men, with the desire of his heart to understand it, not only, but to serve the real interests of a class of persons from their own point of view. You know how it is in friendships; nothing hurts you so much as to have a friend who don't understand why you do a thing, and to have to ask him, "Why, don't you understand me better than that?" That is what hurts.

And the loneliness of the thing consists in the fact that there is a little citadel inside of him somewhere, which nobody else can enter, and that there is something which nobody, not even those nearest and dearest to us, can quite comprehend. We are held apart from each other by our stubborn individuality and nobody can shoot back the bolt from that door. But our happiness consists in the fact that we do for our neighbors, that we love them and help them and will help them, that we love our town and our counties and our cities, that we love the nation, and we are bound together, by an indissoluable tie, to each other.

All of that is sentimental; it does not consist of a body of reasoning. The government of Germany suits the Germans better than the government of America would suit the Germans; and there is just as much reason, I take leave to say, in one love as in the other. But America is built upon our sympathies; it is built upno [upon] our circumstances; it is built upon our lives; it is built upon us—in short[—]and the structure is the structure of our own hearts. And, therefore, no man can give us anything so acceptable as the principles of this beloved home of ours.

That is the reason why America is moving along the whole body politic, in a common interest. It is this common impulse, this insurrectional spirit, this yearning after principles for America to come back and get translated into the politics that is moving the whole body of America at this time, and which will cause a revival of the spirit of politics, which I hope and pray may be embodied in the policies and affairs of the Democratic party.

Printed in the Newton, N. J., *New Jersey Herald and Sussex County Democrat*, Oct. 27, 1910.

From William Francis Magie

My dear Tommy,   Princeton [N. J.] Oct 22, 1910

I cannot let you go into your new life without telling you how much I regret the severance of the bonds which have linked us together so long in the University. My outlook has been so limited by University boundaries that I never thought of one of us as likely to go outside into other work, and your decision to do so & to give up your work here was a shock to my feelings.

I wish you all manner of success in your public career, & I want you to know that however much our views on questions may have differed you have had & will always have my sincere regard and affection.   Yours faithfully   W. F. Magie

ALS (WP, DLC).

From Bliss Perry

Dear Woodrow Wilson: Cambridge [Mass.], 22 Oct 1910

I can't see you go out of the Princeton Presidency and into the Governorship without a word to let you know that I,—like so many other friends of yours who are individually lost in the cloud of witnesses—have been following your recent decisions with the keenest interest and with affectionate good will. I was reluctant to accept the idea of your leaving the Presidency, because one living at a distance can see, as those embroiled in controversy cannot, the immense service which you have rendered to the academic world by your years of leadership. The place which Princeton now holds among American universities is due very largely to your individual efforts. I hoped that you would stay in office until even the stupidest of your local critics could see what you were driving at; but since you have made the other choice, you must let me offer my warmest personal wishes for your happiness and success in politics.

Please give my greetings to Mrs. Wilson, & believe me
                    Faithfully yours   Bliss Perry

ALS (WP, DLC).

To George Lawrence Record

My dear Mr. Record: Princeton, N. J., October 24th, 1910.

I am sincerely sorry that I have been obliged to wait so long before replying to your letter of the seventeenth. The delay has been due entirely to the fact of my necessary absorption in the actual engagements of the campaign.

In order to reply as clearly as possible to your questions, I will quote them and append the answers.

1. "That the public utilities commission should have full power to fix just and reasonable rates to be charged by all public service corporations. Do you favor this?" Yes.

2. "That the physical property of each public utility corporation which is devoted to a public use should be valued by the State. Do you favor this?" Yes.

3. "That such physical valuation should be taken as the assessment upon which such corporations shall pay local taxes. Do you favor this?" Yes.

4. "That such valuation should be used as a basis for fixing rates to be charged by these corporations and that such rates should be so limited as to allow them to earn not exceeding six per cent. upon this valuation. Do you favor this?" No. I think that such valuation should form a very important part of the basis upon which rates should be fixed, but not the whole basis. All the financial, physical, and economic circumstances of the business should be taken into consideration. The percentage of profit allowed should be determined by the commission after full inquiry, and not by statute.

5. "That the present primary law should be extended to the selection of candidates for party nominations for governor, congressmen, and delegates to national conventions. Do you favor this?" Yes, though I should wish a better primary law than the present.

6. "That United States Senators should be elected by popular vote. Do you favor this?" Yes.

7. "To apply this principle, I favor a law compelling all candidates for nomination to the legislature to file a pledge to vote for that candidate of their party for United States Senator who shall receive the highest number of votes under the present primary law. Do you favor this?" In principle Yes; but I fear that a law "compelling" this would be unconstitutional. Surely the voters can exact this pledge, and have the matter in their own hands. A better primary law than the present would facilitate this exaction on the part of the voters by obliging the candidate for the state legislature to state his intention in this matter when accepting his own nomination.

8. "That the names of all candidates at elections should be printed on a blanket ballot, and that all ballots shall be distributed to the voter by mail at public expense, or confined to the polling

place. Do you favor this?" I believe that the ballots should be given out only at the polling places and only by the election officers; and that, while the blanket ballot is the best form yet devised, experience has proved that it is best to put some indication of the source of the nomination after each name. A mere alphabetical list results usually in the election of the top of the alphabet; and there are actually cases on record of would-be candidates who have had their names changed to begin with the first letter of the alphabet in order to increase their chances of election. Amidst a multitude of names, on our long ballots, the ordinary voter needs some guidance.

9. "That primary and election officers should be appointed by some impartial agency, like a court. Do you favor this?" Yes.

10. "There should be a drastic corrupt practices act, forbidding all political expenditures except for the objects named in the act, with drastic penalties for the violation of the act; prohibiting the employment of more than two workers or watchers at the polls on primary or election day representing any one party, or group of candidates; prohibiting the hiring of vehicles for transporting voters; limiting the amount to be expended by candidates; prohibiting political contributions by corporations. Do you favor this?["] Yes.

11. "That every industry employing workmen shall be compelled to bear the expense of all injuries to employees which happen in the industry without wilful negligence of such employees. Do you favor this?["] Yes.

12. "That the County Board of Elections law and the Hillery maximum tax law should be repealed. Do you favor this?" Yes.

13. "Does the Democratic platform declare for the choice of candidates for all elective offices by the direct vote system?" Yes; I so understand it. If it does not, I do.

14. "Do you admit that the boss system exists as I have described it? If so, how do you propose to abolish it?" Of course I admit it. Its existence is notorious. I have made it my business for many years to observe and understand that system, and I hate it as thoroughly as I understand it. You are quite right in saying that the system is bi-partisan; that it constitutes "the most dangerous condition in the public life of our State and nation today"; and that it has virtually, for the time being, "destroyed representative government and in its place set up a government of privilege." I would propose to abolish it by the above reforms, by the election to office of men who will refuse to submit to it and bend all their energies to break it up, and by pitiless publicity.

15. "In referring to the Board of Guardians, do you mean such

Republican leaders as Baird, Murphy, Kean, and Stokes? Wherein do the relations to the special interests of such leaders differ from the relations to the same interests of such Democratic leaders as Smith, Nugent, and Davis?" I refer to the men you name. They differ from the others in this, that they are in control of the government of the State while the others are not and cannot be if the present Democratic ticket is elected.

16. "I join you in condemning the Republican Board of Guardians. I have been fighting them for years and shall continue to fight them. Will you join me in denouncing the Democratic Overlords, as parties to the same political system? If not, why not?" Certainly! I will join you or any one else in denouncing and fighting any and every one, of either party, who attempts such outrages against the government and public morality.

17. "You say the Democratic party has been reorganized, and the Republican party has not. Can a political party be reorganized without changing either its leaders, or its old leaders changing their point of view and their political character? Will you claim that either of these events has taken place in the Democratic party? If yes, upon what do you base that conclusion?" I do not remember saying that the Democratic party had been reorganized. I remember saying that it was seeking reorganization, and was therefore at the threshold of a new era. I said this because it is seeking to change its leaders, and will obviously change them if successful in this election. If I am elected, I shall understand that I am chosen leader of my party and the direct representative of the whole people in the conduct of the government. All of this was distinctly understood at the very outset, when my nomination was first proposed, and there has never been the slightest intimation from any quarter to the contrary since. The Republican party is not seeking to change its leaders, and, therefore, is not even seeking reorganization.

18. "Is there any organized movement in the Democratic party in this State which corresponds to the Progressive Republican movement of which you have favorably spoken?" I understand the present platform and the present principal nominations of the Democratic party in this State to be such an organized movement. It will be more fully organized if those nominees are elected. This is, as I interpret it, the spirit of the whole remarkable Democratic revival which we are witnessing not only in New Jersey but in many other States.

Before I pass to the next question, will you not permit me to frame one which you have not asked but which I am sure lies implied in those I have just answered? You wish to know what

All of this was distinctly understood at the very outset when my nomination was first proposed and there has never been the slightest

and fighting any and every one, of either party, who attempts such outrages
against the government and public morality.

17. "You say the Democratic party has been reorganized, and the Republican party has not. Can a political party be reorganized without changing
either its leaders, or its old leaders changing their point of view and their
political character? Will you claim that either of these events has taken
place in the Democratic party? If yes, upon what do you base that conclusion?"
I do not remember saying that the Democratic party had been reorganized. I
remember saying that it was seeking reorganization, and was therefore at the
threshold of a new era. I said this because it is seeking to change its leaders, and will obviously change them if successful in this election. The Republican party is not seeking to change its leaders, and, therefore, is not
even seeking reorganization.

18. "Is there any organized movement in the Democratic party in this
State which corresponds to the Progressive Republican movement, of which you
have favorably spoken?" I understand the present platform and the present
principal
~~principal~~ nominations of the Democratic party in this State to be such an organized movement. It will be more fully organized if those nominees are elected. This
is, as I interpret it, the sprit of the whole remarkable Democratic revival
which we are witnessing not only in New Jersey but in many other States.

Before I pass to the next question, will you not permit me to frame one
which you have not asked but which I am sure lies implied in those I have just
answered? You wish to know what my relations would be *whose power and influence* with the Democrats you
fear, should I be elected Governor, particularly in such important matters as
appointments and the signing of bills, and I am very glad to tell you. *(over)*
~~They would be entitled to advise me as any other citizen would, but no more entitled,~~
~~and I would treat their advice upon its merits and entirely from the point of~~
~~view of the public interest. I would not only welcome but seek the advice of~~
~~many others. I would not always obey my own judgment and with absolute inde-~~
~~pendence. I have absolutely no connection with or obligation to any political~~
~~leader or organization whatever, and~~ should deem myself forever disgraced
should I in even the slightest degree coöperate in any such *any such* ~~system of~~ transactions as you describe in your characterization of the "boss" system. I regard myself as pledged to the ~~reorientation~~ *regeneration* of the Democratic party *which* I have
~~just~~ forecast above.

19. "Will you agree to publicly call upon the Republican and Democratic
candidates for the legislature to pledge themselves in writing prior to election in favor of such of the foregoing reforms as you personally favor? If
not, why not?". I will not. Because I think it would be most unbecoming in
me to do so. That is the function of the voters in the several counties. Let
them test and judge the men, and choose those who are sincere.

Allow me to thank you for this opportunity to express with the greatest possible definiteness my convictions upon the issues of the present campaign, and also for your very kind expressions of confidence and regard,
which I highly appreciate.

Sincerely Yours

Woodrow Wilson

*Third page of the first draft of Wilson's letter
to George L. Record*

my relations would be with the Democrats whose power and influence you fear, should I be elected Governor, particularly in such important matters as appointments and the signing of bills, and I am very glad to tell you. If elected, I shall not, either in the matter of appointments to office or assent to legislation, or in shaping any part of the policy of my administration, submit to the dictation of any person or persons, special interest, or organization. I will always welcome advice and suggestions from any citizen, whether boss, leader, organization man or plain citizen, and I shall constantly seek the advice of influential and disinterested men, representative of their communities and disconnected from political "organizations" entirely; but all suggestions and all advice will be considered on their merits, and no additional weight will be given to any man's advice or suggestion because of his exercising or supposing that he exercises some sort of political influence or control. I should deem myself forever disgraced should I in even the slightest degree cooperate in any such system or any such transactions as you describe in your characterization of the "boss" system. I regard myself as pledged to the regeneration of the Democratic party which I have forecast above.

19. "Will you agree to publicly call upon the Republican and Democratic candidates for the legislature to pledge themselves in writing prior to election in favor of such of the foregoing reforms as you personally favor? If not, why not?" I will not. Because I think it would be most unbecoming in me to do so. That is the function of the voters in the several counties. Let them test and judge the men, and choose those who are sincere.

Allow me to thank you for this opportunity to express with the greatest possible definiteness my convictions upon the issues of the present campaign, and also for your very kind expressions of confidence and regard, which I highly appreciate.

Sincerely yours, [Woodrow Wilson][1]

CCL (WP, DLC).
1 There is a WWT draft of this letter with numerous WWhw emendations in WP, DLC. Wilson also wrote most of his brief answers in shorthand on the face of Record's letter printed at Oct. 17, 1910.

A News Report

[Oct. 24, 1910]

CAMDEN WILL HEAR WILSON

To Talk There Twice To-night.
Confident After North Jersey Tour.

WILL SOON REPLY TO RECORD

PRINCETON, Oct. 24.—With two weeks more of the campaign for Governor ahead of him, Woodrow Wilson will speak twice to-night in Camden. To-morrow night he will go to Salem; Wednesday he will be in New Brunswick; Thursday he will deliver three talks in Bergen County, at Rutherford in the late afternoon, in Englewood at 8 o'clock and in Hackensack at 9 o'clock; Friday, two talks in Elizabeth and probably one in Bayonne, and Saturday night in Hoboken.

Next Monday had been open until late last week, when Chairman James Hennessey, of the Hudson County committee, obtained consent to have Mr. Wilson speak again in Jersey City. At that meeting Mayor Otto Wittpenn will preside, so as to show personally and publicly that he is heartily in favor of the election of Wilson.

The remainder of next week will be devoted to Passaic, Morris, Middlesex and Essex counties. Mr. Wilson will speak in the Oranges and other suburban towns of Essex November 2. What is planned to be the closing speech of the campaign will be delivered in this city [Newark] November 5, the Saturday night preceding election day.

Dr. Wilson devoted himself to-day to details regarding his removal from Prospect, the home he had occupied as president of Princeton University, the office from which he resigned last Thursday. He also found a big accumulation of correspondence to deal with.

Mr. Wilson will probably send to George L. Record his reply to that gentleman's letter. Mr. Wilson, however, will not give out the letter unless he changes his mind as it is made up at present. He will let Mr. Record make it public if he likes. He believes that the addressee of a letter should be the one to make a letter public. The letter to Mr. Record will constitute a reply also to the specific questions put to him by James G. Blauvelt, of Paterson.

Physically Mr. Wilson has stood the work of campaigning wonderfully well for one who had not previously engaged in it. His voice shows no effect of strain after his speeches. Sometimes of late, during a speech, he suffers from a passing huskiness, but it is only momentary.

Mr. Wilson made two speeches in Sussex, in Sussex Borough and Newton, Saturday, and held receptions in Andover, Sparta, Franklin Furnace, Ogdensburg, Hamburg, Branchville and Lafayette. Although the day was miserably rainy crowds turned out in each place. About 400 persons heard the speech in Sussex and about 1,200 in Newton.

In the former speech he said it was necessary for the people to pay constant attention to the work of the men they elect to office, and he said:

"You can't allow any man to go too long unwatched. If you elect me Governor, keep your eyes on me. Remind me to do the things that during this campaign I have promised to do, so as far as I am able."

Printed in the *Newark Evening News*, Oct. 24, 1910.

A News Report of Campaign Addresses in Camden, New Jersey

[Oct. 25, 1910]

WILSON FREE OF ALLIANCES

Mercilessly Flays Machine Control in Camden,
Hotbed of Machine Politics.

It remained for Woodrow Wilson to give to the city of Camden the largest political gathering in its history, last night. And in that hot-bed of Machine politics he flayed the alliance of the political Machine with the special interests in a manner that must have made some of his Republican auditors wince, for there were among his hearers no small number of officeholders who must have realized fully just what he was driving at, as everybody else understood. So great was the pressure to see and hear this new leader of men that the Democratic managers were forced to arrange for two meetings, and two addresses by this new sort of candidate for Governor, who is setting New Jersey ablaze. He spoke in the Temple Theatre, uptown, and the Broadway Theatre, downtown, and in both the houses the jam was so great that men could scarcely breathe. Uptown an overflow meeting was arranged, the speakers talking to 2000 more persons congregated in Market street, from a platform hastily devised upon a truck. In all some 7000 persons must have gathered, and Mr. Wilson reached at least 4000 of them with the electric thrill of his masterly voice, the magnetism of his presence and the influence of his great mind and heart. And to that immense throng the sturdy man whose courage is so refreshing gave voice to this declaration

Camden, 24 Oct., 1910.

Deterioration of parties and means → machines.
The boss system: patronage — orders.
The grip of party: its object non-partisan

The cleaning up in many States
The issue in New Jersey: reorganization, regen-
~~ganization~~ creation.

If elected, I sh. regard myself as
chosen leader of party and representative of
whole people in conduct of government

Means: Control of corporations
Corrupt practices act
Direct primaries (veto ignored)
Simplification of administration
Judicial appointments
Leadership (on merits of questions)
Pitiless publicity

A renascence of public opinion.

10/24/10.

of independence, a plain, straightforward expression of his attitude toward the men who are supposed to have worked out his selection:

"I want to say, therefore, that I understand the present campaign to mean this, that if I am elected Governor I shall have been elected leader of my party and shall have been elected Governor of all the people of New Jersey, to conduct the government in their interest and in their interest only, using party and party coherents for that service. If the Democratic party does not understand it in that way, then I want to say to you very frankly that the Democratic party ought not to elect me Governor. When I was approached with regard to the nomination for the Governorship I understood it to be distinctly represented to me that the purpose of those who asked my leave to use my name for that purpose was that I should be invited to take the leadership of the Democratic party. If they do not understand it they ought to withdraw the invitation on the eighth day of November.

"I am not claiming that I am qualified for leadership—that is not the point; but I am claiming that I did not seek the leadership, and that I was asked to take it, but that I was asked to take it with the understanding that I was absolutely free from pledges and obligations of any kind. Now, I have been asked if I have said that the Democratic party has been reorganized. No, I have not said that; I have said that the Democratic party is seeking reorganization. It depends on the voters on the eighth day of November whether it gets it or not. That is the issue. If you think I am a suitable leader and that my leadership will produce a reorganization and that I can put that party upon a new footing and give it new objects, then it is clearly your duty to support me; but if you do not think so, then I must just as frankly say that it is as clearly your duty not to support me. The only thing about it, when I say that, is that I don't know what you are going to do if you don't because, on the other side there is no principle, or any kind of reorganization. So, if it is reorganization, a new deal and a change you are seeking, it is Hobson's choice. I am sorry for you, but it is really vote for me or not vote at all."

This declaration came almost at the end of his impressive address uptown, and it brought from the immense audience a great and powerful expression that it had gone home, replying to the criticism of those who take particular delight in alluding to the past records of the Democrats as a piece of what may be expected under the administration of Woodrow Wilson in case of his election. It is supposed also to be the epitome of the answer to George L. Record, the Hudson county "Progressive" candidate for Congress, who queried Mr. Wilson upon nearly all the topics upon which he has made himself very plain in his addresses in the campaign. The presumably unanswerable query put to Mr. Wilson was as to his party's record, and his reply, instantly recognized by the vast assemblage, was regarded as a triumph for the candidate who has previously declared his freedom in no uncertain language.

Nobody in Camden ever saw the parallel of last night's great double demonstration. It simply dazed the leaders of the Republican machine, who had clung to some faint hope that perhaps enthusiastic admirers of the opposing candidate for Governor had been injecting a little effective "color" into their reports of his receptions and the effect of his speeches in other sections of the State. They had no difficulty in discovering that there had been no deception. Camden, confidently looked forward to for its usual 6000 or 7000 majority for Banking Commissioner Lewis, was astir from Pyne Poynt to Line Ditch, and the people went wild in their efforts to see and hear Woodrow Wilson. There was a parade of clubs, and 300 first voters were among the marchers, but when they got to the Temple Theatre only half of them could get in to seats reserved for them. The rest had to join the crowd out on the street. The theatre was so closely jammed that not another nose could be squeezed into an aperture, and the enthusiasm fairly oozed from the crowd.

In the boxes were a number of men and women prominent socially and most of them usually allied with the Republican party, but now devoted to the cause of Wilson and his new kind of campaign. The meeting was called to order by County Chairman William H. Davis, who presented former Judge Howard Carrow as chairman and Mr. Carrow, in the full vigor of his resonant voice, aroused the great crowd to heights of enthusiasm in his introduction of the speaker as the leader of the new thought in American political endeavor, the greatest mind before the people of the nation to-day, a man who had never been identified with politics, except as a teacher of the youth of the land, and who was free of all alliances, "the next Governor of New Jersey!"

As Mr. Wilson stepped to the front of the brightly-lighted and handsomely-decorated stage the great assemblage arose as one man and cheered and cheered the man who loomed so strong before them. It was one of the most demonstrative receptions he had yet received and it moved him deeply. It was some seconds before he could proceed with his address, and then it could be seen that his heart was swelling with the sentiments that swayed him.

"I have met a great many audiences in this State in this campaign, and the interesting thing to me is that they all look alike, which I suppose shows that they are all of the true Jersey breed; but they look alike in this respect, that they do not seem to have come together for a trifling object like mere curiosity; there is a look in their faces as if they thought some new business was astir and some business is astir. Two week[s] from to-morrow the election will come. We are on the home stretch and we are bound for home; we are bound for the place from which the Democratic party has been long excluded, but where, I will venture to assert, it has long belonged. There is an unmistakable increase in warmth and ardor as we approach the day of conquest. There is a necessary examination of our own purposes of mind as to what we intend to do, and I congratulate this body of first voters in front of me, that they are going to cast their votes for the first time in such a free year, in a year of such freedom of choice, in a year when party lines are not sharply drawn, when men are chosen not as between parties, but, I believe in my heart, chosen for the future of America.

"I do not need to tell the citizens of Camden county what the boss system is. You know a boss when you see him, and you have plenty of opportunities to see him. You know, as well as I do, that the boss system has nothing to do with political questions. There was a very astute ward politician in the city of New York who said 'There ain't no politics in politics,' by which he meant that when you are discussing the matter of who are going to have the offices and exercise the power, nobody is interested in public questions; men do not differ with each other as to public policies. Those are things, from the point of view of such politicians, to be talked of on the stump, to take in, to fool, to mislead the dear public, as they call them behind locked doors. The real thing to be discussed is a thing that can be discussed between the two machines without any feeling that there is any political difference between them. It is how to get hold of the spoils of office and keep them. And the boss system is backed in this endeavor by all sorts of power that ought never to be used in the field of politics. There are men here who can bear testimony to the fact that they dare not vote as they think, because of the terrorizing that some political leaders are able to exercise. There are some men here who can testify that they cannot borrow money at certain banks if they do not vote a certain particular political ticket. Give political bosses and political machines offices enough to distribute, business enterprises enough to subscribe to their funds, business connections enough to terrorize great bodies of employes—and they will defy you to turn them out of office. Give them, in addition to that, Grand Juries that never find true bills in political cases and public prosecutors who never try to get true bills, and the system is complete.

"It is generally supposed that men who closet themselves, as they like to say, in colleges, do not know what is going on in the actual world. We do not study politics in college out of books; we study it out of life and out of facts. We know the calibre and the character and the motives of those men and can produce you the witnesses.

"Is this the Republican party of the county of Camden? This county is the home of men who from honorable principles as well as from long tradition have voted the Republican ticket—have voted it because of their character, adhering to it as to family traditions and to the great historical principles of a party which in the past have rendered the country a great service. But do these men accept such things and such organizations as the representatives of the Republican party? This is not the Republican party; it isn't any party. 'There ain't no politics in politics.' These men devoted to the traditions of the party of Lincoln, these men devoted to those great principles which that great party originated to defend, and has sought to defend in all its honest numbers ever since. They have no thought or care for any principle or historic recollections of any kind; they are in the game for what it is worth.

"You know the objects of Machine government. The objects of Machine government are to prevent anything being done that will be inimical to certain interests, and to get everything done which is advantageous to certain interests. By certain interests I mean business interests, not political interests. The Machine is a partnership, an illegitimate and abominable partnership, between business and politics. Now the day when this thing can exist is past. The American people know it, and the American people are not going to permit it a single twelve-month more."

Alluding to the operation of the Machine in legislation and referring to the New York exposure, Mr. Wilson said:

"You know there is only one thing about us that is immortal in this world, and that is our reputation. It does not make any difference after these exposures whether the men are put behind prison walls or not. They have forever violated their faith, and that kind of treatment is being prepared everywhere for that kind of men. Everywhere there has been a cleaning up, a cleaning of house, an absolute repudiation of all politics of that sort from one end of the United States to the other. I don't mean everywhere, but, taking the country by samples in other sections of it, there has been a repudiation of it, and don't you hear the thunder of the wave that comes on? Do you suppose this beach we stand on can remain dry much longer? Do you suppose that tide is going to be stopped because some man lifts his hand and protests and asks it to come no further? If you want to escape being engulfed you better retire from the reach of the sea, and there is no place to go, because the sea is human opinion, the sea is the discovery of seeing things and the overwhelming power is the overwhelming condemnation that will fall upon such men upon their discovery.

"The tide is coming in. Let those who don't know how to swim and keep their heads above water look to it.

"I know how it happens. These things drift in great drifts, as they do in politics; men do not see in which way they are moving, and everybody about them is doing the same thing. Some people think that everything is graft. Now, of course, there isn't graft in everything; we have not grown morally rotten; but there is a subtle kind of growth in a great many things. Whenever you get somebody with influence to do something that somebody else without influence cannot do, that is graft.

"I was sitting in the waiting room of an eminent surgeon one afternoon a few years ago, waiting for my turn to consult him, and I waited there for three mortal hours; and in the meantime I saw several very much more fashionably dressed people than I was take precedence over me, and I was sure that they had no prior engagement with the doctor. Now, that was graft. There is every kind of graft, from the graft which is induced by the handsome dress and the beauty of a distinguished-looking woman to the graft produced by the actual handling of hard cash. All influences that ought not to exist, all inequalities produced by 'working' some fellow, is graft.

"And so every time you wink at a friend and say 'That is all right; I will fix it up for you; I will see that you get in'—you are beginning on the road which ends at the place that I have described, and I warn you—I warn you to keep off, because the American people have their eye on you, and they are getting intolerant of that kind of thing, and you must not carry it too far."

Mr. Wilson made a great hit with his auditors by this humorous, but pointed allusion to his own candidacy: "Now, the chairman has said that the Democratic party has picked out a man whose orbit cannot be calculated. The Republicans are looking at him askance. They say: 'Who is this? A schoolmaster, a gentleman who never before took any part in politics, or offered to take any part in politics, who has enjoyed the luxury for a great many years of going about the country and expressing opinions for which he could not be held responsible.' Now, 'who in the world,' they say, 'can tell what this man is going to do?' There have been many predictions, all the way from the prediction that he would not do anything, to the prediction that if he got there, there would not be anything left of the government, the last prediction having been made by a sage statesman of the city of Camden.[1] Well, I hope that when the Democratic candidate gets there, there will not be anything left of a certain kind of government, the kind of government with which the said sage statesman is most familiar. But I am not in the least surprised they have disturbed thoughts about the Democratic candidate. I know what his intentions are, but I cannot tell what his performances are going to be. You have got to take a sportsman's chance and risk it, but I can promise you this, that it will not be dull; it will be interesting. I doubt if it will be as interesting to you as it will be to me, but it will be interesting. There is one thing to which the candidate himself can testify. He can tell you confidentially that he knows a thing or two, that he is not as innocent as he looks, and that he is not as young as he looks. All of which, turning from jest to earnest, means this, that the Democratic party is attempting a new leadership and a new organization, and the Republican party is not. With such a candidate, so inexperienced in machine politics, and unable to understand them, it is impossible that the Democracy should run politics upon the machine basis. Their chief instrumentality would be too clumsy and bungling; whereas, it is perfectly feasible and highly likely, that the Republican organization would continue business at the old stand and in the old way."

From this his deduction was that the way to break up this unholy alliance is through a corrupt practices' act that will reveal and correct the evil, and a direct primary act that will give the people a chance to choose officers who will execute the laws. To this he added:

"There isn't a single reform that is interesting us in the present campaign that does not swing back upon this boss system of political control and political alliance that we want to break up. But it is not sufficient to have statutes on the books. Statutes don't work themselves. And I would rather have men who intend to serve the public trying to work a body of bad statutes than men who don't mean to serve the public in trying to work a body of

[1] He referred undoubtedly to David Baird.

good statutes. Your salvation does not lie in statutes; it lies in the men, and the men who can serve you are the men who depend upon you for political results. They want to work and not upon the machine.["]

After Mr. Wilson had concluded he was whirled away to the Broadway Theatre and his Temple audience was addressed by former Mayor Katzenbach, of Trenton, and former Mayor Nowrey, of Camden, the candidate for Congress,[2] both of whom were given strong ovations. At the Broadway Theatre Mr. Wilson encountered the same big crowd, only bigger, that [than] his first audience, and it was, if anything, more demonstrative. The meeting was called to order by William C. French,[3] and former Judge Wescott was chairman. Previous to the arrival of Mr. Wilson an address was made by Colonel Alexander Bacon, of New York,[4] and by former Mayor Katzenbach and former Mayor Nowrey, who were then taken to the Temple meeting.

A delegation of 200 students of the University of Pennsylvania, under the leadership of Chatford Smith, of the Medical School, attended the meeting at the Broadway Theatre, having been crowded out of the Temple. These men are enthusiastic followers of President Wilson and joined with the large delegation of Princeton men who are attending the professional schools at Pennsylvania in giving him a rousing reception.

Printed in the *Philadelphia Record*, Oct. 25, 1910; some editorial headings omitted.

  [2] Joseph E. Nowrey, Mayor of Camden, 1902-1905. He was defeated in his race for Congress.

  [3] William Collins French, Camden lawyer and member of the Camden County Democratic Committee, who was appointed by Wilson to the bench of the Camden County District Court in 1912.

  [4] Alexander Samuel Bacon, New York lawyer, vice-president and director of the Webster Piano Co., and colonel in the New York National Guard.

To Harry Augustus Garfield

The Bellevue-Stratford

Dear Garfield,   Philadelphia 25 Oct., 1910

Are you still looking for a Professor of English Literature? I think Axson would like now to get away from Princeton.

I am in the midst of the hardest and most interesting job I ever undertook.

In great haste,

Affectionately Yours,   Woodrow Wilson

ALS (H. A. Garfield Papers, DLC).

Salem, 25 Oct., 1910.

Candidatio?
Doctrine of Election
Experiences of a Candidate
    Attacks personal and inconsistent (2 ∨ ∽)
    E.g. Labor arguments = (Plentiful lack of wit.)
Why are the opposition so sorely put to it?
    Why orders in Camden for additional padding?
Because unfaithful to traditions and policy of
    their party. — A policy becomes a partnership
    This "fifth Phila. district"?
Democratic party may have been betrayed into such
    alliances on occasion, but no such tradition
Now faces a new day — with new Candidates and
    therefore with new programmes.
    Unless you suppose the "leaders" fools and
        the candidate an easy dupe, ∘ ⌣ ⌐)
Parties distinguished not so much by programmes
    as by evidences of sincerity.
If you want — g ∽ — Exercise a sovereign act.
    A sovereign people what?
Here tradition unbroken / ⟋ 10/25/10

A Campaign Speech in Salem, New Jersey[1]

October 25, 1910.

Mr. Chairman,[2] Ladies and Gentlemen: I find that for some reason the novelty of these singular appearances does not wear off. I have entered upon the fifth week of my campaign; I have had many audiences facing me seriously, as this audience is facing me, for a discussion of the really momentous issues of the present campaign, and yet every time I stand up I feel the novelty of it and the singularity of it, and the very deep interest of it. I have never before been a candidate for an office. I am not like the gentlemen in Mississippi of whom I have heard. You know most of the Southern members of Congress after the war bore either illegitimately or otherwise some military title, nobody less than a Major, but a certain member from Mississippi was distinguished as a private, John Adams,[3] for he had never received a higher rank in the Confederate Army. He tells how he went in the home of his childhood where his father lived and where he himself lived only a few years after his birth, and was conversing with an old negro woman who had lived in his father's family, and he asked a few questions about his father. He said, "What did my father do?" She said, "The same as you, same profession as you have, sir, candidating, sir, candidating." Now, I don't feel that I have gone so far as to have myself accused of being a candidate by profession. I am serving my noviatite [novitiate] in that capacity.

I am reminded, in playing the role of a candidate, of a story that I heard. There was once in North Carolina a very eminent man; first he was governor and afterwards he was Senator, and was known to the country as Senator [Zebulon Baird] Vance of North Carolina. He was not, himself, a member of the Presbyterian church, though his wife was, and he said he expected to get into heaven by holding to her skirts. But he was trying to convert his negro, Sambo, and the old darky said, "Oh, no, Massa, I don't like that kind of an election." "Oh," said Vance, "I think that is all right; I think I am one of the elect," and the old darky said, "The fact is, Massa, I didn't know you was a candidate," which I think my clerical friends, if there are any present, on the question of the interpretation of the doctrine of election will agree that they

[1] Delivered in the Grand Opera House.
[2] Morris Hancock Stratton, Princeton 1858, lawyer and veteran Democrat of Salem.
[3] John Mills Allen, congressman from Mississippi, 1885-1901. He retired from Congress in 1901, resumed the practice of law in Tupelo, Miss., and died in 1917.

at least have to be a candidate before they can be elected. And that reminds me of the other story of the negro, who gave his version of the doctrine of elections. He said, "It is like this: man, he votes one way, and the devil, he votes the other way, and the Lord, he votes, and that decides the election."

Now, I have a notion that in every campaign the Lord votes, and I have a distinct anticipation of the way he is going to vote this time, though, for fear my prediction may not be verified, I am not going to tell you on which side He is going to vote. But the Lord is going to decide this election, and I say that without any intention of the least irreverance, because I believe very much more is involved in this election than the fortunes of the parties; I believe that very much more is involved than the fortunes of individuals. New Jersey is only taking part in this campaign, a great movement which has stirred the whole country, a movement for independence and reorganization and purity in politics. And yet it has struck me as a singular thing, not personally an annoying thing, but a singular thing, that my opponents, the Republican campaign speakers have made all of their attacks, so far as I have had time to read them, not upon my position as a representative of the principles of the Democratic party in this campaign, but upon me as a person. Their attacks have been entirely inconsistent with one another, and, therefore, they have been amusing; they have been of such a nature as not to stir my anger in the least, because they have not been true.

You know you do not resent any imputation which is false, which is notoriously false, because you are not afraid anybody will believe it. The things you resent are the things that are true. A distinguished lawyer in South Carolina,[4] a man of great dignity and character, after losing a suit one day was followed from the court room by his client, who abused him for everything that was vile, called him a thief and a liar and everything else that was offensive, but he paid not the least attention, until the client called him a Federalist, and then he knocked him down. Someone said to him: "Why, Mr. Pettigrew, what did you knock him down for? That was the least offensive thing he said." "Yes, confound him," he said, "but it was the only true thing he said." It is only the truth that pinches. A very astute politician once said to his son whom he was trying to instruct in the ways of politicians, "My son, never pay any attention to lies; they will take care of themselves. But when you hear me denying anything you can make up your mind that it is so." There is a great deal of human

[4] James Louis Petigru (1789-1863), South Carolina unionist who opposed nullification and secession.

nature in that principle whether it is a very normal principle or not. So, I am not concerned with the character of these attacks, except to point out how singularly they illustrate the absurdity of the whole thing. For example, these gentlemen began by sneering at me as a learned man. Why I should be sneered at because I am supposed to have learning—which I do not admit, by the way —I cannot understand. But, on the supposition that I am learned, and on the supposition that I have written a history of the United States—which they seem to hold against me—how is it credible that I should say the things which they say that I have said? For example, it has been reported from them, I believe, that I said that no one ought to hold public office who is not a college graduate. Suppose a man who had read American history, or claimed to have read American history, should say a thing like that, what would be the effect of saying such a thing—why, what about George Washington and Abraham Lincoln, who have occupied public office? You do not have to mention any of the other names. The records of our public life are full of the names of men who never attended a college and who rendered not only distinguished but immortal service in the elevation of our politics. The very man who could not make such a statement is a learned man; for he would know that out of the records of human endeavor his statement was given the lie. These gentlemen either have not read American history themselves, or they do not think I have.

Then, take the things that they say that I have said with regard to labor. I am not sensitive with regard to their allegations as to what I may have said concerning labor because the record is there and every laboring man who has come in contact with me knows exactly what my attitude is, and that it is an attitude of consistent friendship and frank friendship. I am not that kind of a moral man that I fear to speak what I think.

I believe that the fundamental principle of all our life in respect to what we do, in [is] the way in which it will effect others. I respect the organization of labor; I believe the laboring man has not only the right to have that organization but that it is indispensable to the establishment and maintainance of such rights, but when the working man does as some individual unions have done—use their power of organization to do something which is detrimental to the whole industry and detrimental to the union itself, I am not a friend unless I be a false one. I am not his friend if I do not tell him of it and I am his friend if I tell him of it, and he has no respect for me if I do not. These are the terms upon which I try to be friendly with everybody, by telling the truth and trying to work out the common interests together. In regard to the singular public criticism of the working man of this country, I do not think they are going to be so stupid as not to know my character and the rest of my life. It is not to refute it, a lie will take care of itself, but only to ask you this question, why are these gentlemen so hard put? Why must these gentlemen make these crude charges in order to effect their objects and stop the momentum of the campaign? Why is it in the city of Camden that the rolls must be padded twenty per cent more than usual? Why is it orders have gone forth there that the methods to prevent the pure use of the ballot have to be resorted to more than ever? Why do these gentlemen resort to those methods unless they are hard put to it, and why are they hard put to it? I speak very plainly because they cease to represent even the Republican party. They have broken with the traditions and policies of the Republican party in the name of those with whom they have combined to do illegitimate business.

What are the traditions and policies of that party? One of the policies of the Republican party of which it is proudest, and of which it has the best reason to be proud, is that its policy has sought—whether wisely or not, I will not now discuss—generation after generation, to build up the material interests of this country; to bring solidity and prosperity to our manufacturing enterprises. For a long time the real spokesmen of the party did devotedly apply themselves to the devotion of that policy. But what has happened in recent years—perhaps I should say in recent months? This has happened: That policy has been turned into a partnership of men taking advantage of the services they have rendered to industry. These men have subsidized industry, and have been subsidized, in turn, by industry for the services industry has rendered to them. Having made the mistake of carrying too far this policy, they have given opportunity for the formation of trusts and combinations, which trusts and combinations, in turn, form partnerships with them. This is not the policy of the Republican party, unless it is its policy turned away in the final process of its development. These men have ceased to serve America and for a long time have been serving particular selfish interests in America. Because they have broken with the past traditions and policies of their party, they cannot any longer depend on their party for success, but resort to desparate subterfuge.

I have tried throughout this campaign to be moderate and fair in the statements I have made. I am willing to concede, I am willing to believe that these gentlemen have been misled themselves, that they have exaggerated a good policy to such an extent and by such subtle and slow stages that they have not perceived where they crossed the line from what was legitimate to what was illegitimate and detrimental to the country, and no matter who says that it is not so, they have ceased to represent the great Republican party of the United States. What is the present condition of that party? It is a condition of confusion, and the vitality of that party resides in men who have created the confusion and brought about insurgency, on the ground not that they were ceasing to be Republicans, but that the Republican party had drifted away from its own true traditions and policies. The most vital men in the Republican party in the nation are taking the position I have just stated of [that] the particular men who are leading the Republican party in New Jersey have ceased to be representative Republicans. For who are the gentlemen who are leading the Republican party in New Jersey now? They are without exception, men who have turned their back with offensive and opprobrious epithets upon the progressives and progressive wing of their own party, and have deliberately allied themselves with all the things that the progressives of the party know will ruin the party if they are not overcome. That is the reason that the Democratic party is setting up as its candidates men who are free from these things, and to appeal to these very independent elements, and to represent, if those elements are ready to be represented, them in a very different direction. They know that their chief difficulty is that they are not bona fide members of their own party—not of the Republican party—I mean the men who have been voting the Republican ticket; they do not constitute the organization; they do their own thinking; they are not to be blindly led this way or that; they are going to choose in this campaign which way they will go; they may choose one way or the other, but they are going to choose upon principle and not upon subterfuge. If they do not believe in what I stand for, they are going to vote against me; but if they do believe in what I stand for, then they are going to vote for me; and nothing that these men are uttering [about] the things that I have said will make any difference one way or the other.

Now, what, on the other hand, is the position of the Democratic party? I have spoken of the Republican leaders as allied with certain special and selfish interests in this state. There have been times, I am sorry to say, when the Democratic party—the Democratic organization—seemed to be allied with those very interests, but those instances were not instances of an organization acting upon the lines of the traditions of that party; they were instances of contagion, the contagion of a modern industrial society. Let us not deceive ourselves. We are proud of America. We believe in the purity and integrity of the American character; we are not afraid of the deterioration of America, either socially or politically; we know how its figure is constantly lifted up. We must admit in all fairness and candor that we have made a fetish for wealth, that we have forgotten none [some] of the essential things that we ought to be proud of, and boasted most of the material power of America. How often do we hear public speakers boast that we can thrash any two European powers. I do not think we could, off-hand, because we are not ready, we haven't a big enough army, but if you give us time enough, of course we could. But I know men who could thrash me, upon whom I look with positive contempt, because I know that my character is better than theirs, and the fact that they have the muscular strength to thrash me, after I have left my authentic marks upon them, does not excite my respect in the least degree. And if the only thing that we have to be proud of is that we have the material strength to overcome any two nations in the world, suppose we have? If that was the only thing to be proud of it would be nothing to boast of. There have been other nations in the world that were able to do this. At the time that Rome was able to thrash all the rest of the world she was not able to control herself and had already begun her own decay and her destruction was at hand. So that material power in itself proves nothing. . . .[5]

There has been a contagion which has demoralized both parties, and that contagion is now obvious. A disease ceases to be dangerous and will not become epidemic when it has been discovered and it is known what will stop it. This disease of our body politic is now recognized everywhere. The contagion is treated; it has been exposed. Look at the investigations which have been going on in neighboring states, investigations of bribery and corruption. Those great committee rooms are like great laboratories in which the germs of a fatal and loathsome disease are being disclosed, and men drew away from them knowing that that is what has been corrupting our body politic. That thing has come to an end. The moral and political sense of this country will not put up with it any longer, they are avoiding the contagion.

Each [Which] party in New Jersey has turned its face in a new direction? Each [Which] party in New Jersey has undertaken to do a new thing and left off doing the old one? Has the

[5] Two sentences have been omitted because they were garbled beyond comprehension.

Republican party done anything unprecedented by the Republican party, I mean the organization? Has the Republican organization beckoned the Republican party to take a new road? Not in any one particular. They are not promising you anything they did not promise you six years ago. They are suggesting as a candidate a man of their own organization, his associates being the same Board of Guardians, and at almost every conference he is called in by the association in determining what the Legislature was allowed to do and what it was not allowed to do. What new thing has the Republican organization offered you?

The Democratic organization is offering you something new. It is offering you a brand new kind of candidate for Governor for one thing. I don't know and I don't like to ask whether you like the kind or not, but you have to admit it is brand new, that there is something very unusual in it, that you don't recognize the earmarks of the usual kind of candidate, and I think you will have to recognize too, quite irrespective of his abilities or disabilities, that it is rather interesting to have a man come entirely from the outside world where he has been doing nothing except understand politics—I think that is a rather big exception—where he has been doing nothing except taking pains to know the facts and to understand the facts, and he comes from the outside and is put up, not at his own suggestion in the least degree, but by their request, to be their representative in an entirely new deal. I do not like the word "new deal" or "square deal," because a deal is either a private transaction in business or else it is the doling out of cards in a game. A deal therefore, is connected with the idea of chance; no matter how square the deal is, you may hold a bad hand; and so I have always objected to the expression "square deal." I would rather have an even deal, so that I would have as nearly as might be as many trumps as the other fellow. But, without quibbling at the use of the word itself, this is an entirely new arrangement, an entirely new adjustment of things. What has taken place is, that they have asked a man from the outside to come in and represent them on the inside, and they have done so absolutely of their own will and initiative. I don't know why, I did not ask them. Partially because I was too modest, and partially—well—it might be inconvenient for me to know all the reasons. But for whatever reason or from whatever motives, they have done that.

Now, what does that mean? Why, it either means what I am about to tell you, or else it was a colossal mistake. The man they picked out was a man who has made it his business to know the facts and to understand them, and a man who, for twenty-five years, has been in the habit of making public speeches. Now, it is a colossal blunder to call in a man who understands and can make public speeches, unless they want everything talked about; and if there [is] anything in the program that cannot be talked about, then they picked out the wrong man. That, to my mind, would mean a colossal blunder; and I believe that at the bottom of most of the errors of our politics in recent years has been the fact that the essential things going on at Trenton have been things that it was not discreet to talk about. The most dangerous kind of government for men who want anything concealed in [is] government with a talker at the head of it, with a man who has, as a schoolmaster, been in the habit of explaining things and making them just as clear as possible. I shall understand if I am chosen Governor of New Jersey, that it will be my business to make everything that is going on at Trenton just as plain as possible to the people of New Jersey. That, ladies and gentlemen, would break down any machine. Therefore, it is inconceivable that those gentlemen have the least desire to have a machine that would break down, so, the situation is this: you are offered a great change in politics under circumstances which make a great change feasible if you vote the Democratic ticket, and you are not even offered a change if you vote the Republican ticket. Am I stating it unfairly? Is not that the literal truth? Now, change is not worth while for its own sake. I am not one of those who loves variety for its own sake. If a thing is good to-day, I would like to have it stay that way to-morrow.

Most of our calculations in life are dependent upon things staying the way they are. For example, if when you got up to-morrow morning you had forgotten all those ordinary affairs which you do almost automatically, which you can do almost half awake, you would have to find out what to to [sic] do to-day. I am told by the psychologists that if I did not remember who I was yesterday, I would not know who I am to-day, and that, therefore, my very identity depends upon my being able to tally to-day with yesterday. If it does not tally, then I am confused and I do not know who I am, and I have to go around and ask somebody to tell me my name and where I came from. I am not one of those who wish to break connection with the past; I am not one of those who wish change for the mere sake of variety. The only men who do that are the men who want to forget something, the men who filled yesterday with something they would not recollect to-day, and so they go about seeking diversion, seeking something, seeking abstraction in something that will blot out recollection, or seeking to put something in them which will blot out all recollection.

Change is not interesting unless it is constructive. If I move out of my present house because I do not like it, then I have got to choose a better house or build a better house, and the change is interesting only when I make improvement, I am not here to use the puerile argument that we are tired of the government given us by the present Republican organization. That is not a sufficient argument, because we might get worse—I must admit that I could not imagine anything very much worse then [than] the present government has given us—but I [am] willing to admit, for the sake of argument, that we could get something worse. So, change is dangerous. It is taking a big risk, unless you know what you are going to get.

Now, do you doubt what you are going to get if the change is made? Have you read the Democratic program? Did you ever read a more sober document than that, or a more explicit document than that program? It is unique among modern platforms in having all the rhetoric left out. At the outset it begins in a most businesslike way. I cannot quote it for you—I cannot quote anything—but it runs in this way: In presenting our candidate for Governor, the Democratic party also states what it will do if the executive and legislative offices of the state are entrusted to them, and it begins to enumerate the things which it will devote itself to, and it enumerates the things in a most explicit way, not only stating that we ought to have a corrupt practices act, but also stating what ought to be in such an act, stating what are legitimate expenses, stating the limit of expenses, obliging those who are managing a campaign to put down and publish the amounts of money they have received and the sources from whom they received them, all of which would be extremely embarrassing if the campaign had not been run in the right way. A large sum of money derived from some sources would create a violent suspicion.

I will venture to repeat to this audience what I said to another audience not long ago. A good many years ago there was a great campaign fund raised in connection with a national campaign, which amounted to $400,000, which was considered a huge sum of money in that day.[6] It would be a mere matter of book-keeping now. But in that day $400,000 was regarded as an ex-

<hr />

[6] During the presidential campaign of 1888, when John Wanamaker, head of a special businessmen's committee, raised $400,000 for the Republican candidate, Benjamin Harrison.

traordinary national campaign fund, and a speaker who was attacking the Republican managers for collecting so large a campaign fund used this illustration: he said, "I do not mean to intimate that it was intended to make direct corrupt use of the $400,000. I mean this, that the gentlemen who contributed it were interested in the present policy of the Republican party and did not want to see it interrupted, and that they expected to get that money back indirectly by preserving that policy." He said, "It is just like this. Down where I live, most people get their water from pumps, and it is notorious that pumps sometimes go dry in the throat at night and won't pump in the morning. The sucker won't suck. Every prudent housewife, therefore, before she goes to bed at night, pumps up a bucket of water and leaves it to stand there over night, and in the morning if the pump won't work, she pours some of the water back into it, and it begins to suck. Now, this $400,000 was contributed to make the pump suck." And he said, "You will notice this interesting thing, that when you make a pump go that way, the first water to come out is the same water that you poured in."

So that you will see how the thing that we are seeking is a whole change in the point of view. We do [not] want political contributions for the sake of making the pump suck. We want political contributions merely for the sake of paying legitimate expenses and letting the people choose between the parties and the candidates—that is all. (Applause) I was about to say when you interrupted me with kind applause that that was all that was intended. What greater thing could it be intended for? For, on the 8th of November next the people of New Jersey are to do that most dignified and that greatest thing that they can do. They are to exercise a sovereign act, the act of determining the character and personnel of their government, the fundamental act of self-government. We speak of a sovereign people. What do we mean by a sovereign people? A sovereign people is one that looks with free eyes upon its own affairs, takes its judgment from no man's dictation, is too great, too conscious of its supremacy and sovereignty to be deceived by or cajoled by any man, that looks calmly upon its own affairs, compares them with the standards to which it would wish them to conform, and then cross-questions those who would serve it and chooses the servants that come nearest to the trustworthiness which is to be demanded of all who would undertake so great a thing as the service of our great sovereignty. That is what we mean by a sovereign people.

I wonder if any man is so ignorant, is so besotted, as not to realize that the corruption of the ballot is the most deadly offense that could be committed against any self-governing community, that so far as that act is concerned, it is the hand of an assassin raised against the sovereign himself—the sovereign seized in the moment of his sovereign act and despoiled of his sovereignty, made a cheat of in the very moment when he was exercising his ultimate and greatest power. Theoretically speaking, if we could be vindictive in such matters, if we could lay aside Christian charity, there is no punishment which would be too severe for a man who would corrupt the ballot and defeat the sovereign act of a great people. When the slightest suspicion rests upon any man of tampering with the ballot then I cease to regard him as worthy of any consideration from any American citizen. Two weeks from to-day you are to exercise this sovereignty. Two weeks from to-day you are to determine in which direction you will turn your government and under what leadership. I leave the question with you with only this intimation, that we have now in our keeping the reputation of New Jersey and the predictions and the great traditions of American freedom.

FPS T transcript (WP, DLC) with corrections from the partial texts in the *Newark Evening News*, Oct. 26, 1910, and the Trenton *True American*, Oct. 26, 1910.

From George Brinton McClellan Harvey

Dear Mr. Wilson,   New York Tuesday [Oct. 25, 1910]

Just a word to say that I consider your letter[1] the most effective political document I ever read.

Have just been reading it aloud to Marse Henry Watterson with joint delight.   As ever   G H

ALI (WP, DLC).
[1] Wilson's letter to Record had just been published in the newspapers.

From Joseph Patrick Tumulty and Mark Anthony Sullivan

Jersey City N J 10/25/10

Your letter is inspiring and makes certain your triumphant election. The New Jersey Democracy gladly accepts your virile leadership.   Joseph P Tumulty
                        Mark A Sullivan

Hw telegram (WP, DLC).

From Henry Otto Wittpenn

Jersey City N J 10/25 191[0]

Heartiest appreciation of your splendid attitude towards progressive policies and your straightforward manly course   hudsons majority should be fifteen thousand

H. Otto Wittpenn

Hw telegram (WP, DLC).

Moses Taylor Pyne to William Cooper Procter

My dear Procter: [Princeton, N. J.] October 25th, 1910.

As you have of course seen from the papers, and heard from West, Wilson is no longer President at Princeton. The thing was done, I think, in a very satisfactory and diplomatic way. According to the newspapers he forced his resignation on a reluctant board, although actually he was most reluctant to put it in and had to be told pretty positively that it had to be done.

We had a hearing some two weeks ago before the Chancellor[1] and we are waiting from day to day to get his decision allowing us to go ahead on the Golf Links. Cram has designed a most beautiful Tower for the Cleveland Memorial which, I am sure, will please you when you see it. It is very different from the Tower which was prepared during his absence in Europe and sent out with the general circular.

We elected John A. Stewart, the Senior Trustee, Acting President of the Board, not that he is to perform any of the routine duties, but because we did not think it advisable for any member of the Faculty, especially one who had been mixed up in the recent troubles, to hold that position, even temporarily. As it is, the Board seems now to be getting together and in a short time I believe that the friction will be entirely removed and we can pull together as a unit. Of course, two or three members of the Board have shown themselves up in a very bad light which will not help their political strength, but that is a matter which neither you nor I need worry about.

I hope, now that things have straightened out, that we shall have the pleasure of seeing you and Mrs. Procter in Princeton, and we should be delighted to have you make us a visit of as long as you care to stay, and if you should happen to come now, after the convocation is over, you will find Princeton very attractive at this time of the year, and we can take some tramps around the country and give you some idea of the hills and streams and woods within easy walking distance of the University.

Mrs. Pyne joins me in warmest regards to Mrs. Procter.

Yours very sincerely,　M. Taylor Pyne.

TCL (M. T. Pyne Coll., NjP).
[1] Mahlon Pitney, Princeton 1879, Chancellor of New Jersey.

From Cleveland Hoadley Dodge
to Henry Burling Thompson

Dear Harry　　　　　　　　　　　New York. Oct. 25th 1910

"We will all forget the past" but I am afraid Wilson is so bitter that he will never forgive Momo[1] & I do not think, that, feeling as he does, we can *now* induce him to accept his salary beyond Oct 20th or stay much longer at Prospect. Momo might have thought of all this before he kicked him down stairs. However we will try.

The worst thing about the situation is that Mr Stewart is worrying so about being President that it is making him sick & his doctor has told him he must not continue. We may persuade him to hold the job, but it is doubtful & if he resigns, that means Momo as acting & *actual* President in the saddle indefinitely, & if no permanent successor is elected so much the better for Momo. Nice, isn't it?

I return Momo's letter & also one from Conklin[2] which do not bother to return　　　　　　Yr's affly　C. H. Dodge

ALS (H. B. Thompson Papers, NjP).
[1] Moses Taylor Pyne.
[2] M. T. Pyne to H. B. Thompson, Oct. 22, 1910, and E. G. Conklin to C. H. Dodge, Oct. 23, 1910, both ALS (H. B. Thompson Papers, NjP). The quotation which opens Dodge's letter is a paraphrase of the postscript in Pyne's letter to Thompson: "P.S. I am delighted to see that we are all anxious to forget the past and pull together—even Cleve."

To George Brinton McClellan Harvey

My dear Colonel:　　　　Princeton, N. J. October 26th, 1910.

Your note of Tuesday gives me a great deal of pleasure. It is delightful to know that you think the letter to Record of the right sort, and I am also mightily pleased that Marse Henry should have liked it.

Gratefully yours,　Woodrow Wilson

TLS (WP, DLC).

To Dan Fellows Platt

My dear Mr. Platt: Princeton, N. J. October 26th, 1910.

I have had only a few hours at a time at home and have been delayed in replying to your important letter of the 21st.[1]

I have read it with the greatest interest and profit and regret that I could not see my way to replying as you suggested to Mr. Record's question 18. I think you will understand from my published letter why.

The suggestions of your letter will be very helpful to me in view of my approaching visit to Bergen County. Thank you very much for what you tell me about the arrangements.

In haste,

Cordially and faithfully yours,   Woodrow Wilson

TLS (photostat in RSB Coll., DLC).
  [1] It is missing.

A News Report of a Campaign Speech in New Brunswick, New Jersey

[*Oct. 26, 1910*]

WILSON SEES A BETTER DAY

New Jersey's Standard Bearer Tells Huge Audience
the Future is Safe.

HUMAN RIGHTS A THEME

New Brunswick, N. J., Oct. 26.—Woodrow Wilson's message to the people of Middlesex county especially, and to the people of New Jersey in general, was one of great cheer for the future of America. He depicted in thrilling eloquence the existing conditions of which the people are so weary, pointed the way to better things and said the future, of which some historian will one day write, is safe.

He had been whimsical in his manner, an unusual thread of humor arousing the spirits of his vast audience, but these passages only led, by way of illustration, to the more serious aspect of his address, and he gave much food for reflection to the 200,000 people of Middlesex county, where for years Republican machine politics held a grip till Senator George S. Silzer shook things up and brought a great change with a succession of Democratic victories.

Mr. Wilson's main theme was the preservation of human rights, which, according to vested interests, are the rights to

New Brunswick, 26 Oct. 1910.

Platform and platform.
 (Promise vs. programmes, — the old vs. the new.

A day of programmes, — of adjustments, the world over
 Rumors from England

What adjustments?
 Once (~ ~) adjustments bit.
 a) Gov'ts and peoples
 b) Man and man (Status to contract)
 Group adjustments, Everything (in particular, corporations) involving, in a sense, Everybody.

Hence new legal safeguards and
 New legal analysis.
 Appearance of radicalism
 Really a new struggle for justice. E.g. Labour.

Parties neither here nor there, — mere instrumentalities, no doubt now to be reformed

Ask candidates, not What are you, but what do
 You purpose to do.

My own answer.

A day of choosing, — for free, clear-sighted, progressive, fearless men.

10/26/10

which they are entitled under the law. "It is a constant unending struggle," he said with impressive emphasis, "a struggle for human rights under the law."

In all of the meetings so far held in 19 counties in the State, Mr. Wilson faced a no more interested nor more enthusiastic audience, and at no time was he in better form. His dominant thought was that, under present political conditions, human rights are held in small cause, but the time is coming when the people of New Jersey and of all of the other States of the United States are to restore the government of their fathers.

From every point of the Opera House where a man could sit or stand an eager face was turned toward the handsomely-decorated stage, where Mr. Wilson, with his escorts, entered, and a mighty cheer arose for this man, whose spare face and gaunt figure grow handsome as one comes to know him. High up in the gallery stood hundreds who could find no seats, while all the aisles and entrances were jammed. But during all of the hour occupied by the candidate in his address there was scarcely a whisper or so much as the shuffling of a foot, so intense was the interest. . . .

Amid the wild cheers and applause which greeted Mr. Wilson as he stepped to the footlights there arose the din of a "locomotive" yell by a bunch of Rutgers students in the orchestra chairs.

"It makes me feel very much at home to face this phalanx in front of me," said Mr. Wilson. "I have been accustomed to seeing young gentlemen like these, but I know by experience they will not absorb it all. A friend of mine, who is a member of the faculty of Yale University, helped me at one time in moments of discouragement by saying that in teaching for 20 years he had come to the conclusion that the human mind had infinite resistance in resisting the influences of knowledge. In that respect the Republican Organization leaders share the characteristics of the human mind. They have not received very much in respect to the movements of politics."

Proceeding, Mr. Wilson unfolded his thought, which was that the people are tired of promises that are broken and want programs that are carried out, and he likened the present spirit of unrest and demand for change to that which gave birth to the Magna Charta. On this line he said:

"I say that we are not interested in platforms as mere promises cast in vague language. We are interested in them only when they seem to be programs, and what interests me about the present time, I must admit, is that everywhere men are interested in great programs. Have you read the papers recently attentively enough to notice the rumors that are coming across the water? Some very unusual and interesting things are happening in England. The English parties are separated, so far as their progressive elements are concerned, as little as the American parties are separated, and what is happening right now is that the liberal and conservative factions are holding a joint conference in order to effect concerted action with regard to a common program.

"And what are the rumors? The rumors are that the program probably includes, not only self-government for Ireland, but self-government for Scotland and the drawing together in London or somewhere else of a Parliament which will represent the British Empire in a great confederated state upon the model, no doubt, of the United States of America, and having its power to the end of the world. What is the program? What is at the bottom of that program? At the bottom of it is the idea that no little group of men like the English people have the right to govern men in all parts of the world without drawing them into real substantial partnership, where their voice will count with equal weight with the voice of other parts of the country.

"This voice that has been crying in Ireland, this voice for home rule, is a voice which is now supported by the opinion of the world; this impulse, which has always remained in Scotland, the spirit of pride in the history of the Scottish people, is a spirit that ought to be respected and recognized in the British Constitution. It means not mere vague talk of men's rights, men's emotions and men's inveterate and traditional principles, but it means the embodiment of these things in something that is going to be done, that will look within hope to the program that may come out of these conferences.

"Do you think that program means anything in that little kingdom of Portugal, that has just now changed its program over night?[1] Do you suppose that the people there are interested in vague phrases? They have listened all their lives to the talk of law and promises of liberty, but they want the substance of the law and the substance of liberty. They had a corrupt government which was not likely to become other than corrupt under the young, easily influenced boy who was King of Portugal. So they insisted upon taking their own affairs in their own hands. They

[1] On October 4, 1910, the Republican party, supported by elements of the army and navy, had begun an insurrection which resulted in the overthrow of the young king, Manuel II. Dr. Teófilo Braga, a prolific historian of Portuguese literature, was installed as provisional President of the new Republic of Portugal. The king took refuge in Gibraltar and eventually in England, where he died in 1932. He was the last king of Portugal.

want the real. They do not want vague promises and phrases. Men are tired of words.

"What is the oldest struggle that we read about, when men began to organize themselves in political States? It was the struggle of the individual not to be too much controlled by government. You know what an unconquerable thing is in you. It is the feeling that you are an individual, and that you will not be subordinated to any other man or any other organization; and, therefore, when government plays too much upon your affairs without your participation and consent you are restless under the bondage.

"If those who conduct the government are not careful the restlessness will spread with rapid agitation until the whole country is aflame, and then there will be revolution and a change of government."

Slowly unfolding this thought of individual rights, Mr. Wilson brought it down to the contest with co-operative organization, citing the building of the railway, its development of the country and then the total dependence of that country upon the railroad. Said he:

"After it is developed, the movement of individuals and freight and everything you want to move, in other words, all your connections with the rest of the world, is in the hands of that corporation. That is the reason why we are so interested in having a Public Utility Commission. We cannot move or handle our goods otherwise, but somehow it is not adjusted to us. We have all sorts of suspicions as to what it is adjusted to, but it is not adjusted to us. Our lives are unjustly inconvenienced by the way it is handled. Don't you see how that illustrates what I am talking about? We haven't got these instrumentalities adjusted for the use we want to make of them and they are so big we are bothered how to handle them. That is the reason that so many people talk in the terms of big corporations. They are all so dependent upon each other that we have to pool our interests and co-operate in every respect.

"That is the Socialistic program. My own objection to the Socialistic program is that it will not work. We are constantly struggling for programs big and little, the biggest is the Socialistic and the smallest of all programs is that of the stand-patter. In his program it is largely negative, it says we have done a lot of things, accomplished a lot of things, most of these have been disappointing, therefore let us not do anything. That is a program that is very popular, that is the program that I have every day when I am tired and want to loaf, that is the program

I am going to carry out at any rate for a few weeks after the campaign is over. I don't mean to stand pat long enough to stagnate and, moreover, I expect to have something to do after this campaign is over."

A tumult of cheers followed that sally. From that on Mr. Wilson unfolded his great thought that the great future need is for action by the whole people to adjust these entanglements and that, so far as he is concerned, he means to devote his days to that adjustment.

"Shall I try to forecast for probabilities of the present Republican organization?" he asked. "How many times do you have to have them forecasted? They were forecasted three years ago, they were forecasted six years ago, and were forecasted nine years ago. Has anything happened that you have noted? What have other States been doing? All sorts of things. What has New Jersey beeng [been] doing? Nothing. Nothing in particular. Forecasts? Why, do you know what happens to you people. Well, if nothing is going to happen, in God's name what are you here for?

"I have not any respect for a large number of persons, as numerous as they are in this hall, who will come together simply to hear a man talk. If there is no dynamic power behind that man's back; if he has not got anything in his head that will make someone hum; if he has not got courage that will defy influences that you are afraid of, why then go home. There is nothing in it. It is just a lot of words. It is just a gentleman who has been accustomed for 20-odd years to making public speeches, doing his stunt, that is all.

"If you think that he is merely the representative of an organization, and that he may or may not know what that organization is going to do, why then adjourn the meeting and come when you can get the organization on the stage and ask it what it is going to do. What are you here for, anyway? Why, you are here for a very important thing. I dare say you wanted to see whether he looked like an honest man, for one thing."

"I believe you are all right," exclaimed a workingman in a front chair, as if suddenly aroused to speak his mind as he looked up into the speaker's gleaming eyes. Cheers and applause greeted the telling point, and Mr. Wilson said: "You will have to form your own conclusions. All I can say is that you will be very foolish if you suppose that all by himself, he can do anything except make the men who oppose him extremely uncomfortable. That I can guarantee."

Printed in the *Philadelphia Record*, Oct. 27, 1910; some editorial headings omitted.

From Robert Davis

Jersey City N. J. Oct 26 [1910]

Congratulations on you[r] magnificent reply to Geo. L. Records it means an increased majority in Hudson county[1]

Robt. Davis.

T telegram (WP, DLC).
[1] Wilson wrote at the bottom of this telegram: "I sincerely app. yr kind tel. and thank you most warmly."

From Harold Godwin[1]

My dear Tommy: Roslyn L. I. N. Y Oct 26, 1910

I am so delighted at your decision to enter public life that I cant refrain from burdening you with a line or two. I wish you an overwhelming success—which you will receive, and feel that the admiration which we, your old friends feel so deeply, will expand expand [sic] from this on so as to embrace within the next year or two the best element of the whole nation. I sincerely hope your health and vigor will be equal to the strain of a campaign in 1912 for the Presidency[.] We shall all be with you now as well as then and wish you God speed.

Sincerely   Harold Godwin

ALS (WP, DLC).
[1] Wilson's classmate at Princeton, former editor and art critic, now retired and living in Roslyn, Long Island.

From John DeWitt

Dear Dr Wilson   Princeton, N. J. 26, Octr 1910

Its strength, clearness, definiteness good temper and many other qualities I will not try to name make your reply to Mr. Record's letter a great political document. I hope it will add enough votes—if indeed you need them—to those already secured to put you with a handsome majority into the Governor's chair. Do not think of acknowledging this note.

Yours very sincerely   John DeWitt

ALS (WP, DLC).

From James Fairman Fielder

My dear Dr. Wilson: Jersey City [N. J.] October 26, 1910.

Let me express my admiration of the position you have taken as the man designated by our state convention as the new leader of our party and of the simple and forcible manner in which you have stated that position in your reply to Mr. Record. Those who have followed your speeches through the state, understood your attitude and to them your letter is only a concise declaration of what you have already said at greater length, but to the independent voter and to those good republican citizens who desire the control of our state government wrested from the hands of the "Board of Guardians," these questions and answers should bring the sure conviction that a man has been found with whom they can safely trust their interests and every one of them, Mr. Record as well, ought publicly to declare their faith in and their intention to support you.

I know you are punctilious in the acknowledgment of letters, but do not acknowledge this one. I should not at this busy time, trouble you with a letter, but the feelings of one who with his democratic colleagues in the legislature, has endeavored to make democratic principles stand for something, must find some vent after reading your splendid letter.

Very truly yours,   James F Fielder

TLS (WP, DLC).

From Joseph Howell[1]

My dear and Hon. Sir: Hamilton Square, N. J. Oct. 26, 1910.

I have read with keen appreciation your reply to the Hon. George L. Record, and drop you these few lines of congratulation for the high and excellent stand you have taken against the "Boss System."

I have been saying to individuals, that Dr. Wilson is a man head and shoulders above the Hon. Vivian M. Lewis, the former being a National character, while the latter is a Local character.

Your letter carries its own illumination, that the masses of the people will have no trouble of judging for themselves.

I am a Republican; but have been fighting this very "Boss System" and its most debasing influences over our elections in this township for the last ten years.

My attitude against it has driven it under cover, and by stealth the work is still carried on, which before had been done openly and with brazen face.

I am heartily glad that a Moses has arisen to lead New Jersey out of the mire of prostitution to "Special Interests," and the "Boss System," and to bribery and to graft; into the open field of civic righteousness.

God speed you in the work. To day I give you my congratulations. November 8th I will give you my vote.

Yours for Victory!   (Rev.) Joseph Howell.

ALS (WP, DLC).
[1] Pastor of the Presbyterian Church of Hamilton Square, N. J.

To Harold Godwin

My dear Godwin,   Princeton, N. J. 27 October, 1910.

I do not remember any message that has given me deeper or more genuine pleasure than yours. I thank you for it with all my heart. I wish that I were not held back by the sheer rush of my present engagements from telling you *all* that I feel when I read such a letter from an old friend.

With affectionate regards,

Faithfully yours,   Woodrow Wilson

WWTLS (WP, DLC).

To Lawrence Crane Woods

My dear Mr. Woods,   Princeton, N. J. 27 October, 1910.

I must stop, even in the midst of the present distracting rush of campaign engagements, to tell you how grateful I am to you for your generous letter of the twenty-fifth.[1] I am thankful that I was in the midst of the campaign and that it absolutely dominated my thoughts. Otherwise I believe that I should have broken down under the mortification of what I discovered last week to be the real feeling of the Pyne party towards me. I want to say, even in this moment of haste, that nothing sustains and reassures me like the affection and respect of men like you, who think straight and whose hearts are hearts of honour.

In haste,

With deep gratitude,

Faithfully Yours,   Woodrow Wilson

WWTLS (WC, NjP).
[1] L. C. Woods to WW, Oct. 25, 1910, TLS (WP, DLC).

Bergen County, 27 Oct., 1910. { Rutherford
                                     Englewood
                                     Hackensack

New Jersey and New York, — Common ground in
   respect of good government (⌐ ⌐ ⌐ ⌐ ⌐)

"Progressive," what? (⌐ ⌐ ⌐ ⌐ ⌐)
   ⌐ ⌐ ⌐ ⌐

   A man with a programme — (⌐ ⌐)

  I. _Efficiency_: Good, i.e. economical and busi-
       nesslike and genuine, government —
       Direct primaries
  II. _Purity_: Corrupt practices act
  III. _Justice_: Equal taxation
          Rate regulation
          Corporate regulation in general
          Justice to the laborer

Is the Democratic party progressive?
Am I a "progressive"?

10/27/10

A News Report of Three Campaign Addresses in Bergen County, New Jersey

[*Oct. 27, 1910*]

BERGEN INDORSES WOODROW WILSON

Three Towns Turn Out En Masse to Welcome Leader of New Kind of Politics.

Hackensack, N. J., Oct. 27.—In three great gatherings of deeply-stirred Bergen county people to-night Woodrow Wilson was given one of the most emphatic indorsements of his great campaign. He addressed immense audiences at Rutherford, at 5 o'clock; at Englewood, at 8 o'clock, and in Hackensack at 9 o'clock. In each of them he made a telling speech, differing materially in all of them, while centralizing his thought upon the main feature of his new kind of campaign, the need for action to secure good government.

"It's an astonishing thing," he said, "that the only thing that stands between us and good government are the people who do the governing." From that point the deduction was plain and straight, that it is necessary to elect good men to office to get good government. He said New Jersey was lagging behind her sister States in the struggle. "Not behind Pennsylvania," he added humorously.

He ascribed a good deal of the lethargy heretofore prevalent to the habit of men thinking in New York, where their business is, and voting in New Jersey, where their homes are, and in this strong commuter county, with its score or more of rich towns on the railroads out of New York, his sentiments and his proposed remedies for intolerant conditions were applauded to the echo.

Bergen county usually is Republican on election day by from 800 to 1500, and the State managers have been counting upon it to present Banking Commissioner Lewis with the usual majority, but, if the receptions accorded Mr. Wilson and the hearty approval of his strong principle by audiences in which sat hundreds of Republicans count for anything, the county is sure to give a substantial Democratic majority. Old party adherents, like former Senator Henry D. Winton, the veteran editor of this city, say they never saw such crowds at political meetings. At Rutherford 900 persons jammed the town hall, at Englewood more than 1200 assembled in the Lyceum, and in this city as many more squeezed into the armory, while in all three places scores were unable to get in.

When Mr. Lewis was in the county last week he drew not

more than one-fourth the number of listeners and the county Republican managers are in a panic, and the impressiveness of Mr. Wilson's sterling and strong personality and vigorous campaign have made most of the commuters of this section turn out to see him in unprecedented numbers. Conditions seem to be ripe for a sensational political turnover next month.

In his Rutherford address Mr. Wilson frequently was interrupted by applause when he made this pointed allusion to the spirit of independence in politics, which has a strong grip on this county: "I know, or I think I know, what your real political sympathies are. I know that probably a large majority of you call yourselves Republicans, but do you realize that it is no longer a descriptive term. What kind of Republicans are you?

"There are many breeds of Republicans nowadays; there are all sorts and varieties. It used to be perfectly possible to describe with comprehensive accuracy a Republican by the traditional principles of his party, but there are Republicans who interpret those principles now in terms of one set of politics, and other Republicans who interpret them in terms of another set of policies, and there are all varieties. For example, even the word 'insurgent' does not describe any body because there is one kind of insurgent in California, there is another kind in Kansas, there is another kind in New Hampshire, there, apparently, is still another kind in Maine. And, therefore, when you speak of yourself as a Republican, I have to ask that you go into particulars and state what kind of a Republican you are, holding what purposes, what ideals of government, what opinions with regard to the present conduct of the government, both in this State and in the nation.

"I think I can make a very fair guess as to what kind of Republicans most of you are. I think it is a fair guess to say that you are progressive Republicans, and I don't want you to be so vain as to suppose that all the progressives are in the Republican party. Frankly, gentlemen, what we are trying to do in this campaign, so far as I understand it, is to form a league of progressives to get something out of the government of New Jersey, without stopping to think what our party labels are, to pay ourselves the compliment of not going by the label, but going by the contents.

"Now, what is a progressive? I understand a progressive to be a man who insists upon bringing about all the adjustments of interests which have not been brought about and also insists upon returning to the primitive, righteous, pure and reasonable processes of popular government. In other words, I understand a progressive is a man who wishes certain reforms of our economic policy, together with certain radical reforms of our political methods, because you can't get the policy without the methods.

"Is the Democratic party progressive? It is astonishing how long it takes to make some people realize that certain things have been said. A gentleman prominent in the politics of this day addressed a letter to me recently, in which he asked me my opinion about things, upon every one of which I had expressed my opinion in public. I was not in the least inclined to make the least trouble about collecting my opinions and putting them in one letter for him, but that is all that I did. Now I want also to remark that all of those opinions are in the Democratic platform, and that not two-thirds of them are in the Republican platform. You have to distinguish when you are talking about Republican platforms, because the platform of the party is one thing and the platform of the candidate is another. The candidate has expanded his platform speech by speech until it has very extensive dimensions; but he hasn't carried the platform of the party with him."

Mr. Wilson explained what it was that the progressive element of all parties was after, which, summed up, was efficiency in government, purity in politics and that fundamental thing that underlies all government—justice. In his Englewood address the candidate dwelt at some length upon the great movement speeding through the country to secure better and freer independent men for important offices of government.

"The evidence is," said he, "that here, there, in every portion of the country, the Democratic party has been putting up new men as its candidates, men not hitherto connected with the active conduct of party organizations at all, men who are, so to say, drawn from that outside body of opinion which is not labeled with party designation and which has swung to the modern movements of purposes. The Republican party organization has done this to a very much less degree. If you will take the nominations made for the governorship throughout the country you will find the Republican nominees are usually men, no matter how admirable their character, who have been connected with the processes of party organization.

"What does it mean that the Democratic party in New Jersey has chosen an independent candidate, if it does not mean that the Democratic party in New Jersey sees that a new day has come, and that the old game is up? What does it mean that the Republican organization has nominated one of their own number, an admirable man, but a man trained in their own processes and of their own number, to be the Governor of the State, except that they expect to continue the old game?"

The day was one more astonishment for the candidate, who has had some chance to become accustomed to astonishments, but this one was different from all the others. He arrived at the Hudson Terminal at 4 o'clock and there, in the busy underground city of the stupendous modern enterprise, he ran plump into fully 100 Bergen county men, mostly Democrats, but many Republicans, ready to conduct him to the three points where he was to speak. . . .

A special tunnel train carried the candidate and the big Reception Committee under the Hudson and up to the Erie station, where a special car awaited to take them to Rutherford, the first stop in the county, and Mr. Wilson was for once a commuter with a fine chance of feeling what it means to that great army of Jerseymen to have a sudden boost in their railroad fares,[1] with no chance for a shot at anybody to get back. Rutherford was reached on schedule time, 5 o'clock, and the party marched up the street from the station back of a fife and drum corps, with little sprinkles of rain falling, which failed to phase the candidate. . . .[2]

Printed in the *Philadelphia Record*, Oct. 28, 1910; some editorial headings omitted.

[1] The New Jersey railroads had raised their commutation fares 20 per cent late in the summer of 1910.

[2] A news report of his address at Hackensack is printed at Oct. 28, 1910.

From Richard Vliet Lindabury

My dear Doctor: Newark, N. J. October 27, 1910.

That Record letter was immense! It appears to have completely satisfied the Independent Press and the Independent Voters,—in fact it could not do less. I saw the editor of "The News"[1] this morning who told me he thought it was the greatest political document he had ever read. His enthusiasm was no less than mine which is boundless. There is no longer any lukewarmness in the News office. The editor told me that from now on they proposed to make a special effort to win and hold the labor vote. I understand that the attitude of the Hoboken Observer—which has been a little shaky—is now the same as the News and that you may expect from this time on the enthusiastic support of that paper. Although a Democratic paper, The Observer has always been independent and has stood for progressive principles. It therefore has much influence among the independent voters and I am told that its support will ensure the votes of most of the Independents and the Progressives in Hudson County. Everything just now looks so bright and promising that I wish the election were to be held next Tuesday. However, there is no reason to fear that you will lose ground during the remainder of the campaign. The editor of The News told me this morning that he thought you would have a tremendous majority and I incline to the same view. Anyhow, the fight is won and there is no longer any occasion for anxiety. I do not believe that it will be necessary—and I have some doubt if it would be advisable—for you to say much more on the subject of your independence. You have so thoroughly established that point now, that no one will any longer doubt it and I fear that too much reiteration of it might weaken it; but you are not making mistakes in this campaign and must not think that I regard advice or caution on this or any other subject necessary. In fact, I begin to feel that suggestions from me are almost presumptuous.

Do not take the trouble to answer this letter.

I am,   Yours sincerely,   R. V. Lindabury

TLS (WP, DLC).
1 That is, the *Newark Evening News.*

From John Augustus Roebling II[1]

Dear Sir: Bernardsville New Jersey Oct. 27, 1910

I inclose check for 750.00 to be used as you think best towards the expenses of your campaign.

With much satisfaction at the prospect of your election, I am,
Very truly yours,   John A. Roebling

ALS (WP, DLC).
1 Son of Washington Augustus Roebling, vice-president of John A. Roebling's Sons Co. John Augustus Roebling devoted his time to his private chemical laboratory in Bernardsville, N. J.

From Walter Moore Dear[1]

My dear Doctor: Jersey City, N. J. Oct. 27th, 1910.

Permit me to congratulate you upon the clear cut and forcible expression of opinion as shown in your letter in answer to the questions propounded to you by Mr. Geo. L. Record.

I never, for one instant doubted your attitude on these important questions of the day, but nevertheless it is a keen source of personal satisfaction to your many friends, among whom I class myself as one, to find that you have so publicly evidenced your attitude on political matters with which every clean thinking and broad minded American citizen must agree.

I believe it is not exaggerating to state that your straight forwardness and unequivocal attitude has won you thousands of friends and votes. While personally, I feel no doubt as to your election, still we must all recognize the other alternative and with this in mind I can only commend you for setting an example which will always redound to your credit and elevate the plane of political aspirants who in the future shall seek the suffrage of their fellow-citizens.

With best wishes for your success, I remain,

Yours sincerely, Walter M Dear

TLS (WP, DLC).
[1] Princeton 1897, business manager of the Jersey City *Jersey Journal.*

From Edwin Camp[1]

My dear Sir: [Atlanta, Ga.] October 27, 1910.

Georgians and The Georgian are intensely interested in your campaign for the governorship of New Jersey, and I am not sure but that your campaign is being watched with more eagerness than even those in our neighboring states. Atlanta loves to claim you as an erstwhile citizen and I am sure that if you win there will be general rejoicing in your victory as the victory of a native son.

We have at our disposal only very unsatisfactory portraits of yourself and if you will be so good as to have some one in your office send us a recent photograph, we shall be deeply obliged to you. Yours very truly, Edwin Camp

TLS (WP, DLC).
[1] Managing editor of the *Atlanta Georgian and News.*

From Thomas Marcus Donnelly[1]

Dear Dr. Wilson: Jersey City, N. J., October 27, 1910.

I am one perhaps of tens of thousands who closely read and thoroughly digested the communication issued a short time ago by Mr. George L. Record, Congressional Candidate from the Ninth New Jersey District, in which certain questions were asked pertinent to the future policy of the Democratic Party and your position on progressive legislation, through which it is alleged the rights of the people and future prosperity of the nation largely depend.

Your reply as published on the 25th inst. was just as closely read as were the interrogatories and I cannot refrain from expressing to you my humble congratulations upon the firm and clear stand you have taken and upon the way and manner you have met this issue.

Your expressions have been commented upon by many people within my hearing and it appears to be a decided conclusion that the campaign is over and the people are anxiously awaiting November 8th to create a "Wilson" tidal wave which will sweep this State like a mighty flood and carry the "Sage of Princeton" to the Governors chair by a majority unheard of in the annals of this Commonwealth.

I am a candidate on the Democratic Ticket, for election to the Assembly. If successful, as I expect to be,[2] it will give me much pleasure to give you every possible support in your endeavor to put into operation the ideas you have expressed, because, as I believe, they are paramount to future success and the happiness of our people.

Asking to be pardoned for consuming your time and predicting success I am, with best regards,

Yours very truly,   T. M. Donnelly.

TLS (WP, DLC).
[1] National secretary of the Order of the Foresters of America; president of the Fraternal Organizations of New Jersey, for whom he acted as a lobbyist; and president of the Square Deal Democratic Association of Hudson County.
[2] He was elected.

A News Report of a Campaign Address in Hackensack, New Jersey

[Oct. 28, 1910]

WILSON WITH COMMUTERS

Hackensack and Rutherford Greeted Him in Force.

HACKENSACK, N. J., October 28.—One of the significant features of the Woodrow Wilson meeting in this city, the county seat of Bergen County, last night, was that the crowd gathered to hear the Democratic candidate, in the Second Regiment armory, numbered nearly fifteen hundred, and was three times as large as the audience which heard Vivian M. Lewis in the same building a week or so ago. Carrying comparison further it may be said that, whereas Mr. Lewis's audience was unemotional, those who heard the Democratic candidate last night offered him hearty response in the way of cheers, handclapping, and friendly comments throughout his speech.

In addition to his Hackensack speech Mr. Wilson spoke at smaller towns in the county, and at all places was received with enthusiasm and by audiences which overflowed buildings engaged for the occasions. The nature of Mr. Wilson's campaigning yesterday came by way of decided contrast to the candidate's experiences of the last three weeks. Heretofore he had for the most part been in sections of the State wherein residents live their own lives, are unswayed by extraneous affairs, and look upon visits to great cities as holiday events to be undertaken infrequently. Yesterday he was among those who work in New York and sleep in New Jersey—among the commuters. . . .

In Hackensack he got a howl from the audience when he stated that his answers to the questions in George L. Record's letter had merely been taken from speeches he had already delivered, and that he had thus "got on Record." Mr. Wilson does not usually do a thing like that, but the temptation suddenly confronting him was too powerful to resist, and as every one laughed with him no harm was done.

In talking of railroads and their relation to the public, he referred to the commuters as "the medium of exchange as between communities."

Speaking of corporations, he said:

You know that the chief difficulty of our modern society is that we have not adjusted ourselves to its new conditions. The law of the United States, the law of each of the United States, is, for the most part, still not effective for all time. Once individuals dealt with one another; you know very well that in our time that is the least important part of our economic life. We now deal with each other by organization. The central organization of the whole economic body is the corporation. Now, a corporation isn't anybody in particular; a corporation is not for a long period of time together the same persons. For example, if I should happen— something which has not yet happened to me—to have enough money to invest in the stock of a corporation, and I should go to a broker and ask him if he had any of that stock for sale at an agreed price, and I should buy it, I would be buying what is theoretically, not practically, but theoretically a partnership in that business, for I would certainly be one of the minority stockholders, and the rights of the minority stockholder are very difficult to see with the naked eye.

But theoretically, in theory or at law I should be buying a partnership of that business. The board of directors would not know that anything had happened; they are willing at the meetings of the corporations to admit a new partner. This partnership is dissolved and formed and re-formed all the time by the sale and transferance of its securities and its voting power, but some gentlemen see to it that a certain block of the stock is not tampered with, but the junior partners are constantly changed. We have no part or lot in the management of the business; that is changed constantly. That is an entirely model [novel] situation so far as the law is concerned. Who is the corporation? Who constitutes the corporation? Nobody knows, and it is the same set of persons who get together. In dealing with corporations you are dealing with shifting sections of society; in other words, you are dealing with society itself. Our modern law is not adjusting itself to these conditions. That is why we are talking about regulating corporations.

Mr. Wilson makes two speeches to-night in Elizabeth.

Printed in the New York *Evening Post*, Oct. 28, 1910; some editorial headings omitted.

A Campaign Address in Elizabeth, New Jersey[1]

October 28, 1910.

I wonder if you realize how great a change has taken place in American politics since the adjournment of Congress. It is very difficult to throw our minds back to the state of affairs which existed before the last Congress of the United States adjourned. At that time the politics of the country and the policy of the country were in the control of a small group of men at one end of the capitol combined in action and purpose with a small group of men at the other end of the capitol. It is possible to name a little handful of Senators who were the masters of the Senate and a little handful of representatives clustered about the speaker of the house who were masters of the house.

The President of the United States after the adjournment of Congress admitted in the public speech that it was impossible for him to guide the policy of his party without the consent and the co-operation, not of the rest of the party, but of this little group of men. He said that in order to get the policies which he thought absolutely necessary through this house, it was necessary to give these men what they wanted in the matter of the tariff.

And what did they want? Did they want to promote the interests of the country? Did the President himself intimate that

[1] Delivered in Proctor's Theatre. This was the main address of the evening. As following reports will disclose, Wilson spoke earlier at a reception and dinner in his honor in Elizabeth, and, after this affair, he spoke at Elizabethport.

Elizabeth, 28 Oct., 1910. (II)

The change "over Summer", in men and methods
(Except in New Jersey)
Exit Single Bosses, House Bosses
Enter new men, new forces, in both parties, but
    particularly in Dem. party

What does it mean? New leadership, of course, but
    also new methods, new politics, if the people
    keep awake and get into the game.

    The close of the boss system (Define partnership)
    The beginning of the settlement of public ques-
            tions on their merits.
            The question henceforth, with regard to
                    public men, not whom have they served,
                    but what do they think?
    The re-allignment and reillumination of parties.

    IF THE PEOPLE THINK AND SUPPORT.

Question of the campaign, Which way lies the most
    open road to reform?
    Conversion by pressure and compulsion vs. a
            fresh start, a new approach

The object, STATESMANSHIP,
    The standard, THE COMMON INTEREST.

                                    10/28/10

they wished to promote the interests of the country? He intimated nothing of the kind, for he knew that the country was aware that these gentlemen were arranging a tariff policy for the country with regard to certain groups of men in the manufacturing and commercial world.

You have been reading no doubt the magazines and newspapers since the Payne-Aldrich tariff bill was passed, how it has been disclosed that most of the clauses contained in them what has been called, in bitter jest, a joker the meaning of which has not been disclosed to the houses themselves, and which altered the tariff and adjusted it in a way in which the interests would never dare to argue their case in public the way they granted it adjusted.

Upon the floor of the Senate, Senators were unable to get explanations from the chairman of the finance committee, Mr. Aldrich of Rhode Island, concerning some of the most important features of the bill, and submitting to his refusal to give them information. That was only a very short time ago. Have you realized how short a time ago? Now, it is not only ancient history, but it is history impossible of repetition.

These gentlemen have—at least one of them[2] has—retired or announced his retirement from public life. He was able to see the signs of the times, and knew it was more graceful to retire when you may than when you must. A gentleman at the other end of the capitol, the indomitable speaker of the last house of Representatives, has been showing a spirit which I must say, as a sportsman, I admire. He has not admitted his defeat, and he has defied his enemies and he has been deserted by his friend[s].

If I had stood by Mr. Cannon in the fight he made against the House of Representatives last spring,[3] I would not have deserted him this autumn. Either he was right or he was wrong. If he was right, the men who stood by him ought to stand by him now, and ought not come, when they feel the wind of public opinion blowing hot against him, and say that under no circumstances would they vote for Mr. Cannon as speaker.

I want to say very frankly that I do not understand, and I have conptempt [contempt] for, that kind of politics. But you know what it means. It means that Cannonism in these few months has become impossible, and men know it.

See how the plot of the play has changed. These men have had

[2] Senator Aldrich.
[3] See G. L. Record to WW, Oct. 17, 1910, n. 12.

their brief time upon the stage and the play has read, "Exit, Aldrich. Exit, Cannon." Why have they withdrawn? They have withdrawn because, as I have just said, the plot of the play demands it. There is no place for them any longer in our politics. The public opinion of this country has awakened, and it is impossible that those men should play the part again that they have played in the past.

What is the part that they have played? I have already intimated; it is the part of private arrangement. I do not know anything duller than the politics of this country has been in recent years, and I do not know anything more interesting than the politics of this country right now. It is infinitely dull to go like driven cattle to the polls and pretend that you [are] exercising the sovereign right of ballot, to give to man a chance to do something that they never tell us about, and that we cannot understand.

That is a beautiful exercise of independence on the part of self-governing people, when our representatives are told in unmistakable terms that what they are voting for is that business of private arrangement, which is none of their business. Now, I have talked with gentlemen, with my fellow citizens, about this sort of thing. They have shrugged their shoulders and said that the legislative business chiefly affects the large money interests, and you cannot blame them for seeing that they are represented in our legislature. You cannot blame them for seeing that they are represented?

Are these [men] that we go through the motions of electing our representatives or the representatives of special interest[s]? They are the representatives of private interests—a great many of them—and not of the public. But something has happened during the summer. I didn't notice anything particular or unusual about the weather last summer, but this autumn looks like another age in the politics of America.

Look at the personnel of the play as changed. Look at the extraordinary number of new men or made-over men that have come to the front. Now, I do not want to display any lack of modesty as a Democrat, and I want to call your attention to the fact that most of the new men have appeared on the Democratic side, and that most of the prominent men in the Republican ranks are made over. For example, take the leading Insurgent. I have nothing to say against Mr. Record. He did me a great service.

But take the leading Insurgents of the Middle West. They are men who used to follow the leadership of Mr. Aldrich without question: but they have broken away from the leadership, and I suspect—I won't speak with undue confidence—but I suspect that they are following the people rather than leading them. They have heard things, and they have felt currents in that great wide western country which they do not dare resist, and they have made themselves, whether they would or not, spokesmen of the new spirit that is in America. But whether we regard them as genuine converts, or unwilling converts, they are converts, and their very conversion is proof of the point that I am making, that they have recognized that new spirit when men can face in a different direction and have another attitude than they have hitherto had in matters of politics.

What does it all mean? Why, it means that one thing that we ought to know, which only one party has recognized in New Jersey, the change. There is no apparent change whatever on the part of the leaders of the Republican party in this State. They held a convention on the twentieth day of September in the city of Trenton at which strenuous efforts were made to apprise them of the change of climate. They were urged to put into the platform and to express in their nominations the new spirit of the Republican party, and they refused to do so and heaped insult upon insult upon those who suggested it, and since that nomination their chief spokesman has been the spokesman for the unorganized Republican party, for I want to say that the Republican party in most parts of this country has renewed itself, as the Democratic party has renewed itself—except in New Jersey. There are no symptoms upon the surface of these changes which I have [been] speaking of so far as the organized Republican party in this State is concerned. The symptoms are all on the Democratic side.

Well, what does it mean? Well, if you wish to put the lowest construction upon it, it means that the Democratic party has been [seen] the handwriting on the wall; it means that the Democratic party knows enough to get in under cover when it rains. But I don't believe that that is all there is to it, because the Democratic party has not sought a leader whose habit is to get under cover. There are symptoms that the Democratic party wants new leaders and actually wants to be led; led in a different spirit from that which has obtained hitherto: led in the spirit of a new age, led in the spirit of new processes, of new politics altogether.

Now what does this all mean? Why it is a very happy thing to state what it means. It means the end of the boss system. By the boss system I don't mean merely the system of organized politics, for parties, in order to be co-operative, must be organized, and we must not heap contempt upon the men who do the hard work in maintaining that organization.

The boss system means that the boss is used for private ends. That is the heart of the boss system. The boss system does not mean the organization, but that the organization determines the policies, not from the point of view of the public, but from the point of view of certain private interests.

What is it that is galling to a member of the legislature? To find that the organization to which he belongs in his home county has this kind of a grip upon him. It is because he is told that he must vote for a particular bill. He had not been told anything about that bill when he was elected. He supposed he was elected as a representative of the people, but it seems not. The bosses have let him know that he will sacrifice their friendship, that he will no longer enjoy their political contributions if he does not order his men to vote for them.

His men! Why his men? Because he can prevent their renomination if he chooses and they are in his grip. Because they have done something in violation of the party? Not at all. Because they have done something which the boss does not like. There is where the pinch comes. Not because it is politics at all, but because it is private business. That is the boss system.

Have you not noticed how little politics there is in the boss system for public policy, for the things we discuss? Discussion! Why, that is the dress parade on the platform. It does not follow that because gentlemen walk up and down the stage and pledge you when they go to the State capitol they are going to vote as they talk, as much as they may wish to do so, because their political fortunes are sometimes held in the hollow of a man's hand, because of the private understanding that man has had with particular interests.

That is the terror of the boss system, for it is not politics at all and absolutely deprives us of representative government. Very well, that act is over; the curtain has fallen. That kind of so-called politics has been smoked out and we are so hot on the trail of it that capture of it is instantaneously probable. It is not seen in the open; it [is] seen only when it is in its burrow; and when politics consists of burrows and underground passages and places of concealment then it is neither interesting nor profitable. It is both interesting and profitable when it is brought out into the open and becomes a matter of common knowledge and common discussion.

Now this change means the discussion of public questions on their merits. You are to have a novel experience—the settlement of public questions on their merits, on the basis of real solid permanent public opinion, of people whose lives are affected by everything that is best and purest in the way of legislation, so that hereafter you will ask your representatives not "Whom do you serve?" but "What do you think?"

That is a refreshing change, and if you should happen to find that they don't think at all, then you will have to dispense with their services to get somebody who can think. I was told by the superintendent of a great system of railways the other day that the trouble was not to get men in any number who would do what they were told, but to whom you could tell a thing and not forever have them come back and ask you how to do it; men who could adapt themselves to circumstances; men who could meet exigencies; men who are not forever at your apron strings; men who undertake a job with intelligence, and any duty they are assigned to.

That is the kind of intelliegence every intelligent employer requires, and that is what the public are looking for in their representatives, not men who will constantly be coming back for tips and say, "Such and such a bill is going to be up next week, how shall I vote on it?" but men who know how to discuss the merits of such a bill and know their antecedents and know what is being done in othere states about it who will submit to some kind of intelligent and enlightened leadership and who are willing to serve in public discussion as well as private, realizing that every piece of business is public not private business.

This is what is happening and this is the most interesting incident about this whole campaign. There is coming about an entire realignment of purposes and re-illumination of parties. Did you ever know in your experience a time when men were less blindly following a party hope than they are this year? And the reason is perfectly obvious. I am willing to admit that both parties have in the past had the particular bad habits that I have been talking about. The interesting circumstance about the present moment is that the past records of the parties do not serve for our guidance.

If you are looking for a habit you have got to look forward and not backward, and if you are looking for a new habit and forming a new habit you have to make an independent choice. There is nothing else for it. The question you will have to ask yourselves on the 8th of November is this, so far as New Jersey is concerned, where do you see the road most open to reform? Does it seem to you most open and likely on the Republican side, or does it seem to you most open and likely on the Democratic side?

I don't wish [you] to decide that question after what I shall say in any partisan spirit whatever. I simply ask you to put that question candidly to yourselves, not on the ground of the relative ability of the candidate[s], or at any rate of the gubernatorial candidate[s], not on the basis of any comparison of their character, certainly not on any comparison of their looks, for I believe it is the universal opinion that the Republican candidate is better looking. But I base all intrinsic human probabilities upon where does the open road lie? Does it lie in following a man who has been trained in the habits of an organization that is unreformed and probably unreformable, or in following a man who has never belonged to any organization, who has been invited to lead with absolute freedom, and who intends to lead.

(At this point a man called out from the audience, "The very best Republican[s] in the country will vote for you." "You are evidently very partial," replied Mr. Wilson, "and I thank you very much.")

Leaving individual personal merits entirely out of the question it does seem to me this is an opportune time in which to turn for a new deal, always provided however, always provided you do your part. If the people themselves don't think, if the people themselves don't see through public questions and make a point of supporting those who show the best disposition to serve them and the most enlightened method in serving, then there is nothing in the politics of a free people.

You are not to entrust your government to someone and take your eyes and your attention and interest off of it, even if the men you entrust in that fashion did what they thought right. They would be without the necessary guidance, for the men who represent you must constantly know what you are thinking about: they must constantly be in touch with your thoughts and your knowledge, and with your determination, with your devotion to those things which are for the public interest, for we are seeking a very rare and a very great thing.

We are seeking to substitute for politics old and ancient and handsome things which we call statesmanship. A very clever writer once defined a statesman as a man of ordinary opinions and of extraordinary ability. Now, in my opinion, it is absolutely necessary for a statesman to be in constant touch with the general body of opinion and if he does not share that opinion, if he cannot form it, if he cannot lead it, if he cannot inspire it, then he is no statesman at all. He may be a prophet; he may be a great thinker; he may be a very inspiring person, but he is not a statesman.

A statesman is a man who, with his intimate connection whether he knows it or not, is with the great average body of thinking men. Men do think in this country; they do observe the course of affairs; they are full of the ardor of hope that they have entered upon a new age, and they are ready therefore, to breathe that breath which distilled will make public opinion; which understood will make statesmen and which will lift the level of politics until America will feel again the exhilaration of the age in which politics is a great altruistic undertaking, in which men's veins will throb with all those unselfish purposes which after all underlie all the great accomplishments of the human race, for the standard of statesmen is the common interest, and the common interest cannot be thought out interest by interest.

If capitalists think only of the interests of capitalists, and if merchants think only of the interests of commerce, if men in retail trade think only of the retail trader in the particular community, if the workingman thinks only of the interest of the workingman, we cannot make any progress. Each class must think also of the interest of the rest; they must try to come to a common understanding, in a common sympathy, with a common thought and purpose, and then if we can get a spoke[s]man, an honest man, to lead them, we will recover the prestige and hope and accomplishment of American politics.

Is it not a heartening prospect? Is it not like recovering some of the breath of that age in which America becomes a nation, when men thought not only in the terms of neighborhoods and trades and occupations, but that of the leadership of the world? What was in the writings of the men that founded America—to serve the selfish interests of America? Do you find that in their writings? No; to serve the cause of humanity, to bring liberty to mankind. They set up their standards here in America in the tenet of hope, as a beacon of encouragement to all the nations of the world, and men came thronging to these shores with a hope that never existed before, with a confidence they never dared feel before, and found here for generations together a haven of peace, of opportunity, of equality. God send that in the complicated state of modern affairs we may recover the standards and recover the achievements of that heroic age.

FPS T transcript (WP, DLC).

From Charles Williston McAlpin

My dear Dr Wilson   Princeton, New Jersey Oct 28, 1910.

Please accept the enclosed contribution[1] to your campaign fund with my love and best wishes for your success. I want to have a small share in this epoch-making fight

Faithfully and Sincerely Yours   C W McAlpin

ALS (WP, DLC).
[1] Of $250, as D. F. Collins to WW, Nov. 11, 1910, TLS (WP, DLC), reveals.

From Henry Burt Ware[1]

Dear Sir: Salem, N. J., October 28th, 1910.

I enclose you herewith two circulars, one entitled "The deeds of Lewis the words of Wilson," the other purporting to be a declaration to "the working men of New Jersey," and issued by "The Progressive Voters of Labor, Luke McKenny, Secretary."[2]

These circulars have been distributed from house to house in this city and have been sent to the various labor organizations, and it would seem that they are having the desired effect. Salem is essentially in favor of organized labor; it is a glass manufacturing city, and while a great part of the workmen are members of our party, yet above everything else they are strong for their rights and resent anything that might be construed as opposition to their rights to unionize and co-operate with each other for their mutual rights and protection.

It was a pleasure for me to hear your address in the Opera House in our city last Tuesday and I thoroughly agree with you in the statement of your position in regard to labor. But owing to the fact that our opponents are taking this method of fighting you in this section I would suggest for your respectful consideration that you make some declaration in writing explanatory of these addresses of yours in the past wherein it is alleged that you showed such an unfriendly attitude towards labor. Making use of short excerpts from your speeches without a synopsis of the whole article or even its context puts one in an unfair light. The public I believe have faith in you and I therefore think that you should definitely explain your position. The [Salem] "Sunbeam" is a most excellent paper, and my wish is that you favor me with a statement of your position in order we may publish it, and give it such other publicity that it deserves.

Trusting that you will favor me with an early reply, I remain,

Yours, very truly,   Henry Burt Ware

TLS (WP, DLC).

[1] Attorney and master in chancery of Salem, N. J.

[2] These missing enclosures are described in W. Blackburn to WW, Oct. 15, 1910, n. 2.

From Charles Apffel Eypper[1]

My dear Sir: Guttenberg, N. J., Oct. 28th, 1910.

The Democratic party is to be congratulated in having nominated you as its candidate for Governor.

Since your declaration of principles in reply to the letter of Mr. Geo. L. Record, I feel that the entire state is to be congratulated in having the very rare opportunity of voting for a man, who, it is evident, will be truly the peoples representative, a condition practically unknown in this great country of ours, establishing thereby the beginning of a new era in political history.

Unfortunately your candidacy will aid in carrying into office some of the less reputable candidates on our ticket, especially in our county,[2] but we all feel that in your election the good accomplished will more than compensate for such shortcomings in our representation as will be produced by their election. Permit me to assure you that our little town will give you, comparatively speaking, as large a majority as any town in the state and, that, without the aid of any boss driven votes of which we feel proud to say we are free.   Very truly yours,   Chas A Eypper

TLS (WP, DLC).

[1] Mayor of Guttenberg, N. J., and a real estate and insurance broker of that town.

[2] Hudson County.

A News Report of an After-Dinner Talk in Elizabeth, New Jersey

[Oct. 29, 1910]

MANY ATTENDED RECEPTION AT ELKS

Dr. Wilson Guest of Honor at Informal Affair Given by General Collins

The reception and dinner tendered to Dr. Wilson and to the members of the county committee and the city executive committee by Gen. D. F. Collins last evening in the Elks' Club will linger as a pleasant memory in the minds of those who were privileged to attend long after the campaign is over. It partook of the nature of a big happy family gathering. One hundred and fifty guests were present, including prominent democratic workers from all parts of Union county and from neighboring cities.

From Dr. Wilson's arrival in the city at 4:45 o'clock until 6:15, an informal reception was in progress in the club rooms and the guests enjoyed the pleasure of meeting the candidate and of mingling together under the influence of his warm personality. The success of the affair was complete when the guest of honor had expressed his deep appreciation in a short after-dinner speech. . . .

Dr. Wilson was introduced by General Collins and said: "After having received the warm reception you have tendered me I feel that I am speaking to a body of friends and not to an audience. I particularly appreciate the delightful touch of intimacy that has pervaded this occasion. Although a great deal has been said about the debased uses to which the power of political parties has been in many instances turned I fully realize the importance of party organization and I honor the men who through disappointment, discouragement and defeat have held together their party organization. It is a great credit to their loyalty and patriotism and I do not hold it in any disregard.

"I am particularly indebted to you for I know that it was the vote of the delegation from this county that completed my nomination. I am highly honored by the confidence you placed in me. I anticipated the things that would be said about me before my metal was tested in any way. A man coming from the halls of a university is naturally regarded as a sort of remote, abstract person with little red blood in his veins. He is regarded not only as an amateur, but an amateur whose knowledge comes solely from books. There is nothing surprising in that. In view of these things you realize more now how I appreciate your trust. I am not here to make a speech but simply to express those feelings that have lain close to my heart. I hope in the months to come to be able to deserve in some measure the confidence you have displayed in me."

Printed in the Elizabeth, N. J., *Evening Times*, Oct. 29, 1910.

A News Report of a Campaign Address in Elizabethport, New Jersey[1]

[Oct. 29, 1910]

TELLS WHERE INTERESTS LIE

2,000 Cheer as Mr. Wilson Discusses Issues at Downtown Meeting

A heart to heart talk with 2,000 downtown democrats and a few hundred more who evidently came to be converted won

1 Delivered in St. Patrick's Parish Hall.

Elizabeth, 28 Oct, 1910. (I) Labour

Politics coming out of corners into the open
    Chief obstacles overcome when that is the case
Our object, to get together.
How get together on the labour qu.?
    By seeing what the rights of labour are
What are they? *For they need the law*   They are dealing with portions of Society
    The right to organize (— — — — !)
    To Sanitation, and the like
    To limitations of the length of day — — — —
    To insurance vs. injury and loss of life !
    To the individual and collective rights wh. may
        at any time be threatened.
In brief, protection and justice.
The same rule for all of us. — the Common in
    terest —
The same process for all of us, — the Common
    judgment.

10/28/'10

Woodrow Wilson the heartiest reception he has probably received
during his campaign for the governorship. Getting down to "the
level" of his audience he pointed out to them what he believed
their interests were and showed them in forceful, pointed phrases
that what was good for all was good for one.

His speech had particular reference to the workingman, to
organized labor, to corporations and to legislation which would
protect the toiler from the unreasonable monopolies. He also hit
at the private method of conducting government.

Ae [As] he entered the hall in the lead of General Collins and
other leaders three hearty cheers greeted his ears, the audience
rising as one man and shouting itself hoarse with welcoming
cries. His departure from the hall was the occasion for a similar
demonstration and for another three cheers. As he entered the
automobile which conveyed him to the station another three
cheers rang out, and he arose to bow to the hundreds of persons,
both men and women who were unable to enter the Court street
hall, but patiently waited to catch a glimpse of the candidate.

Mr. Wilson entered the hall just as Colonel Alexander S. Bacon
of New York was speaking. Mr. Bacon stopped at once and gave
the signal for the enthusiastic reception to the Princeton scholar.
There was nothing artificial or bombastic about this reception.
It could plainly be seen that it was from the heart of everyone
present. Not only was he given rousing cheers and applause before and after the speechmaking, but at various intervals of his
address when he made some particular reference [to] some
issue dear to the hearts of the men in the audience. . . .

"It is a great deal of pleasure for me to meet a body of men
like this," said he by way of introduction. "This is not an ordinary
campaign. It is not a question as to who has the offices. For my
part I don't care a rap for them, except that I can do something
that will be of service to men like yourself. Take away that right
and you deprive me of one of the greatest pleasures of my life.
The mere dignity of holding office is not a question in this
campaign. It has been too much of a question as to who would
get control of the offices not what good could be accomplished
or done.

"In a month we have turned a corner in our policies, or rather
we have chased men out of a corner and made them make up
their mind as to what kind of men they were. Politics in recent
years was an agair [affair] of 'corners.' " Here Mr. Wilson imper-
sonated the "whispering" style of government. "Some people who
didn't want to talk loud about something wrote letters about it.
Some talked over the long distance telephone. I am told that a

certain association takes pains to know all the conversations over the long distance telephone. This association offers to newspapers what they could learn of these conversations. Don't use the long distance telephone or write a letter. Go see the man. These statements are not exaggerations as a great deal of our policies happened that way in recent years.

"A committee waited on Mr. Aldrich and asked him why certain clauses were put in the tariff bill. They were practically told to mind their own business.

"The United States government asked the German government for information as to the amount of wages paid in the principal industries and got it. This information wasn't seen by anyone but Mr. Aldrich's committee. Why? Because it upset Mr. Aldrich's arguments; it was privately arranged.[2]

"When you think of that it's like you're talking of long ago. How long is it since the president made a speech at Winona to the effect that he was not a free agent, but that he had to accept the dictation of a certain coterie. Everybody knows that the game is up, and that a thing like that can't be done again. The public has wakened up. It is a well known fact that that sort of policy is impossible. The very breath of the policy is privacy. There isn't going to be any more of that kind of privacy. What was this privacy about? About the interests that were going to be served, or for the service of party interests.

"It is fatal to any country to have legislation made for any party. The task of the present moment is the task of getting together; more a task of heart understanding.

"Why is this warfare between labor and capital? Could capital exist without labor? Could labor exist without capital? Could anyone exist by trying to destroy the thing upon which each depends? It seems unnecessary to have warfare. Capital studies the interests of capital; labor the interests of labor. Capitalists should study the interests of the employe so that he may be justly protected against injury. That is what I mean when I say 'get together.' That is the 'common interest,' not the party interest. Nobody is true to his own interests who is opposing anybody else's true interests.

"I know that many down here are working men. I know that the American working man has a spirit of fair play. He wants a fair show, that's all he wants. I never knew a working man yet who wouldn't yield to the truth and do the sane thing if he was convinced he was not in the right.

"We want to break up private interests and private confer-

2 See n. 5 to the address printed at Jan. 21, 1910, Vol. 20.

ences. To understand a question is to get down to the point of view of the other fellow, see what creates the difference and how much difference exists. The way to study the labor question is to study the interests of the laboring man. You can't settle it by thinking that the labor man is trying to get something he ought not to get.

"Why do the labor men find it necessary to argue now when they didn't in former years? I'll tell you why. Long ago the laboring man served under one employer. He knew him intimately. He dealt with his employer as a mand [man] and as a friend. But the labor man no longer works for the individual. He works for a great body of men called a corporation. He never sees them. They have no sympathetic relations with him. They don't know what it means. They no longer have close sympathies.

"What is a corporation? A corporation is part of the whole community. What are stockholders? Stockholders are persons together for two weeks at a time. He who buys stock has voting power. Anybody who has money can get into corporations, except one or two. You cannot deal with corporations because they are changing their lists of stockholders all the time.

"We should make laws for corporations because they are a piece of the community. The workingman should have the freest and fullest right of organization.

"He should have the right to do anything that is legitimate when dealing with a piece of the community. Everything is legitimate about that, provided nothing is done that is contrary to the interests of the whole community.

"Now if I were to talk to you about something that interested myself alone I couldn't talk loud enough to make you listen. But if I talked about something that interested 10,000 I would have many listeners.

"An example of how the rights of the laboring man should be protected would be the introduction of proper sanitation; the guarding of machinery, proper ventilation, the proper relation between the physical life and work you are doing. There should be no confinement in working places where the atmosphere is almost stifling. If your employer lived with you in that atmosphere you wouldn't have need of organizing. You would get what you want without organizing.

"We have devised a law providing for employer's liability. It is not a law which will say that the employer should be liable for damages, but an arrangement where you won't have to sue. For in most instances if you sue you won't get it. This is an arrangement which will operate like insurance where you can get your fixed rate without waiting. This law is going to be a tax on all of us so far as the thing manufactured is concerned. But it is only fair we should get together and do the fair thing.

"Let us hope that we will have a democratic legislature to go to to fix things that are out of joint. That's what the government is for.

"If you don't consult the government you'll get left. The trouble is that one man doesn't see the thing from the viewpoint of the other man. The trouble with kings is not that they are despotic, but that they get their legs pulled all the time.

"What we advocated in this campaign is to get accessibility to your government. What we want is to get men to lead that government, men who will listen to you and won't always be thinking how it will affect the 'organization' in the next election.

"If I was elected governor there is not a single man or body of men I would not be willing to consult with. I tell you though that if a man came to me in his own interests I would oppose him even if I saw it would lose me votes at the next election. Good government is a vital thing. Like friendship, it is made possible through the association of open minds and honest purpose. Men do not always make wilful mistakes.

"Let us all get in the games, study each other's interests.

"Old campaigns were conducted by the candidates lying about each other. It doesn't make a difference to the person lied about, but it does make a difference to the voter. He has to see things as they are.

"No man for himself. Every man for New Jersey. New Jersey because we live here, because we get justice here, because we get our living here. We are not going to try for some millenium that is tardy in coming, but we will see what we can do for each other. That is the way I want to serve you. I understand what some of you want and I am going to learn to understand what all of you want."

Printed in the Elizabeth, N. J., *Evening Times*, Oct. 29, 1910.

To David Paulson Foster *et al.*

My dear Friends: [Princeton, N. J.] October 29, 1910.

Your request that I should continue my lectures in Jurisprudence has given me the greatest pleasure and gratification, and I wish with all my heart that it were possible to comply with it. I feel, however, that even if it were possible for me to continue my lectures, my time would be so broken in upon, my service in the classroom so irregular and unsatisfactory, that it would be of no advantage to you, and I should myself be mortified to have the thing badly done.

I have thought it my duty to resign not only the Presidency of the University, but my professorship also, though by a misunderstanding it was not so interpreted at the last meeting of the Board, and therefore I have to reply to your generous request, that I am no longer connected with the teaching body of the University which I have so long loved and served.

Will you not accept from me my warmest assurances of gratitude for your kindness and of regard for you collectively and individually? It would be a pleasure to serve you further if it were possible. Sincerely yours, Woodrow Wilson.

Printed in the *Daily Princetonian*, Nov. 16, 1910.

To Charles Williston McAlpin

My dear McAlpin: Princeton, N. J. October 29th, 1910.

I need not tell you how warmly I appreciate your contribution to the campaign fund or how it strengthens my heart that it should come with affection and with confidence in me.
Affectionately yours, Woodrow Wilson

TLS (photostat in RSB Coll., DLC).

A News Report of Three Campaign Addresses in Hudson County, New Jersey

[*Oct. 29, 1910*]

HUDSON EXCEEDS FORMER WELCOME

Woodrow Wilson Centre of Three Tremendous Outpourings on His Return.

PLEADS FOR OPEN DOOR

Wants the People Brought Into Close Contact
With Their Own Government.

Hoboken, N. J. Oct. 29.—In a return visit to Democratic Hudson county to-night Woodrow Wilson found himself in the midst of a fresh demonstration of the following of the common people. All unexpectedly he was called upon to address three meetings, one at West Hoboken, one at West New York and a third here, every one of them attended by immense numbers of people, and

HOBOKEN, 29 October, 1910.

THE PEOPLE AND THE GOVERNMENT.

The people have been shut off from their gov't.
1) By the processes of nomination
2) By the uses made of the power of the Machine
   It was only necessary, and always necessary, to "see" somebody.
3) By consequently organized influences
4) By lack of frank and exhaustive public debate
5) By lack of a spokesman.
   The changing conception of the function
   and privilege of the Governor of the State.
The "House of Governors".

Growth of publicity in the processes of our governments.

PUBLIC OPINION: How to use it:
By finding out and publishing the facts
By public discussion
By systematic pressure
By independent voting.

10/29/10.

all showing the utmost interest in the speaker's arguments and line of reasoning. It was a trying experience for the candidate, but he bore up well under it, and displayed in all his addresses the same great strength and courage and valor.

Mr. Wilson was met at the University Club, New York, by former State Comptroller William C. Heppenheimer, City Chairman Griffin[1] and a committee of local Democrats, who brought him across to New Jersey in an automobile, arriving at St. Michael's Hall, West Hoboken, for the first meeting, to the accompaniment of music of several bands, fireworks and much cheering.

He spoke there half an hour, and then was started over to St. Joseph's Hall, West New York, where there was a brilliant electrical illumination, with more fireworks. After a 20-minute address there he was brought to the main meeting, in St. Mary's Hall, in this city, where a great and demonstrative crowd had gathered, and his appearance was the signal for a mighty cheer, the waving of flags and hats, and, despite the lateness of the hour, the big crowd evinced an interest that was wonderful to see.

"There is a very remarkable thing in this campaign, gentlemen," said Mr. Wilson. "I have been struck by nothing so much in the audiences that I have faced as the evident sincerity. This is no ordinary campaign—it is evident that the people have come out in order to do something, to accomplish something. I don't wonder you feel as you do. We have drifted very far away from a government by the people. We have a great many things between us and the government that belongs to us.

"I think I can tell you what I mean by that statement. You know that when a bill is introduced in the Legislature, whether it be the Legislature of New Jersey or the Legislature of New York, or the Congress at Washington, the first thing that happens to that bill is that it goes to a committee. That committtee is appointed by the Speaker, who is chiefly connected with a great political organization, which great political organization is connected with certain business interests, and then, when the bill comes to be considered, it is generally considered by the committee and not by the Legislature. Are you admitted? Is the public admitted to the deliberations of the committee? Not at all.

"Those deliberations are private in most instances. Of course, the committee holds hearings and allows persons who are interested in the subject matter of the legislation to come and be heard, either in person or by attorney, but those are public hear-

1 Patrick Robert Griffin, chairman of the Hoboken Democratic Committee.

ings. The deliberations of the committee are another matter. They are private, and most of the things that happen to bills happen in ways that the public can not find out. Most of the bills that are intended for public interest are smothered in committee, and it requires an investigation which you cannot conduct to find out why they are smothered.

"Something is between you and legislation, and when you come to debate upon the floor—either of the national Legislature or the Legislature of the State—you know what has recently happened in Washington, what we call Cannonism, is the control of legislation by the Speaker, one man who appoints all the committees, dictates to those committees what they shall do with the bills and won't allow anybody to get on the floor to oppose them who has not had a previous understanding that he will be recognized, so that you can get up and shout your throat out at 'Mr. Speaker,' and you won't be seen, although you are under the nose of the Speaker, shaking your finger at him in the space right before his desk.

"He does not see you; he does not hear you; but he recognizes somebody over there in the distance who has had a previous understanding with him that he would be recognized. If you want any time for debate you have to go and dicker with the chairman of the committee and get him to share his time with you—as if it were his time and not the time of the people—in order that you may exercise your right of debate. It is all a game, tied up in private understanding.

"Now, these understandings may be perfectly honorable; they may be intended for the public good; but my point is that they are private and not public, and that the debates on the floor of Congress, and, for the most part debates on the floor of the State Legislature, do not amount to anything and are not worth reading because they do not amount to anything.

"Who reads the debates of Congress? The newspaper editors and men who want to comment on the affairs of Congress. I have received the Congressional Record, I cannot tell how many years, and I sometimes read it, but when I do read it, I know that is not the business. When I want to find out what is going on in Washington I ask somebody who knows what is being said in the committees. What was at the bottom of all this tariff legislation, of which we have got so sick and tired? Why nobody in the Senate knew what [lay] back of that legislation except the Committee on Finance, and then only those members of the Committee on Finance who happened to be Republicans knew it. The Democratic members of the committee could not get at the true inwardness of that legislation, and Senator Aldrich, the chairman of the committee, answered questions or not as he pleased, when questions were propounded to him by members of the Senate, representatives of great sovereign States on the floor of that body. That is not representative government. I don't care what the reason was for it. I would a great deal rather have things said aloud than said behind closed doors.

"What is the remedy for it? There are a good many remedies for it, and one of the remedies I have and talk about is the services that an inquisitive and talkative Governor can render. A Governor who wants to know what is going on behind all the closed doors has opportunities to find out and will greatly relish talking about it aloud. There are a good many men on the Democratic ticket with me in the several counties of this State, men who have been and who I hope will be in the Legislature of this State, who are just as dead in earnest about letting the people of this Commonwealth have a grip upon this Legislature as anybody else. Some of them can talk most eloquently. I don't have to talk for them; I have come here to let you see what kind of a chap I am."

"Three cheers for Dr. Wilson," yelled a man in the audience, and the crowd let loose with startling vim.

"Now you know a very interesting thing has happened. During the latter part of the month of November there's going to meet in Frankfort, Ky., a body of Governors, all the Governors in the United States. You know they were twice heard. Mr. Roosevelt and Mr. Taft called them together. Now they have formed an association of their own and are not going to wait for the President to call them together again. They have a chairman, a secretary and a permanent organization, and they are going to hold annual meetings. What for? To compare notes, to see how their several Commonwealths co-operate in respect to those matters about which the State Legislatures are most interested. Don't you see how interesting that is? What are they going to do?

"Are they going to go home and twiddle their thumbs? Aren't they going home with opinions in their heads? Aren't they going home with ambitions to serve a great people, with a consciousness of what immense issues are involved, and with the desire in their hearts to submit wise counsel, gathered from such sources?

"There is, if the Governors of these States are wise enough to exercise it, a great leadership in store for them of the most legitimate sort, not given them by the law, but given them in their several commonwealths as they are about to control public opinion. That is what I call bringing the people back to their government, giving them a spokesman, giving them direct contact with the things that are going on generally. That is what I call government by public opinion, which is what our arrangements are for. Let that thing get once started and you will find that there are no locks on committee doors; you will find that everything will slowly creep out into the open.

"We want the contact of public affairs with public opinions. That is what we are after in this State, and that is what we are going to get. We are going to get it, no matter what happens, because it does not depend even on the next 8th day of November. This tide is rolling so that nobody can get out of its way. There is no dam that can stop it; there is no subterfuge that can escape it. This thing is going to rise and overwhelm everything that is antagonistic."

Printed in the *Philadelphia Record*, Oct. 30, 1910; some editorial headings omitted; with corrections and additions from the partial text in the Jersey City *Jersey Journal*, Oct. 31, 1910.

From William H. Morrow[1]

My dear Doctor Wilson: Belvidere, N. J. October 29th, 1910

This morning the local 'schoolmaster' of Blairstown,[2] always hitherto a republican, and former assessor of his township, came to see me on a business matter, and it gave me much pleasure to hear from him that not only Doctor Sharpe, principal of Blair Hall Academy, but all the resident members of his faculty have expressed their purpose to vote for you at the coming election.

This is the more gratifying, showing as it does, the present tendency of thoughtful men towards progressiveness and freedom of action in that it comes from a body of men who are connected with an institution almost wholly maintained by the Blair family, none of whom has ever been known to vote anything but the republican ticket. And the schoolmaster himself said that not only out of respect for the profession, which seems to have had a wonderful exaltation since Griggs' unfortunate satire, but because of his conviction of duty in the matter as well, he purposed not to be behind others of his calling, and would cast his vote and use his influence towards others for your election. And he named a good many who are of his way of thinking.

From every part of this county comes to me the same expression, and from the same class of people.

I know there are some disagreeable features connected with a campaign such as you are conducting,—and you *are* leading the people as well as the party to a higher level of true politics,—but there is another side to the conflict, and that is the demonstration by [that] men who think for themselves and who help others to think for themselves, too, are standing by your side and approving the magnificent stand you have taken for a purer and better way of administering governmental affairs.

No one can help realizing that we are to pass through a readjustment of affairs,—that order must be brought out of the existing disorder,—that present conditions have been brought about by incompetent and unfit men who have had hold of the body politic's affairs and have used their power for purely selfish purposes and have brought discredit upon all the departments of the state government, judicial as well as legislative and executive, and that some one previously wholly unconnected with machines,—the machinery of both parties, must be placed at the head of the state to suggest, to advise, to mould the sentiment of the people in the struggle through which we are of necessity to pass that out of it all [we] may come to the very best solution of the problem.

And this is why the best element of society,—the people who read and study and think and know something of the state's condition, are turning to you in so great numbers, and I do not think there can be the peast [least] doubt as to the result.

The "charming lady"[3] of whom you spoke in the court-house, and of course she is charming to me, asks me to have you come to our house after the election is over that she may entertain you and come to know you better than she did six years ago.

Yours very Truly,   Wm. H. Morrow

TLS (WP, DLC).

[1] Lawyer of Belvidere, N. J.

[2] The Rev. Dr. John C. Sharpe, headmaster of Blair Academy.

[3] Mary Wilhelmina Wychoff Morrow.

An Interview

[Oct. 30, 1910]

WOODROW WILSON SEES HOPE IN AN AWAKENED PUBLIC

Exposure of Widespread Political Graft Is Encouraging
Because It Shows That People Are Unwilling
to Stand Corruption Any Longer.

By EDWARD MARSHALL.

Are we hopelessly mired in public corruption?

Is the whole country honeycombed with graft?

Was there ever before in the world's history a similar prevalence of official wickedness?

Is our country singular among the countries of the world in the unfortunate character of its public servants?

Are we merely passing through an evolutionary period, peculiar to all people who work out new systems of government, or are we just naturally and regularly bad?

What ails the public men in the United States, anyway?

Is there any hope for betterment, or are we all mad with the money lust, so that conditions will grow worse instead of better?

These and a few other questions I put to Woodrow Wilson, President of Princeton University, candidate for Governor of New Jersey, militant reformer. And the answer or answers were most comforting. . . .

I found that he was not in the least alarmed by the conditions indicated in these exposures. I found that the prospect of having to deal at first hand with similar conditions in his own State not alone did not appall him but left him most cheerful.

"The general situation," said he, "affords no cause for despair; on the contrary, it excites and justifies hope."

"That widespread corruption is now being exposed," he went on, "is far from furnishing proof of a hopeless demoralization in our politics. There are no ills confronting us of which we cannot hope to rid ourselves. That we are hearing of them constantly shows that we are demanding full reform wherever viciousness exists. That many scandals are being made public is an evidence that we are throwing off abominable practices with wholesome and abundant vigor."

Dr. Wilson is a long, lank man, neither careless nor very careful in his dress. I don't believe there is much muscle on his bones, but those bones are very large. When he stands his coat fits loosely on his shoulders. Maybe his tailor measured him for it; but I fancy that instead he told him to go in and take a look at the two pegs in his clothes closet where he hangs it up of nights. His cheek bones are high, like a Multnomah Indian's, and he runs to chin excessively.

Dr. Wilson's face is definitely four-cornered, with hard bone not far beneath the skin at any of the corners. His hair is thin and graying, and may possibly be combed regularly. There is a wrinkle just between his heavy eyebrows deep enough to be a knife scar, and the lines which curve down and outward from his nose, callipering his mouth, are very definite and deep.

I presume the man had dimples there when, fifty-three years since, he was a baby one year old, and I presume his mother worried because he had so very large a mouth. I can imagine, also, that she worried somewhat because his ears stuck out. But these things now give great strength to his face, although not even a campaign manager would try for women's votes for him with the announcement that the man is handsome. Campaign managers can lie, but none would go that far.

It is a kindly face, however; about as far from that which one would pick out as belonging to a college President as any I have recently encountered. I can imagine how the many wrinkles which enmesh his eyes and those faint lines indicated upon his forehead could deepen into an extremely fearsome frown for undergraduates who had transgressed, or for the grafters who do not make him despair.

I ought to say about this time that all the nice things he insisted on about poor human nature in his talk with me surprised me somewhat; but I felt certain he knew what he was talking about. For Woodrow Wilson is no dreamy scholar. He wears eyeglasses, not spectacles.

This indicates a detail of him which is worthy of some emphasis, because he is already spoken of for a bigger job than Governor of New Jersey. Many enthusiastic Democrats are saying that if he wins out and then makes good down in mosquito land he will be timber fit to brace a Democratic National platform as a Presidential nominee. I heard that talk in Princeton, and the day before I had heard it in a small town in New York State. Since then two newspapers have come to hand, each spreading it —one from a city in Michigan and one from Mississippi.

When I protested at the statement that the envelope full of clippings telling of corruption, which I had carried down with me as ammunition, was a bunch of signs of hope, he said:

"Why, certainly they're signs of hope. The fact that all these facts are being finally made public is the best of signs. We are hearing everywhere of graft. Graft, graft, graft—the word echoes and re-echoes in the public prints and on the public platforms. This does not mean that there is more graft in proportion to our population than there was in the 'good old days,' but that now we are unwilling to put up with it and are ferreting it out and getting at the grafters.

"There always have been grafters. They were most dangerous, however, when their grafting could be hidden with success. Those days have passed. Everywhere where there has been a graft scandal it has scotched the grafters even if it has not carried to them actual concrete punishment. In many cases it has done the latter, too. And every scandal has resulted in more careful scrutiny of other places in which scandal might be breeding.

"Scrutiny safeguards. We are beginning to scrutinize. We are getting over some of our careless ways. Scrutiny and care—they will be the purifiers.

"Do not mistake me," he continued. "I am not belittling any of the sins which are revealed. The revelations being made on every hand of the venality of officials and the maintenance of business by corruption should fill the whole Nation with sorrow and shame; but, as I have said, this ought not to discourage us, but to make us feel more confident than ever that better things and purer times are coming.

"The discovery and punishment of corruption and sins against public morals of every kind are proof that the moral energy of the communities that uncover and condemn them is more vigorous than it has been. And there are no cases in which the sinners, being once uncovered, are not punished, although there may seem to be such cases. A 'whitewashing' by a Judge or jury does not give a man immunity. 'Whitewashed' men are often more utterly disgraced than are convicted men.

"The 'whitewashed' man can seldom face his fellow-men again with any comfort in his soul. That such men break beneath the strain, as they almost invariably do, is proof enough that the majority of the community is good—that they, the occasional grafters, are surrounded by honest men who give contempt and reprobation to the offender against public morals. Such contempt and reprobation men cannot endure as easily as they can endure prison stripes. Ostracism in a crowd is worse than solitary confinement."

"Then the epidemic is of exposure, not of grafting?"

"Certainly. Grafting has always been practiced more or less—not, I believe, more of late than in olden times."

"Was there grafting, then, for instance, in the time of Washington?"

"History, I think, does not record the time when there were not dishonest men. But history does not record, and history will not record, the time when honest men were not in the majority."

"Then you see no cause for discouragement at all?"

"Of course not. Everything, upon the other hand, is most encouraging."

A moment later Dr. Wilson presented an extremely striking illustration of his view of the existing situation. It expressed the viewpoint of the President of Princeton University—and, I am told, is characteristic of him in its picturesque forcefulness.

"A hollow in the ground," said he, "is filled with all sorts of corruption. Naturally it becomes offensive. Men cover it and hide it. The public then does not see it, and is unconscious of its presence; but its unhealthful influence is there and harms the folk who live near it, giving them all manner of diseases, coming whence they know not. The fester, being hidden, works its evil secretly.

"A man comes by who is inquisitive, suspicious, investigative. He takes a spade and turns back the rich sod which covers the concealed corruption. Having been there a long time, and having been extremely bad to start with, the whole community is startled, and offended, by the stench which instantly arises when the pit is opened. They have been suffering from the insidious influence of the concealed offense for years, but now for the first time know about it. It had its origin in bygone times.

"Another man in a nearby community hears of this episode and looks about him, wondering if some of the illness in his neighborhood may not have been caused by similar hidden horrors. He finds reason to believe that that has been the case, digs, to make certain, and, in turn, finds filth. And then another and another, another and another dig. Each finds filth, for it was buried, hidden, in the days when that was common custom.

"Well, the whole country gasps. The stench is very great. A mighty cry arises that this is a most vicious age and that the earth is very vile. But, as fast as these unpleasant places are uncovered, corrective measures are resorted to which cleanse them, and the secret damage which they have been doing is brought to an end. Therefore the people who asserted that the discovery of the filth meant that the country was becoming dangerous to live in were all wrong. Its discovery meant, really, that it was becoming safe to live in. For its discovery meant that it would be eliminated and its baleful influence brought to an end."

I have not here transcribed President Wilson's exact words. Just before I left for Princeton I was obliged to discharge my regular stenographer and when I reached the college town a hotel clerk found for me one who was not competent to take in shorthand the exceedingly crisp utterances of the scholarly nominee for Governor. I did not learn of this incompetence till the time came for the transcription of the notes.

But what I have written is about what President Wilson said. He made it very clear that he did not believe the graft exposures which are nowadays so much in evidence are signs that we are any worse than were our fathers and grandfathers, but, rather, signs that we have been progressing in our slow, uncertain way, toward that perfection which, it has been written, shall obtain at last. For instance, I inquired of him:

"But do not all the instances of muncipal corruption, for example, which are lately being brought to light indicate that our political condition really is very serious?" I was working desperately to make him give vent to one pessimistic thought at least.

Instead of expressing pessimism he smiled pleasantly—a smile which indicated that he had no fears whatever for the welfare or the morals of the people as a whole.

"Of course we are in a serious situation," he replied. "All nations are. This world is serious. But it is my conviction that our present situation is far more serious for the grafter than it is for the honest people of the Nation. Correction is in progress all along the line."

"As we grow older will graft decrease among us?"

"I feel certain of it. Yes, graft will certainly decrease as we grow older, for as we grow older we shall grow to know better how to handle it. Humanity improves. It does not retrograde."

"Lord Northcliffe,[1] to whom I talked the other day, attributed most of our faults, as a Nation, to the fact that we are mixing blood. He said that we are mixing the worst blood of Europe and making of it unpleasant average blood in the United States. Do you agree with him?"

"I believe our mixed blood will compare favorably with the unmixed blood of any European nation. I do not believe that mixed blood in our people has the slightest thing to do with such political corruption as occurs here. It is my belief, although I do not know, of course, that there was as much grafting in the old days as there is in these."

"In the days, for instance, of the Revolution?"

Now I waited for his answer with anxiety; for Woodrow Wilson is the author of "George Washington," an elaborate and eloquent appreciation of the Father of our country and his confrères in the launching of our institutions. The very paving stones on certain streets of Princeton are held holy by all, save drivers and chauffeurs, because they've been in place since 1776. The Sons of the Revolution are as popular in Princeton as the sons of ironmasters are on Broadw[a]y, in New York City. But nothing bitter happened. He nodded his head gravely in assent.

"Yes, in the days of the Revolution. There was graft in those days, too. Graft is not a novelty. There have been good men and bad men in all ages, with the proportionate number of good men steadily increasing. It will continue to increase."

[1] Alfred Charles William Harmsworth, Baron (later Viscount) Northcliffe, British publisher, whose newspaper empire at this time included the *Evening News*, the *Daily Mail*, and *The Times*, all of London.

"Have you any especial remedy to suggest for such evils as at present either actually canker us or threaten us?"

"No special concrete remedy can be devised for human nature's tendency toward graft. I do not think that tendency is greater in this country than in others. I am not willing to speak definitely upon that score, because of lack of knowledge; but no doubt it is to general moral education that we must look for the correction of the evil as it now is found, and this is now in progress and is having its results.

"It may be to the effect of this trend toward an effectual moral education for the young that these exposures which bring graft so fiercely into the public attention at this time are due. That, doubtless, is the case to a degree. Yes, I am sure that the mere fact that the exposures are in progress is an evidence that the education which our schools and colleges are giving in good morals is having its effect upon the rising generation."

I asked here if he could not suggest a list of books for the youth who cannot take advantage of a course at Princeton or another college—a list of books which fathers could advise their sons to read—a list of books which would help keep a youngster honest.

"No," said he, "I could not make a list of that sort. You cannot really teach men to be honest in the activities of life by giving them a list of books to read. Books help toward mental discipline, and furnish needed technical information. But the great educators are the lives of good men and successful. All this news of graft exposure is food education for the youth of the United States. It is example which must teach the young man which way is the best to choose; example far, far more than printed precept; example and the friction of his mind against more mature minds which are able. That is real education. The information which books furnish is the mere stuff on which to base it."

"Do you find the recent revelations in New York City—revelations that the poor have been robbed viciously for years through short weight and short measure by small tradesmen, and that the Government has been robbed likewise by importers, suggestive of any general condition?"

"It has been tolerance which has made this possible. The people, themselves, have tolerated the robbery, largely through sheer carelessness. Officials, chosen from the people, have thought it safe to tolerate it and get paid for it, perhaps. But the tolerance is growing less and less, and when the people cease to tolerate it, graft will automatically cease."

"Lord Northcliffe found a reason for alarm in that the small American business man seems to be as great a grafter, in proportion, as some so-called magnates of the trusts."

"My reply to such a criticism of American conditions would be the wholly obvious statement that the small and large are so closely interlaced in business life that they cannot be separated. If the wholesaler is a grafter, then the retailer will be, of course; but there are fewer wholesale grafters than there were, and, therefore, fewer retail grafters. Instances of both will become rarer with the passage of time and our development.

"The people should not be alarmed but pleased because they find so much talk of exposure in the newspapers. Editors should not allow themselves to become pessimistic because, day after day, night after night, new items come to them which tell of vice uncovered in official life. It is an era of exposure and an era of exposure means the dawn of better things.

"The newspaper reader, and especially the newspaper editor, finds his attention fixed on details. The aggregate of tales of graft in a day's newspaper may be appalling. It may make the man who reads or prints it feel amazement and alarm. Yet, when he comes to analyze it, he will find that that day's aggregate of revelations concern not the grafting of that day alone, but the grafting of a long period. The grafting has been going on for years. This era of exposure is bringing it to light all at once.

"The result, apparently, is a tremendous mass of current crimes of this sort. But, in truth, the crimes are not the crimes of this day, but the crimes of this day and the crimes of many yesterdays made public simultaneously. Here are items in the newspapers which tell of recent graft, in the next column there are items telling of the graft of fifteen years ago, now for the first time uncovered. Carelessly we lump them and assign to current days the aggregate. In doing this we are unjust to ourselves. We are much better, really, than we have lately been believing ourselves to be.

"New York's recent discoveries of false bottoms in its potato measures, of false sides in its pint cups, are not significant of anything but good. Retail cheating is as old as retail trade. It were foolish to be horrified by the announcement that it notably exists. Of course it notably exists. It always has existed, and it always will exist as long as it is tolerated by its victims. They are the ones to put a stop to it—and they can stop it absolutely. That they have begun to stop it at all these things attest, and that is a good sign. How can you think it otherwise?

"No, I am an optimist. In the speeches which I have made recently referring to corruption I have been doing what I could to help along the present admirable movement which is everywhere, throughout the country, going on toward graft exposure, graft correction. It is one of the good signs, it is one of the reasons why we should rejoice, that such speeches are the sort of speeches candidates are finding it most wise to make in seeking public office. They are optimistic signs. No signs could be more so."

"Then, finally," said I, "you do not think we ought to be too greatly worried?"

"Worried?" said Woodrow Wilson, smiling very brightly, very pleasantly. "Of course not. We should be elated."

With that I packed my doleful graft clippings in my bag. They had outlived their usefulness, and, for me at least, had ceased to have further significance. I had come a black pessimist. I went away an enthusiastic optimist. I defy any one to come under the influence of the Woodrow Wilson smile, to say nothing of the Woodrow Wilson logic, and go away otherwise than as an optimist.[2]

Printed in the *New York Times*, Oct. 30, 1910.
[2] There is an undated typed copy of a memorandum for this interview in WC, NjP, and a WWsh draft entitled "Mem. for Interview" in WP, DLC.

A News Report of a Campaign Address in Bayonne, New Jersey

[Nov. 1, 1910]

"I AM THE FRIEND OF LABOR," SAYS WILSON

Gubernatorial Candidate Tells of His Plan for an Employer's Liability Act.

Bayonne had more politics last night than ever it had before in the same space of time. Both the candidates for Governor, Woodrow Wilson, Democrat, and Vivian M. Lewis, Republican, were the principal speakers and each was accorded a hearty and boisterous ovation. Mr. Wilson delivered his address, or rather his two addresses, at the Democratic Club, Broadway and Twenty-seventh Street, and Mr. Lewis spoke at the Republican Club, two blocks farther north. Each club had a band of music playing and set off fireworks and red fire and at times skyrockets from the rival buildings almost crossed each other as they ascended high in the air.

BAYONNE, 31 October, 1910.

The Government for all, not for some.

                                    The common cause.
Object, TO GET TOGETHER.

How get together on the labour qn.?
    By sympathy and the wide outlook
    By comprehending what the rights of labour are

The change in all conditions.
    Labourers now dealing with portions of Society,
        not with "employers" in the old sense.
    They, therefore, need and are entitled to The
        Law.

The Rights of Labour:
    To organise (and to have the countenance of·
        the law in doing so).
    To sanitation and physical protection
    To limitation of the labour day, especially
        in certain occupations.
    To insurance against injury and loss of life
        (employers' liability)
    To all individual and loocoltive rights wh.
        may at any time be threatened by the pro-
        cesses of society.
    In brief, protection and justice.

Same rule for all, — the common interest.

Same process for all, — the common judgment.

                                    Comp. Eli. speech
                                    - 10/28/10

The rally at the Democratic Club was declared by old-timers to be about the biggest and most enthusiastic that the party ever held in the city and veteran Republicans were strong in their statement that the reception accorded Mr. Lewis was about the best ever. There was no doubt but that both Mr. Wilson and Mr. Lewis were decidedly pleased with the crowds that greeted them and the cheers and applause with which their speeches were received. At the Democratic rally were many Republicans and at the Republican ratification were many Democrats. Women were conspicuous in both gatherings.

It was estimated that 800 persons jammed themselves into the Democratic Clubhouse. They filled every chair, they crowded the aisles, they stood ten deep in the rear and they formed a solid mass down the stairs and into the main corridor. Hundreds unable to get into the buildings were content to stand out in front and were rewarded when an overflow meeting was held. Recorder Hugh Mara called the attention of Mr. Wilson to the crowd outside after the candidate had started to leave the hall after speaking, and Mr. Wilson graciously consented to make an extra speech for which he was repaid with tumultous applause.

Rev. Peter E. Reilly, pastor of St. Henry's R. C. Church, sat on the platform along with prominent Democrats, and in the audience were Rev. Mitchell Bronk, pastor of the First Baptist Church, and Rev. C. X. Hutchinson, pastor of the First Methodist Church. Workmen composed a large part of the audience and some of them bore evidence of having just came from work. They listened with unusual attention to the speech by Mr. Wilson, for it had to do with the labor question. . . .

"I want to speak to this crowd of men to-night on the subjects of labor.

"Not because my views have been misrepresented, because I know workingmen enough to know that they are not going to be misled by things of that sort. I know their independence, and I know that they are not going to be deceived by gross and wilful misrepresentation; but I want to speak of labor, because I believe I am going to be elected Governor of New Jersey and because I want you men to understand how I look at the subject of labor, so that when we come to deal with this complicated and important question in later months we may know how we are dealing with one another.

"Now, why is it that we have a labor question at all? It is for the simple and the very sufficient reason that the laboring man and the employer are not intimate associates now, as they used to be in an age now so far past that we have forgotten it. Most of our laws were formed in the times when the employer and the employe knew each other, knew each other's characters, were associated with each other, dealt with each other as man with man. You know that that is no longer the case. You in most instances are serving a great corporation. You not only do not come into personal contact with the men who have the supreme command in those corporations, but it would be out of the question for you to do it.

"Now, what are we going to do about it? Suppose you go back in your fancy to dealing with individual employers, for instance; but you are not dealing with the individual employer, and therefore the law is justified in going into factories, and obliging those who are managing them to conduct them in a proper way, by insisting upon proper ventilation and proper conditions for doing the work of the factory. What are we doing? Large artificial corporations are employing large numbers of men upon whose health and strength and morality depends the health and strength and morality of the community itself. Who make up the community anyhow? Nine-tenths of every community is made up of men who do the work. I get impatient hearing them talk about laborers, as if laborers were somebody set off by themselves, to be paraded and looked at. Four men out of every five I meet, and probably more, are laborers; they are doing the work of the world; they are putting their hands to crude instruments that are difficult to handle, and are producing the work of the world. I don't like to cut society up into sections and say, 'These are laborers and these are employers.' Most of employers that have not been laborers are not worth their salt, anyhow. It is merely a question of which part of the work you are doing. If you have proved capable in the part of the work you have been doing, and have become the boss of a gang, or a superintendent, that means that your intelligence has lifted you to another place, in which there is still work. I regard myself, not as a laboring man in the ordinary sense of the word, but certainly as a working man, certainly as a man who does work; and I belong to a class in which the hours cannot be limited; I generally have to work not only all day, but until late to bed time. And I have never heard it yet suggested that there should be a union of college presidents to stop it. We not only have to work, but we have to work overtime, whether we want to or not; but it is all part of the work of society. My work has been the work of enabling young gentlemen to understand the very things I am talking about now. That is what I have been engaged in for a great many years. So I say I am tired of hearing this talk that divides society up into sections.

"You cannot cut and carve it so that you can really distinguish one part from another; and the labor question is a question of society, of how many are going to tackle the tasks and work of the world, and how they are going to be related to it; and as nine-tenths of the men of the world are working men, that society has to protect, it has to protect this nine-tenths, to see that its health does not suffer, to see that its morals are protected, for it is a pretty difficult thing when a man, after working for a long time in a badly ventilated room, that his morals should be lowered, not only, but that it should spoil his morals. If I am not all right physically, I don't act normally in respect of the things I do when I get out of the shop. Society has to protect itself. The corporation is one term by which we describe one piece of society, and the workingman is a term by which we describe another piece of society, and therefore we must devote ourselves to such legislation as will make these parts work together, and dovetail into each other without friction; and because they do not, that is why you have the labor question. Not only that, but another thing follows from it: If you oblige the laboring men to deal with these sections of society I have called corporations, let him deal with one man at a time, but when a man is dealing with an association that consists of a thousand men, the characters of which we cannot get at, because they may live in distant cities, their work spread all over the United States and their offices in another section, that is not a possible proposition; therefore, the right of the laboring man to organize is not only a right, but in some sense it is a necessity. I have never found any man who was jealous in regard to the interests of the laboring man, much less jealous of his forming organizations whenever he pleased for any legitimate purpose.

"Nobody—no wise and just man—is jealous of the proper use of organization. But the interesting thing is that organization cannot accomplish what society as a whole can accomplish through legislation. Look at some of the present legislation in New Jersey. There are laws in New Jersey which oblige the owners of factories where there is dangerous machinery to shield the men that drive that machinery, by which the workingman may be protected. I am sorry to say that these laws have not been strictly enforced. And if they are [not] enforced, what happens? Suppose the machinery is not properly guarded, and suppose some man is injured; does the law compensate him for the injury? Not at all. But what happens? The money goes, not to the man who was injured, or to the family of the man who has lost his life, but it goes into the public treasury. That is no comfort to him, nor any help to his family. It may be sort of a mental comfort that they have had to pay for it, but that is very slim comfort, and does not last very long. So that our laws, while it is proper to put penalties upon those who do not properly protect their machinery, do not get at the matter.

"We are now speaking on the question of the protection of the workingman himself. That is the reason we cannot get a proper employers' liability act. You know that we have an employers' liability act, but it was so ingeniously drawn that I have yet to find the lawyer who can interpret what it means. I suppose somebody can work it out, but nobody has yet found the spring. I have read it myself, and I am accustomed to interpreting the meaning of the English language, but I don't know what it means. I read it and read it and I think there must be something the matter with the punctuation, something has gone wrong about it; it does not mean anything that I can make out, and the several parts seem so to offset each other that it is meant to establish an equilibrium and doesn't get anywhere. Therefore, we can see that we have not got any employers' liability act. We want one that will work, not only, but we want one that will work without being worked.

"By that I mean that an act never so clearly drawn, never so clear in its definition as to liability and the amount of liability to be paid by the employer in the case of accident, is not satisfactory if it is necessary for the employe to sue the employer for the sum for which the employer is liable. It ought to be a law which will work like accident insurance—which will work, in that sense automatically; you don't have to sue an accident ins[u]rance company, unless it is particularly cantankerous, for the amount that is due you. The thing is set down by schedule. If you lose an ear, so much, and if you lose a hand, so much; if you lose a foot, so much, and if you are in bed so many weeks, so much, and all the rest of it. You are divided up and catalogued and then there is a price list in the catalogue. Now, that may be personally mortifying, but it's wise. One does not like to have his privacy invaded in that way, but, nevertheless, the results are satisfactory; you get the money. There is nothing embarrassing about the money.

"Now, that's my conception of an employers' liability act. Moreover, you must realize this. We talk about the cost of living. Very well. If the employers of this State are going to insure you against accident, you know perfectly well—I do not say that there is anything to be criticized about it—but you know that what they produce will cost a little more, because they will have to pay for that insurance; but I say that is all right, because we are legislating on the theory that we are doing a just thing, and if it is a just thing to do, then it is a just thing to pay for. I think to draw an act and get a just thing done, and then to make somebody else pay for it, is a pretty poor business. We are legislating for all of us. Very well. Let us all pay for that just thing in proportion to our means. That, it seems to me, is a perfectly fair proposition and the cost won't be very great. You have only to judge by the premiums paid on accident insurance, which are not great. I have forgotten the proportion[s], but they are not much, and you can judge by that. The insurance companies can afford to do it at a comparatively small charge, and so can employers. What then would happen would be that the employers would themselves insure themselves against loss in insurance companies, and that would enter into the increased cost of production—the premium that he would pay for insurance—and that is a perfectly business-like, and, I should judge, a very satisfactory arrangement—provided, you see, the State has a right to oversee insurance companies—provided it was seen that with this increase in business there was not an unreasonable increase in the rates.

"I have illustrated thus for you, gentlemen, what my attitude is toward the so-called labor question. There is not any aspect of it, any part of it, which does not come down to this: How can society justly protect those who cannot protect themselves? That is what it all comes to. There is one standard for all of us, and that is what is right and just to the common interests. It is manifestly to the common interest that the splendid body of American workmen should be protected as much as it is fair for law to protect them. Where else would our American prestige go. We lead the world in all the greater kinds of workmanship. We cannot lead the world very long unless we are to see that justice is done to our great body of workingmen. If I did not sympathize with the workingmen, if I did not have a heart under my jacket, I shoould [should] at least have sense enough to see that it is a business question. It is not only a question of sympathy, but it is a question of justice and of business. The rule for protection and justice, the common standard, is the common judgment. We have got to get together. And that is the political side of the question.

"Has the Republican organization shown any desire—I do not ask that as a partisan, I ask it as a matter of fact—have they shown any desire to legislate for the common interests, including the workingman? If they have I have not seen any evidence of it on the statute books in the last six or eight years. On the contrary, I have seen just the opposite."[1]

Printed in the Jersey City *Jersey Journal*, Nov. 1, 1910.
[1] Following this address, Wilson spoke along these same lines in St. John's Hall in Jersey City. The *Newark Evening News*, Nov. 1, 1910, printed the best report of this speech.

To the Board of Trustees of Princeton University

Gentlemen: Princeton, N. J. November 1st, 1910.

I take the liberty of submitting to you my resignation as Mc-Cormick Professor of Jurisprudence and Politics, to take effect as of October 20th, 1910. It was owing to a mere oversight on my part that this was not included in my resignation of the Presidency at the meeting of the Board on October 20th. I took it for granted that the resignation of the Presidency included the resignation of my professorship. Finding since the meeting that it was not so interpreted by the Board itself, I now beg that you will accept my resignation as Professor.

I feel that it would be impossible for me to perform the duties of the professorship in a way that would be satisfactory either to myself or to my classes. It seems to me absolutely necessary that I should withdraw from all university work.

I need not say with what regret I do this, but I do wish to say that it has given me deep gratification during recent years to serve as Professor on a foundation so generously provided by friends of the University who have served it so thoughtfully and admirably. It was a constant pleasure to me to be known as the McCormick Professor.

With much respect,
                    Sincerely yours,   Woodrow Wilson

TLS (Trustees' Papers, UA, NjP).

To Henry Smith Pritchett

[Dear Mr. Pritchett: Princeton, N. J., Nov. 1, 1910]

I have severed my connection with Princeton University and have given up teaching, after twenty-five years of service, to enter public life.

I feel that in such circumstances I should tender to you my resignation.[1] I do so with genuine reluctance and only out of a sense of duty.

I wish to express my sense of the privilege I have enjoyed in having been permitted to share in the administration of this great and beneficent trust, and wish also to congratulate the founder and the board on the great good it has accomplished.

Sincerely yours,   Woodrow Wilson

Printed in the New York *Sun*, Dec. 5, 1911.
1 As trustee of the Carnegie Foundation for the Advancement of Teaching.

A Campaign Address in Passaic, New Jersey[1]

November 1, 1910.

Mr. Chairman,[2] Ladies and Gentlemen: I conceive it a great honor to be greeted in Passaic by an audience like this. It is indeed inspiring and makes anything that I may try to say worth while. I have found myself very much interested as I sat here waiting for the proceedings to begin, in my surroundings. This noble hall, used I understand, for the first time to-night, except on the occasion of its formal opening, and used for an occasion like this, for a use like this. Having been, during the greater part of my life, a school master, devoted to public service of the nation, and of the young of the nation, it is an added touch of inspiration in facing this audience that I should face it in this room; and I do not feel that my task this evening is radically different from what I should have undertaken had I met this audience in this room at any time.

Princeton University is one of the few universities which has been frank enough to maintain a chair of politics, wishing to redeem it from the degradation sometimes put on it, and to associate with the word "politics" the serious study of the government of States, and, by the use of human power, in the ratification of human affairs, and therefore from month to month there goes on in the class rooms of that University discussion of such matters as we shall discuss here to-night, for I have not come here to discuss any question in a partisan spirit or from a partisan's point of view, but to expound to you, as candidly as I know how, the questions that involve the welfare of New Jersey. For, after all, this is a singular campaign; it does not belong to that ridiculous comedy of politics which we see when men are merely struggling for office. There is nothing more dull, there is nothing less worth while, there is nothing more laughable than the mere struggle of men to occupy public office. If public office is the object of politics, then politics is not worth the serious con-

1 Delivered in the auditorium of the Passaic High School.
2 The news reports did not identify the chairman.

PASSAIC, 1 November, 1910.

A study in dynamics.

1) We wish new laws: e.g., Public utilities
                                    Direct nominations
                                    Employers' liability
                                    Corrupt practices
                                    Water conservation
   Why can we not get them? Public opinion is
      ready: who is not ready?
   Take the question, for example, of water con-
      servation, or
   The question of canal facilities.

2) We wish a new spirit in affairs.
      Why cannot we get it? I have tried to
         put things on a high plane. Is it
         possible these gentlemen are fight-
         ing, not on public questions, but
         for _possession_?

3) We want new men, evidently; for we get bad
      laws. Things are in some way tied and
      embarrassed at Trenton.

In brief, we want new government, based on new
      conceptions.
      What conceptions? The ancient conceptions
         of the Republican party, that parties
         are a means of policy, a means of ser-
         vice.
The use of parties.   11/1/10.

sideration of men who are interested in the betterment of communities and in the achievement of things. I conceive myself to have come here to-night in order to expound, if I may, what I might call the dynamics of politics. We are not interested in the mere filling of offices; they are easily filled; we can get volunteers for that at any time. But we are interested in getting something done for the State of New Jersey, and that is not easy to do, and there are not abundant volunteers for that undertaking. We are interested in applying force in the direction in which we want to move, and we are interested in the movement as much as we are interested in the force. The force is the force of parties, the force of men united to vote together to a common end. But the force is not half so interesting as the thing it is applied to accomplish. It is applied to accomplish public policies; and the interesting thing of the present campaign is that we have not made up our minds about most of the important matters that affect the immediate, present welfare of New Jersey, from the point of view of politics.

Opinion is ready. Who is not ready? Why, if we know the direction in which we want to move, is there any difficulty or doubt as to the choice we should make regarding the means of moving in that direction? We have made up our minds. It is another interesting thing to notice the indications that we have made up our mind. You don't find any unanimity upon public questions, if you look at the two platforms of the two parties, except on two points. The Democratic platform and the Republican platform promise the same thing on two important matters, but upon the rest all the promises, all the undertakings and all the programs are to be found in the Democratic platform. But since these two platforms were adopted the Republican candidate for Governor has added, time after time, until he has almost moved to make it unanimous as to what we desire to do and what he desires to do and what he hopes, along with the Democratic candidates, may be accomplished at the next session of the State Legislature.

We have made up our minds, then, about what? Why, for one thing, we have made up our minds about the public utilities commission. We all want a public utilities commission, and we want a public utilities commission that will have some definite and effectual powers. That is unanimous. But we have not considered this matter very carefully in its details.

What, after all, is our main object in having a public utilities commission? Many of you are commuters, and you will say that your main object in having a public utilities commission is to regulate rates. Yes, but the regulation of rates rests upon a great many other things which are fundamental to the regulation of rates and which things interest a community just as much as the regulation of rates interests us. The main function of a public utilities commission, properly clothed with power, is to display to the public, by inquiry, full information concerning the affairs and the finances of the public utility corporations; to be a board which can hear complaints concerning all kinds of lack of service and all kinds of discrimination in service, have the same kind of right that the Interstate Commerce Commission at Washington has to rectify abuses and to correct inequalities of service; to check all those preferences which may be shown to be inequitable to individuals or to localities, and then building upon these regulations, building upon the information to establish equitable rights [rates], rights [rates] which will be equitable alike to the common carrier, to the water company, to the gas company, and to the electric light company, and equitable to the communities which they serve. That is the full program. I don't believe there is any ground for serious debate by anybody on that question. Opinion is ready. Who is not ready?

Then there is another matter about which we have made up our minds. We have made up our minds that we want a very effectual direct primaries act, one that will be very much more effectual than the one we now have. The one we now have has gone a certain distance and has rendered us some satisfaction, but why do we want a direct primaries act? I am afraid because most of us don't take the trouble to inform ourselves; because ordinarily we are very content to go along in a sleepy and inattentive fashion in the matter of our government.

I was saying to an audience in another place made up very largely of gentlemen who did their business in New York, that it was very fortunate that the issues of this campaign had been introduced and discussed in the New York papers; else they might not have known what was going on in New Jersey; for their attention, in most instances is concentrated upon the matters which are in the New York papers, and they do not pay a very active attention to the matters which center upon the communities in which they live in New Jersey; I do not think that most American communities can congratulate themselves upon a very active and vigilant participation in self government. It cannot be that we want direct primaries because we have such a keen appetite for the business of politics, for we have not shown that keen appetite. No; the desire for direct primaries is based upon a certain uneasiness and jealousy. We see that the business of choosing candidates for office and delegates to conventions and all the other persons who have been chosen in the processes of politics, has been concentrated and monopolized in the hands of managing politicians. We want to see an open, not a shut game. We won't always, I imagine, make a very active use of the direct primary, but we know that we can use it if we choose, and that we can put the machine out of business whenever it occurs to us to do so. I dare say that the machine politicians will regard the direct primary as most of us do regard the lightning rod. It will, in most instances, carry the lightning off; but we never know when we are going to get struck, and, therefore, we regularly say our prayers; we are regularly attentive to all the possible accidents and dangers of a very uncertain game. That is the reason, I suppose, that we want direct primaries. Opinion is made up. Who is not ready, if opinion is?

Then we want another matter in which we are very much interested, perhaps more interested in other communities than you are in Passaic, but we want a very thorough going workmanlike employers' liability act, not because we regard the working man—as I have so many times said in this campaign—as a separate class that have separate interests, but because we regard the working man as part, a very essential and fundamental part of our great industrial community, who have the same right to protection that the rest of us have; because we want to put our great industrial processes upon such a footing that those who cannot otherwise take care of themselves shall be protected against undue injury from those industrial processes. We are carrying on the industries of a great nation by the sweat of the brow and skill of the hand of hundreds of thousands of good men, and we have got to see to it that they do not suffer in the processes, who [which] are the processes that sustain us all. Opinion is ready about that. Who is not?

Then there are other matters that we are greatly interested in. There is a matter that I take it you are particularly interested in. There has been a long history of the Passaic River. One can get a sniff of that history as he comes along the road. It is lifted to heaven out of the very waters of the stream. It has a solidity— that stream has—unknown elsewhere in the fluid world. If you seek high up the stream in order to find pure waters, you find those waters going astray. You find those waters beckoned to and led off by a certain water company which says: "This way, if you please. We have some private business to transact with you. Will you follow us? We are going to sell you wholesale and retail to certain communities who are waiting for you in the levels below." In the meantime, there are all sorts of things that lawyers call riparian rights, which are lying neglected and unused and un-asserted in those same levels below. Now, that has a legislative history back of it. I am not here to utter an indictment against the men who passed the legislation that made the diversion of the water of the Passaic possible. We were a pretty benighted people once upon a time about questions of that kind, and I am perfectly willing to admit that these gentlemen were merely benighted if that sits better on their stomach.

But nevertheless there was a time when a thing very dangerous for all this section of New Jersey was done—a thing dangerous to its health, a thing dangerous to its very existence. Why, if there had not been abundant rainfall in the month of June, what would have been the effect on this community and the community that lies about us, the great urban area of New Jersey, as the result of those recent droughts? It makes one sick at heart to think of the consequences that might have ensued. Now, are we in our folly always going to wait upon providential rainfalls when Providence did not give us any license to wait on it and at the same time make fools of ourselves? That Cromwellian motto, "Trust in God and keep your powder dry," was just as important in one clause as in the other. God does not trust a soldier who does not keep his powder dry. I remember a very pertinent question being asked an old Puritan in the days of the early settle-ment of the country, who professed himself absolutely confidant of the providence of God. He had a fatalistic confidence in the providence of God. He believed that nothing could happen but what was intended by God to happen. He was asked very per-tinently: "Why do you carry a gun, if you are going to die when your time has come?" He said: "Well, I might see an Indian whose time had come." He regarded himself as an instrument in the hands of Providence. We are all instruments in the hands of Providence, and there is no quarrel against Providence if we are improvident of our resources and of the things that have been put at our disposal.

Now, by some means, by some wise processes of common counsel this part of New Jersey has got to get command again of its water sheds and of its water supply. It has got to be done legally; it has got to be done justly; it has got to be done with fair compensation to everybody concerned, who have through mis-take or error or policy acquired any rights, but it has got to be done. We cannot afford to let this great urban area run much longer the dangers that it is now running. Neighboring com-munities are co-operating to spend millions of money to put in a trunk line sewer, to relieve the condition at any rate of the contamination of the streams, but that is not going to increase the water supply; that is not going to safeguard the communities as they should be safeguarded. Then, in the meantime, there is the Morris Canal, with a lot of water in it, owned by a certain railroad company, that hardly permits it to be used for transportation as it was intended to be used, and portions of which that railway company diverts and sells to a water company. Everywhere we turn we see this same improvidence, this same private mastery of public resources. That is the serious part of it. No doubt those rights were legally acquired. I do not pass any judgment upon that, particularly since the matter is still pending in the courts. But that is neither here nor there. The courts may say that they were properly and legally acquired, but the point is that they ought never to have been suffered to be acquired; and it is going to need very wise and unselfish and unprejudiced statesmanship and self-control on our part to get control of these resources again, so that we shall not suffer the dangers that we are now suffering. Have we not seen the need of this urban development of this part of the State which is going on and on and on? We are to need greater and greater amounts of this indispensable necessary of life, necessary to drink, necessary to cleanliness, necessary for us in so many of the fundamental functions of life. We are all agreed about that.

Then there is another matter we are all agreed upon. We are agreed that we do not think that we have sufficiently safeguarded against corrupt practices in politics. We think that too much money is subscribed, that it is subscribed by the wrong persons, and that it is spent for the wrong things; and we want to get at that.

But I have illustrated sufficiently. My point is this: that if we are agreed, what do we wait for? If opinion is ready, who is not ready? Why, evidently, if we are to judge by the history of the past six or eight years, the political organizations are not ready. There has been no serious debate about these things, or there need not have been, these dozen years. But if the debate is over, where is the jury? Why are they out so long? Why are they hung? What are they doing? Are they conferring privately with anybody? Have they lacked for food and starved? Where are they? Did I not say to you at the beginning of this address that it was a suit in political dynamics? Well, here is the power; now why don't you move something? Why is the shock just striking air and not driving the car of public opinion? Something is the matter. Somebody is unwilling to move. Somebody is unwilling to yield to public opinion. Something is holding somebody back.

And we are tired of it; we are sick and tired of it. It may be habit, it may be ignorance, it may be anything that isn't criminal, but no matter what it is, we are tired of it, and we have had enough of it. What do we want then? We want these laws and we cannot get them. But, more than that, we want a new spirit in politics; we want a new aim and conception of what the whole thing is.

I have always tried, gentlemen, in this campaign to hold things to the high level of the discussion of public questions, but some gentlemen on the other side have been unwilling; they have insisted upon keeping things down to the low and ignoble level of personalities. Why? Is it possible that these gentlemen do not want to discuss public questions? Is it possible that they do not know how to discuss public questions? Is it possible that they think that has nothing to do with it, and are merely trying to keep possession? Is possession their notion of politics, or is action their notion of politics? That I conceive to be the center and heart issue of this campaign. What is it about? Is it about getting possession of the government of the state, or is it about doing something with the government of the state, when you have got possession? Now, I must tell you frankly that I am not interested in getting possession of the government of the state. For one thing, it is an extremely and almost unnecessarily complicated government. I foresee that it will take about twelve months to know its intricacies and cellars and attics and closets, and that there will be skeletons in some of the closets, and there is a possibility of exploring the premises. That is not interesting. It is a great factory, in which the human spirit must produce something. That is the reason I am interested in it. And if the human spirit cannot be made to do something with it, it ought to move out and get another habitation. For we don't live in this free land to go through the motions of politics, but to get the views of statesmanship, the substantial views of politics; and therefore I suppose—I say it with reluctance and with, at any rate, feigned regret—we need new men, because we get bad laws by some kind of bad luck; we get good laws indifferently administered by some kind of misfortune, and inasmuch as the laws have all their vitality in the men who administer them, I am driven to the conclusion that we need new men.

There is a very handsome clause in the constitution of Massachusetts which has been repeated in the constitutions of many other commonwealths, which sounds very finely and sonorously on the tongue. It is that this is a government of laws and not of men. But after you have rolled that fine phrase under your tongue, you know that it don't taste right, that as a matter of fact every government is a government of men and not of laws. Laws don't run themselves, laws don't administer themselves. Institutions live in the character and consciences and achievements of the men who conduct them. Your institutions are alive when the men who administer them are alive; their character is high when the men who administer them shine with sincerity and with resoluteness of purpose. Government is personal, gentlemen, the responsibilities of government are personal. You cannot put it on the government of New Jersey that it has not yielded the things you want; you have to put it on the men who have conducted the government of New Jersey. You may put it upon them politely or opprobriously, but you have to put it upon them, for they constitute the government of New Jersey.

The ship resides in the spirit of the captain on the bridge, and without him it goes adrift, it falls off with the currents, the charts are as if they were of no use without that guiding mind to know just where the ship is, where it is going and where it stands with all the forces of nature. What we want, then, is to recover an old conception, perhaps long enough gone out to be quite a new conception, of politics. What conception? Why, the conception of the Republican party. The rank and file has always had that government [conception] since the formation of the party. The conception that the Democratic party has always had since the days when its founders uttered those general principles which still quicken our pulses by the representation and services of the people; the conceptions once uttered in the phrase which has lived because sprung from living thought, that "public office is a public trust," that the objects of parties is to accomplish the welfare of the people; that the central word of all political action is the word "service." How can we speak with freedom in a political campaign in a hall dedicated to learning, to that impartial, impersonal, unprejudiced thing that we call and revere as learning? Because learning is an expression of truth that is in the human mind for that reverence of the thing that is so, of contempt for and rejection of, the thing that is false.

Men differ in respect of their policies. There must be parties, but parties must be based upon the conception of service, and although they may have opposite conceptions they must be held with the force and sincerity of conviction.

What are political parties for, gentlemen? They are to unite together men of like convictions, men of like sincere impulses, in order that abandoning their minor differences of opinion, agree to put together their conclusions and pool their interests; they shall move forward in one common direction, believing that they see upon the horizon the guiding light that makes the direction, the direction of hope, the direction of confident expectation. Parties are to link human spirits together in a great altruistic unselfish enterprise, of lifting and purifying men and their affairs, the rectification of wrong, the establishment of justice, the promoting of all progress and all enlightenment. That is what parties are for. The use of parties therefore must be through the men who conceive such things, conceive them in such ways that they cannot escape the compulsion of their own spirits. How did America come to have gatherings like this? How did America come to have this conception of the united will? By first having the conception of the individual will; by first having the conception of the integrity and the indomitable courage and independence of the independent spirit. How it mortifies any man to feel that he is put upon, that he has been deceived, that he has been drawn into the company which professed to be of his principles and acted in a way contrary to his principles! How he condemns his company when he has been so deceived, and draws away!

I have received letters during this campaign from men who have said, with bitter cynicism, that they did not believe there was any public man who could be trusted, and when I had asked for the ground for that bitter belief, they have said that they had not found a public man in their day who kept his promises and lived up to his convictions. I do not agree with that judgment. I think it is founded upon a distempered thought; but if such a thing—even if it were true—the truth strikes like a dagger at the heart of America, for America was founded in order that men might keep troth with themselves; might keep their own self-respect, might feel that they were not in slavery to any man's opinion, to any party, any dispensation; that they were free to deny anything that their minds could not accept, and to live according to the light of their own consciences and their own judgment. That is the ground work of all American life. Whenever there is a great political campaign, therefore, we are met to concerted action together upon this ground of freedom, this opportunity for service, and we are met together in order to study the use of parties. On the eighth of November, a week from to-day, we shall again go to the polls to decide that high question. God grant we may decide it in the spirit of free men and true citizens.[3]

FPS T transcript (WP, DLC) with corrections and additions from a CS T transcript in NjHi and from the partial text in the *Philadelphia Record*, Nov. 2, 1910.

[3] Following this address, Wilson spoke at Carlstadt, N. J. A news report of this speech is printed at Nov. 2, 1910.

From Edward Casper Stokes

Dear Sir: Trenton [N. J.], November First, 1910.

A series of questions recently asked you by George L. Record contains the following:

"In referring to the Board of Guardians, do you mean such Republicans as Baird, Murphy, Kean and Stokes?"

"Wherein do the special interests of such leaders differ from the relations to the same interests of such Democratic leaders as Smith, Nugent, and Davis?"

In answer to this you say: "I refer to the men you name. They differ from the others in this, that they are in control of the government of the State, while the others are not and cannot be if the Democratic ticket is elected."

Another of Mr. Record's questions is:

"I join you in condemning the Republican Board of Guardians. I have been fighting them for years, and will continue to fight them. Will you join me in denouncing the Democratic overlords as parties to the same political system? If not, why not?"

Answer: "Certainly. I will join you or any one else in denouncing and fighting any and every one of either party, who attempts such outrages against the government and public morality."

Your answers to these questions taken together constitute a charge that not only the men responsible for your nomination, and who with your consent are conducting your campaign, have aided special interests, and have been or are attempting outrages against the government and public morality, but also that certain members of the Republican party, among whom I am named, have been guilty of a similar offense.

This charge, in so far as it refers to myself, I absolutely deny. I have taken an interest in public affairs in New Jersey as a citizen and as an official for over twenty years, and I have served no special interests but the interests of the people.

I have never been a member of any Board of Guardians—an organization that never existed save as a myth, created by those whose political fortunes depend upon fighting wind mills rather than real evils.

Your association of my name in this connection is of course a statement made by you as a candidate for office and not as a historian.

I was honored by the people of New Jersey with the highest office in their gift, after a legislative apprenticeship of eleven years, and I served three years in the executive position to which you aspire. I deny that during my terms as a member of the Legislature, and during my administration as Governor there was any outrage perpetrated by the Republican state leaders of New Jersey against "the government and public morality."

Franklin Murphy, one of the Republican leaders to whom you refer, has also been honored by the people of the State, and likewise served three years as its Governor. I held an important position under his administration and am familiar with the history thereof, and I deny that any outrage was perpetrated by Republican leaders against the "government and public morality" during his administration.

Such a charge as you make I am sure you will promptly withdraw if you will acquaint yourself with the legislative history of this state since the Republican party took control of its affairs by the command of an indignant people.

The charge of "outrage against the government and public morality" might well apply to the days of race track and coal combine supremacy, and attempted Senate steals perpetrated under the leadership of the very men who engineered your nomination and who are the controlling factors in your campaign. Those were the days when, to quote a happy phrase in your Camden speech, "the boss system means the boss is used for private ends." They ceased on election night in November 1893 when the voters of this state said, "we will have no more of such Democratic rule."

The history of the State since that hour has been written by the Republican party, and it is a record of reform, of advanced and progressive legislation, for which the party offers no apologies, and which the people of this state have ratified time and again at the polls.

For brevity's sake, I pass over the period of "Repeal and Reform," made necessary by previous Democratic legislation, and call your attention to some recent measures which could not have been passed had the party been dominated by a boss system for private ends:

The railroad tax acts increased the tax on the railroads from $1,595,121.14 to $5,050,095.01; gave additional revenue for the State and is yielding annually from two and a quarter to two and a half million dollars for the cause of education,—a field in which you have rendered incomparable service.

The corrupt practice acts—of the existence of which you are apparently not aware, as you have repeatedly denied them in your speeches—forbid all form of bribery, the corrupt use of money at the primaries and at the polls, and if enforced, will provide clean and honest elections.

The Civil Service act lifts patronage from the plane of partisanship to the plane of merit.

The potable water acts—two passed under my administration and one under Governor Fort's—conserve the waters of the state for the use of the people and protect them against the possible greed of corporations.

The forestry commission act conserves the forest lands of the state for the use and benefit of the people and protects the sources of our water supply.

Another act provides that the inland lakes of New Jersey may be acquired for the state and held as public parks for the free and common benefit of all.

These three enactments are a part of the state policy of conservation which New Jersey inaugurated before conservation became popular as a national issue.

The reform of the petit jury system places our juries beyond the control of political pull and aids in the administration of impartial justice.

The act providing for a gradual increase in franchise taxes on public utility corporations is turning into the local treasuries over $824,273.29 per annum—a source from which not a penny was realized under Democratic administration.

Reform in our primary law has banished from our primary elections violence and disorder that once prevailed, and given us a primary under State supervision where votes are honestly cast and honestly counted.

The direct primaries for the nomination of officials to be elected by the voters of the county and the Senatorial primary, providing as near a popular nomination for United States Senator as may be until the Constitution of the United States is changed, are measures in advance of those of many of our sister states, and strengthen the power of the people in the selection of candidates, and were passed solely in the interest of popular government.

The railroad and public utility commissions were created in accord with modern legislation for the control and regulation of corporate enterprises—a policy which had its beginning in the passage of the Sherman anti-trust act by a Republican Congress and a Republican President.

The act prohibiting the watering of stock and the issuance of securities, except for actual cash, or property of actual cash value, is one of the most effective remedies for this evil yet adopted by any of our states, and has recently received editorial praise in the Newark News—a paper not unfriendly to your candidacy.

The limited franchise act prevents subservient municipal boards from granting franchises to corporations in perpetuity, and thus enables the people who own the franchises to renew them at stated periods on more advantageous terms as they become more valuable through the growth in population.

These are but a few of the sum total of the Republican legislative acts of recent years. They indicate, however, the spirit of that legislation. It has been legislation solely in the interests of the people. Not one of the above acts would have met the approval of a boss system such as you describe or would have been favored by the "special interests." Nor do they constitute "outrages against government and public morality."

If there had been an alliance between the Republican party and selfish business interests, these acts could not have been passed. Their passage is proof that such an alliance does not exist. Had special interests or the boss system controlled the Republican party, it never could have written this legislation. To say that such legislation as this was passed in spite of the bosses, even if true, is the highest compliment that could be paid to the Republican organization and the Republican management of affairs. A party that can pass such legislation, notwithstanding the opposition of the bosses, deserves credit for its fidelity to public service and is worthy of continued confidence.

The Republican party in this state has kept abreast of the times; it has given this state advanced and progressive legislation on current topics, and its face has always been turned in the right direction. As McKinley said, "It is the direction, not the length of the step, that counts."

The Republican party of New Jersey has not served special interests; it has not been dominated by a boss system; it has not failed in its duty to the people; it has not stood pat; it has been progressive; it has moved every year and every administration along the lines of just popular demand, and its work has met with continued favor at the hands of the voters of this state.

I mention the fact that I have aided and promoted most of this legislation, merely to refute your implied charge that I have been associated with those who have aided special interests, and "committed outrages against the government and public morality."

This legislation has been Republican legislation, and it stands to the credit of the patriotic spirit of the Republican party of New Jersey that serves itself only by serving the people of this state.

In view of the fact that your reference to me was given publicly through the Press, I avail myself of the same source for reply.

Very sincerely yours,   E. C. Stokes

TLS (WP, DLC).

A News Report of a Campaign Speech in Carlstadt, New Jersey

[Nov. 2, 1910]

PICTURESQUE CAMPAIGNING

Woodrow Wilson's Night Visit
To Carlstadt, N. J.

PASSAIC, November 2.—After addressing an audience of seventeen hundred persons in the new high school building in this city, Woodrow Wilson was hurried last night in a motor car across the river to the town of Carlstadt in Bergen County. Carlstadt is one of New Jersey's oldest Dutch settlements, and here in many homes may be found the habits, manners, and customs of the dyke-bound fatherland. . . .

Mr. Wilson is one of the most adaptable speakers who ever faced an audience, but it was clear that these dwellers on the marsh "stumped" the speaker at the outset. They listened eagerly; they wanted to applaud, but, frankly, for the first five minutes a great many of the burghers did not know what he was talking about. It was really delightful to watch and to hear the Princetonian as he changed the aim of his rhetorical shafts to the end that eventually he would find the vulnerable spot in the auditory armor.

Well, he went along until finally he confided to his hearers that this game of running for Governor was not all it was cracked up to be. This by way of emphasizing his statement that he was not a candidate for the fun of the thing, but for a serious purpose.

"You know," he said, "I have been going all over the State in an automobile. Well, I feel now, after nearly six weeks of talking, that I am running out of gasolene. I feel as though I have to run on the drippings."

There was a roar of laughter. Mr. Wilson followed it up by holding out two fingers—he was speaking of the two rival tickets. What was the difference between the two? he asked. They looked the same and if the utterances of his opponent were sincere both tickets meant the same. What then was the difference? Why, all the difference in the world: one ticket would work and the other wouldn't. There was another outburst of laughter and thereafter, with the key to the hearts of his audience in hand, all was plain sailing for the candidate.

He got talking about the elements of strength which aliens from foreign lands have injected into our national life, referred to the ancestry of the people who had founded Carlstadt, and told of an old town in the homeland which twenty years ago had 30,-000 inhabitants and now had 10,000, because all the youth and strength and ambition had been translated to this country.

"And those 10,000 people in the old country are being supported in every way by the 20,000 sons and daughters who left the old town and came to the United States."

Mr. Wilson's picture had been carefully and eloquently drawn, and his reward was serious faces and not a few damp eyes in the audience. He pointed out that these people who had come to America must assume their share of the political thought of the country of their adoption, and that they should so conduct themselves with reference to the ballot that the things which had made them prosperous and free here should never cease to exist.

He elicited loud laughter when he compared English candidates who "stand" for office with Americans who "run" for office, and, concluding with a general statement that the main issue for the people of New Jersey in this campaign was to ascertain what their rights were and then how to get them, he left the platform with the audience howling and completely won.

Reference thus extended to the meeting in Carlstadt seems warranted because it was the most unique meeting thus far held in the campaign and established Mr. Wilson's ability to deal successfully with an audience of any sort.

Printed in the New York *Evening Post*, Nov. 2, 1910; some editorial headings omitted.

A Campaign Address in Montclair, New Jersey[1]

November 2, 1910.

Mr. Chairman,[2] Ladies and Gentlemen:

I would indeed be insensible if I did not appreciate a cordial greeting such as you have given me. It encourages me immensely at the opening of a speech at which I am a little daunted, because I know the character of Montclair audiences and I would fain commend Democratic doctrines to their approval. I feel, as I look

[1] Delivered in the auditorium of the Hillside Grammar School.
[2] Harold MacDonald Anderson, chairman of the Montclair Democratic organization and on the editorial staff of the New York *Sun*.

THE ORANGES, 2 November, 1910

        I. MONTCLAIR.

"Progressive" government,

  Means 1) A programme, and in parts that pro-
    gramme is well known.

    But it extends beyond Public utilities,
  Direct nominations, Employers' liability,
  Corrupt practices acts, Water conservation,
  and taxation based on actual values. It is
  a <u>principle</u> of free government and of conservation in the widest sense.

    Moreover all sorts of people profess be-
  lief in the programme. It is therefore necessary that we should have also

    2) Progressive methods: publicity, dis-
  cussion, organized opinion, the pressure of
  systematic agitation, and independent voting. And

    3) Men in office who are in love with
  both the conceptions involved and with the
  free processes by which they are translated
  into action.

  Renaissance of that most difficult thing, Gov-
    ernment by organised opinion, and by men who
    have opinions and upon whom opinions can <u>re-
    gister</u>.

      <u>Direct access to government.</u>

        11/2/10.

over an audience like this, that something has happened in New Jersey.

We have tried to introduce a new kind of political campaign, and it seems to take; for we are not interested in commending a party to you; we are not interested in commending persons for office; but we are deeply interested in commending certain political purposes to you; we are deeply interested in discussing the means of advancing the welfare of the commonwealth to which we should be devoted. We have heard a great deal in recent months of Progressive Republicans and of Progressive Democrats, and of progressive men of this, that and the other creed or persuasion. I suppose that the implication is that there are also retrogressive Republicans and retrogressive Democrats and men of every sort or other who wish to stand still or to pull things back to a period which we hope we have left behind us. But whatever our understanding of the meaning of these designations may be, this thing is clear—that only those who profess progressive principles are now likely to attract the attention or to hold to themselves the purposes of this free country. There is no means of health except progress. Nothing can be kept—nothing that lives—can be kept at a single point without disease and decay. When you speak, therefore, of a Progressive Republican, I understand you to mean a man who wishes to carry forward to the uses of a new age the ancient principles of an old party. When you speak of a Progressive Democrat, I understand that you mean not a man who will always be standing upon a literal interpretation of quotations out of Thomas Jefferson, but who will try to carry forward in the service of a new age, in the spirit of Thomas Jefferson, in the spirit of this man who tried to comprehend the things of the people and to serve them by political combinations and concerted action.

What we want therefore, and what I dare say a company of men like this is united in wanting, is a progressive government. But it is one thing to use these general terms and to be sure that you want to make progress, and it is another thing to know what progress is and wherein it consists. The fact that a man is moving all the time does not prove that he is progressive; it depends where he started and in what direction he is going. Once, when I was inveigled into seeing one of those terrible contests that were formerly sometimes held in Madison Square Garden, of races that lasted for days when the poor worn-out creatures were turning lap after lap, I said to myself, "Here is a picture to dwell on—these men making mile after mile and never making an inch of progress." It does not follow that because you are moving you are moving forward; and that because you are accidentally moving forward you know where you are going. I have seen men stumble on the right track, and I have seen men keep to the right track by sort of an indulgent Providence, but neither sort of man is the leader of progress. Progress consists of things that spirited men sometimes loose [lose] interest in; of movement from day to day, foot by foot, through a long series of practical details. We never invented and never shall invent the airship in politics; we have to keep our feet on the ground, to accommodate ourselves to slow movement and a united life in order to make progress.

It is not uncommon to satisfy ourselves with a progressive programme, and one of the things that interests me about the Democratic platform in the present campaign is that it contains the progressive items of a progressive programme. It contains all the things we know we want; it contains the things we ought to have in regard to creating an adequate commission with adequate powers for the proper control of our utility corporations; it contains a very explicit declaration in reference to an efficient corrupt practices act; it also contains an explicit declaration in respect to a direct primaries act; and it declares in favor of water conservation and all kinds of conservation so necessary to the sustenance and enjoyment of our modern life. It declares for each one of the items with which we have become so familiar in discussion in this campaign. The Republican programme, I am sorry to say, is not so complete. The Republican candidate has adopted the whole of this programme, but the Republican organization has not, being more modest and holding back. And the difficulty about being reassured by the circumstances that their candidate has adopted a broader platform is that I have never heard it suggested that there is any danger of their candidate leading their organization or the party. I have never heard it suggested that there is any danger of his forcing their hand or forcing their action or making his program their program. And not because he lacks force of character, not because he lacks admirable qualities, but because he has always been habituated to follow after them, and not to lead ahead of them. It is no indictment of him; it is simply an inference from the well known circumstance of his career.

We therefore can have no quarrel, in a company like this, with the program of the Democratic party and the program of the Democratic candidate, for his program and the program of the Democratic party are one and the same. But, as we have learned by sad experience, programs are not sufficient. Anybody can write out a program, though I must say it would be very indiscreet to write out as explicit a program as the Democratic platform and not stand by it. But anybody can write out a program, and we can carry out and exhaust the program; and then will we be satisfied? Is that all we are after? That is not all I am after. That is not all that a company of thoughtful people like this is after; that will not satisfy them. Have we laid out a little program that in two or three years of mere keeping faith we can fulfill and establish? Then shall we merely by resolution demand this, that or the other thing for any particular part of the community? That is not what we are after. We are after realizing our purposes in action. But there is something greater than action, and that is the spirit and process of light behind it. I consider this to be a year—and it is a most exhilarating year in consequence—of renaissance of American impulse for right government in politics. That impulse will not spend and exhaust itself upon a single program and a single platform; it will go on with accumulating force until men shall stand most to see that American citizens have recovered control of their own government, or begun to.

The processes by which you recover control of a government are not merely voting into office a set of men who promise to do particular things, and making them do them by fear of being anathematized if they don't. There is nothing in that; there is nothing hopeful in a programme like that. You can whip any party under fear of eventual defeat into doing the will of the people if they know what the will of the people is and if you keep whipping them into action; but to whip them and force them isn't anything to satisfy the ambition of a man who would lead a great people or a great people who would be led. What we want is to recover the fundamental processes of America in an age when it will be a greater achievement to recover them than it ever could have been in any preceding age. A simple community can do the task of America with comparative ease; but a complicated community—a community divided into many classes by its economic organization—can recover and operate its processes only with infinite difficulty.

There is one sentence in de Tocqueville, in his *Democracy of America*, which constantly rises to my thought as I address audiences in this campaign. He said that he marvelled at the variety of information and the excellence of discretion which were required of the ordinary body of American citizens to conduct so great a government. If that were true in the early days of Andrew Jackson when de Tocqueville wrote, how much more is it true in this complicated age of ours? There is not any one interest, gentlemen, in our age which includes all classes of our people—I mean any one economic interest. There is not any one interest upon which you can base a policy and have the country comprehend it. When you come to a mere mechanical, bargaining, combination of interest, what have you got? Merely the harnessing and linking together of several kinds of selfishness in order to make something that is not selfish, and the compound does not produce what you want it to produce.

I know that there is a certain amount of truth in that process, which I was trying to illustrate the other night by way of criticism of a remark of Thomas Carlyle, who, in a cynical mood said that the real problem of popular government is how to add a multitude of knaves to make an honest people. Now, without undue immodesty, I believe that even on his hypothesis, that even out of a multitude of knaves, I can show how we can make an honest people, provided the knaves are numerous enough and are engaged in a sufficiently large miscellany of occupation. I can illustrate it in this way: Suppose a crowd of people such as you and I have seen are sitting around the field watching for a game of football to begin; they are so far away from the arena in which the game is to be played that nothing said there can be heard by anybody sitting on the side. Suppose that two men, not expected to do rough things, but dressed as citizens, should come out into the open arena and there suddenly fall to blows. How outraged we would be. We would say: "Put them off! This is intolerable, that two men should come out and fight in public. They ought to be ashamed of themselves." But, if you had been one of those men, and the other had said to you what he did say, you would certainly have hit him. Don't pretend, therefore, that you are superior to those persons who have made an exhibition of themselves, but reflect that the reason that you are so judicial, the reason that you remember your manners so excellently, is that it was none of your quarrel. Now, if you get a people numerous enough to have it true with regard to the conquest [contest] of any two interests, that it is with regard to most of them none of their quarrel, you have got an impartial jury and you have made out of a multitude of knaves an honest people.

I do not admit the premises. I do not admit that any body of people are a multitude of knaves. I suspect, from certain transactions that I have been engaged in, that some men have knaves concealed about them, but that is not a very large section of their personality, and it can be subdued; it can be subdued particularly by the watchfulness and manoeuvres of their fellow men; but for the most part, I believe that disinterested motives are very common, provided you give them a field in which to work. Now, the enormous task of our day is for the majority of us to forget our special interest long enough to be disinterested, to take action with regard to the welfare of the whole. That is the splendid programme of the progressive, to put things forward by justice, by fairness, by a concern for all interests, by a combination of all interests, by a union of all interests, until men shall think in the terms of the common weal and not in the terms of special interests or partisan advantage.

How are you going to do it? That is what interests me. I believe that the present specific programme can be carried out. It cannot be carried out, I am afraid—let me say parenthetically—if you send me to Trenton all by myself. Unless you elect a Democratic ticket, I submit I shall have a very lonely eminence, and shall be obliged to indulge in a lot of futile talk, because things have to be done by the body; they cannot be done by the individual; and the individual does not want to make himself a common scold. He wants co-operation, and I believe from conferences with my fellow Democrats on the Democratic ticket, that they are ready to give me their co-operation. I believe that this programme can be carried out.

But what beyond that? That is what interests me. What beyond that? Why, that all depends upon you, not upon us. There is abundant evidence in a company like this that you have for the time being got into the game, but are you going to stay there? Are you just an audience, or are you part of the play? Have you just been drawn in by the management to be supers on the stage, or does the plot rest in your minds and hearts? Are you making the pace? If you are not, there is nothing in it. It is not even interesting. How are you going to stay in it? Why, by very ancient and very interesting methods. Have you ever reflected how much we have got by that old-fashioned thing that we call political agitation? I do not mean political excitement; I do not mean getting agitated; but I mean the systematic stirring up of opinion. That is what I mean by agitation. As a matter of fact, we leave most of that to the newspapers. Now, some of the newspapers stir things up in the general interests, and some do not—I am not going to discriminate by names, because I would get into trouble —but you know newspapers, and they are of all kinds. Some of them are private pieces of property, used as such, and some are public instruments used as such. Have you not indulged yourselves long enough by leaving political agitation to the editors of newspapers? They know how to do it admirably well. Sometimes they do stir up political talk in a way that is wholesome to see, but the real impulses of this kind must come from the body of thinking men, and they must think even outside of the columns of newspapers; they must give the newspapers something to write about; they must have a method among themselves that will make it impossible for any newspaper to be dull upon any political subject.

Now, the first progressive thing in political agitation is publicity. Exercise inveterate curiosity about what is going on. Insist upon knowing what is going on, and make a row if you don't know what is going on. Insist upon it that there is nothing conceivable about government that is private. Think what a revelation that thing in itself would be! I don't know what your experience has been, but if you have ever tried to deal with political organizations—whether you have been told so in so many words or not—you have had it intimated in some way to you that you had better mind your own business; that you elected these gentlemen to govern, and they are going to govern, and that they are running this thing, and if you have anything to say you must wait until the next election; and then you must say it only in the terms of the names of the persons you wish to occupy office. Now, there is no distinct virtue in a list of names. You do not get anything that way. And platforms? Why, platforms have come to be merely convenient rhetorical accompaniments of the election of persons to office. At any rate, they have in this state. I have not read a platform in this state that meant anything in a long time, to judge by what followed after the election.

Now, you want to insist upon it, in the first place, that everything be known that is going on. If there is a bill which you know is pending in the legislature and it has disappeared, find out which committee it has been referred to, and make the members of that committee and particularly the chairman of that committee tell you why that bill does not come up for consideration again. You have a right to know. Ask them why, when the bill has been introduced in the very beginning of the session, it does not come out until so near the time of adjournment that something happens to it to smother it before the adjournment comes. You have the absolute right to know these things. You have not been inquisitive enough. You have not asked. The minute you ask, the bill will come out of committee, because the reasons for delay are generally not public reasons but private reasons, and you have got to smoke out everything that is private in your politics. You can do that by systematic discussion. You can do that by holding meetings in the interest of particular measures or a particular series of measures, or a particular interest—like the great conservation of the watershed of this northern part of New Jersey, for example. There is a great big subject that you have allowed all sorts of private things to be done about in legislation at Trenton and have never so much as asked impertinent questions about it.

Why don't you hold meetings and insist that your particular representative in Trenton attend the meetings in public and tell you what is being done in regard to these matters? Nothing dissipates the things that are wrong like the mere heat of the sun. If you merely let the light in, then you have at least let the light in. As the Irishman who was digging a hole through the cellar wall [was] asked, "Pat, what are you doing—letting the light into the cellar?" replied, "No: I am letting the darkness out." Now dig alongside of those cellars that we know as legislative committees and let the darkness out and you will be astonished at the pace legislation will take on.

A body of men like this sitting before me, holding meetings of that kind, would act like dynamite on legislation, for you have to be systematic about it; you have to bring to bear systematic pressure. Flashes in the pan won't do. You have to keep at it, form an association and put inquisitive men in as officers; keep them inquiring and keep publishing what they find out; hold meeting after meeting; and then do the final thing which gives every private plan such chills down its spine that it can't survive—that is, vote the way you think. The salvation of every community is independent voting. Why, if I could get a body of men together and call them a political party and then let them do as they pleased and count on them by label, I wouldn't have to do anything else for the rest of my life to deserve my fate. But if there is a larger number to decide the election and they are men upon whom I cannot count, then I have given valuable service; and by no other process whatever.

A progressive government! Yes, indeed, a progressive government, but progressive because no man can possibly cast a horoscope, because things must be adjusted to the public interest, in order that men may have the confidence of their fellow citizens. That is the process of liberty—independent thinking and voting, the constant pressure of public opinion. If you can't keep awake somebody ought to be employed to make noise enough to wake you up.

There is a certain characteristic that obtains in this part of New Jersey. A good many of you do business in New York. The fortunate part of this campaign is that the New York papers have been discussing the Jersey campaign, and therefore you have known that something was going on in New Jersey. Try to do a little more thinking in New Jersey. I am very much interested, as I know you are, as to how the election is to go in New York; I am also interested to know how the election is going in California; but it is none of my business how the election is going in New York and it is all of our business how the election is going in New Jersey. We have to make our choice how it is going in New Jersey.

But the method is not enough; you have to carry the method to this point, that you have to elect men to office who represent the method, men who are in love with that method, men who are in love with publicity, men who are in love with discussion, with the settlement of things on a genuine basis; men who don't want to occupy office simply for the sake of occupying office; men who don't care a peppercorn for an office that does not carry with it the confidence and support of their fellow citizens. So far as that is concerned it would be more comfortable to occupy some other office if the difficulty is merely pecuniary, because you can find offices with better salaries.

Your wife and your children do not approve of political office; it has all sorts of uncertainty about it and is a routine job. But it is immensely exhilarating and worth while if it is designed to lead the community to shape its affairs in the common interest. That is the highest privilege that can come to any American, no matter how humble a political place he may occupy, to be the real representative of thoughtful and spirited men in advancing the public interests.

I do not see how anybody can read American history without feeling his pulse quicken at a conception like that. The most extraordinary passage in history, to my mind, is the American Revolution, not because it obtained the freedom of America, for other races have obtained freedom, but because, without newspapers, by the private correspondence of public spirited men opinion was formed and lifted and energized throughout the whole coast, so that men who had never seen one another felt each other's pulses beat in generous phrases, though miles apart, mile upon mile by mere messengers; and those men toiling day and night at the formation of opinion were making, forming the spirit of the nation. And when America was born, she was born fully equipped as a self-conscious and self-confident people; no longer thirteen separated colonies, but one nation, knit together by the force of great men, and banded together for a great and generous purpose. That was the American Revolution.

Go into the Department of State at Washington and see those sixty odd scrap books containing so much as has been collected there of the correspondence of General Washington, and see how everything is there, from a torn scrap of writing paper upon which he issued an order to a Sergeant to bring a barrel of flour and a cow across the Charles River in a boat, and tells him where he may find the boat tied, up to those letters in which he discusses the formation of the constitution of a free people, and then you will know that in those volumes you are touching the vital stuff of the American Revolution, and that Washington lives there in those dynamic letters that moved communities to action. And Washington was not the only one; the letters of every great man in that day were engines of power to move and to form a people.

Now nothing less than that is what we are trying to recover out of the welter and confusion of our modern politics. I am no mere optimist; I do not dream that this thing is to be done by a turn of the hand, that it is to be done by the ballots that are cast in a single election, that that is going to turn New Jersey into a united patriotic body of citizens. The journey will be infinitely long and tedious, full of disappointments and all sorts of mistakes and errors of judgment; but the longer and harder it is, the more gracious the privilege of struggling in it, that we shall be men trying a man's experiment, and when the achievement shall come, it will be a very happy thing as we withdraw from the scene to hope that future generations will look back to us and thank God that we at last and at least began it.

FPS T transcript (WP, DLC) with corrections and additions from a CS T transcript in NjHi and from the partial text in the *Philadelphia Record*, Nov. 3, 1910.

Two Letters from Cyrus Hall McCormick

My dear Woodrow: Chicago 2 November 1910.

I have not trusted myself to write you about the turbulent condition of things as they developed after I left Princeton, but I will be glad to talk this over with you whenever I have an opportunity. I told you in perfect good faith just what I thought the situation was from the conversations I had with many, but it turned out that either I was decidedly mistaken in my diagnosis of the feeling, or that some people had quite radically changed their minds in the meantime. However, the less said about this now the better until we can talk with each other heart to heart on the subject.

Your compeign in New Jersey is attracting attention everywhere and your course is being praised on all hands.

With very warm regards to Mrs. Wilson,

I am   Affectionately yours,   Cyrus H. McCormick

My dear Woodrow: Chicago 2 November 1910.

While I would not for a moment add to the pressure of invitations upon you under the old condition of things, I realize that
now after November eighth it will be very different than heretofore as to your time and the drafts upon your energies. I have
no doubt that you will be elected, but I do not know in that event
just what you will think it best to do with the few days at your
command after November eighth. It is quite likely that you will
be so tired after the many addresses you have been giving that
you will not want to appear here for another one such as the
Committee of Citizens is asking you to make on the seventeenth
in commemoration of the centennial of Theodore Parker's birth,
—therefore, all I can say is that if it fits in with your own wishes
and desires, every one here will be most delighted to give you a
splendid welcome, but if it adds one jot to your burdens or cares,
then I would be the first to suggest *that you decline the invitation.*
It is only because I do not know just how your engagements will
stand after the eighth that I add my word to that of many others
of the great pleasure it will give us if you feel that you would like
to come.[1]

I am   Very sincerely yours,   Cyrus H. McCormick.

Of course you will come to us if you accept the invitation.

TLS (WP, DLC).
[1] See WW to C. H. McCormick, Nov. 4, 1910.

From Philip Hilton Fraser[1]

Dear Wilson: New York City, November 2, 1910.

The *Times* today gives a brief summary of your speech yesterday at Passaic.

The persual [perusal] of it gives me immense pleasure.

I am more than ever gratified at the prospect of your election
as Governor of New Jersey—on which I desire to offer my hearty
congratulations

I am a Republican but if I were a citizen of New Jersey, party
lines would not prevent me from casting a ballot for you, because

your election will not only enhance your prestige, but also extend the usefulness of Old Nassau as a school for statesmen.

Keep your wagon hitched to the stars, all the while looking out for the ruts under the wheels! And the path of glory and of public service will not end in the governor's chair at Trenton.

With every best wish for your success,

Yours Sincerely   Philip H. Fraser

ALS (WP, DLC).

[1] Wilson's classmate at Princeton; insurance broker in New York.

A News Report of a Campaign Address in Orange, New Jersey

[Nov. 3, 1910]

SUBURBS GIVE EAR TO WILSON

Two big audiences heard Woodrow Wilson in Essex County last night and received him with flattering outbursts of enthusiasm. One was in Montclair, where Democratic leaders said that almost two-thirds of the crowd was made up of Republicans. The other was in Orange, where, according to the Democratic leaders, about one-third was composed of men hitherto identified with the opposing party. . . .

In Orange the meeting was held in Columbus Hall. There the crowd was even greater than in Montclair. Men stood both on the main floor and the gallery and the stage and wings were crowded as well. Probably 1,800 persons were in the place. In the audience were a number of clergymen, including three or four Catholic priests, and Thomas A. Edison and his family. Mayor Arthur B. Seymour, of Orange, was the chairman. . . .

At the Orange rally Senator [Harry V.] Osborne had been describing wrongs in the State government when Mr. Wilson arrived. As the latter appeared on the stage the Senator cried: "None of these things will happen when Mr. Wilson is Governor."

In presenting Mr. Wilson, Mr. Seymour said he would not consume three-quarters of an hour in introducing him, as the chairman of a Republican meeting had done the night before when presenting Mr. Lewis. This sally got the crowd into a jovial frame of mind and it burst into cheers when Mr. Seymour at once named Mr. Wilson.

Mr. Wilson said he, as a candidate, would not be boastful about what he could accomplish; all he could do would be to tell what he means to do. He said:

Government doesn't consist in promising things and not doing them, and then coming back three years later and promising them again. If I should break the promises I have made I would not want to come back and look you in the face again.

The Democratic party has a platform and a candidate that match. The Republican platform and the Republican candidate don't match. On one side you have a candidate with a party and a party promise back of him; on the other side you have a candidate without party pledges back of him.

When electing me you should elect the whole Democratic ticket. Then I'll be able as Governor to do something. If Mr. Lewis should be elected, the presumption to be taken from the past is that he will lead the party the same way he has led in the campaign.

The candidate described the need of working for the interest of the whole body of the people, and taking a cue from the speech of Mr. Townsend,[1] ridiculed Republican action upon their claim that the tariff is fundamental. He said:

"The tariff principle and Aldrich-Payne tariff law are as different as a plant and a flower that has gone to seed."

Reference was made by Mr. Wilson to the need of effective laws for employers' liability, direct primaries, water conservation, factory regulation, protection of women and children, and for economy in State administration. He added:

You have heard about a surplus in the State treasury. Well, part of that "surplus" is a fake, but let me say that a government that shows a big surplus is a wretchedly-run government. A big surplus tempts to the establishment of new offices so as to spend the surplus. With a surplus no attempt is made to cut down expenditures. Any business man would be ashamed to have his business run as that of the State is run, so extravagant is it.

You know that at one time sheriffs were paid by fees, some of them going up to $30,000 a year, but the salary system was put into effect instead. Then came the addition of deputies, and more deputies, until some sheriffs are now said to be drawing salaries without doing any work. I would sooner have a sheriff doing real work on a fee basis than not doing any on a salary basis.

Mr. Wilson urged publicity in legislative affairs and concluded by saying that "this campaign means giving the people access to their own government."

Printed in the *Newark Evening News*, Nov. 3, 1910; some editorial headings omitted.
[1] Edward Waterman Townsend, Democratic candidate for the seat in the House of Representatives from the 7th congressional district; author of several novels, plays, and a textbook on American government. He was elected in 1910 and re-elected in 1912.

An Interview

NEW KIND OF CANDIDATE

Dr. Woodrow Wilson A Novel Figure
In New Jersey Politics.

Princeton, N. J., Nov. 3.—There are many things that charm about Woodrow Wilson, the Democratic candidate for Governor in New Jersey, but it is not hard to pick out the chief among them. It is his absolute sincerity.

If he is elected—and there does not seem to be much doubt of that—it will be to this trait that he owes his victory most. His brains, his fine mind, his high character, his great reputation, his really wonderful speeches and his winning personality have contributed much, but "in the last analysis," as the magazine writers say, it is his sincerity that counts. . . .

Today, at his home in Princeton, I asked Dr. Wilson this question:

"Doctor, what induced you to take the nomination and why do you want to be Governor?"

"I didn't want it," was the reply. "For many years I have been telling these young men here at Princeton that the duty of every educated man is to take an interest in public affairs and respond when he is called upon to do his share toward good government. When I was asked to take the nomination with the understanding that if elected I should be absolutely free from all obligations of any sort, and with the further understanding that the platform upon which I was to run would be satisfactory to me in every respect, I could say nothing but yes. There was nothing else for me to do but accept. It would have been churlish to decline to do my part under the circumstances, and impossible after what I had been preaching here for years; but I did not want it."

Dr. Wilson does not go around over the State telling the voters that the nomination was forced on him and that he had no desire to be Governor. When he decided to make the fight he put all that behind him, and he is fighting to win, but it is a fact that New Jersey never had a Gubernatorial candidate who wanted the job less than he.

"What issue, in your judgment," he was asked, "has appealed most to the people in this campaign?"

"That," said Dr. Wilson, "is rather a hard question to answer. I would say, however, that the expectation of having real independent State government and of having enacted into laws measures which they have long wanted is the thing which appeals strongest. By independent government I mean government that is wholly divorced from the special interests and has no connection of any sort with them. The people have not been used to that sort of government or that sort of politics, and I believe they want it."

"You are opposed, then, to political organizations or machines?"

"Not at all" was the emphatic reply. "I think a political organization is absolutely essential. You could never hold a party together without a party organization. What I do not believe in, however, is a political organization with a business end. A political organization ought to have nothing to do with anything except politics. In explaining my views on this subject I sometimes quote an old Tammany friend of mine who used to say, 'There ain't no politics in politics.' And that has been the trouble. The usual political organization or machine has its connection with the special interests which are legislated for and protected ahead of the public. Such an organization should be smashed with a club. I am for the political organization that has nothing to do with anything but politics and which is led by men who have no interest in the organization other than to promote party success. I am opposed to the political organization that, through its leaders, deals with the special interests."

"Where, Doctor, should the leaders of the organization come from?"

"The organization leaders," was the reply, "should be the men who have been elected to office by the people. No others have a right to lead. In this way only can the people select their own party leaders."

This is new doctrine from a candidate for office who was nominated by the organization and is being supported by it, but the strange part about it is that, although Dr. Wilson has expressed these views from the stump, it does not diminish the enthusiasm with which the organization is supporting him. In view of the fact that the Democratic machine in New Jersey has been generally supposed to have "a business end," and that its leaders were distinctly not chosen by the people, it can be judged that Dr. Wilson is rather a courageous sort of a candidate.

Another earnest conviction of Dr. Wilson, which in itself would mean a wonderful change, is in the righteousness and necessity of publicity in all public matters.

"I believe in publicity," he said. "If publicity were given to the many public matters that are now concealed, there would be an end to the connection between business and politics. The best way to insure publicity is for the people to develop and acquire an inveterate curiosity about public matters. They have a right to know why a certain bill is held in a committee instead of being reported, and who is holding it. They have a right to know why other bills are passed without being considered. They have a right to know who is responsible when a bill is lost altogether—simply disappears—and if they insist upon knowing they will get the information. I want to see the people wake up to the importance of inquiring into what is done in the Legislature, and I think, not only here, but all over the country, there is a general increase in interest along these lines among the people. Public officials should discuss public questions with the people as often as possible. I believe the Governor should lay before the people of his State as frequently as he can the facts he has in his possession as to legislative and administrative matters in which they are or ought to be interested. There has been in the past too much of a tendency upon the part of the people to leave their politics to editors of newspapers instead of stirring them up themselves. Some newspapers are public instruments and, being used as such, are capable of great good. There are others which are private pieces of property, and are so used. What the people need is a keener interest of their own in politics. Let them develop abnormal inquisitiveness to find out what is being done by the men they elect to office, and let them raise a row if the information is not forthcoming. They have a right to know and I should like to see all over this State and the others associations of citizens formed, with extremely inquisitive persons at their head, for the purpose of investigating and finding out how things are going in politics. The minute the people themselves begin to sit up and take a real interest in what occurs after the election there will be a big change. And I believe this time will come."

Dr. Wilson, when asked as to whether he thought the Democrats would carry New Jersey, said he had been in the thick of the fight so much that he had not as clear an idea of the situation as others who were on the outside, but that everything he had heard certainly encouraged the Democrats to think they would win.

"I have," he said, "attended a great many political meetings in past campaigns, but I have never seen as much interest and enthusiasm as this time. It shows, I think, that the people are aroused and interested as they have not been in former years. I think, too, they like the kind of campaign the Democrats have made. We have not abused the other side and we have not dealt in personalities. We have let the other side monopolize that method of campaigning and have tried merely to put the issues squarely before the people. We have a specific, strong platform, containing specific promises. We have pledged ourselves to the enactment of these promises if given the power. In my speeches I have not attempted to discuss national issues. The tariff I have referred to only as an illustration and have told the people frankly that as Governor there was nothing I could do toward altering the tariff and that, therefore, it was none of my business to discuss that issue."

Dr. Wilson is a man of average height, but slender. He is smooth-shaven, with a strong, kindly face, creased with "smile" lines, and a long, lean, firm jaw that could never belong to a weak man. His eyes are gray, shrewd and calm. Sometimes they twinkle. He does not dress like a statesman and there is no pretense, pose or personal vanity about him. He is as sturdy and square off the platform as on and is thoroughly companionable. He is philosophical, even-tempered and loves to listen to a good story as much as he likes to tell one.

While he does not inspire awe, no one who meets and knows him has any doubt about his being of Presidential size, or that, as Governor of his State, he will be a big national figure.

F. R. K.[1]

Printed in the Baltimore *Sun*, Nov. 4, 1910; some editorial headings omitted.

[1] Frank Richardson Kent, until his death in 1958, one of the most influential American political journalists of the twentieth century through his widely syndicated column, "The Great Game of Politics," begun in 1922. At this time he was in the early stages of his long career with the Baltimore *Sun*.

A News Report of Campaign Addresses in Madison, Dover, and Morristown, New Jersey

[*Nov. 3, 1910*]

WILL VOTE AS THEY THINK—WILSON

Even Snow Fails to Lessen Warmth of His Reception.

Morristown, New Jersey, Nov. 3.—Cold rain, and later wet snow coming down by bucketsfull, did not bother Woodrow Wilson in this his last week of campaigning. At Madison he made his first speech in Morris county.

Dr. Wilson found all the Drew Theological Seminary and about 200 others, including a great many women, waiting to hear him. The theological students massed in the gallery, set up a concerted cheer long before his arrival. And after he had been introduced and stood ready to speak he had perforce to listen while they chanted:

"Oh Woodrow Wilson, Oh Woodrow Wilson,
"The brightest man New Jersey ever saw!
"Oh Woodrow Wilson, Oh Woodrow Wilson,
"Oh Wilson, Wilson, Wilson, that is all."[1]

"The refrain of that song might seem rather shocking from students from a theological seminary," said Mr. Wilson, with a warning laugh, "but I am glad you know the brand when you see it."

Then he spoke for twenty minutes, resolving his whole campaign into the elements.

He told the folk of Madison that since both candidates pledged the same forms, it was simply a choice of men.

["]I believe Mr. Lewis's professions are sincere. I have no doubt he would use all the force at his command to accomplish them," said Mr. Wilson, earnestly. He reminded his hearers that Lewis is associated with an organization that does not stand for these reforms.

"Mr. Lewis's position," he continued, "is, therefore, intellectually possible, but is impossible for practice. When you come to make the choice of men," Mr. Wilson went on, "You must apply certain tests, such as the ability of the men to resist political inaction, to stand ground against opposition, to wage successful and purposeful war, to sustain the State even though an individual suffers, to withstand office seekers and the biased urging of friends."

Mr. Wilson spoke a moment of the party in politics. "A party is neither for reward or discipline," he said, gravely. "You cannot afford to regard a party as any other than a public instrumentality for accomplishing public policies."

Very frank, very significant to the audience, were Mr. Wilson's next words.

"I know the processes by which it was determined that I should be nominated," he said. "I know this, too, that the men who came to me came to me only because they thought I might lead the Democratic party to the people's service. If I had not known this I would never have taken the nomination."

"The campaign is coming to an end," said Mr. Wilson, "and I for my part, have just about enough steam to finish it. But on November 8, whatever the result may be, I do rejoice to believe that men in this State will vote as they think."

The inch or so of fallen snow, the wet and cold boded badly for Mr. Wilson's meeting in Dover this evening. He found 400 folks waiting to hear him at the Baker Theater. Mr. Wilson, commenting upon the fact that Morris is a Republican stronghold, said that only men who hold real views, and hold them strongly, are susceptible of conversion anyway.

They applauded timidly when he promised that if he became Governor there will be made some of the most interesting political history even right here in New Jersey. Speaking of labor, Mr. Wilson won applause by saying that we shall know certainly we have broken the back of the political business machine when we find ourselves taking care of people whom it is not to our immediate advantage to take care of.

"Why, if I were a sporting man and taking chances I'd take a chance on a change," cried the candidate. "I'd at least feel I wasn't betting on a certainty," he added.

The candidate hurried to Morristown and spoke to an audience of 800. He had a hearty reception from the crowd, and spoke for a half-hour, traversing the matter of his whole campaign and trying to sift it and make his purpose clear.

Printed in the Trenton *True American*, Nov. 4, 1910; some editorial headings omitted.
[1] As has been noted earlier, this was the slogan of a popular whiskey.

A Campaign Address in Morristown, New Jersey[1]

November 3, 1910.

Mr. Chairman,[2] Ladies and Gentlemen:

Colonel Bacon has quite destroyed my sense of identity, and I can see where his error began; he spoke of me at the outset, after I came in, as a lion; he has mistaken the beast; I am a tiger. It is therefore evident how he got all his description mixed in the last part of his speech. It has been my misfortune to interrupt Colonel Bacon in several of his addresses, which I regret exceedingly, for I am always sorry to have him stop. I feel about speaking as a noted English author once said he felt about his books, that in order for him to thoroughly enjoy them it was necessary that they be written, either in whole, or in part, by somebody else. So it is with me; I would a great deal rather hear the speeches that other people make, especially at this juncture of the campaign.

Because as the campaign draws to a close I find myself feeling in a sense the solemnity of it. It was great fun at first; it was great fun to come out and be critically scrutinized as a closeted school-master who was trying to play an unaccustomed part, but as I

[1] Delivered in the Lyceum Theatre.
[2] Charles D'Urban Morris Cole, general attorney for the American Telephone and Telegraph Co.

MORRISTOWN, 3 November, 1910.

Fundamental Matter: Men to do things, and to administer the government from day to day against
temptation.

What temptations?

/. Private understandings of all sorts. Some
'interest', real or fancied, will be
affected by every change in the law.

2. Pressure for office: the practice of party
reward and discipline, rather than of
personal merit and fitness.

Hence the importance of civil service
reform.

The crux, judicial appointments.

3. To let obstacles prevail and follow the
lines of amiability and least resistance.

Government personal. Parties intended, not to
share and disperse responsibility, but to support men and measures

This the significance of the direct primary.
They put a greater strain than ever
on the virtue and initiative of the e-
lectorate. The machine may use them
with greater success than anyone else.
Who is to organize and get out the
vote?

Necessary not only to put men in but also to
sustain them with great bodies of conviction,—with active, not inactive and spasmodic, opinion.

The universal protection= The tonic air of public
opinion and of publicity.

No better year for this than the year 1910.

What this year may mean.

11/3/10

have faced audience after audience and have seen the eagerness of the faces that I have faced to discuss not candidates, not the fortunes of parties, but the fortunes of a commonwealth and the probabilities of such policies as would lift the commonwealth to a new level of accomplishment, I felt how serious a matter it is to stand for office amongst a people who are expecting great things of those whom they may elect to office; for I have never been deceived, ladies and gentlemen, about the character of government. Government consists of the men who compose it, and I cannot imagine anything more solemn than the sense that a great body of your fellow citizens have deliberately trusted you with a great enterprise in which they expected you to be their spokesman and representative. We have discussed before many audiences this year the issues of the campaign. I have taken pride in pointing out that the platform of the Democratic party is not a body of rhetorical phrases but a definite program of what they wish to do for the state, and I have again and again called the attention of the audiences we have addressed to this interesting difference between the Republican case and the Democratic case. In the Republican case the candidate and the platform do not match; in the Democratic case they do. I have not advanced a single position in these speeches that is not to be found explicitly stated in the Democratic platform, whereas Mr. Lewis, displaying more and more as the campaign has advanced his own liberal tendencies and opinions, has added item after item of personal conviction on his part that is not to be found in the Republican platform. Apparently, therefore, I have a party behind me, and Mr. Lewis has not; but inasmuch as I am arguing, to my great embarrassment, for my preference over Mr. Lewis, you will see that I am precluded from arguing it on the basis of our opinion, on the basis of what we individually stand for.

What basis is left, therefore, for argument? Nothing but the personal basis, and that is extremely embarrassing. Mr. Lewis has been in active public life a long time; I have never been in active public life; I have only taken pains to understand public questions, and therefore there is no basis that I can think of except one for commending myself to your suffrages. That one is not my personal ability, not my personal character, but my—if I may so express it—impersonal connection. I have not been bred in a political organization and Mr. Lewis has been bred in a political organization. What I want to point out to you as the main theme of what I have to say, is that not only the fundamental matter in government is to find men who can be trusted in the administration of affairs, but men who can be expected in the administration of affairs to resist temptation. I don't mean the gross kind of temptation; I don't mean the temptation of money. I think to most self-respecting men there is no temptation in money, in money evilly got. But there is a very great temptation in those things that tug at the heart strings. I can imagine that a man bred by long custom to co-operate with a particular body of men in party questions would find it very difficult to accomplish things according to his own judgment. That is the subtlest temptation that concerns us; and what I want to intimate to you, without desiring to cast aspersions on anybody's character, for that is not part of the argument, is that we have had programs of action before, and made rather explicitly by the Republican leaders, but they have never been carried out after, or have never been carried out. The most interesting thing in answering that question is that we don't know why they have not been carried out; nobody can tell you why they have not been carried out, which means that politics are now based on private understandings which are none of our business. If you will give me some other rational explanation, and if anbody can tell me except by intimation why their programs are not carried out, I am warranted in coming to the conclusion that it is not something which can be discussed in public. There may be reasons for that, for there are things which I am free to admit it is not in the public interest to discuss publicly, because they would be misinterpreted and misunderstood, but what I seriously object to is any government conducted upon the basis of private understanding with anybody.

We are trying to change the character of politics in this campaign, and we are trying to change it in this fundamental particular which cuts to the heart of everything politically. We are not trying to put political organizations out of business, for that would be to put parties out of business. You have to have great bodies of men banded together for political purposes. But the kind of political organizations we are trying to put out of business are those kinds of organizations which have connection with particular interests, and which, whether innocently or guiltily, work in terms of the special interests. If you try to settle any public question in terms of the special interests you are sure to settle it wrong; if you try to settle the question of the tariff on wool from the point of view of the woolen interests, and only from the point of view of the woolen manufacturers, you will inevitably settle it wrong. If you try to settle the steel tariff from the point of view of men in the steel industry, you will settle it wrong, unless it happens that the men in the steel or the woolen industry are cast in the frame and mold of statesmen and who see that their prosperity is bound up in the prosperity of the country. In that instance, if they can give you advice which squares with the interests of the country and at the same time increases their prosperity, they are safe advisers. But if you are looking at it only from the point of view of present and immediately present profits of any industry, and look at only one industry at a time, then you will be inevitably led astray. The trouble with a great many of our public men is that they are led in a particular direction according to the nearest and strongest pressure. It is pressure on the mind as well as on the conscience, and pressure on the judgment. I have many a time felt that pressure myself. I have argued that it was not for the interest of the country, and I have been told by men who know more about it than I did that I did not know what I was talking about, and, knowing in detail that I did not know what I was talking about, I could not answer their argument. I have sometimes looked up the facts afterwards and have found out that I was right and they were wrong, and sometimes I have found that they were right and I was wrong; and your judgment gropes, is at a loss, feels the pressure, a pressure that holds strong and masterful men. That is a dangerous influence in politics, for it has in it this element, that it is not based on the common interest but upon a special interest.

Then there is another kind of temptation that public men are open to—that is, another kind of pressure—I mean the pressure of force. I suppose that the most common conception among certain men is that their parties reward and discipline, that they reward men who have worked for the party and discipline those who have opposed it. If I could tell you some of the things that go on in some of the communities in this state, you would see the force of that illustration. I know some men who cannot get a license unless they vote and continue to vote according to the beliefs and plans of the men from whom they get their licenses. I know of men who can indulge in any disregard of law so long as they stand in with persons who are influential in the making up of Grand Juries. I know of all sorts of intricacies and underground processes by which parties are maintained as instruments of control, for the control of other men's lives and fortunes.

We passed a law some time ago which obliged workers at the polls to keep at least a hundred feet away from the voting place. Why? Because they stood by the polls and handed tickets out and when their employes came along they did not dare take any other ticket, and they were watched until they put these tickets in the box, and they knew that their wages depended on obeying

orders. Obeying what orders? The orders of the political organization. That is one of the things that a civil service reform law is
for. A civil service reform law does not, I suppose, greatly
enhance the efficiency of the service. There is something a little
ridiculous about filling offices by examination tests, because it
is very difficult to set tests along a line which has anything to
do with the duties the man who is given office is to perform.
I have never had any confidence in test examinations; they are
a crude way of ascertaining, not whether a man knows anything
or not, but whether he has made preparation for the examination
or not. Many an ignorant man has received a college diploma
because he has run the gauntlet, by intellectual dexterity, of
examination. So there is a great deal of justifiable ridicule heaped
upon civil service reform based on examination. But the real
object of it is the manner of holding public office on a footing
that cannot be controlled by men who are not superior to the
persons appointed to office. It is an interesting circumstance that
we have constantly to admit that English politics are purer than
American politics, but English politics began to be pure only
when they were put on a civil service examination basis, and
there was never anything in English politics that was not corrupt
before that, and English politics were like American politics before they had civil service reform; they used their power as a
means of political reward and discipline. One of the strongest
passions in the human mind is to punish a man for not agreeing
with you. You know the story of the Englishman who said it was
so absurd for the French to call bread "*pain*," and the Frenchman
said it was no more absurd than for the Englishman to call it
"*bread*"; and the Englishman replied, "Oh, but it is bread you
know." An Englishman thinks it reductio ad absurdum to intimate
that everything an Englishman says is anything less than rational. I must admit that feeling myself of persons who disagree
with me, who are either very perverse or very ignorant.

I can very well understand the temptation of sending a man
officially to Coventry to resist the enlightening process of your
own mind, and yet if you give a political leader that power of a
political organization, that power would throttle the very organs
of breath in the body politic. There is nothing more serious than
that. The crux of the whole difficulty in politics in states—particularly in states like New Jersey—lies in the judicial appointments,
in the legal appointments, in the appointments of prosecutors
and of judges, particularly county judges. If you allow men to get
the notion that organizations are meant for the maintenance of

power then, as compared with the more gross corruption of money bribery, you have sunk to a deeper level than it is possible to sink in any other way; so that your moral is a simple moral,— that government consists in the state of mind and the attitude towards you and towards affairs of the men whom you put into office.

Government, gentlemen, is personal, it is not impersonal. That is the lesson that we are trying to learn all along the line. I stated in one of the early speeches of the campaign with regard to the disregard of law by corporations, that guilt is personal, and some of the newspapers took it up as if it were a discovery. I thought it was a commonplace, and I thought it was very obvious; and I stated it merely for the convenience of my argument. Of course guilt is personal. I do not do wrong by proxy. I do wrong when I originate it or yield to it for myself. If I keep on in it, I am going to be damned and nobody else; I am going to be damned by some process or other, no matter what your theological beliefs are, because the most exquisite damnation is that knowledge of yourself that you have done the thing. You do not have to postpone your experience of hell until you die, as the great poet Dante shows, because in his Inferno are many persons who, at the time of writing the book, were still alive, but he knew where they were, and I doubt if they questioned his conclusions when they read the poem. All evil doing is, of course, personal, and guilt, therefore, is of course personal. By the same proof government is intensely personal. It consists in certain freedoms and in certain bondages, and what we are trying to break up now in this interesting year of grace in which I speak is political bondage. We are trying to get away from the idea that parties are intended for the dispersion of responsibility, to come around to the idea that parties are intended for the support of responsible representatives who are expected to read [rede] them in definite policies. If you conclude that I am not a suitable leader, I should not argue the matter with you at all; I might privately agree with you. But I could not agree with you if you tried in any way to escape the conclusion that on the eighth day of November you have got to choose a leader. I am sorry if you do not like either of the candidates, that your choice should be so limited, but that is due to the circumstance of the method of the nomination; you might have waked up earlier and through the process of our imperfect primary law,[3] you might have put somebody else in nomination who

___

[3] The existing primary law of New Jersey, enacted in 1903, did not provide for the direct nomination of gubernatorial candidates. However, it did permit

was more in your mind; but inasmuch as you have got to this stage, there is not any other choice that you can make, and there is only one basis upon which you can make a choice, and that is the probability whether the one man will lead or not, or whether the other will lead or not.

Leadership is a very subtle matter. Leadership is based, first of all, upon knowing what you are talking about, and secondly in making yourself so troublesome to those who oppose you that, if only for the sake of peace, they will let you have your way. A very astute gentleman once defined popular government as a method of making it a very anxious and uncomfortable business because of a constant watchfulness and force of public opinion. What we are trying to do therefore, is first of all, to awake as we have awakened—I do not mean we in New Jersey, but all over the nation as speakers have awakened public opinion, and then to put upon public opinion the responsibility of choosing its spokesman. Parties are intended for the systematic support by organizations— by legitimate organizations—of the men whom the majority conceive to be in the right; and that is all they are for. You do not get lost [laws] by agreeing that they are necessary, as I can prove to you from the last six years of history of New Jersey; for we have all been agreed that certain laws were necessary in the last six years, and yet we have not got them. It has been admitted at election time that they were necessary, but in the meantime, they have been smothered in the legislature, that is, they have lost their ways, they have disappeared in the labyrinth somewhere down in Trenton; they have got smothered, as the local expression is in Trenton. They have been smothered in committee, and that is because opinion has not got upon the warpath. You have not expressed yourselves in insistent judgment. Why, gentlemen, there is not anything that cannot be accomplished in America by a sincere man, there is not anything that cannot be accomplished by a man who seriously intends the public interest and who is found to be disinterested. America loves a bold man; America loves a fearless man, loves him so much that even when he is mistaken it will follow him if it believes that he is bold and sincere; loves him for his own sake, for his character, for his intrepidity, for the very fact that he is self convinced and has got the momentum of moral force. Such a man sometimes may even be dangerous. I have often felt that it seemed to me a mistake on the part of providence—if I may say so without ir-

---

candidates for convention delegates to have printed on the official ballot, after their names, the name of the candidate for office whom they would support in convention. See Noble, *New Jersey Progressivism before Wilson*, pp. 133-34.

reverence—not to have made all fools knaves, because some fools are admirable persons, and loving them for their characters we follow them in their error. American politics has illustrated that again and again, that because he is bold, we do not scrutinize his opinion critically. We have got to pay a very high price for liberty and political success in this country. We have got to exercise a critical examination and at the same time that we criticize a man we have got to love him and believe in him. That is the hardest combination for the American people to effect—to be critical and at the same time to repose entire confidence in the man whom they are criticising. Criticism is necessary as a tonic to him. I want to make this single suggestion—the only antiseptic in politics is vigilant public opinion; the only thing that is tonic and that will keep things pure is the effect of critical opinion upon the men whom we choose as leaders. There never was a time when America seemed more certainly bent upon doing this interesting and difficult thing than it is this year. New Jersey has hitherto, although the rest of the country was astir, resisted the contagion, but this year something has happened that has admitted the contagion to our own air. Politics is becoming interesting here and men are looking with open eyes without prejudice or prepossession at questions as they are, are examining candidates as they are—though I must admit, to the great embarrassment of the candidates—but nevertheless applying the pitiless judgment of candid thought to things with regard to which they have not hitherto looked as partisans, with prejudices and prepossessions. Think, for example, of meeting a man, as I often did in previous years, who voted on present questions because the Republican party conducted the Civil War. That is an interesting but not a rational basis of action, because the Civil War is over. Even elderly men amongst us have found that these passions have subsided in them. There is no longer the bitter feeling; there is no longer any bitter feeling about the matter, particularly on the part of the men who were engaged in the actual struggle; and yet there are men who have been voting the Republican ticket because of traditions that run back into the ages as antiquated as if they preceded the settlement of America; for America in the last generation has utterly changed all her economical and political landmarks. This is a new age in which a very few persons control so large a part of the wealth of America. We will have to try very hard to keep a steady poise under the pressure of such extraordinary circumstances, under the pressure of so extraordinary influences. Therefore it seems to me that this is the day in which America is trying to recover her pristine naturalness and simplicity of conduct in public affairs, coming at it without the mists that have gathered and formed about former questions in former days and directing our attention immediately to the issues that are before them.

The campaign draws to an end, and with it, as I have said at the outset, the solemn impression of what we are about. We are about to perform the characteristic thing for which America was established; we are about to express the judgment of a free people about their own affairs, the choice of a free people with regard to the men whom they choose to be their leaders and representatives in public questions. I wonder if there has ever come into your imagination the picture of what happens on election day. Look away from the polls in your own district, and forget all those petty discouraging things which happen in your own ward. Just think on the eighth of November of those millions of people in 48 states, all gathering at the voting place. Full of what? Full of hope, that little flame of hope.

How impossible it seems to quench it. Politicians have tried to quench it by their neglect and folly, again and again and again, but it burns on with a serene flame which shows how immortal all processes of life are. They blaze up in us whether we would or no. Again and again, through disappointment, through everything that is likely to dampen the energies, we crowd to the polls, hoping for what? Hoping for something that we have not got, for someone who will think in terms for [of] the common good, for someone who puts his country before his party, hoping that the day will come when men conceive programs as those men conceived them when they made America, in the interest of mankind.

FPS T transcript (WP, DLC) with corrections and additions from a CS T transcript in NjHi.

From Charles Williston McAlpin

Princeton, New Jersey,
My dear Dr. Wilson: November 3, 1910.

I have the honor to hand you herewith a copy of the actions taken and resolutions adopted by the Board of Trustees of Princeton University at an adjourned meeting held this day.

The special committee appointed to prepare resolutions in recognition of your distinguished services to the University presented the following resolutions which were adopted unanimously.

"In accepting the resignation of Dr. Woodrow Wilson, as President of Princeton University, the Board of Trustees desires to place on record its high appreciation of the service which he has rendered to the educational life of the University and the higher education of the country at large during these eight years of his administration.

It was singularly fortunate that, when in 1902 a vacancy occurred in the office of President, there was in the Faculty of Princeton one of her sons who, through his culture, his scholarship, his contact with affairs, and his knowledge of education, was conspicuously fitted to assume the duties of this high position, and the Board is satisfied that, in its selection of him as the University's head, it acted with a wisdom that has been justified by the position which his educational policy has given Princeton among the Universities of the land.

He came to his work at a time when the University, in common with other Universities, suffered under the burden of an unorganized mass of studies. With the loyal help of the Faculty, he brought the curriculum to an effectiveness that has steadily increased throughout his administration, and has placed before the student the opportunity of a training which conserves the broad foundations essential to an education that is productive of lasting results. In the present day, when vocational instruction seems to have caught the fancy of an emphatically practical age, this development of Princeton along cultural lines is not the least of the services he has rendered to the University.

When he assumed his office, there was here, as in other Institutions, a conception of education which fell short of affording the student the mental discipline needed to fit him for his place in the world of culture and citizenship. With the generous aid of the University's friends he established that system of preceptorial training which has made Princeton marked among Universities and has turned toward her the expectation of the thoughtful and aggressive educators of the country. Through this innovation in method, he has changed study at Princeton from the formal duty of the class room and the examination hall to the vital task of the student's life, and has not only brought the student to realize that education consists primarily in the discipline of his mental powers, but has inspired him with those ideals of character and conduct which have constituted the distinctive force of the educational principles for which his administration has stood.

The Princeton over which he was called to preside, in spite of the generous provision which had already been made for its scientific work, lacked the facilities for study which the enormous increase of the fields of Science had come to demand of all University work. Through the munificence of those who saw this need, the University is today as conspicuous in the opportunities it offers for scientific research as for the study of letters, and stands abreast of the foremost Institutions which aim at the production of a broad and effective scholarship. While he has recognized that discipline of mind is needful in every line of study, he has coveted for Princeton the largest powers to broaden that discipline beyond the narrow provincialism of any one department, convinced that the student of letters will be better fitted for life if he shall consider for himself the problems of the laboratory and the student of science better trained for his work if he shall bring himself under the influence of letters, philosophy, and art.

Eight years ago the Graduate work of Princeton was small in compass and unmarked in results. Through the cooperation of those who have devoted themselves to this commanding side of the University's life, there is today in its Graduate Department, the promise of a rare opportunity for serious intellectual work. In the accomplishment of the tasks involved in such work it has been his belief that the University would find its greatest possibilities of service to the world, and through the realization of these possibilities its highest reward.

To these problems of the University President Wilson brought the best powers of his finely trained mind, and spared himself no effort, not only to accomplish his educational policy within the University life, but, as it was accomplished, to make known to the educational world the distinctive place among its Institutions which Princeton was thus securing.

Knowing that he has accepted nomination for the chief office of this State in obedience to his convictions that a high conception of citizenship left him no other course, the Board desires to express to him its assurance of a sincere interest in the career which he has chosen and a confidence that, whatever the future may bring to him, it will disclose him to others, as his colleagues here have known him,—the man profound of thought, clear of vision, gifted of speech that makes truth plain to all who hear him, and controlled by ideals that must inspire all to whom he makes them known."

Your resignation as McCormick Professor of Jurisprudence and Politics was presented to the Board, whereupon the following resolution was adopted unanimously.

RESOLVED, That the salary of Woodrow Wilson, as President of the University, be continued until the end of the first term of the present academic year, that he be invited to continue to occupy the premises at Prospect and that he be requested in so far as he may find it possible in such duties as may devolve upon him, to continue his present Professorship of Jurisprudence and Politics, which he has made of such service to the student body.

And it was further

RESOLVED unanimously, in view of the report of the Committee and the action of the Board thereon including its request to Dr. Wilson to continue to hold his Professorship—that the resignation of Dr. Wilson as Professor of Jurisprudence and Politics be referred to the Committee on the Curriculum with power.

The By-Laws were then suspended by unanimous consent, and the Board in recognition of your scholarly studies in the fields of letters, History and Constitutional Laws and in appreciation of your distinguished service to education in general, and, in particular, to this University during your Presidency, conferred on you the degree of Doctor of Laws *honoris causa.*

I have the honor to remain with deepest respect,

Most sincerely yours,   C. W. McAlpin[1]

TLS (WP, DLC).

[1] Enclosed was an illuminated manuscript with the university seal and reproducing the first resolution.

From James Calvin Hemphill[1]

My dear Dr. Wilson: Richmond, Virginia November 3, 1910.

You may be interested in the enclosed editorial article from The Times-Dispatch.[2]

Very sincerely yours,   J. C. Hemphill

TLS (WP, DLC).

[1] At this time editor of the *Richmond Times-Dispatch.*

[2] The editorial, entitled "Wilson: That's All," predicted Wilson's election to the governorship and, quoting a correspondent of the Baltimore *Sun,* claimed that Wilson would have no less than a 20,000 majority. "The Republicans," the editorial continued, "have quit talking about Wilson as 'College Professor.' They have found out that he wears woolen socks and not silk stockings; that he is a man all the way through, in spite of his being a gentleman; and it is because of his integrity of character, his strength of conviction, his loyalty of purpose, and his unusual ability, that the people of New Jersey will make him their Governor." The editorial concluded that if the Democratic party nominated Wilson or someone like him in 1912 "it is as certain as anything can be that the next President of the United States will be a Democrat."

From Henry Smith Pritchett

My dear Wilson: New York November 3, 1910.

You cannot know with what regret I have received your two letters of November 1,[1] announcing your resignation from the Board of Trustees of the Foundation, notwithstanding the fact that I realize your action is absolutely right under the circumstances. I have felt that my association with you in this work has meant not only an educational comradeship, but a friendship which meant much more. I find that as one gets to the fifty year line he finds a deepening pleasure in those friendships which involve not only good will, but confidence in the intellectual processes of his friend. I hope that your resignation from the board will not mean that I shall not see you now and then and have a chance to talk over with you problems of common interest. You know, I am sure, how heartily I am interested in your success.

I will not bring up the matter of the pension[2] until I get your letter in regard to it, which, I take it, might better wait until after the election and after our annual meeting. In sending it give me the details of your twenty-five years' service, such as are called for on the ordinary blank. It is not necessary for me to tell you that the executive committee will consider any such suggestion in the most friendly spirit.

                    Yours faithfully,   Henry S. Pritchett

TLS (WP, DLC).
    ¹ They are missing in the files of the Carnegie Foundation for the Advancement of Teaching and of the Papers of Henry Smith Pritchett in the Library of Congress.
    ² This is the first evidence that Wilson was contemplating applying for a Carnegie retirement pension. All of Wilson's correspondence relating to his application are missing in the files of the Carnegie Foundation for the Advancement of Teaching. There are many documents and notes relating to this matter in Vols. 23 and 24.

From Matthias Cowell Ely

Dear Governor   Hoboken, N. J. Nov 3 [1910]

We thank you very much for your letter of yesterday. We look for a majority for you of 15,000 in Hudson County and 25,000 in the State. How much more it will be no man can tell.

                    Yours Respt   Matt C Ely

ALS (WP, DLC).

From George Hammond Sullivan[1]

My dear sir,   New York, Nov 3rd, 1910

One of my clients, a lady residing in Chicago and a personal friend of yours[2] desires to further your success by contributing to your Campaign Fund seven hundred and fifty dollars.

I take pleasure in enclosing my check for that sum to your order.

I wired to you today seeking instructions in case you desired contributions to be paid to some one else for the expenses but not hearing as yet and realizing that time presses I send it direct to you.

I am   Very truly yours   George H. Sullivan

ALS (WP, DLC).
[1] Of the New York law firm of Sullivan and Cromwell.
[2] [Nancy] Nettie Fowler (Mrs. Cyrus Hall, Sr.) McCormick.

From David M. Flynn,[1] with Enclosures

Dear Doctor Wilson: Princeton, New Jersey Nov. 3, 1910.

I have taken the liberty to send a copy of the enclosed to the following papers and feel that the insinuation contained in the circulars[2] put out by those opposed to you will fall flat. No political trick of this kind to catch the Catholic vote has ever been effective in this state and it usually reverts against those who attempt to arouse religious bigotry.

With much respect,   David M Flynn

Princeton Press.	Hoboken Observer.
Trenton Times,	Elizabeth Times.
Philadelphia Record.	Paterson Guardian.
Newark Evening News.	Passaic Daily News.
Newark Star.	Paterson News.
New York Evening Post.	New Brunswick Times.
Jersey City Journal.	Perth Amboy News.

TLS (WP, DLC).
[1] Cashier of the First National Bank of Princeton and colonel in the New Jersey National Guard.
[2] The circulars contained a collection of quotations from Wilson's *History of the American People* which seemed to suggest anti-Catholic sentiments on Wilson's part. The circulars were unsigned and concluded, "No word of censure or condemnation drops from the pen of this unbiassed historian as he records these infamies." According to a news report in the *Newark Evening News*, Nov. 3, 1910, the circulars were sent to Roman Catholic clergy and laity. The report also said that, according to Democratic campaign officials, the source of the circulars was William Harrigan, Sheriff of Essex County, a Democrat opposed to Wilson.

David M. Flynn to James Kerney

Dear Sir: Princeton, New Jersey Nov. 3, 1910.

You have doubtless seen the circular referred to which has been mailed to the Catholic clergy and many of the laity throughout the state. As a Catholic who feels that he knows Woodrow Wilson I resent the insinuation that the circular purports to convey. You may use your own judgment about publishing the enclosed letter.   Sincerely,   [David M Flynn]

TCL (WP, DLC).

David M. Flynn to James Kerney

Princeton, N. J., Nov. 3, 1910.

It is to be regretted that some malicious individuals, with the evident intent of injuring the candidacy of Woodrow Wilson, have issued a circular, (which, by the way, bears the earmarks of a political campaign document), in which they try to make it appear that Doctor Wilson was biased by Anti-Catholic sentiment in his "History of the American People"; they have published a few extracts cut out of the context without their concomitant explanations.

The parties responsible for the circular must very much underrate the intelligence of the clergy and laity of the Catholics of New Jersey if they imagine this eleventh hour misrepresentation will arouse religious bigotry, influence, or detract from the real issues of the campaign.

Those who know the bigness and broadmindedness of Woodrow Wilson in his dealings with the many Catholic students of the University as well as his cordial relations with the Catholic life of Princeton, his home town, have the utmost confidence in his sense of justice and fairplay. This weak attempt to prejudice the Catholic voter should meet with the merited repudiation of all fairminded citizens. No bigotry or narrowness is tolerated in this country longer than our own prejudice nourishes, or allows it to grow in the field of selfish discontent.

The International Catholic Truth Scoeity [Society] recently made a thorough investigation of the charges, sending out a series of letters to those who would be in the best position to know. This society, which speaks with authority from the Church in all such matters, says, "In reply to our letters relative to the attitide [attitude] of Woodrow Wilson towards the Catholic Church, we have only received answers in his favor."

David M Flynn

TCLS (WP, DLC).

To Cyrus Hall McCormick

My dear Cyrus,   Princeton, N. J. 4 November, 1910.

I have time for only a word, but it is a word of warm affection and appreciation. Thank you with all my heart for your letter.

As for the Parker memorial celebration, I have made engagements for that very time to deliver addresses which will yield me enough to defray the extra expence I have been put to by my campaing [campaign]. My chief disappointment is that I shall not be able to visit you.

As always, Affectionately Yours, Woodrow Wilson

WWTLS (WP, DLC).

To George Hammond Sullivan

My dear Sir,   Princeton, N. J. 4 November, 1910.

I was absent from home when your telegram of yesterday reached Princeton. This morning I find your letter with its enclosure, a cheque for seven hundred and fifty dollars, a contribution to my campaign fund.

I warmly appreciate the interest of your client in my campaign, and I hope that you will convey to her my deep sense of obligation. I am honoured that she should have thought of me in this way, and wish that I might have the pleasure of expressing to her directly my gratitude for her generousity.

With much respect,

Sincerely Yours, Woodrow Wilson

WWTLS (Nettie Fowler McCormick Papers, WHi).

A Campaign Address in Perth Amboy, New Jersey[1]

November 4, 1910.

Mr. Chairman,[2] Ladies and Gentlemen:

I am sincerely obliged to you for the warmth and cordiality of your greeting. I cannot make as much noise as you can, but

---

[1] Delivered in the Donahoe Auditorium.
[2] The news reports do not identify the chairman.

I can assure you that I am as glad to see you as you are to see me. I have never been to Perth Amboy before and I now know what I have missed by not being here. I have found, even in the short time that I have been here, such interesting evidences that this is a thoroughly progressive community, and it has been a very delightful and interesting thing to me, even on such a night as this, to be upon streets that are well-paved and beautifully lighted, and the whole thing seems to be typical of what I have heard of Perth Amboy though I have never seen it.

Perth Amboy is one of the first places in the State to have a nonpartisan school board. I cannot imagine anything that should be nonpartisan if not a school board. I have been, as you have been told by some of my political opponents, a schoolmaster for a good many years, and I have never seen any propriety by any possibility of introducing partisanship into teaching. It is singular that it first occurred to Perth Amboy that that was the case, and that you should have had the leadership in constituting your board in the proper way, and I congratulate you upon that evidence of progressiveness; but one does not have to go far afield in order to find out why a community like this is progressive.

You know that in the history of great nations those have been most powerful that have had the greatest combination of strong bloods in them. I know that a great many people, not knowing history and not knowing what really constitutes the strength of nations, have been jealous of our process of compounding a nation out of a store of national elements, not knowing that that was the way America was compounded at first, and that in a community like Perth Amboy the American process is being repeated all over again, of the contribution of scores of nations to a rich compound that makes for new imagination, new impulses and new purposes, a nationality rich in its elements and powerful in all purposes. I look upon a community like this as a picture of America in the making, and there is no better means of making America the proper compound of strong national elements than by meetings like this; provided you come together in order not merely to discuss the question as to which man you will put into office, but to discuss the question of what service you will render by your vote to the great state of which you constitute a part.

The only thing worth discussing is not the fortunes of individuals, not the fortunes of parties, but the promotion of a common interest that is to achieve the bettering of our interests, by getting together in a common enterprise, and by seeing enough to see our communities as a whole, to seek to lift them to the levels to which we would seek to see them lifted. That is what this campaign is about. This campaign is not intended to support the fortunes of parties. If the Republican party can serve the commonwealth of New Jersey better than the Democratic party, that is the only question you need answer. If the Democratic party can serve the commonwealth better than the Republican party, that is the only question that you need be interested in, but always the question is, which will serve the commonwealth best, not which party will prosper most in its own fortunes by filling the offices in the State.

Don't you see, therefore, that as public men we have to do the very thing that is done, and done very wisely, in a mixture of races? Men flock to America from many continents and from many countries; they come with all sorts of predispositions, with all sorts of prejudices, and with all sorts of habits. They unite together in a single community and find themselves engrossed in that thing that we call the American spirit, in that sentiment that we call the national sentiment of America. No man can tell how it comes. It comes in no very describable form and fashion, but it rises slowly in our hearts in a single generation. Men do not forget their ancient connections and their homes in foreign lands, they still love the dear people whom they have left there at home, but nevertheless feel that they are part of America; no matter where they come from, they imbibe the new spirit and become Americans.

You have particular manufacturing interests in this community, but you should not center your thoughts on these interests and on these alone, no matter how short a time you sojourn in this particular division of America which we love under the name of New Jersey. You should try to get some of the spirit of New Jersey in you; not a spirit that is antagonistic to your neighbors; not a spirit that is antagonistic to the homes you have left; not a spirit of jealousy of New York or of disdainfulness of Pennsylvania—though it is hard not to be disdainful of the politics of Pennsylvania—but a spirit of comradeship and a feeling that America cannot be sound unless all of you are sound, that America cannot be pure and patriotic unless New Jersey is pure and patriotic, unless she helps to lift the common levels and to take a patriotic and disinterested step forward. That, it seems to me, is the privilege of public life, the privilege to know that we are a progressive community.

I alluded tonight, not by way of mere local compliment, to your well paved and well lighted streets; I wanted to use it as an illustration. You don't make these public improvements for one merchant or any one of a group of merchants; you don't make them for any one factory or any one group of factories, you don't make them for any one man or group of men in the community; you are proud of those things because they have a common use, and they serve you in the way of satisfaction in a public spirit. The light upon your streets means that you in your own minds have conceived the necessity of general illumination and general betterment and the general common service for which the money that you spend is spent freely and without grudging. All of these things make a picture of what is inside of the minds of men, as well as evidence of things accomplished; and a progressive community is not one which only makes progress, but is thoughtful of something besides the present. You cannot make progress unless you look at the road ahead of you—I mean by that that you cannot make prudent progress unless you look at the road ahead of you. If you had been going about the state in automobiles over roads at night, as I have been in this campaign, you would be more interested in the road ahead of you than you would be in the road behind you. And a progressive community has to have its light ahead of it, penetrating every fog, disclosing every obstacle, uncovering every danger ahead, and know where to turn and the road signs.

What does that mean? Why are the people interested all over the country in the question of conservation? What does it mean? Keeping certain gentlemen from stealing mineral lands and appropriating the public lands in Alaska?[3] Yes, it means that, but not that only. It means keeping men from appropriating money that they ought not to appropriate except for the public benefit, in and around Perth Amboy also. Don't confine your conservation to Alaska. The whole business of conservation lies all around you, and it is just as much your business to conserve the public health as to conserve the water resources and all those things that should be as common and as useful as the air. When you have tuberculosis, contagion of any kind; when you sweep through the streets and factories, you are interested in the deepest conservation of all conservations, that deal with the health of men. That is what public affairs are for; they are the study of things

3 Wilson was referring to the famous controversy between Richard A. Ballinger, Secretary of the Interior, and Gifford Pinchot, head of the Forest Service in the Department of Agriculture. This celebrated fight began in late 1909 and involved Ballinger's approval of the acquisition of Alaskan coal lands by a syndicate of investors headed by Clarence Cunningham and Daniel Guggenheim. Although a congressional committee cleared Ballinger of charges of misconduct in early 1910, the incident was used by insurgent Republicans and progressives to discredit the Taft administration's conservation policy. For a full account of the affair, see Alpheus T. Mason, *Bureaucracy Convicts Itself: The Ballinger-Pinchot Controversy of 1910* (New York, 1941).

for everybody in every respect; they are not merely for promoting political projects.

I sometimes think that political projects are the lesser part of the matter; but they are for promoting all the common interests that pertain to the health of the body and spirits of men. It is just as important to America that she is a land of religious freedom, and to let every man follow the dictates of his own conscience as it is to walk the streets unmolested without proper police protection. I would a great deal rather be free in my thoughts than in my body; I would a great deal rather lie bedridden, with a free mind than to go where I please respondent to other men's opinions. We must conserve all these things; we are conserving the spirits and fortunes of our fellow-men when we take the proper views of public affairs; that is what a progressive community means.

Now I dare say that Perth Amboy is progressive in many of these ways, but she is not [as] progressive as she might be, not as thoughtful in detail as she may become, but nevertheless progressive; progressive under a mayor[4] whom she loves, who, as I have just seen, is greeted on the streets like a beloved comrade. You cannot be progressive unless you hang together, and you cannot hang together unless you believe in the men whom you follow. That is the fundamental prescription for political and social success and co-operation. Very well, being progressive, Perth Amboy is interested in having a progressive state to live in and share fortunes with. Now, is the state of New Jersey progressive? There are all sorts of definitions of progressiveness, and I have not found a man who did not want himself called a progressive, but we will have to let somebody else do the defining. I have heard of progressive Republicans and progressive Democrats, and progressive this and progressive that, but I cannot tell them apart by looking at them. I can tell them apart only by what they do. I cannot tell them apart by what they profess to believe in; I can only tell them apart by what they do in correspondence with their professions.

Now, the present Republican organization of this state might call itself progressive until it was out of breath, and I could not believe it because it has never progressed. If you wish me to regard you as moveable, I must trouble you to move. Unless I have ocular demonstration, or proof that you are mov[e]able, I cannot believe it. Now, every three years the Republican machine says that it is progressive, but it has not budged an inch. It

4 Albert E. Bollschweiler, who was elected in 1906 and re-elected in 1908. He was also engaged in the manufacturing of tubs and wash basins.

may be getting up steam; it may have sent for gasoline; its sparker may be out of order, I do not know what is the matter with it, but I know it has not moved, and therefore I begin to have my suspicion whether it is movable except by dynamite.

On the eighth of November we are going to try dynamite. It may then move in separate and scattered parts, but it will move, and the dynamite is going to be your own convictions, your own conclusions, as to what sort of men you want and what you want them to do; for it is not half as interesting to choose the men as it is to get the things done. The interesting part of this whole business is going to come in watching the men you choose; I say that with uncomfortable anticipation. I expect to be watched, because I expect to be elected. The interesting part of it may be now for you, but it will be then for me. All I have had to do in the campaign has been to go about and make speeches to cordial and indulgent audiences. It is easy enough to have men sit and look at me as you look at me with cordiality and sympathy. Under such circumstances I can talk all night, but when you are looking at me critically after the election, and when what I say counts for very little, but what I do counts for a great deal, then there may be times when I will get nervous, but I am going to control my nerves and see if something can be accomplished, always with your assistance.

Do not deceive yourselves into supposing that if you put up a talkative gentleman for governor, things will necessarily happen. You have got to put up a legislature that will have to help, not a legislature that will sit still, but gentlemen who will feel as if there was electricity in the seats of their chairs, the kind of electricity that comes of an electrified opinion that throbs, that thrills everywhere in the whole air of the commonwealth and makes it impossible for any man to be comfortable who is not doing what he said he would do. If you keep behind this opinion, your momentum will be irresistible, and if you do not there may be some of us who will go to sleep and do nothing and forget—merely forget—in the dignity of elevation of office.

How are you going to tell whether New Jersey is progressive or not? I have given you one test, which shows that New Jersey has not progressed under the recent Republican administration. There has been singular unanimity of opinion as to what ought to be and singular unanimity in not doing it. That is a curious contradiction. It has come to such a pass in this campaign that I have not anything left to discuss, because step by step the Republican candidate has dogged my words and has taken for [first] this position and then added that, and has then another, and then still another, until he has acquiesced in the whole of the program set forth in the platform of the Democratic party and has left his own platform so far behind that he is not within hailing distance of it now, so that there is not anything for me to discuss—at any rate, with Mr. Lewis. It is unamnimous [unanimous].

Very well, how are we going to tell what is going to happen? If Mr. Lewis is elected, of course he will be in a very awkward situation, because he will be all by himself, he is doing this thing alone, he is playing a single hand. I will at least have the advantage of standing solidly on a whole platform not made by myself but made by my party; and if I do not get their support there will be a great deal of reckoning to be done with their constituents. They are all in the same box. These gentlemen are going to [be] just as nervous after the eighth of November as I am. Now, there is nothing for the Republican managers to be nervous about after the eighth of November if Mr. Lewis gets elected. They have not said anything that will embarrass them. Well, that is not literally true, either. They have said things about me which, if they have any manner[s], ought to embarrass them; but I shan't remind them about that, because they are perfectly innocent; men always amuse themselves in that way when they know they are going to get licked. If they are going to get any fun that way, they are welcome to the consolation. But we want to know whether we are going to have progress or not.

I want to ask just this question. Why have promises repeatedly been made to you and never been kept? Are these gentlemen utterly insincere? I do not believe they are. I know some of these men and I do not believe that they are insincere, that is to say, in the ordinary sense of the term; but I do suspect that they regard the campaign as a dress parade, after which the play is over. They really believe, gentlemen, that the way to serve this country is to promote the interests of big business and then depend on big business to take care of us. I am not saying that in satire at all. That is what they believe; they believe that if they promote the great business interests of this commonwealth, for example, represented by certain groups of capitalists, they have sufficiently promoted the interests of New Jersey and that these big interests will take care of us.

Now, I differ from them as widely as the poles are separated from each other. Under my theory of government I believe that the way to make a prosperous people is to promote the prosperity of the individual, and when the people are prosperous they will take care of big business. I turn the matter exactly around. I remember a wise French writer said that a poor kingdom made a poor king, and I believe that a poor people make a poor body, and that the way to have prosperity is to have it general and not have it particularly.

This is what happens. They promise you a particular piece of legislation. As soon as the legislature meets, a bill embodying that legislation is introduced into the legislature. It is referred to a committee, and you never hear of it again. What happened? Nobody knows what happens. I am not intimating that corruption crept in; I do not know what crept in. The point is that I, as a citizen of New Jersey, not only do not know but it is intimated to me that it is none of my business. My reply is that it is my business, and it is the business of every man in New Jersey, and that we have a right to know all the particulars of the reason. There is not any legitimate privacy about matters of government. Government must, if it is to be pure and correct in its processes, be absolutely public in everything that affects it. I cannot imagine a public man with a conscience having a secret that he would keep from the people about their own affairs. I know how some of these gentlemen reason. They say that the influences to which they are yielding are perfectly legitimate influences, but if they were disclosed they would not be understood. Well, I am very sorry, but nothing is legitimate that cannot be understood. If you cannot explain it properly then there is something about it that cannot be explained at all. I know from the circumstances of the case not what is happening but that something private is happening, and that every time one of these bills gets into committee, something private stops it, and it never comes out again unless forced out by the agitation of the press and the courage and revolt of brave men in the legislature.

I have known brave men of that sort. I could name some splendid examples of men, who, as representatives of the people demanded to be told by the chairman of the committee why the bill was not reported, and when they could not find out from him they investigated and found out for themselves and brought the bill out by threatening to tell the reasons on the floor of the House. Those are private processes. These are processes which stand between the people and the things that are promised them, and I say that until you drive all of these things into the open you are not connected with your government; you are not represented; you are not participants in your government. Such a scheme of government by private understanding deprives you of representatives, deprives you of representation, deprives you of a representative institution.

There are things that are going on in the city of Camden at this present moment, and in Atlantic City at this present moment. Deliberate secret preparations are being made to vote voters who do not exist in this state. I want to say that the people of New Jersey, through their representatives, are not going to stand for Philadelphia gang methods in the city of Camden, and that sooner or later the authorities of New Jersey are going to insist upon seeing the voters who are said to be legitimately registered upon these lists. I say that because I know what is going to happen. These gentlemen in Camden apparently do not, but they have stopped listening so long to the movement of public affairs that I do not wonder that they are deaf. Don't they hear that murmur crossing the continent all the way from California, that murmur which will presently become the roar of the voices of determined men who are coming back, millions strong, to take possession of their own government again?

Then there will be a day of reckoning for these gentlemen, and they will wish they had never been born—not because of punishment, but because of discovery. These men do not mind doing these things as long as they are not discovered, but when they are discovered, as they have been discovered, their infamy is certain and permanent. I do not envy them the prospects!

I have seen many plays, and I have been thrilled by many parts in plays that I have seen, but I have never envied the man playing the villain. I would like to play any part that I might be engaged in well and successfully, but I would hate to go out of the wings with hisses following me. Now the hissing that these gentlemen will hear presently will not exist in the actual air, but it will hiss in their consciences for many a long day. What have they been doing? They have been attacking the very heart of all liberty, the very citadel of self-government—the purity and integrity of the ballot. They are not going to succeed and therefore I am only sorry for them.

But I have illustrated for you two of the things that are standing between you and self-government—private understandings and deliberate frauds at the polls. How long are you going to stand it? What are you going to do about it? Do you want big business beneficiently to take care of you, or do you want to take care of yourselves? Are you wards or are you men? Do you want the court to appoint guardians for you or are you old enough to take care of yourselves? If you know how to speak for yourselves you will speak at the polls next Tuesday. I have not the slightest doubt of the result. Not because of any excellence that there may be in, at any rate, the head of the Democratic ticket; not because of any virtue, any special virtue, that there may be in the Democratic party; but because the man is blind who does not see the signs of the times.

What are the signs of the times? Why, that men are absolutely ignoring party labels in 1910 as they never did before in any other year anywhere, and that they are going to vote for the man they prefer without regard to party altogether; and inasmuch as the American people is fundamentally a sporting people and want to take the most interesting chance, I think they are going to bet on the new horse. I cannot be mistaken in this, because I have gone from one end of this State to the other and I know what I have read in the audiences I have met. I have not read interest in me—that is not the point; I have not read interest in the Democratic platform, because there have been scores of Democratic platforms before that you have not been interested in. The present Democratic platform is more interesting, however, because it is more explicit. But the point is that you are scrutinizing men and platforms and coming together, as you have to-night, to hear things discussed, in order to help you make up your mind as to what you are going to do with your ballot when it comes to the day of voting. But when men gather for a purpose; when, as in this campaign, in a degree never before witnessed, ladies are drawn to political meetings, then you know that something is happening, besides what happens on street corners. Ordinary politics is supposed to be the gossip of the street corners. Now they are matters of conviction at home, and when that gets to be the case, look out for the signs of the times.

I heard a gentleman say the other night something that interested me very much. He has been a leading Democratic figure in a community that has been, from a Democratic standpoint, at any rate, hopelessly Republican for many years, and he said, "I do not know what to make of things now. The Democratic party is in danger of becoming fashionable, and if it does become so, I will not know how to behave. I will have to move, but I will have to move on to something else, because I am accustomed to be in the minority." He had been living in perpetual minority; he had never been able to control anything in his community. Now these are the signs of the times. Not in the narrow sense fashionable, but in the sense that men are flocking to the Democratic platform for the very best of reasons, that they think there is something in it.

As I was saying the other night to a little group of persons: Suppose somebody handed you a Republican and a Democratic ballot upside down, would you be satisfied simply to draw? If you knew one was Democratic and the other Republican and wanted something to happen, which would you draw? Why, if you drew the Republican ballot and wanted something to happen you would show that you had just moved into the state, because that ballot has not made anything happen for a great length of time, and therefore you would show that you did not know how to reckon the probabilities.

If you want something to happen you would invariably draw the Democratic ticket, and I will tell you why. If nothing else happens, this will happen: that you will have several interesting years, for if the Democratic program is not carried out then there is going to be trouble in the Democratic family. Nothing more satisfies [than] gossip, there is nothing more piquant and interesting than a family row, and if this family does not keep to its program, does not keep its family arrangements and engagements, there is going to be the biggest kind of a row that you ever heard of, because if it wants to continue a family on the premises it has made, it has to do something or it must go out of business permanently. It has been out of business for a good while. Is it credible to you that it wants to risk everything and go out of business permanently? I never heard of a political party that wished permanently to be in the minority and yet I say to the Democratic party, both in the State and the nation, that if it does not fulfill the expectations of the country, it is going to be in the minority for another generation; and I want to say, as a man, that in those circumstances it will deserve nothing better.

We want progress then. We want movement which is progress and we want intelligent movement, and we know in what direction we are to move. We have made up our minds about a lot of things. For example we have made up our minds that we want an Employers' Liability law. We have an Employers' Liability law from a recent legislature, but that kind of an employers' liability that there is not a lawyer in the state of New Jersey that knows what it means. We want at least an intelligible and workable employers' liability law. This law we have now was not intended to work, just between you and me; and I must say that it was most skillfully and successfully drawn for that purpose—it is one of those statical, instead of a dynamic act, which stands still instead of moving.

We want a genuine act. Something that will work. Why? Because we are after the labor vote and are courting the labor vote? Not at all. I would be ashamed of any man that courted any particular interest. I would be just as ashamed of courting the labor vote as I would of courting the Wall Street vote. It is none of my business, as a public man, to serve either Wall Street or labor. But it is my business to serve them both and to serve everybody. An employers' liability act is not intended to serve the special interests of a particular class of men, namely the ordinary working man. It is intended to keep up the levels of community.

What constitutes communities anyhow, I would like to know. Why, the majority of any community is made up of workingmen. Suppose that you want to maintain the physical and spiritual levels of a community taken as a community, where would you most naturally begin? By safeguarding the health and the interests of those who constitute the major part of it. Now, an employers' liability act is a means of insurance against accident in the midst of a society most of whose working men are engaged in dangerous occupations, I might say, handling extremely powerful machines and tools which some slight miscarriage or accident will make deadly to their personal safety.

Suppose that you do not provide for this, suppose that you let the working men take the consequences of accidents, what do you do? The head of the family gets maimed. That whole family is, in nine cases out of ten, rendered helpless. Then what do you do? They go through a period of infinite privation. Then their hope and courage slowly ooze out until there is hardly anything left of pyhsical [physical] or heart vigor in them. Then they are taken care of by charity. In the first instance, you let them sink below their level of self-respect, and then you complete the demoralization by taking care of them by somebody's benevolent kindness. That is not the way to maintain the spirit and strength of a community.

Let a man know that the community is interested to maintain him at a self-respecting level if he suffers injury at the hands of that society; then you have raised the moral tone, you have tightened every screw up, you have adjusted every part, you have removed the friction as much as possible, and you have coordinated and assembled all the parts of the machinery and the whole society is invigorated. These are the grounds upon which I am in favor of these acts, not of concession but of justice.

By the same token, I am interested in seeing that there is proper sanitation maintained in factories, and that there is proper regulation in regard to women and children, upon whom more than on any other part of the community the ultimate health of the community depends; I am interested to see that there should be proper regulation of the conditions and the length of labor. These things are the modern methods of safeguarding the health and energy of the state itself; and, therefore, I am interested in all of these things. We are all agreed upon them. Very well. Why have we not got them, and when shall we get them? I put it to you to decide.

You have a very important part in deciding what New Jersey shall do. I challenge you, not as manufacturers, not as merchants, not as workingmen, not as citizens of Perth Amboy, but as citizens of the Union, as members of mankind, as those who are interested in every handsome process of liberty, to summon your will to answer your convictions and to vote as you think on the eighth of November.

FPS T transcript (WP, DLC) with corrections and additions from the partial texts in the *Philadelphia Record*, Nov. 5, 1910, and the New York *Evening Post*, Nov. 5, 1910.

From Hiram Woods

Dear Tommy: Baltimore. Nov. 4 1910.

I guess I am in the same box as lots of the men who feel closest to you personally, and who love you most. When the news came of your resignation there was at first a heart-felt disappointment that even a call to civic duty, which you rightly say no man has the right to decline, should take you from the Presidency. I believed, and so did others, that the battle was virtually won, simply because the new Princeton owes its inspiration to you, and is essentially a part of you. We think down here that THIS Princeton is worth saving, and a lot depends on who is at the helm. However, this is "past history" now. What the relief must be to you those who are nearest to you must and do know. You could not have stood the mental state you were in last March a great-deal longer. Still, just how Princeton will come out under what seems to be the inevitable "conservative" or "midway" successor no one can foresee, nor is it worth while to discuss. Much as we feel the loss for Princeton, your old crowd is relieved to have you out of the rushline for your own sake, and to see you where we have known for years you would make good. I am writing you today because of the enclosed which I cut from The Sun of this morning.[1] I have followed you around New Jersey since the campaign opened. The people have caught on to your essential traits, and I look for a big majority on Tuesday. At any rate, I want to offer my hearty wishes for that result. Bob Henderson[2] spent Wednesday night with me, and told me he had seen you for a moment at Princeton. I had hoped to be with him and Ned[3] there, but Bob's machine broke down the first day out and my "ride" consisted largely in watching attempts at repairs. I had to come home before they were made. I hope to go to the game on the 12th,[4] and Mrs. Woods will be with me. We may stay in Princeton ower [over] Sunday. I hope we can catch a look at you while there. In any event, old man, this article inspired me to do what I ought to have done long ago, and would have done but for the never-ending demands on my time for one thing or another, and my chronic disposition to put off letter-writing. Don't trouble to answer this with all that is on you now. With love to the family, As Ever,

Affectionately Yours: Hiram Woods.

TLS (WP, DLC).
    [1] It was the interview in the Baltimore *Sun* printed at Nov. 3, 1910.
    [2] Robert Randolph Henderson.
    [3] James Edwin Webster, another of Wilson's classmates and an attorney in Bel Air, Md.
    [4] The Princeton-Yale football game. Princeton lost, 5 to 3.

From [Nancy] Nettie Fowler McCormick

Dear Dr Wilson   New York Nov 4, 1910

Your addresses are delightful. You have a new and captivating literary form, in which to clothe your new and unsurpassed method of appeal to public conscience.

I hear professional men here praise your canvas, and stand up for your election. I long for your success!

Princeton's resolutions yesterday are fine.[1]

Have been kept here by some illness.

Faithfully Yours   Nettie F. McCormick

Have sent a little check for your campaign fund

ALS (WP, DLC).
    [1] That is, the resolutions of the Board of Trustees printed in C. W. McAlpin to WW, Nov. 3, 1910.

From Marie Louise Norris Gollan

My dear Dr. Wilson   New York. November 4th, 1910

Have you a moment to waste on a tiny note of admiration.

My Judge, who is in Bermuda holding his assizes, has followed with keen interest your brilliant campaign, by the clippings of your speeches I have sent him.

He is rather inclined to bore me about my ardent partisanship— a reflection of his *own*! In his last letter he writes "What a pity it is I can't stand for a constituency at home and have you to canvass for me. Such wholehearted partisanship as yours would ensure as well as deserve success. I hope with you for W. W.'s success and when he does win—with you I don't say *'if'*—please wire him my heartiest congratulations. One might even go further and congratulate New Jersey still more heartily but I suppose that would be lèse democratie." His own words are so much more characteristic than a cold wire, I can not resist sending them to you.

With our united congratulations

Yrs. very Sincerely   Louise Norris Gollan

ALS (WP, DLC).

From John Sharp Williams[1]

My dear Sir: Benton, Miss., Nov 4 1910

I don't often "slop-over"—too lazy or too cynical, I don't know which, but I want to congratulate you on your article in last North American Review—"The Lawyer & the Community."[2]

Maybe one reason I admire it so extremely is because I have been long harping on the same string in & out of Congress. Crimes can be put an end to only one way—by punishing the flesh & blood which commits them, whether by ordering them, or obeying orders. Let even subordinates learn that it is not "The Boss" who is boss but the Law, and if a subordinate be discharged because of refusal to obey an order violative of law, let him have damages actual & punitive. You will succeed in public life because you have the knack of striking off "key-note" sentences. God grant that you may redeem tariff-bought New Jersey.

Yours   John Sharp Williams

ALS (WP, DLC).

[1] Former congressman (1893-1909) and United States senator-elect from Mississippi.

[2] Woodrow Wilson, "The Lawyer and the Community," *North American Review*, CXCII (Nov. 1910), 604-22. It is printed at Aug. 31, 1910.

From John Bassett Moore[1]

My dear Mr. Wilson: New York, Nov. 4, 1910.

Having lately returned from South America, where I served as a delegate to the Fourth International American Conference, at Buenos Aires, I have been deeply interested in our recent political developments and especially in your inspiring campaign, to the expenses of which I beg leave, in token of regard for yourself and of devotion to the cause, to make the enclosed contribution,[2] which can be turned over to your treasurer, whose name and address I lack.

Believe me to be

Ever sincerely yours, John B. Moore.

ALS (WP, DLC).

[1] Hamilton Fish Professor of International Law and Diplomacy at Columbia University.

[2] The amount of Moore's contribution is unknown.

From William Cavanagh Gebhardt

My dear Dr. Wilson: Jersey City [N. J.], November 4, 1910.

Please accept my sincere congratulations upon the splendid fight you have made to be elected Governor. You will recollect the conversation which I had with you in your room at the hotel in Flemington. I took up the matter in accordance with our conversation of that night, and I think I am safe in saying that practically every clergyman in the State is today quietly working for you, as well as practically every Local Option man. I have not changed my views with reference to the liquor interests. I think they are quietly against you and will remain so. All the reports I can get very strongly indicate your triumphant election, and I hope and pray that the reports now coming in are correct and that you will be elected on Tuesday next by a large majority. I am very sorry indeed that I have not been able to take as active a part in the fight as I wanted to take. I have offered repeatedly to speak in any part of the state, and expected to be called upon to do so day and night, but up to the present time I have received only one invitation outside of my own county, and that is for Belvidere on next Monday night.

Very truly yours, Wm. C. Gebhardt

TLS (WP, DLC).

From Harry Augustus Garfield

Dear Wilson: Williamstown, Mass. Nov. 4, 1910

Your note from the Bellevue-Stratford reached me shortly before I left to attend the meeting of New England College Presidents, from which I have just returned.

What you suggest interests me very much. The chair of English Literature has not yet been filled, and I shall most assuredly consider Axson. I know and value most highly his fine personal qualities and his ability as a lecturer. I do not know so much about him as a teacher. Concerning the last, I shall not embarrass you by asking questions, but you can perhaps tell me, when the rush of the campaign is over, something of Axson's literary ambitions and plans. It would be a great delight to Mrs. Garfield and me to have him with us here.

You may be sure I am reading everything I can lay hands on concerning your campaign. To a resident of New Jersey I wrote, in answer to his question, that, were I still a resident of the State, I should not hesitate to cast my vote for you. My judgment in the matter is, I think, dispassionate, but it would be easy to deceive myself.

With best wishes for your success, I remain,

Affectionately yours,   H. A. Garfield.

TLS (WP, DLC).

To Harry Augustus Garfield

My dear Garfield: Princeton, N. J. November 4th, 1910.

Thank you for your letter of November 4th. The thing that Axson is particularly famous for here is his teaching and the way he gets hold in intimate fashion upon his men, to their great stimulation, but I would rather you would take testimony of some-one else on that point than from me.[1]

I need not tell you how happy your words about my candidacy make me. To have the support of your judgment in a matter of this sort is immensely cheering to me.

In haste,   Affectionately yours,   Woodrow Wilson

TLS (H. A. Garfield Papers, DLC).
[1] Axson did not accept the position at Williams, if, indeed, it was offered to him.

To John Bassett Moore

My dear Mr. Moore,   Princeton, N. J. 5 November, 1910.

Your letter of yesterday has given me much cheer and great pleasure, and I thank you for it with all my heart. Your wish to contribute to the campaign fund is very generous, and I need not tell you that I appreciate it very warmly.

I sincerely hope that you are well, and that you enjoyed the International Conference.

In haste,

With warm regard,

Sincerely Yours,   Woodrow Wilson

WWTLS (J. B. Moore Papers, DLC).

A News Report of a Campaign Address in Carteret, New Jersey

[Nov. 5, 1910]

RAILROAD MEN GREET WILSON

Give Democratic Nominee One of the Most Novel Welcomes of Campaign.

HEART-WARMING ENTHUSIASM

PERTH AMBOY, Nov. 5.—Railroad men of Middlesex County last night gave Woodrow Wilson what was without doubt one of the most whole-hearted receptions that he has received during his campaign for Governor. In fact, he got two, one at Port Reading, on his way to Carteret, and the second in Carteret. There, it seemed that all the 581 men who voted in the Borough of Roosevelt last year had gathered. This followed a meeting here, at which almost three thousand persons heard the candidate, in the Donahoe Auditorium, which seats 2,200 persons.

The candidate, accompanied by Mayor Joseph A. Hermann, of Roosevelt, went from this city to Carteret through Port Reading. At the yards there a score of Reading Railroad locomotives were massed, and as the auto approached the engineers tied down the engine whistles. Then arose a concentrated din that prevented one from even thinking.

To get the auto to halt railroad men stood in the roadway with red lanterns and burned red fire. In windows were red, white and blue lamps. In the falling rain the scene was most picturesque. Men in jumpers and carrying dinner pails crowded around the auto to shake the candidate's hand, and Mr. Wilson was kept busy bobbing from one side of the machine to the other trying to gratify his admirers.

Unusual as was this, the candidate received another surprise when he arrived at Carteret. In a long, low, narrow hall were gathered more than 500 men, the first rows of seats being filled with railroad men clad in their jumpers. Across the ceiling were strips of red, white and blue bunting, and the railroad men had lighted red, white and blue lanterns, which they massed when Mr. Wilson entered. The cheers that greeted him, in the closed hall seemed almost as voluminous as the more strident locomotive whistles that he had heard a few minutes before. And the enthusiasm was unfettered by any social formalities; it was spontaneous, whole-hearted and human.

"Such receptions as these," said Mr. Wilson afterward, "touch a man's heart and make him feel that he would like to do a whole lot of things for the people." . . .

With another composite audience before him at Carteret, Mr. Wilson referred to "the infinite variety of blood and genius" brought to this country by various nationalities. He took occasion to refer also to freedom of religious belief, saying: "This is the freest place in the world for a man to think, especially of his religion and his God—although I am afraid that there are some men who don't think of God at all in politics."

The candidate censured the Republican party for failure to keep its promises, and declared that if it could be proved that it had kept them, he would retract the criticism, and he said:

"We don't want to be looking always at a game in which no runs are scored. You don't want automatic pitching; you want to see some action and some results."

This made a hit right off the bat with the crowd, and Mr. Wilson scored a run when he referred to the good a public utilities commission could do for Carteret, where the last train in of an evening is around 6 o'clock. He made still another tally when he urged an efficient employers' liability law. When the present one had been formulated, he said, that in it "the English language had gotten tangled up" so that it could not be understood. There was a suspicion in some minds that this was done deliberately so that the law could not be made workable.

Printed in the *Newark Evening News*, Nov. 5, 1910; some editorial headings omitted.

A News Report of Four Campaign Addresses in Essex County

[Nov. 5, 1910]

WILSON'S LAST CALL GREATEST

Wins Responses to His Appeals to Essex Crowds That Prove Him Leader.

Newark, N. J., Nov. 5.—Letting down the curtain on the first act of the stirring drama of American history, in which he is the new-risen star, Woodrow Wilson to-night was accorded a mark of approval that must ring in his ears and linger in his eyes till the lights go out forever upon his stage of action.

No mortal man ever won the hearts of an awakened people like this man did those in a vast audience in the Krueger Auditorium where, earlier in the campaign, he scored a triumph no less brilliant. No man in New Jersey has so gripped human interest, so aroused the spirit, so lifted the human mind, and it has all been so clear, so simple, so direct, so impelling that any fair-minded

GLEN RIDGE,   5 November, 1910.

                        BLOOMFIELD,

                                        East ORANGE.

                YYYYYYYYYYYYYYYYYYYYYYYY

        Or Objects:

                The SIMPLIFICATION of politics

                The PURIFICATION of politics

                The ACCOMPLISHMENT of a certain DEFINITE
                PROGRAMME of progressive policies.

        The Means to the end:

                Definte leadership, clear and accepted;

                Team work vs. isolation of the leader and a
                        futile struggle, - a game for party ad-
                        vantage, party "points".

                                        11/5/10

man must of necessity be fully convinced of his absolute sincerity and unflinching courage.

Mr. Wilson made four speeches in Essex county to-day, three this afternoon in the suburban sections of Newark, and the final appeal to-night to nearly 3000 eager, interested persons, and in all of them the ruling note was the awakened impulse of the new American, the rehabilitation of the old American, the readjustment of the government to the needs of the people, as against the behests of special privilege. It was refreshing, therefore, to watch and to hear with what a storm of unanimity the thinking people agreed that that is the great question of to-day. . . .

The brilliant wind-up of the campaign included afternoon speeches at Glen Ridge, Bloomfield and East Orange, where many prosperous commuters live and where political independence is so strong that it chooses a man of the Colby type every little while. In all of his speeches Mr. Wilson thrilled his intelligent hearers, who jammed all three of the halls, with the patriotic impulse that sways his own great mind.

It was perfectly evident that, of the nearly 3000 persons who listened to him to-day, he had not before had a more sympathetic nor appreciative audience, and he seemed to draw fresh inspiration, for all three of the addresses were different, and it was difficult to pick the strongest. Speaking to the 1500 persons who crowded every bit of space in Commonwealth Hall at East Orange, Mr. Wilson was describing that what really is happening in the whole country is that the people are seeking new leaders in whom they can trust, and this, he explained, accounts for the tremendous power over the people which Theodore Roosevelt enjoys.

Mention of the name of the Colonel elicited a round of cheers, which showed that a majority of his hearers were Republicans, though, beyond all question, in quick sympathy with the speaker. "There are so many hidden passages, so many back doors and hidden processes in this system," said the candidate, referring to the prevalent political system and its business alliance, "that we believe that somebody is working a game. That is the reason the Democrats have proposed to send me to Trenton to find out what is going on, to disclose to the people of New Jersey what is their own business."

Mr. Wilson arrived here soon after 2 o'clock and was a few minutes ahead of time at the first stop at the Town Hall, in the handsome public schoolhouse at Glen Ridge. The hall was crowded with interested persons, of course. It would be a singular thing to see a small Wilson audience. A short address was made by James K. Milod,[1] one of the bright candidates for Assembly in Essex, who said it was quite extraordinary for so many people of Glen Ridge to gather for a Democratic meeting. With an instantly responsive audience, Mr. Wilson was in fine form, and he made a rattling address, bristling with good, effective points.

"Politics as now operated," he said, "is a complete system, and we on the outside don't understand all its deep intricacies, but we propose to get on the inside and understand it all." He made a sharp rap at "Cannonism" in Congress and said that it also exists in the New Jersey Legislature, that system of legislation by committee.

"You've got to treat diseased politics," he said, "as we have learned to treat tuberculosis, by having people live out doors and even sleeping in the pure air."

Printed in the *Philadelphia Record*, Nov. 6, 1910; some editorial headings omitted.
[1] James P. Mylod, lawyer of Newark, who was elected.

The Final Address of the Campaign Delivered in Newark, New Jersey[1]

NOVEMBER 5th, 1910

Mr. Chairman,[2] Ladies and Gentlemen:

It sounds like the cheering on the home stretch. Your greeting is certainly most cordial and most welcome. I almost all but began the campaign in this room, and for the last six weeks I have been hard at it, up and down the State, and now I came back to report progress.

With your permission and indulgence I should very much like to pass, in brief review, the six weeks through which we have just gone. It has, I think, we can all agree, been a very notable campaign, a campaign which has had many features in it that are likely to lift the hope and restore the confidence of men who believe in government by the people.

I started out six weeks ago at a meeting in Jersey City, or rather at three meetings, at which I was bidden to repeat myself by outlining what seemed to me the Democratic opportunity—the opportunity of the Democratic party, because no one else has seemed ready to recognize it and avail themselves of it—the opportunity to lead a great people seeking leadership in the effort

[1] In Krueger Auditorium.
[2] Jacob Haussling, Mayor of Newark.

to restore their government to its processes, to its ancient processes.

Why, gentlemen, there has not been any such opportunity in a generation in this country as in this year to set the people of the Union an example as to what [part] the people of a free common-wealth should have in the government and control of their own affairs. Do you know that all over this country there is a search, a search for principles, not a search for expedients, not a search for selfishness, not a search by men who are seeking to get something that will be for their own selfish aggrandizement, but a search for someone, some body of men, some party of men, who will set up again the ancient standards of principles which men used to gather about and follow in this country.

Politics in recent years has degenerated in New Jersey, as else-where, into a struggle for control, into an effort to preserve the integrity and power of an organization which held the people at arm's length, and all over the country there has been the starting of opinion, the starting and gathering of revolt against the processes of politics, because they are the processes of selfishness and not the processes of patriotism.

I want to give honor where honor is due, and I want to say something about some of my Republican fellow citizens.

You know what happened in Washington. There was no in-timation that there was any split or division in the Republican party until the present unspeakably selfish legislation known as the Payne-Aldrich bill was passed or brought up. Then what hap-pened? Certain men who were Republicans said that this piece of legislation was not in conformity even with the professions of the Republican party; it was not a measure for protection, but a measure for patronage; that it was seeking to give favors where favors were not needed, and that its object was not the industrial object of America. That was said by United States Senators, men who have gone out in the West and made a political revolution. All the while, standing by them is that same Democratic party, mustering thousands of strong men over the country, where there were Democrats waiting for the Republicans to come to their senses, waiting for the Republicans to see that this was not patriotic accomplishment, but self aggrandizement. So that it is nothing but the simple truth to say that the Democratic party, in respect of its principles, has been waiting for the country to re-cover its just point of view and see the public interest in its true light. We have been saying all along of this policy that it would have sufficed had a plea for the prosperity of the country nevertheless been used, [however, it was] manipulated and manoeuvred for private and selfish advantage, until it no longer represented the interests of the American people, but only the interests of some selfish combinations of men.

Was it not then the golden opportunity for Democracy to come into its own, to step forward and take the leadership of an awakened people in the return to sensible and safe policies? Not only that, but to the methods of right politics?

What are the right methods of politics? They are the methods of public discussion; they are the methods of public opinion; they are the methods of open leadership, open and above board, not closeted with boards of guardians, or anybody else, but brought into the open, where honest eyes can look upon them and honest eyes can judge of their integrity.

If there is nothing to conceal, then why conceal it? If it is a public game, why play it in private? That is the Democratic inquiry—that is the inquiry of the United States. If it is a public game then come out into the open and play in public.

You have got to treat diseased politics as we have learned to treat tuberculosis, by making all the people who suffer from it live out of doors; not only to spend their days out of doors and walk around, but to sleep out of doors; always to be in the open, where they will be accessible to those fresh, nourishing and revivifying things which are the only antiseptics in such circumstances.

That was the thought with which we opened, if we wanted to restore politics to their former publicity, to their former freedom, to their former openness and to their former candor and their old processes of leadership. But we had a program, and we have a very definite program, indeed; we had a program that consisted of a catalogue of reasonable and progressive measures. It was not necessary that the candidates of the Democratic party should be asked whether they believed in this, that or the other specific measure; it was in the platform.

You did not have to question the candidate for Governor on the Democratic ticket; you did have to question the Republican candidate, because his platform did not contain anything worth mentioning, and he has, stage by stage, added to the items, that liberal policy which he proposed, and his party—his party managers, I mean—his party organization—has been extremely reticent as to whether they agree with him or not.

The Democratic candidate has a party behind him, and the Republican candidate has not a party behind him.

The program contains that list of measures which is so familiar to you that it is hardly worth while to run them over by mention of the whole catalogue; you know what it includes, it includes some of the most important features; it includes a public utilities commission with genuine powers of regulation; it includes equalization of taxation; it includes the business-like and economical reorganization and administration of the State government; it includes direct primaries; it includes an extension of the civil service; it includes the prevention of corrupt practices in elections, which, by the way, is abundantly evident as a necessity.

I can show you registry lists, for example, in the city of Camden which would be all the argument you needed for a revision of all your laws with regard to the ballot and the protection of its purity.

For example, your present law does not require you to appear in person to register, but you may be registered by affidavit. Well, you can register ghosts by affidavit; you can register all the thugs in the city of Philadelphia by affidavit; you can put them down as living at fictitious residences and have seventy men live where but two men actually live. All of that by the assistance of your present laws.

And then you have not attempted to define what are legitimate campaign expenses; you have not attempted to limit them to pledge campaign managers and candidates for office to publish itemized accounts of what they spend, and, what is more important, itemized statements of where they got the money.

But you want more than that. You want an employers' liability act that will work. You have got one now that does not work and was not intended to. You want not only that, but you want the reasonable protection of that great body who sustain the health and energy of our community—I mean by that, the workingmen. You want their proper protection by the sanitary inspection of factories and the enforcement of laws of sanitation, the proper limitation of labor, proper conditions of labor, and the proper limitation of the labor of women and children, because nowhere else does the health of the community rest so much as with the women and children.

These then are the great questions of conservation about which we have been so careless and so improvident. Why, if it had not been for the abundant rains in the month of June, the northern watershed of New Jersey would have bred diseases without limit because of bad legislation and the lack of very needed legislation—legislation which improvidently allowed a private company to divert the waters of the Passaic River, and then allowed other persons to pollute what was left, until it has come about that there is no more solid body of water anywhere to be found. If you carried it much farther, you could walk across it, if you don't mind soiling your shoes.

All these things are the familiar catalogue of what we want.

In order to have a proper foundation for equal taxation, we should have revaluation of those things about which we talk so much and know so little—I mean the valuation of great corporations. I surround my statements with cautious limitations when I know what I am talking about. Not only do you not know anything about the processes of taxation in this commonwealth, but there is not anybody who does. Your tax assessors copy the assessments of those who preceded them, and the whole matter of assessment and taxation is in a state of utter chaos in this commonwealth, and therefore the sooner we find out where we are, the sooner we can get at justice and the sooner we can reach a point where we can discuss this question with knowledge.

These are the programs of men who want justice done and want the ends of government stirred [served] in the most economical and efficient manner.

I am not going to keep you hear [here] to listen to a discussion one by one of the issues of this campaign because they have been discussed until everybody has been brought, at any rate, into a professed agreement. You cannot startle a man with a question to which he will not make answer in the most orthodox fashion so that the question that you are to determine in this campaign is: Whom are you going to trust to mean what he says? That is all. Very well then; what has happened? I want to speak very plainly to this audience tonight. I have now been into every county of the State, and I have seen audiences that would move the heart of any man, thronging in numbers and rallying around, not a party, not a person, not to accomplish some selfish purpose or interest, but to enjoy the expereince [experience] of hearing the genuine intersets [interests] of the genuine commonwealth candidoy [candidly] discussed. I have tried, throughout this campaign, to be as candid and as fair as I know how to be. I have tried always to dwell upon the merits of every question; I have tried to point out to the audiences that I have faced what they wanted to hear, and not only what they wanted to hear but what it was right to do in the circumstances.

What has been done on the other side? Has the level of the campaign been lifted by the methods of my opponent? Have you hear[d] them discuss the questions in a frank and open mood? Have you not seen them diligently inventing stories against their opponents? Have you not seen them filling the public prints with personal matters which are without foundations of facts or justice? What do these gentlemen suppose public questions to be? Have they forgotten what American politics is? Have they forgotten that this is a question of what communities must do, and that it is neither here or there what individuals are?

I have not been conducting this campaign on the ground that I was the fittest person in the State of New Jersey to enjoy the confidence of my fellow citizens. That has not been in my speeches and it has not been in my thought. I have been trying to explain to you matters of policy, and I am met by aspersions of character. Now, these gentlemen have not discussed public questions. Have they forgotten how to discuss public questions? Have they forgotten that the people of this commonwealth are entitled to hear public questions expounded? Is government so much a matter of habit, a matter of private arrangement, that they do not feel the necessity of trying to explain it to the people?

We have been building, building and building, while they have been tearing down, tearing down, tearing down. Every acid that can eat they have been sprinkling abroad, and no balm that can heal, no tonic that can put fresh vigor in the body politic, no hope to lift the people to candid and energetic leadership. I do not speak of these things because I have been hurt, for I have not. These gentlemen have earned nothing except what it is very cheap to earn, my entire contempt.

But it is neither here nor there what I think of them. The question is what do you think of them. If they cannot fight the battle of knowledge and of principle, let them get out of the arena. There are no challengers in this contest for the things that they know how to do; there are no challengers for such contests as they are accustomed to; the only challenge is as to what they are going to do, and they have not met the challenge.

What has been the result? Look at the response of the people of this State in this campaign. Look at the response of the people of this State from Cape May to Sussex, and see what the people of New Jersey want. The people of New Jersey have not been sitting in private conference like some of those gentlemen. They have been discussing their affairs in the open way; they have been looking around the country, and they know that the rest of the country has heard that New Jersey is awake, and that she has stopped taking the drugs that have been offered her; that she has stopped waiting for people who never do what they promised to do; that whereas the men who would lead her on the Republican side reject, and reject with scorn, most of the men who speak liberally. Liberal principles, nevertheless, are to the liking of the people, and only those who lift the banners of liberalism will have the people as their followers. That is what the people of New Jersey have meant as they have trooped out, rain or shine, not to follow the Democratic party—we have stopped thinking about parties —to follow what they now know as the Democratic idea, the idea that the people are at last to be served.

Do you know what the American people are waiting for, gentlemen? They are waiting to have their politics utterly simplified. They are realizing that our politics are full of secret conferences, that there are private arrangements, and they do not understand it. They want to concentrate their force somewhere. They are like an unorganized army saying, "The thing is wrong. Where shall we congregate? How shall we organize? Who are the captains? Where are the orders? Which is the direction? Where are the instruments of government?" That is what they are waiting for. It is an opportunity of effort, and not only that, it is a terrible opportunity.

Don't you know that some man with eloquent tongue, without conscience, who did not care for the nation, could put this whole country into a flame? Don't you know that this country from one end to the other believes that something is wrong? What an opportunity it would be for some man without conscience but with unlimited power, to spring up and say: "This is the way. Follow me," and lead them into the paths of destruction. How terrible it would be.

What is our duty then? Our duty is sobriety and patience, but leadership nevertheless is always the means of centering our affairs where it can be used for the recovery of our rights. Why, I have grown sick at heart to hear men discuss the interest of this industry or the interest of that industry, the interest of the employer, and the interest of the workingman, as if they were different interests. Why is it that we are face to face with this subject of the relation of the employer to the employee. Just suppose for a moment that the employer wished to see the thing from the point of view of the employee, that he wished his employee to know the exact conditions and details of his business and his account books, that he wanted to take him into his confidence and share with him the product of the business upon some equitable scale, and suppose that the workingman, equally fair-minded, wanted to meet the employer, to see the figures that he showed him, and wanted to co-operate with him, to know that such and such were the figures, and that such and such wages were fair compensation, would there be any labor question?

That is why we want a Public Utilities Commission—not to squeeze the railway corporations and the corporations that supply us with water, gas and electricity, not to put them out of business, not to make what they undertake impossible because unprofitable —but a commission whose inquiries can lay the whole state of the business before us, so that we may know what is just, so that we may be convinced by the inquiry of disinterested persons that the rates charged are reasonable rates, and then we will pay them without grumbling.

But let it continue to be said, as it is now said, without the means of contradiction or of knowledge, that such and such a corporation is earning such and such enormous dividends, and charging such and such rates, and there will continue to be misunderstanding—misunderstandings which are dangerous to the body politic and which prevent the accomplishment of anything in the process of adjustment, the process of justice, which is at the foundation of good government. See what you have a chance to do, gentlemen. You have a chance to choose somebody for leader whom you will trust to lead you morally. You have a chance to choose somebody for leader whom you will trust to lead you moderately, not passionately, wisely, with knowledge, if he can go in the direction of general understanding in a general movement forward.

Now, I am free to admit that the methods by which we choose leaders in this country are whimsical methods. In many countries there are methods that are parliamentary methods, where men have opportunity to prove their metal, and, having proved their metal, they have become leaders. You cannot make a man a leader by election, and you cannot keep him from being a leader by not electing him. If you want to prove the last proposition, look at some of our big cities and ask who are the bosses of those cities. In many instances I could point out men who do not occupy any public office at all, men whom the people never elected. And therefore they cannot put them out of anything; they are men of genius and men who have assumed leadership, and it is their genius that has put them where they are; and although men of genius, in some instances they are men of cunning, and you cannot put them out of business except by substitution, finding a better leader to whom the people will flock with heartiness and cheer that the others will be thrust to one side.

Now, when parties choose leaders, how do they choose them? Well, in America we elect delegates to a convention, and the convention gets together, and, by one process or another—sometimes by one process and sometimes by another—they choose a leader. If they choose somebody who has been in public life a long time, they have at least some gauge by which to calculate his orbit; but if they choose somebody from the outside, then it is just a process of guessing; it is just as if they said, "We will bet you that this man turns out to be a leader." You don't know whether he will or not, and the man himself don't know whether he will or not.

But I need not apologize to you for your own methods. These are the methods by which you pick your leaders. Now, by these methods two leaders are picked out from whom you are to choose. The Republican convention picked out one whom they thought was a good leader, and the Democratic convention picked out one whom they guessed would be a good leader.

Now, I cannot verify either guess, and the only way you will know, and the only way I will ever know whether the Democratic guess was good or not is by trying. I have had a good deal to do with various companies of men in America, and I have found that they are good sports, and I believe you are going to take a sporting chance.

But what does leadership mean, gentlemen? Here is the case: When you vote a ballot, just for curiosity, if you have the time, provided they let you stay in the booth long enough, count the names on the ballot and ask yourself candidly how many of these men you know anything about. I saw a ballot once—and I must confess it was the longest ballot I ever saw—that had seven hundred names on it, and I don't believe that any conceivable man could vote a ballot like that with intelligence. You have to fill all the offices there are, from top to bottom, by election, and you are so used, when you go through the process, to doing the same thing, that you don't know whether you accomplish anything or not.

In the precinct I vote in in Princeton, there is one of those wretched voting machines, and you work a lever one way or the other, you work it one way for one party and the other way for the other party, and I have often thought, so far as my knowledge of the ticket was concerned, that I might as well pull one lever as the other. I have to vote in a blind kind of way what I think is the probability as to what the one set of men will stand for or what the other set of men will stand for.

Now, what happens in those circumstances? There is nothing that the people of this country follow so much as the leadership of somebody whom they have chosen to do something, somebody to explain to them what is going on, somebody who will come out in the open and propose policies to them and try to convince them of the wisdom and usefulness of those measures. So, just as I said a moment ago, as the people of this country have been following the wrong kind of leaders, there would be absolutely no resisting under a right leader.

If you once got a leader in whose integrity and honesty you thoroughly believed in, he could lead you against any combination or machination that was set up against him, and you would thank God that at last they knew what they were about. You hear of debates in the legislature on this, that and the other subject, the push of this thing and the pull of that; one man says that [it] is necessary that a certain bill should pass and another man says that it would be iniquitous that such a bill should get through; one represents one district in the state and another represents another district in the state, and there is no common spokesman; it may be that each is trying to grind his own axe, and they can't choose somebody to come out and tell them what it means for the whole state, and let them judge for themselves.

Did you never reflect upon this interesting circumstance? Ther[e] is only one person elected by all the voters of New Jersey; there is only one person elected by all the voters in the United States? If I were to sum up all the criticisms that have been uttered against the honorable and distinguished gentleman who is now President of the United States, it would be summed up in this, that the people are disappointed that he has not led them; they looked to him to form processes of affairs and he refrains. I don't know why he refrains. I have, for myself, no criticism to make of the refraining, but the disappointment of the people is perfectly evident, because he refrains, and they long to see somebody go in there and do it, put upon Congress itself the pressure of opinion of the whole United States.

Now, that is the only thing that will disentangle the complicated affairs of New Jersey, to put somebody in the governorship who will bring to bear on legislation the pressure of opinion of the whole of New Jersey. That is not only legitimate pressure, but it is a pressure that bears the most authentic stamp of legitimacy in America. The President or the Governor who would try to accomplish his ends in respect to a legislative program by the use of patronage and by appointments to office does not deserve the confidence of any man. His only instrument, and his absolutely irresistible instrument, if he knows how to use it, is the instrument of public opinion. If he can get the people of the commonwealth to go with him and stand back of him, then there is no force in Washington or anywhere else that can withstand him. That, I understand to be the meaning of this campaign.

First of all, as I said, is the rehabilitation, the re-establishment of ancient policies of government, and then concentration of public opinion in some particular leader. I believe that is the thing you ought to do. Now, choose your leader. By doing so you will also choose your party, you will also choose your program. All the choices are involved in that, but that must be your choice; and I warn you that if you do not want the trouble of making up your minds to support a set of policies, then don't elect me; there is no use in it. There is no use in beginning anything that you are not going to stay in yourselves until it is finished.

The Governor does not constitute the government of New Jersey; the members of the legislature and the other officers of the State do not constitute the government of New Jersey. Every drop of vitality and energy there is in the government, every drop of vitality and energy there is in New Jersey comes from the people of New Jersey, and if the people don't find the means of expressing themselves, then the whole process of election is futile. You need not take the trouble to vote unless your vote does mean that there is dynamic force in every vote deposited in the ballot box.

We decide things now by ballot; we don't decide them by bloodshed; we decide them by that magnificent irresistible force, the force of the concerted purposes of men. Oh, if men would only realize the power that is in unselfish purpose. Selfish purpose has no power in it except to destroy, because not everybody's interest is the same, and when you and men of the same interests with yourself exert power, then you simply create the antagonism of men with other interests, and by the time you have all the interests stirred up you are going to have a grand melee and nothing accomplished. There is no propulsive and corrective force in that. The only force that you can imagine that accomplishes anything is unselfish force. The moment you commence to think in terms of the interest of New Jersey, not only will New Jersey be served, but your own interests and the interests of New Jersey will be extended, your lives broadened and made worth while.

Why do men come together in a manner like this? Are you all in the same occupation, are you all seeking the same purpose, are you all selfishly interested in the same enterprise? Is this body of men come together to promote the interests of a particular occupation or calling? If not, why do you come together? Why don't you hold separate meetings? Why don't you congregate in halls of particular clubs, unions and societies? Why have you all come together here? Because you are fellow citizens; because you are united in a single community and in a single common-

wealth; because there are scores of things that you are interested
to see done, that cannot put a cent in your pockets, but that can
improve your health, extend your enterprise and quicken the
energy of the whole community.

Now, the most cunning members of every community are the
thieves in the community. Now, since the thieves are always
naturally cunning and ingenious, why don't they overcome us?
Because you know the old adage, that "thieves will always fall
out." The only men who can hang together are men of honest
purpose, and the only purposes that can keep us together for
action are disinterested purposes. That is the reason that the
organization that fears scrutiny meets behind closed doors.

The reason, therefore, is that the spirit of hope, of unselfish
purpose, is abroad. Men are tired of being governed by interests
that are not interests of the people, and are coming to look about
like free men, like free citizens, and to ask themselves what the
commonwealth desires, what the nation needs; for America has
undertaken to hold the lamp of progress up to the nations, not
only to guide her own feet with a little lamp of her own kindling,
but to guide the feet of all men who seek that which is just. When
we think of the long struggle, we may be disheartened, but let no
man who knows the destiny of the human race lose heart now.

We have begun a fight that it may be will take many a generation to complete—the fight against special privilege, but you know
that men are not put into this world to go the path of ease; they
are put into this world to go the path of pain and struggle. No
man would wish to sit idly by to whistle a tune and lose the opportunity to take part in such a struggle. All through the centuries
there has been this slow, painful struggle forward, forward, up,
up, a little at a time, along the long incline, the interminable way,
which leads to the perfection of force, to the real seat of justice
and of honor. There are men who have fallen by the way, blood
without stint has been shed, men have sacrificed everything in
this sometimes blind, but always instinctive and constant struggle; and America has undertaken to lead the way. America has
undertaken to be the haven of hope, the opportunity of all men.

Don't look forward too much. Don't look at the road ahead of
you in dismay. Look at the road behind you. Don't you see how far
up the hill we have come? Don't you see what those low and damp
myasmatic levels were from which we have slowly led the way?
Don't you see the rows of men come, not upon the lower level,
but upon the upper like the rays of the rising sun?

Don't you see the light starting, and don't you see the light
illumining all nations? Don't you know that you are coming more

and more into the beauty of its radiance? Don't you know that the past is forever behind us, that we have passed many kinds of evils that are no longer possible, that we have achieved great ends and have almost seen the fruition of free America. Don't forget the road you have trod, but remembering it and looking back for reassurance, look forward with confidence and charity to your fellow men, one at a time as you pass them along the road, and see those who are willing to lead you, and say: "We do not believe you know the whole road. We know that you are no prophet; we know that you are no seer, but that you can see the end of the road from the beginning, and we believe that you know the direction and are leading us in that direction, though it costs you your life, provided it does not cost you your honor."

And then follow your guide, trusting your guides, imperfect as they are, and some day when we are all dead, men will come and point at the distant upland with a great show of joy and triumph and thank God that there were men who undertook to lead in that struggle.

What difference does it make if we ourselves do not reach the uplands? We have given our lives to the enterprise, and that is richer and the moral is greater.

FPS T transcript (WP, DLC) with corrections and additions from a CS T transcript in NjHi and from the partial text in the *Philadelphia Record*, Nov. 6, 1910.

From Walter Hines Page

Dear Mr. Wilson: New York, Nov. 5. '10.

I wish you to bear witness to my self-restraint and self-denial. When I might have been insisting on your writing magazine articles, as soon as it became evident that you wd. be nominated, I said: "No, don't add even to his correspondence now—that's unfair. For relief and forbearance now, he will gladly write articles later—after he has got the governor's chair warm."

And so I didn't even send my congratulations. Instead, I went back over into N. J. where I used to live & made speeches for you —a superfluous bit of activity, but a joyful bit for all that.

And now my thanks—we all owe you hearty thanks—for a campaign done with meaning & sincerity & eloquence—the good old times of politics come again. If the truth were told, I suspect that the old times had no match for it. It is refreshing, lifting—even bully!   Very heartily   Walter H. Page

ALS (WP, DLC).

From Edgeworth Bird Baxter[1]

[Princeton, N. J.]

My dear Doctor Wilson,   November 5th., 1910.

I hope I am not guilty of an impropriety in expressing the very earnest hope that you will find it possible to comply with the wish of the Trustees, and retain your Chair of Jurisprudence in the University. Coming into contact with some fifty of your students, as I do, I am in a position to see how effective is your instruction; how deeply you have interested the class at large; how much you succeed in arousing them to serious thought. I know how few are the men who can do that in such a subject. And viewing Jurisprudence as I do—as one of the essentials of liberal culture—I cannot resist expressing the hope that you will not be forced to add to the larger loss we sustain in surrendering you as President the vacation of your invaluable lectureship.

Very sincerely yours,   E. B. Baxter.

TLS (WP, DLC).

[1] Princeton 1890, formerly a lawyer in Augusta, Ga., and at this time Instructor in Philosophy and Instructor in History, Politics, and Economics at Princeton.

From Ralph Waldo Emerson Donges[1]

My dear Dr. Wilson: Camden, N. J. November 5, 1910.

From the present indications, I fear the situation in Camden County will not be properly taken care of, by reason of a lack of funds to pay challengers and workers about the polls. The work already done is splendid, and it will be a great misfortune if it is not followed up by the necessary efforts on election day to make it effective. Failure to do this will set us back ten years in our efforts to arouse the interest and confidence of Democrats here. I dislike very much to bring this matter to your attention, and do so only because I believe the situation demands it. Will you use your efforts to have sent here sufficient to cover the expense incurred by us, in good faith, for legitimate purposes?   Sincerely yours,   Ralph W. E. Donges

TLS (WP, DLC).

[1] Lawyer of Camden and vice chairman of the Democratic State Auxiliary Committee.

To An Unknown Person[1]

[Princeton, N. J., c. Nov. 6, 1910]

Earnest appeal comes from one of the best men in Camden for funds for challengers and workers. Fears failure will set effort

to arouse interest and confidence of Democrats there [back] 10 years and make effective beginning end only in disappointment.
Woodrow Wilson.

Transcript of WWsh telegram written on R. W. E. Donges to WW, Nov. 5, 1910.
¹ Probably James R. Nugent.

From Melancthon Williams Jacobus

Hartford [Conn.]

My dear Dr. Wilson: Sunday afternoon [Nov. 6, 1910].

On the eve of Election day, which is to bring to you the deserved triumph of your notable campaign I simply wish to send you my greetings and best wishes

You have brought politics in New Jersey to its feet and have shown how clear and vital the student of political history can make to the people the problems of the day and hour. If the moral upheaval of these last two years is to result in a real conservation of our National institutions, it must be along the lines you have laid down.

You have made yourself independent of everything save the people; make them independent of everything save yourself and your administration will lead you inevitably to the highest honor they can bestow upon a living man.

Yours faithfully   M W Jacobus

ALS (WP, DLC).

From Charles Andrew Talcott

My dear old boy: Utica, N. Y. Nov. 6, 1910.

I am glad New Jersey is to be all right. I have taken great interest as well as a great deal of pride in your campaign and your success seems to me certain. I can't tell you how much I hope for it. Up here I am running against a gentlemen who had 5500 to the good two years ago. That majority will be considerably reduced this year and some of my friends say they think it will be entirely wiped out. I will let you know the result as soon as I learn. It was very kind to write me right in the midst of your campaign. Your note gave me great encouragement.

With best hopes and best wishes,
Yours as ever,   Charles A Talcott

TLS (WP, DLC).

To James Calvin Hemphill

Princeton, N. J.

My dear Major Hemphill: November 7th, 1910.

Thank you sincerely for the editorial you sent me in your kind note of November 3rd. It is too generous, but it gives me the deepest pleasure and puts ginger into me, you may be sure.

In haste,

Cordially and faithfully yours,   Woodrow Wilson

TLS (J. C. Hemphill Papers, NcD).

To Walter Hines Page

My dear Mr. Page: Princeton, N. J. November 7th, 1910.

Your card of the 5th has given me the deepest pleasure, as I need hardly tell you. It cheers me mightily after the struggle of the campaign to be so praised for merely doing my duty. The praise is stronger than I deserve, but I accept it gratefully as a token of generous friendship.

Cordially and faithfully yours,   Woodrow Wilson

TLS (W. H. Page Papers, MH).

From William Goodell Frost

My Dear Dr. Wilson: New York Nov. 7th, 1910.

Hail to you in your new career!

As a candidate you have benefited the whole country, and as governor you will benefit it still more—not all you desire, but enough to reward your heart and to point the onward march.

Now governors, and candidates, are subject to many applications. I take my early place in the line of your suitors.

Since we met at the Harvard inaugural[1] I have suffered many months of banishment due to physical breakdown, but am back with a chance to put some more finished touches on Berea's work for the Southern mountains.

We need more friends—the cause (more clear and eloquent now than when we spoke in Brick Church)[2] is still generally unknown.

We are to have meetings, under distinguished auspices, in January in Philadelphia, New York and Boston, and we earnestly desire you for a speaker at all three appointments.

Our "case" in this application to you is *our need*. Berea needs friends, and unless she gets more "right soon" my best years will be frittered away in things not spiritual, and her highest aims will fail.

Beside this it is certainly to be said that the urging of such a cause is not aside from but a part of the great public service to which you are called. You will serve more than Berea; more than the mountains, by doing this good deed.[3]

With admiration and faithful regard,

Sincerely yours,   Wm. Goodell Frost.

ALS (WP, DLC).
  [1] At the inaugural of Abbott Lawrence Lowell, October 6-7, 1909.
  [2] The text of Wilson's address on this occasion is printed at Jan. 29, 1899, a news report of it at Jan. 30, 1899, both in Vol. 11.
  [3] See WW to W. G. Frost, Nov. 15, 1910, n. 2, Vol. 22.

From Charles Allen Culberson[1]

My dear Sir,   Washington, D. C. Nov. 7th, 1910.

Let me congratulate you on the splendid campaign you have made. We hope for your election tomorrow, but whatever may be the result your name is writ high on the roll.

Very truly yours   C. A. Culberson

ALS (WP, DLC).
  [1] United States senator from Texas.

From Joseph Albert Dear, Jr.

My dear Doctor   Jersey City, N. J. Nov 7/10

It will be all over tomorrow, but whatever the result may be, though I cannot see how you can be defeated, I want to thank you as a Jerseyman for the campaign you have conducted. It has been a good thing for the state to have had you as a nominee. I do not recollect a campaign where the issues have ever been made to stand or fall so much upon the personality of the candidates themselves and upon their ability to convince the voters of their own ability to carry out their promises. I think it fine that in this way the campaign should have been such a personal one. Such campaigns tend to insure good nominees.

I did not get an opportunity to read your reply to Mr. Record until Sunday a week ago when I was on my way home from a trip out west. Believe me, I think it was some of the best Sunday reading I ever enjoyed—and I have taught and do yet in a Sunday school.

I want to offer you my thanks and my sincere congratulations

Yours with best wishes   Joseph A. Dear

ALS (WP, DLC).

From Marion Woodville Woodrow[1]

My dear Cousin: Columbia, S. C. Nov. 7, 1910.

Allow me to congratulate you on the brilliant campaign you have just brought to an end. No matter what may be the result at the polls to-morrow, nothing can dim the glory of the past few weeks or destroy the good you have done.

Mother[2] and I have followed your campaign with the greatest interest, as my Father would have done, if he had been spared to us so long. He would have been very proud of you, of your bold, sturdy, unflinching advocacy of truth and righteousness. To me it has been almost like hearing him speak again, you have said publicly so many of the things he used to say to me.

I sincerely hope the people of New Jersey and later the people of the United States will give us the opportunity to enjoy seeing a real statesman as the chief executive first of a State and then of all the States.

With love and best wishes from Mother and me both,
        Your affectionate cousin,   Marion W. Woodrow.

ALS (WP, DLC).
[1] Wilson's first cousin and daughter of James Woodrow.
[2] Felexiana Shepherd Baker Woodrow.

From William W. St. John[1]

Dear Sir: Trenton, N. J. November 7, 1910.

I am so confident that tomorrow's voting will result in the election of yourself as Governor and enough Democratic candidates for the Legislature to make the law-making body Democratic on joint ballot, that I am anticipating events in this letter.

If the Democrats win enough members to control the Legislature in a joint session, that result will bring the question of the United States Senatorship to the front as the most immediate problem to be settled in New Jersey political affairs. But should the Senatorship be a problem? Has it not, in fact, been settled by the people themselves, by exactly the same method and with the same proportion of representative voting as was, say, your nomination as a candidate for Governor? Is it not the truth that at least as many Democrats who voted for delegates to the State convention who proposed making you the gubernatorial nominee of their party, at the same time, through the direct primary, voted in favor of making James E. Martine the candidate of the Democratic party for the United States Senator?[2]

Does not party honor and party loyalty require acquiescence in the selection of Mr. Martine equal with the acquiescence that came from Democratic affiliations with respect to your own candidacy arising from similar political initiative and power?

Now, if these questions are to be answered in the affirmative, and an affirmative answer is the only one that will accord with both political logic and truth, there is no point of view to take other than to recognize the claim that Mr. Martine should be elected United States Senator.

I need hardly call your attention to the fact that there are many in the State who believe that Mr. Martine will not be elected Senator. On the other hand there are thousands who are ready and determined to make the hardest kind of a fight to compel the Legislature to abide by the results of the direct primaries on the Senatorship. As perhaps you may already know, such influential newspapers as the Newark Evening News, the Jersey City Journal, the Hoboken Observer and the Trenton Times, not to say anything of many other smaller papers, are committed to the principle of accepting the result of the direct primary voting on the Senatorship.

In my judgment the most effective force in behalf of vitalizing this great principle of permitting the people to say who shall serve them in the United States Senate, even in the admittedly inadequate form in use in New Jersey, is the *public opinion*.

This leads me up to the suggestion that I wish to make to you. In the event of your election as Governor you will undoubtedly be called upon to make some public statement. Whatever you say will be read with intense interest and will be potent in forming public sentiment. In view of this may I not urge upon you the advisability of expressing yourself, after election, in such a way as will leave no doubt as to where the incoming Governor will stand on the question of the Senatorship? I urge you to hold to the view that the Senatorial question has been disposed of by the people themselves and that the action of the Legislature in disposing of this subject in a constitutional manner is merely a perfunctory proceeding; and with this question out of the way there is nothing to prevent the next administration, in both executive and legislative departments, from getting down at once to the solution of the problems of statecraft with which we are confronted.

A few words from you along the lines that I suggest, declared immediately after election day, would be one of the most stimulating influences to public opinion that can be called into use.

I hope that you may in conscience be able to take the stand I have outlined. First, it is right; Secondly, a little thought would seem to me to convince you that it is also expedient.

If the power of public opinion does not prevail to shut off opposition to the election of Mr. Martine as Senator, it means, contrariwise, that political infidelity, chicanery and double dealing, not to say anything of baser influences, will permeate the Legislative body at the beginning of your administration. Such a condition means strife, bitterness and scandal the misfortune of which does not need to be forecasted by me to you.

The great mass of the Democratic voters take you at your word with respect to the declaration that if elected Governor you will be the leader of the party—of the people in fact. It is in this view that I appeal to you to make your leadership felt at the earliest possible moment on this very grave question of the disposition of the United States Senatorship.

As I have already stated, I am confident of your election as Governor. This result, I hope, may mean that I will come to know you personally since my newspaper work is confined exclusively to the State House and runs almost entirely along political lines.

Trusting that you may regard my suggestions favorably, I remain,　　　　　Sincerely yours,　W. W. St John

TLS (WP, DLC).
[1] One of the founders of and associated with the Elizabeth, N. J., *Evening Times*, 1901-1909; co-organizer of the Trenton News Bureau; at this time a political writer of Trenton.
[2] St. John had organized the campaign for Martine, and he and Martin Patrick Devlin had persuaded him, much against his will, to run in the Democratic senatorial primary. See James Kerney, *The Political Education of Woodrow Wilson* (New York and London, 1926), pp. 78-80.

From David Bryant

Wilmington N. C. Nov. 8 [1910]

I am praying for your election as Governor of New Jersey.
　　　　　　　　David Bryant
　　　　　　　　"Your Fathers Old Servant"

T telegram (WP, DLC).

From Charles Andrew Talcott

Utica N Y Nov 8 10

Warmest congratulations　　you have certainly a great victory.[1]
I have a small one here.　　　　　Charles A Talcott

T telegram (WP, DLC).

[1] The final election results were Wilson, 233,682; Lewis, 184,626; Killingbeck, 10,134; Charles A. Repp, Prohibition candidate, 2,818; and J. C. Butterworth, Socialist-Labor candidate, 2,032. Wilson's plurality was 49,056; he received 54 per cent of the vote, in contrast to Lewis's 43 per cent.

Wilson's victory was hailed as a "political revolution" by the Trenton *True American*, Nov. 10, 1910, and while this may have been an overstatement, his victory was of landslide proportions. His plurality was exceeded in recent history only by Edward C. Stokes in 1904. Stokes' plurality of 51,644 was due largely to the more than 80,000 majority for Theodore Roosevelt in that year.

Wilson's vote was an almost exact reversal of that for John F. Fort in 1907. Fort carried fourteen counties, Frank S. Katzenbach, Jr., seven. Wilson carried fifteen counties, and Lewis won only in the six traditionally Republican counties of Atlantic, Camden, Cape May, Cumberland, Passaic, and Salem. Even in these counties, Wilson nearly won Camden, Cape May, Cumberland, and Salem. His largest margins of victory came in Essex and in heavily Democratic Hudson County; ironically, his smallest was in his home county of Mercer, which he carried by 147 votes.

In most areas of the state, Wilson outpolled local candidates. The Democrats gained four additional congressional seats, elected four of the seven contested state senatorial positions, and swept the Assembly, with forty-two of the sixty seats. Also significant was the total vote cast for governor in the election. In this non-presidential year, 433,292 persons cast ballots, approximately a 10 per cent increase over the gubernatorial election of 1907.

From Roger Charles Sullivan

Chicago Ills Nov 8 10

Congratulations on your grand success.

Roger C Sullivan

T telegram (WP, DLC).

From Roland Sletor Morris

Phila Pa Nov 8 10

The democratic Club of Phila joins me in heartiest congratulations   we have not been so happy since ninety-two

Roland S Morris

T telegram (WP, DLC).

From Thomas Bell Love[1]

Dallas Tex Nov 8 1910

Permit me as an humble Texas democrat to congratulate you upon your splendid campaign and to express my sincere gratification at your election as Governor of New Jersey. I am for you for President of the U.S. in 1912   Thos B Love.

T telegram (WP, DLC).

[1] Former member and speaker of the Texas House of Representatives; Commissioner of Insurance and Banking, 1907-10; prominent Texas Democratic prohibitionist and progressive; at this time vice-president of the Southwestern Life Insurance Co. of Dallas.

From Raleigh Colston Minor[1]

Dear Mr Wilson,   [Charlottesville, Va.] Nov. 8, 1910

I do not yet know which way your election is going, but I am hoping most heartily that it is going your way. In any event, I want to congratulate you sincerely on the campaign you have made,—both the substance & the form of it. Always courteous and kindly even in your severest arraignments, always the gentleman, you have distinctly raised the standard of political fights not only in your own State of New Jersey but throughout the country. Yet, notwithstanding your mildness & moderation, you have never failed to show the courage of your convictions nor the intelligence and penetration that have evolved them. I hope that you will soon have the opportunity to serve your country in much wider fields.

With cordial regard, I am

                        Very sincerely   Raleigh C. Minor

ALS (WP, DLC).

[1] Professor of Law at the University of Virginia; son of Wilson's law teacher at the university, John Barbee Minor.

From George Brinton McClellan Harvey

Deal N. J. Nov 8 1910

So far so good   hearty congratulations upon results of your wonderful canvass.   George Harvey

T telegram (WP, DLC).

From George Sebastian Silzer

New Brunswick N. J. Nov. 8 [1910]

Accept my heartiest congratulations   the people of New Jersey are also to be congratulated for they are now assured of better Government. I know better than many how much it was needed. I hope we may again truthfully say president Wilson

                        Geo S Silzer

T telegram (WP, DLC).

From Josephus Daniels[1]

Raleigh N. C. Nov 8 1910

My wife[2] joins me in hearty and sincere congratulations   your victory will hearten all men everywhere who are tired of Government by favoritism   Josephus Daniels

T telegram (WP, DLC).
  [1] Editor and publisher of the Raleigh, N. C., *News and Observer*, prominent North Carolina Democratic politician. Secretary of the Navy, 1913-21.
  [2] Addie Worth Bagley Daniels.

From Franklin Knight Lane[1]

My dear Mr. Wilson: Washington November 8, 1910.

Permit me to extend my congratulations upon your election. Although the result has not yet been announced I am confident of your success. Your campaign has been watched here with a great deal of interest, and as a Democrat and one who ran as Democratic nominee for Governor of California in 1902, permit me to say that the members of our party are extremely proud of the character of the canvass that you have made, and I trust that it may be within my power sometime to help you to still higher honors.   Sincerely yours,   Franklin K. Lane

TLS (WP, DLC).
  [1] At this time a member of the Interstate Commerce Commission; Secretary of the Interior in the Wilson administration.

From Victor Louis Mason[1]

My dear Doctor Wilson: New York City, Nov. 8/10.

I voted against you and worked fairly to defeat you, because I believe in Viv. Lewis who is a personal friend, and while I am bitterly disappointed over his defeat I am delighted that you have won.

Please accept my sincere and warm congratulations over your great and clean victory.   Faithfully yours,   V L Mason

ALS (WP, DLC).
  [1] Vice-president of the Development Co. of America, assistant secretary of the Republican National Committee, and president of the Passaic Board of Trade.

From Edward Herrick Griffin[1]

                                        Baltimore, Maryland
My dear Dr. Wilson: November 8, 1910.

May I send you a word of hearty congratulation—not merely because of your success but because of the means through which you achieved it?

You have set a new standard of campaign speaking in this country. Never before have I read campaign speeches so reasonable and just and sincere as yours, so free from personalities and cant and claptrap. I hope the lesson will not be lost.

I was very sorry that you resigned at Princeton, and was inclined to think that you were making a mistake. But your decision seems to be justified by the event.

With all good wishes, I am

Yours very sincerely,   Edward H. Griffin

ALS (WP, DLC).
[1] An old friend from Wilson's Johns Hopkins days, Professor of the History of Philosophy and Dean of the College Faculty at the Hopkins.

From Lindley Miller Garrison[1]

My dear Dr. Wilson: Jersey City, N. J. November 8, 1910.

Your election is a demonstration of the inherent sanity and wisdom of the people, and for this they are to be congratulated.

Your opportunity is a great one, and you have the capacity and courage to measure up to it; and for that, both you and the people are to be congratulated.

I am sincerely glad.   Yours,   Lindley M. Garrison

TLS (WP, DLC).
[1] At this time Vice-Chancellor of the New Jersey Court of Chancery; Secretary of War in Wilson's first administration.

From Bessie Louise Dickson[1]

My dear Dr. Wilson,   Princeton [N. J.] Election Day. 1910.

Please accept these few blossoms with my heartiest congratulations, and the wish that God may bless and prosper you in all your undertakings. I cant express to you how keenly I feel the loss to Princeton, and my own personal loss. Your help, sympathy, and encouragement have indeed been appreciated. You have always been an inspiration to me in my work here, and your spirituality ever helpful.

I never shall forget the real friendship shown me at a crisis in my life. I thank you for all. My prayers will follow you always, Believe me

Very sincerely yours   Bessie Louise Dickson.

ALS (WP, DLC).
[1] The nurse and superintendent of the Isabella McCosh Infirmary at Princeton University.

From William C. Liller

My dear Governor: Indianapolis, Ind. November 8, 1910

Governor [Thomas R.] Marshall, Senator-elect John W. Kern and Indiand [Indiana] Democrats join with me in extending you

their heartiest congratulations over your magnificent victory and
extend best wishes for a successful administration.

Personally, it is a matter of the greatest pleasure and gratification.

With kindest regards and best wishes,
                           Sincerely your friend,   Wm. C. Liller

TLS (WP, DLC).

From Caesar Augustus Rodney Janvier

My dear Wilson: Phila., Nov. 8th, 1910

Please accept my very sincere and cordial congratulations, not
only on the victory you have one, but on the sort of campaign
you have made. Not that either thing was at all a surprise to
those who know you, but that *any*one is to be congratulated on
such work as you have done.

I believe you would value my congratulations more highly if
you could *possibly* know how much of regret your leaving Princeton has brought me! I am as near to despair about it as it is right
for a Christian to be—possibly nearer! But I do earnestly hope—&
pray—that it may all turn out for good not only for you and for the
country, but even for Princeton—tho' I do *not* see how this last
can be!

Please extend my warm congratulations to Mrs. Wilson and
to your daughters.
                           Cordially your friend,   Rodney Janvier.

ALS (WP, DLC).

From Franklin Potts Glass

                                   Birmingham Ala Nov 8 10

Hurrah for Princeton and Tommie Wilson. Prepare for 1912
and look out for Alabama.   F P Glass

T telegram (WP, DLC).

From James Alfred Hoyt, Jr.[1]

Dear Dr. Wilson: Columbia [S. C.] 12 p m Nov. 8, 1910.

We are exceedingly rejoiced over your splendid victory but
even more over your campaign, which has impressed the entire
country. You can have no conception of the deep interest taken in

it all down here by the people generally, to say nothing of those who know you or your family.

It is safe to say you can count on South Carolina in 1912 if you will consent to stand for the presidency, and you must consent. May your administration as governor fulfill the rich promise of your campaign and candidacy.

If we can only hold for two years what we have now won!

With best of wishes,   Sincerely,   Jas. A. Hoyt

Don't bother to acknowledge this.

ALS (WP, DLC).
  ¹ Clerk of the House of Representatives of South Carolina, editor of the *Columbia Record*, and a cousin of Mrs. Wilson.

From Joseph Patrick Tumulty

Jersey City N J Nov 8-9 10

In this hour of democratic triumph hudson county by twenty four thousand majority voices its approval of the principles you so courageously espoused during the campaign   The opportunity carries with it the gravest obligations and I sincerely trust that the fulfillment will redeem [redound] to the prosperity of the state and to the credit of your administration

Joseph P Tunulty

T telegram (WP, DLC).

A Victory Statement

[Nov. 9, 1910]

GOVERNOR WILSON AT PEOPLE'S SERVICE

In Concise Statement New Democratic Head of New Jersey Makes Known His Position—Happy in Capacity of Servant

PRINCETON, Nov. 9.—Dr. Woodrow Wilson, Democratic Governor-elect, today issued the following statement:

"I feel very deeply the great honor that the people of New Jersey have conferred upon me. I feel quite as deeply the responsibility it imposes upon me and upon my colleagues on the Democratic ticket. I shall, of course, put every power I possess into the service of the people as Governor of the State. It will be my pleasure and privilege to serve them, not as the head of a party, but as the servant of all classes and of all interests, in an effort to promote the common welfare.

"I regard the result of the election as a splendid vindication of the conviction of the Democrats of this state that the people desired to turn away from personal attacks and party maneuvers and base their political choices upon great questions of public policy and just administration."

Printed in the *Trenton Evening Times*, Nov. 9, 1910.

To James Smith, Jr.

My dear Senator Smith,   Princeton, N. J. November 9, 1910
    Your generous telegram[1] has given me a great deal of pleasure. I feel very deeply the confidence you have displayed in me, and the deep responsibility to the people which our success has brought with it. I hope with all my heart that I may be able to play my part in such a way as to bring no disappointment to those who have trusted me.
    With much regard and deep appreciation,
                        Sincerely yours,   Woodrow Wilson

TCL (received from Henry W. Bragdon).
    [1] It is missing.

To Simeon Eben Baldwin

                        Princeton, N J. Nov. 9, 1910.
    Aloow [Allow] me to extend to you my heartiest congratulations   I rejoice in your success.   Woodrow Wilson.

T telegram (Baldwin Family Papers, CtY).

To Charles Andrew Talcott

My dear Charlie,   Princeton, N. J. 9 November, 1910.
    Hurah! and Hurah!. The first thing I looked for in the morning paper was the result in your district, and the news made me glad down to the bottom of my heart. God bless you and make this the first chapter in a new career of distinction and honour, such as you have always been fitted for, and trained for.
    Thank you for your telegram. It was generous and bro[u]ght me cheer. It is a big and rather thankless job that lies ahead of me.
    In haste,   Affectionately Yours,   Woodrow Wilson

WWTLS (WC, NjP).

From Vivian Murchison Lewis

Paterson N. J. Nov. 9 [1910]

Accept my heartiest congratulations may your administration be almost [a most] successful and happy one.

Vivian M. Lewis.

T telegram (WP, DLC).

From Robert Bridges

Dear Tommy: New York. Nov 9, 1910

It is a great victory, better than my biggest hopes for you. Certainly it abundantly justifies your decision, and nobody can be more pleased than I am. Nobody ever made a cleaner campaign than you did, or made more reasonable people do reasonable thinking. I wanted to say it—but you know how I feel.

Charley has telegraphed me that he wins by 1500—and that too in face of the fact that Stimson[1] seems to have carried the same district by 800. I have just written him that your election, and his, is the only consolation that I, as a Roosevelt Republican, have in the results.

May all good fortune attend you. You have a great chance which you have abundantly earned by your own efforts. Its your personal victory.   Faithfully Yours   Robert Bridges

ALS (WP, DLC).
[1] Henry Lewis Stimson, unsuccessful Republican candidate for Governor of New York.

From Cleveland Hoadley Dodge

Dear Governor   New York. Nov 9th 1910

HOORAY

Isn't it perfectly bully. I never was happier than last night when each succeeding "bullyton" made your majority larger than the one before.

You *know* what I feel & what I think of you so I won't say any more except to tell you how glad I am you are going off for a good change[1]—I hope it will be a complete rest. How you have stood the tremendous strain I cannot understand. I am so proud of knowing you as all men (& women) are singing your praises.

Don't think of house or professorship till you get back—though Dodge Lodge can be made ready at short notice

When you do get back, before you get started on any political work it is important that I should see you regarding one or two matters which came up during your campaign which it would be well for you to know about, before you take any active steps. It is nothing at all disagreeable—rather the contrary & it will keep.

Please give our warmest regards to Mrs. Wilson—what a proud & happy woman she must be.

God bless you old man   Yrs affly   C H Dodge

Now for 1912

Had I better write Mr Reid[2] to engage Dorchester House for me 1913-1917

ALS (WP, DLC).
  [1] Wilson had planned a post-election vacation in Bermuda; however, as will be seen, the impending struggle over the senatorship caused him to cancel the trip.
  [2] Whitelaw Reid, United States Ambassador to Great Britain.

From John Thompson Kerr[1]

Dear Wilson   Elizabeth, N. J. Nov. 9, 1910.

My sorrow over the loss to Princeton by your resignation of the presidency is swallowed up in my joy over the gain to the State & nation by your election as Governor yesterday. I will not take your time to tell you in detail how much I have admired the high level of thought & conduct maintained by you during the campaign, but I must detain you long enough to express my delight in it. It was a pleasure for a born Democrat to enter again upon the exercise of his natural right of voting for a Democrat that is a Democrat of the highest order. You have a difficult way before you. I trust you. May God bless you & all good men keep you. I remain, with great esteem,

                    Sincerely yours   Jno. T. Kerr.

ALS (WP, DLC).
  [1] Wilson's classmate at Princeton, pastor of the Third Presbyterian Church of Elizabeth, N. J.

From Alfred Lewis Dennis[1]

My dear Wilson   Newark, N. J. 9th Nov. 1910.

I hope you will accept my sincere congratulations upon your stirring victory. Your brilliant campaign demonstrates the inherent power of sound ideas clearly and candidly stated and enthusiastically believed in, combined with that irresistably compelling attraction of personal character of the highest type. The people are now back of you and will follow you as their leader, but only so long as they believe in you. Be logical and do right and they will never desert you.

Public men seldom perceive what a power over the people is given to a man by simple righteousness and intellect. I will not bore you with other observations now, but I shall watch your career with warm interest and wish you the greatest measure of success   Sincerely yours   Alfred L. Dennis.

ALS (WP, DLC).
[1] Wilson's classmate at Princeton; head of the Newark office of Post and Flagg, stockbrokers.

From Henry Burling Thompson

Greenville P. O. Delaware
Dear Wilson: November Ninth, 1910.

It is with unalloyed and sincere delight that Mrs. Thompson[1] and I congratulate you on your election. You have made a magnificent campaign and are justly rewarded. You have put the whole political situation and political discussion on a higher plane than they have been since slavery days.

I have followed you from day to day throughout the entire campaign with unqualified approval and pleasure, and I cannot tell you how much delight it gives me to say all of the above; and you know that I can only wish and pray for your success in the new field in which you have so ably started.

Very sincerely yours,   Henry B Thompson

P.S. Now let us beat *Yale*

TLS (WP, DLC).
[1] Mary Wilson Thompson.

From David Benton Jones

My dear Mr. Wilson: Chicago November 9th, 1910.

You see I have changed from "Doctor" as I saw in the paper that you objected to that title. I have just sent you a telegram of congratulation.[1] Here in the west you have made a very marked impression by your method of campaigning. It is evidently as effective as it is unusual. I had no doubt you would make it so.

I saw by the papers that you were expected here on the 18th of this month. If so, I shall be delighted to have you stay with us, as we move into the city early next week. As you may find time, if you will let me know what road and train you expect to arrive on, I shall meet you at the station.

Please give my warmest greetings to Mrs. Wilson.

Very sincerely yours,   David B. Jones.

TLS (WP, DLC).

[1] D. B. Jones to WW, Nov. 9, 1910, T telegram (WP, DLC).

From Edward Wright Sheldon

New York Nov 9 10

Please accept my warmest greetings   New Jersey has distinguished itself.   Edward W Sheldon

T telegram (WP, DLC).

From Melancthon Williams Jacobus

Hartford Conn Nov 9 1910

Hearty congratulations on your great victory and they [the] best of wishes for the two years that are to come at Trenton and the longer years that are sure to follow at Washington.

M W Jacobus.

T telegram (WP, DLC).

From Cyrus Hall McCormick

Dear Woodrow: Chicago 9 November 1910.

I see by today's press notices that you are expected to be in Chicago on 18 November to speak for the "Business Service Lecture League." If I am at home, I should of course like to have you with us, tho my house on Huron Street is undergoing repairs and I am living at Lake Forest. If you are to be here only one night, perhaps you would prefer to go to the University Club, in which case I would be glad to put you up there.

I am going East today, so I will leave this letter to be signed for me, and will ask you, in writing, to put on the outside of your envelope "For F. A. S.," so that Mr. [Frederick A.] Steuert, my secretary, may receive the letter and attend to the matter in my absence.

I telegraphed you this morning[1] how elated we all are at your sweeping victory. I take it that this is a very handsome personal compliment to you, and in the line of some of the unfortunate occurrences of the last few weeks, I am very much pleased at the outcome, deeply as I regret the almost irreparable loss to Princeton in your leaving.

With kind regards to Mrs. Wilson, I am,

Very sincerely yours,   Cyrus H. McCormick.   S.

TLS (WP, DLC).
1 C. H. McCormick to WW, Nov. 9, 1910, Hw telegram (WP, DLC).

From Joseph Pulitzer

Menton [France, c. Nov. 9, 1910]

I congratulate you your state and our republic upon your splendid victory and I must thank you warmly for the intel[l]ectual delight your great speeches have given me. Speeches truly democratic not because they serve the democratic party but because they strengthen democrats institutions against libels and lawlessness.   Joseph Pulitzer.

T telegram (WP, DLC).

From Edwin Anderson Alderman

Personal.

My dear Dr. Wilson: Charlottesville [Va.] November 9, 1910.

No man in America, I dare say, has watched with more interest and sympathy the progress of your campaign than the President of the University of Virginia, from motives of personal interest, of professional pride, and of institutional pride. I have been engrossed in thought of you and your success in the great struggle in which you are engaged, and have been much about the country during its progress.

You have set a standard of campaigning that has acted like a tonic upon the dull minds of many of our political leaders. The keen analysis, the good humor, the self-respect, the frankness, the dignity, the abstinence from personalities, and the plain, practical common sense of your appeals have lifted you, more than mere success at the polls, to a place among the small but inspiring list of national leaders of our re-organized party of opposition. Of course the University of Virginia is for you heart and soul—everybody in it and everybody around it. That is, of course, local and sentimental.

I believe you have a great opportunity for national leadership in a new era of American politics. I believe you are the one man upon whom our reorganized democracy can rely for successful leadership in meeting the essential problems that face Republican government at this time. What I fear, and I speak confidentially, is that the people in Congress will tangle up and mar the situation, so far as democracy is concerned, before the presidential election of 1912 comes squarely before the people.

A tremendous responsibility belongs to you, to Harmon, to Baldwin, and the new group of leaders. Your administration in New Jersey will be wise and will demonstrate your power as a political executive. The idea I have in mind is that you and the new leaders should get together, invite into your council some wise men and take the situation in hand. You ought to control the programme, in so far as you can do so, of democracy in the interval between now and the battle for the presidency in 1912.

I have put this clumsily; I heartily wish I could see you, for I have been in conference, recently, with some important people in New York, on politics, education and finance, and I think I know the South from Louisiana to Virginia pretty intimately.

Do not over work yourself and get knocked out physically. I am keen about that just now, for the doctors are about to send me away for a little rest on account of overstrain and overwork. Happily, I am organically sound and will quickly pull out of it.

My congratulations and assurances of pride and faith.

Fraternally yours,   Edwin A. Alderman, President.

TLS (WP, DLC).

From George Lawrence Record

My dear Doctor Wilson: Jersey City, N. J. Nov. 9, 1910.

I congratulate you upon your election and the great majority by which it was accomplished. I am satisfied that you will appreciate both the opportunity for service, and the responsibility which the opportunity entails. You have an immense task before you, and if I can be of any service at any time, I hope you will feel free to call upon me.

Respectfully yours,   George L Record

TLS (WP, DLC).

From Henry Smith Pritchett

Personal.

My dear Wilson,   New York Nov. 9, 1910

It is a fine victory and it comes as a result of a campaign which does you great credit. Accept my congratulations and good wishes. No other friend will take more pleasure than I in your performance and in your triumph.

Your real test comes now. If you succeed in conducting your office courageously, and above all, wisely, in this next year and a half a notable opportunity to serve the nation is open to you.

Let me make one friendly suggestion. You are enough of an orator to be carried along by the sweep of your own speech. It is a fine quality and the source of great power. It has however the danger that it betrays its possessor into saying things on his feet which go further than his cool judgment would permit. If you can keep a sharp eye on this it will save you some difficult situations.

Please do not trouble to answer this. I know you are overwhelmed with letters and telegrams. Just consider that I am at your service at any time for anything a friend can do.

Always Cordially Yours,   Henry S. Pritchett

ALS (WP, DLC).

From Sylvester Woodbridge Beach[1]

My Dear Wilson: Princeton, N. J. 11.9.10

I sat up last night until I was assured of your triumph, and then went to bed to sleep in peace. Accept my heartiest congratulations in which I am sure tens of thousands all over our land join.

As ever   Faithfully Yours   Sylvester W. Beach

ALS (WP, DLC).
[1] Wilson's minister, pastor of The First Presbyterian Church, Princeton.

A Telegram and a Letter from Richard Heath Dabney

University of Va Va Nov 9 [1910]

Hip Hip Hurrah   your Va friends are shouting with joy
                        R. H. Dabney

Hw telegram (WP, DLC).

My dear Woodrow: Charlottesville 9 Nov., 1910.

Although I sent you a hurrah-telegram this morning to tell you that your Virginia friends were shouting for joy at your great victory, I cannot refrain from also scratching you a line tonight just to let off a little of my pent-up steam. You can just "betcherlife" that Ole Virginny is stepping high and "swellin' wisibly" with pride at the splendid campaign and glorious triumph of her son; and you may be equally sure that there is no Virginian whose joy is more keen and intense than mine. For I cannot but feel that this election, followed by the gubernatorial record that you will be sure to make, is a stepping stone to the White House. I know, of course, that Harmon, Dix, Foss,[1] Baldwin or some other among the victors may be regarded as more "available" in 1912. As against the first three of the above-named, you are, of course, handicapped by the fact that the electoral vote of N. J. is smaller than that of either O., N. Y. or Mass. Yet Harmon will be handicapped by the hostility of Bryan, who though a dead cock in the pit, so far as his own aspirations are concerned, may conceivably have enough influence left to make the party afraid to nominate a man whom he strongly opposes. Foss may fail to get the nomination because many will think it impossible for the Dem. party to carry Mass. in a presidential campaign; while Dix will find it hard to make a record that will shine in comparison with that of Hughes. I have no doubt that Harmon, Foss & Dix are all strong men—all probably of presidential size —yet please hide your blushes when I frankly state that I think I know a fellow whose dimensions are still more ample, one who, I *know*, is of presidential size. And I believe that that *'Illimitable' Idiot*,—that *Very Ass*—will be just as "available" to attract the independent vote of New York, Connecticut & Massachusetts as of New Jersey. He is just the kind of fellow to catch that self-same vote; &, if he can get a fair chance to let the country see what sort of man he is, he will have a "mighty" good chance of capturing the Dem. nomination in 1912 and taking his seat in the chair of George Washington on March 4th, 1913. Shall I attend that inauguration? Well, just watch me & see!

Of course it is a glorious thing to have dealt a staggering blow to that blatant Fraud, Roosevelt. I was overjoyed when he beat the Old Guard in the Repub. Convention.[2] For, had he been beaten *then*, he & his worshippers would have shouted *now* that the Dem. victory was due to the fact that the Repubs had rejected the Only Honest Man, & would have demanded that he be accepted as the Moses to lead the party out of the Wilderness in 1912. But, as it is, T. R. was the whole shooting match in the campaign, & the defeat in N. Y. is *his* defeat,—a much greater defeat than his party would have experienced had he not made himself its dictator. My belief is that he will for some years be the same sort of incubus on the Rep. party that Bryan has been on the Dem. But the hey-day of his power is past. He is on the

toboggan & will reach the bottom at last. He will never be President again. But that *you shall* be President is the ardent hope of
Yours faithfully,   R. H. Dabney.

ALS (WP, DLC).
¹ Eugene Noble Foss, at this time a Democratic congressman from Massachusetts, had just been elected governor of that state.
² See n. 6 to the campaign address printed at Oct. 5, 1910.

From George Brinton McClellan

My dear Governor   New York, N. Y. Nov 9/10

Accept my very sincere & heartfelt congratulations upon your gallant victory. As there was no Roosevelt issue in New Jersey, your victory was personal, & to you yourself belong the credit & the honor. I wish you all success & happiness possible on the attainment of what God willing will be only the first step upward, of your political career.
I am   Yours ever   Geo B McClellan

Please don't bother to answer this. I shall do myself the pleasure of seeing you soon to shake your hand.

ALS (WP, DLC).

From Thomas Davies Jones

Chicago Ills Nov 9 10

Heartiest congratulations upon your splendid victory.
Thos D Jones

T telegram (WP, DLC).

From Charles Wellman Mitchell

Baltimore Md Nov 9 1910

Hiram [Woods] joins me in heartiest congratulations on your splendid victory   C. W. Mitchell.

T telegram (WP, DLC).

From Robert Randolph Henderson

Dear Woodrow,   Cumberland, Md. [c. Nov. 9, 1910]

Since "yours is the world and everything that's in it," another congratulation can not mean much to you, but it does to me

and its for *my* pleasure I am sending this. I can not contain myself for joy. Nothing so fine has happened in American politics
in my recollection. I hope to live to see you President. God bless
you and yours.   Affectionately   Robert R. Henderson

Don't think of answering this.

ALS (WP, DLC).

From Edgar Allan Poe[1]

My dear Dr. Wilson,   Balto. Md. Nov. 9th [1910]

Among the many democratic victories of yesterday none was
so gratifying to those of us in Maryland as your splendid one.

We followed your method of campaigning with admiration
and it is most reassuring to feel that an appeal to the intelligence
& honesty of the voters has met with a so ready & complete
response. It should be a lesson in the future for all candidates for
public office. Your many admirers are confident that it is only a
short time now before the opportunity to cast a vote for you will
not be dependent upon the question of a legal residence within the
State of New Jersey.   Sincerely yours   Edgar Allan Poe

ALS (WP, DLC).
[1] Princeton 1891, great-nephew of the author, at this time City Solicitor of
Baltimore; Attorney General of Maryland from 1911 to 1915.

From John Watson Foster

My dear Dr,   Washington, D. C. Nov. 9-10.

I send you my hearty congratulations. I rejoice that the Democratic party made a man of your character & caliber its standard
bearer, and I wish you great success in your office.

Mrs. Foster[1] joins me in congratulations to Mrs. Wilson also.
                    Very truly   John W. Foster.

ALS (WP, DLC).
[1] Mary Parke McFerson Foster.

From William Jennings Bryan

                    Lincoln Nebr Nov 9 10

Congratulations on your election. May your adminstration be
crowned with signal success. Permit me to join the officials of
the nebraska state teachers association in extending to you as

[a] cordial invitation to speak under the auspices of this association at Lincoln Friday evening November twenty fifth[1]

William Jennings Bryan

T telegram (WP, DLC).
[1] Wilson declined this invitation.

From John Wanamaker

Dear Mr. Wilson: New York, Nov. 9th, 1910.

Your State, and the country generally, is to be congratulated for the victory yesterday which resulted in your election as Governor.

When I read your first statement regarding your willingness to serve your State, it commanded my admiration, and when you were nominated at the Convention for Governor I said to a friend, "I am inclined to get a residence in Camden," "that I may have the privilege of voting for Woodrow Wilson for Governor." I read many of your wonderful speeches and now I write this by typewriter that it may be more easily read in these days when you may be overwhelmed with congratulations.

I beg you to believe in my personal friendship and my great satisfaction, Republican as I am, that you have set a new standard of citizenship by the work that you have done and by your willingness to undertake the greater work of the Governorship.

With assurances of high regard, I remain,

Yours very sincerely, Your Friend John Wanamaker

TLS (WP, DLC).

From Edwin Augustus Stevens

My dear Tommy, Hoboken, N. J. Nov. 9th, 10.

This is to congratulate you on your splendid victory. You have your work cut out for you & the best wishes of your friends for success.

Remember I am at your service if I can be of use, but am not looking for anything.

Very Truly Yours, E. A. Stevens

ALS (WP, DLC).

From Frederick Jackson Turner

Cambridge Mass Nov 9 [1910]

Hearty congratulations   you are bringing princeton into the nation's service   Frederick J. Turner

Hw telegram (WP, DLC).

From Theodore Whitefield Hunt

My dear old friend—Governor-Elect!   Princeton, N. J. 11 9 '10

You have my heartfelt congratulations & best wishes! I rejoice especially in that your excellent gifts & commanding merits have at last been vindicated.

To Mrs Wilson, also, I must send my congratulations, whose loving & courageous support during these months of academic dissension has cheered your heart in every kind of trial. In this day of your common rejoicing, I rejoice with you both.

Aff Yr   T. W. Hunt.

ALS (WP, DLC).

From William Burhans Isham

My dear Tommy,   [New York] Nov 9/10

You do not know how glad I am that you are *It*. My felicitations go with this. I am sorry you are not a Princeton resident. Much more that you are not the president but I am heartily glad you won out & rejoice with you & Mrs. Wilson[.] My love to you & God bless you dear Tommy.

faithfully   Wm. B Isham

ALS (WP, DLC).

From Thomas Nelson Page

Dear Mr. Wilson: [Washington] Nov 9th 1910

I wish to express to you my warm congratulations on your admirable canvass and its splendid issue. May your success be but the beginning of a career which shall redound to the good of the whole People.

Sincerely yours   Thos. Nelson Page

ALS (WP, DLC).

From Daniel Moreau Barringer

Dear Woodrow: Philadelphia, Pa. November 9, 1910.

Before I enter upon the day's work, or even open my mail, I want to write to you and tell you how sincerely glad I am to know that you have been elected Governor of New Jersey. You must be gratified to know that there is so much rejoicing this morning on this account among your old-time, I was about to say boyhood, friends, for after all we were not much more than boys when we were in College. May God give you strength and health to nobly play the great part which now seems your destiny.

Affectionately yours,   Daniel Moreau Barringer.

TLS (WP, DLC).

From William Hughes

Paterson N. J. Nov 9 [1910]

I congratulate the state, the Democrats and you. I never had a doubt at as to the result after hearing you speak at the convention   Will write you about the county later.

Wm Hughes.

T telegram (WP, DLC).

From Thomas Riley Marshall

Indianapolis Ind Nov 9 [1910]

I welcome you into the company of governors who think that principles are worth maintaining. Congratulations

Thos R. Marshall

Hw telegram (WP, DLC).

From Alexander Thomas Ormond

My Dear Wilson   [Princeton, N. J.] Nov 9th 1910

I wish to congratulate you on the splendid triumph of yesterday's election. Your canvass has been a campaign of education in the truest sense and the result of yesterday proves the people of New Jersey to be good learners. Though a Republican by tradition I think one of the finest results of yesterday's vote was the choice of a Democratic legislature thus giving you a body of lawmakers that will be, politically, amenable to your counsel. God speed you and give you strength and courage for the great work that is before you during the next three years.

Yours very sincerely   A T Ormond

ALS (WP, DLC).

From John Wesley Wescott

Dear Dr. Wilson: Camden, N. J., November 9, 1910.

Isn't it just glorious! Now for firm and progressive construction. Mistakes in form and letter are likely, but, to a brave mind like yours, errors in respect to principle, policy and truth are impossible. The whole country cries for a master mind. You will be called.

Personal affection, arising instantaneously from your contact with the people, was no less potential in securing your election than your mental and moral fitness for the great work ahead of you.

I noticed with concern how you wilted under the strain of the campaign. Rebound is often as serious as impact. Go somewhere for rest. Don't trouble to acknowledge this letter, but believe me

Affectionately yours,   John W. Wescott.

TLS (WP, DLC).

From Alexander Mitchell Palmer[1]

Stroudsburg Pa Nov 9 [1910]

Please accept my warmest congratulation on your magnificent victory   the state and the country are alike to be congratulated

A Mitchell Palmer

Hw telegram (WP, DLC).
[1] Lawyer and United States representative from the 26th congressional district of Pennsylvania. He served as Attorney General in the Wilson administration, 1919-21.

From Francis Fisher Kane

Dear Dr. Wilson: Philadelphia November 9, 1910.

No man can be happier than I this morning, and the principal source of my happiness is the news from New Jersey which reached us last night at the Democratic Club. I hope [Roland S.] Morris's telegram will reach you with the hundreds of others that must have been pouring in. Your victory at this time was essential to the Democratic Party and equally necessary to the counrty [country], but by your campaign alone you had already performed a great public service. Your Governorship will mean the redemption of New Jersey, and the Democratic success in the Presidential Campaign of 1912.

Last, but not least, what a vindication it is of your work at Princeton! The people have declared their approval of democracy in college life and college management. I think the Trustees will take the lesson to heart. Oh, but the news is good!

Yours sincerely,   Francis Fisher Kane.

TLS (WP, DLC).

A Telegram and a Letter from John Franklin Fort

Trenton N J Nov 9 10

Permit me to extend congratulations. The people have committed to you the affairs of a great state and I am sure you appreciate the responsibility of the trust and will loyally fulfull it   John Franklinf Fort

T telegram (WP, DLC).

[Trenton, N. J.]

My dear Doctor Wilson: November ninth 1910.

I wired you my congratulations this morning and I wish to follow the telegram with this note.

You made a splendid campaign—clean, intellectual and honorable, and the result showed the wisdom of it. The candidate who deals in personalities or attempts to evade the issues in these times is sure of defeat.

It will be my pleasure to give you any information that I can in relation to the Executive Office, or any of the departments of the State, and I will be very glad to do so at any time.

On the twenty-ninth of this month the Conference of Governors is to be held at Frankfort, Kentucky,—part of the session being at Louisville. The Conference includes not only Governors but Governors-elect. The last Legislature of this State provided in the appropriation bill for the expenses of the Governor and Governor-elect in attendance upon that Conference, which will last from the twenty-ninth of November until the second of December, practically taking the entire week to go and return.

It is my purpose to attend, as I have found these Conferences to be exceedingly useful and instructive, and I hope that you will not permit any engagement to interfere. Mrs. Fort will accompany me and I trust you will go and take Mrs. Wilson.

If you can go, please advise me, and the Adjutant-General will arrange for transportation and the like.

Another matter is the matter of residence in Trenton. I asked the Legislature some time ago to provide a residence for the next Governor. They offered to do so for me and appropriated funds for it, but I felt that having asked for it I could not accept and the appropriation was allowed to lapse. At the last session, the Legislature authorized the purchase of the Green properties adjoining the Capitol on the East, and either of these places would make a good residence for the Governor,[1] and I would like very much to go through them with you. There is sufficient appropriation made to furnish and the State House Commission was authorized to do so.

I want to make your advent into the office as congenial and as pleasant as possible and carry out any suggestions which you may have to make.

I shall be in Princeton on Saturday, lunching with Professor [Henry Dallas] Thompson, and I will try and see you.

With kind regards, I am,

Yours very sincerely, John Franklin Fort

TLS (WP, DLC).
[1] New Jersey never constructed a governor's mansion. Morven in Princeton was given to the state by former Governor and Mrs. Walter Evans Edge in 1950; in 1953 it became the official residence of the governor.

From Henry Jones Ford

Princeton, New Jersey
My dear Dr. Wilson: November 9, 1910

My hearty congratulations upon the result and its auguries for the future. I take peculiar satisfaction in the event as a stage in the fruition of ideas and principles whose development I have followed sympathetically for many years, with confidence that the time would come at last when they might be applied in practice. It seems to have arrived.

I have considered the matter about which you spoke to me and I do not know of any one I could recommend for a post that deserves to be made valuable in confidential agency.[1] It has occurred to me that I myself might be able to serve you in that capacity, and if so I should esteem it a pleasure and an honor.

Nota bene. This is an offer and not an application. It calls for no consideration whatever save as your interest and convenience may suggest in making your arrangements. In any event, I shall remain   Sincerely and cordially yours   Henry J. Ford

ALS (WF, DLC).
1 The office of secretary to the governor.

From William Frank McCombs

New York Nov 9 1910

The people of New Jersey should be congratulated on your magnificent victory. They [The] people of the United States will follow the fine precedent established by New Jersey and confer upon you the supreme executive honor in 1912

William F McCombs.

T telegram (WP, DLC).

From Robert Stephen Hudspeth

Jersey City, N. J. Nov 9 1910

Sincerely congratulate you upon your great fight and victory the people of New Jersey have come into their own through you

R. S. Hudspeth

T telegram (WP, DLC).

From Brand Whitlock[1]

Toledo O Nov 9 1910

I congratulate you sincerely on your election and wish you all success.   Brand Whitlock.

T telegram (WP, DLC).
1 Mayor of Toledo since 1905, muckracking novelist, and American Minister to Belgium during Wilson's administration.

From Robert Lansing[1]

Watertown N Y Nov 9 [1910]

Congratulations upon your personal victory and the triumph of Democratic principles   Robert Lansing

Hw telegram (WP, DLC).
1 Lawyer specializing in international law; most recently counsel for the North Atlantic Coast Fisheries Arbitration at The Hague; Counselor of the State Department, 1914-15; and Secretary of State, 1915-20.

From David Lawrence[1]

My dear Dr. Wilson: Washington, D. C., Nov. 9, 1910.

My sincerest congratulations to you on your election. All of the Washington correspondents with whom I have come in contact since joining the Washington staff of The Associated Press recently seemed to think your election assured from the start though none believed so large a plurality would result. The Democratic landslide[2] was generally predicted here. Gossip among the political writers mentions you frequently in respect to 1912.

Any time that I can be of personal service to you by reason of my residence in Washington, I shall hope to hear from you. Please don't bother acknowledging this.

Very sincerely yours,   David Lawrence

TLS (WP, DLC).

[1] Princeton 1910, correspondent of the Washington bureau of the Associated Press.

[2] The November elections produced a Democratic landslide throughout most of the country. For the first time since 1892, the House of Representatives went Democratic, with a net change of fifty-three seats, from 175 Democrats in the Sixty-first Congress to 228 in the Sixty-second Congress. The Democrats controlled the House by sixty-six votes when Congress convened in 1911 and elected Champ Clark of Missouri as Speaker. In the Senate, the Democrats gained nine seats, and although the Republicans retained party control, forty-nine to forty-two, a coalition of Democrats and insurgent Republicans took charge of legislative policies. Several previously Republican states—Massachusetts, Connecticut, New York, New Jersey, Ohio, Indiana, Colorado, and Oregon—elected or re-elected Democratic governors. The only exception to this nation-wide trend was the West Coast, but even there the progressive Republican, Hiram Warren Johnson, was elected Governor of California, and a Democrat, Oswald West, was elected Governor of Oregon. Even in states that remained Republican, such as Pennsylvania, the Democrats ran strongly. Contemporary observers and subsequent historians attributed this dramatic political shift to several factors—popular dissatisfaction with the Payne-Aldrich Tariff, divisions within the Republican party, growing progressive sentiment in the nation, and, above all, popular rejection of the Taft administration.

From Walker Whiting Vick

New York Non [Nov.] 9 [1910]

Have been waiting to complete Rutherford returns before telegraphing you have carried the borough of Rutherford. This is first time a democratic gubernatorial candidate has carried borough in twenty years. My family join heartily in sincerest congratulations and best wishes for your administration.

Walker Whiting Vick

T telegram (WP, DLC).

From John Bach McMaster[1]

My dear Dr Wilson,   Philadelphia Nov. 9th 1910

To follow your recent campaign has been a great pleasure. Democrat government is a success when men of your type will run for office and the people will elect them. May all your effort for good government bear abundant fruit, and may we of Pennsylvania have an opportunity to vote for you in 1912. Sincere congratulations.

          With great respect   John Bach McMaster

ALS (WP, DLC).
[1] Professor of American History, University of Pennsylvania.

From Harry Augustus Garfield

Dear Wilson: Williamstown, Mass. Nov. 9/10

You have my heartiest best wishes. I did not believe you would lose, & now that victory has actually perched on your standard I realize how much I desired that you should not. You will be too much overwhelmed with things political to read letters. I therefore add nothing of the impression which yesterday's battle makes upon me, beyond my rejoicing that you have won.

I wish we might see you here. Perhaps, as you said at Lyme, you may find the time.

Mrs. Garfield[1] joins me in all this & remembrances to Mrs. Wilson.   Affectionately Yours,   H. A. Garfield.

ALS (WP, DLC).
[1] Belle Hartford Mason Garfield.

From James Rudolph Garfield[1]

                              Cleveland [Ohio]
My dear Governor Wilson: November 9, 1910

I am glad that I can so address you. My heartiest congratulations upon your election. You will now have a great opportunity to see the practical application of what you so admirably stated in your address before the American Bar Association "Lawyers will construct for you a very definite policy, and construct it to admiration; they have not often shown themselves equally fitted to liberalize it or facilitate the processes of change." I hope you will find in your legislature "lawyers who are also statesmen" * * * "lawyers who can think in the terms of society itself, mediate between interests, accommodate right to right, establish equity, and bring the peace that will come with genuine and hearty co-operation, and will come in no other way."

With best regards to Mrs. Wilson and yourself,

Sincerely yours,   James R. Garfield

TLS (WP, DLC).
  ¹ Son of President James Abram Garfield, brother of Harry Augustus Garfield, head of the Bureau of Corporations and Secretary of the Interior in the administration of Theodore Roosevelt. At this time he was practicing law in Cleveland.

From Eugene Noble Foss

Boston Mass Nov 9 1910

Thanks for your telegram   I congratulate N. J. on your election   Eugene N. Foss.

T telegram (WP, DLC).

From George Mason La Monte

My dear Dr. Wilson: Bound Brook New Jersey Nov. 9. 1910

I am glad to add my word of rejoicing to the many pouring in upon you. For the first time in years Somerset has gone *Democratic*.

I hope the work of the winter will be such as to justify confidence in our programme.

Yours very truly   Geo. M. La Monte

ALS (WP, DLC).

From John Ralph Hardin

My dear Dr. Wilson   Newark. Nov. 9. 1910.

Kindly accept my congratulations on the splendid outcome of the campaign. While I rejoice in the triumph that has come to you, over and above all I find satisfaction in the ratification by the people of the State of the things you stood for and stand for. I am confidently expectant of great permanent advantage to the public interests by reason of your service in the office to which you have been called.

Yours very Sincerely   John R. Hardin

ALS (WP, DLC).

From Jacob Gould Schurman[1]

My dear Mr. Wilson: Ithaca, New York November 9, 1910.

Accept my cordial congratulations on your election as Governor of New Jersey.

I am profoundly sorry to have you leave the educational field in which you have already done such invaluable work and in which so much more of the same kind might reasonably have been expected of you in the future.

On the other hand, I rejoice that men of your type are going into practical politics, and devoting themselves to public service. And I especially congratulate you on the campaign you have conducted. It was not only high-toned and dignified, but intellectually instructive and patriotically stimulating and uplifting. I read nearly all of your speeches as they were reported in the New York City papers, and I greatly admired the richness of your material and effectiveness of your presentation, your downright honesty and sincerity, the entire absence of claptrap, and the extraordinarily high plane on which you kept your discussions.

While I congratulate you with all my heart on your triumph at the polls, I most earnestly and sincerely wish you the greatest success in the high office to which you have been called.

With kindest regards to you and Mrs. Wilson I remain
                    Very sincerely yours,   J. G. Schurman

TLS (WP, DLC).
[1] President of Cornell University.

From George Green Yeomans[1]

My dear "Governor,"   Chicago Nov. 9. 1910

I dont believe you have a friend who takes a more sincere delight in your successful plunge into politics than I do, and you may be sure that none of the congratulations which will be extended to you are more hearty or more heart felt than mine.

I have followed your campaign closely in the daily press—and it was magnificent—just what we who know you had a right to expect—an inspiration for those who stand for clean politics—and your splendid majority is an encouragement to those who still believe that the people recognize and appreciate honesty and sincerity of purpose in their public officials.

I think you know that the fellows in the west have been right at your back in the "late unpleasantness" and have admired your course throughout and we are glad that the *whole* people appreciate you more than the little bunch whose horizon is limited by the tops of the nearest hills.

Out here on the prairies I sometimes think we get a little wider view.

May you have a very full measure of success in your new adventure—and may this prove to be only a step to a call higher up. For the glory of '79—

Faithfully Yours,   Geo G. Yeomans

ALS (WP, DLC).
¹ Wilson's classmate at Princeton; at this time assistant to the president of the Wabash Railroad Co.

From Henry Lee Higginson

Dear President Wilson: Boston. November 9, 1910.

The University must be sorry to lose you, but, at any rate, we are very glad of your election. You are just the kind of man we want, and if you are willing to undertake the work, we are more the gainers.

On the whole, the election came out well, although we have had the misfortune to elect a very ordinary, ignorant man as Governor, and he has allied himself with the worst gang that has ever been in Massachusetts. There has been a foolish personal dislike of Draper,¹ who is an honest, able man, and who has been abused about high prices, with which he has nothing to do, and about the tariff, which he cannot change. Foss is a blatant, vulgar man, who had been seeking office in every direction,— just the kind of man we do not want, and you are just the kind of man that we do want.

Now, do not answer this letter, for you will get a million. I only want to express my pleasure at your election.

Yours truly,   H. L. Higginson

TLS (WP, DLC).
¹ Eben Sumner Draper, who had just been defeated for re-election as Governor of Massachusetts on the Republican ticket by Eugene Noble Foss.

From John Joseph Wynne¹

The Hon. Woodrow Wilson.   [New York] November 9, 1910

Hearty congratulations on your splendid triumph, and gratitude also for your elevating campaign work. It is especially pleasing to feel that attempts to misrepresent your attitude to any religious body have failed lamentably.

In the name of my associates here,

Respectfully   John J. Wynne

ALS (WP, DLC).
[1] The Rev. John Joseph Wynne, S.J., one of the editors of *The Catholic Encyclopedia* . . . (15 vols., New York, 1907-12).

From John Holladay Latané[1]

                    Lexington, Rockbridge County Virginia
Dear Dr. Wilson: November 9, 1910.

Your campaign has interested me more than anything that has taken place in Democratic politics for years. I have followed it closely, and can not refrain from congratulating you on the splendid manner in which you have conducted it, no less than on the outcome. You have given the entire country a demonstration of the political sagacity which your friends and former students have always believed you to possess.

I have often hoped that you would sooner or later enter the field of active politics and I am delighted that you have at last made your appearance under such auspicious circumstances.

Your friends in Virginia are ready to start your presidential boom right now.

With best wishes for your success and with sincere regard, I am,   Yours very truly,   John H. Latané.

TLS (WP, DLC).
[1] A student of Wilson's at The Johns Hopkins University and at this time Professor of History at Washington and Lee University.

From Isidor Straus[1]

Dear Doctor Wilson: New York. Nov. 9, 1910.

My brother Nathan joins me in heartiest congratulations. You have covered Democracy all over with glory. The tremendous landslide throughout the country bespeaks for our party, unless it is foolish enough to stultify itself within the next two years, the high probability of having the White House occupied by a Democrat, and the names that will come to everyone's lips will be those of the men who have succeeded in wresting the gubernatorial honors of their states from the opposition.

With all good wishes, I am,

                    Sincerely yours,   Isidor Straus

TLS (WP, DLC).
[1] Partner in the department store firms of R. H. Macy and Co. of New York and Abraham and Straus of Brooklyn, as well as a director of various banks and financial institutions.

From Leo Stanton Rowe[1]

My dear President Wilson: Philadelphia Nov. 9, '10.

You have placed everyone who is striving to put our political life on a higher plane under deep obligations. The magnificent victory of yesterday is an inspiration to every patriotic citizen. Your election is a further demonstration of the fact that the American people will make the right choice if they are guided by real leaders. You have done the country a great service, and which is the forerunner of a long series.

I congratulate you, and above all I congratulate the people of New Jersey on the standard that has been set to the other states of the Union.   Yours sincerely,   L S Rowe

TLS (WP, DLC).
[1] Head of the Department of Political Science at the University of Pennsylvania. He later served in the State and Treasury departments in the Wilson administration.

From Charles Joel Fisk[1]

Plainfield, N. J.
My dear Sir: November ninth, Nineteen Hundred Ten.

Although I have always been a Republican and was one of the men that worked diligently in the interests of Vivian M. Lewis throughout the last campaign, I want to be among one of the first to congratulate you on your election as the next Governor of New Jersey.

I believe you and my brother Pliny Fisk,[2] were in Princeton College at the same time, although not in the same Class, and I want you to feel that you may count upon me now and throughout your administration for the loyalty, support and respect due from a citizen of New Jersey to the Governor of the State.
        Very sincerely yours,   Chas J Fisk

TLS (WP, DLC).
[1] Mayor of Plainfield, N. J., affiliated with Harvey Fisk and Sons, a prominent New York investment banking house allied with the Morgan interests.
[2] Pliny Fisk, Princeton 1881, senior partner of Harvey Fisk and Sons.

From Theodore Marburg[1]

Dear Mr. Wilson: Baltimore, Md. Nov. 9, 1910.

Accept my hearty congratulations on your victory. I feel that at this moment personnel is of more importance to us in America than public policies or possible tinkering with the machinery of government, whether it be municipal, state or national. On the whole our laws are good and our institutions are sound. What is needed is the right men to administer them and on this score your victory should be welcomed by Republicans as well as Democrats throughout the country.

We are loath to accept as final your declination to participate in the projected conference of this society[2] in Washington Dec. 15-17. May I ask you to hold the matter in abeyance and come to us if at the last moment you find the time and have the inclination to do so? Thus far the following gentlemen have consented to address the conference: the President of the United States, the Secretary of State,[3] Senator Elihu Root, Charles W. Eliot, Simeon E. Baldwin, Richard Bartholdt,[4] Charles Noble Gregory,[5] William Dudley Foulke[6] and Francis B. Loomis.[7]

The Secretary of State has been so good as to transmit for us, through the kindness of Ambassador Whitelaw Reid at London, invitations to eminent Englishmen whose presence we hope to secure. We are likewise enlisting the co-operation of Ambassador [Robert] Bacon at Paris and Ambassador [David Jayne] Hill at Berlin in the hope of getting several prominent French and German publicists and statesmen here so that the meeting may be international in character. The cause is of such vast importance to the leading countries of the world that we deemed ourselves justified in asking the sacrifice of time and comfort which is involved in the foreign visitor's coming so far to us.

We know that you have the cause very much at heart. Your presence would help to center attention upon the conference and aid us materially in realizing one of the prime motives of the conference, namely, the cultivation of a public sentiment here and abroad which will ensure the success of the movement to establish the court. Sincerely, Theodore Marburg

TLS (WP, DLC).

[1] Secretary of the American Society for Judicial Settlement of International Disputes, author of several books on international affairs, and Minister to Belgium, 1912-13.

[2] There is no other correspondence about this invitation, but Wilson declined to attend. The American Society for the Judicial Settlement of International Disputes met in Washington, December 15-17, 1910. The speakers included President Taft, Andrew Carnegie, Senator Elihu Root, former Secretary of State John Watson Foster, Joseph Hodges Choate, former Ambassador to Great Britain, and the French Ambassador, Jean Jules Jusserand. For news reports of the conference, see the *Washington Post*, Dec. 16-18, 1910.

[3] Philander Chase Knox.

[4] United States representative from St. Louis, chairman of the group of congressmen associated with the Interparliamentary Union for the Promotion of International Arbitration.

[5] Dean of the College of Law, State University of Iowa, known for his work in international law.

[6] Editor of the Richmond, Ind., *Evening Item*, author of several literary and historical works, and active in various reform causes.

[7] Francis Butler Loomis, diplomatist and foreign trade adviser, who held several positions in the McKinley and Roosevelt administrations, including a brief tenure as acting Secretary of State in 1905.

From William Sulzer

My dear Governor: New York, Nov. 9-1910

Sincere congratulations on your magnificent victory. I know your administration will be a great success, and will keep the good old State of New Jersey in the Democratic column for years to come.

With best wishes believe me,

Sincerely your friend,   Wm. Sulzer

TLS (WP, DLC).

From W. C. Payne[1]

My dear Sir: Washington, D. C. [c. Nov. 9, 1910]

The National Independent Polit[ic]al League of Colored voters receive the news of your election as governor of New Jersey with great delight and admiration, and as one of its national officers, I extend congratulations.

The League has laid plans, which must yet be more encouraged, to continue organizing for the campaign of 1912.

Beginning with the first of January next we shall publish "The Voice of Independence"[2] to promote intelligent political education among Colored people, which is something they have not received until very recently, and has not been carried far as yet.

I take it that you are one very logical person to be urged to accept the leadership of your party in 1912. And regardless of your personal ideas on that subject at this time, I consider it my duty to show our people the importance of urging it upon you.

Since I am to organize and also edit the League organ, I desire your photo or "cut" that I may show the man as well as give the reasons.

Again I congratulate you, and pray God to crown your head with wisdom.   Very truly yours,   W. C. Payne

ALS (WP, DLC).

[1] Assistant national organizer of the National Independent Political League.
[2] No copies of this newspaper have survived.

From William Hunter Maxwell

Honorable Sir: Newark, N. J., Nov. 9, 1910.

I take this means to congratulate you upon your splendid victory.

All thinking men must be proud of the result.

Let us hope that the people of New Jersey will respond to your leadership, with the same spirit and interest with which you responded to their call.

Very Truly Your's,   Wm. H. Maxwell.

TLS (WP, DLC).

From Rudolph Edward Schirmer

My dear Wilson: [New York] Novr 9/1910

I send you my very heartiest congratulations on your election to the governorship of New Jersey. As a life long democrat, a loyal Princetonian and a contemporary of yours I take great pride and satisfaction in yr. success, which I feel sure is the forerunner of still greater honors to come.

My last conversation with C C Cuyler was about you and it largely foreshadowed what has happened & what I hope is still to come.

May you be given strength to confront all yr. responsibilities.

I grasp you warmly by the hand and say Godspeed

Yours faithfully   Rudolph E. Schirmer

ALS (WP, DLC).

From Edward Webster Bemis[1]

New Brighton, N. Y.
My dear Doctor Wilson: November 9, 1910.

Every Hopkins graduate, independent of politics, and everyone who, like myself, has had the pleasure of knowing you personally and of using your textbooks in college work, must take special pride and great pleasure in your victory yesterday. When to this, as in my case, is added sympathy with your point of view, so far as has been possible at a distance to follow it, the rejoicing is keen indeed.

You will be interested in knowing that at the City Club dinner last night, the entire group who assembled until midnight to receive the returns, including such men as the Filenes[2] of Boston, Maltbie[3] of the Public Service Commission, [George] McAneny,

President of the Borough of Manhattan, [Oswald Garrison] Villard of the Evening Post, etc., were enthusiastic over your election, and over the promise of the future.

In the multitude of congratulations which you are receiving, you need not bother to reply to this.

Very sincerely yours,   E W Bemis

TLS (WP, DLC).

[1] An old friend from Wilson's student days at the Johns Hopkins; at this time Special Investigator of Public Utilities, New York City.

[2] Abraham Lincoln Filene and Edward Albert Filene of Boston, who were both involved in reform causes and in programs to benefit the employees of William Filene's Sons Co., the family department store in which they were partners.

[3] Milo Roy Maltbie of New York, specialist in public utilities regulation, at this time a member of the Public Service Commission of New York.

From Henry Mayer Goldfogle[1]

My dear Governor: New York, Nov. 9, 1910.

Accept my hearty congratulations on the victory you won yesterday. I wish you a successful administration of your office.

The entire Democracy is indebted to you for the gallant fight you made.   Very truly yours,   Henry M. Goldfogle

TLS (WP, DLC).

[1] United States representative from the 9th congressional district of New York.

From Frank Miles Day

My dear Dr. Wilson: Philada. Nov. 9th, 1910

Your election is a source of the most profound satisfaction. It means so much not only for New Jersey but for right thought and action in our politics generally that it gives heart to all who have been hoping and striving for better things. One even writes the word "politics" without that sense of shame that one has usually felt in using it.

With best wishes and sincere regards I am

Very truly yours   Frank Miles Day.

ALS (WP, DLC).

From William Osler[1]

Dear Wilson   Oxford. Nov 9th [1910].

Hearty congratulations! The Platonists are everywhere rejoicing

With best wishes   Sincerely yours   Wm. Osler

ALS (WP, DLC).

[1] Regius Professor of Medicine at Oxford University.

From Magnus Fraser Peterson[1]

West Thorpe, Bowdon, Cheshire.

Dear Dr. Woodrow Wilson   Nov. 9. 1910.

I see from today's papers that you have been elected Governor of New Jersey. Most heartily do I congratulate New Jersey. I do not know anything about American politics, but I know that they can only be the better for your entrance into their arena. At first when I heard of your candidature I experienced something of a shock. Then I remembered John Morley and I have been thinking of you as the American Morley ever since. This does not mean that I (or you either) approve or disapprove of Morley's political opinions, though "opinions are constitutional" (you see I know something of your speeches) but that I believe that the man of letters is none the less but all the more qualified for public affairs, because he is a man of letters, & that I rejoice at the presence in the counsels of the nation of an "honest" man wielding moral force.

I have been trying to think of you in the lulls of the political storm sitting at your own table (an oval table of mahogany wood, I believe, & without a cloth) with your family and particularly on one occasion with our common friend—Fred Yates. Did he give you my message? The night before he left he, his wife & I walked "under Loughrigg" toward Pelter Bridge (twilight was falling & the owls were preparing to hoot); and I told him to give you my warmest remembrances and to ask you to come over next summer. Are you coming? Surely now that you are a Governor, you can do what you like! Otherwise I and all your friends here see little good (for us) in your being a Governor.

Will you tell Yates that I walked over under that Scar one evening & Mrs. Yates read me his delightful letters (This explains my knowledge of your mahogany table: there is nothing occult— no table rapping—about my knowledge) Also that Mrs. Yates came to see us and that she was looking as clear-eyed as ever. I wish I could join you two for an evening around that mahogany table. I want to get my legs under your mahogany. Who knows, I may do that yet. The doctors have ordered me six months complete rest from parochial work because of throat trouble & six weeks of that time I have to spend in absolute silence. (Don't you wish that this had been prescribed for some of your politicians?) But they promise me that the throat will get alright. I will do my best to get ready for you next summer.

We have had, as the school boy says, "heaps" of Americans in Grasmere this year. I kept looking for a Woodrow Wilson but

never found him. Surely, you won't disappoint me another year.
    With warmest remembrances, believe me
                    Yours very sincerely   M. F. Peterson
ALS (WP, DLC).
    [1] At this time rector of St. Oswald in Grasmere, England.

From William Henry Steele Demarest[1]

                                    New Brunswick, New Jersey.
My dear Dr. Wilson: November 9th. 1910.
    I have just wired you my congratulations and good wishes.[2]
You have been very emphatically and widely assured of the
feeling of the people of the State toward you and I do hope that
you will have a very happy and successful administration.
    I write you now in haste to ask whether it might not be pos-
sible for you to come to New Brunswick to-morrow, Thursday
evening, to meet the Rutgers Alumni of New Brunswick and
vicinity who will be assembled in modest observance of the
Charter Day of the college. We shall have dinner at 7 o'clock
in the College Hall and a hundred or more of our representative
men will be there. I realize that it is asking much of you after
the strenuous campaign which you have so successfully carried
out but it would mean very much to us individually and as a college if you could come. To reduce the trip to its smallest terms,
you could leave Princeton at 5:45 and reach New Brunswick
at 6:22; could leave New Brunswick at 9.07 and reach Princeton
at 9:45. It will gratify us all more than I can tell if the way be
clear for you to accept.
    With highest regards,
                    Faithfully yours,   W. H. S. Demarest.

Our Exercises in the afternoon are at 4 with address by Dr.
[Andrew Sloan] Draper, Commissioner of Education, New York,
on "Motive in Education."[3]

TLS (WP, DLC).
    [1] President of Rutgers College.
    [2] It is missing.
    [3] Wilson wrote in shorthand at the top of this letter: "Am worn out. Would not
dare come tomorrow evening."

From William Bailey Howland[1]

Dear Sir: New York November 9, 1910
    The Periodical Publishers' Association, representing practically
all the leading National periodicals of the country, has com-

missioned me as its President to extend to you a very cordial invitation to be our guest, and address the Association, on the occasion of our Annual Banquet, which is to be held at the Waldorf-Astoria, in New York City, on Friday evening, January 6th, 1911. At the first annual banquet of this Association we had the honor of welcoming the then President, Mr. Roosevelt, as our guest, and in successive years have had the further honor of the presence of ex-President Cleveland, Governor Hughes, and our present Chief Magistrate, Mr. Taft. For the present year our only living ex-President, Hon. Theodore Roosevelt, has accepted an invitation to be our guest of honor. I sincerely hope that it may be possible for you to honor us with your presence as a speaker on what we hope will be a very memorable occasion.[2]

I venture to enclose, merely for the sake of information, a copy of the invitation and menu of last year.

With great respect, I am

Yours sincerely,   William B. Howland

TLS (WP, DLC).
[1] Publisher of the New York *Outlook*.
[2] Wilson declined the invitation.

From Charles Henry Parkhurst[1]

My dear Sir: New York City. Nov 9th 1910.

Please accept my hearty congratulations on your election to the Governorship of New Jersey.

Although I have not the pleasure of an intimate personal acquaintance with you, yet I have followed your campaign with intensest interest, and I consider that the entrance of a man of your quality and statesmanship into the arena of political life augurs well for the future of New Jersey and the country.

Yours with high esteem   C. H. Parkhurst.

TLS (WP, DLC).
[1] Famous crusader against vice and crime in New York through his presidency of the Society for the Prevention of Crime and pastor of the Madison Square Presbyterian Church since 1880.

From Darwin Pearl Kingsley[1]

My dear Dr. Wilson: New York, N. Y. November 9, 1910.

My only excuse for writing you a note is the fact that I am an American citizen, and, although a Republican, very happy this morning over the fact that it has been possible for you to emerge as one of the great leaders of the Democratic Party.

In common with many American citizens, I have deplored the fact that our most representative men have not been attracted to public life. Your election as Governor of New Jersey will reach in its effects far beyond the borders of your State. That you could succeed will be an object lesson to other men of a similar type.

Republican as I am, I do not know when anyone's success at the polls has brought me any more genuine satisfaction than yours.

It is a little early to talk about 1912, but I think all fair-minded Republicans will admit that at the present hour there is no figure in that party standing as a Presidential possibility, which compares with your position as a Democrat before the Nation.

Very truly yours,　D. P. Kingsley

TLS (WP, DLC).
[1] President of the New York Life Insurance Co.

From Ashton Cokayne Shallenberger[1]

Lincoln Neb Nov 9 10

Accept my heartiest congratulations on your election　I wish you[r] administration great success　let me join in invitation of Nebraska state teacher association to speak at Lincoln friday evening Nov twenty fifth　　　Ashton C Shallenberger

T telegram (WP, DLC).
[1] Democratic Governor of Nebraska.

From Robert Garrett

Baltimore Md Nov 9 1910

Hearty congratulations　trust you will have equal success during term.　　　Robert Garrett

T telegram (WP, DLC).

ADDENDUM

To Joseph Finch Guffey[1]

My dear Mr. Guffey: Princeton, N. J. March 21st, 1908.

I expect to be in Pittsburgh[2] in time to attend such a luncheon as you suggest, but I am going to say frankly that I very much doubt the advisability of such a conference as seems to be in your mind. I think there is at present a distinct danger of the formation of definite parties in regard to the future of Princeton and I think that we should be very careful indeed not to seem to gather groups interested on the one side or the other.

You see I am assuming, in view of the very reassuring conversation I had with you when you were in Princeton, that your purpose would be to gather together at lunch men whose minds were at least hospitable to the reforms which I have proposed. At the request of the Trustees, I withdrew the quad plan from present consideration, and while I feel that we must return to that plan if anything thorough is to be done, I fear that it would have at least the appearance of bad faith on my part if I were to press it for consideration in any way whatever for the time being.

I know that you will appreciate the weight of what I am saying and that you will not think for a moment that I fail to appreciate the very patriotic motives and very thoughtful kindness of your suggestion for a lunch.

I hope that this will not cut me out from seeing the Princeton men when I am in Pittsburgh. I should feel that I had been cheated of a great pleasure, and I particularly hope that I shall see you.

With warmest regard,
Always cordially and faithfully yours,
Woodrow Wilson

TLS (photograph in J. F. Guffey, *Seventy Years of the Red-Fire Wagon From Tilden to Truman Through New Freedom and New Deal* [n.p., 1952], p. 16).

[1] Student at Princeton, 1890-1892; nephew of James McClurg Guffey; Pittsburgh businessman and oil producer; Democratic senator from Pennsylvania, 1935-47.

[2] To attend the meeting of the Western Association of Princeton Clubs on May 2.

INDEX

NOTE ON THE INDEX

THE alphabetically arranged analytical table of contents at the front of the volume eliminates duplication, in both contents and index, of references to certain documents, such as letters. Letters are listed in the contents alphabetically by name, and chronologically within each name by page. The subject matter of all letters is, of course, indexed. The Editorial Notes and Wilson's writings are listed in the contents chronologically by page. In addition, the subject matter of both categories is indexed. The index covers all references to books and articles mentioned in text or notes. Footnotes are indexed. Page references to footnotes which place a comma between the page number and "n" cite both text and footnote, thus: "624,n3." On the other hand, absence of the comma indicates reference to the footnote only, thus: "55n2"—the page number denoting where the footnote appears. The letter "n" without a following digit signifies an unnumbered descriptive-location note.

An asterisk before an index reference designates identification or other particular information. Re-identification and repetitive annotation have been minimized to encourage use of these starred references. Where the identification appears in an earlier volume, it is indicated thus: "1:*212,n3." Therefore a page reference standing without a preceding volume number is invariably a reference to the present volume. The index supplies the fullest known forms of names, and, for the Wilson and Axson families, relationships as far down as cousins. Persons referred to in the text by nicknames or shortened forms of names can be identified by reference to entries for these forms of the names.

INDEX

Abbett, Leon, 343n9
Aberdeen, Scotland, 216
Abernethy, Lloyd M., 342n6
Afro-American Industrial and Benefit Association, 275n1
Afro-American League, 21n1, 275n3
Afro-American Ledger (Baltimore), 47n1, 275n2
Alaska: public lands, 546,n3
Albany, 360
Albany Evening Journal, 252n6
Alderman, Edwin Anderson, 595-96
Aldrich, Nelson Wilmarth, 175, 215,n5, 243, 244, 249, 255, 272, 280, 456,n2, 457, 468, 475
Alexander, Archibald (1855-1917; Princeton 1875), 6:*12,n2; 150,n1
Alexander, Archibald Stevens (Princeton 1902), 6-7,n1, 18-20, 112-14, 354, 389
Alexander, Caroline Bayard Stevens, 150,n1,2
Alexander, Henry Eckert, 8-9, 22-23, 24, 26, 27, 33-34, 37, 40, 53n1, 54, 57-58, 62, 158-59, 164, 167-68, 200-1, 219, 225-26, 243-44, 275, 292; Mrs. (Elizabeth Kirkwood), 54
Alexander, Lucien Hugh, 328,n1
Allen, Charles Dexter, 168,n1, 171
Allen, Charles Sterling, Mrs. (Anjenett Holcomb), 26
Allen, John Mills, 423,n3
Allen, Yorke, 300-1,n1
American Academy of Arts and Letters, 109,n2
American Bar Association, 51, 64-81, 300n2, 386, 609; *Report of Twenty-Third Annual Meeting . . .*, 81n
American Press Association, 300
American Society for Judicial Settlement of International Disputes, 615,-n1,2
American Tobacco Company, 206
America's Cup races, 38,n2
Anderson, Charles W., 47
Anderson, Harold MacDonald, 508,n2
Andover, N.J., 413
Arnold, Harris A., M.D., 239,n2
Asbury Park, N.J.: Hippodrome, 328; WW campaign speech, 328-34
Associated Press, 608, 608n1
Association to Prevent Corrupt Practices at Elections, 155,n2
Atkins, Gaius Glenn, 4,n1
Atlanta Georgian and News, 451n1
Atlantic City, N.J., 21, 29, 47, 551; Steeple Chase Pier theatre, 310n1; WW campaign speech, 310-20
Atlantic County, N.J., 584n1
Auburn Theological Seminary, 367,n2
Austen, Jane, 225
automobiles, 207, 209

Axson, Margaret Randolph (Madge), see Elliott, Edward Graham, Mrs.
Axson, Stockton (full name: Isaac Stockton Keith Axson II), brother of EAW; 2:*386n1; 52, 174, 243n2, 421, 558-59

Bacon, Alexander Samuel, 421,n4, 467, 527
Bacon, Benjamin Wisner, 4,n2
Bacon, Charles Reade, 220,n1
Bacon, Robert, 615
Baird, David, 219n2, 260, 278,n2, 305, 346, 378, 409, 420, 503
Baker, Alfred Brittin, 117,n1
Baker, Jacob Thompson, 283,n2
Baker's Hotel, Washington, N.J., 383
Baldwin, Simeon Eben, 109,n3, 117, 133, 144, 386, 590, 596, 598, 615
Ballinger, Richard Achilles, 546n3
ballots, 432-33
Baltimore *Sun*, 102, 525n, 539n2, 555,-n4
Barber, Isaac, M.D., 393n1
Barber, Thomas, M.D., 393,n1
Barnes, William, 252,n6, 258, 259n11
Barr, John Watson, Jr., 39,n1
Barringer, Daniel Moreau (Princeton 1879), 603
Bartholdt, Richard, 615,n4
Baxter, Clarence Hughson, 158,n1
Baxter, Edgeworth Bird, 577
Bayonne, N.J., 19; Democratic Club, 485, 487; First Baptist Church, 487; First Methodist Church, 487; St. Henry's Church, 487; WW campaign speech, 485-92
Beach, Sylvester Woodbridge, 16:*301,-n1; 597,n1
Beach Haven, N.J., 8
Bean, Walton, 342n5
Bee (Washington), 47n1
Bellevue-Stratford Hotel, Philadelphia, 558
Belmont Hotel, New York City, 321, 362n1
Belvidere, N.J., 558; Allen's Drug Store, 384; Court House, 384; WW campaign speech, 384
Bemis, Edward Webster, 617-18,n1
Berea College, 579
Bergen County, N.J., 7, 11, 22, 41, 52, 141, 142, 149, 173, 436, 452, 507; WW campaign speeches, 446-49; mentioned, 412
Berlin, University of: Theodore Roosevelt Professorship, 48,n4
Bermuda, 164, 556, 591n1
Bernardsville, N.J., 354
Berrien, Andrew J., 219,n3, 226
Beveridge, Albert Jeremiah, 219,n5, 343n11

Big Business, 395, 549, 551
Birrell, Augustine, 51
Blackburn, William, 335,n1
Blair, Francis Preston, Jr., 335
Blair Academy, 476,n2
Blair family, 476
Blairstown, N.J., 384
Blairstown Hotel, Blairstown, N.J., 384
Blairstown Seminary, 384
Blauvelt, James Gillmor, 256n9, 260-64,n1, 412
Bloomfield, N.J., WW campaign speech, 563
Bobbitt, Benjamin Boisseau, 299,n2, 324
Bok, Edward William, 118
Bollschweiler, Albert E., 547,n4
Borden, Robert Laird, 155,n3
Boss Ruef's San Francisco . . . (Bean), 342n5
Boston: Union Club, 40n1; WW in, 40, 40n1, 46, 51, 61
Boston Suffrage League, 21n1
Bound Brook, N.J., 361; WW campaign speech, 354-61
Bowen, Herbert E., 53
Bowlby, Harry Laity, 90-91
Braga, Teófilo, 439n1
Bragdon, Henry Wilkinson, 103n
Branchville, N.J., 413
Branson, Roswell H., 154,n2
Brayton Hotel, New York City, 164n1
Bremner, Robert Gunn, 133, 153-54
bribery, 302, 393, 443
Bridges, Robert, 1:*284,n1; 298, 337-38, 591
Bridgeton, N.J.: WW campaign speech, 276-81, mentioned, 244, 322
Briggs, Frank Obadiah, 219n2, 244,n3, 249,n5, 290,n1, 296, 330, 351
Brodhead, Calvin Easton, 83-84,n1, 84-85
Brodhead, William E., 85n
Bronk, Mitchell, 487
Brougham, Herbert Bruce, 97-98
Brown, Oliver Huff, 324
Bryan, Alison Reid, 201,n2
Bryan, William Jennings, 21n1, 24n1, 86, 598, 600-1
Bryan, William Swan Plumer, 201,n1
Bryant, David, 583
Buenos Aires: Fourth International American Conference, 557, 559
Bureaucracy Convicts Itself: The Ballinger-Pinchot Controversy of 1910 (Mason), 546n3
Burgess, John William, 48,n4
Burlington, N.J., 290n1; WW campaign speech, 269-74, mentioned, 244
Burlington County, N.J., 403; County Fair, 269
Butterworth, J. C., 584n1

Cadwalader, John Lambert, 353, 362n1, 364-66
Caldwell, N.J.: birthplace of Grover

Cleveland, 309,n3, 309; Democratic Union, 306, 309; Kingsley School, 310; Monomonock Inn, 306,n1; WW speeches, 306-10
California, 608n2
Camden, N.J., 420, 426, 551; Broadway Theatre, 421; Line Ditch, 416; Pyne Point, 416; registry lists, 567; Temple Theatre, 413, 416, 421; WW campaign speech, 413-21
Camden County, N.J., 278n2, 417, 418, 577, 584n1
Cameron, Simon, 62,n1
Camp, Edwin, 451,n1
Canada, 254
Cannon, Joseph Gurney, 215,n6, 221, 243, 244, 249, 249n2, 255, 280, 344,-n12, 456, 457, 474, 564
Cape May County, N.J., 281, 283, 285, 286n4, 569, 584n1
Cape May Court House, N.J.: WW campaign speech, 281-87
capitalists, capitalism, the capitalistic system, 268, 395, 401, 468
Capps, Edward, 166-67,n2; Mrs. (Grace Alexander), 167,n1
Carlisle, Pa., U.S. Indian Industrial School, 53,n1
Carlstadt, N.J.; WW campaign speech, 507-8
Carlyle, Thomas, 513
Carnegie, Andrew, 615n2
Carnegie Foundation for the Advancement of Teaching, 492-93, 540, 540-n1,2
Carrow, Howard, 416
Cary, Hunsdon, 117-18,n1
celibacy, clerical, 319
Central Railroad Co. of New Jersey, 343n9, 354
Century magazine, 322,n1
Chambers, Benjamin Bright, 336,n1
Chapman, Edward Mortimer, 4,n3
Charles River, 518
Chattanooga, Tenn., WW in, 64-81
Chicago, 21, 343n11; Business Service Lecture League, 163n1; Committee of Citizens, 519; University Club, 594
Chicago Tribune, 343n11
Choate, Joseph Hodges, 615n2
Christie, Samuel M., 179,n1
Civil War, 227, 535
Clark, Champ, 608n2
Cleveland, Grover, 10, 86, 129, 160, 309-10, 345, 345n13, 621
Clinton, N.J., 383
Close, Gilbert Fairchild, 13
Coke, Sir Edward, 135
Colby, Everett, 341, 352, 563
Cole, Charles D'Urban Morris, 527,n2
Cole, Clarence Lee, 310n2, 315
Cole, George B., 383
Collier's Weekly, 40n1
Collingwood Hotel, New York City, 87

Collins, Dennis Francis, 296, 464, 465, 467
Collins, Gilbert, 147,n2
Colorado, 608n2
Columbia, S.C., 201
Columbia River, 12
Columbia University: Kaiser Wilhelm Professorship, 48n4
Congregationalist and Christian World (Boston), 5n, 31,n1
Congressional Record, 474
Conklin, Edwin Grant, 116-17, 136-37, 435,n2; Mrs. (Belle Adkinson), 117,-n2
Connecticut, 598, 608n2
conservation, 44, 88n3, 95, 126, 271, 402, 505
Cornish, Johnston, 383, 384
Corona (Dodge yacht), 38,n2
corporations, 45, 60, 71f, 88n3, 93, 95-96, 99, 119, 122, 126, 134, 139, 140, 153, 165, 186-87, 199, 204, 206, 207-10, 216, 222, 228, 233, 277, 298, 304, 305, 325, 326, 330, 331, 340-41, 342-n5, 345, 359, 371, 374-75, 407, 453-54, 469, 488, 489, 503, 505, 533, 568, 571
corrupt practices, 155,n2, 172, 195, 232, 244n1, 256, 343n10
corruption, 231-32, 302, 479-80, 485
Cosmopolitan Magazine, 342n7
Coxe, Alfred Conkling, 298,n1
Cram, Ralph Adams, 434
Crisis (N.A.A.C.P. organ), 275n3
Croker, Richard, 342,n8
Croly, Herbert, 322
Cromwell, Oliver, 498
Crusader (Baltimore), 156n1
Culberson, Charles Allen, 580,n1
Cumberland County, N.J., 277, 584n1
Cummins, Albert Baird, 219,n5, 251
Cunningham, Clarence, 546n3
Cuyler, Cornelius Cuyler, 617

Dabney, Richard Heath, 1:*685,n1; 138, 597-99
Dalrymple, Alfred N., 261,n3
Daniels, Josephus, 585,n1; Mrs. (Addie Worth Bagley), 585,n2
Daniels, Winthrop More, 7:*205,n3; 10-11, 174, 321, 337
Dante Alighieri, 217, 533
Dartmouth College, 21n1
David, King, 319
Davidson College, 201
Davis, Robert, 7, 18, 19, 26, 27, 43, 62, 63,n1, 85, 86, 90, 261, 341,n3, 345, 346, 347, 378, 388, 389, 409, 442, 503
Davis, William H., 416
Davis, William J., 341,n3
Day, Frank Miles, 618
Deal, N.J., 27, 88, 89
Dear, Joseph Albert, Jr., 23-24, 116, 580
Dear, Walter Moore, 450-51,n1

Deeds of Lewis; the Words of Wilson, 463
Delaware and Raritan Canal, 403,n3
demagogues, 570
Demarest, William Henry Steele, 620,-n1
democracy, 268, 269; in college life, 605
Democracy in America (de Tocqueville), 512
Democratic party and Democrats, 10, 21, 85, 144, 161, 183-85, 190-91, 193, 211, 212, 217, 223, 227, 237, 239, 255, 285, 294, 300, 335, 343n11, 344n12, 345n13, 373, 387, 396, 398, 427-28, 448, 474, 479, 501, 565-66, 586, 592, 595, 598, 605, 608n2, 613, 621, 622
Democratic party and Democrats in Maine, 119,n1, 123, 128, 136
Democratic party and Democrats in Massachusetts, 598
Democratic party and Democrats in New Jersey, 5, 6-7, 10, 11, 18, 19, 19,n7, 24n1, 39, 40n1, 43-46, 57, 63, 64, 82, 84, 86, 87-88, 89, 94-96, 100, 101, 103, 106, 112-14, 118-20, 125, 130, 131, 133, 134, 138, 139, 142, 145, 146, 158, 159, 161, 164, 167-68, 168n2, 179, 181, 183, 184, 185, 189, 197, 201, 202, 204, 214, 217, 219, 221, 223-24, 227, 236, 240, 247, 249, 260, 286, 287, 290n1, 295-96, 304, 311, 312-13, 314, 326, 332, 345-48, 352, 354, 356, 357, 362, 364, 369-70, 378, 380, 381, 383, 388, 395, 396-98, 404, 405, 409, 411, 413, 415, 417, 419, 420, 424, 429, 430, 431, 436, 448, 449, 451, 452, 457, 458, 461, 475, 495, 503, 504, 505, 510, 511-12, 514, 521, 523, 524, 529, 545, 547, 549, 552, 553, 563, 564, 566, 570, 572, 577, 581, 583, 584n1, 589, 603, 608n2, 610, 616; "Overlords", 266, 346, 347, 409, 503; proposed 1910 platform, 43-46; 1910 platform, 87-88,n3, 94-96, 139, 202, 204, 205, 275, 511, 512, 522, 525, 529, 552
Democratic party and Democrats in New York, 608n2
Democratic party and Democrats in Pennsylvania, 103
Dennis, Alfred Lewis, 592-93
Denver, 130
Des Moines *Leader*, 251
Devlin, Martin Patrick, 141,n1, 153, 583n2
Dewalt, Arthur Granville, 103
DeWitt, John, 365, 366, 442
Dickinson, Clinton Roy, 169,n1
Dickinson, Jonathan, 169n1
Dickson, Bessie Louise, 587,n1
Dillow, Thomas H., 82-83
direct primary, 157, 195, 204, 271, 272, 332

Dix, John Alden, 275n2, 322, 322n1, 598

Dixon, Warren, 63

Dodge, Cleveland Hoadley, 1:*210,n3; 38, 112, 137-38, 139, 292, 295-96, 321, 385, 385n1, 435, 591-92; Mrs. (Grace Parish), 38,n1, 385,n3

Dodge, Henry Nehemiah, M.D., 354,n1

Dolliver, Jonathan Prentiss, 219,n5

Donges, Ralph Waldo Emerson, 577,n1

Donnelly, Thomas Marcus, 451-52,n1

Dorsey, Joseph, 156,n1

Douglas, Stephen Arnold, 161

Dover, N.J.: Baker Theatre, 526; WW campaign speech, 526-27

Draper, Andrew Sloan, 620

Draper, Eben Sumner, 612n1

Drew Theological Seminary, 525-26

DuBois, William Edward Burghardt, 21n1, 47n1, *275n3, 292

Dullard, John Power, 153,n1, 167

dummies in corporations, 122, 134

Durham, Israel, 342n6

Dye, Forrest R., 62, 159

East Orange, N.J.: Commonwealth Hall, 563; WW campaign speech, 563

Easton, Pa., 393

Edge, Walter Evans, 313,n3, 606n1; Mrs. (Camilla Sewall), 606n1

Edinburgh, 49

Edison, Thomas Alva, 122, 520

Edward VII, 48

eggs, 358

Eliot, Charles William, 615

Elizabeth, N.J.: Elks' Club, 464; Proctor's Theatre, 454; WW after dinner talk, 464-65; WW campaign speech, 412, 454-62

Elizabeth Evening Times, 465n, 470n, 541, 583n1

Elizabethport, N.J.: St. Patrick's Parish Hall, 465n1, 467

Elliott, Edward Graham, 2:*417n1; 11:*198,n1; 39-40, 51,n3, 84, 87; Mrs. (Margaret Randolph Axson; Madge), sister of EAW, 2:*417,n1; 39-40, 48, 51n3, 84, 87

Ely, Matthias Cowell, 26,n4, 540

England: politics, 439

Englewood, N.J., 141; Lyceum, 141, 446; WW campaign speech, 446-49

Erie, Pa., 161

Essex County, N.J., 7, 89, 113, 161n2, 171, 341, 380, 412, 541n2, 561, 564, 584n1

Eypper, Charles Apffel, 464,n1

Fagan, Lawrence, 18, 23,n5, 26,n3

Fagan, Mark Matthew, 19, 19,n2

Farrand, Max, 7:*172,n3; 309n2

Farrand, Wilson, 152, 362n1, 365-66

Fay, Thomas P., 299,n1

Federal power, 381

Felt, Zephaniah Charles, 12, 38; Mrs. (Nora Belle Harker), 12,n1

Ferguson, William T., 21,n1, 28-29, 47, 162, 238-39, 275, 292

Fielder, James Fairman, 97, 442-43

Filene, Abraham Lincoln, 617,n2

Filene, Edward Albert, 617,n2

Fine, Henry Burchard, 7:*223,n3; 112, 385

Finley, John Huston, 7:*271,n1; 137,-n1

Firth, Joseph H., 383

Fisk, Charles Joel, 614,n1

Fisk, Pliny, 614,n2

Fitzgerald, John Joseph, 327, 338

Flemington, N.J., 382; Court House, 377n4, 381; Flemington Opera House, 369,n1, 381; WW campaign speeches, 369-77, 377; WW in, 558

Florida crackers, 227

Flynn, David M., 541-42,n1

Ford, Henry Jones, 11:*262,n2; 606-7

Fort, John Franklin, 219n2, 505, 584n1, 605-6; Mrs. (Charlotte E. Stainsby), 606

Fortune, Timothy Thomas, 275n4

Fosdick, Raymond Blaine, 16:*138,n1; 238,n1

Foss, Eugene Noble, 598,n1, 610, 612n1

Foster, David Paulson, 381-82,n1, 470-71

Foster, John Watson, 600, 615n2; Mrs. (Mary Parke McFerson), 600,n1

Foulke, William Dudley, 615,n6

Fowler, Charles Newell, 219,n5, 249,-n2, 301, 383

Frankfort, Ky.: Conference of Governors, 475-76, 605-6

Franklin Furnace, N.J., 413

Fraser, Philip Hilton, 519-20

Fraternal Organizations of New Jersey, 452n1

Frazer, David Ruddach, 362n1, 366-67,n1

Freehold, N.J.: Armory Opera House, 334,n4; WW campaign speech, 334

Freehold Transcript, 218n, 334n

Frelinghuysen, Joseph Sherman, 7,n5

French, William Collins, 421,n3

Frost, William Goodell, 579

Future of Democracy (Daniels), 322,-n3

Gallagher, Charles Henry, 27,n2, 34

Garfield, Harry Augustus, 14:*486-87,-n1; 421, 558-59, 609, 609n1; Mrs. (Belle Hartford Mason), 559, 609

Garfield, James Abram, 609n1

Garfield, James Rudolph, 609-10,n1

Garrett, Robert, 11:*113,n2; 3, 25-26, 622

Garrison, Lindley Miller, 587,n1

Gauss, Christian Frederick, 111

Gaynor, William Jay, 9n2, 144, 238

Gebhardt, William Cavanagh, 110-11,-n1, 156-57, 354, 558

General Theological Seminary, 105,n2
George W. Norris: The Making of a Progressive, 1861-1912 (Lowitt), 344-n12
German-American Alliance of New Jersey, 295
Germany, 48; government, 405; report on wages, 468
Glass, Franklin Potts, 588
Glazebrook, Otis Allen, 98
Glen Gardner, N.J., 383
Glen Ridge, N.J.: Town Hall, 563; WW campaign speech, 563-64
Gloucester County, N.J., 245, 254
Gloucester County Democrat (Woodbury, N.J.), 259n
Godwin, Harold, 1:*249,n3; 442,n1, 444
Goldfogle, Henry Mayer, 618,n1
Gollan, Henry Cowper, 556-57; Mrs. (Marie Louise Norris), 556-57
Goltra, Edward Field, 17, 294
Gompers, Samuel, 322,n2, 379
Gordon, James Gay, 267
Gordon, Sloane, 300,n3
Gorman, Arthur Pue, 345n13
governors: meeting in Frankfort, Ky., 475
graft, honest and dishonest, 303,n3, 304, 342, 399-400, 419, 443, 479, 480, 481, 482, 483, 484, 485
Graft as an Export Trade in Pittsburgh (Russell), 342n7
Grandison, Charles N., 171-72,n1
Grant, Ulysses Simpson, 367
Grasmere, 619
Grasty, Charles Henry, 102,n1
Green, Henry Woodhull, 152
Gregory, Charles Noble, 615,n5
Griffin, Edward Herrick, 586-87,n1
Griffin, Patrick Robert, 473,n1
Griggs, John William, 276, 277, 280, 283, 301, 305, 357-58, 476
Griscom, Lloyd Carpenter, 252n6
Grover Cleveland: A Study in Courage (Nevins), 345n13
Guardian (Boston), 21n1, 47n1, 275n5
Guffey, James McClurg, 623n1
Guffey, Joseph Finch, 623,n1
Guggenheim, Daniel, 546n3
Guinn, Walter, 52,n1
Guttenberg, N.J., 464

Hackensack, N.J., 11, 141; Second Regiment Armory, 446, 452; WW campaign speech, 446-49, 452-54
Hackettstown, N.J.: American House, 384; WW campaign speech, 383-84
Hahn, Simon, 7,n3
Hamburg, N.J., 413
Hamill, James Alphonsus, 19,n4
Hampton, N.J., 383
Hand, Robert E., 286,n4
Handy, Parker Douglas, 138
Haney, Conrad, 176,n3,4
Harbaugh, William H., 148n1

Hardin, John Ralph, 610
Harlan, John Maynard, 8:*179,n3; 266, 389
Harlow, Samuel Allen, 110,n1
Harmon, Judson, 9n2, 29, 71, 144, 275n2, 300,n3, 386, 596, 598
Harper & Brothers, 51,n1
Harper's Weekly, 28,n6
Harrigan, William, 62,n2, 541n2
Harrison, Benjamin, 431n6, 505
Hartford, Conn.; Owl Club, 168,n3, 171
Hartford Theological Seminary, 143
Harvard University, 167, 258, 259, 579,n1
Harvey, George Brinton McClellan, 11:-*369,n2; 5, 6, 17, 24-25, 27-28, 35n1, 35, 37n1, 40-42,n1, 46, 52-53, 54, 61, 85, 87-90, 148, 166, 243, 245, 292-93, 297, 320, 327, 338, 433, 435, 585
Haussling, Jacob, 564,n2
Hazen, Azel Washburn, 107; Mrs. (Mary Butler Thompson), 107,n1
Hearst, William Randolph, 85n1
Helm, Nathan Wilbur, 320,n2
Hemphill, James Calvin, 539n1, 579
Henderson, Robert Randolph, 1:*270,-n1; 555-56,n2, 599-600
Hendrickson, Charles Elvin, Jr., 346,-n15
Heney, Francis Joseph, 342,n5
Hennessey, James, 412
Henry, [James] Bayard, 152, 362n1, 366
Heppenheimer, William C., 473
Hermann, Joseph A., 560
Higginson, Henry Lee, 612
Hilfers, Henry F., 82,n1
Hill, David Jayne, 615
Hillery, Thomas J., 340n2, 408
History of Tammany Hall (Myers), 343n10
Hoboken, N.J., 18, 19, 43, 112; Naegeli's Hotel, 295; St. Mary's Hall, 473; WW campaign speech, 473-76, mentioned, 412
Hoboken *Observer*, 18,n1, 19, 20, 23,n5, 26, 113, 449, 541, 582
Hoff, Joseph Stanislaus, 97,n1, 102-3, 120, 219
Hope, N.J., 384
Hopkins, Harvey Sylvester, 396,n2
hosiery, 215-16
Howe, Edward, 51-52
Howell, Clark, 327,n1
Howell, Joseph, 443-44,n1
Howland, William Bailey, 620-21
Hoyt, James Alfred, Jr., 588-89,n1
Hudson County, N.J., 7, 19, 37n1, 63,n1, 90, 97, 113, 147, 172, 173, 275, 297, 341, 346n15, 380, 412, 415, 449, 464, 540, 584n1; Square Deal Democratic Association, 452n1; WW campaign speeches, 471-76
Hudspeth, Robert Stephen, 607

Hughes, Charles Evans, 146, 195, 341,-n4, 598, 621
Hughes, William, 57,n2, 145, 153-54, 213, 302, 603
Hulbert, Allen Schoolcraft, 26
Hulsizer, Abraham Chalmers, 369,n2
Hunt, Theodore Whitefield, 6:*528,n1; 377-78, 602
Hunterdon County, N.J., 354, 369n2, 381, 382
Hunterdon County Democrat (Flemington), 377n
Hutchinson, C. X., 487
Hutchinson, Paul, 393

If Wilson only Could and Would, 335-n2
Illinois: legislature, 343n11
Illinois Manufacturers Association, 266, 389
Indiana, 608n2
Inferno (Dante), 533
Inglis, William Otto, 40n1, 53, 54, 62, 293
initiative, referendum and recall, 142, 149, 269, 352
insurance scandals in New York state, 341,n4, 392, 393, 399, 418
Insurgency in Philadelphia, 1905 (Abernethy), 342n6
insurgents, 306, 457-58
"interests," *see* Wall Street
International Association of Machinists, 335n1
International Catholic Truth Society, 542
Interparliamentary Union for the Promotion of International Arbitration, 615n4
Ireland: self-government, 439
Isham, William Burhans, 602

Jackson, Andrew, 512
Jacobus, Melancthon Williams (Princeton 1877), 12:*400,n2; 6, 30-31, 109, 142-43, 321, 362n1, 578, 594
Janvier, Caesar Augustus Rodney, 588
Jefferson, Thomas, 510
Jersey Central Railroad, 343n9, 354
Jersey City, 8, 19, 23, 42-43, 173, 241, 341; Die Wilde Gans Club, 147; Grand View Hall, 191n1; St. John's Hall, 492n1; St. Patrick's Hall, 191-n1; St. Peter's Hall, 181; WW campaign speeches, 181-91, 310, 412, 492n1
Jersey City Herald, 94n
Jersey Journal (Jersey City), 23-24n1, 42,n1, 191n1, 218n, 228n, 243,n1, 244n1, 256,n8, 265,n1, 293, 451n1, 476n, 492n, 541, 582
Johns Hopkins University, 587n1, 613-n1, 617
Johnson, Hiram Warren, 608n2
Johnson, Robert Underwood, 109,n1, 322,n1

Johnson, Samuel, LL.D.. 253
Johnson, William Mindred, 7,n6
Joline, Adrian Hoffman, 6:*683,n1; 39,n1
Jones, David Benton, 12:*288,n1,5; 10, 29, 132, 144, 162-63, 173-74, 386, 389, 593-94
Jones, Thomas Davies, 7:*614,n4; 163, 321, 362n1, 385, 599
joy-rides, 207
Judson, Harry Pratt, 8:*426,n1; 144-45,n1
jurisprudence, 577
Jusserand, Jean Adrien Antoine Jules, 615n2

Kane, Francis Fisher, 266-67, 604-5
Katzenbach, Edward Lawrence, 27,n3, 132
Katzenbach, Frank Snowden, Jr., 23,-n3, 24,n2, 27,n2,3, 33-34, 34n1, 35n1, 37,n1,2, 40, 52, 54, 90, 96, 101, 103, 103n1, 104, 106, 120, 121, 137, 141, 174, 213, 229n1, 295, 329,n3, 330, 331, 354, 409, 421, 584n1; Mrs. (Augusta Mushbach), 27,n4
Kean, John, 90,n1, 200,n1, 219n2, 244, 249,n4, 260, 330, 346, 503
Kelly, Edmond, 174,n2, 175, 179
Kenny, Edward, 346,n15
Kent, Frank Richardson, 525,n1
Kern, John William, 587
Kerney, James, 23,n4, 31, 34-35, 35n1, 142n1, 542, 583n2
Kerr, John Thompson, 592,n1
Kidder, Peabody & Co., 40n1
Killingbeck, Wilson B., 267-69,n1, 288, 351-53, 386, 584n1
Kingsley, Darwin Pearl, 621-22,n1
Kinkead, Eugene Francis, 17, 19, 213, 249n3, 341
Knox, Andrew, 172,n1
Knox, Philander Chase, 615,n3

La Barre, George B., 54,n3, 167
labor and labor unions, 5, 45, 60-61, 63, 82-84, 85, 88, 89, 113, 114, 133, 141, 153-54, 179-80, 254-55, 280, 287-88, 297-98, 322-23, 335, 335n2, 336-37, 350, 392, 394, 395, 401, 425-26, 449, 463, 467, 468-69, 487-89, 491, 527, 553-54, 560, 567, 570
Labor Standard (Orange, N.J.), 55n1, 61n
Lafayette, N.J., 413
Lafayette College, 393
La Follette, Robert Marion, 343n11
Lakewood, N.J.: WW campaign speech, 325-26
La Monte, George Mason, 131, 361, 610; Mrs., 361
Lane, Franklin Knight, 586,n1
Lankering, Adolph, 295,n1
Lansing, Robert, 607,n1
Latané, John Holladay, 613,n1
Laverty, Edgar, 323

law and lawyers, 64-81
Lawrence, David, 608,n1
Lawrenceville School, 84
Laws of New Jersey, 340n1
Lea, Luke, 343n11
Learned, Florence J., 48,n1
Lebanon, N.J., 383
Lee House, Phillipsburg, N.J., 385
legislative committees, 473-74
Lehigh Valley Railroad, 403,n3, 499
Lethbridge, Edgar E., 346,n14
Letters of Grover Cleveland, 1850-1908 (ed. Nevins), 345n13
Lewis, Griffith Walker, 313n3
Lewis, Vivian Murchison, 7,n4, 20, 43, 62, 90, 114,n2, 158, 217, 219,n1, 226n1, 229, 230, 244, 249, 250, 265, 274, 293, 301, 311, 312, 313, 324, 329, 331, 335n2, 352, 370, 380, 390, 392, 393, 416, 443, 446-47, 452, 463, 485, 487, 495, 511, 520, 521, 526, 529, 549, 584n1, 586, 591
Libbey, William, 7:*176,n1; 229n1, 234
Library of Congress, 293
Lincoln, Abraham, 62n2, 161-62, 180, 196, 275n2, 292, 329, 330, 404,n4, 418, 425
Lincoln, Thomas (1853-1871), 162,n1
Lincoln, Neb., 622
Lindabury, Richard Vliet, 35n1, 140, 274, 354, 356, 378-79, 388, 449
Link, Arthur Stanley, 91n1
Lippincott, Job Herbert, 145-46, 274-75
Lizzie (caretaker at Dodge Lodge), 385
local option, 354
Lodge, Henry Cabot, 275n2
London: Dorchester House, 592
Long Branch, N.J., 218n7, 227; Ocean Park Casino, 228n1; WW campaign speech, 227-28
Long Branch Record, 299n2
Loomis, Francis Butler, 615,n7
Lorimer, William, 343-44,n11
Love, Thomas Bell, 584,n1
Lovett, Edgar Odell, 10:*552,n7; 159
Lowell, Abbott Lawrence, 5:*170n2; 109, 143, 580n1
Lowitt, Richard W., 344n12
Lucerne County, Pa., 211
Lyme (and Old Lyme), Conn., 4, 5, 13, 14, 15, 17, 22, 24, 25, 26, 34, 35, 36, 38, 39, 40, 41, 46, 50, 51, 53, 58, 59, 84, 87, 88, 107, 143, 225; Congregational Church, 84

McAdoo, William Gibbs, 108, 265, 298
McAlpin, Charles Williston, 13, 13-14, 49-50, 463, 471, 536-39; Mrs. (Sara Carter Pyle), 13,n3
McAneny, George, 617-18
McBride, Andrew Francis, M.D., 302
McCarter, Robert Harris, 1:*132,n3; 131-32
McCarter, Thomas Nesbitt, Jr., 27,n1, 139

McClellan, George Brinton (1826-1885), 86
McClellan, George Brinton, Jr. (Princeton 1886), 137, 599
McCombs, William Frank, 108, 294-95, 607
McCorkle, Walter Lee, 105,n1
McCormick, Cyrus Hall, Sr., Mrs. (Nettie Fowler), 541,n2, 543, 556
McCormick, Cyrus Hall, Jr. (1859-1936; Princeton 1879), 5:*767,n3; 10, 140, 152, 321, 353, 362n1, 385, 518-19, 543, 594-95
McCormick family, 492
McDermit, Frank M., 263n4
McFaul, James Augustine, 90,n4
McGill, Alexander Taggart, Jr., 343n9
McIlvaine, Anne, 53,n2, 54n1, 62
McIlvaine, William Brown, 10
McIntire, Michael F., 22,n1, 23
Mack, Norman Edward, 101, 102
MacKay, David L., 287-88, 297-98, 322-23, 336-37
McKenny, Luke, 335n2, 463
McKinley, William, 506
McMahon, Robert Fulton, 11
McMaster, John Bach, 609,n1
MacVeagh, Isaac Wayne, 152, 293-94, 320,n1
Madden, Walter, M.D., 23,n2, 219, 226, 232
Madison, N.J.: WW campaign speech, 525-26
Magie, William Francis, 1:*360,n6; 406
Magna Carta, 328, 438
Maine: Democratic landslide in 1910, 119,n1, 123, 128, 136
Maltbie, Milo Roy, 617,n3
manifest destiny, 317
Manuel II, King of Portugal, 439n1
Mara, Hugh, 487
Marburg, Theodore, 614-15,n1
Marelli, Henry, 301
Marshall, Edward, 477
Marshall, Erwin E., 106,n1, 167
Marshall, Howard, 324-25,n1
Marshall, Thomas Riley, 587, 603
Martin, William Parmenter, 313n3
Martine, James Edgar, 263,n4, 581-83,n2
Marx, Franklin, 86,n1
Maryland, 600
Mason, Alpheus Thomas, 546n3
Mason, Victor Louis, 586,n1
Massachusetts, 598, 608n2, 612; constitution, 500
Master of Manhattan: The Life of Richard Croker (Stoddard), 342n8
Mather, Sir William, 49
Maxwell, William Hunter, 161,n1, 617
Mercer County, N.J., 25n2, 34, 37n1,2, 39, 40, 90, 97, 104, 168, 219, 229, 349, 584n1; Democratic Committee, 97, 102, 103; Democratic League, 35n1n1

Meyers, James Cowden, 107-8,n1
Middle West: insurgents, 457-58
Middlesex County, N.J., 354, 412, 436, 560
Milod, James K., 564,n1
Milwaukee: City Club, 163n1; Pabst Theatre, 163n1
Minor, John Barbee, 1:*581,n3; 585n1
Minor, Raleigh Colston, 585,n1
Mitchell, Charles Wellman, M.D., 1:-*249,n4; 599
Mobus, Frank, 131
Modern Battles of Trenton (Sackett), 343n9
Monmouth County, N.J., 227, 324
Montclair, N.J.: Hillside Grammar School, 508; Montclair High School, 310; WW campaign speech, 508-18
Montclair Times, 169n1
Montgomery, John Alexander, 104,n1
Moore, John Bassett, 557-58,n1,2, 559
Moravians, 384
Morgan, John Pierpont I, 35n1
Morgan, Junius Spencer, 48
Morison, Elting Elmore, 252n6
Morley, John, 619
Morris, Roland Sletor, 584, 604
Morris Canal, 403,n3, 499
Morris County, N.J., 412, 525
Morristown, N.J.: Lyceum Theatre, 527,n1; WW campaign speech, 527-36
Morrow, William H., 383, 476-77,n1; Mrs. (Mary Wilhelmina Wychoff), 477,n3
Mowry, George Edwin, 158n1, 344n12
Murphy, Franklin, 90,n2, 212, 219n2, 346, 409, 503, 504
Mutual Life Insurance Co. of New York, 26, 51, 152,n2, 294
Myers, Gustavus, 343n10

Naegeli's Hotel, Hoboken, N.J., 295
Nashville, WW in, 114
Nation (New York), 322,n3
National Afro-American Council, 21n1, 275n3
National Association for the Advancement of Colored People, 275n1,3
National Colored Democratic League, 275n3
National Independent Political League of Colored Voters, 21n1, 47,n1, 275-n2,4,5, 387, 616
National Institute of Arts and Letters, 109,n2
Nebraska State Teachers Association, 600-1, 622
Negro-American Political League, 21n1, 275n1
Negroes, 21, 21n1, 28-29, 47, 47n1, 106, 156, 161, 162, 171-72, 183, 206, 238-39, 255, 275-76, 292, 333, 335n2, 387, 390, 392, 423, 583, 616
Nevins, Allan, 345n13

New Brunswick, N.J.: Opera House, 438; WW campaign speech, 436-41
New Brunswick Times, 541
New England College Presidents, 558
New England Suffrage League, 275n5
New Jersey: administrative reorganization, 94-95; Assembly, 313, 324, 372; automobile laws, 45, 96, 305; ballots, 262-63, 339, 407-8, 531-32, 567, 571; boss system, 303n2, 340, 346, 408, 411, 417, 420, 443, 458-59, 504, 506, 571; campaign contributions, 31; campaign expenses, 567; canals, 225, 359, 403; civil service, 45, 96, 505, 532, 567; coal-combine scandals, 343,n9, 345, 504; cold storage bill, 324; Commissioner of Roads, 234; commuters, 446, 449, 453, 516; conservation, 44, 88n3, 95, 126, 402, 505; constitution, 250; Corrupt Practices Act and corrupt practices, 45, 83n3, 96, 111, 126, 272, 313-14, 326, 332, 339-40, 359, 408, 420, 499, 504, 511, 567; County Board of Elections law, 340n1, 408; County Board of Taxation law, 264, 340n1; county clerks, 264; Democratic party, *see* Democratic party in New Jersey; direct nominations, 45, 96, 100; direct primaries, 31, 111, 126, 127, 258, 250,n10, 261-62, 307, 359, 420, 496-97, 505, 511, 521, 567, 582; eighthour law, 45, 95; election frauds and corruption, 345, 403; election laws, 326; electoral reform, 307; employers' liability, 31, 45, 95, 195, 256-57,n9, 280-81, 305, 307, 340, 408, 469-70, 489-90, 490-91, 497, 521, 553, 554, 561, 567; factory regulation, 521; Forestry Commission act, 505; gas companies, 312, 340, 341; Geran law, 340n1; Governor, 503-4, 573, 574; Governor's Mansion, 606,-n1; Governor's Secretary, 606-7; grand juries, 418, 531; Hahn Investigating Committee, 7,n3; Hillery maximum tax act, 340n2, 408; horse-racing and betting, 343n9; incorporation laws, 45, 88n3; inland lakes act, 505; inland waterway, 316, 324, 327; Legislature, 229, 230, 231, 234, 251, 303, 339, 343n9, 346, 347-48, 358, 360-61, 370, 374, 388, 475, 504, 523, 534, 548, 564, 573, 574, 581, 582, 605, 606; limited franchise act, 506; liquor laws and home rule, 45, 57, 63; machine government, 418; *Manual of the Legislature*, 369n3; *Minutes of the Votes and Proceedings of the 131st General Assembly*, 8n3; "mother of corporations," 100, 134, 204; natural resources, 44, 88-n3, 95, 505; ocean highway, 324; personal registration, 263; petit jury reform, 505; Pierce bill, 325; popular election of U.S. senators, 31, 263,

339, 348; Potable Water acts, 505; primary election officers, 262, 408; primary law, 123, 339, 407, 505, 533,n3; Public Service Commission, 44, 88, 93, 119, 196, 204, 207-8; public service corporations, 44, 88n3, 207n2, 228; Public Utilities Commission, 31, 42-43, 111, 207n2, 226, 233, 247, 263-64, 305, 311, 312, 316, 324, 325, 331, 339, 369n3, 407, 440, 495-96, 505, 561, 567, 571; racetrack scandals, 343,n9, 345, 504; railroads, 42-43, 63, 311-12, 340, 340n2, 402-3, 449,n1, 453, 571; railroad commission, 207,n2, 505; railroad tax acts, 504; rate-making, 307, 311-12, 324-25, 332; Register of Deeds, 264; registration laws, 325; Republican party, see Republican party in New Jersey; Robbins bill, 325; sanitation laws, 567; school fund, 44,n1, 95; Senate, 324, 504; sheriffs, 521; ship canal, 225; State Board of Assessors, 264; State Board of Riparian Commissioners, 264; State House Commission, 606; State Treasury, 521; State Water Supply Commission, 276, 277, 280; stock-watering act, 505; taxation and tax-system, 44, 95, 100, 257, 304, 375, 567, 568; trolleys, 226, 312, 340, 341; vote-buying, 167-68; U.S. Senators, 200-1, 263, 505, 581-83; water rights, 44, 88n3, 95; watersheds and water supply, 316, 341, 359, 402, 498-99, 516, 521, 567
New Jersey Car Advertising Co., 341n3
New Jersey Herald and Sussex County Democrat (Newton, N.J.), 405n
New Jersey Historical Society, 502n, 518n, 536n, 576n
New Jersey Progressivism before Wilson (Noble), 207,n2, 219n1, 256,n9,-10, 340n1, 533,n3
New Jersey State Federation of Labor, 55,n2, 56n1, 57, 59, 60, 82, 83, 256n9
New Nationalism, 322, 322n1, 337, 381
New Rochelle, N.Y.: People's Forum, 322-23, 335n2
New York Age, 239n1, 275n3
New York City: Belmont Hotel, 321, 362n1; Brayton Hotel, 164n1; Brick Presbyterian Church, 579,n2; Carnegie Hall, 320,n3; City Club, 617; Collingwood Hotel, 87; Hudson Terminal, 449; Lawyers' Club, 5n1, 356,n1; Madison Square Garden, 510; Madison Square Presbyterian Church, 621n1; robbery of poor, 483, 484; sight-seeing buses, 207; Southern Society, 105n1, 265, 298,n1; street railways, 343n10; Tammany Hall, 303n2, 342n8, 344n12, 523; University Club, 473; Waldorf-Astoria Hotel, 265, 621
New York Evening Journal, 85n1
New York *Evening Post*, 81,n1, 85,

168,n2, 274n, 320, 322n1, 377n, 381n, 385n1, 454n, 508n, 541, 555n, 618
New York *Evening Telegram*, 323
New York Herald (Paris edition), 166
New York Law School, 147,n3
New York Press, 180
New York state, 598; anti-racetrack legislation, 393; beet sugar manufacturers, 343n10; dairy interests, 343n10; insurance scandals, 341,n4, 392, 393, 399, 418; Legislature, 343-n10, *Report of the Joint Committee . . . to Investigate Corrupt Practices in Connection with Legislation, and the Affairs of Insurance Companies . . .*, 343n10; old guard Republicans, 252n6, 598; racetrack interests, 343n10; reformers, 360; street railway companies, 343n10; Superintendent of Insurance, 343n10
New York *Sun*, 225-26, 287, 299, 335-n2, 493n
New York Times, 98, 101n, 124n3, 362n1, 485n, 519
New York *World*, 5,n1, 85, 134-36, 148
Newark, 146, 171; Krueger Auditorium, 202n1, 564; Presbytery, 367; WW campaign speeches, 202-12, 412, 564-76
Newark Evening News, 5, 6, 40n1, 53, 56,n1, 125, 128, 175n1,3, 176, 212n, 219n1, 288n, 290n1, 306n, 310n, 340n1, 361n, 388, 388-89, 396n, 413n, 433n, 449,n1, 450, 492n1, 505, 521n, 541, 541n2, 561, 582
Newark Evening Star, 17,n1, 541
Newton, N.J.: Newton Public School, 396; WW campaign speech, 396-405, 413; Woodrow Wilson Club, 396n2
Niagara Movement, 21n1
Nichols, Isaac T., 277
Noble, Ransom Elwood, Jr., 207,n2, 219n1, 256n9,10, 340n1, 533,n3
Noonan, Joseph M., 42n1, 42-43, 54-55, 56, 58, 63-64, 85-86, 108, 265-66
Norris, George William, 344n12
North American Review, 557,n2
Northcliffe, Alfred Charles William Harmsworth, Viscount, 482,n1, 484
Norton, Charles Dyer, 124,n2,3, 132
Nowrey, Joseph E., 421,n2
Nugent, James Richard, 106-7, 141, 142, 173, 243, 261, 290-91, 290n1, 292, 296, 345, 347, 361, 367, 378, 388, 389, 409, 503, 577,n1

Oakland, N.J., 43
Ocean County, N.J.: WW campaign speeches, 325-27
O'Connell, Joseph L., 239-41
Ogdensburg, N.J., 413
Ohio, 598, 608n2
Old Lyme, Conn., *see* Lyme, Conn.
Orange, N.J.: Columbus Hall, 520; WW campaign speech, 520-21

Oranges, N.J., 171, 412
Order of Foresters of America, 452n1
Oregon, 608n2; Oregon law, 141,n2
Ormond, Alexander Thomas, 6:*528,-n2; 603-4
Osborn, William Church, 172
Osborne, Harry V., 520
Osborne, Thomas Mott, 47
Osler, Sir William, M.D., 618,n1
Ossining, N.Y., 38
Outlook (New York), 243,n2, 244n2, 620n1
Oxford, N.J.: WW campaign speech, 384

Page, Arthur Wilson, 6n2
Page, Thomas Nelson, 602
Page, Walter Hines, 2:*96,n4; 5-6, 576, 579
Palmer, Alexander Mitchell, 604,n1
Palmer, Stephen Squires, 362n1, 385
Parker, Alfred L., 24,n1
Parker, Alton Brooks, 5,n2, 322,n1
Parker, Theodore, 519, 543
Parkhurst, Charles Henry, 621,n1
party government, 223
Passaic, N.J., 133, 154; Passaic High School, 493, 507; WW campaign speech, 493-502
Passaic County, N.J., 7, 264, 380, 412, 584n1
Passaic Daily News, 541
Passaic River, 497-98, 567
Paterson, N.J., 153, 158; Paterson National Bank, 43; Paterson Opera House, 301; WW campaign speech, 301-6
Paterson Guardian, 158, 158n1, 281n, 541
Paterson News, 541
Patterson, Samuel Alexander, 328,n2
Patton, Francis Landey, 3:*114,n3; 26,n1
Payne, Sereno Elisha, 175
Payne, W. C., 616,n1
Payne-Aldrich tariff, 126, 175, 194, 219, 252, 255, 275, 327n1, 369n3, 456, 521, 565, 608n2
Peck, Mary Allen Hulbert (Mrs. Thomas Harbach Hulbert; Mrs. Thomas Dowse Peck), 17:*29,n1; 26, 38-39, 48, 50-51, 64, 163-64
Pennsylvania: politics, 446, 545; Supreme Court, 342n7
Pennsylvania, University of: students, 421
Pennsylvania Magazine of History and Biography, 342n6
Pennsylvania Railroad, 290, 312, 403,-n3
People Awakened: The Story of Woodrow Wilson's First Campaign (Bacon), 220n1
Periodical Publishers' Association, 620-21
Perry, Bliss, 8:*179,n3; 406

Perth Amboy, N.J., 544f; Donahoe Auditorium, 543n1, 560; WW campaign speech, 543-55
Perth Amboy News, 541
Peterson, Magnus Fraser, 619-20,n1
Petigru, James Louis, 424,n4
Phi Kappa Psi fraternity, 105
Philadelphia, 567; Bellevue-Stratford Hotel, 558; Democratic Club, 584, 604; Durham ring, 172,n2, 342,n6; gang methods, 551; gas scandal, 342,n6; United Gas Improvement Co., 342n6; WW in, 421
Philadelphia & Reading Railroad Co., 343n9
Philadelphia Negro (DuBois), 275n3
Philadelphia *North American*, 9,n1,2, 158, 164, 165, 198-99, 243, 267,n1,4
Philadelphia Record, 191n, 218n, 220-n1, 221, 225, 243, 267n4, 287n, 320n, 385n1, 421n, 441, 449n, 476n, 502n, 518, 541, 555n, 564n, 576n
Phillipsburg, N.J., 383; Lee House, 385; Ortygian Hall, 382, 390; WW campaign speech, 390-96
Pinchot, Gifford, 546n3
Pitney, Mahlon, 1:*360,n5; 16, 20, 27, 434,n1
Pittsburgh: city councils, 342n7; graft and bribery, 342n7; Voters' League, 342n7; WW in, 623
Pittsfield, Mass.: Elmwood Court, 48-n1; Wednesday Morning Club, 48,n5
Plainfield, N.J., 173; Reform Club Hall, 193,n1; WW campaign speech, 193-98
Platonists, 618
Platt, Dan Fellows, 11-12,n1, 22, 36, 41, 52, 56-57, 58, 140-42, 149, 172-73, 436
Pleasantville, N.J.: WW campaign speech, 325
Plunkitt, George Washington, 303,n2; *Plunkitt of Tammany Hall . . .* (Riordan), 303n2
Poe, Edgar Allan (Princeton 1891), 600,n1
Political Education of Woodrow Wilson (Kerney), 583n2
political organizations, 523
political parties, 372f, 501-2, 530-33, 534
Poole, Monroe Van Brackle, 324
Port Reading, N.J., 560
Port Reading Railroad Co., 343n9
Porter, James Jackson, 16,n2
Portugal: politics, 439,n1
Power and Responsibility: The Life and Times of Theodore Roosevelt (Harbaugh), 148n1
Princeton, N.J., 13, 323; Dodge Lodge, 385,n2, 591; First Presbyterian Church, 597n1; Morven, 606n1; Mrs. Wright's boarding house, 132,n1; Trinity Church, 117n1
Princeton Press, 84n, 541

PRINCETON UNIVERSITY

see also Wilson, Woodrow,
PRINCETON UNIVERSITY

Albert Baldwin Dod Hall, 169; alumni, 81-82, 149; alumni trustees, 39,n1; American Whig Society (1:*75,n1), 170; Chancellor Green Library, 364; Class of 1910, 98, 102, *1910 Locomotive*, 98n, 102; Class of 1914, 169; Cleveland Tower, 434; Cliosophic Society (1:*75,n1), 170; *Daily Princetonian*, 169, 171n, 178n, 471n; Department of Classics, 30; exclusion of black students, 171-72; faculty, 434, 537; Graduate College: controversy mentioned, 3, 25, Golf Links site, 434, William Cooper Proctor offer, 12, Isaac Chauncey Wyman bequest, 12, 36; Graduate Department, 538; Isabella McCosh Infirmary, 587n1; McCormick Professorship of Jurisprudence and Politics, 471, 492, 493, 538-39, 577; Marquand Chapel, 151; Murray-Dodge Hall (7:*61n1), 169, 176; Musical Clubs, 170; *Nassau Literary Magazine*, 16, 16,n4, 33n; Opening exercises, Sept. 22, 1910, 151-52; Philadelphian Society (7:*61,n1), 169, 170, 176; Preceptorial System, 537; Press Club, 16; Princeton Alumni Wilson League, 82n1; Prospect, 125, 167, 225, 289, 362n1, 385, 385n1, 412, 435, 539; Quadrangle plan, 623; Trustees, 39, 100, 136, 143, 146, 149, 166, 353, 362, 362n1, 377-78, 385n1, 434, 492, 577, 605, 623, Committee on Curriculum, 539, resolution on WW resignation, 536-39, 556,n1, minutes quoted, 364-66; Western Association of Princeton Clubs, 623n2; Wilson's resignation, *see* Wilson, Woodrow, PRINCETON UNIVERSITY, *resignation as president*; Yale football game, Oct. 12, 1910, 556,n4; Princeton University mentioned, 3, 6, 10, 11, 12, 14, 16, 21, 22, 24, 25, 27,n2, 30, 31n1, 36, 39, 49, 53, 55, 55n2, 81, 82, 86-88, 89, 90, 100, 104, 108, 109, 111, 112, 116, 121, 122, 129, 130, 132, 134, 136, 137n1, 141, 146, 147, 149, 151, 153, 154-55, 160, 166-67, 169, 169-71, 171, 174, 178, 193, 201, 238, 289-90, 301, 334, 336, 362, 362n1, 367, 369, 377-78, 406, 412, 434, 452, 478, 480, 483, 492, 520, 522, 555, 587, 592, 595, 602, 603, 605, 614, 617, 623

End of Princeton entry

Pritchett, Henry Smith, 20, 39-40, 160, 492-93, 540, 596-97

Procter, William Cooper, 362n1, 385, 434-35; Mrs. (Jane Eliza Johnson), 434, 435

progress, 510-11

Progressive Voters of Labor, 335n2, 463

Progressives and Progressive party, 344,n12, 447-48, 449, 547

Promise of American Life (Croly), 322

protection, *see* tariff

Providence, R.I., Central Congregational Church, 4n1

Prussia: Ministry of Education, 48n4

public domain, 242

Pulitzer, Joseph, 595

Pyne, Moses Taylor (Momo), 5:*132,-n2; 152, 353, 362n1, 366, 385, 385n1, 434-35, 435,n1,2, 444; Mrs. (Margaretta Stockton), 435

Ragan, Adolphus, 14,n1

railroads, 42-43, 63, 126, 134, 242, 311-12, 340n2, 402-3, 449,n1, 453, 571

Reid, Whitelaw, 592,n2, 615

Repp, Charles A., 584n1

Reading Railroad, 560

Record, George Lawrence, 244n2, 249,-n3, 258n10, 259, 274, 275, 290, 290-n1, 291, 293, 296, 297, 338-47, 348, 379n1, 380, 406-11, 412, 415-16, 433n1, 435, 436, 442, 443, 449, 450, 451, 453, 457, 464, 503, 580, 596

Records of the Federal Convention of 1787 (ed. Farrand), 309n2

Red Bank, N.J.: Frick Lyceum, 213,n1; WW campaign speech, 213-18

Reform of Legal Procedure (Storey), 386n2

reformers, 360

Reilly, Peter E., 487

Republican party and Republicans, 9, 21, 21n1, 46, 88n3, 96, 124, 125, 126, 129, 141, 145, 174, 183, 185, 194, 197, 211, 212, 214, 215, 218, 219, 223, 227, 248-49, 253, 256, 272, 276n2, 284, 292, 300, 329, 330, 339, 342n6, 343n11, 344n12, 357, 367, 427, 431n6, 432, 448, 454, 474, 501, 535, 565, 591, 598, 603, 608n2, 621

Republican party and Republicans in California, 447

Republican party and Republicans in Kansas, 248, 447

Republican party and Republicans in Maine, 447

Republican party and Republicans in New Hampshire, 447

Republican party and Republicans in New Jersey, 7, 7n4,7, 9, 11, 16, 18, 19, 20, 23, 27, 37, 50, 57, 107, 114, 161, 168, 214, 217, 219n1, 226, 231, 232, 235, 236, 240, 241, 244, 244n2, 247-50, 251, 252, 255, 258, 259, 260-61, 272, 273, 275, 278-79, 283, 284-87, 290n1, 293, 303, 311, 312-13, 314, 315, 324, 326, 327, 329, 331, 343n9, 345-48, 351, 352, 354, 357-59, 369-70, 369n3, 380, 388, 389, 390, 392, 393, 394, 395, 396, 398, 404, 409, 411, 413, 416, 418, 419, 420,

Republican party and Republicans in New Jersey cont.
424, 426, 427, 429, 430, 431, 438, 441, 446, 447, 448, 449, 457, 458, 461, 491, 495, 503-5, 510, 511, 520, 521, 529, 530, 545, 547-49, 552-53, 561, 566, 568-69, 572, 584n1; "Board of Guardians", 219,n2, 226, 230-31, 266, 272, 301, 303, 303-4, 315, 346-47, 347, 359, 378-79, 380, 408-9, 429, 443, 503; card index of expected campaign contributors, 226, 232; insurgents, 447; New Idea progressive Republicans, 7,n7, 19, 172, 214,n3, 219n1, 256n9, 275, 297, 301, 346, 347, 380, 409, 510
Republican party and Republicans in New York State, 252n6, 598
Republican party and Republicans in Ohio, 248
Republican party and Republicans in Pennsylvania, 608n2
Review of Reviews (New York), 175, 300,n1,2,3
Revolution, American, 369, 482, 517-18
Richmond, Archibald Murray, 146,n1
Richmond, Charles Alexander, 146
Richmond (Va.) *Times-Dispatch*, 539,-n2
Riordan, William L., 303n2
Roebling, John Augustus II, 450,n1
Roebling, Washington Augustus, 450n1
Rogers, G. Tracy, 343n10
Rogers, James Slocum, 153,n1
Roman Catholic Church and Catholic voters, 180, 319, 541-42
Rome, 428
Romeo and Juliet (Shakespeare), 335-n2
Roosevelt, Theodore, 47n1, 124, 129, 132, 136, 147,n1, 154, 160, 176, 252-n6, 275n2, 284,n3, 294, 322, 322n1, 475, 563, 584n1, 591, 598, 599, 609-n1, 621
Roosevelt Borough, N.J., 560
Root, Elihu, 166, 615, 615n2
Rothwell, Laura P., Mrs., 115
Rowe, Leo Stanton, 614,n1
Roxbury, N.J., 385
Ruef, Abraham, 342,n5
Russell, Charles Edward, 342n7
Rutgers College, 438; Alumni Association, 620
Rutherford, N.J., 141, 608; Town Hall, 446; WW campaign speech, 412, 446-49

Sackett, Clarence, 502n, 518n, 536n
Sackett, William E., 343n9
St. Hubert's, N.Y., 13,n4, 49-50
St. John, William W., 581-83,n1
Salem, N.J., 463; Grand Opera House, 423,n1, 463; WW campaign speech, 423-33, mentioned, 412, 463
Salem County, N.J., 584n1
Salem Sunbeam, 463

Salmon, Edward Seiler, 105-6,n1
Salter, Harry Broughton, 226,n1
San Francisco: traction graft, 341-42,-n5
Scarboro, N.Y., 38
Schirmer, Rudolph Edward, 617
Schmitz, Eugene E., 342n5
Schurman, Jacob Gould, 611,n1
Scotland: self-government, 439
Scott, William H., 21n1
Scribner, Charles (Princeton 1875), 104, 144
Scudder, Edward Wallace, 175-76,n1, 388-89, 449,n1, 450
Scully, Michael Welsh, 131,n1
Scully, Thomas Joseph, 213,n2
Seaview, Wash., 12
Seventy Years of the Red-Fire Wagon from Tilden to Truman Through New Freedom and New Deal (Guffey), 623n
Seymour, Arthur B., 520
Seymour, Horatio, 335
Shafer, Robert, 16,n5
Shakespeare, William, 335n2
Shall We Work or Be Worked? Being an Appeal to the Colored Republican Voters of Essex County . . ., 161n2
Shallenberger, Ashton Cokayne, 622,n1
Sharpe, John C., 476,n2
Shaw, Albert, 3:*214,n1; 300
Shaw, William B., 300
Shea, Joseph Bernard, 81-82
Sheldon, Edward Wright, 1:*240,n7; 143, 298, 353, 362n1, 385n1, 594
Sherman, James Schoolcraft, 252n6
Sherman Antitrust act, 505
Silzer, George Sebastian, 7,n2, 35n1, 37n1, 97, 436, 585n1
Smith, Chatford, 421
Smith, James, Jr., 7, 23, 27, 34, 35, 40n1, 52, 57, 62, 88,n4, 90, 99, 141, 142, 200,n1, 261, 345, 345n13, 347, 348, 349, 367, 378, 388, 409, 503, 590
Snitcher, Harriet Peck, 48,n6, 50
Snyder, J. M., 383
Socialists, Socialism, 63, 268, 352-53, 386-87, 440, 584n1
Somerset County, N.J., 354, 610; Democratic Committee, 131
Somerville, N.J., 361, 380; Armory, 354; WW campaign speech, 354-61
Sons of the Revolution, 482
Souls of Black Folk (DuBois), 275n3
Source of His "Wisdom," 335n2
South, The, 335n2
Sparta, N.J., 413
Speer, Robert Elliott, 334,n1
Speyer, James Joseph, 48n4
Sprigg, James Cresap, 62-63, 309, 310
Springfield Republican, 35
statesmanship, 461-62
Steck, David W., 17n
Sterling (of Lyme, Conn.) 52n1

Steuert, Frederick A., 594
Stevens, Edwin Augustus, 150n1, 198, 601; Mrs. (Martha Bayard Dod), 150n1
Stewart, George Black, 367,n2
Stewart, John Aikman (1822-1926), 7:*602,n1; 362n1, 364, 366, 434, 435
Stimson, Henry Lewis, 252n6, 591,n1
stock-watering, 99
Stockbridge, Frank Parker, 309n, 309-n2, 320n, 334n, 433n, 462n, 502n, 536n, 555n, 576n
stockings, 216
Stockton, Bayard (Princeton 1872), 131
Stoddard, Lothrop, 342n8
Stokes, Edward Casper, 90,n3, 219n2, 263,n5, 277, 293, 346, 409, 503, 503-7, 584n1
Stone, Melville Elijah, 243,n1, 245
Storey, Moorfield, 386,n1,2
Stoy, Franklin Pierce, 47,n2
Stratton, Morris Hancock, 423,n2
Straus, Isidor, 18n1, 613,n1
Straus, Nathan, 18,n1, 613
Straus, Oscar Solomon, 18n1
Street Railway Association of the State of New York, 343n10
Strong, Theodore, 260,n2, 378
Study in Boss Politics: William Lorimer of Chicago (Tarr), 343n11
Sugar Trust, 206, 304,n3
Sullivan, George Hammond, 541,n1, 543
Sullivan, Mark Anthony, 19,n5, 57, 346,n15, 433
Sullivan, Roger Charles, 99, 584
Sulzer, William, 616
Suppression of the African Slave-Trade to the United States of America, 1638-1870 (DuBois), 275n3
Sussex Borough, N.J., WW campaign speech, mentioned, 413
Sussex County, N.J., 396, 404, 413, 569
Sweny, William H., 59
Swift, Jonathan, 253, 317

Taft, William Howard, 21n1, 47n1, 115, 124,n3, 132, 175, 251, 252, 253, 275n2, 284n3, 454, 456, 468, 475, 546n3, 573, 608n2, 615, 615n2, 621
Talcott, Charles Andrew, 1:*240,n3; 298, 338, 578, 583, 590, 591
Tammany Hall, 303n2, 342n8, 344n12, 523
tariff, 46, 88n3, 96, 175, 194, 196-97, 206, 214-16, 251, 253-56, 280, 327, 327n1, 338, 344n12, 345n13, 454, 456, 468, 474, 475, 521, 525, 530, 557, 612
Tarr, John Arthur, 343n11
Tarrytown, N.Y., 38
Theodore Roosevelt and the Progressive Movement (Mowry), 148n1, 344n12
Thompson, Henry Burling (Princeton 1877), 49, 104, 138, 299, 385n1,

435, 435n2, 593; Mrs. (Mary Wilson), 593,n1
Thompson, Henry Dallas (Princeton 1885), 606
Thompson, Samuel Huston, Jr., 130, 149
Thompson, Suzanne Dawes, 13,n2
Thorpe, James Francis, 53n1
Tocqueville, Alexis Charles Henri Maurice Clérel de, 512
Toms River, N.J., WW campaign speech, 325-26
Toronto, 341
Townsend, Edward Waterman, 521,n1
Trenton, 25, 33, 167, 226, 228, 430; Central Labor Union, 23n1; Democratic League, 24n1; Green properties, 606; Masonic Hall, 351n1; Taylor Opera House, 91n1, 104, 229; Trenton Fair, 217; WW campaign speech, 229-38
Trenton Evening Times, 23,n1,4, 26,-n2, 31, 52, 53, 54,n1, 55n2, 91n, 94n, 100n, 120, 125n, 142n1, 191n, 198n, 238n, 541, 582, 590n
Trenton State Gazette, 62
Trenton Sunday Advertiser, 34,n1
Trenton True American, 5, 9, 16n, 22, 23, 24n, 24, 26,n2, 28n3, 33-34, 37,-n1, 40, 54, 58, 61n, 62n2, 94n, 96n, 120n, 152n, 181n, 259n, 290n, 327, 351n, 433n, 527n, 584n1
trolleys, 226, 312, 341, 343n10
Trotter, William Monroe, 21n1, 275,n5
Trowbridge, Augustus, 13
trusts, 45, 60, 268, 269, 426
Tucker, William Jewett, 31,n1
Tuckerton, N.J., WW campaign speech, 326
Tumulty, Joseph Patrick, 19,n6, 141, 346,n15, 433, 589
Turmoil and Tradition: A Study of the Life and Times of Henry L. Stimson (Morison), 252n6
Turner, Frederick Jackson, 6:*58,n1; 602
Tuttle, William T., 383
Twentieth Century Socialism . . . (Kelly), 174,n2, 175, 179

Union County, N.J., 83, 464
United States: Confederation, 73; Congress, 358, 454, 474, 505, 564, 573, 596; Constitution, 250, 505; Corrupt Practices act, 96; Department of State, 518; flag, 120; House of Representatives, 344n12, 345n13, 454, 456, 608n2; Industrial Commission Report, 323; Interstate Commerce Commission, 496; President, 573; Senate, 343,n11, 345n13, 348, 349, 388, 407, 454, 456, 475, 582, 608n2, Committee on Finance, 474, direct election of senators, 31, 88n3, 96, 126, 204, 263, 339, 348; Supreme Court, 69, 147-48,n1

United States Indian Industrial School, Carlisle, Pa., 53,n1
universities, 305

Vance, Zebulon Baird, 423
Vanderlip, Frank Arthur, 38, 59; Mrs. (Narcissa Cox), 38
van Dyke, Henry [Jackson, Jr.], 10:-*9,n2; 16,n4,5
Van Syckel, Bennet, 274,n1
Van Valkenburg, Edwin Augustus, 9,-n1, 158, 164-65, 198-200, 241-42, 267
Vick, Walker Whiting, 115-16,n1, 608
Villard, Oswald Garrison, 58-59, 618
Virginia, University of, 595, 597-98
Virginia State Bar Association, 117
Voice of Independence, 616,n2
Voorhees, Foster, 277, 378
Vreeland, Williamson Updike, 154-55

Waldorf-Astoria Hotel, New York City, 265, 621
Waldron, John Milton, 21n1, 275,n1,3, 292, 387
Wall Street and "the interests," 5, 29, 55n2, 98-99, 335n2, 554
Walters, Alexander, 21n1, 47n1, 275,-n2,4
Wanamaker, John, 431n6, 601
Wanamaker, [Lewis] Rodman, 267,n4
Wanamaker, Thomas Brown, 267,n2,4; Mrs. (Mary Lowber Welsh), 267,n3
Ware, Henry Burt, 463,n1
Warren County, N.J., 382-85
Washington, Booker Taliaferro, 21n1, 275n3,5
Washington, George, 138, 180, 184, 196, 309, 404,n4, 425, 480, 518, 598
Washington (D.C.) *Evening Star*, 275-n2
Washington (D.C.) *Herald*, 275n2, 387n1
Washington (D.C.) *Post*, 275n2, 615n2
Washington, N.J., 382-83; Baker's Hotel, 383; WW campaign speech, mentioned, 383
Watson, Gertrude, 48,n1
Watterson, Henry, 433, 435
Weaver, John, 342n6
Webster, James Edwin, 1:*249,n2; 555,n5
Weehawken, N.J., 43
Welch, William Henry, M.D., 129-30
Werts, George Theodore, 258n10, 343n9
Wescott, John Wesley, 103,n1, 137, 152, 421, 604
West, Andrew Fleming, 6:*528,n3; 13, 25, 36
West, Oswald, 608n2
West Hoboken, N.J.: St. Michael's Hall, 473; WW campaign speech, mentioned, 473
West New York, N.J.: St. Joseph's Hall, 473; WW campaign speech, mentioned, 473
White, Charles A., 343n11
whitewashed men, 480

Whitlock, Brand, 607,n1
Wilder, William Royal, 1:*253,n2; 129, 150
Wildwood, N.J.: Hippodrome, 281n1, 283; WW campaign speech, 281-87
Wilhelm II, Emperor of Germany, 48
Wilkes-Barre, Pa., 211
Wilkins, Walter Maurice, 98,n1, 102
Williams, John Sharp, 557,n1
Williams College, 421, 558, 559n1
Williamson, Edgar, 55-56,n1, 59-61, 61n1, 83, 85, 89, 115, 180
Wilmington, N.C.: First Presbyterian Church, 115
Wilson, Alice, niece of WW, 115
Wilson, Edwin Clinton, 162n1; Mrs. (Elizabeth McCalmont), 161
Wilson, Eleanor Randolph (*afterwards* Mrs. William Gibbs McAdoo), daughter of WW and EAW, 6:*407,n1; 225
Wilson, Ellen Axson (Mrs. Woodrow Wilson I), 10, 13, 49, 84, 101, 107, 130, 146, 167, 225, 378, 385, 519, 588, 589n1, 592, 594, 595, 600, 602, 606, 609, 611
Wilson, James (1787-1850), grandfather of WW, 223
Wilson, John Adams, first cousin of WW, 8:*427-28,n1; 161-62
Wilson, Joseph R., Jr., brother of WW, 1:*3,n8; 114-15; Mrs. (Kate Wilson), 115
Wilson, Joseph Ruggles, father of WW, 1:*3,n1; 223; Mrs. (Janet Woodrow), 1:*3,n1,2, 225, 478
Wilson, William Lawrence, 20-21,n1
Wilson, William Lyne, 345n13

WOODROW WILSON

APPEARANCE

There is something in his makeup that suggests the timber of which superior men are made, 124

The President of Princeton . . . is an old-young man, 134

He has what is sometimes called "a strong face." The brow is both high and broad, the eyes deep set, the nose long and the mouth quite straight and not very large . . . , 135

When you look at the face in profile it is decidedly aquiline . . . The mouth is large and full-lipped, but drawn into a straight, firm line. When he smiles he shows fine, large teeth. The eyes are blue-gray, clear and penetrating, undimmed by the glasses, 220

His cheek bones are high, like a Multnomah Indian's, and he runs to chin excessively, 478

. . . not even a campaign manager would try for women's votes for him with the announcement that the man is handsome, 479

Woodrow Wilson, cont.
His eyes are gray, shrewd and calm.
Sometimes they twinkle, 525

HEALTH

Mr. Wilson has stood the work of campaigning wonderfully well, 412

INTERVIEWS

6n2, 14-16, 17,n1, 31, 34, 35, 98-100, 120-28, 133-36, 179-81, 220-25, 477-85, 522-25

OPINIONS AND COMMENTS

his philosophy of education, 32-33
always the warm friend of organized labor, 60-61
Publicity is one of the purifying elements of politics. The best thing that you can do with anything that is crooked is to lift it up where people can see that it is crooked, and then it will either straighten itself out or disappear, 232-33
I come of a Scotch-Irish stock that cannot help fighting to save its life. I always think I am right, and although I try to be courteous to the men I differ from, I am always sure they are wrong . . . , 250

POLITICAL CAREER

Candidacy and nomination for governor of New Jersey, 3, 5, 6, 7, 8, 9, 10, 11, 12, 13, 14-30, 31, 33-38, 39-46, 49-50, 52-64, 81-91
Nominated for governor by the Democratic State Convention, Sept. 15, 1910, Taylor Opera House, Trenton, 91n1
Speech accepting the Democratic gubernatorial nomination, 91-94, 118-20
Platform of the New Jersey Democratic party, Sept. 15, 1910, 87-88,n3, 89, 91, 94-96, 99, 139 (proposed platform, 43-46)
Congratulatory messages upon nomination for governor: from Archibald Stevens Alexander, 112-14; Caroline Bayard Stevens Alexander, 150; Charles Dexter Allen, 168; Alfred Brittin Baker, 117; Simeon Eben Baldwin, 133; Clarence Hughson Baxter, 158; Edward William Bok, 118; Robert Gunn Bremner, 133; Robert Bridges, 298; Herbert Bruce Brougham, 97-98; Edward Capps, 166-67; Hunsdon Cary, 117-18; Edwin Grant Conklin, 116-17; Richard Heath Dabney, 138; Joseph Albert Dear, Jr., 116; Arthur Granville Dewalt, 103; Clinton Roy Dickinson,

Woodrow Wilson, cont.
169; Cleveland Hoadley Dodge, 112; Joseph Dorsey, 156; James Fairman Fielder, 97; Henry Burchard Fine, 112; Christian Frederick Gauss, 111; William Cavanagh Gebhardt, 110-11; Otis Allan Glazebrook, 98; Charles Henry Grasty, 102; Samuel Allen Harlow, 110; Azel Washburn Hazen, 107; Joseph Stanislaus Hoff, 97, 102-3; William Hughes, 145; Melancthon Williams Jacobus, 109, 142-43; Robert Underwood Johnson, 109; David Benton Jones, 132; Harry Pratt Judson, 144-45; Edward Lawrence Katzenbach, 132; Frank Snowden Katzenbach, Jr., 96; Richard Vliet Lindabury, 140; Job Herbert Lippincott, 145-46; Edgar Odell Lovett, 159; Abbott Lawrence Lowell, 109; William Gibbs McAdoo, 108; Robert Harris McCarter, 131-32; Thomas Nesbitt McCarter, Jr., 139; William Frank McCombs, 108; Walter Lee McCorkle, 105; Cyrus Hall McCormick, 140; Norman Edward Mack, 102; Isaac Wayne MacVeagh, 152; William Francis Magie, 406; Erwin E. Marshall, 106; James Cowden Meyers, 107-8; John Alexander Montgomery, 104; Franklin Murphy, 212; Joseph M. Noonan, 108; James Richard Nugent, 106-7; William Church Osborn, 155-56; Bliss Perry, 406; Dan Fellows Platt, 140-42; Henry Smith Pritchett, 160; Charles Alexander Richmond, 146; Edward Seiler Salmon, 105-6; Charles Scribner, 104; Michael Welsh Scully, 131; Bayard Stockton, 131; Henry Burling Thompson, 104; Samuel Huston Thompson, Jr., 130; Walker Whiting Vick, 115-16; Williamson Updike Vreeland, 154-55; William Henry Welch, 129-30; William Royal Wilder, 129; Walter Maurice Wilkins and the Class of 1910, 98; Edgar Williamson, 115; John Adams Wilson, 161-62; Joseph R. Wilson, Jr., 114-15; Henry Otto Wittpenn, 155; Charles Albert Woods, 128; Lawrence Crane Woods, 157-58
Campaign speeches: Jersey City: Die Wilde Gans Club, Sept. 20, 1910; news report, 147-48; mentioned, 128,-n1
Speech opening his campaign, Jersey City: St. Peter's Hall, Sept. 28; text, 181-91; mentioned, 199,n1, 265, 564
Jersey City: St. Patrick's Hall, Sept. 28; mentioned, 191n1, 239
Jersey City: Grand View Hall, Sept. 28; mentioned, 191n1
Plainfield: Reform Club Hall, Sept. 29; text, 193-98

Woodrow Wilson, cont.

Newark: Krueger Auditorium, Sept. 30; text, 202-12

Red Bank: Frick Lyceum, Oct. 1; text, 213-18; mentioned, 227,n2

Long Branch: Ocean Park Casino, Oct. 1; news report, 227-28

Trenton: Taylor Opera House, Oct. 3; text, 229-38; mentioned, 243, 260, 267, 274

Woodbury: Green's Opera House, Oct. 5; text, 245-59; mentioned, 243

Burlington: Auditorium, Oct. 6; news report, 269-74

Bridgeton: Criterion Theatre, Oct. 7; news report, 276-81; mentioned, 287-88, 322, 336

Cape May Court House, Oct. 8; news report, 281-87

Wildwood: Hippodrome, Oct. 8; news report, 281-87

Paterson: Paterson Opera House, Oct. 11; news report, 301-6

Caldwell: birthplace of Grover Cleveland, Oct. 12; news report, 309-10; mentioned, 309n3

Caldwell: Monomonock Inn, Oct. 12; transcript, 306-9

Atlantic City: Steeple Chase Pier Theatre, Oct. 13; transcript, 310-20; mentioned, 310n1

Ocean County: Pleasantville, Tuckerton, Lakewood, Toms River, Oct. 14; news report, 325-27

Asbury Park: Hippodrome, Oct. 15; transcript, 328-34; mentioned, 320, 338

Freehold: Armory Opera House, Oct. 15; mentioned, 320, 334,n4

Remarks to Democratic leaders of Mercer County, Masonic Hall, Trenton, Oct. 18; news report, 349-51,n1

Bound Brook: home of G. M. La Monte, Oct. 19; news report, 354-61

Somerville: Armory, Oct. 19; news report, 354-61

Flemington: Opera House and Court House, Oct. 20; news reports, 369-77, 377n4, 381

Warren County, Oct. 21; news report, 382-85

Washington, N.J.: Baker's Hotel, Oct. 21; news report, 383

Hackettstown: American House, Oct. 21; news report, 383-84

Blairstown: Blairstown Hotel, Oct. 21; news report, 384

Hope: Village Green, Oct. 20; news report, 384

Oxford: Allen's Drugstore, Oct. 20; news report, 384

Belvidere: Court House, Oct. 20; news report, 384-85

Woodrow Wilson, cont.

Phillipsburg: Ortygian Hall, Oct. 21; news report, 390-96

Newton: Newton Public School, Oct. 22; news report, 396-405

Camden: Temple Theatre, Broadway Theatre, Oct. 24; news report, 413-21

Salem: Grand Opera House, Oct. 25; transcript, 423-33; mentioned, 412, 463

New Brunswick: Opera House, Oct. 26; news report, 436-41; mentioned, 412

Bergen County: Rutherford, Englewood, and Hackensack, Oct. 27; news report, 446-49; mentioned, 412

Hackensack: Second Regiment Armory, Oct. 27; news report, 452-54; mentioned, 412

Elizabeth: Proctor's Theatre, Oct. 28; transcript, 454-62; mentioned, 412

Elizabethport: St. Patrick's Parish Hall, Oct. 28; news report, 465-70

Hudson County: West Hoboken, West New York, Hoboken, Oct. 29; news report, 471-76; mentioned, 412

Bayonne: Democratic Club, Oct. 31; news report, 485-92; mentioned, 412

Jersey City: St. John's Hall, Oct. 31; mentioned, 492n1

Passaic: Passaic High School, Nov. 1; transcript, 493-502; mentioned, 507

Carlstadt, Nov. 1; news report, 507-8; mentioned, 502n3

Montclair: Hillside Grammar School, Nov. 3; transcript, 508-18; mentioned, 520

Orange: Columbus Hall, Nov. 2; news report, 520-21

Madison, Nov. 3; news report, 525-26

Dover: Baker Theatre, Nov. 3; news report, 526-27

Morristown: Lyceum Theatre, Nov. 3; news report, 527-36

Perth Amboy: Donahoe Auditorium, Nov. 4; transcript, 543-55

Carteret, Nov. 5; news report, 560-61

East Orange: Commonwealth Hall, Nov. 5; news report, 563

Bloomfield, Nov. 5; mentioned, 563

Glen Ridge: Town Hall, Nov. 5; news report, 563-64

Final address, Newark: Krueger Auditorium, Nov. 5; transcript, 564-76; mentioned, 412, 561

Elected Governor of New Jersey, Nov. 8, 1910, 584n1; Victory Statement, 589-90

Woodrow Wilson, cont.

Congratulatory messages on election as Governor: from Edwin Anderson Alderman, 595-96; Simeon Eben Baldwin, 580; Daniel Moreau Barringer, 603; Sylvester Woodbridge Beach, 597; Edward Webster Bemis, 617-18,-n1; Robert Bridges, 591; William Jennings Bryan, 600-1; Richard Heath Dabney, 597-99; Josephus Daniels, 585n1; Frank Miles Day, 618; William Henry Steele Demarest, 620,n1; Alfred Lewis Dennis, 592-93; Bessie Louise Dickson, 587,-n1; Cleveland Hoadley Dodge, 591-92; Charles Joel Fisk, 614,n1; Henry Jones Ford, 606-7; John Franklin Fort, 605-6; Eugene Noble Foss, 610; John Watson Foster, 600; Harry Augustus Garfield, 609; James Rudolph Garfield, 609-10,n1; Robert Garrett, 622; Lindley Miller Garrison, 587,n1; Franklin Potts Glass, 588; Henry Mayer Goldfogle, 618,n1; Edward Herrick Griffin, 586-87,n1; John Ralph Hardin, 610; George Brinton McClellan Harvey, 585n1; Robert Randolph Henderson, 599-600; Henry Lee Higginson, 612; James Alfred Hoyt, Jr., 588-89,n1; Robert Stephen Hudspeth, 607; William Hughes, 603; Theodore Whitefield Hunt, 602; William Burhans Isham, 602; Melancthon Williams Jacobus, 594; Caesar Augustus Rodney Janvier, 588; David Benton Jones, 593-94; Thomas Davies Jones, 599; Francis Fisher Kane, 604-5; John William Kern, 587; John Thompson Kerr, 592,n1; Darwin Pearl Kingsley, 621-22,n1; George Mason La Monte, 610; Franklin Knight Lane, 586,n1; Robert Lansing, 607,n1; John Holladay Latané, 613,n1; David Lawrence, 608,-n1; Vivian Murchison Lewis, 591; William C. Liller, 587-88; Thomas Bell Love, 584,n1; George Brinton McClellan, 599; William Frank McCombs, 607; Cyrus Hall McCormick, 594-95; John Bach McMaster, 609,-n1; Theodore Marburg, 614-15,n1; Thomas Riley Marshall, 587, 603; Victor Louis Mason, 586,n1; William Hunter Maxwell, 617; Raleigh Colston Minor, 585,n1; Charles Wellman Mitchell, 599; Roland Sletor Morris, 584; Alexander Thomas Ormond, 603-4; Sir William Osler, 618,n1; Thomas Nelson Page, 602; Alexander Mitchell Palmer, 604,n1; Charles Henry Parkhurst, 621,n1; W. C. Payne, 616n1; Magnus Fraser Peterson, 619-20,n1; Edgar Allan Poe, 600; Henry Smith Pritchett, 596-97; Joseph Pulitzer, 595; George Lawrence Record, 596; Leo Stanton Rowe, 614,n1; Rudolph Edward Schirmer,

Woodrow Wilson, cont.

617; Jacob Gould Schurman, 611,n1; Ashton Cokayne Shallenberger, 622,-n1; Edward Wright Sheldon, 594; George Sebastian Silzer, 585n1; James Smith, Jr., 590; Edwin Augustus Stevens, 601; Isidor Straus, 613,n1; Nathan Straus, 613; Roger Charles Sullivan, 584; William Sulzer, 616; Charles Andrew Talcott, 583; Henry Burling Thompson, 593; Joseph Patrick Tumulty, 589; Frederick Jackson Turner, 602; Walker Whiting Vick, 608; John Wanamaker, 601; John Wesley Wescott, 604; Brand Whitlock, 607,n1; Hiram Woods, 599; John Joseph Wynne, 612,n1; George Green Yeomans, 611-12

Mentioned for president in 1912, 10, 18, 40,n1, 99, 108, 109, 115, 117, 129, 133, 138, 162, 168, 171-72, 298, 320n1,2, 328, 442, 479, 525, 539, 581, 584, 585, 588, 589, 592, 594, 596, 597, 598-99, 600, 602, 603, 605, 607, 609, 612, 613, 622

PRINCETON UNIVERSITY

Baccalaureate Sermon, Unprofitable Servants, June 13, 1909; text in Vol. 19, pp. 242-51; mentioned, 288, 297, 322, 323, 335n2, 337, 379
Resignation as President: news announcement, 101; mentioned, 122-23, 143, 160, 321; proposed Pyne resolution and letter, 353; WW letter of resignation, 362, 364, mentioned, 377-78; trustee action, 364-66; WW resigns McCormick professorship, 492; trustee resolutions on accepting resignation, LL.D. conferred, 537-39, mentioned, 556
Remarks at the Opening Exercises, Marquand Chapel, Sept. 22, 1910; news report, 151-52
Address to the Class of 1914 at Murray Hall, Sept. 24, 1910; news report, 169-71
True University Spirit, address to Philadelphian Society in Murray Hall, Sept. 27, 1910; news report, 176-78
Remarks to student demonstration, Oct. 10, 1910; news report, 289-90
Jurisprudence lectures, 381-82, 470-71

PROFESSIONAL ACTIVITIES

LL.D. degree voted by trustees of Princeton, 539
Carnegie retirement pension, 540,n2

PUBLIC ADDRESSES AND LECTURES

Nature of Democracy in the United States, address before the Owl Club,

Woodrow Wilson, cont.
Hartford, May 17, 1889; text in Vol. 6, pp. 221-39; mentioned, 168
Leaderless Government, address to Virginia Bar Association, Hot Springs, Aug. 5, 1897; text in Vol. 10, pp. 288-304; mentioned, 117,n2
Civic Patriotism, address at Passaic Board of Trade dinner, Dec. 3, 1903; news report, Vol. 15, pp. 61-64; mentioned, 133,n3
The Individual and the Organization, address before the People's Forum, New Rochelle, N.Y., Feb. 26, 1905; news report, Vol. 16, pp. 14-15; mentioned, 322-23, 335n2, 337
The Clergyman and the State, address at General Theological Seminary, New York City, April 6, 1910; text, Vol. 20, pp. 328-35; mentioned 105,-n2
Address to the Princeton Alumni Association of Western Pennsylvania, Hotel Schenley, Pittsburgh, April 16, 1910; news reports, Vol. 20, pp. 363-68, 373-76; mentioned, 31n1

The Lawyer and the Community, address to the American Bar Association at Chattanooga, Aug. 31, 1910; text, 64-81; mentioned, 51, 85, 300-n2, 386, 557, 609

Speech to City Club of Milwaukee, Nov. 17, 1910; text in Vol. 22; mentioned, 163,n1
Lecture in Pabst Theatre, Milwaukee, Nov. 17, 1910; text in Vol. 22; mentioned, 163,n1
Address to Business Service Lecture League, Chicago, Nov. 19, 1910; text in Vol. 22; mentioned, 163,n1, 593, 594
Address to Illinois Manufacturers Association, Chicago, Dec. 12, 1910; text in Vol. 22; mentioned, 389,n1

READING

I haven't had time in the last eight years, since I came here [to Prospect], to arrange my library. . . . I don't have time, either, to keep up with the present books, though I get some idea of the best of them from what my friends tell me, 136

RELIGIOUS LIFE

The Function of the Country Church, address at the dedication of the new meeting-house of the First Church, Old Lyme, Conn., July 1910; mentioned, 4

Woodrow Wilson, cont.
THEATER AND AMUSEMENTS

golf, 51, 136; horseback riding, 136

WRITINGS

George Washington (1897), mentioned, 482
History of the American People (1902), mentioned, 228, 425, 541n2, 542
Life and Education, *Nassau Literary Magazine,* Oct. 1910, 32-33; mentioned, 16,n3
proposed volume of essays for Harper & Brothers, 51,n1

End of Woodrow Wilson entry

Wilson: The Road to the White House (Link), 91n1
Wilson whiskey, 302,n1, 526,n1
Winans, Samuel Ross, 30,n1, 151-52; Mrs. (Sarah Macdonald), 30, 31
Winona, Minn., 252,n7, 468
Winsor, Robert, 40n1
Winton, Henry D., 142,n3, 446
Wisconsin: public service commission, 93; railroad law, 141
Witherspoon, John, 369
Wittpenn, Henry Otto, 7, 8,n1, 16, 19, 37n1, 42, 42n1, 63, 90, 112, 155, 412, 434
Woodbury, N.J., WW campaign speech, 245-59; mentioned, 243
Woodhull, Josiah Townsend, Jr., 16-17,n1
Woodroe, Mrs. (of West Virginia), 107
Woodrow, James, maternal uncle of WW, 1:*41,n1; 581, 581n1; Mrs. (Felexiana Shepherd Baker), 1:*42n1; 581,n2
Woodrow, Marion Woodville, 581,n1
Woods, Charles Albert, 128,n1; Mrs. (Sally Wannamaker), 128,n2
Woods, Hiram, M.D., 1:*133,n3; 555-56, 599; Mrs. (Laura Hall), 556
Woods, Lawrence Crane, 157-58, 385n1, 444
Workingmen, Read and Reflect! 335n2
World's Work, 6n2
Wyman, Isaac Chauncey, 12
Wynne, John Joseph, 612,n1

Yale University, 167, 259, 438; Divinity School, 4n2; football game with Princeton, Oct. 12, 1910, 556,n4; William Lucius Storrs lectures, 386,-n2
Yates, Frederic, 16:*437,n1; 59, 87, 619; Mrs. (Emily Chapman Martin), 59,n2, 619
Yates, Mary, 59,n2
Yeomans, George Green, 611-12